£30

ABOUT THE EDITORS

Brian Fynes is a Lecturer in Manufacturing in the Department of Business Administration at the Michael Smurfit Graduate School of Business, University College Dublin and European Union Post-Doctoral Research Fellow in the Centre for Operations Management at London Business School. His research interests focus on the moderating impacts of buyer-seller relationships on manufacturing practices and performance and he has published articles in the *International Labour Review,* the *European Management Journal, De Qualitate,* and the *Journal of Irish Business and Administrative Research,* as well as contributing chapters to a number of books. He is also co-author of *Flexible Working Lives.*

Sean Ennis is a Lecturer in Marketing at the University of Strathclyde in Glasgow. His main research interests are in logistics management, channel strategy and entrepreneurship, focusing in particular on the marketing-entrepreneurship interface. He has published in a number of journals such as *The International Review of Retail, Distribution and Consumer Research* and the *Irish Marketing Review.* Previously he lectured at the College of Marketing and Design in Dublin. He has also published in edited books such as *Research at the Marketing/Entrepreneurship Interface.* He has served in the past as Vice-Chairman Education for the Marketing Institute of Ireland and participated in the redesign of the Graduateship programme. His PhD research investigated the way in which small indigenous businesses in the electronics sector utilise planning in strategy development.

Irish Studies in Management

Editors:

W. K. Roche
Graduate School of Business
University College Dublin

David Givens
Oak Tree Press

Irish Studies in Management is a series of texts and re-
search-based monographs covering management and business studies. Published by Oak Tree Press in association
with the Graduate School of Business at University College
Dublin, the series aims to publish significant contributions
to the study of management and business in Ireland, especially where they address issues of major relevance to Irish
management in the context of international developments,
particularly within the European Union. Mindful that most
texts and studies in current use in Irish business education
take little direct account of Irish or European conditions,
the series seeks to make available to the specialist and general reader works of high quality which comprehend issues
and concerns arising from the practice of management and
business in Ireland. The series aims to cover subjects ranging from management, accountancy, marketing, economics,
industrial relations/human resource management and international business. Studies of public policy and public affairs of relevance to business and economic life will also be
published in the series.

COMPETING FROM THE PERIPHERY

CORE ISSUES IN INTERNATIONAL BUSINESS

Edited by
Brian Fynes and Sean Ennis

Oak Tree Press
Dublin

Oak Tree Press
Merrion Building
Lower Merrion Street
Dublin 2, Ireland

A catalogue record of this book is
available from the British Library.

ISBN 1-86076-027-9

Printed in Ireland by Colour Books Ltd.

CONTENTS

ABOUT THE CONTRIBUTORS

Antti Ainamo is a Research Fellow in the Department of Marketing at the Helsinki School of Economics and Business Administration

Frank Barry is a Lecturer in the Department of Economics at University College Dublin

Jim Bell is a Senior Lecturer in International Marketing at the University of Ulster at Jordanstown

Ken Bernard is a Lecturer in the Department of Marketing at the University of Strathclyde, Glasgow

John Bradley is Research Professor at the Economic and Social Research Institute in Dublin

Seán de Búrca is a Lecturer in the Department of Marketing at the Michael Smurfit Graduate School of Business, University College Dublin

Delma Duggan is a Research Fellow at the Economic and Social Research Institute, Dublin

Sean Ennis is a Lecturer in the Department of Marketing at the University of Strathclyde, Glasgow

Brian Fynes is a Lecturer in the Department of Business Administration at the Michael Smurfit Graduate School of Business, University College Dublin and EU Post-Doctoral Research Fellow at the Centre for Operations Management at London Business School

Jim Hamill is Reader in Marketing in the Strathclyde International Business Unit within the Department of Marketing at the University of Strathclyde, Glasgow

Dylan Jones-Evans is Professor of Small Business Management in the Business School at the University of Glamorgan, Wales

Michael McDermott is a Senior Lecturer in the Strathclyde International Business Unit within the Department of Marketing at the University of Strathclyde, Glasgow

Alastair McPherson is an EU Post-Doctoral Research Fellow at the Business Research Programme in the Michael Smurfit Graduate School of Business, University College Dublin

Alan McKinnon is Professor of Logistics in the School of Management at Heriot-Watt University, Edinburgh

Rory O'Donnell is Jean Monet Professor of European Business in the Department of Business Administration at the Michael Smurfit Graduate School of Business, University College Dublin

Andy Pike is a Lecturer in the Centre for Urban and Regional Development Studies at the University of Newcastle-upon-Tyne

Paul Ryan is a Research Associate at the Judge Institute of Management Studies at the University of Cambridge and a Lecturer in the Department of Business Administration at the Michael Smurfit Graduate School of Business, University College Dublin

Örjan Sölvell is Associate Professor and Director of the Institute of International Business at the Stockholm School of Economics

James Taggart is a Senior Lecturer in the Strathclyde International Business Unit within the Department of Marketing at the University of Strathclyde, Glasgow

Jenny Taggart is a Research Associate in the Department of Economics and Management at the University of Paisley

John Tomaney is a Lecturer in the Centre for Urban and Regional Development Studies at the University of Newcastle-upon-Tyne

James Wrynn is Senior Lecturer in Business Policy at the College of Marketing & Design in the Dublin Institute of Technology

Ivo Zander is Assistant Professor at the Institute of International Business at the Stockholm School of Economics

PREFACE

When we invited contributions for this book we were cognisant of the fact that a number of perspectives had to be addressed within our basic framework. As our primary objective was to analyse comprehensively how countries, industries and firms compete from peripheral regions, we realised the necessity for contributors to cover both policy issues and models of best practice.

As a consequence, the various chapters in this text reflect upon and assess a broad range of policies and practices from across a number of peripheral regions in Europe. The early chapters consider the policy perspectives at both European Union and national level. These are followed by contributions which assess the way in which national governments, through their agencies and institutions, seek to provide support in areas such as inward investment, export promotion, research and development and innovation. The final chapters provide some empirical case evidence of how certain industries and firms overcome the problems of competing from the periphery.

In order to fulfil our objectives, we recognised the need to invite contributions from researchers from disciplines such as economics, logistics, human resource management, international marketing, innovation and technology, manufacturing, international business strategy, regional development and competition policy. As a consequence, the contributors come from some of the leading research centres in Europe. Thus, while the treatment of the subject is essentially European in nature, the contributions provide significant insights for the broader global arena.

In our opening chapter, we examine the concept of peripherality, highlighting the diverse interpretations made by scholars in the literature. We highlight the importance of core-periphery issues in the context of political, social and economic developments in Europe. We consider the theoretical frameworks from various disciplines and caution against the danger of adopting a simplistic, uni-dimensional view of peripherality. This caveat provides a pertinent backdrop for the subsequent contributions.

In the next chapter, *Seán de Búrca* identifies a core-periphery structure as a common thread in world trade as far back as the fifteenth century even though economic leadership has shifted from country to country. He reviews the concept of peripherality by juxtaposing its common characteristics and regional imbalance against the advantages of operating from the core and argues that there are potential inherent economic disadvantages associated with a peripheral location. As a result, a number of barriers to development in peripheral regions can arise and may have a significant impact on regional economic development. The role of distance in the internationalisation of the firm is also considered in order to ascertain whether or not the expectations derived from spatial theory are supported in practice.

Rory O'Donnell addresses the considerable uncertainty about the correct concept, unit of analysis and measure of competitiveness or competitive advantage. He reviews the multiplicity of concepts, measures and theories of competitiveness, and addresses some important conceptual and definitional issues which arise in the study of the competitive advantage of peripheral regions and countries. The chapter includes a discussion of the three levels at which international competition can be analysed and outlines an important distinction between measures of competitive *performance,* competitive *potential* and management *process.* By examining recent extensions of Porter's framework, he demonstrates that each of the conceptual and measurement issues discussed in the chapter arise in a particularly acute form in the study of peripheral competitive advantage.

In the following chapter *John Tomaney* and *Andy Pike* review the impact of European Union (EU) policy on peripheral regions. They argue that despite the evolution of regional policy within the EU, its contradictions with other EU policy areas has conflicted and undermined its aim of promoting economic and social cohesion. In reviewing the impact of EU policy on peripheral regions within a wider context of the impacts of the process European integration on these regions, the authors conclude that contradictions between regional and other EU policies within peripheral regions are undermining the potential for economic and social cohesion

Frank Barry, John Bradley and *Delma Duggan* highlight similarities in economic structure across the EU periphery, as well as identifying important differences between the individual peripheral economies. They argue that the process of structural changes appears to be at a much more advanced stage in Ireland than in the other small peripheral economies, and speculate that Greece and Portugal will undergo similar structural changes in coming decades. They also discuss the likely effects of the Single European Market and the Structural Funds programmes on the peripheral countries.

The institutional arrangements for supporting the export promotion activities of three small peripheral nations: Ireland, a long-standing member of the EU; Finland, which recently joined the EU; and Norway, which has declined membership of the EU on several occasions, are examined by *Jim Bell.* He argues that, in each case, valuable insights can be gained from their approaches to stimulating export activity among small indigenous firms. His analysis also considers national export promotion within an EU context and speculates on its future shape and direction in light of the completion of the Single European Market (SEM) and EU competition policy.

James Wrynn focuses on the role of Foreign Direct Investment (FDI) from the perspective of the host country. His analysis of the Irish experience in this context examines the political, historical and economic background to economic development and economic policy. He then documents the sequence of events which led to a complete reversal of policy resulting in Ireland pursuing a most active policy of encouragement of FDI and examines the details of FDI policy implementation and performance.

Alastair McPherson considers the relationship between investment in the human capital of the periphery, inward FDI and changing human resource and industrial relations practices. In considering the factors underpinning a high capital strategy, he addresses the argument that national economies that do not adjust their industrial relations arrangements to a more co-operative model will be unable to compete. This chapter also reflects on the role of overseas investors as a factor in stimulating human resource development and whether strategies for human resource development are likely to fit with emerging trends in the organisation of production. In concluding, the merits of the 'flexible specialisation' approach as an industrial model conducive to peripheral human resource development objectives are considered in the light of more critical appraisals of organisational and human resource trajectories.

In examining the economy of the Republic of Ireland, *Dylan Jones-Evans* discusses the role of technology in the development of the peripheral regions of Europe, concentrating, in particular, on the role that can be played by small technology-based firms and the university sector. He demonstrates that the indigenous technological capability of industry within a peripheral economy such as the Republic of Ireland remains low, mainly as a result of a weak entrepreneurial high-technology sector, and the under-utilisation of the university sector in developing linkages with this indigenous industry.

Jim Hamill considers the impact of the recent boom in cross-border mergers and acquisitions on national competitiveness. He extends the earlier discussion of FDI impact by examining the host country effects of this surge in international take-overs, based on the experience of the UK. The choice of the UK is par-ticularly relevant given its pole position as the leading target country for cross-border acquisitions in Europe. He concludes from his analysis of UK and EU merger policy that the question of external acquisition of UK companies has not been a major con-cern of policy makers and that existing merger control legislation is inadequate to deal with the issue.

James and *Jenny Taggart* examine how the perspectives of multinational subsidiaries in a peripheral region of the European Union compare with an analysis of subsidiary strategy, and how the two might interact with the core-periphery tension to impact on the subsidiary's degree of independence from headquarters control. They review the basic economic parameters that affect the core-periphery continuum and appraise the concepts underly-ing our understanding of strategy-making at subsidiary level, and a brief survey of evidence from Scotland. In addition, the position of five multinational manufacturing subsidiaries in Ireland are analysed with specific reference to the strategic factors that affect subsidiary independence.

The logistical implications of manufacturing in peripheral re-gions is addressed by *Alan McKinnon*. He argues that the concept of peripherality needs to be adapted to take account of the com-plexity of modern logistic networks. In analysing the experience of Scottish manufacturers, he assesses the logistical penalties asso-ciated with peripherality and supplements an analysis of trans-port cost differentials with a more broadly-based review of the logistical challenges confronting 'peripheral' manufacturers. His review of current trends in logistics concludes with an assessment of their effect on the attractiveness of peripheral regions to manu-facturing investment.

This theme is taken up by *Paul Ryan* who reports on an exploratory investigation of the European automobile industry, which encapsulates most of the conditions of regional production and neo-modern production methods. In this chapter he examines whether, on the one hand, peripherally located supplier firms are employing just-in-time delivery systems and are endeavouring to develop closer relations with their powerful assembler customers or, on the other, are dismissed as distant and unviable and thus are expelled from the supply chains of the assemblers. His conclusions are framed in the context of expectations regarding future trends in the spatial organisation of production.

Örjan Sölvell and *Ivo Zander* examine the evolution of Swedish multinational enterprises and demonstrate how Sweden, although a geographically peripheral country in Northern Europe, has developed many world-class centres of industrial activity. They argue that such centres, or clusters of interrelated industries, have played a critical role in this regard. Using Hollywood as an illustration, they contend that perceived peripheral disadvantages can be overcome by developing specialist industrial expertise. With increased market integration in Europe, they expect to see not only increased competition between firms, but also between industry clusters in different parts of Europe.

Antti Ainamo describes, in a historical perspective, Finland's strategy of 'catching up' with the core in the context of national systems of innovation. In tracing Finland's industrial strategy of competing from the periphery as a series of stages of economic development, he assesses its economy-wide strategic changes, illustrating these changes with a description of the impact of Nokia Corporation's firm-level strategy on the Finnish economy as a whole. His conclusions present a number of public policy implications for similar economies.

Ken Bernard considers the applicability and application of perceived models of international business development in markets which are developing in Eastern Europe. Specifically, he considers the conundrum of the extent to which the liberalisation of political and economic relationships will produce more opportunities than threats for the rest of European business and whether those changes will be seen more in the form of new customers, or of competitors or of suppliers/subcontractors. The chapter includes a discussion of a recent research project which examined the extent to which the development of relationships between firms in Eastern and Western Europe, and the interactions between them, conforms to the norms of academic literature, market entry strategies and barriers to entry.

In a similar vein, *Michael McDermott* considers the impact of peripheral location from the Portuguese perspective. This chapter highlights the huge challenges which still have to be met in Portugal and the initiatives underway to ensure they are overcome, and focuses on seven industries that have already been accorded priority status, ranging from traditional industries to new sectors growing largely because of and in response to inward investment. This analysis includes a particular focus on the auto-components sector and how it is expected to play a crucial role in transforming Portugal's industrial structure away from the traditional, basic, labour-intensive industries towards modern, capital- and technology-intensive sectors.

ACKNOWLEDGEMENTS

Any book which addresses a complex subject area such as that of competing from the periphery must, of necessity, draw upon the collective knowledge, wisdom and experience of many researchers from different backgrounds and disciplines. We feel, as editors, privileged to have worked with the authors who have contributed to this text. It is fair to say that we both have learned a lot about the subject area as a consequence of working closely with what, in many respects, is such an eclectic group. We would like to sincerely thank everyone who has participated in this venture. Although it was hard work, it was also enjoyable.

We would like to thank Professor Bill Roche, Dean of the Michael Smurfit Graduate Business School, University College Dublin, and Director of the Business Research Programme, for his intellectual support and advice. When we first suggested the idea of a book to him, he was most positive in his encouragement. He also committed financial resources to the symposium which we organised for the contributors in September 1995. This was an invaluable means for us, as editors, to structure the book and learn from the presentations given by the individual authors. Without such support our task would have been much more difficult.

The European Commission's funding of Post-Doctoral Research Fellowships in the area of peripheral studies at the Business Research Programme, University College Dublin, provided an initial stimulus for the progression of the project from the concept stage right through to the end-product.

We would also like to thank Professor Rory O'Donnell, Jean Monet Professor of European Business, Michael Smurfit Graduate Business School, University College Dublin, for his ongoing advice and comments.

To Professor Frank Bradley, Dean of the Faculty of Commerce, University College Dublin, for his support during the project.

To Dr. Jim Hamill, Reader at the Strathclyde International Business Unit, for his advice during the early phase of the project, in particular for his recommendations as to potential authors who might contribute to the book.

We also wish to acknowledge the European Commision's funding of a Research Fellowship for Brian Fynes under the Human Capital and Mobility Programme at London Business School.

We wish in particular to acknowledge the contribution of David Givens of Oak Tree Press. He responded patiently and quickly to any problems or difficulties experienced by us and, as a consequence, made our job that much easier.

This book is dedicated to Noreen and Liz for their patience and understanding.

1

PERIPHERALITY: CONCEPTS, ISSUES AND ALTERNATIVE FRAMEWORKS

Brian Fynes and Sean Ennis

1.1 INTRODUCTION

The background to this book originated from a paper (Fynes, Ennis and Negri, 1995) which we presented at a conference organised by the Centre for Quality and Services Management at University College Dublin. Our paper examined the strategic changes which Microsoft Ireland had made to their production, logistics and marketing operations within the European market. The subsequent discussion which took place among the participants focused on the way in which the company had managed to move their logistics and customer services hub from continental Europe to Dublin. This led to various delegates commenting on the perceived difficulties of competing from a peripheral region such as Ireland and how Microsoft Ireland managed to overcome these obstacles throughout Europe. It was during this session of lively debate that the idea emerged for a book which would reflect, in a scholarly fashion, on the broad range of factors which impact on the capability of companies to compete successfully, or otherwise, from such areas, often euphemistically referred to as 'less favoured regions'.

Our preliminary examination of the literature revealed a number of significant contributions towards an understanding of peripherality. We examine these in more detail later in this chapter. That such a myriad of articles and reports has emerged in the last decade is not surprising. Within Europe, countries such as Ireland, Portugal and Sweden have had to assess their competitive position in the light of major developments such as the creation of the Single European Market, the move towards European Monetary Union, the enlargement of the European Community and the social, economic and legal changes which have taken place in

Eastern Europe. The question which emerges is whether or not regions such as Ireland, Scotland, Wales, Portugal and Greece can operate as self-sustaining regional economies within this dramatically altered boundary or, alternatively, will they disintegrate in a fragmented manner and be economically and socially disadvantaged as the impact of these changes percolates through over the coming decade or so? This issue is exacerbated by the fact that the four largest countries in the European Union (EU) — Germany, France, Italy and the UK — account for 73 per cent of the population and over 66 per cent of the population of Western Europe (O'Donnell, 1994a). Perhaps a more pertinent statistic is that these economies produce 78 per cent of the EU Gross Domestic Product (GDP), with Germany alone producing over 25 per cent. OECD figures (1993) reveal that GDP per head in so-called peripheral countries such as Ireland, Portugal, Greece and Spain is considerably lower than the core countries within the EU such as Germany, UK and France. This ranges from an index low of 44 in Greece to 110 in Germany. O'Donnell (1994a) concludes that

> these data reveal a distinct geographical divide in Western Europe: less prosperous countries all lie on the southern or western periphery. This suggests that some systematic factors differentiate the Western European 'core' from its periphery (p. 50).

The foregoing analysis highlights one of the central challenges which the EU, since its original emergence as the European Economic Community (EEC) in 1957, has continuously, both explicitly and implicitly, had to address: namely, how to achieve closer economic integration between the members of the EU, while at the same time attempting to overcome the imbalances and disparities which exist in the various countries. This task has been made more difficult by the fact that throughout the 1970s and 1980s there has been a singular lack of commitment on behalf of many member states to create an environment which actively embraced the notion of integration. Evidence of this could be gleaned from the unpalatable fact that the economic performance of the EEC was worse than the two other key trading regions: Japan and the US. A report by Albert and Ball (1982) concluded that 'the main obstacle to the economic growth of European countries is what we must call "non-Europe"'. O'Donnell (1994a) interprets this as meaning the low level of co-operation and the weakness of common policies. The issue of lack of co-operation was typically manifested in the implementation of non-tariff barriers, which 'bended' but did not contravene the rules as laid down by the EU. The net consequence of this was a weakening, in overall terms, of the EU competitive position.

The response from the European Commission was the concept of the internal market, as advocated by Jacques Delors, in 1985. It is in the context of this development that this book draws upon a number of influential authors who have researched in a wide range of areas on the specific issue of competing from the periphery. We argue that the aims of the objectives of the Single European Market (SEM) have created both opportunities and challenges for companies of all sizes who operate from the so-called 'peripheral' regions. A quick glance at the main aspects of the move to complete the internal market crystallises this observation:

- welding together the twelve (as of 1985) individual markets of the member states into one single market of 320 million people

- ensuring that this single market was also an expanding market

- ensuring that the market was flexible so that resources, both of people and materials, and of capital and investment, flowed into areas of greatest economic advantage (O'Donnell, 1994a, p. 59).

In order to move towards a completion of the internal market, the Commission identified a number of measures which would have to be fulfilled. In essence, this meant that a number of barriers — physical, technical and fiscal — would have to be removed. While most of the measures were acted upon by the member states prior to the December 1992 deadline, a number of the more contentious ones still remain in place; the main ones being indirect taxation, the suppression of border checks and company law. O'Donnell (1994a) argues that while the programme which was instigated to complete the internal market was a significant step towards the goal of integration, it remains a moot point as to whether it will ensure a single market. One ongoing problem arises from the wide diversity of cultures, buying preferences and attitudes to nationalism which prevail within the member states. This is perhaps best illustrated by the differing attitudes of certain countries

to the concept of a single European currency or to the establishment of a European Central Bank. The exchange rate crises experienced within the EU during 1992 and 1993 reinforced the
view held by many commentators that the move to full economic
monetary union was unlikely to be as smooth as envisaged by
Delors and other proponents of the concept. Likewise, the recession experienced by Germany, mainly as a consequence of taking
over the former East Germany, also was perceived as a critical
factor in slowing down the transition to monetary union. The current public displays of argument between the 'Euro-sceptics' and
the pro-European lobby within the Conservative government in
the UK only serves to reinforce the confusion over whether even-
tual monetary integration of Western Europe will actually occur.

The net effect of these developments on companies located in
peripheral regions remains difficult to assess. O'Donnell (1994a)
posits the view that the SEM programme will not lead to greater
protectionism; indeed, he argues that certain aspects of the internal market can be of distinct benefit to companies from outside.
This is evidenced by the fact that the EU would not appear to
have such a well-defined set of industrial policy goals as to allow
it to pursue a policy of 'European Champions'. Given the likely
further enlargement of the EU over the coming decade, much of
the implication for firms competing from the periphery remains
unclear. In essence, there is no simple mechanism for analysing
the competitiveness of firms which compete from the periphery.
The primary goal of this book is to synthesise the ideas of a number of researchers in a number of interrelated disciplines on the
question of competing from the periphery. It is to be hoped that
the reader will gain a deeper insight into the complexity of the
issue under investigation, but it would be disingenuous of us as
editors to put forward a position statement which argues that
there are clearly defined benefits or disadvantages accruing from
competing from the periphery.

1.2 THE CONCEPT OF PERIPHERALITY

The background to any discussion on peripherality centres on the
original premise that in any economic system there will be an underlying imbalance in performance between regional areas. That
such a situation can occur is, in itself, not surprising. Evidence
presented earlier in this chapter reinforces this position in the
EU. The issue of geographical remoteness from the core area of

activity has received the most attention from researchers. Thus, it is argued that companies which are located in those areas which are the hub for production sourcing and research and development, and are closely linked to the prevailing customer base, are in a far stronger competitive position than those firms which are located a long distance away from such activities. De Búrca, in Chapter 2, provides a detailed assessment of the literature in this area. If one accepts the logic of such a view, then it can be argued that a clear imbalance emerges between regional areas.

Much of the policy developments which have taken place within the European Community in the past decade or so have sought to redress this imbalance. Krugman and Venables (1990) note that a major EU objective is to make the nations and regions of the community more similar in two senses:

- the poorer regions should catch up in income to the wealthier areas, and

- the inflation and macroeconomic performance of the most troubled economies should improve toward the standard of the best performance — to allow for monetary union among other things.

This move towards convergence or, in the longer term, cohesion explicitly recognises that such imbalances exist. Whether such a situation occurs solely because of geographic remoteness and distance is a moot point. McKinnon, in Chapter 12, provides evidence which suggests that a peripheral region, such as Scotland, need not suffer a serious logistical handicap. Given the trends towards just-in-time, sub-contracting, the centralisation of inventory and the increasing level of foreign inward investment in similar regions such as Ireland, Wales and the north-east of England, it becomes apparent that the handicap of distance can be overcome, to some extent, by other locational advantages.

The notion of *agglomeration* is one which has also received attention in the literature. This is based on the principle of cumulative causation, which suggests that a region can acquire an initial competitive advantage either due to economies of scale (which arise as output increases) or where the cost of production is lower because of the proximity of other firms in the region. The cumulative effect emerges as, and when, output increases, costs fall and other regions find it increasingly more difficult to catch up. O'Donnell (1994b) observes that when the strong region attracts capital and labour from weaker regions, this will further enhance its productive potential and, because of agglomeration, strengthen its competitive advantage. This tendency for firms to concentrate in large central economies depends, to a large extent, on three factors: economies of scale, transport costs and the size of the manufacturing sector. These are referred to in the literature as *centripetal forces*. In contrast, *centrifugal forces*, such as high urban land rent, can impact on a region which has been based on agglomerations. Amin and Malmberg (1992) note that such agglomerations can provide a range of benefits upon which a system of vertically-disintegrated and 'knowledge'-based production can draw. This includes such factors as a reduction in transaction and transport costs; the build-up of a local pool of expertise and know-how; a culture of labour flexibility and co-operation resulting from dense social interaction and trust; and the growth of a local infrastructure of specialised services, distribution networks, and supply structures.

Thus, by creating, nurturing and developing a business environment which is based on particular product specialisms, a self-contained regional economy can emerge. A number of such areas which have appeared such as Silicon Valley, the 'Silicon Glen' in Scotland, the M4 Corridor and Grenoble.

This school of thought has much to commend it. Firstly, in areas where sovereignty over knowledge, product and process development and sourcing rests with the manufacturer, it is not unrealistic to expect a close degree of networking with suppliers and customers. Scott (1988) argues that where this high level of specialism exists, such 'linkages are likely to be mediated by face-to-face contact, thus encouraging spatial agglomeration'. De Búrca, in Chapter 2, provides a detailed assessment of the contribution of network theory to the debate on peripherality.

Amin and Malmberg (1992), however, argue that an unreserved acceptance of the localisation theory is an over-simplification. They point to the fact that regions such as Silicon Valley are likely to fragment internally in much the same way as the cutlery districts in Yorkshire did in an earlier decade during this century. Perhaps more fundamentally, the conditions for success which may exist in one area are not capable of being transferred as smoothly or as quickly to another.

The trend towards localisation can be juxtaposed with the trend towards globalisation. In this respect, Amin and Malmberg (1992) point to the ever-increasing influence of transnational corporations over both local and national economies. They argue that one of the implications which emerges is that 'the meaning of place is becoming defined within the hyperspace of global corporate activity'. In essence, this means that the ultimate survival of organisations which are linked to such trans-national corporations (TNCs) is, to some extent, outside their control, and very much framed within a wider context. The critical question arises, however, as to whether the linkages which may emerge between local firms in peripheral regions and the TNC act as a driver of change for altering the relationship, or, if more strategic decision-making areas are re-allocated? The evidence from the literature is conflicting. Wrynn, in Chapter 7, presents an assessment of the performance of linkage programmes, and the reader is directed towards that chapter for a fuller discussion of the topic. It is not proposed that we examine the issue in detail at this juncture. However, writers such as Turok (1993) suggest that the quality of linkage is related to the focus of the relationship: whether it is viewed by the TNC as being collaborative, over the longer term, or directed towards tactical, short-term issues such as cost-cutting. Turok's empirical research indicates that problems of unreliability in the areas of quality and delivery can militate against greater sophistication emerging within such linkages.

Amin and Malmberg (1992) discuss the case of Benetton, a company which has been highlighted extensively in the literature as one of the modern 'network' organisations. While much of the production task is sub-contracted to a large number of small local companies, strategic tasks such as dyeing are done internally. All key decisions are retained within the family firm. He also notes that while many industry sectors embrace the concept of collaboration, partnerships and long-term agreements, they do so with a small minority of companies. These companies are able to enjoy the benefits of working closely with TNCs. However, this reduces the opportunity for the secondary suppliers and may ultimately threaten their survival and growth prospects.

Within this discussion on the concept of peripherality and the trends towards agglomeration and networking, it is perhaps pertinent to consider the developments which have taken place in the area of information technology and their resulting implications for companies located in peripheral regions.

The adoption of technologies such as Electronic Data Interchange has allowed companies to manage transfer of data both backwards and forwards in the supply chain more swiftly, accurately and cost-effectively than has hitherto been the case (Fynes and Ennis, 1994). It could therefore be argued that the adoption of such techniques might mean that it becomes easier for companies located in less-favoured regions to work in a more interactive fashion with other companies, and in the process redress the imbalance.

Yet again the evidence from the literature is mixed in this regard. Castells (1989) found that the role of telecommunications is strengthening the competitive role of major business around the world and that the 'effects of new technologies vary according to their interaction with economic, social, political and cultural processes'. It would therefore be dangerous to use a uni-dimensional development such as telecommunications to argue that the problem of competing from the periphery is reduced: it can only be assessed in relation to the other variables which impact on competitiveness.

So far the discussion has centred on the concept of peripherality from the traditional core-periphery relationship, the theory of agglomeration and the developments in the area of networking. The words distance and geography feature, either explicitly or implicitly, in much of the literature. While this is understandable, it ignores other categories of peripherality that may exist. It also ignores the changing perception which both individuals and companies have of distance itself. After all, developments in transportation have reduced both the lead times and costs associated with distribution of products. As referred to earlier, McKinnon provides some evidence to suggest that this has happened in the case of Scotland where the tapering of transport costs over distance can work to the advantage of firms located in that region.

The issue of cultural peripherality is considered by Bernard in Chapter 16, where he argues that far from being some sort of 'fringe entity', Eastern Europe is at the very centre of European history and culture. It also appears that while each country in the region has its own language which bears little resemblance to any mainstream language, it counteracts this problem by adopting a second language such as German or English to allow it to compete more effectively.

Psychological peripherality can and does exist. For instance, the 'Iron Curtain' meant that for many years people from countries to the east were virtually isolated from the west, with little first-hand experience of visiting either region. It can be argued that while the subsequent removal of such a barrier led to business people identifying potential opportunities, both sides were operating under a number of misconceptions about each other, resulting from either a lack of knowledge or basic ignorance.

The preceding discussion has identified the main ideas surrounding the concept of peripherality. It is submitted that the subject is a complex, multi-faceted one which many commentators too easily treat as a uni-dimensional topic under the traditional core-periphery categorisation. The next sections of this chapter explore the theoretical approaches developed in the literature.

1.3 ALTERNATIVE THEORETICAL MODELS OF PERIPHERALITY

A considerable number of disciplines exist which contribute to the theoretical underpinning and conceptualisation of the study of peripherality. Spatial theory, economic geography, trade theory, international economics, regional growth theory and competition theory provide the researcher with a diversity of perspectives for addressing the subject area. In this section, we consider some of the recent contributions to theoretical development in this area.

In terms of spatial theory, Krugman (1991, p.1) has defined economic geography as 'the location of production in space; that is, the branch of economics that worries about where things happen in relation to one another', and suggests that the theory of international trade has, to a large extent, ignored potential insights from both economic geography and location theory. He contends that the best way to understand how the international economy works is to start by examining what happens *inside* nations: if we want to understand variation in national growth rates, the best place to start is by looking at differences in regional growth.

Conceptualising market structure is one of the primary reasons why spatial phenomena are neglected in the mainstream economics literature. This, Krugman (1991) argues, is because on the one hand, economists tend to remain loyal to the constant-returns, perfect-competition paradigm, while on the other hand, geographers have ignored the issue of market structure and have concentrated on the geometric dimensions of market areas and optimising facility location.

Krugman contends that *concentration* is the most pervasive feature of the geography of economic activity and is the most compelling evidence of the existence of increasing returns. Increasing returns suggests that countries trade with each other because there are inherent advantages arising from specialisation. Although until the 1980s international economics emphasised comparative advantage (whereby countries trade in order to take advantage of their differences) as the dominant paradigm, Krugman notes that is no longer the case. As the lines between international economics and regional economics become increasingly blurred, newer trade, growth and business cycle theories are beginning to provide explanatory power in our understanding of increasing returns, imperfect competition, history and self-sustaining phenomena. In addition, Krugman cautions that the circular relationship in which the location of demand determines the location of production, and vice versa, may act as a highly conservative force which further entrenches core-periphery patterns. He concludes that economic analysis based on the factor endowments, technology and tastes may be somewhat constrained; instead, an economy's form is largely shaped by historical contingency.

Krugman and Venables (1990), in modelling the forces at work in determining the relative competitiveness of industry located at the centre and at the periphery, found that there were strong forces at work tending to pull manufacturing industry towards the central economy at the expense of the periphery. Their analysis reveals that if trade barriers are very high, then markets in both the centre and the periphery will be served by local firms. Prices thus need to be somewhat higher in the peripheral economy, as only then can firms in that market cover their costs. However, as trade barriers are reduced, this price differential is narrowed, resulting in a reduction in the number of firms in the periphery. Consequently, production moves to the centre, and the periphery becomes a net importer of manufactured goods. They note, however, that lower barriers to trade could also make it more attractive to move production out towards the periphery if such economies are labour-abundant and production is labour-intensive. In such circumstances, the relative factor endowments become a key determinant of the direction of trade flows.

Krugman (1992) has also explored the dynamic implications of models of economic geography. Arguing that any model of economic geography must exhibit a tension between centripetal and centrifugal forces, he identifies three strands of literature that provide a theoretical basis for his analysis.

Firstly, there is a rich literature on 'market potential' (Harris, 1954) which proposes that the desirability of a region as a production site depends on its access to markets and that the quality of that access may be measured by an index of market potential (M_j) which is the weighted sum of the purchasing power of all regions, with the weights depending inversely on distance:

$$M_j = \Sigma k Y_k \, f(D_{jk})$$

where Y_k is the income of region k, D_{jk} is the distance between j and k and f is some declining function. Harris (1954) suggested that the traditional manufacturing belt in the US persisted because of the circular relationship in which industrial concentration tended both to follow and to create market access. The theoretical weakness of this argument, Krugman notes, is the absence of microeconomic foundations: while an index of market potential may be useful in deciding on location, there is no clear explanation of how the market works in practice.

A second literature strand (Pred, 1966; Dixon and Thirwall, 1975) focuses on cumulative causation and suggests that agglomerations, in nurturing large local markets, are able to attract new industries, thereby further enhancing the position of local markets: the dynamics of the process are thus self-sustaining.

Central place theory, (Christaller, 1933; Lösch, 1940), although ignoring circular causation, is the third relevant strand of literature in the dynamics of spatial development. This contribution addresses the trade-off between economies of scale and logistics costs and contends that the efforts of firms:

> to make the best of this tradeoff should lead to the emergence of a lattice of production sites roughly evenly spaced across the landscape perhaps in a hierarchical structure in which the activities with larger scale economies or lower transport costs are concentrated in a smaller number of higher-level sites (Krugman, 1992, p. 9).

Krugman's own analysis attempts to model the role of market access (in determining manufacturing location), the role of forward and backward linkages (in producing agglomerations) and the proposal that an economy is a self-organising phenomenon that evolves a self-sustaining locational structure. While acknowledging the limitations of his model, he concludes that its results are 'strongly suggestive' in terms of explaining relationships between the modelled variables.

More recently, Jacquemin and Sapir (1995) have used cluster analysis to assess the implications of a deeper and faster economic and monetary integration amongst a hard core of five EU countries. They suggest that the creation of such a core would help to deepen the process of integration, but would also possibly lead to a rift between northern and southern members. Indeed, they argue that it may not be desirable for southern member states to integrate rapidly with the hard core northern cluster, given their idiosyncratic economic structure and the danger of asymmetrical sectoral shocks. Rather, they may wish to stay on the fringe and 'free-ride' on the core's stability. The key concern, however, is to ensure that further integration remains available to all members and that the rules for managing the relationships between the 'ins' and 'outs' are clearly established: this concern, the authors suggest, requires conceptualisation and analysis 'that extend far beyond the realm of economics' (p. 10).

An additional perspective is provided by Krugman and Venables (1995a) in their analysis of the impact of globalisation on real national incomes. The conventional free-trade argument is that while global integration may hurt particular interest groups it will normally raise the overall level of real income of just about every nation. Opponents of this argument contend that greater integration usually produces national winners and losers and that integration nurtures inequality which divides into a rich core and a poor periphery, and that that wealth centre is at the periphery's expense. In their model, they find evidence for both arguments and suggest that the global economy must achieve a threshold level of integration before the forces that result in a core-periphery dichotomy can become established. When this happens the rise in core income is partly at the expense of the periphery; however, as integration continues, the advantages of the core are diminished and the subsequent rise in peripheral income may be at the core's expense.

Krugman and Venables (1995b) have also attempted to analyse international trade theory without mentioning countries: instead of assuming that trade takes place between nations and regions, they have developed a model in which economic space is assumed to be continuous and in which the resulting seamless world spontaneously organises itself into industrial and agricultural zones because of the tension between the forces of agglomeration and disagglomeration. Using contributions from biological theory (Turing, 1952), they found that strong linkages and low transport costs generated low frequency agglomeration (i.e. a few large manufacturing regions), whereas weaker linkages and high transport costs generate higher frequency agglomeration. They conclude that the evolution of global spatial structure is characterised by punctuated equilibrium: long stretches of stability interrupted by episodes of continuous change.

If one is to draw inferences from these recent contributions, it is that scholars increasingly challenge the limitations of conventional paradigms. Instead, they are now using radically different disciplines in their analysis of core-periphery relationships.

In conclusion, we believe that these contributions add significantly to the level of understanding about what is a complex, multi-faceted subject area. Much of what has previously been written by academics and practitioners implies that competing from the periphery inherently places countries, regions, industries and firms at a disadvantage.

Whether or not these claims are rhetoric or reality is at the heart of much of the debate within the following chapters.

References

Albert, M. and Ball, R. J. (1983), *Towards European Economic Recovery in the 1980's*. European Parliament Working Document, Luxembourg: European Parliament.

Amin, A. and Malmberg, A. (1992), 'Competing Structural and Institutional Influences on the Geography of Production in Europe', *Environment and Planning A*, Vol. 24, pp. 401-416.

Castells, M. (1989), *The Information City*, Oxford: Basil Blackwell.

Christaller, W. (1993), *Central Places in Southern Germany*, Jena: Fisher. English translation by C. W. Baskin, London: Prentice Hall.

Dixon, R. and Thirwall, A. P. (1975), 'A Model of Regional Growth Differences Along Kaldorean Lines', *Oxford Economic Papers*, Vol. 27, pp. 201-214.

Fynes, B. and Ennis, S. (1994), 'EDI in Retailing: Implementation and Prospects in Ireland', *The International Journal of Retail, Distribution and Consumer Research.* Vol. 4., No. 4, October. pp. 411-426.

Fynes, B., Ennis, S. and Negri, L. (1995), 'Service Quality at the Manufacturing-Marketing Interface: From Kaizen to Service-Driven Logistics' in *Understanding Services Management,* (Eds. W.J. Glynn and J.G. Barnes), Dublin: Oak Tree Press, pp. 370-392.

Harris, C. (1954), 'The Market as a Factor in the Localization of Industry in the United States', *Annals of the Association of American Geographers,* 64, pp. 315-48.

Jacquemin, A. and Sapir, A. (1995), *Is a European Hard Core Credible? A Statistical Analysis,* Centre for Economic Policy Research, Discussion Paper 1242, London.

Krugman, P. (1991), *Geography and Trade,* Gaston Eyskens Lecture Series, Leuven: Leuven University Press and Cambridge, MA: MIT Press.

Krugman, P. (1992), *A Dynamic Spatial Model,* Working Paper No. 4219, Cambridge, MA: National Bureau of Economic Research.

Krugman, P. and Venables, A. J. (1990), *Integration and the Competitiveness of Peripheral Industry,* Centre for Economic Policy Research, Discussion Paper 363, London.

Krugman, P. and Venables, A. J. (1995a), *Globalisation and the Inequality of Nations,* Working Paper No. 5098, Cambridge, MA: National Bureau of Economic Research.

Krugman, P. and Venables, A. J. (1995b), *The Seamless World: A Spatial Model of International Specialization,* Centre for Economic Policy Research, Discussion Paper 1230, London.

Lösch, A. (1940), *The Economics of Location,* Jena: Fisher. English translation (1954), New Haven: Yale University Press.

O'Donnell, R. (1994a), 'The Economic Environment' in *The European Business Environment,* (Eds. N. Nugent and R. O'Donnell), London: Macmillan, pp. 47-90.

O'Donnell, R. (1994b), 'The Evolution of the Theory of Regional Development' in *European Integration and Regional Policy.* (Eds. S. Fountas and B. Kennelly), Centre for Development Studies, Social Sciences Research Centre, Galway.

Pred, A. (1966), *The Spatial Dynamics of US Urban-Industrial Growth,* Cambridge, MA: MIT Press.

Scott, A. J. (1988), 'Flexible Production Systems and Regional Development: The Rise of New Industrial Spaces in North America and Western Europe', *International Journal of Urban and Regional Research,* Vol. 12, pp. 171-186.

Turing, A. M. (1952), 'The Chemical Basis of Morphogenesis', *Philosophical Transactions of the Royal Society,* 237, pp. 5-72.

Turok, I. (1993), 'Inward Investment and Industrial Linkages: How Deeply Embedded is Silicon Glen?' *Regional Studies,* Vol. 27, No. 5, pp. 401-417.

2

CORE-PERIPHERAL RELATIONSHIPS AS THE NEXUS IN WORLD TRADE TRENDS

Seán de Búrca

2.1 INTRODUCTION

Global economic growth has evolved dramatically since 1945 as a result of changing patterns of trade, the dynamism of the Pacific Rim and a changing European architecture. In addition, the changing attitudes to the regulation of trade and moves towards closer integration and internationalisation have all combined in a complex web of interdependency. In analysing international trade performance, numerous theories of development, international trade, and regional economies have provided partial explanations. This chapter discusses one dimension to international perform-ance, the concept of peripherality.

The first part of this chapter focuses its attention on how a core-periphery structure can be identified as a common thread in world trade as far back as the fifteenth century. Even though eco-nomic leadership has shifted from country to country, core-periphery relationships are still evident. However, what is not evident or agreed among scholars and practitioners alike, is the impact of core-periphery relationships on economic development.

The second section examines the concept of peripherality by juxtaposing the common characteristics of peripherality and re-gional imbalance against the advantages of operating from the core. The central thesis is that there are inherent economic disad-vantages associated with a peripheral location. As a result, a number of barriers to development in peripheral regions can arise and may have a significant impact on regional economic develop-ment.

Finally the chapter concludes by discussing the role of distance in the internationalisation of the firm and by reviewing the available empirical evidence confronting that body of spatial theory that purports to explain the geography of international trade, with a view to ascertaining whether or not the expectations derived from theory are supported.

2.2 HISTORICAL EVOLUTION

Economic history provides a rich source of examples illustrating how economic development within any geographic area has been unevenly distributed. For example, a north-south pattern of regional development is evident in the economic history of Italy, Germany and the USA, with the industrialised north linked to a more rural south. Indeed, the industrial heart or core of Europe sometimes referred to as the European Golden Triangle extends from London across to Hamburg and south to Paris, down the Rhine and Rhône valleys to the southern parallel from Marseilles across through Milan to Turin. Outside of this triangle are the peripheral regions which include Ireland, Portugal, Spain, Greece, southern Italy and northern Scotland. This core-periphery structure is not a recent phenomenon, in fact, a core-periphery structure emerges as far back as the fifteenth century. A brief historical review of world trade highlights this core-periphery pattern.

Early patterns of long-distance trade focused on luxury goods and rare items and the volume of this trade was very small. However, international trade activity increased dramatically in the late fifteenth and early sixteenth centuries in a small core of European maritime nations principally England, the Netherlands, France, Spain and Portugal. These countries, reflecting the prevailing political philosophy of the day, 'mercantilism,' measured their wealth in terms of their ability to regulate their external trade, acquire overseas colonies and increase their holdings of precious metals (mainly gold and silver). Initially, the core of international trade centred on Spain, and to a lesser extent, Portugal. Both of these countries had colonies in the Americas, which provided a rich source of materials and subsequent markets for their manufactured goods. However, by the middle of the seventeenth century this trade dominance had shifted to England, the Netherlands and France as the core, with Spain and Portugal declining to semi-periphery with their colonies in the Americas becoming the periphery (Dicken, 1986).

Trade developed over the next century along the tripartite geographical structure of core, semi-periphery and periphery. This pattern was interrupted by the industrialisation of Britain, which gradually became the core. The nature and geographical pattern of world trade changed to one where Britain (the core) exported manufactured goods throughout the world and imported raw materials, especially from its colonies. Dicken (1986, p. 13) contends that a new pattern of geographical specialisation had emerged in the form of a new international division of labour:

> where the core produced most of the world's manufactured goods, the periphery were the source of materials and foodstuffs for the core nations and also markets for manufactured goods from the core.

As a result, Britain came to dominate world trade. However, Britain's industrial leadership did not go undisputed. During the last quarter of the nineteenth century industrial production shifted to the United States and Germany, who pursued protective policies to nurture their industrial development. Even though economic leadership shifted from country to country, the core-periphery relationship was maintained, to a large extent, by the exercise of colonial power by most of the core nations. Indeed, Dicken (1986, p. 15) argues that:

> despite such historical shifts in the centre of gravity of the world economic system, the roles of core and periphery in the geographical divisions of labour became increasingly clearly demarcated. Industrial production was pre-eminently a core activity. Industrial goods were both traded between core nations and also exported to the periphery. Conversely, the periphery's role was a dual one. First, it supplied the core with primary commodities — raw materials for transformation into manufactured products in the core; foodstuffs to help feed the industrial nations. Second, it purchased manufactured goods from the core, particularly capital goods in the form of machinery and equipment.

2.3 POST-WAR CHANGES IN INTERNATIONAL TRADE

World trade has not continued uninterrupted. Periods of rapid growth of production and trade and of geographical expansion were punctuated by periods of stagnation and recession. The Second World War in many ways provided a new beginning. The world economic order reflected the new political realities, particularly the sharp distinction between East and West. The West reflected the economic system and political dominance of the United States, while the East created its own economic system under Soviet dominance. Apart from these two core power blocs was the so-called 'Third World', which proved to be another variable with implications for the development of subsequent trade patterns. In addition, three international constitutions, namely, the International Monetary Fund (IMF), the World Bank and the General Agreement on Tariffs and Trade (GATT) were set up to provide the international framework in which to rebuild the world economy. The IMF and World Bank arose out of the Bretton Woods conference. The primary purpose of the IMF was to encourage international monetary co-operation among nations through a set of rules for world payments and currencies on the basis of fixed exchange rates in which the United States dollar played the central role. Much of the finance for reconstruction came as 'Marshall Aid'. The purpose of GATT was to reduce tariff barriers and to prohibit other types of trade discrimination. In essence, GATT reflected a desire not to return to the protectionist policies of the 1930s. These institutions were to play a vital role and had a major influence in shaping the world economy.

The increase in growth rates after the war and up to the early 1970s exceeded any previously experienced. The distinguishing feature of growth patterns during this period was that trade increased more rapidly than production. This reflected the increased internationalisation of economic activities. However, there was considerable variation in these growth rates from country to country.

The post-war economic boom continued up to the early 1970s and came to an abrupt end with the OPEC decision in October 1973 to raise oil prices by 400 per cent. However, not all commentators would accept the singular impact of the OPEC decision in causing world recession. Indeed, commodity prices and labour costs had risen sharply since the mid 1960s.

Although a broad core-periphery structure was still evident, its form had changed. In particular, substantial changes in the relative positions of the old established core economies occurred, particularly the shift from British to United States dominance, coupled with the rise of Germany and the emergence of Japan as a leading manufacturing nation, and the rapid growth of manufacturing production and trade in a number of countries on the periphery. One notable outcome of these changes was that manufacturing was no longer almost exclusively a core activity as it had tended to be in the previous last two hundred years (Dicken, 1986). Apart from Japan, new industrial countries (NICs) particularly those in Asia have achieved the most spectacular growth rates. Accordingly, the centre of gravity of the world manufacturing system has begun to shift towards the Pacific.

More recently, the dynamism of the Pacific Rim is gradually breaking down the old economic order that was dominated by the older industrialised countries. What is emerging is a more diversified world order in which, for the first time, developing countries will have a significant economic weight. The World Bank forecasts that, over the next ten years, developing countries and the new transition economies will grow by nearly 5 per cent a year, compared with an average rate of 2.7 per cent in the richer industrial world.

Already, we are witnessing a significant shift in European architecture. Europe's centre of gravity is shifting due to projected enlargement. Scandinavian countries and Austria have recently joined, and further enlargement is likely to include the countries of Central Europe.

The recent Vision 2010 Trade and Market Development Report (1995) pointed to a number of trends in world trade which, it argues, will have a considerable impact on the centre of economic gravity. Specifically, moves towards closer integration, such as the North American Free Trade Area (NAFTA) and the Asia-Pacific Economic Co-operation (APEC) forum, are significant not only in the size of the market they create but in their ability to act as a magnet for other countries to join them, and thus contribute to the shifting centre of economic gravity towards the countries of their region.

In addition, the Vision 2010 report points to the changing attitude to regulation and trade. Governments have intervened extensively in trade with both a protectionist and export-promotion intent. However, by the year 2010, it is argued that traditional forms of trade intervention will have substantially disappeared. The current GATT Uruguay Round and future rounds will ensure that import restrictions and tariffs will decline to insignificant levels. The establishment of the World Trade Organisation and the more effective dispute-settlement mechanisms agreed in the Final Act of the Uruguay Round are important guarantors of this development.

This section traced the geographical shifts in the centre of economic gravity. Even though economic leadership shifted from country to country, there is evidence to support the hypothesis that a core-periphery structure can be identified as a common thread through the history of world trade. Although there are clearly elements of continuity, some quite dramatic changes have occurred, such as the shift towards the Asia-Pacific region, and within Europe, towards the East. Accordingly, the relatively simple core-periphery structure based on the traditional division of labour is now being transformed into a newer, more complex structure. Moreover, a number of studies have advocated that these geographical shifts exacerbate the disadvantages of peripherality. Accordingly, the next section examines the concept of peripherality, identifying the common characteristics and discusses the proposition that there are inherent economic disadvantages associated with the periphery.

2.4 CORE-PERIPHERY RELATIONSHIPS

This section examines the concept of peripherality by juxtaposing the common characteristics of peripherality and regional imbalance against the advantages of operating from the core. As a result, a number of barriers to development are highlighted and their impact on economic development discussed.

The concept of peripherality is primarily discussed and debated in terms of geographical remoteness from the core. The central thesis highlighted in the literature on peripherality is that there are inherent economic disadvantages associated with a peripheral location. As a result, a number of barriers to development in peripheral regions can arise and may have a significant impact on regional economic development.

Analysing core-periphery relationships is usually motivated by the assumption that there are advantages of operating at the centre. Accordingly, it is important to define the concept of centrality and to articulate the advantages commonly associated with it. Centrality can be loosely and somewhat simply defined as the areas where important economic activities are concentrated. Cuddy and Keane (1990, p. 381) refer to the core as areas where 'the dynamic sectors of production, the key economic decision-making units and the entities that wield market power are concentrated'.

The Irish Trade Board (1992) identified in studies of various countries and regions a number of common characteristics of peripherality. These studies were principally concerned with understanding why differences existed between the core and the periphery. A number of common characteristics emerged from these studies indicating why peripheral countries are inherently economically disadvantaged compared with the countries at the core. Specifically, smaller countries in the periphery have not developed a cohesive, horizontal and well-structured production base and therefore, the demands on government industrial policies are far-reaching. The majority of enterprises in these regions are small and many of the larger enterprises are controlled by foreign capital. In addition, the indigenous sectors in these peripheral regions are dominated by traditional labour-intensive industries which are highly exposed to growing competition from low-wage countries, which rules out any competitive advantages. Selwyn (1979) suggests that a culture of dependency is evidenced in these periphery countries, which also manifests itself in a loss of dynamism and a comparative lack of innovation as new ideas are mainly imported from the core. Indeed, information flows tended to be uni-directional from the core to the periphery. In addition, the Selwyn study found that internal linkages tended to be weak and that there was evidence of greater government involvement in economic development in the periphery.

Furthermore, the Irish Trade Board (1992) suggests that central location in an economy bears a number of significant advantages for manufacturing and services companies. The most obvious of these are the direct advantages related to market access. Its study contends that market access is a fundamental issue for any business and easy access not only minimises distance costs to the widest possible market area, but is also conducive to the achievement of economies of scale as the productive capacity of firms is increased to service larger markets. Likewise, Kilby (1980) highlights the importance of transport costs and argues that the need to minimise transport costs has favoured the Golden Triangle countries in the EU and has operated to the disadvantage of the peripheral industrial countries.

A number of other studies provide supporting evidence to the above contention. Goddard's (1983) study highlights the cost and quality of telecommunications between the core and periphery countries. The PIEDA (1984) study provides additional evidence and identifies additional costs associated with remoteness from

the core. This research concludes that these other costs revolve
around the difficulties of maintaining market contact and ensuring input supply at a distance. Indeed, it is argued that centrally-
located firms have an additional competitive advantage derived
from the greater ease of access to buyers and suppliers. As a result, central location enables such firms to maximise customer
contact and market knowledge and, consequently, to be more responsive to changes in market conditions.

A number of other advantages are identified in the Irish Trade
Board's report (1992, p. 8). Specifically, the report argues that the
impact of agglomeration economics, with the concentration of economic activity in the centre, generated its own momentum. The
report contends that:

> the growth of a leading sector industry attracts sub-supply in-
> dustries and support services which themselves develop and
> diversify. The close functional linkages which grow between
> firms and the ready access to buyers, suppliers and services
> (including financial services and capital markets) contribute
> to cost savings, product development and other marketing
> advantages.

In addressing this issue, Keeble et al. (1988) argue that innovations are often first adapted at the centre before spreading to
more peripheral regions at a later stage. These authors offer a
number of reasons to explain this view. They suggest that central
location gives maximum access to national and international information networks and that new product launches are less risky
in central areas where potential customers are more accessible,
generally wealthier and more open to new ideas. They also contend that core regions tend to contain above average concentrations of highly qualified workers, research scientists and technologists. In Ireland, NESC (1989) supported this view and highlighted that research in other countries had shown that firms in
peripheral regions undertake significantly less innovation than
firms in more central regions.

The Irish Trade Board (1992, p. 10) also draws attention to the
impact of the core on labour market characteristics. The report
concludes that:

> the concentration of economic activity and product development
> at the centre is inevitably paralleled by a concentration of
> skilled manpower. This pattern of industrial development at the

centre . . . activates high skill levels and provides opportunities
which encourage migration to the centre from other regions.
Technical knowledge is also enhanced and high level research
and development, marketing and corporate decision-making
functions also tend to be concentrated in the centre.

All of the above studies suggest that there are inherent economic
advantages associated with operating at the centre and, on the
other hand, there are inherent economic disadvantages associated
with operating at the periphery. The conclusion that may be
drawn from the above evidence is that inherent economic disadvantages are associated with operating at the periphery and that
these can give rise to a number of barriers to economic development. The main contention is that the speed and direction of economic development in these regions is largely dependent on the
extent to which these barriers can be overcome.

The advantages of centrality coupled with the common characteristics of peripherality, can inhibit developments in peripheral
regions. In fact, the barriers to the development of peripheral regions can be considered as the converse of the advantages of centrality and are major factors in the shaping of peripheral regions
and their economies. The main barriers are related to distance
costs and the absence of scale economies. Such costs are often
borne as additional costs by suppliers. Cuddy and Keane (1990)
identified a number of direct and indirect costs as a result of remoteness. The direct costs include transport, telecommunications,
postal, information-gathering, and storage costs.

Transport costs are the most obvious additional direct costs associated with distance from the market. The greater the distance
to markets, the greater the costs involved, and, therefore, the
greater the disadvantage. These costs are not just related to the
movement of goods, but also to the movement of personnel and to
the physical cost of keeping in touch with the market on both the
input and the output side. Of course, not all authors would agree
that transport costs are such an additional barrier. Indeed, research on the transport operations of Scottish-based manufacturers, for example, appear to challenge the traditional view of peripheral regions as being severely handicapped by their location
(McKinnon, Chapter 12).

Telecommunications, postal and information-gathering costs
are also related to distance from markets. Distance costs related
to peripheral locations can inhibit the cultivation of direct per-

sonal relationships between buyers and sellers and may place restrictions on the ability of firms to gather vital information on
changing market trends and customer requirements. The Irish
Trade Board (1992) suggests that this distance factor is a significant barrier, not in terms of the actual difficulties which it creates,
but in relation to *perceived* difficulties. Indeed, the perceptions of
distance-related problems in servicing markets and customers
may exist on both the demand and supply sides. The contention is
that buyers in the market centre may be reluctant to buy for a
variety of reasons including perceived risks of breakdown in
supplies and doubts about quality control. On the other hand,
suppliers at the periphery may also lack confidence in attempting
to break into what they perceived as the large, sophisticated and
technically demanding market centre. The major implications for
companies on the periphery are that they may have to expend
substantial expenditures of time, effort and money by management and marketing executives to overcome these perceptions. In
addition, the cost of storage can be an additional cost, because a
higher average stock may have to be held if the plant is distant
from the market and the ability of firms to implement a 'just-in-
time' regime is questioned as the distance from the market
increases.

Besides the obvious direct costs associated with distance to
market, Cuddy and Keane (1990, p. 383) highlight a number of
indirect costs that are not as obvious. They suggest that, because
of the limited local market in peripheral regions, the growth of the
firm is constrained, even where monopolistic structures exist. The
main impact is the loss of the economies of scale and, as a result,
the impairment of economic efficiency.

As a result, these authors conclude that:

> firms in peripheral regions in general tend to lag behind in
> technological dynamism and innovation. They tend to concen-
> trate on production at the end, rather than at the beginning, of
> the product cycle.

This contention is addressed elsewhere in this book (see Jones-
Evans, McPherson and Taggart and Taggart).

2.5 ECONOMIC IMPACT OF PERIPHERALITY

The general characteristics of peripheral regions and the barriers
to their economic development are summarised above. At this

point it is appropriate to consider the evidence on the economic impact of peripherality. The Irish Trade Board (1992), in its study, considered the broad impact of major current developments such as the completion of the Single European Market, European Monetary Union, GATT and CAP reform, and further enlargements of the EU are considered. Each of these developments were analysed in the study and the conclusions are outlined below.

With respect to the impact of the Single European Market, the study concluded that, sectors in Ireland identified by the EU as being the most sensitive to the '1992' process have a large presence of foreign-owned, multinational-controlled firms, and that there is no guarantee that these foreign-owned firms will avail of the opportunities created by the Single European Market by expanding production in their plants in Ireland. Similarly, the EU has concluded that there will be a reduction in costs for both the public and private sectors, but the implications of their analysis is that the balance of gains will favour the more central regions. In the field of transport, however, the liberalisation of transport services should be of benefit in terms of expanded access links and a possible downward pressure on air and sea fares.

The study considered the impact of completing monetary union and suggested that further movement towards economic and monetary union would require a resource transfer of such scale as to make such a budget unattractive and unacceptable to member states.

With respect to the impact of GATT and CAP Reform the study concluded that not only would losses be incurred by primary producers but also the reforms are likely to inhibit the expansion and development of the food industry in Ireland by accentuating the seasonality of farm production.

The authors of the study further argue that if the EU membership grows to include more Eastern European countries, the centre of gravity would position Ireland in a more extreme peripheral position especially as far as intangible distance costs are concerned. In conclusion, the study suggested that the major challenge ahead for the EU is to ensure that the gap between the peripheral regions and the centre is not widened by the internal market.

The above set of arguments would seem to suggest that there are indeed inherent economic disadvantages associated with peripheral location.This is, however, only one side of the argument and there is little consensus among scholars on this issue. Indeed, empirical evidence confronts the contribution of spatial theory that purports to explain the geography of international trade. In particular, a number of studies and reports indicate that distance (transfer cost) is not a very important factor. The next section examines the evidence confronting these theories on geographical location, particularly in the context of the role of distance in international business.

2.6 DISTANCE AND INTERNATIONALISATION.

The conventional wisdom suggests that there are inherent economic disadvantages associated with the periphery. This can only be assessed by examining the available empirical evidence confronting these theories with a view to assessing whether or not it supports the expectations derived from them. In doing so, it is first necessary to discuss the role of distance in the internationalisation of the firm.

This section examines the evidence confronting these theories on geographical location paying particular attention to the role of distance. The concept of distance and in particular the notion of psychic distance has featured extensively in a number of theories purporting to explain or account for the internationalisation of the firm. Two such approaches towards how firms internationalise, the stages theory of the internationalisation process and the network perspective on internationalisation, are discussed here. These theories explicate the role of distance in the internationalisation of firms.

The stages theory of internationalisation posits that firms proceed in a consistent stepwise fashion along some organisational continuum as they develop their international activities. In attempting to internationalise, various aspects of direct physical barriers become significant. In particular, the location of the firms involved in the transactions is seen to have an impact on the process of international marketing. Tornroos (1989) examines the concept of distance on a number of levels:

- physical distance barriers

- cultural features and distance

- cognitive and psychological features

- different levels internationally and distance.

As the internationalisation process of a firm proceeds, physical distances can form a critical obstacle for the marketing process between firms. Tornroos (1989, p. 128) states the case as follows:

> In physical terms industrial businesses often spend large amounts of time, money, and personnel on creating efficient logistics systems between the firms concerned, and especially for the firms individually. The seller is often obliged to concentrate on the role of transportation and physical distribution to find ways of creating systems which satisfy the buyer. . . . For many firms the reliance on external sources is quite important. This means that the interaction process is not influenced only by the selling and buying firms, but also other influences.

Besides the physical distribution management, logistics, time management and reliance on external firms, physical distance can also create cultural, communication, and other problems in carrying out interaction activities between firms. The cultural distance variables may be outlined in terms of the problems in the interaction process and the atmosphere between the interacting parties. Johanson and Wiedersheim-Paul,(1975, p. 308) suggest that the concept of psychic distance may prove useful here. These authors define the concept of psychic distance as follows:

> factors preventing or disturbing the flows of information between firms and market. Examples of such factors are differences in language, culture, political systems, level of education, and the level of industrial development.

Several studies of international business place considerable emphasis on the role of physical and psychic distance in international business. Indeed, these studies have indicated that internationalisation of the firm is a process in which the firms gradually increase their international involvement (Johanson and Wiedersheim-Paul, 1975; Johanson and Vahlne, 1977). Johanson and Vahlne (1977) developed a model of the internationalisation process of the firm that focuses on the development of the individual firm and particularly on its gradual acquisition, integration, and use of knowledge about foreign markets and operations and on its successively increasing commitment to foreign markets. The basic assumptions of the model are that lack of such knowledge is an important obstacle to the development of international operations and that the necessary knowledge can be

acquired mainly through operations abroad. The model is based
on empirical observations from studies in international business
at the University of Uppsala which show that Swedish firms often
develop their international operations in small steps rather than
by making large foreign production investment at single points in
time (see Sölvell and Zander, Chapter 14). Typically, firms start
exporting to a country via an agent, then, at a later stage, establish a sales subsidiary, and eventually, in some cases, begin production in the host country. With respect to the development of
operations in individual countries, Johanson and Wiedersheim-
Paul (1975) distinguish between four different stages: firstly, no
regular export activities; secondly, export via independent representatives (agents): thirdly, sales subsidiary and finally host-
country production/manufacturing

Of particular interest in the above stages is the relationship
between each stage and psychic distance. Agency establishments
are made primarily during the early stages of internationalisation
which are generally closely related to psychic distance. However,
extension by sales subsidiary or production/manufacturing could
be expected to be influenced primarily by the market size as it
generally requires a larger minimum resource commitment than
an independent representative.

Studies of export companies in Sweden (Forsgren and Johanson, 1992) provide evidence of how the concept of psychic distance
is correlated with geographic distance. This research indicates
that almost all sales subsidiaries have been established through
acquisition of the former agent or have been organised around
some person employed by the agent. Most of the establishments
were occasioned by various kinds of economic crises in the agent
firms. Sales to a market by the agent had preceded establishment
of a sales subsidiary. Similarly, local production was generally
preceded by sales subsidiaries. The international development of
these firms seems to be in accordance with the incremental internationalisation process view discussed above, with psychic distance playing a significant role at the agency-development stage.

Explanations of the internationalisation of the firm have also
been considered from a network perspective. This perspective
starts from the assumption that international business takes
place in a network setting, where different business actors are
linked to each other through direct and indirect business
relationships. As a result, managing international business, is a
matter of establishing, developing and maintaining the firm's

positions in the international business networks (Johanson and Mattsson, 1988).

It is important at this point to distinguish between these two approaches to internationalisation as the theoretical foundations of the network perspective give rise to a different set of assumptions and characteristics. The next section describes these assumptions and outlines the characteristics of the network perspective.

2.7 THE NETWORK PERSPECTIVE

The network perspective has a number of theoretical foundations principally empirical studies of the Industrial Marketing and Purchasing (IMP) Group (Håkansson, 1982), social exchange theory and resource dependence theory which give rise to a number of assumptions. A basic assumption in the network perspective is that the individual firm is dependent on resources controlled by other firms. Because of the interdependences of firms, the use of an asset in one firm is dependent on the use of other firm's assets (Johanson and Mattsson, 1987). This dependency between firms has to be co-ordinated. Co-ordination takes place through firms interacting in the network, in contrast to the traditional market model where co-ordination is achieved by organisational hierarchy or through the price mechanism.

In the atomistic perspective typically assumed by economics, individual actors are depicted as making choices and acting without regard to the behaviour of other actors. This ignores the social context within which the social actors are embedded (Knoke and Kuklinski, 1982). The network perspective places greater emphasis on contextuality and time and incorporates two significant assumptions about social behaviour. Knoke and Kuklinski, (1982, p,173) describes these assumptions as follows, firstly:

> any actor typically participates in a social system involving many other actors, who are significant reference points in one another's decisions,

and thus their relationship may affect each other's perceptions, beliefs and actions, and secondly:

> by emphasising the relationship between actors, within which individual actors are embedded, allows social phenomena that

has no existence at the level of the individual actor to be detected.

Therefore, a firm's activities are not performed in isolation. They are more or less embedded in the wider web of business activities. These business activities are co-ordinated through interactions between firms. This interaction process develops over time.

The traditional business literature places the single firm as the unit of analysis. The firm is assumed to have a distinct boundary which separates it from its environment. In contrast, the network model assumes that business takes place in a network setting where different business actors are linked to each other through direct and indirect relationships. The network of relationships is the unit of analysis, not the individual firm.

The network perspective assumes that there is no distinct boundary between the firm and its environment. The environment is not transparent to managers. Rather than viewing the environment as a set of separate political-legal, competitive, cultural and social forces, managers perceive their meaning of these forces through enactment (Forsgren and Johanson, 1992). This enactment occurs through the everyday interaction between firms and is not based on single discrete decisions. The interaction involves individuals within firms on every level and lacks the traditional dominant top-management perspective. These individuals have different interests, and within the context of interacting with other individuals, have considerable opportunities to pursue their self-interest. Therefore the firm as a whole entity is not assumed or taken for granted; rather it is the relationship between firms that is important.

Another basic assumption of the network perspective is that networks are essentially heterogeneous in nature (Hagg and Johanson, 1983). The sources of heterogeneity are rooted in matching heterogeneous resources to heterogeneous demands given that individuals or individual firms needs can be met in a variety of different ways. An additional source of heterogeneity lies in the firms involved in the network. Each firm is individual in its structure, employer preferences, history, resources and the role it chooses, or may be forced, to play in the transformation process will be determined partly by these factors (Easton, 1992).

In conclusion, the combined assumptions of the network perspective presents an alternate platform to the analysis of how business is co-ordinated. The dependency assumption between firms motivates firms to co-ordinate their interactions in relationships. Therefore, all these activities are considered in the context of these relationships. These relationships cannot be made overnight and take time to develop. The development of those relationships is activated by individuals at all levels in the firm and not just by top management. Everyday interaction between individuals, focusing on current activities and not single discrete decisions, are the means by which relationships are developed. The unit of analysis is the network of relationships the firm has, and the firm is not considered separate from its environment. These assumptions give rise to an unique set of characteristics. In particular, the characteristics of a network are described as sets of connected exchange relationships between actors controlling business activities (Cook and Emerson, 1984).

The emphasis on connection is important because networks emerge and develop as a consequence of interactions. Business activities are co-ordinated through interactions between firms in the network. When firms interact with each other they exchange resources, products and services. Through interaction, they influence and adapt to each other's ways of performing activities. This interaction process develops over time, parties have to learn about each other's ways of doing and viewing things and how to interpret each other's acts (Håkansson and Johanson, 1988).

Relationships form the context in which interactions take place. Johanson and Mattsson (1985) distinguish between inter-firm relationships and interaction behaviour. The relationship elements of behaviour tends to be long term in nature, and comprises the processes by which firms adjust products, production and routines, whereas interactions represent the day-to-day exchanges of a business.

Once all parties in buyer-seller relationships recognise the need for greater co-operation in an equal-partner relationship, each side can begin the change process by addressing the activities where it best can contribute. A necessary prerequisite for this is familiarity with each other's processes, so that joint efforts are constantly made to improve operations and thus reduce costs, whilst allowing for the price increases that are outside their control (Fynes and Ainamo, 1996).

Relationships are the *sine qua non* of the network perspective and consist of four elements: mutual orientation, dependency, bonds and investments (Easton, 1992). Inter-firm relationship is a mutual orientation of two firms towards each other. This implies that the firms are prepared to interact with each other and expect each other to do so (Johanson and Mattsson, 1987). A number of reasons have been identified to explain this mutual orientation. Hagg and Johanson (1983) suggest that relationships allow a more effective acquisition of resources and sale of product.

Another rationale for mutual orientation concerns a firm's ability to exploit network access (Easton, 1992). Such relationships allow access to resources consisting of physical, financial and human assets.

Dependence is the second element used to describe networks as relationships and in some senses may be regarded as the price a firm may have to pay for the benefits that a relationship bestows. It also brings with it the problems of power and control (Easton, 1992).

The third element describing the characteristics of networks as relationships is the bond between firms. Bonds of various kinds are developed between firms: technical, planning, knowledge, socio-economic and legal. These bonds can be exemplified by product and process adjustments, logistical co-ordination, knowledge about the counterpart, personal confidence and liking, special credit arrangements, and long-term contracts (Johanson and Mattsson, 1987).

Johanson and Mattsson (1986) identify investment as the fourth element of networks as relationships, and define investments as being processes in which resources are committed in order to create, build or acquire assets which can be used in the future.

If relationships are the *sine qua non* of the network perspective, then, according to Cunningham and Homse (1986), the character of business relationships is a consequence of the interaction strategies of the parties. Firms have different interaction strategies towards each other depending on the nature of the relationships. Interacting with each other to develop or solve a technical problem is different to the interaction that takes place when emphasising sales volume. Therefore, both interaction strategies and relationships are intertwined.

The four elements described above are interrelated and imply that a firm's activities are cumulative processes. Because of the cumulative nature of business activities, the network position of a firm is an important concept. Mattsson (1984) defines a position as a role that the organisation has for other organisations that it is related to, directly or indirectly. Such positions are the result of mutual orientation, dependency between firms, different kinds of bonds and investments.

Position is inherently a dialectical concept, in the sense that it provides the development possibilities and constraints of the firm in the network. A firm's current position is determined by earlier activities in the network both by the firm itself and by other firms. Thus, history is important. Mattsson (1984) outlines four characteristics of position:

- the role the firm has for the other firms

- the identity of the other firms with which the firm has direct relationships and indirect relations in the network

- the importance of the firm in the network

- the strength of the relationships with the other firm.

The position concept provides a metaphor to describe network dynamics and change. A change in position for any one firm will change the relative positions of other firms. Network positions are also the result of the different power some actors have over the activities. Power (the ability to influence the decisions or actions of others) is the central concept in network analysis (Thorelli, 1986). Many relationships are asymmetrical with respect to power. The power structure dictates the way in which the network both operates and develops.

The Swedish pulp and paper cluster is a good illustration of how a Swedish firms have built world-leading positions throughout a large number of related industries, including a dense network of manufacturers of speciality inputs, machinery, and services as well as buyer industries such as liquid packaging (see Sölvell and Zander, Chapter 14).

The assumption that business networks consist of lasting exchange relationships does not suggest that network structures can be characterised as static. On the contrary, the structure changes continually: as new relationships are established, existing relationships can be further developed or terminated. Gradual changes are made and accumulate over the years, resulting in a radical change to the structure of the network. These changes reflect the dynamic characteristics of networks. Therefore, while network structures are considered stable, they are not static. Instead, they evolve gradually in response to changes external and internal to the network.

Two dialectical processes in networks are competition and co-operation (Easton, 1992). While the network perspective emphasises co-operation, the reality is that in every exchange relationship there is potential conflict between the actors. Hagg and Johanson (1983) argue that potential conflict or competition in the traditional sense is replaced by rivalry for the control of resources.

This rivalry is necessary because for a network to exist there must be at least a partial overlap in domain (Thorelli, 1986). Thorelli defines the domain of any organisation in terms of five dimensions:

- product (or service) offered the environment

- clientele served

- functions performed

- territory

- time.

Should there be total domain overlap, then we have a case of head-on competition. Therefore complete overlap implies competition, while partial overlap implies networking.

Indirect relationships are another important characteristic of networks to be considered. Easton (1992) defines indirect relationship as the relationship between two firms which are not directly related but which is mediated by a third firm with which they both have relationships.

Mattsson (1986) identifies seven dimensions which can be used to characterise indirect relationships. They include distance from a focal firm; vertical or horizontal nature; complementary or competitive; narrow or wide connection; the strength, kind and content of the direct bonds concerned; the interdependency of the direct relations concerned and the value added of a focal firm's direct relationship. The importance of indirect relationships can be seen in the way they affect the structure of the network. Firms control resources directly and indirectly, so in every network there is a power structure where different firms can influence the action of other firms, which ultimately affects the development of the network. The dynamic combination of direct and indirect business relationships leads to the important conclusions that markets are more or less stable networks of business relationships (Hagg and Johanson, 1983).

The assumption that there is no distinct boundary between the firm and its environment gives the network the characteristic that boundaries are arbitrary and depend on the perspectives, intentions and interpretations of the actors (Håkansson and Johanson, 1986). Boundaries can be drawn for analytical purposes on the basis of technology, product, process, country or focal organisation.

Networks are opaque. Everybody is aware of the existence of business relationships but no one can have a clear view of other relationships that they own. This is particularly true of indirect relationships. It is difficult to view relationships from the outside because they are subtle phenomena, in that intentions, interpretations and expectations are important. Håkansson and Johanson (1986) claim that the opaqueness of networks has to do with the complexity and fluidity of the interaction; actors have a clear view of their own interaction and bonds with other actors even if the views of interacting actors are not necessarily consistent.

Finally, the network approach can be further distinguished by comparing the approach to the traditional marketing-mix model. The exchange partners to the network approach are active and mutually dependent, in contrast to the passive, independent approach of the marketing-mix model. Both buyer and seller initiate exchange in the network approach. The main emphasis is to establish, develop, maintain and sometimes breakup relationships as against the optimisation focus of the marketing-mix approach.

The network model implies that it is more relevant to use the concept of psychic distance at the level of the firm. There is a psychic distance between two firms from different cultural settings and this distance is affected by their interaction and it affects their interaction with each other. Thus the distance is a relationship specific factor. The interaction between, for instance, a buyer and a seller leads to the development of an atmosphere in which the psychic distance is one component. This atmosphere is dependent on the character of the specific relationship rather than on general differences on a country level (Hallen and Wiedersheim-Paul, 1982).

In summary, the above two theories or approaches to internationalisation attempt to explicate the role of distance in the internationalisation of the firm. Psychic distance plays a significant pole at the agency development stage in the stages theory of internationalisation. In contract, in the network perspective to internationalisation, the concept of psychic distance is treated as a relationship specific factor at the level of the firm rather than as some general difference on a country level.

2.8 SPATIAL THEORY AND INTERNATIONAL TRADE

Thus far the role of distance has been considered in the context of two theoretical explanations of the internationalisation process., In order to assess the impact of the role of distance, however, it is necessary to review the available empirical evidence confronting the body of spatial theory that purports to explain the geography of international trade, with a view to examining whether or not the expectations derived from these theories are supported.

A number of spatial theories are described below which provide a partial explanation of the geography of international trade. However, when these theories are confronted with empirical evidence there is limited support for their theoretical contentions.

One such body of theory that attempts to explain the effect of geographical location is the gravity model. This model predicts that the volume of trade should be inversely related to the distance (transfer cost) which separates trade partners. The simple assumption is that firms will supply near markets in preference to more distant ones. Such behaviour at the level of the firm should be evident in the aggregate trade patterns of regions and nations, interaction being strong between areas which are close to each other, and weak where trade partners are distant from each other (Chisholm, 1995).

The gravity model is based on the simple assumption that prices vary according to the distance products have to travel, and that for similar or identical commodities customers are assumed to be price-sensitive. Therefore, everything else being equal, firms will have an advantage if they are near their suppliers and customers. However, the empirical evidence on distance costs portrays a somewhat different picture. Linnemann's (1966) comprehensive attempt to measure international trade flows shows the impact of the distance variable in international trade to be rather small. Johnston (1976), confirming Linnemann's findings, also highlights the instability of the observed-distance effect over time. In addition, the European Commission has published data on the bilateral trade flows between the 12 EU countries in 1958 and 1989 which provides evidence confirming the negligible effect of distance. Chisholm (1995) points to two important conclusions which may be drawn from this evidence. Firstly, the theoretical considerations of the gravity model are less significant than they would lead one to expect. Secondly, an important reason for the apparently minor impact of distance on trade volumes may be found in the somewhat limited role of price in the competitiveness of manufactured products and the limited impact which distance has on ocean freight rates. It appears that non-price characteristics are important, even dominant, in determining the competitiveness of products. What this evidence appears to suggest is that relative location does not greatly matter. Thus the limited empirical research on the gravity model in international trade indicates that distance (transfer cost) is not a very important factor.

Besides the gravity model, two other bodies of spatial theory theoretically suggest that there are inherent advantages to centrality. The first of these, the spatial consequences of economic integration, holds that the formation of an economic union such as the EU will favour countries and regions that are central in the sense that numerous and important barriers to trade have been removed. Reviewing the empirical evidence on the theory of economic integration, Chisholm (1995) concludes that the centralisation thesis derived from the theory of economic union receives scant support. He claims that in practice the expected benefits are hard to quantify and appear to be smaller than many would wish us to believe. If that conclusion is accepted, it follows that peripheral regions or countries have little to fear from economic integration solely on account of their relative location. El-Agraa (1990) suggests that the real significance of economic integration may lie in the political and not the economic arena.

The second body of spatial theory known as cumulative causation postulates a continuing process of growth in central areas that occurs to the detriment of peripheral regions. Fundamental to this theory is the idea of scale economies, and especially external economies of scale. However, when confronted with empirical evidence (Commission of the European Communities, 1991, 1993; Keeble, 1989; Keeble et al., 1986) focusing on the changes over time in the geographical pattern of GDP per capita, unemployment rates and factor prices, as well as information on migration flows, the conclusion that may be drawn is that the prediction derived from cumulative growth theory is not fully substantiated. Neo-classical economic thinking lends support to this conclusion by drawing attention to the relative mobilities of the factors of production, to differences in the cost functions facing firms, and

hence to the role of prices in the allocation of resources between
sectors and places.

2.9 CONCLUSIONS

This chapter focused its attention on how a core-periphery structure can be identified as a common thread through the history of
world trade. Even though economic leadership shifted from country to country, there is evidence to support the hypothesis that a
core-periphery structure can be identified as a common thread
through the history of world trade. However, the traditional, simple core-periphery structure, based on the division of labour, is
being transformed into a newer, more complex structure.

There exists a school of thought which supports the hypothesis
that there are inherent economic disadvantages associated with
operating at the periphery. The conclusion that may be drawn
from these studies is that inherent economic disadvantages are
associated with operating at the periphery and that these can
give rise to a number of barriers to economic development. The
main contention is that the speed and direction of economic development in these regions is largely dependent on the extent to
which these barriers can be overcome.

The central thesis highlighted in the debate on peripherality is
that there are inherent economic disadvantages associated with
peripheral location. As a result, a number of barriers to development in peripheral regions can arise, and may have a significant
impact on regional economic development. The main barriers relate to distance costs and the absence of scale economies. Besides
the direct costs associated with distance there are indirect costs
that are due to the limited local market in peripheral regions.

In considering the broad impact of major current developments
such as the completion of the Single European Market, European
Monetary Union, GATT and CAP reform, and further enlargements of the EU, the overall conclusion from this body of evidence
would suggest that there are indeed inherent economic disadvantages associated with peripheral location.

There are two sides to the debate, however. In fact, there appears to be little consensus among scholars for the above conclusions. Indeed, when that body of spatial theory that purports to
explain the geography of international trade is confronted with
empirical evidence there seems to be scant support for the theoretical propositions. In addressing the role of distance in interna-

tional trade two theories of internationalisation were discussed
that place considerable emphasis on the role of physical and psychic distance in international trade. The stages theory of internationalisation provides evidence of how the concept of psychic distance is correlated with geographical distance. On the other hand,
the network model implies that it is more relevant to use the concept of psychic distance at the level of the firm, and that distance
is a relationship-specific factor rather than a country-level
phenomenon.

In testing the theoretical framework which suggests that distance is an important factor in international trade, a number of
spatial theories were confronted with empirical evidence. The
overall conclusions were, firstly, that the theoretical considerations of the gravity model were less significant than they would
lead one to expect. Secondly, an important reason for the apparently small impact of distance on trade volumes may be found in
the somewhat limited role of price in the competitiveness of
manufactured products and the small impact which distance had
on ocean freight rates.

With respect to the spatial consequences of economic integration, the main conclusion after reviewing the empirical evidence is
that, in practice, the expected benefits are hard to quantify and
appear to be smaller than many would wish us to believe. If that
conclusion is accepted, it follows that peripheral regions or countries have little to fear from economic integration solely on account of their relative location and that the real significance of
economic integration may lie in the political and not the economic
arena.

The diversity of perspectives is addressed by Keeble (1991, p.
53) who concludes that the core-periphery model is overly
simplistic:

> The complexity and variety of economic forces currently at
> work in Europe's regions are too great to be encompassed by
> any single all-embracing theory of economic change. The
> outcomes of these forces at the regional level are moreover not
> inevitable, but contingent upon many factors, not least social
> and political responses by local communities, institutions and
> governments. The result is a regional mosaic of development
> trajectories within Europe, in the evolution of which both
> macro-economic forces and local socio-economic characteristics
> are important.

It is quite clear that the thesis which holds that there are inherent economic disadvantages associated with periphery location is not substantiated. The debate continues. This chapter is a further attempt to clarify the issues involved.

References

An Bord Trachtála (1992), 'Exporting to Europe: An Analysis of the Competitive Position of Ireland's Peripheral Location', Dublin: The Irish Trade Board.

Chisholm, M. (1995), *Britain on the Edge of Europe*, London: Routledge.

Commission of the European Communities (1990), 'One market, one money. An evaluation of the potential benefits and costs of forming an economic and monetary union', Luxembourg: Office for Official Publications of the European Communities.

Commission of the European Communities (1991), 'The Regions in the 1990s. Fourth periodic report on the social and economic situation and development of the regions of the Community', Luxembourg: Office for Official Publications of the European Communities.

Commission of the European Communities (1993), 'Report on progress with regard to economic and monetary convergence and with the implementation of community law concerning the internal market', Luxembourg: Office for Official Publications of the European Communities.

Cook, K. S. and Emerson, R. (1984), 'Exchange Networks and the Analysis of Complex Organisations', *Research in the Sociology of Organisations*, Vol. 3, Greenwich, CT: JAI Press, pp. 1-30.

Cuddy, M. P. and Keane, M. J. (1990), 'Ireland: A Peripheral Region' in *The Single European Market and the Irish Economy* (Eds. Foley, A. and Mulreany, M.,) Dublin: IPA, Chapter 17.

Cunningham, M. T. and Homse, E. (1986), 'Controlling the marketing-purchasing interface: resource development and organisational implications', *Industrial Marketing and Purchasing*, Vol. 1, No. 2, pp. 3-27.

Dicken, P. (1986), *Global Shift: Industrial Change in a Turbulent World*, London: Harper and Row.

Easton, G. (1992), 'Industrial Networks: A Review' in *Industrial Networks: A New View of Reality*. (Eds. Axelsson, B. and Easton, G.) London: Routledge, pp. 3-27.

El-Agraa, A. M. (1990), 'The theory of economic integration' in *Economics of the European Community* (Ed. El-Agraa, A. M.), Hemel Hempstead: Philips Allan, pp. 79-96.

Forsgren, M. and Johanson, J. (1992), *Managing Networks in International Business*, Philadelphia: Gordon and Breach.

Fynes, B. and Ainamo, A. (1996), 'Organisational Learning in Buyer-Supplier Relationships: A Case Study of Apple Ireland', Working Paper No. 96-1, Centre for Quality and Services Management, Graduate School of Business, University College Dublin.

Goddard, J. B. (1983), 'Study of the Effects of Less Favoured Regions of the Community', Luxembourg: Office for Official Publications of the European Communities.

Hagg, I. and Johanson, J. (1983), 'Firms in Networks', Stockholm: Business and Social Research Institute.

Håkansson, H. and Johanson, J. (1988), 'Formal and Informal Cooperation Strategies in International Industrial Networks' in *Cooperative strategies in International Business* (Eds. Contractor, F. J. and Lorange, P.) Lexington, MA: Lexington Books, pp. 369-379.

Håkansson, H. (ed.) (1982), *International Marketing and Purchasing of Industrial Goods. An Interaction Approach*, Chichester, UK: John Wiley and Sons.

Hallen, L. and Wiedersheim-Paul, F. (1982), 'Psychic Distance in International Marketing'. Working Paper 1982/3, Department of Business Administration, Uppsala University, Sweden.

Hammarkvist, K. O., Hakansson, H. and Mattsson, L.(1982), *Marketing for Competitive Power*, Malmø: Liber.

Johanson, J. and Mattsson, L. (1988) 'Internationalisation in Industrial Systems — A Network Approach' in *Strategies in Global*

Competition (Eds. Hood, N. and Vahlne, J.E.), New York: Croom Helm, pp. 287-314.

Johanson, J. and Vahlne, J. E. (1977), 'The Internationalisation Process of the Firm — A Model of Knowledge Development and Increasing Foreign Market Commitments', *Journal of International Business*, Vol. 8, No. 1, pp. 23-32.

Johanson, J. and Wiedersheim-Paul, F. (1975), 'The Internationalisation of the Firm: Four Swedish cases', *Journal of Management Studies*, October, pp. 305-322.

Johanson, J. and Mattsson, L. (1985), 'Marketing and Market Investments in Industrial Networks,' *International Journal of Research in Marketing*, Vol. 2, No. 3, pp. 185-195.

Johanson, J. and Mattsson, L. (1987), 'Interorganisational Relations in Industrial Systems: A Network Approach Compared with a Transaction Cost Approach', *International Studies of Management Organisation*, Vol. 17, No. 1, pp. 34-48.

Johnston, R. D. (1976), *The World Trading System: Some Enquiries into its Spatial structure*, London: Bell.

Keeble, D. E. (1989), 'Core-Periphery disparities, recession and new regional dynamisms in the European Community', *Geography*, Vol. 74, pp. 1-11.

Keeble, D. E. (1991), 'Core-Periphery disparities and regional restructuring in the European Community' in *Europaische Regionen im Wandel* (Ed. Blotevogel, H.), Dortmund: Dortmunder Vertrieb für Bau- und Plannungsliteratur, pp. 49-69.

Keeble, D. E., Offord, J and Walker, S. (1988), 'Peripheral Regions in a Community of Twelve Member States', Luxembourg: Office for Official Publications of the European Communities.

Kilby, M. L. (1980), 'Industrial Instrument: Must Britain Always Lose Out', Association of British Chambers of Commerce.

Knoke, D. and Kuklinski, J. H. (1982), *Network Analysis*, London: Sage, pp. 9-21.

Linneman, H. (1966), *An Econometric Study of International Trade Flows*, Amsterdam: North Holland.

Mattsson, L, (1984), 'An Application of a Network Approach to Marketing: Defending and changing Market Positions' in *Changing the Course of Marketing. Alternative Paradigms for Widening Marketing Theory* (Eds. Dholakia, N. and Arndt, J.), Greenwich, CT: JAI Press, pp. 263-288.

Mattsson, L. (1986), 'Indirect Relationships in Industrial Networks: A Conceptual Analysis of their Significance,' 3rd IMP International Seminar, IRE, Lyon, France.

National Economic and Social Council (NESC) (1987), 'Ireland in the European Community', Dublin: NESC.

PIEDA (1984), 'Transport Costs in Peripheral Areas', Scottish Economic Planning Department, ESU Research Paper, No. 9.

Selwyn, P. (1979), 'Core-Periphery Relationships' in *Underdeveloped Europe: Studies in Core-Periphery Relationships* (Eds. Seers, D., Schaffer, B., and Kiljanen, M.), Hassocks: Harvester Press.

Thorelli, H. B. (1986), 'Networks: Between Markets and Hierarchies', *Strategic Management Journal*, Vol. 7, No. 1, pp. 37-51.

Tornroos, J. (1989), 'Relations Between the Concept of Distance and International Industrial Marketing' in *International Marketing Strategy* (Ed. Paliwoda, S.), London: Prentice Hall.

Vision 2010 Trade and Market Development Report (1995), 'Market Opportunities and Trade Policy in the Year 2010', Dublin: The Irish Trade Board.

3

THE COMPETITIVE ADVANTAGE OF PERIPHERAL REGIONS: CONCEPTUAL ISSUES AND RESEARCH APPROACHES

Rory O'Donnell

3.1 INTRODUCTION

In considering the competitiveness of peripheral regions and countries in Europe, we confront a range of analytical and practical problems. Among these, is considerable uncertainty about the correct concept and measure of competitiveness or competitive advantage. Even at the level of nations, it is relatively rare to find the concept of competitiveness defined in a rigorous way. Indeed, a range of measures of relative international competitiveness are widely used in the media, official documents and discussions of economic policy. The most popular of these is the change in relative unit labour costs. But most discussions also include within the concept of national or regional competitiveness, the ability of a country or region to meet the needs of its population for high and rising incomes and employment. Despite the absence of a clear definition, and a widespread use of single-factor measures, such as unit labour costs, it is strongly believed that a range of other factors — such as technology, innovation, management, marketing, skills and finance — influence a country or region's competitive advantage. Indeed, this range of 'explanations' of competitiveness or competitive advantage is reflected in a wide range of policies which governments, regional authorities and the European Union now pursue. Indeed, in some countries and regions, we see policy intended to enhance competitive advantage, shift from one factor to another — sometimes in response to fads in economic or business literature. This multiplicity of concepts, measures and theories of competitiveness, suggests that, in approaching the competitiveness of Europe's periphery, we begin with a careful review of concepts and theories. Without careful consideration of the range of meanings and explanations of competitive advantage, research and policy analysis are unlikely to impose a structure on the multiple factors which undoubtedly influence the relative economic performance of Europe's peripheral countries and regions. Consequently, this chapter is concerned with identifying the appropriate concept, or concepts, of competitive advantage and outlining alternative approaches to the study of its determinants.

Section 3.2 addresses some important conceptual and definitional issues which arise in the study of the competitive advantage of peripheral regions and countries. The first of these is whether competitive advantage refers to trade alone. It is argued that international business involvement takes a range of forms and all of these have relevance to the measurement and understanding of competitive performance and potential. A second, and more difficult, question concerns the concept of *national* or *regional* competitive advantage. Competition takes place between firms, not nations or regions. It is firms which have competitive advantages and disadvantages. This might suggest that national or regional competitiveness is simply a product of the competitiveness of *local firms*, and this is, indeed, the solution proposed by Porter (1990). Others believe that the concept of competitive advantage has no correlate at the national level and, for this and other reasons, entirely dismiss studies of national competitiveness as meaningless (Krugman, 1994; Harris, 1993). Alternative views on the relevant unit of analysis are considered, and their application to small countries and peripheral regions is assessed. It is argued that it is not valid to assume, as Porter does, a complete identity between the competitive advantage and performance of *local firms* and the prosperity of *society*. In addition, contrary to Porter's methodology, it is advisable to include all firm activities — including those of trans-national corporations (TNCs) — in the study of peripheral competitive advantage.

Section 3.2 also contains a discussion of the three levels at which international competition can be analysed — the macroeconomic/developmental, the mesoeconomic/industrial and the microeconomic. It is shown that these three levels are not the same as, and should not be confused with, the three spatial scales — the regional, the national and the international. Identification of three levels of analysis and three spatial scales allows a classification of the numerous approaches to the study of competitive advantage. This identification of a broad framework of possible research approaches serves two purposes. First, it situates the study of the competitiveness of peripheral regions in the wider study of international competitive advantage. The second is to suggest that alternative approaches are valid, and should each be seen as making a contribution to our knowledge. By this method, it is hoped to avoid fruitless arguments about *the* correct definition of competitiveness and *the* correct approach to its analysis.

The international debate of competitive advantage, or competitiveness, has been characterised not only by alternative definitions and conflicting explanations, but also disputes about measurement. Section 3.3 outlines an important distinction between three different categories of measure of competitiveness. These are measures of competitive *performance,* competitive *potential* and management *process.* The distinction between these three, and the classification of a wide range of measures by means of it, greatly clarifies many of the contradictory claims in the recent literature on competitiveness.

The limitations of Porter's approach, identified in Section 3.2, suggest that it requires considerable modification in the study of smaller, peripheral countries and regions. Section 3.4 outlines the way in which Porter's framework has been extended in recent research. One major extension concerns the role of TNCs in shaping the competitive advantage of certain countries and regions. Dunning suggests that trans-national business activity be added to Porter's framework, and identifies ways in which it may impact on the determinants of competitive advantage. A second major extension of Porter's framework concerns the reliance of strong firms in smaller and peripheral countries on foreign, as well as domestic, sources of competitive advantage. This has led several authors to suggest that Porter's diamond be reformulated as a 'double diamond', in order to capture the inter-relationships between smaller or peripheral countries and the major markets and economies. This approach suggests an alternative interpretation of the observed economic structure in smaller and more peripheral regions. This alternative interpretation is outlined in Section 3.4.

In conclusion, Section 3.5 highlights the way in which exploration of these conceptual issues is motivated by a concern with peripherality. However, this involves a rejection of a conventional approach to peripherality — which focuses exclusively on distance and transport costs — and adoption of a broader approach which

reflects recent developments in the study of regional development
and economic agglomeration. It is shown that each of the conceptual and measurement issues discussed in the chapter arise in a
particularly acute form in the study of peripheral competitive
advantage.

3.2 THREE ISSUES IN THE STUDY OF COMPETITIVE ADVANTAGE

3.2.1 Competitive Advantage in Doing What?

There is a strong tradition of thinking that competitive advantage
refers to strength in international trade. In part, this reflects a
conflation of competitive advantage with comparative advantage
— which, of course, does refer exclusively to trade. The tendency
to think of competitive advantage in terms of trade is reflected in
many of the widely used measures of competitiveness, such as
export market shares or the balance of payments. In research on
the competitive advantage of peripheral regions, there is a case
against confining the study to a region's competitive position in
international trade. International economic involvement takes
many forms and all of these are part of what Stout calls international competition (Stout, 1987).

Given the significance of international and inter-regional investment, there are many reasons why a study of peripheral
competitive advantage which confined itself to trade could fail to
identify the correct issues. First, FDI strongly shapes the international pattern of production. This might not matter if FDI had
grown steadily in line with international trade and was evenly
spread throughout the trading world. In fact, FDI has taken quite
distinct patterns in space, time and across industries. Second, the
growth of FDI has led to the growth of the trans-national corporation (TNC). It is widely agreed that theories of trade and trade
competition are inadequate to explain the existence and behaviour of TNCs and, given their significance in many peripheral
regions, this provides another reason not to confine the study of
competitiveness to trade (Pitelis and Sugden, 1991; Dunning,
1988). A third reason not to think of competitive advantage in
terms of trade alone is that the growth of FDI and multinational
corporations (MNCs) influences trade and trade patterns
(Dunning and Norman, 1985).

An aspect of foreign direct investment which may soon be particularly relevant to the study of the competitive advantage of peripheral regions is outward investment by the region's firms. This *may* reflect competitive disadvantages to production in the periphery, but it might equally be an indicator of the increased competitiveness and strength of peripheral firms. However, it is also likely to *influence* the region's competitive advantage — either negatively or positively (Dunning, 1991). This further illustrates the need for careful conceptualisation and measurement of competitiveness.

There is evidence for the growth of forms of international business involvement other than trade and direct investment. These include joint ventures, licensing agreements, management contracts, turnkey operations and international subcontracting. If FDI investment involves the transfer of a package of resources — including money capital, ownership, control, management and technology — these new forms of involvement include some but exclude others (Grimwade, 1989). The two most significant are joint ventures and licensing agreements.

What are the implications of these developments for the study of competitive advantage? First, it suggests that consideration must be given to the periphery's competitive advantages and disadvantages in home production, trade of various sorts, inward investment and outward investment. As Stout (1987) notes 'the overall volume of trade is nowadays a poor measure of the importance of the strength of international competition'. The correct subject matter of investigation is international competition, or what Dunning calls 'international production'. International production encompasses trade, the location of economic activity and multinational enterprise. Porter adopts a somewhat similar definition of the subject matter in *The Competitive Advantage of Nations*:

> Most previous theories have set out to explain either trade or foreign investment. A new theory must explain instead why a nation is home base for successful global competitors in a particular industry that engage in both (Porter, 1990).

It will be seen below that the variety of forms of international business involvement has implications not only for the scope of research on the competitiveness of peripheral regions, but also for the analytical approach.

3.2.2 Competitive Advantage of What?

The Problem Stated

The question naturally arises: what do we mean by the competitive advantage of a peripheral region or country? Competition takes place between firms, not nations or regions. It is firms which have competitive advantages and disadvantages (see Section 3.4). Does this imply that the only valid subject of inquiry is the competitive advantage of peripheral *firms*? And, if so, what is the relation between this and the prosperity of a peripheral region or country? This section is concerned with the relevant unit of analysis for the investigation of competitive advantage and how this relates to the idea of the competitive advantage of a nation or region. It is argued that there are, indeed, difficult and, in many respects, unresolved issues in this area.

In considering whether the firm or the nation is the relevant unit of analysis, two, subtly different, questions are involved. The first is whether the competitive advantage of particular firms, industries or industry segments, implies or is synonymous with, prosperity for a particular nation? The second is whether, and how, national characteristics influence the competitive advantage of the relevant firms, industries and industry segments? The difference between these two questions can be illustrated as follows:

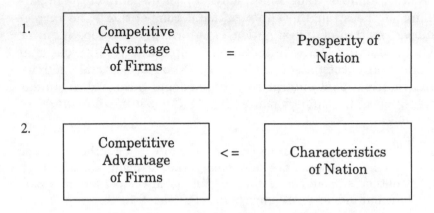

The concern in this section is primarily with the first of these questions. In a later section, *theories* which explain competitive advantage by reference to firm, regional or national characteristics will be noted.

The first of these questions itself has two aspects:

(1a) Does corporate success imply social prosperity?

(1b) Does internationalisation alter the relationship between corporate success and social prosperity?

The answer to the first of these questions (1a) provided by economic theory — contained in the fundamental theorems of welfare economics — reveals little about the properties of a private enterprise economy as we know it. Work on Schumpeterian competition implies a general presumption that capitalist competition will generate prosperity for society, but recognises that innovation — the key to competition and prosperity — will occur unevenly, in both time and space. Examples of these contingent relationships between the competitive advantage of firms and national prosperity are outlined by Kay (1993). He argues that 'there is no necessary equivalence between the creation of added value by the corporation and wealth creation in the economy at large' (Kay, 1993, p. 322). Instances can be cited in which firms can appropriate added value which they have not created, and in which firms create wealth which they cannot effectively appropriate. Kay identifies four primary sources of competitive advantage: innovation, architecture (systems of relationships), reputation and possession of strategic assets. He argues that the social benefits of corporate added value depend on which of these is its source. 'Where added value is the product of reputation, or architecture, there is a broad identity between the private and social value of corporate activity' (*ibid.*). In the case of innovation, the difficulties of appropriation mean that firms may not fully benefit from the wealth they create. Likewise, nations might have competitive advantages (or perhaps just distinctive capabilities) which firms cannot easily exploit in commercial competition. Overall, it cannot be presumed that corporate success is synonymous with social prosperity.

The Implications of Internationalisation

Porter's *Competitive Advantage of Nations* has established the terms in which the implications of internationalisation are now debated. He does not consider the general question of whether, and when, corporate success implies social prosperity (1a). Assuming that it does, his focus is on the sources of prosperity and identification of *what* business activity, indigenous or foreign-owned, is most significant to national economic success. Porter's answer to question (1b) is implicit in his insistence that the correct question is: 'why does a nation become the *home base* for successful international competitors?' (Porter, 1990, p. 1). He defines the home base as the nation in which the essential competitive advantages of the enterprise are created and sustained:

> The home base will be the location of many of the most productive jobs, the core technologies, and the most advanced skills. The presence of the home base in a nation also stimulates the greatest positive influences on other linked domestic industries, ... While the ownership of firms is often concentrated at the home base, the nationality of shareholders is secondary. As long as the local company remains the true home base by retaining effective, creative, and technical control, the nation still reaps most of the benefits to its economy even if the firm is owned by foreign investors or by a foreign firm (Porter, 1990, p. 19).

As it happens, Porter's answer to the second main question — do national characteristics influence the competitive advantages of firms and industries? — is that 'differences in national economic structures, values, cultures, institutions and histories profoundly influence competitive success' (Porter, 1990, p. 19). This suggests that the definition of *what* phenomena to study in order to understand national prosperity is not entirely separate from the subsequent explanation of those phenomena. Porter argues that competition is ultimately between firms, but *countries* have competitive advantage in specific industries and industry segments, in the sense that the influence of the national element or environment is not particularly on firms, but on industries and segments of industry. Consequently, his theory of *what determines* competitive advantage further defines the relevant unit of analysis:

> The basic unit of analysis for understanding national advantage is the industry. Nations succeed not in isolated industries, however, but in *clusters* of industries connected through vertical and horizontal relationships (*Ibid.*, p. 73).

This is more than a definition and should only be adopted if the *theory* which motivated it is considered worthwhile.

It is clear that Porter's concept of 'home base' embodies a number of distinct hypotheses:

- that firms do have a 'home base' or nationality

- that the competitive advantages of firms are synonymous with the competitive advantage and prosperity of the nation which is their home base

- that the competitive advantage of firms is determined by characteristics of the nation, and this works via the impact of national factors on industries.

Porter's approach suggests that the study of the competitive advantage of peripheral regions and countries should focus on the advantages of firms whose 'home base' is in those regions — but include both their export and foreign direct investment activities.[1]

Porter's concept of home base is supported by a number of other authors, who suggest that leading multinationals are strongly influenced by their parent company's nationality, and that what are seen as 'global' or 'stateless' corporations are, in fact, 'national firms with international operations' (Hu, 1992; Grant, 1991). In explaining the significance of *national boundaries*, various factors are invoked. Porter argues that external economies 'do not cross national boundaries easily' (Porter, 1990, p. 144). Hu considers that 'social memory functions in a nation but not between nations' (Hu, 1992, p. 118). Likewise, Kay suggests that:

> although scientific knowledge observes no national boundaries as it observes no corporate boundaries, the transfer of expertise is always easier between those who work in geographical proximity to each other, meet each other regularly, share the same educational background, and speak the same language. In this way, the individual innovations which form part of the competitive advantage of individual firms in the United States, Germany, and the United Kingdom — countries with strong scientific capabilities and traditions — create a national competitive advantage which adds up to more than the sum of its parts (Kay, 1993, p. 329).

While this lends support to aspects of Porter's approach, it does not necessarily imply the unique relevance of *national* firms.

However, others consider Porter's core proposition — that national competitiveness and prosperity are synonymous with the success of national firms — to be problematic. They identify cer-

---

[1] However, as will be seen in Section 3.4, Porter's critics argue that his studies actually ignore the off-shore activities of locally-based firms.

tain firms, such as Shell, BP and Exxon, whose nationality is
certainly indefinable, and note that the 'nationality problem
becomes more acute in defining the effective nationality of firms
originating in small and medium-sized countries' (Graham and
Krugman, 1989). In addition, they argue that there are negligible
behavioural differences between US firms and foreign firms in
terms of import propensity, quality of jobs, R&D activity etc. These
empirical observations are the starting point for Reich's rejection
of the idea of the nationality of firms and criticism of Porter's
work. In his view, Porter's acknowledgement that 'a nationality of
shareholders is secondary ... renders most of the remainder of his
book irrelevant' (Reich, 1990). This leads Reich to reject almost all
analyses of US competitive advantage and to argue that America's prosperity, like that of all other nations and regions, depends
on the quantity and quality of employment *located in* the country.
Reich's own analysis contains an argument which leads him to
prefer *inward* over *outward* FDI. Thomsen has taken the idea of
the irrelevance of corporate nationality further than Reich and, on
this basis, questions his preference for inward over outward investment (Thomsen, 1992).

*The Unit of Analysis in the Study of Peripheral Competitive
Advantage*

The implications of these arguments for the study of the competitive advantage of peripheral regions and countries would seem to
be the following. First, there is no analytical/definitional solution
to the problem of unit of analysis. The relationships between
corporate and social prosperity are contingent and the correct
unit of analysis depends on the theoretical and practical approach
adopted. Second, if the investigation includes the study of firms
and industry segments, there is a case for initially including *all*
firm activities, whether local- or foreign-owned and, in the case of
locally-owned firms, whether located in the region or elsewhere.
This constitutes clear rejection of Porter's procedure. Third, in
approaching the competitiveness of peripheral regions, we should
not rely on the US debate. Both the globalisation thesis
(Thomsen/Reich/Graham/Krugman) and the 'home base' proposition (Porter/Hu) may be incorrect. TNCs in peripheral regions and
countries are unlikely to behave in the same way as TNCs in the
United States (Cantwell, 1989). But this does not reinstate Porter's perspective in its entirety. Porter's case for the idea of 'home
base' is founded on the argument that 'the process of creating

skills and the important influences on the rate of improvement and innovation are intensely local' (Porter, 1992, p. 158) and that many external economies, a central force in Porter's theory, 'do not cross national boundaries easily' (*ibid.*, p. 144). If it were the case that the openness and external orientation of peripheral economies and societies meant that such local processes of innovation failed to occur and that many external economies, do, in fact, cross national boundaries easily, then even *locally-owned* firms may not have a home base in Porter's sense.[2]

3.2.3 Level of Analysis and Spatial Scale

Having identified the need to look beyond trade, and to include TNCs in the study of peripheral competitiveness, a third issue concerns the choice of level of analysis and spatial scale. International production can be analysed at three different levels: macroeconomic/developmental, mesoeconomic/industrial and microeconomic (Cantwell, 1991). A macroeconomic or developmental analysis would examine broad national and international trends and relate the pattern of production, investment and, ultimately, competitiveness, to the stage of development and the position of a given peripheral country or region within the international system. Mesoeconomic or industrial approaches focus on the competitive interaction between firms in an industry. Finally, analyses at the microeconomic level look at the growth of individual firms. Various theories have been developed at each of these levels of analysis, and some of these will be identified below.

It is important to note that these three levels of analysis do not, in general, refer to spatial levels like the regional, the national and the global or international. Each type of analysis could, in principle, be undertaken at the various spatial levels. For example, a mesoeconomic study of the interaction of firms in an industry could be undertaken within a region, a state, or as a study of the international industry in question. The range of possible research approaches is illustrated in Table 3.1.

---

[2] Similar anxiety about these issues can be found in the work of a number of authors: Grant, 1991; Dunning; 1991 and OECD, 1991.

TABLE 3.1: LEVEL OF ANALYSIS OF INTERNATIONAL PRODUCTION
AND POSSIBLE SPATIAL SCALES

	Regional	*National*	*International*
Macroeconomic/developmental			
Mesoeconomic/industrial			
Microeconomic			

Echoing the earlier discussion of the unit of analysis, there is a
strong case for keeping an open mind concerning the relevant
spatial scale. Indeed, the relevant spatial scale will differ depending on what aspect of peripheral competitiveness is being considered. For example, it would be futile to conduct an analysis of the
'Irish computer assembly industry', since the Irish 'industry' is
simply a particular segment of an industry which only exists at
an international scale. Likewise, the relevant spatial unit will
differ depending on whether it is competitive *performance* or the
determinants of competitive advantage which are the subject of
inquiry. For example, a given firm may have a strong competitive
advantage in an industry which is global, but the *explanation* or
source of that competitive advantage may be characteristics of the
region in which the firm resides. The essential point is that care
must be taken in moving between categories which are not essentially spatial ones, such as the firm or the industry, and categories
which are essentially spatial, such as the region or the country.

This identification of a broad framework of possible research
approaches has two purposes. The first is to situate the study of
the competitiveness of peripheral regions in the wider study of
competitive advantage, in order to identify differences and over-
laps between alternative approaches. The second is to suggest
that alternative approaches are valid, and should each be seen as
making a contribution to our knowledge. By this method, it is
hoped to avoid fruitless arguments about *the* correct definition of
competitiveness and *the* correct approach to its analysis. Some of
the relevant ideas and theories — at different levels of analysis
and spatial scales — are identified in Table 3.2.

This suggests that there are reasons to take note of various
explanations of peripheral competitiveness, some of which cite
regional factors as relevant and others of which emphasise national or international forces. Given my emphasis on the openness

of peripheral regions and countries, the significance of TNCs and the limited strength of home-based firms, the emphasis here is on regional approaches. Indeed, the 'internationalisation of Porter's diamond' — which is necessary for the study of peripheral regions and countries (see below) — creates a certain overlap between regional, national and international approaches.

TABLE 3.2: RELEVANT THEORIES IN THE STUDY OF COMPETITIVE ADVANTAGE

	Regional	*National*	*International*
Macroeconomic/ developmental		• Theory of income distribution and regulation • Cultural factors • Factor endowments	• Theories of international development and division of labour
Mesoeconomic/ industrial	• Theory of territorial industrialisation • Porter's theory of clusters • Industrial districts • Theory of innovation	• Porter's theory of competitive advantage • Theory of innovation	• Theories of international competitive industries • Theory of technical change
Microeconomic	• Theory of collective business organisation	• Theory of organisational capability • Theory of innovative enterprise	• Theories of the TNC

Theories of Regional Competitive Advantage

The past decade has seen a renewed interest in the region as a focus of economic, business, social and political analysis. This work includes theories of territorial industrialisation (Storper and Walker, 1989), Porter's theory of clusters, the theory of industrial districts (Harrison, 1992) and new formulations of regional economics (Krugman, 1991). Some of these are listed in Table 3.2. The important themes in this renewed interest in regional analysis include clustering, innovation, institutions and globalisation. While clustering has long been the most pronounced pattern in the process of industrialisation, this is, as Storper and Walker note, 'rediscovered once a generation'. The focus on the regional level is related to a renewed research interest in innovation, which strongly suggests that innovation and technical change are location-specific (Dosi, 1988; OECD, 1991). This, in turn, is related to increased interest in the way in which competitive advantage is grounded in culture and institutions (Enright, 1993; Saxenian, 1994). The renewed focus on the region has also been prompted by globalisation. This, apparently paradoxical, result is partly explained by Enright's observation that 'there is a fundamental difference between the globalisation of industries and companies and the globalisation of the sources of competitive advantage' (ibid.). Globalisation, by internationalising markets and making firms more footloose, has the effect of making local conditions more, and not less, important to economic development. Both Storper (1995) and Courlet and Soulage (1995) provide surveys of the way in which diverse analytical approaches — focusing on institutions, industrial organisation and transactions, and technological change and learning — have reasserted the significance of the region in competitive advantage.

3.2.4 Conclusions

This section has examined three conceptual and definitional issues which arise in research on the competitive advantage of peripheral regions and countries. It has been shown that, in these cases, competitive advantage cannot be confined to trade performance. Other forms of international economic involvement are significant enough to demand that we focus on what Dunning and others call 'international production', and Stout calls 'international competition'.

Part of the difficulty of defining and researching competitive advantage reflects the complexity of the relationship between firms' competitiveness and regional or national economic prosperity. Several views of the nature of this relationship were reviewed and three conclusions were reached. First, there is no clear *a priori*, or conceptual, resolution of these complexities. Second, it is necessary to reject Porter's approach by including TNCs in the study of peripheral competitiveness. Third, the debate in the US on the relationship of firm nationality to national competitive advantage cannot be transferred, unaltered, to the peripheral context.

Some of the difficulty in thinking about competitive advantage reflects the existence of theories of competitiveness which operate at different levels of analysis and different spatial scales. In order to reduce confusion arising from this, this section distinguished between these two dimensions and identified some of the theories which are available. In particular, it has noted that various researchers have focused on regional, national and international factors. These theories by no means exhaust those available.

3.3 MEASURES OF COMPETITIVENESS

3.3.1 Three Dimensions of Competitiveness
The lack of clear definitions of competitiveness or competitive advantage has meant that a wide range of measures are used by different authors in different contexts. Implicit in the use of each measure is a particular idea of where competitiveness resides and what factors influence it. Some focus on competitiveness at the level of the firm and suggest quantitative measures of costs, prices and profitability, and qualitative indicators of non-price factors. Others consider competitiveness at the level of the nation and measure trade performance, cost advantages or qualitative assessments of countries' international business ratings. In surveying these different approaches, Buckley et al. conclude that ideas about the complex concept of competitiveness varied greatly. Some see it as the ability to perform well, others as the generation and maintenance of competitive advantages, for the rest it is the process of managing decisions and processes in the correct way (Buckley et al., 1988a). This leads them to categorise the various measures into three groups.

- competitive *performance*

- competitive *potential*

- competitive *process*.

This suggests that the various measures in each category describe different stages of the competitive process. *Potential* measures the inputs into the operation, *performance* measures the outcome of the operation and *process* measures the management of the operation. They suggest that this variety is appropriate since 'competitiveness cannot be considered as a static concept, but rather as an ongoing process' (*ibid.*). They illustrate the value of using measures in all three categories by considering the limits of each category on its own. Performance measures, on their own, ignore the sustainability of competitiveness and fail to capture the regeneration and maintenance of competitive potential. On the other hand, measures of competitive potential give no indication of whether this potential is turned into performance. Finally, qualitative measures of the management or competitive process would, on their own, tend to ignore much of the hard data through which the competitiveness of countries, regions, industries and firms can be compared.

Moving beyond the classification of measures to causation, it is probable that potential, process and performance interact in various ways. Figure 3.1 shows Buckley, Pass and Prescott's conception of these inter-relationships. This reinforces the view that competitiveness is multidimensional and that single measures alone will fail to capture the nuances of competitive advantage.

FIGURE 3.1: THE INTER-RELATIONSHIP BETWEEN MEASURES OF COMPETITIVENESS

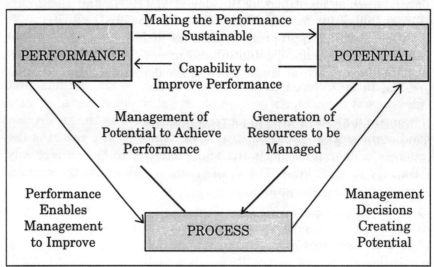

Source: Buckley et al. (1988a).

A distinction between these three measures of competitiveness, and the classification of a wide range of measures by means of it, greatly clarifies many of the contradictory claims in the recent literature on competitiveness. The attempt to develop approaches to competitiveness which are broader than, or different from, relative unit labour costs has frequently led to protracted debates on whether measures, such as unit labour costs, are adequate (OECD, 1981). The approach adopted by Buckley et al., suggests that, even if one desires to develop a theory of competitive advantage based on, say, technology and innovation, there is a case for measures of potential, such as costs, and measures of performance, such as export shares.

In classifying and using measures of competitiveness it is important to define both the level or unit analysis and the time horizon. Buckley et al., adopt an approach to the unit of analysis which is similar to that developed in Section 3.2 above. Although competition takes place between firms, and competitiveness is an attribute of firms, the mutual interaction between firms and the environment in which they operate justifies measurement and analysis at levels other than the firm, such as the country or region, the industry and the product. The time horizon is important because binding constraints on competitiveness in the short run become flexible over a longer time period (Buckley et al., 1988a). Table 3.3 lists some of the widely used measures of competitiveness, as identified by Buckley et al. (1988a and 1988b). It is clear that many measures can be used at national, industry and firm level, while, appropriately, there is little overlap across the categories performance, potential and process. The strengths and weaknesses of each of these types of measures are identified by Buckley et al.

3.3.2 Relevance of all Three Dimensions

There are a number of reasons why study of the competitive advantage of peripheral countries and regions should incorporate performance, potential and process. First, any analysis of the causes of competitiveness will necessarily include more than one of these categories. Much confusion has been generated in the discussion of competitiveness by confusing measures of performance and measures of potential. It is also common to express a particular *theory* of competitive advantage by insistence on a particular *measure* of competitive performance. While it is appropriate that each theory should suggest particular measures, it is better if theoretical arguments are presented explicitly rather than being implicit in an assertion of the correct or true meaning of competitiveness.

Competing from the Periphery

TABLE 3.3: MEASURES OF INTERNATIONAL COMPETITIVENESS

Level of Analysis	Performance	Potential	Management Process
Country	• Export market share • % total output in manufacturing • Balance of trade • Export growth • Profitability	• Comparative advantage • Cost competitiveness • Productivity • Price competitiveness • Technology indicators • Access to resources	• Commitment to international business • Government policies • Education/ Training
Industry	• Export market share • Balance of trade • Export growth • Profitability	• Cost competitiveness • Productivity • Price competitiveness • Technology indicators	• Commitment to international business (trade associations, etc.)
Firm	• Export market share • Export dependency • Export growth • Profitability	• Cost competitiveness • Productivity • Price competition • Technology indicators	• Ownership advantage • Commitment to international business • Marketing aptitude • Management relations • Closeness to customer • Economies of scale and scope
Product	• Export market share • Export growth • Profitability	• Cost competitiveness • Productivity • Price competitiveness • Quality competitiveness • Technology indicators	• Product champion

Source: Buckley et al. (1988a).

Second, as Buckley et al., say, the three elements of competitiveness are interrelated. Changes in potential are likely to induce changes in management process and, ultimately, performance. Performance can feed back into the firm's future potential and this potential can be enhanced by the strategic use of the management process (see Figure 3.1). These two-way processes pose difficulties for research on the competitive advantage of peripheral countries and regions. The large number of possible casual relationships must be narrowed down in some way if practical observations and propositions are to be derived.

Third, Buckley et al., emphasise that competitiveness is a relative concept. It must be measured relative to some other time, some other firm, industry or country, or some alternative state of affairs. Each of these types of comparison has methodological implications. To identify relative competitiveness between two dates, two firms or two countries, it is necessary to hold many other factors constant — insofar as this is possible.

3.4 APPROACHING THE STUDY OF PERIPHERAL COMPETITIVENESS

3.4.1 The Impact of Trans-nationals on Peripheral Competitive Advantage

An important issue in any study of competitive advantage of peripheral countries and regions is the role of inward and outward foreign direct investment. As noted above, Porter's procedure is one which, by and large, excludes foreign-owned firms from the study of national competitive advantage. While this procedure may have some rationale in the countries studied by Porter, it is problematic in the case of peripheral countries and regions. Indeed, even in some of the countries studied by Porter, the internationalisation of the economy has posed particular questions. For example, the study of Sweden had to ask particular questions about the international activity of Sweden's leading firms and their implications for the Swedish 'home-base' (Sölvell, Zander and Porter, 1991). Although the Swedish pattern of internationalisation is quite different from that in other parts of the European periphery, the question of the role of TNCs in national competitive advantage is a general one.

A number of authors have suggested that Porter's approach to TNCs limits the generality of his work. Dunning, for example, argues 'that more explicit attention should be given to the ways in which the trans-nationalisation of business activity could affect the nature and character of the diamond of competitive advantage of the countries involved' (Dunning, 1992, p. 142). He proposes to 'internationalise Porter's diamond' by including the activity of

TNCs as an additional exogenous variable affecting the diamond. In elaborating this idea, he provides a number of hypotheses which will prove useful in analysing the implications of inward direct investment for the competitive advantage of peripheral regions and countries (Dunning, 1993).

In order to explore ways in which trans-national business activity might influence each of the four determinants of competitive advantage, Dunning begins by identifying the unique characteristics of *inward* direct investment. First, it is likely to provide a different package of resources and capabilities from that provided by domestic investors. Second, the uses made of those assets are likely to be different, partly because of the foreign ownership of the firm and partly because of the distinctive effects of transnationality *per se*, such as those that relate to the international management of resources and capabilities and the spreading of risks. Having identified the particular characteristics of inward direct investment, Dunning lists five ways in which the competitiveness of a country or region might be improved:

- by the country's or region's firms producing more efficiently

- by innovation, in products, processes or organisational structures

- by reallocation of resources, to better accord with the country's comparative dynamic advantage

- by capturing new foreign markets

- by achieving structural adjustment to changes in global demand and supply conditions (Dunning, 1994).

It is clear that inward investment can, *potentially*, contribute to national or regional competitiveness in each of these ways. Dunning sees this as an interaction between the *existing* competitive advantage of a nation or region and the TNCs which locate within it — an interaction which shapes the region's *future* competitive advantage in a variety of ways. Thus, he suggests we 'internationalise Porter's diamond' and modifies Porter's schematic presentation as illustrated in Figure 3.2. As can be seen, Dunning proposes that foreign direct investment be added as a new 'auxiliary factor' which can affect each of the four determinants of competitive advantage. In addition, foreign direct investment can shape the actions of host governments and what Dunning calls the 'mentality of competitiveness' within the host country or region.

FIGURE 3.2: INTERNATIONALISING PORTER'S DIAMOND OF COMPETITIVE ADVANTAGE

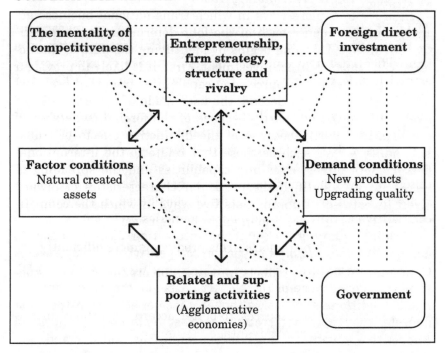

Source: Dunning (1994).

Dunning's 'internationalisation of Porter's diamond' presents a general framework for thinking about the possible impact of TNCs on the competitiveness of peripheral countries and regions. He focuses this approach by suggesting that the actual impact of trans-national business activity on national or regional competitive advantage will depend on the value of three contextual variables:

- the nature of TNC activity
- the existing competitive advantage of the country or region
- economic policies of host governments or authorities.

In order to explore the first of these variables, he identifies four types of foreign direct investment:

- natural resource-seeking

- market-seeking

- efficiency-seeking

- strategic (created) asset-seeking.

The first two — resource-seeking and market-seeking investment — represent the main motives for an initial foreign entry by a firm. The latter two embrace the main modes of expansion by established foreign investors. He argues that, in the 1960s and 1970s, most FDI was of the first or second type. By contrast, in the 1980s and early 1990s, FDI has been increasingly of the third and fourth type. Consideration of the different ways in which these four types of FDI impact on Porter's four determinants of competitive advantage, thereby upgrading competitiveness (in five different ways), summarises a large body of research. It suggests a range of hypotheses which should be considered in studying the competitive advantage of peripheral countries and regions.

Reading Dunning's account, an interesting pattern seems to emerge. The most *definite* impact on competitive advantage seems to arise from natural resource-seeking and market-seeking FDI, in particular because of their effect on factor conditions and demand conditions. However, although these effects seem the most definite, they may not create the most *dynamic upgrading* of competitive advantage, since factor conditions and demand conditions are the more basic of Porter's determinants. The effect of efficiency-seeking and strategic asset-seeking FDI seem less *certain*, but potentially more significant in upgrading competitive advantage. Since 'the local value added of a foreign affiliate is positively correlated with its age', efficiency-seeking and strategic asset-seeking FDI will tend to have a more significant impact on the local economy. Indeed, Dunning argues that — where FDI helps the dynamic comparative advantage of host countries — it is likely to have the most beneficial effect when it is directed to those parts of the value chain in which the potential for upgrading productivity is the greatest. This seems more likely to be the case with efficiency-seeking and strategic asset-seeking FDI. Dunning suggests that, in the right circumstances, efficiency-seeking FDI can assist those countries to restructure their economic activities more in line with their dynamic comparative advantages; reduce the costs of structural adjustment; and foster more demanding purchasing standards by firms and consumers.

Strategic asset-seeking investments are designed to acquire resources and capabilities that an investing firm believes will sustain or advance its core competencies in regional or global markets. He notes that these may range from innovatory capability and organisational structures, to accessing the foreign distribution channels and the superior appreciation of consumer needs in unfamiliar markets. Consequently, this type of investment can integrate the competitive advantage of the acquired firm with those of the acquiring firm and increase competition between domestic firms. While this suggests a *possible* significant impact on the dynamic competitive advantage of a region, Dunning notes that 'this type of FDI, unlike the other types, may be undertaken with a specific purpose of transferring the assets acquired from the host to the home country, and this may work to the disadvantage of the competitiveness of the former country' (Dunning, 1994, p. 38).

In considering the way in which TNC activity influences the fourth determinant of competitive advantage — related and supporting industries — Dunning notes that:

> Porter does not attempt to measure the significance of clusters as a facet of the diamond, or whether it has become a more or less important facet with the passing of time. Nor does he give much attention to the conditions that make for successful clusters. Clearly, not all firms need to be part of a network of vertical or horizontal linkages. Moreover, not all linkages need to be in the same, or similar, locations (Dunning, 1992, p. 160).

Dunning identifies a number of hypotheses and possibilities which should be considered when analysing the impact of TNC activity on clustering of related industries in the peripheral regions. Although a TNC is *par excellence* a network of inter-related activities, there is no general law about its impact on spatial clustering in any given country or region. Sometimes, the economies of common governance are best exploited in the same location, and sometimes in different locations. Second, it must be asked whether TNCs are tending to *create* their own clusters of foreign-based activity in the Irish economy. While much foreign investment is attracted to *existing* agglomerations of activity, there is evidence — in South Wales, Scotland and the Dusseldorf area — of foreign investment *creating* new clusters.

Although it is not his main focus, Dunning's analysis of the possible impact of TNC activity on competitive advantage, contains ideas which may be of particular relevance to the competitive advantage of peripheral countries and regions. The focus of this volume is the *geographic* periphery of Europe. Dunning relates his 'internationalisation of Porter's diamond' to the changing spatial characteristics of FDI. Indeed, he suggests that the significance of the spatially-related variables which shape FDI have changed considerably over the past two decades. 'As their share of total production costs declined, so did the drawing power of natural resources and unskilled labour, while that of created assets and the opportunities of networking with local firms rose' (Dunning, 1994, p. 42). In particular, he suggests that intending investors now usually place their need for state-of-the-art facilities for the *cross-border transmission* of information, technology and finance at the top of their locational priorities. An effective and trustworthy legal framework comes a close second. At higher levels of economic development, the quality of a country's educational and technological infrastructure becomes more critical (*ibid.*). Dunning generalises and conceptualises these observations in terms of organisational and transactions costs: 'as the organisational and transaction costs of economic activity have become relatively more important ... countries that can offer a business environment that is conducive to minimising these costs are *ceteris paribus,* likely to gain an increasing share of inbound investment' (*ibid.*). He cites two recent surveys, one on the determinants of Japanese FDI in the UK manufacturing sector, and one on the location of international offices. In both surveys, 'transaction and co-ordinating cost variables . . . were ranked considerably higher as investment determinants than more traditional production cost related variables' (*ibid.*).

Dunning also argues that TNC activity influences Porter's subsidiary determinant of competitive advantage, government. In particular, the growth of TNC activity shapes the policy of small countries and, it can be argued, increases the significance of government policy in influencing competitive advantage. This is so, because the configuration of TNC activity is less dependent upon the availability and cost of unimproved natural resources, and more dependent upon the knowledge base and infrastructure facilities of economies in which they are producing, or contemplating producing. Governments strongly influence the extent, quality and cost of those factors by their education, science and technology, industrial, trade, environmental, transport, communications and fiscal policies.

> The combination of the footloose nature of much modern industry (especially within integrated regions, such as the European Community) and the increasing significance of government influence on the transaction costs of such activity — and especially of high value activities in which TNCs tend to have a competitive advantage — is something which deserves more attention than Porter has chosen to give it in his book (Dunning, 1992, p. 163).

This is, undoubtedly, of particular relevance to competitive advantage of peripheral regions and countries.

3.4.2 The Reliance of Peripheral Firms on International Diamonds

The discussion above has identified a number of limitations of the conceptual framework developed by Porter. These concern the correct unit of analysis, the role of foreign direct investment, the emphasis on export market shares and the concept of 'home-base'. Together, they suggest that the study of the competitive advantage of peripheral countries and regions requires a careful review of concepts and theories and, in particular, needs to draw on a wider range of theories of corporate, regional and national competitiveness. The application of Porter's methodology to smaller and more peripheral countries — such as Canada, Mexico, New Zealand and Austria — has led researchers to somewhat similar conclusions. This, in turn, has led to an important reformulation of Porter's diamond, which would seem to be relevant to the study of the European periphery. This section summarises the motivation for, and main features of, the idea of a 'double diamond' or 'multiple diamonds' of competitive advantage.

Work by Rugman and D'Cruz (1993) on Canada, and Cartwright (1991) on New Zealand, suggested that Porter's framework did not adequately explain the competitive advantage of these countries. In these countries, Porter's reliance on the export shares of national industry groups, as the major indicator of competitive strength, was misleading. Porter's methodology takes little account of the overseas operations of Canadian multinationals. Its exclusion of foreign subsidiaries in Canada and New Zealand — which he does not regard as sources of competitive advantage — 'rules out the broad nature of the foreign-owned subsidiaries' contributions to the development of Canada's manufacturing base' (Rugman and D'Cruz, 1993, p. 94). Thus, Porter's methodology 'is biased towards the selection of industries that

export from the home-base and against those that compete
through off-shore production or which export from the home-base
to off-shore value-adding subsidiaries' (Cartwright, 1993, p. 58).
Likewise, Porter's approach to the role of natural resources —
which are clearly of major significance in both Canada and New
Zealand — is unsatisfactory. His view, that reliance on natural
resources is as bad as reliance on unskilled labour or simple
technology, obscures the fact that 'Canada has developed a number of successful mega-firms which have turned Canada's comparative advantage in natural resources into proprietary firm-
specific advantages in resource processing and further refining'
(Rugman and D'Cruz, 1993).

It is clear that a major challenge is to incorporate these factors
— all of which are important in European peripheral regions and
countries — into a conceptual approach to competitive advantage.
Rugman and D'Cruz suggest that Dunning's idea, of adding multinational activity as a third outside variable (see Figure 3.2) 'is
an ingenious idea but itself raises problems' (*ibid.*). An alternative
is to add multinationality to Porter's third determinant of competitive advantage, firm structure, strategy and rivalry. However,
this is not entirely satisfactory either, since it overlooks the fact,
emphasised by Dunning, that 'MNEs are influenced in their competitiveness by the configuration of the diamond other than their
country's and that this, in turn, may impinge upon the competitiveness of home countries' (Dunning, 1990, p. 11). Recognising
this, Rugman and D'Cruz conclude that 'it is questionable that
multinational activity can actually be added into any, or all, of the
four determinants, or included as a third exogenous variable'
(Rugman and D'Cruz, 1993, p. 26).

These limitations of Porter's framework in the analysis of
smaller economies, has led these authors to suggest a reformulation of the diamond. Working in the Canadian context, Rugman
and D'Cruz suggest that the competitiveness of Canadian industries can only be understood in the context of a wider North
American diamond. Thus, they suggest a 'double diamond' model
of international competitiveness, as illustrated in Figure 3.3
(Rugman and D'Cruz, 1993; Rugman and Verbeke, 1993). On the
one hand, this suggests that Canadian firms are not limited to
their home base in drawing strength from factor conditions, demand conditions, structure, strategy and rivalry, or related and
supporting industries. On the other hand, it suggests that North
American standards of performance are a minimum requirement

for the competitive success of Canadian businesses. This approach has direct implications for the interpretation of Canadian competitive advantage and for policy approaches to upgrading it.

FIGURE 3.3: THE 'DOUBLE-DIAMOND' OF COMPETITIVE ADVANTAGE

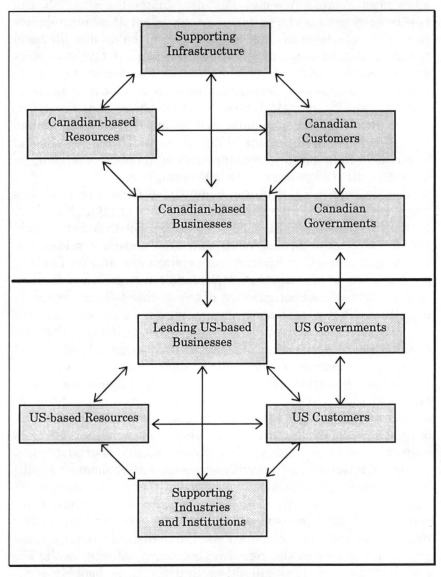

Source: Rugman and D'Cruz (1993).

First, it confirms that Canada is likely to be strong in resource-based sectors; this is not a weakness of Canada's economic structure, provided that dependence on export of resource-based products is linked to the wider, North American, diamond of competitive advantage. Second, it implies a different view of one of Canada's most successful sectors, automobile components; this can now be seen as part of a powerful Windsor-Detroit motor industry cluster. At the level of strategy and policy, the double diamond approach suggests that existing and potential strategic clusters within Canada are likely (a) to contain foreign-owned enterprises in Canada and (b) to be heavily linked with a wider North American diamond. Porter and his colleagues consider that these empirical points can be accommodated within the diamond framework (Porter and Armstrong, 1992). A careful interpretation of this debate may be an important starting point for the study of the competitive advantage of Europe's periphery.

The concept of a double, or multiple-linked, diamond has yielded a powerful reinterpretation of Porter's study of New Zealand. In New Zealand, 24 of the 25 industries with highest world export shares are resource-based, and 21 of these are land-based. Cartwright shows that Porter's four determinants in New Zealand are incapable of explaining New Zealand's successes and failures in the international economy. In his view, this reflects a general inability of Porter's diamond theory 'to predict or prescribe the characteristics of internationally competitive industries that are resource-based and export-dependent' (Cartwright, 1993, p. 65). For example, several of New Zealand's most successful sectors — such as the dairy industry — have very small home-based markets, such that domestic 'demand factors' offer little pressure for competitive advantage. Likewise, these industries tend to have co-ordinated exporting strategies. 'This co-ordination achieves economies of scale and scope in international operations and enhances international bargaining power, but it disagrees with Porter's prescription of strong rivalry between exporters in each industry' (*ibid.*). In addition, these industries are strongly involved in offshore investment, and see this as essential to their presence in international markets. Cartwright illustrates these points in the case of the New Zealand dairy industry in the US food ingredient market. He shows that the home-base determinants of competitive advantage, as suggested by Porter's methodology, are highly unfavourable:

By comparison with the 'diamond' theory benchmark, this industry is apparently strategically 'unhealthy'. Home-base demand conditions offer no stimulation, government has removed the possibility of competition between exporters, factor creation emphasises upstream value activities, and related and supporting industries have not developed strongly (Cartwright, 1993, p. 67).

However, in reality, several segments of this industry are actually international leaders. Cartwright suggests that this can be understood by constructing a 'diamond' for the US food ingredient segment in which New Zealand's casein and whey protein industry competes. This shows several of the determinants, including fierce competition from Danish and Irish firms, to be enhancing the competitive advantage of the New Zealand Dairy Board. Cartwright concludes that:

Insight into the determinants of competitiveness is achieved only by study of *both* home base and off-shore industry structure and conduct. In the example, the two 'diamonds' are strongly complementary and the sources of international competitiveness of the New Zealand dairy industry in this segment can be understood only by reference to both 'diamonds' and the linkages between them (*ibid.*).

It is clear that this extension from a home-base diamond to multiple, linked diamonds has major implications for the study of the competitive advantage of peripheral countries and regions.

The concept of a double diamond has also been used effectively in studies of Mexico and Austria. In his research on Mexico, Hodgetts (1993) justifies the approach on the basis of three criticisms of Porter. First, he takes issue with Porter's view that inbound foreign investment is never a solution to a nation's competitive problems, and outward direct investment has a very limited role in competitive upgrading. Second, he is unhappy with Porter's view that reliance on natural resources (the factor-driven stage) is insufficient to create world-wide competitive stature. Third, he draws on Dunning's critique of Porter's neglect of TNCs. Consequently, he argues that in applying Porter's framework, one conclusion is irrefutable:

Different diamonds need to be constructed and analysed for different countries, and these diamonds often require integration and linkage with the diamonds of other economically stronger countries, thus creating a double diamond paradigm (Hodgetts, 1993, p. 46).

His study suggests that this approach is useful in understanding Mexico's two strategic clusters — the petroleum cluster and the automotive cluster. The development of the petroleum cluster requires intense interaction, not only with the American market, but also involving extensive use of foreign contractors, foreign technologies and compliance with international environmental standards. The emerging Mexican automotive cluster is incomprehensible without recognition of the role of leading US firms, General Motors, Ford and Chrysler. Yet, within the operations of these firms, Mexico would seem to have distinct competitive advantages. Similar issues arose in the Austrian Porter study. Bellak and Weiss (1993) conclude that the concept of clustering should be extended to a supranational level in the context of a small nation like Austria.

3.5 CONCLUSION

This chapter has reviewed conceptual issues and research approaches which arise in the study of the competitive advantage of peripheral regions. Although this has led to some general exploration of the concept of competitive advantage and the limits of Porter's framework, the analysis is, in fact, intended to explore the implications of peripherality. To see this, it is important to appreciate that the concept of peripherality which informs this chapter is not the conventional one in which peripherality is conceived solely in terms of distance and transport costs. The issue of peripherality is, of course, simply the inverse of the issue of economic and social agglomeration. To understand why a given region is peripheral, is to understand why other regions are central, i.e. are the sites of significant economic agglomeration. It follows that the study of peripherality cannot be undertaken separately from the study of economic agglomeration or regional development. Indeed, this implies that the best developments in regional economics and geography must be applied to the study of peripherality.

In recent years, there have been significant changes in the theory of regional development, and this allows a new, wider, conception of peripherality (O'Donnell, 1994). We still find a formidable list of arguments which suggest that there are forces making for concentration of advanced economic activity. Nevertheless, most recent theories of regional development do share a rejection of deterministic cumulative causation. The existence of strong tendencies to regional concentration of economic activity is no longer understood as implying that industry will definitely concentrate and that regional fortunes will definitely diverge. Many now reject the idea that the process of regional change, or the process of economic development, is a steady journey along a path of either concentration or dispersal. Under the influence of neo-Marxist and neo-Schumpeterian work, it is now viewed as an inherently uneven process which can move in bursts of progress and sharp reversals. This unpredictability and contingency is reflected in the more interesting recent research in regional economics, the economics of trade and integration and development economics. It is recognised that although there are tendencies to concentration (and, to a lesser extent, tendencies to dispersal), there is, in fact, a *shifting hierarchy* of leading and lagging regions. Much recent regional analysis is concerned to explore the factors which mediate any underlying tendencies to divergence or convergence. Technical change is one of the factors most frequently considered. Where traditional theory focused on the relationship between productivity growth, cost reduction, and export growth, the recent work is concerned to explore the sources of productivity growth and the relationship between technology, economic organisation and spatial change. The traditional focus on external factors, particularly demand, has been enhanced by increased interest in indigenous factors, in both leading and lagging regions. Indeed, these are now seen to include a wide range of indigenous economic, social, institutional and political factors.

These developments in regional theory are, in turn, giving rise to new conceptions of peripherality. These suggest that the impact of peripherality cannot be measured by looking purely at distance and transport costs. As Begg and Mayes (1994) point out, this has two, somewhat offsetting, effects. On the one hand, it means that the mere fact of being remote from a geographical core does not imply that an economy is necessarily marginalised, in the sense of being inhibited from effective participation in the economic system to which it belongs. On the other hand, it implies that geography matters, for reasons other than transport and travel. They suggest that peripherality may be found in other aspects of separation — such as information — and in demand conditions, supply conditions and technological change. It is this non-conventional conception of peripherality which informs the discussion of conceptual issues in this chapter.

The three conceptual issues raised in Section 3.2 are directly motivated by the issue of peripherality. In peripheral regions and countries, it is particularly inappropriate to reduce competitive advantage to international trade, since FDI and other forms of international or inter-regional interaction are very important. Careful definition of the unit of analysis in the study of competitive advantage — firm, region or nation — is particularly important in the case of the periphery. Indeed, as noted in Section 3.2.2, in peripheral regions, even locally-owned firms may not have a home base in Porter's sense. The need to distinguish clearly between the level of analysis (macroeconomic, industrial, microeconomic) and the spatial scale (regional, national, international) arises precisely because the periphery is itself a spatial concept.

The discussion of measures of competitiveness, in Section 3.3, relates to the issue of peripherality in two ways. First, the conventional approach to peripherality — focusing on distance and transport costs — would limit the measurement to one dimension of competitiveness, i.e. competitive potential. The identification of three distinct and relevant dimensions of competitiveness strongly suggests that an exclusive focus on transport costs would be mistaken. Equally, the broader conception of peripherality, outlined above, underlines the relevance of the three dimensions, and types of measure, discussed in Section 3.3.

Finally, the extensions of Porter's framework, outlined in Section 3.4, strongly reflect the conceptual issues explored in Section 3.2. Both reflect attempts to explore the applicability of Porter's framework to smaller, more peripheral, more resource-dependent, economies. The first (discussed in Section 3.4.1) concerns the high incidence of trans-national investment in peripheral economies, and its implications for national or regional competitive advantage. The second issue (discussed in Section 3.4.2) concerns the fact that peripheral enterprises seldom base their competitive advantage solely on characteristics of the peripheral economy or society. All of these considerations suggest that, while particular difficulties undoubtedly arise, the study of peripheral competitive advantage should not be seen as an entirely separate subject from the study of competitive advantage *per se*. Indeed, the major goal of this chapter has been to locate the study of competitive advantages of the periphery in the wider context of competitiveness research.

References

Begg, I. and Mayes, D. (1994), *The Implications of Peripherality for Northern Ireland*, NIEC Report 111, August, Belfast: Northern Ireland Economic Council.

Bellak, C. J. and Weiss, A. (1993), 'A note on the Austrian "diamond"', *Management International Review*, Vol. 33, special issue 1993/2, pp. 109-134.

Buckley, P. J., Pass, C. L. and Prescott, K. (1988a), 'Measures of international competitiveness: a critical survey', *Journal of Marketing Management,* Vol. 4, No. 2, pp. 175-200.

Buckley, P. J., Pass, C. L. and Prescott , K. (1988b), 'Measures of international competitiveness: empirical findings from British manufacturing companies', *Journal of Marketing Management*, Vol. 6, No. 1, pp. 1-13.

Cantwell, J. (1989), *Technological Innovation and Multinational Corporations,* Oxford: Basil Blackwell.

Cantwell, J. (1991), 'A survey of theories of international production' in *The Nature of the Transnational Firm* (Eds. Pitelis, C. and Sugden, R.), London: Routledge.

Cartwright, W. R. (1991), 'Did the Porter project get it right?', *Management*, Vol. 10, No. 2, pp. 15-19, Auckland.

Cartwright, W. R. (1993), 'Multiple linked "diamonds" and the international competitiveness of export-dependent industries: The New Zealand experience', *Management International Review*, Vol. 33, special issue 1993/2, pp. 55-70.

Courlet, C. and Soulage, B. (1995), 'Industrial dynamics and territorial space', *Entrepreneurship and Regional Development*, No. 7, pp. 287-307.

Dosi, G. (1988), 'Sources, procedures and microeconomic effects of innovation', *Journal of Economic Literature*, September, Vol. 26, pp. 1120-1171.

Dunning, J. H. (1988), *Explaining International Production,* London: Harper Collins.

Dunning, J. H. (1990), *The Globalization of Firms and the Competitiveness of Nations*, Lund, University of Lund, The Crawford Lectures, 1989.

Dunning, J. H. (1991), 'The eclectic paradigm of international production: a personal perspective' in *The Nature of the Transnational Firm* (Eds. Pitelis, C. and Sugden, R.), London: Routledge.

Dunning, J. H. (1992), 'The competitive advantage of countries and the activities of transnational corporations', *Transnational Corporations*, Vol. 1, No. 1, February, pp. 135-168.

Dunning, J. H. (1993), 'Internationalizing Porter's diamond', *Management International Review*, Vol. 33, special issue 1993/2, pp. 7-17.

Dunning, J .H. (1994), 'Re-evaluating the benefits of foreign direct investment', *Transnational Corporations*, Vol. 3, No. 1, February.

Dunning, J. M. and Norman, G. (1985), 'Intra-industry production as a form of international economic involvement' in *Multinationals as Mutual Invaders* (Ed. Erdilek, A.), Beckenham: Croom Helm.

Enright, M. J. (1993), 'The geographic scope of competitive advantage', Working Paper No. 60, Harvard Business School, Division of Research.

Graham, E. M. and Krugman, P. R. (1989), *Foreign Direct Investment in the United States*, Washington, DC: Institute for International Economics.

Grant, R. M. (1991), 'Porter's *Competitive Advantage of Nations*: an assessment', *Strategic Management Journal*, Vol. 12, pp. 535-548.

Grimwade, N. (1989), *International Trade: New Patterns of Trade, Production and Investment*, London: Routledge.

Harris, R. G. (1993), 'The selling of competitiveness', *Canadian Business Economics*, Spring 1993.

Harrison, B. (1992), 'Industrial districts: old wine in new bottles?' *Regional Studies*, Vol. 26, No. 5.

Hodgetts, R. M. (1993), 'Porter's diamond framework in a Mexican context', *Management International Review*, Vol. 33, special issue 1993/2, pp. 41-54.

Hu, Y. S. (1992), 'Global or stateless corporations are national firms with international operations', *California Management Review*, Winter 1992.

Kay, J. A. (1993), *The Foundations of Corporate Success: How Firm Strategies Add Value*, Oxford: Oxford University Press.

Krugman, P. (1991), *Geography and Trade*, Cambridge, MA: MIT Press.

Krugman, P. (1994), 'Competitiveness: A dangerous obsession', *Foreign Affairs*, March/April.

O'Donnell, R. (1994), 'The Evolution of the Theory of Regional Development' in *European Integration and Regional Policy* (Eds. Fountas, S. and Kennelly, B.), Galway: Social Science Research Centre.

OECD (1981), 'The notion of international competitiveness: A discussion paper', Directorate for Science, Technology and Industry, Paris, OECD.

OECD (1991), Background Report Concluding the Technology/Economy Programme, C/mim(91) 14, Paris: OECD.

Pitelis, C. and Sugden, R. (1991), *The Nature of the Transnational Firm*, London: Routledge.

Porter, M. (1990), *The Competitive Advantage of Nations*, London: Macmillan.

Porter, M. and Armstrong, J. (1992), 'Canada at the crossroads: dialogue', *Business Quarterly*, Vol. 56, No. 4, Spring, pp. 6-10.

Reich, R. (1990), 'But now we're global: a review of Michael Porter's *The Competitive Advantage of Nations*', *Times Literary Supplement*, August 31-September 6.

Rugman, A. M. and Verbeke, A. (1993), 'Foreign subsidiaries and multinational strategic management: an extension and correction of Porter's single diamond framework', *Management International Review*, special issue, Vol. 33, 1993/2, pp. 71-84.

Rugman, A. M. and D'Cruz, R. (1993), 'Internationalizing Porter's diamond', *Management International Review*, Vol. 33, special issue 1993/2, pp. 17-41.

Saxenian, A. (1994), *Regional Advantage: Culture and Competition in Silicon Valley and Route 128*, Cambridge, MA: Harvard University Press.

Sölvell, O. Zander, I. and Porter, M. E. (1991), *Advantage Sweden*, Second Edition, Sweden Norstedts: Juridik.

Storper, M. (1995), 'The resurgence of regional economies, ten years later: the region as a nexus of untraded interdependencies', *European Urban and Regional Studies*, Vol. 2, No. 3, pp. 191-221.

Storper, M. and Walker, R. (1989), *The Capitalist Imperative: Territory, Technology and Industrial Growth*, Oxford: Basil Blackwell.

Stout, D. K. (1987), 'Competition in international trade' in *The New Palgrave: A Dictionary of Economics* (Eds J. Eatwell, M. Milgate and P. Newman), London: Macmillan.

Thomsen, S. (1992), 'Integration through globalisation', *National Westminster Bank Quarterly Review*, February.

4

THE IMPACT OF EUROPEAN UNION POLICY ON 'PERIPHERAL' REGIONS

John Tomaney and Andy Pike

4.1 INTRODUCTION

The question of social and economic conditions in the regions of the European Union (EU), in theory at least, has been integral to the project of European integration. Issues of regional convergence and divergence have been closely related to the conditions in individual regions and with the fortunes of the EU as a whole. The emergence of 'core' and 'peripheral' regions has been a preoccupation of the EU and a high proportion of the array of policy-making competences and resources at EU level are focused especially on responses to problems in Europe's peripheral or Less Favoured Regions (LFRs). However, those EU policies which have no territorial focus are not without their implications for such regions — what Gröte (1992, p. 14) calls 'territorial externalities' — and the extent of their impact is such that they may compromise the aims of regional policy. The debates about 'widening' or expanding the EU and 'deepening' integration between its Member States and their regions have further complicated the extent and interdependency of core and peripheral regions and the management of the EU budget. Together, these policy conflicts and the broader market-led framework within which they exist have complicated the issue of competing from the periphery and reinforced the lack of a 'level playing field' upon which peripheral regions can participate on an equal footing.

In essence there are two views on the likely impact of European integration on the development prospects of peripheral regions. The first view emerging from the official analyses of the EU sees further integration having a largely positive effect. The clearest expression of the EU approach to cohesion is that given by Delors (1989). Delors rejects the idea that there are inevitable winners or losers in the process of integration. Peripherality, for instance, is no longer seen as a serious problem on the grounds that transport costs are becoming, on average, less important in the location of industrial production. New developments in tele-communications and increased capital mobility are seen as repre-senting an opening up of the locational choices of firms with the implication that this might benefit the LFRs. Delors concludes that the most important factor determining the distribution of industrial activity is effective supply-side policies, and for this reason he rejects regional employment and capital subsidies. The former, he argues, gives the wrong signal to those responsible for labour competitiveness while the latter encourages inefficient in-vestment. Besides, both measures are seen to contravene the market ethos that underpins the single market. Delors also re-jects the case for automatic fiscal transfers between European regions. He does not believe the EU should offer guarantees of equal standards of public welfare of the type that justify inter-regional transfers in federal states such as Germany and Austra-lia. Thus, he argues for a greater policy emphasis on upgrading local entrepreneurship, training efforts, environmental improve-ments in urban areas and local initiatives which promote innovation.

The contrary position, however, states that instead of integra-tion leading to equalising centrifugal movements of firms and in-vestment towards the peripheral regions, economic integration is likely to stimulate a spatial reconfiguration of business activity in favour of core areas because these areas already enjoy greater comparative advantages. Because the expected gains arising from European integration are mainly generated endogenously, the various processes of resource of re-allocation will tend to promote the accumulation of economic resources in core regions which de-rive their strength not so much from their geographical location as from their possession of the determinants that shape and re-new competitive advantage. Such regions will derive a dispropor-tionate share of the benefits of integration (Martin, 1993).

Chief among the advantages of the core regions are strong technological capabilities. For instance, O'Donnell (1993) respond-ing to Delors notes that, while it may be true that distance-related costs are becoming, on average, less important in determining the location of production, it is too simplistic to infer that tele-communications and transport improvements, because they technically reduce the friction of distance, will cause a dispersal of economic activity and therefore contribute to convergence via regional specialisation. This would be to ignore a powerful countervailing factor, namely the dynamic external economies that operate in many sectors as well as the forces of accumulated technological expertise within the most dynamic companies — accumulated technology which is to some extent location-specific insofar as research and technology capability tends to be clustered in core regions. Thus, rather than decentralising activities to lower-cost regions, large firms in particular might remain firmly rooted in supply-rich regions in order to continue to reap the advantages of existing economies of scale and agglomeration (see Krugman, 1991). This observation is particularly important given the centrality of the promotion of scale economies in the single-market agenda.

This chapter therefore presents a review of the impact of EU policy on peripheral regions within a wider understanding of the impacts of the process of European integration on these regions. The issue of social and economic cohesion and the evolving policy framework of structural funds is detailed. The development of other EU policy areas, their implications for peripheral regions and relation to reforms in the structural funds are then discussed. The paper concludes by arguing that contradictions between regional and other EU policies within peripheral regions is undermining the potential for economic and social cohesion.

4.2 FROM ROME TO MAASTRICHT:
SOCIAL AND ECONOMIC COHESION IN EUROPE
AND THE EVOLVING POLICY FRAMEWORK

The aim of social and economic cohesion has been a concern of the European Community (EC) since its earliest days. The Treaty of Rome enjoined the EC 'to promote throughout the Community a harmonious development of economic activities, a continuous and balanced expansion . . . an accelerated raising of the standard of living' (Article 2). Since then, the European Union has developed a particular concern with spatial disparities, in terms of Gross Domestic Product (GDP) per head, unemployment, investment, Research and Development (R&D) expenditure and convergence and divergence between the regions of the Union. 'Structural policies' designed to assist the weaker regions of the EU to adapt to the conditions of an increasingly integrated economy have been developed in response. The scale of these structural policies has grown with each enlargement of the EU as the scale and diversity of regional problems has increased. During the 1980s, the renewed effort to complete the internal market with accompanying changes in industrial, competition and Research and Technological Development (RTD) policies and moves toward Economic and Monetary Union (EMU) were accompanied by further expenditure increases — and substantial reform — of the EU's structural policies. Underpinning these policies has been an acknowledgement at least that the process of European economic integration poses particularly severe problems of industrial adaptation for weaker regions. Enhanced structural policies are deemed necessary to assist the weaker regions to adapt to new competitive conditions which are the intended consequence of economic integration.

4.2.1 EU Structural Policy

Spatial disparities are primarily tackled by the EU's various Structural Funds (SFs) which grew in size and importance during the 1980s. The three SFs include the European Social Fund (ESF), the European Regional Development Fund (ERDF) and the European Agricultural Guidance and Guarantee Fund-Guidance Section (EAGGF-GS). The ESF was established under the provisions of the Treaty of Rome, although its scope and resources remained limited for a long time. With the rapid increase in unemployment in the 1970s, the resources of the ESF were expanded and its role defined as that of supporting the vocational training of workers forced out of crisis-hit sectors, particularly agriculture. As such, most ESF expenditures in the early days were directed at regions such as the Italian *Mezzogiorno*. The ERDF was established at the time of the EC's first enlargement in 1974. The accession of the UK and Ireland extended the scale and nature of the regional problem within the EU. In particular the UK brought with it a number of weak industrial regions. The UK's problems in this regard were particularly acute, but similar problems of concentrated industrial decline emerged in most northern Member States during the 1970s, and the problem of 'converting regions in industrial decline' became an important task of the ERDF. During the 1980s the accession of Greece and later Spain and Portugal brought new concerns with cohesion, as did intensifying problems in the declining industrial regions. The Structural Funds were reformed in 1979 and 1984 as the Commission sought to increase the available resources and to improve the effectiveness of the Funds. A more far-reaching reform of the Structural Funds occurred in 1988. This reform differed from the previous ones insofar as it was one aspect of the renewed impetus to economic integration, represented by the signing of the Single European Act (SEA).

The SEA was itself partly a response to Europe's low levels of growth in 1980s. The SEA and the accompanying White Paper sought to 'complete' the internal market by the end of 1992 through a series of measures designed to 'free' capital movements and harmonise standards, policies and taxes of Member States. Underpinning this programme was an analysis which held that a major cause of the lack of dynamism of the European economy, relative to that of Japan and the USA, was the enduring fragmentation of the European economy into national markets. While the original treaties establishing the European Community had removed many tariffs and quotas and established a common external tariff, many non-tariff barriers to integrated trade remained. Specifically, the '1992 programme' legislated for the removal of frontier controls between Member States, the harmonisation of product specifications and service regulations, the removal of local preferences in public procurement and greater controls over state aid, the abolition of exchange controls and the harmonisation of VAT rates.

The European Commission's research indicated that the removal of these impediments to the free movement of goods services, capital and people — referred to as the 'Costs of Non-Europe' (Cecchini, 1988) — would allow more efficient allocation of resources at the European scale, thus stimulating renewed growth. In practice, significant restructuring and rationalisation of European business was expected as a result of these measures. It was believed, however, that the weaker regions of the Community would need special assistance to adjust to the new conditions of competition and to ensure they participated in the new growth opportunities. For instance, the European Commission's own analyses pointed to the degree to which employment in LFRs was dependent on industries involved in public procurement and which were expected to experience intense rationalisation (CEC, 1991a). A concern with mitigating the effects of these developments was the major impetus behind the 1989 reform of the SFs.

At the same time the 1989 reform was used as an opportunity to overhaul the way in which the funds operated. The principal effect of the reforms was to achieve greater co-ordination of the hitherto separate Funds and to focus their efforts around five clear objectives (Table 4.1). In particular, the intention was to focus the greatest level of assistance on the 'lagging regions', which are mainly located in the southern periphery of the EU (Table 4.2).

TABLE 4.1: STRUCTURAL FUND BUDGET (1989-93)

Objective	Nature of Objective	MECU (1989 prices)	%
1.	Lagging Regions	38,300	63
2.	Regions in industrial decline	7,205	12
3.	Long-term unemployment	7,450	12
4.	Youth training/employment	3,415	6
5.	(a) Adaptation of agricultural structures	2,975	5
	(b) Development of rural areas	1,150	2
Total		60,495	100

Source: CEC (1990c)

TABLE 4.2: EC STRUCTURAL FUND OBJECTIVES

Objective	Nature of Objective	Funds Involved
1.	Development of lagging regions	ERDF, ESF, EAGGF-GS
2.	Conversion of regions in industrial decline	ERDF, ESF
3.	Combatting long-term unemployment	ESF
4.	Increasing youth employment	ESF
5.	(a) Adjustment of agricultural structures	EAGGF-GS
	(b) Development of rural areas	ERDF, ESF, EAGGF-ES

Source: CEC (1989)

The 1989 reform was supported by a decision to double in real terms the EC's allocation to the three Structural Funds between 1988 and 1993 under the provisions of the so-called 'Delors I' package which overhauled the finances of the EC.[1] In addition, regions were obliged to undertake what, in effect, was a comprehensive system of regional planning in order to obtain support from the Funds. These measures, by assisting improvements in the infrastructure and skills base of regions, were expected to offset any job losses in LFRs arising from the harsher competitive environment in Europe generated by the 1992 programme. In this way it was presumed LFRs would become more attractive locations for new investment and indigenous entrepreneurship, and would share the anticipated increased growth generated by the single market.

The 1989 reform is emblematic of the emphasis on a supply-side agenda that dominates Commission thinking and underpins the policies of the Commission's Regional Policy Directorate (DG XVI). The Fourth Periodic Report on the regions, for example, suggested that the LFRs should 'seek to exploit specific regional competitive advantages to serve specialised product markets' and, in particular, LFRs should 'establish niche positions based on the exploitation of local advantages' (CEC, 1991a, pp. 70-71). Similarly, the Commission is of the view that new location factors, including the growing importance of executive 'lifestyle' factors and the viability of advanced telecommunications and information technology, are opening up new possibilities for the decentralisation of economic activity away from the European core.

4.3 INDUSTRIAL POLICY, COMPETITION POLICY, RTD POLICY, MONETARY POLICY AND SOCIAL POLICY

Regional policy is but one element of the EU's competency. Equally important to understand are the contradictions that arise from the workings of industrial, competition and RTD policy within the EU. This section examines each of the 'horizontal' policy areas in turn in order to assess their 'territorial externalities'.

---

[1] A further aspect of the Delors I package was a reform of the Common Agricultural Policy. It was recognised that the structure of the Community budget, in key respects, worked against the aim of cohesion. Support for farm prices was not allocated in relation to cohesion objectives, but according to farm output. So, for instance, prosperous Denmark is a net beneficiary under CAP, whereas Spain sees little benefit. Delors I sought to redress the situation, but CAP remains an anti-cohesion force.

4.3.1 Industrial Policy

Within the EU, industrial, competition and RTD policies have become ever closer in their mutual reinforcement and operation.
The focus of EU industrial policy has shifted from the interven-
tionist approach, at least in certain sectors (coal, steel), between
the 1950s and 1970s, toward a market-led stance since the 1980s.
This strategy has been explicitly non-interventionist but with a
residual focus on limited horizontal, supply-side measures. The
completion of the Single European Market (SEM) has been the
centrepiece of this policy and has been promoted both as 'the best
example of industrial policy' and 'the perfect training ground for
learning global competition' (Bangemann, 1992, pp. 20, 36).
Statements have since focused on 'industrial policy in an open
and competitive environment' emphasising that 'enterprises
themselves must bear the major responsibility for adapting to
change, but public authorities can assist the process by putting in
place the suitable environment for business to flourish' (CEC,
1991b, p. 3). Competition is interpreted both in the 'passive' sense
of controls over monopoly and abuse of market power, and in the
'dynamic' sense as rivalry as a stimulus for upgrading and competitiveness. Industrial policy has therefore emphasised the importance of 'adjustment' and the Commission for the European
Communities' (CEC) role as a catalyst, accelerating and facilitating this market-led process (Ramsey, 1992). This residual interventionism is directed toward the creation of 'Euro-Champions',
as opposed to national firms, capable of competing globally with
the US and Japan from their 'home'-base SEM, bolstered by RTD
policy (Ramsey, 1992). This policy has met with a critical reception in some quarters, particularly with regard to the reality of
the 'external threat', internationalisation processes complicating
the distinction between 'our' and 'their' companies and the industrial and economic logic of creating new industrial champions
with such a dominating role in the EU (Grahl and Teague, 1990;
Amin and Tomaney, 1995). The most recent *Growth, Competitiveness and Employment* White Paper (CEC, 1993b) in its preamble
at least, notes 'recovery must be achieved by developing work and
employment and not by endorsing basically Malthusian solutions'
(CEC, 1993b, p. 1) but remains wedded to the market-led agenda.

This version of EU industrial policy has implications for peripheral regions. First, it lacks a regional focus and its objectives
conflict with those of cohesion (Amin and Tomaney, 1995). Sadler
(1992, p. 1727), for example, highlights the 'regional dilemma'

facing the EU in the 1990s, since industrial policy is fixated with competition as part of the Single Market and with technological collaboration, both of which elements reinforce the hand of the largest EU firms to shift production around the regions of the EU thereby posing threats to the regions. Second, the horizontal application of EU industrial policy has revealed shortfalls in scope necessary to address the sector-specific needs of industry in their particular localities. While Bangemann (1992, p. 13) notes that a '"horizontal approach" to industrial policy does not try to help selected sectors, it attempts to improve competitiveness from the bottom up and is increasingly gaining support in the European Community', it is true that this approach is explicitly based on restricting policy to the promotion of supply-side interventions on the one hand and creating generic conditions for competitiveness on the other hand. This approach developed in response to the alleged failure of more active forms of intervention. Such policies are criticised as a waste of financial resources and promoting weakness in the productive base (Bangemann, 1992).

Horizontal industrial policy that ignores the specific requirements of particular sectors can have, at best, dampening, or at worst, negative effects in peripheral regions. It has meant that strategic issues, often specific to the material nature of individual sectors, have been poorly addressed by such industrial policies. For example, inward investors have been attracted but the policy framework for regulating 'local content' defines 'local' at the EU scale rather than national or regional, in accordance with SEM objectives, and any purchase local institutions might have had over increasing local supply linkages is immediately compromised (see Sadler, 1992).[2] In the energy sector during the 1980s, previously dominant policy was aimed at promoting medium-term goals relating to EU reliance upon energy imports (especially within LFRs such as Ireland, Portugal and Spain) with the intention of maintaining security of supply. However, shorter-term cost considerations and the Single Market initiative came to the fore ahead of sectorally-specific strategic considerations and the needs of LFRs with the aim of creating 'a more efficient pattern of

---

[2] The method of calculating local content was also changed from ex-works price to ex-works cost to prevent non-production costs such as advertising and packaging being included to boost local-content figures and to reflect more accurately the costs of production and prevent the import of high value-added components from outside the EU (Sadler, 1993).

investment and use of capacity' through free competition (Sadler, 1992, p. 1717). Elsewhere, services, which make up an increasingly large component of the EU economy, have been largely a 'non-issue' for EU industrial policy (Gröte, 1992). Given the recent growth in services and the *laissez-faire* approach of the Commission this is perhaps not so surprising. How fruitful this market-led approach will prove to be, however, particularly in peripheral regions dependent upon public services, is questionable.

4.3.2 Competition Policy

In a market-led context, the competition policy necessary to create and uphold the functioning of the free market has dominated other measures. EU competition policy has implications for peripheral regions in four areas. The creation of the internal market has liberalised the movement of both labour and capital through dismantling technical and non-tariff barriers to trade and the harmonisation of technical standards and taxation. This extension and deepening of the single market has unleashed powerful destabilising and centripetal tendencies from which 'core' regions and major multi-national players have been best placed to benefit (Amin, Charles and Howells, 1992). Further, in relation to trade policy, a (now somewhat dated) study concluded that the regional impact of trade with third countries outside the EU has been to worsen the economic situation in peripheral regions, favour prosperous Northern European regions and only to help peripheral regions when vulnerable sectors remained protected (CEC, 1984).

Despite the breadth of liberalisation legislation, however, there is strong evidence to suggest that one of the key targets of reform — public procurement — is still being utilised by some member states as a shelter of protectionism and an instrument of national industrial policy. In the railway equipment sector, for example, Abbott (1993, p. 685) notes that 'there is a widespread feeling that the Continental railway administrations are not taking seriously the European directive on competition, EC 95/3/1, which came into being at the end of this year, but are seeking to reserve rolling stock orders for their national manufacturing industries'. Examples of this phenomenon are extensive: in France SNCF placed an order for 288 doubledeck vehicles for the Paris Regional Express system with GEC-Alsthom, with an option for another 252 vehicles in future, while the Berlin transport authority placed an order 690 metro cars with a consortium of German manufacturers. In Belgium, SNCB placed eight years of work with the

Belgian equipment industry just days before the 1992 rules came into effect. In late 1994 the German rail utility, DBAG, placed DM7.4 billion (£3 billion) worth of orders entirely with German manufacturers, in the process saving threatened plants from closure and illustrating the disjuncture between theory and practice in the Single Market and the way in which core economies are maintaining their ability to protect home industries (Tomaney, 1995).

The reduction of national state aids to industry has also been an integral component of EU competition policy. Although precise estimates are difficult to ascertain within Member States, they are thought to vary between 5 and 10 per cent of domestic income (Lintner and Mazey, 1991). Article 92 of the Treaty of Rome affords the CEC the capability to restrict member states from giving subsidies or other aid 'which distorts or threatens to distort competition by favouring certain undertakings or the production of certain goods'. In the context of the internal market, state aids are considered to protect uncompetitive industries and 'distort' trade patterns and investment flows by 'artificially' subsidising production costs. The reduction of these state aids have had particular implications for peripheral regions due to their concentration in the sectors and the Member States and regions which are more dependent on state aid. In the automobile sector, between 1977 and 1987, nearly 30 billion ECU of aid was granted to producers in Europe, the majority of which was concentrated on the four 'national champion' producers British Leyland (now BMW-owned Rover) (UK), Renault (France), Alfa-Romeo (Italy) and SEAT (VW-owned) (Spain) (Sadler, 1993). Rather than encourage staged adjustment in the automobile sector, for instance, the underlying principle of policy was that 'over-reliance on state aid to solve the problems of industrial adjustment *vis-à-vis* third country producers undermines the competitiveness of the Community car manufacturers by hindering the economically healthy influence of market forces' (Official Journal of the European Communities, 1989). Car manufacturers operating in peripheral regions, such as parts of Spain or the West Midlands, UK, have therefore disproportionately shouldered the effects of the reduction of state aids. In aggregate terms, peripheral Member States have also been disproportionately affected. Total aid granted to the Member States fell to an average of 89 billion ECU between 1988-90 from 92 billion ECU in the period 1986-88 and the highest concentrations of aid in manufacturing industry were found in Italy, Portugal and Ireland (CEC, 1993c) (Table 4.3).

TABLE 4.3: STATE AID TO MANUFACTURING INDUSTRY: ANNUAL AVERAGES 1988-90 AND 1986-88

Country	As a % of Value-added		Million ECU*	
	1986-88	1988-90	1986-88	1988-90
Belgium	4.3	4.1	1,175	1,211
Denmark	1.9	2.1	316	333
Germany	2.7	2.5	7,869	7,865
Greece	24.3	14.6	2,074	1,072
Spain	6.8	3.6	4,491	2,499
France	3.8	3.5	6,479	6,106
Ireland	6.4	4.9	447	368
Italy	6.2	6.0	10,760	11,027
Luxembourg	2.3	2.6	37	48
Netherlands	3.1	3.1	1,101	1,225
Portugal	2.2	5.3	245	616
United Kingdom	2.6	2.0	4,101	3,133
EUR 12	4.0	3.5	38,835	35,503

* 1986-88 averages are at 1989 prices.

Source: CEC (1993c, p. 214).

EU competition policy has also led to the relaxation of regulation for transborder co-operative ventures (through the 'block exemption') and (de)-regulation of merger and acquisition controls. Again, this had specific impacts for peripheral regions. Love (1994), for example, highlights the inherent contradiction between the Commission's stated aim of reducing regional inequalities and promoting cohesion and the reliance on a mergers policy as a key part of the Single Market programme that has no mechanism for dealing with the uneven regional economic consequences of takeovers. This has reduced member state options in helping the process of industrial adjustment and, some claim, has acted as a positive incentive amongst business to create joint ventures and other strategic alliances (often with non-EU partners) to avoid such controls. Moreover, the conflict of industrial logic and strategies more motivated by concerns of 'financial engineering' — changes in the ownership of corporate assets which generate only shareholder value and fulfill no productive purpose — are also poorly addressed by EU competition policy implications for the regions in which the takeover targets are based. In their analysis of the failed Hanson-ICI takeover Adcroft et al. (1991) argued that 'when Europe needs employment, value added and import saving, intervention in traditional industries, like bulk chemicals, would be a more progressive way of building Europe'. While the Hanson-ICI deal did not go ahead, the case illustrates yet further the shortfalls in EU industrial policy and the failure to understand its consequences for peripheral regions dependent on the employment, output and investment in the chemicals industry.

4.3.3 RTD Policy
The key element of the residual 'interventionism' of CEC industrial policy has been RTD policy. Its aims have been, first, to build the European Technology Community (ETC) through promoting collaboration between member states for 'pre-competitive' RTD projects and, second, to enhance the competitiveness of European industry relative to the US and Japan. Increasingly, however, a regional dimension coupled with linkages to local endogenous/indigenous growth potential has featured as a complementary component of structural funds through Community initiatives such as STRIDE (Science and Technology for Regional Innovation and Development in Europe) and STAR (Special Telecommunications Action for Regional Development) (Logue, 1995). EU RTD policy is based on the Framework Programmes which include numerous initiatives including BRITE-EURAM (Basic Research in Information Technology for Europe — European Research in Advanced Materials), ESPRIT (European Strategic Programme for Research in Information Technology) and RACE (Research in Advanced Communications for Europe). Currently, funding for the Fourth Framework Programme (FPIV) (1994-98) has been more than doubled from the Third Framework Programme (FPIII) (1990-94), rising from 5.7 million ECU to 12.3 million ECU (current prices) (CEC, 1993a). Criteria for funding is again functional rather than territorial and based on 'equal access to all programmes and equal opportunities for all participants. . . the projects that receive support are selected on the basis of quality' (CEC, 1994, p. 1). Previously, EU RTD policy focused on

so-called 'pre-competitive' collaboration that brought institutions together from across Europe in projects still relatively far from the market. This emphasis allowed the utilisation of EU funds in a manner that did not conflict with the desire of competition policy to avoid subsidising near-market activities. More recently, however, a shift towards nearer-market, product-oriented research has been encouraged, particularly through the intergovernmental, non-CEC initiative the European Research Co-operation Agency ('Eureka'), mainly as a consequence of the pressures to achieve commercial outcomes from RTD investments.

Several implications arise for the regions from RTD policies. Not only has RTD policy failed to reduce the technology gap, it has increased it through the overconcentration of resources in larger firms with their RTD centres based in core regions and within the institutions of core regions — the so-called 'islands of innovation' (Amin, Charles and Howells, 1992). The low level of participation in RTD initiatives amongst the Objective 1 regions is evident from Table 4.4.

The development of the 'European Technology Community has been shaped by Europe's leading 12 multi-national 'Euro-Champions' (such as GEC, Philips, Siemens, Thomson) and, as a consequence, it is not surprising that they have substantial involvement in RTD programmes (Junne and Van Tulder, 1988). Their involvement in the scrutiny and awarding of ESPRIT projects, for example, led to 70-80 per cent of all contracts between 1981 and 1983 being awarded to the big 12 multi-nationals (Mytelka and Delapierre, 1987). In addition, these firms typically have their RTD centres in a small group of technologically advanced and/or metropolitan regions, including Île-de-France, Rhône-Alpes, Provence and Côte d'Azur (France), Greater London and East Anglia (England), Milan, Pisa and Rome (Italy) and Madrid and Barcelona (Spain) (Gröte, 1992). Small and medium-sized enterprises (SMEs), which provide more of national output in the Member States of the South, have had relatively less involvement, particularly given the higher share of innovations that come from SMEs relative to their share of total R&D expenditure (Peterson, 1991). This situation has become less pronounced in more recent Framework initiatives but a bias still exists.

TABLE 4.4: ABSOLUTE PARTICIPATION RATE OF FIRMS FROM
MEMBER STATES WITH OBJECTIVE ONE REGIONS IN 4 EUROPEAN
RTD PROGRAMES

Country	European RTD Programme				Total
	ESPRIT	COMETT	BRITE	SPRINT	
Greece	20	24	10	5	59
Ireland*	28	21	8	8	65
Portugal	13	26	11	7	57
Italy	89	45	38	13	185
Italy (Objective 1 Regions only)**	(7)	(5)	(4)	(4)	(20)
Spain	17	59	29	18	123
Spain (Objective 1 Regions only)***	(1)	(14)	(9)	(4)	(28)
Total (Objective 1 Regions only)	69	90	42	28	229
Total Countries Listed	167	175	96	51	489
Total EU Projects	219	149	117	42	527

* Plus Northern Ireland (UK); ** Abruzzi, Basilicata, Calabria, Campania, Molise, Puglia, Sardegna and Sicily; *** Andalucia, Asturias, Castilla-Leon, Castilla-La Mancha, Communidad Valenciana, Ceuta y Melilla, Galicia, Canarias and Murcia.

Source: Adapted from Gröte (1992).

When firms and institutions from peripheral regions have participated in Framework projects they have often taken one of two types of role. First, such institutions and SMEs from LFRs are sometimes included as 'sleeping partners' to produce 'cohesion-friendly' bids more likely to win Framework money. Or, second, the participation of institutions from peripheral regions in international collaborative programmes has often fractured more local, or even national, linkages that existed previously. This further weakens the local technology infrastructure and often means that other potential local partners become excluded from international collaborative networks since Framework programme rules limit the amount of funding that can be paid to individual member states (Pike and Charles, 1995). The ETC is therefore more like an exclusive club for certain firms and regions. The complementarity between RTD and regional policy has also been weak.

Germany, for example, receives only 4 per cent of the total contributions of the Structural Funds but gets 22 per cent of the total
contributions of the RTD programmes whereas Spain receives
16.5 per cent from the structural funds and only 1 per cent from
RTD policies (Saublens, 1988). RTD policies incorporating an
explicit regional dimension have also not been without their
problems. STRIDE, for example, has tended to favour capital investment in infrastructure without corresponding revenue to run
facilities, and in more 'basic' forms of research that often find a
poor reception amongst technology-oriented needs of local industry, the shift towards 'softer' 'info- (rather than infra-) structural'
approaches in the new Regional Technology Plans (RTPs) is evidence of these problems. EU RTD policy therefore acts to per-
petuate or possibly widen the 'technology gap' (measured in terms
of government and business investment in R&D and employment)
between Europe's regions which is currently estimated as twice
the 'cohesion gap' (in terms of income and employment)
(Landabaso, 1995). However, these regional impacts of RTD policy
have often been overlooked or have become smothered by internal
wrangling between DGs (Gröte, 1992).

4.3.4 Monetary Policy

Economic and Monetary Union (EMU) is the next, and arguably
most problematic, stage after the Single Market for European integration. EMU has been enshrined in the Maastricht Treaty and
aims to capitalise on the theoretical benefits of monetary integration in moving from fixed exchange rates to a single currency, including increased trade due to risk and transaction cost reduction
as well as the increased transparency of prices, more efficient resource allocation through heightened mobility of capital and labour, insulation from external shocks to the EU economy, having
the EU single currency become an international reserve currency[3]
and improved effectiveness of economic policy-making through
centralisation as well as the stimulus to political integration
(Lintner and Mazey, 1991). The main problems of loss of control
over the objectives of economic policy and tools of economic

---

[3] A single European currency would allow Member States to enjoy the advantages of *seigniorage*, that is, the ability to finance balance-of-trade deficits
by having other countries hold the Euro-currency as part of their reserves
(Lintner and Mazey, 1991).

management have proved intractable points of debate between Member States.

The changes in monetary policy in the direction of EMU have dramatic implications for peripheral EU regions. First, the tendency for capital and labour in an enlarged SEM to gravitate towards the core and more developed regions could be accentuated by EMU (Gröte, 1992; Hankel, 1994; Hughes Hallet and Scott, 1992). Wages in peripheral low-productivity regions will tend to rise towards the levels in high-productivity regions without the corresponding closure of the productivity gap. This would set in train out-migration of capital from peripheral regions and further intensify their decline. This view of the exacerbation of regional differentials is confirmed by the Delors Committee on Economic and Monetary Union (1989) with the need for compensatory measures (regional and social policies) that 'enhance the process of resource allocation in those economic sectors and geographical areas where the working of the market forces needed to be reinforced or complemented' (Gröte, 1992, p. 21). This has led to calls for a significantly bolstered EU regional policy as an integral component of EMU but retains the focus on market-led solutions and displaces the responsibility for amelioration of the problems caused to Structural Policies by EMU.

Second, the operation of the ERM (Exchange Rate Mechanism) of the EMS (European Monetary System) as part of EMU irrevocably fix exchange rates together. The flexibility of devaluation for the currencies of weaker LFRs or smaller Member States is therefore removed. National governments can no longer alter the exchange rate to adjust for differences in competitiveness and the burden of adjustment is manifest on levels of employment, investment and growth as the weaker economies use deflationary monetary and fiscal policies to control inflation and balance of payments constraints.[4] 'Competitive devaluations' by weak or 'softer' currencies (Lira, Peseta and Sterling) are viewed by those with strong or 'harder' currencies (Deutschmark, French Franc) as potentially undermining the whole European project, but for others it may represent the only way of reducing the deflationary burden on weaker manufacturing economies and improving

---

[4] Crucial also are the rates at which currencies are fixed, the recent Italian and UK ejection from the ERM and the corresponding surge in their exports are testament to the problems of being fixed at an overvalued exchange rate.

(albeit short-term) the competitiveness of peripheral region exports (Tett, Fisher and Hill, 1995).

Lastly, the 'convergence criteria' necessary to underpin economic policy co-ordination tend to be deflationary and aimed at getting the supply-side in order. They include tight limits for levels of public debt and deficits, inflation and interest rates.[5] These criteria constrain demand-side activity and impose infeasible public debt reductions, drive down GDP, reduce tax revenue and produce substantial employment losses (Holland, 1995). The implications for the peripheral regions are stark. In particular, the need to reduce public debt and fiscal deficits is particularly damaging. The removal of exchange-rate autonomy means that fiscal policy would become the main means for securing the regional distribution of income and employment. But, here the stringent fiscal discipline which is stipulated in the Maastricht Treaty in the run-up to monetary union poses a severe threat to the very regions which will have the greatest burden of adjustment in relation to the convergence criteria. Clearly the most serious threat posed is to weak regions in Member States with weak fiscal capacity and which are running large deficits. For instance, in the early 1990s, Greece has a deficit of 15 per cent of GDP, while Italy has a public debt of 100 per cent of GDP (Begg and Mayes, 1993). In addition, the concentration in the industrial structure of nationalised or formerly state-owned industries in LFRs has meant they have suffered disproportionately from reductions in state expenditure in both the private and public sector.

Given these concerns a further increase in funds for EU structural policy was therefore associated with the signing of the Maastricht Treaty. Maastricht reiterated the EU's commitment to economic and social cohesion. A new financial package, known as 'Delors II', was proposed. A new budget was needed anyway after 1993, but the Commission argued that extra finance would be needed to meet the objectives outlined in the Treaty (CEC, 1992). These objectives were defined by the Commission as economic and social cohesion, enhancing the competitiveness of European industry (mainly through an enhanced RTD policy) and external action (i.e. support for Eastern Europe, North Africa and humanitarian aid).

---

[5] To meet the Maastricht conditions, the Member States must reduce their current budget deficits to 3 per cent of GDP and their gross debt to 60 per cent of GDP.

The proposal for increased financial resources was justified by the Commission on a number of grounds. Firstly, it was acknowledged that the task of meeting the convergence criteria might prove particularly burdensome for weaker Member States. Secondly, it was recognised that monetary union would prevent weaker Member States from adjusting exchange rates as a basis for coping with internal or external economic shocks (see Delors, 1989). Thus, there was a chance that the European convergence criteria would simultaneously strain public finances and restrict the scope of macroeconomic policy choices in the latter states.

The combined effect of these new pressures on LFRs, it was argued, warranted an increase in resources to ease the fiscal constraints on weaker Member States and regions (CEC, 1992). The Maastricht Treaty, therefore, proposed the creation of a Cohesion Fund to support environmental improvements and the development of trans-European networks in the poorest Member States. This funding, plus increased funding proposed under the 'Delors II' package, would in the case of Objective 1 regions double funds by 1997. The Commission argued that the previously successful reforms of the SFs illustrated the potential of structural policies. However, as Scott notes:

> Despite this, the Delors II package quickly ran into trouble. Unsurprisingly, the protagonists in the debate roughly split along geographical lines. The poor countries in the EC's southern periphery, in which the overwhelming share of Objective 1 regions were located, demanded full implementation of the proposals insofar as raising the finance available to the structural policies was concerned, while the rich, northern countries complained of fiscal profligacy on the part of the Commission and insisted that the financial commitment to cohesion should be reduced (1994, p. 79).

In the event, the package of financial reforms agreed at the Edinburgh summit in 1992 failed to meet the Commission's initial ambitions. The overall level of resource agreed was closer to that proposed in 'Delors II', but the period for intervention was extended to 1999. In practical terms the Objective 1 regions saw a doubling of funds, while funding for the other structural objectives was lower than that envisaged in 'Delors II'.

4.3.5 Social Policy

The EU's concern for social and economic cohesion has been focused on its periodic attempts to develop a European social policy.
Similar to other domains, the attention to the 'social dimension'
has a history at least as old as the EU itself. The Treaty of Rome
first gave expression to this concern when it called on Member
States 'to promote improved working conditions and an improved
standard of living for workers' (Article 117). Article 118 of the
Treaty entrusted the European Commission with the task of promoting co-operation in matters relating to employment, working
conditions, social security, occupational safety and health, training
and collective bargaining. Although attempts to add a 'social
dimension' to European integration are long-standing, such
attempts have proved more politically contested than the development of structural policy, with fewer tangible results as a
consequence. However, such policies have also had implications
for peripheral regions in particular, since they have failed to
strengthen the international role of labour to the same extent as
EU industrial and competition policies have bolstered the hand of
capital within the EU.

Created under Article 123 of the Treaty of Rome, the ESF element of the Structural Policies was the initial but rather loosely
defined instrument of EU social policy. Despite rising from 5.5 per
cent of the EC budget in 1973 to 7.2 per cent in 1989 it remained
dwarfed by the scale of the problems of unemployment and re-
training. Social and employment policies have been developed in
tandem to augment EU action concerning social policy. In the
early 1960s, concern within the Commission and member states
over the 'social dimension' of European integration and the need
for a 'social union' culminated in the Social Action Programme
(SAP) aimed at 'the improvement of living and working conditions' and the 'increased involvement of management and labour
in economic and social decision-making' (CEC, 1974). Other developments, such as the draft Vredeling Directive (named after the
Commissioner responsible) concerning formalised employee consultation and representation procedures which was never implemented due to hostility, have proved only dead-ends. The dialogue
over social policy within the EU until the mid-1980s was marked
by the reluctance of Member States to cede control over social and
employment policies and by the utilisation of pronounced UK
hostility to hide national inaction (Lange, 1992). The debate was
further dominated by the rhetoric of the market-led agenda of

reducing the 'burdens' of costs and rigidities allegedly associated with social policy on European industry.

More recently, the 'social dimension' has become more important with the need to establish the safeguard of a 'level playing field' of social conditions within the SEM. Although the original White Paper on the completion of the Internal Market did not address the question of social policy the Commission presented a new action programme to the European Parliament at the beginning of 1985 which, among other things, outlined the social measures designed to accompany the completion of the Single Market (CEC, 1985). According to the Commission the Single European Act would contain not only economic measures but would be accompanied by measures aimed at improving working conditions, facilitating 'social dialogue' and, generally, promoting social and economic cohesion through the reform of the Structural Funds. The 'Social Charter', which, on behalf of the UK, Margaret Thatcher infamously refused to sign, was the mechanism through which minimum standards for labour market regulation were to be implemented (CEC, 1990a). It represented little more than a statement of principles and aspirations and had no legal authority. The weakness of the action programme and the unlikelihood of its more controversial measures being passed prompted IG Metall, the largest German union, to describe the Social Charter and the Action Programme not unfairly as a 'non-binding wish list' (quoted in Silvia, 1991, p. 639). Similarly, the 'Social Chapter' of Maastricht, which altered the provisions of the Treaty of Rome and from which the UK again gained an 'opt-out', called for upward harmonisation of living and working conditions, improved health and safety at work, the promotion of 'social dialogue' between management and labour at the European level and equal pay for men and women. The promise of intent again went unmatched by the reality since unanimous voting dominated qualified majority voting on key issues which effectively buoyed national sovereignty in such areas and, as Streeck (1994) argues, the portrayal of increased trade union influence was overshadowed by the Commission's real agenda of furthering employer support for the integration project. More recently, this direction of development of EU social policy has been further reinforced by the Delors White Paper on *Growth, Competitiveness and Employment* (CEC, 1993b) which, alongside its focus on tackling unemployment, emphasises the need to reduce non-wage labour costs and to increase labour flexibility.

The piecemeal evolution of EU social policy has been particularly pronounced between Member States and the implications for peripheral regions have been stark. The CEC (1987) still notes that social policy is functional in aim in contrast to the primarily territorial focus of regional policy. The regional impact of the ESF has since been claimed to be both complementary to the ERDF and of little significance (Vanhoven and Klaasen, 1987; Cappellin, 1988). Several points can be made. First, any attempts to build a social dimension have not been wholeheartedly adopted by Member States, often with the explicit aim of seeking advantage from remaining outside EU-level social legislation. Herein lies the origins of the 'social dumping' debate and the shifts in economic activity toward regions with lower thresholds of labour regulation and standards of social provision. The UK government's hostility to the extension of EU competence in the social policy domain in part is bound with its policy of attracting inward investment from other areas of the EU and elsewhere. UK regions have been promoted as benefiting from low levels of wages, social costs, corporate taxation and the availability of grants. The UK government presents itself as having 'opted-out' from the Social Chapter of the Maastricht Treaty but, crucially, 'opted-into' the Single Market.

Two of the most infamous recent relocations of investment which provide some support for the above analysis of the UK role are those of Digital from Galway, Ireland, to Ayr, Scotland, and Hoover from Dijon, France, to Cambuslang, Scotland. Differential arrangements for workplace consultation, through works councils for example, are therefore touted rather than tolerated between places. It has been noted that such shifts are often between peripheral regions and are encouraged by the combination of EU and national Structural Funds (Tomaney, 1994). Marquand (1994) too, has stressed also that such undercutting of regulatory standards between regions represents an unsustainable 'race to the bottom' in terms of social conditions and economic remuneration. A distinction can therefore be drawn between high-wage/high skill economies underpinned by investment, innovation and state support (e.g. Germany, Scandinavia, Northern Italy), and low-wage/low-skill economies like Portugal, Greece and, increasingly, Britain, based on price competitiveness and limited or reduced state intervention (Nolan, 1994). At the same time, however, it should also be recognised that the UK's actions may suit other Member States: while casting the UK as the villain of the piece, they are able to use the existence of the competitive threat of a deregulated UK labour market as means to restructure their own 'over-regulated' labour markets (Amin and Tomaney, 1995).

Second, in keeping with the contradictions between EU policies, EMU will further undermine the attempts to create a social union. In Germany, for instance, despite the problems generated by unification, a key compensation for the new *Länder* was access to the welfare provision of the federal German state. In addition, for Hankel (1994, p. 56) the exit of Italy and the UK from the EMS highlighted this fundamental contradiction between plans for monetary union and the EU's stated aim of cohesion: 'The members states hit hardest by recession and unemployment needed to protect their job markets, and they preferred to fight for them on a national basis rather than stabilise the EMS exchange rate'. It is this contradiction which will plague efforts to create a 'Social Europe' into the next century. For the present, the dominant agenda appears to be that of endorsing only those aspects of EU social policy which do not conflict with market-based strategies for economic recovery. The weakness of the 'Social Dimension', both in terms of content and enforceability, will have the effect of separating nations and regions with old economic surpluses and strong social legislation to underwrite progressive employment and welfare rights from those which do not have such capability. The social divide in the EU, therefore, seems set to grow.

4.4 EU POLICY EXTERNALITIES IN THE REGIONS AND COMPETING FROM THE PERIPHERY?

Current EU regional policy reveals both the possibilities and limits of tackling regional disparities through structural policies. On the credit side, the Structural Funds have been a stimulus to innovation in the design and implementation of regional policy. The reforms of the Structural Funds in the 1980s represented a major advance in so far as they extended principles of programming. The 1989 reform, in particular, required regions to move toward a comprehensive system of regional planning in the LFRs — a development which has been reinforced since. The new framework regulations for the operation of the Structural Funds enacted in 1993 went further and developed the principle of 'regional partnerships', with a clear consultative role for the social partners, as the basis on which planning should occur. As a consequence, in many European regions, where regional institutions are weak (such as the UK) the existence of EU regional policy has been the catalyst to the development of local planning structures which are essential if regional structural problems are to be effectively tackled.

It is clear that the development of strong sub-national political and administrative structures is necessary for the successful development and implementation of structural policies (Amin and Tomaney, 1995; Begg, 1995). Simple subsidies on capital or labour, while sometimes necessary, are insufficient to ensure the development of longer-term solutions to the problems of the LFRs. It is even clearer that market forces alone will not ensure successful adaptation of regional economies. Thus, the simple model of structural change and resource allocation based on market signals, as accepted by both the monetarist and Keynesian orthodoxy, is insufficient for the task of upgrading productive structures. There is persuasive evidence that successful structural policies are often those adopted by institutions small enough to develop an intimate understanding of the microeconomics of regional development, but large enough — and with the necessary political legitimacy — to act upon them (e.g. Matzner and Streeck, 1991).

Notwithstanding these successes and the expansion of the SFs during the 1980s, serious weaknesses remain with the EU approach to cohesion and regional development. A major area of concern is that despite the changes in their operation and the doubling of the size of the SFs, the measures and financial resources involved remain insufficient in relation to the scale and nature of the EU's entrenched regional problems and the threats posed by further integration. In the period 1989-93, during which the single market was completed, total expenditure on SFs amounted to 60.3 billion ECU, equivalent to only 0.24 per cent of the EU's GDP. This figure seems particularly modest when set beside the alleged welfare gains of 216 billion ECU which the Cecchini report predicted would arise from the single market. Indeed, in the 1970s, the MacDougall Report on the role of public finance under European Integration argued that a federal Europe of reduced disparities would need inter-regional resource transfers of around 20 to 25 per cent of GDP, while a 'looser' federation would require expenditures of around 5 to 7 per cent of Community GDP (MacDougall, 1977).

It also has to be asked whether any positive gains resulting from EU regional policy in facilitating cohesion are complemented by EU policy actions designed to enhance European competitiveness. Here, the evidence tends to suggest that action in other areas of EU policy is likely to advantage Europe's larger firms and advanced regions. The EU's RTD policy, for example, which is aimed at supporting expensive pre-competitive research is an important part of the effort to improve the competitiveness of European industry. However, the available funds are more easily absorbed by large companies, whose R&D centres typically are located in Europe's prosperous regions, with the unintended outcome that the EU's RTD policy will militate against the aim of cohesion.

Similarly, the EU's liberal stance within Competition Policy on merger controls within and across borders is likely to encourage market concentration at Europe-wide level by facilitating acquisitions and take-overs. This is a development which will strengthen the interests of the largest firms in Europe. Already, there is evidence that, in the context of a unified market, multi-locational firms have begun to restructure operations, leading to the concentration of research and management tasks in advanced regions, and the nationalisation of capacity in the LFRs (Amin, Charles and Howells, 1992; Tomaney, 1994).

The Commission hopes that such outcomes will be compensated by the overall extra growth that will result from scale economy gains, as large companies win new market share. The achievement of scale economies is central to the alleged welfare gains suggested by Commission analyses — some 80 per cent of gains are expected to flow from this source (Cecchini, 1988). Yet, much research exists to suggest this is a highly optimistic scenario. Studies of mergers in operation suggest few if any real examples of synergy or increased efficiency (Ramsey, 1995). Moreover, it is by no means certain that 'European' companies will be the prime beneficiaries of the SEM. Ramsey's evidence shows that the SEM has attracted investment from Japan and the USA almost on the scale that it has induced from internal cross-investment. In addition, since many large European companies are already global players their investment plans are increasingly dictated by a logic of globalisation rather than Europeanisation. It is not likely, therefore, that increased productive capacity will be created within the EU following the first round of rationalisations in LFRs.

The intensification of competition as a consequence of the single market is likely to accentuate the process of cumulative causation through which established centres of innovation and competitive advantage enjoy a virtuous circle of growth, while other regions become locked into trajectories of dependent development, or are denuded of the resources necessary for endogenous growth. In addition, there is no guarantee that improvements to the local skill-base or infrastructure-base in LFRs will automatically bene- fit local industry: they may benefit inward investors looking for a low-cost location that is well serviced by advanced communication links or they may pull in cheaper goods from the advanced re- gions, threatening the survival of local firms and leading to profit repatriation.

These problems of regional divergence are likely to be compli- cated by monetary union. For some commentators, monetary un- ion provides no additional threats to the LFRs beyond those raised by the single market programme (CEC, 1990b; Holland, 1993; O'Donnell, 1992). Indeed, the European Commission sees monetary union as contributing to cohesion, arguing that while partial dismantling of trade barriers will result in economic activ- ity locating closer to the market centre, complete integration will increase the attractiveness of peripheral locations 'where variable costs are lower' (CEC, 1990b, p. 214). Holland, argues that, 'with the trend to multinational investment and pricing, Maastricht only formalises the facts' (Holland 1993, p. 33), suggesting that the effectiveness of currency devaluation as a national policy measure has become limited. For other commentators, however, the road to monetary union, as laid down in the Maastricht Treaty, poses a set of threats for the LFRs (Begg and Mayes, 1993; Hankel, 1994; Hughes Hallet and Scott, 1992; Scott, 1994). They stress that the requirements of monetary union go far beyond those of the internal market programme (which does not require close co-ordination of fiscal and other economic policies or the fixed exchange rates demanded under economic and monetary union). It is argued that convergence requirements designed to make monetary union possible will risk aggravating existing dis- parities by placing further fiscal pressures on the LFRs and ac- centuating the forces of 'cumulative causation' which favour the core regions of the EU (Begg and Mayes, 1993; Doyle, 1989).

These fears are partly supported by the recent experience of German monetary union. The introduction of the DM to the for- mer GDR in 1990, *inter alia*, precipitated a major social and eco- nomic collapse, contributing to the outbreak of neo-Nazi racial violence. By mid-1993, the new German *Länder* had lost 35 per cent of their jobs and production had fallen by 25 per cent. In the industrial sector nearly 50 per cent of jobs were cut and production was down by 40 per cent (Hankel, 1994). For Wilhelm Hankel, former head of the Hessische Landesbank, the lessons of German unification are clear:

> When there are real differences in cost and productivity, especially on this scale, the nominal convergence of prices, interests and exchange rates required by monetary union can be achieved only at the cost of social crisis (1994, p. 52).

Even among those who see monetary union as posing no additional threats to the LFRs, there is a recognition that structural policies alone are unlikely to be sufficient to establish a trend toward social and economic convergence. Thus, O'Donnell (1992) notes that in existing economic and monetary unions, normal budgetary contributions and expenditures constitute the most significant redistributive mechanism between individuals and regions. Drawing on the theory of fiscal federalism, he argues for a 'new assignment of policy functions' which gives an expanded role to the Community budget, stating that it is necessary for many policy functions to be conducted at the highest level if they are to be effective. Whatever the logical merits of O'Donnell's approach, its political feasibility seems doubtful. The negotiations surrounding the 'Delors II' package revealed only too starkly the reluctance of richer member states to increase expenditure on structural policies, let alone develop a system of automatic fiscal transfers. Put together, economic and monetary union, EU competitiveness policies and the inadequacies of the structural policies are likely to have limited impact in terms of reducing regional disparities in Europe.

References

Abbott, J. (1993), 'Procurement 1993: Are the continentals playing ball?', *Modern Railways*, November, p. 685.

Adcroft, A., Cutler, T., Haslam, C., Williams, J. and Williams, K. (1991), 'Hanson and ICI: The Consequences of Financial Engineering', Occasional Papers on Business, Economy and Society, No. 2, University of East London.

Amin A. and Tomaney J. (1995) (Eds.), *Behind the Myth of the European Union*, London: Routledge.

Amin, A., Charles, D. and Howells, J., (1992), 'Corporate restructuring and cohesion in the new Europe', *Regional Studies,* Vol. 26, No. 4, pp. 319-31.

Bangemann, M. (1992), *Meeting the Global Challenge: Establishing a Successful European Industrial Policy*, London: Kogan Page.

Begg, I. and Mayes, D. (1993), 'Cohesion, convergence and economic and monetary union', *Regional Studies*, Vol. 27, No. 2, pp. 149-165.

Begg, I. (1995), 'Threats to Cohesion' in *Behind the Myth of the European Union* (Eds. Amin A. and Tomaney, J.), London: Routledge, pp. 110-124.

Cappelin, R. (1988), 'Interdependenza tra politiche regionali e politiche economiche no-regionali nella Comunita europea', *Economia Pubblica*, 3, March, pp. 97-112.

CEC (1974), 'The Social Action Programme', *Bulletin of the European Communities*, 10, pp. 370-380, Brussels: Commission for the European Communities.

CEC (1984), *The Regional Impact of the Community's External Policy* (Kirschen Study), Brussels: Commission for the European Communities.

CEC (1985), *Completing the Internal Market: White Paper from the Commission to the European Parliament*, Luxembourg: Commission for the European Communities.

CEC (1987), *The Regions of the Enlarged Community — Third Periodic Report on the Social and Economic Situation and Development of the Regions of the Community*, Brussels: Commission for the European Communities.

CEC (1989), Regulation 2052/88 — Tasks of the Structural Funds; *Official Journal of the European Communities* L185, 15th July 1989.

CEC (1990a), *Charter of Fundamental Social Rights for Workers* (The Social Charter), Brussels: Commission of the European Communities.

CEC (1990b), 'One market, one money', *European Economy*, 44, Brussels: Commission of the European Communities.

CEC (1990c), *The New Structural Policies of the European Community* (European File 7-8/90), Luxembourg: Office for Official Publications of the European Community.

CEC (1991a), *The Regions in the 1990s*. (The Fourth Periodic Report on the social and economic situation and development of the regions of the Community), Luxembourg: Commission of the European Communities.

CEC (1991b), 'European Industrial Policy for the 1990s', *Bulletin of the European Communities*, Supplement 3/91, Brussels: Commission of the European Communities.

CEC (1992), *From the Single Act to Maastricht and Beyond: The Means to Match Our Ambitions*, COM(92) 2001. Brussels: Commission of the European Communities.

CEC (1993a), *Official Journal of the European Communities*, C230/4, 26th September, Brussels: Commission for the European Communities.

CEC (1993b), *Growth, Competitiveness and Employment: The Challenges and Way Forward for the 21st Century*, Brussels: Commission for the European Communities.

CEC (1993c), *XXIInd Report on Competition Policy, 1992*, Brussels: Commission for the European Communities.

CEC (1994), *EC Funded Research and Technological Development: An Insight into the Handling of Project Proposals. An Introduction to Contract Negotiation*, Luxembourg: Commission for the European Communities:

Cecchini, P. (1988), *The European Challenge, 1992* (The Cecchini Report), Aldershot: Wildwood House.

Committee for the Study of Economic and Monetary Union (1989), *Report on Economic and Monetary Union in the European Community* (The Delors Report), Brussels: Commission for the European Communities.

Delors, J. (1989), 'Regional implications of economic and monetary integration' in *Report on Economic and Monetary Union in the European Community*, (Ed. Committee for the Study of Economic and

Monetary Unions), Brussels: Commission of the European Communities, pp. 63-68.

Doyle, M. F. (1989), 'Regional Policy and European Economic Integration' in *Report on Economic and Monetary Union in the European Community*, (Ed. Committee for the study of Economic and Monetary Unions). Brussels: Commission of the European Communities, pp. 69-80.

Grahl, J. and Teague, P. (1990), *1992: The Big Market,* London: Lawrence and Wishart.

Gröte, J. R., (1992), 'Diseconomics in space: traditional sectoral policies of the EC, the European Technology Community and their effects on regional disparities' in *The Regions and the European Community: The Regional Response to the Single Market in Underdeveloped Areas* (Ed. Leonardi, R.), London: Frank Cass, pp. 14-46.

Hankel, W. (1994), 'Maastricht's EMU is too much, too soon' in *Is European Monetary Union Dead?* (Philip Morris Institute, Paper No. 3), Brussels: Philip Morris Institute, pp. 48-61.

Holland, S. (1993), *The European Imperative: Economic and Social Cohesion in the 1990s,* Nottingham: Spokesman.

Holland, S. (1995), 'Squaring the circle: Maastricht convergence, cohesion and employment', *European Labour Forum*, 15, Summer, pp. 12-23.

Hughes Hallett, A. and Scott, D. (1992), *Monetary Union and the Regions* (Final Report to the Confederation of Scottish Local Authorities), Edinburgh: CoSLA.

Junne, G. and Van Tulder, R. (1988), *European Multinationals in Core Technologies*, Chichester: John Wiley and Sons.

Krugman, P. (1991), *Geography and Trade*, Cambridge, MA: MIT Press.

Landabaso, M. (1995), 'The Promotion of Innovation in Regional Community Policy: Lessons and Proposals for a Regional Innovation Strategy', Paper for International Workshop on Regional Science and Technology Policy Research, RESTPOR '95, Himeji, Japan, February.

Lange, P. (1992), 'The politics of the Social Dimension' in *Euro-Politics: Institutions and Policymaking in the 'New' European Community* (Ed. Sbragia, A.), Washington, DC: Brookings Institute, pp. 225-256.

Lintner, V. and Mazey, S. (1991), 'Monetary integration in the European Community' in *The European Community: Economic and Political Aspects* (Eds. Lintner, V. and Mazey, S.), London: McGraw-Hill, pp. 55-71.

Logue, H. (1995), 'The Role of Research and Technology Development in the Regions', Paper for International Workshop on Regional Science and Technology Policy Research, RESTPOR '95, Himeji, Japan, February.

Love, J. H. (1994), 'EC mergers regulation and regional economic cohesion', *Environment and Planning A,* 26, pp. 137-152.

MacDougall, D. (1977), *Report of the Study Group on the Role of Public Finance in European Integration* (Volume 1: General Report). Brussels: Commission of the European Communities.

Marquand, D. (1994), 'Reinventing Federalism: Europe and the Left' in *Reinventing the Left* (Ed. Miliband, D.), Cambridge: Polity Press, pp. 219-229.

Martin, R. (1993), 'Reviving the Economic Case for Regional Policy' in *Spatial Policy in a Divided Nation* (Eds. Harrison, R.T. and Hart, M.). London: Jessica Kingsley.

Mytelka, L. K. and Delapierre, M. (1987), 'The alliance strategies of European firms in the Information Technology industry and the role of ESPRIT', *Journal of Common Market Studies*, 26, 2, pp. 255-272.

Nolan, P. (1994), 'Labour market institutions, industrial restructuring and unemployment in Europe' in *Unemployment in Europe* (Eds. Michie, J. and Grieve Smith, J), London: Academic Press, pp. 61-74.

O'Donnell, R. (1992), 'Policy requirements for regional balance in economic and monetary union' in *Economic and Social Cohesion in Europe* (Ed. Hannequart, A.), London: Routledge, pp. 21-52.

O'Donnell, R. (1993), *Ireland and Europe: Challenges for a New Century* (ESRI Policy Research Services Paper No. 17), Dublin: Economic and Social Research Institute.

Official Journal of the European Communities (1989), *Community Framework on State Aids to the Motor Industry*, 89 C 123/03.

Peterson, J. (1991), 'European technology policy — Policy communities and the politics of meso-corporatism', Mimeo.

Pike, A. and Charles, D. (1995), 'The impact of international collaboration on UK university-industry links', *Industry and Higher Education*, Vol. 9, No. 5, pp. 264-276.

Ramsey, H. (1992), 'Whose Champions? multinationals, labour and industry policy in the European Community after 1992', *Capital and Class*, 48, pp. 17-39.

Ramsey, H. (1995), '*Le Défi Européen*: multinational restructuring, labour and EU policy' in *Beyond the Myth of the European Union* (Eds: Amin A. and Tomaney, J.), London: Routledge, pp. 174-200.

Sadler, D. (1992), 'Industrial policy of the European Community: Strategic deficits and regional dilemmas', *Environment and Planning A*, 24, pp. 1711-1730.

Sadler, D. (1993), 'National and international regulatory frameworks: the politics of European automobile industry production and trade' in *Towards a New Map of Automobile Production in Europe? New Production Concepts and Regional Restructuring* (Eds. Hudson, R. and Schamp, E.W.), Berlin: Springer.

Scott, A. (1994), 'Financing the Community: the Delors II package' in *The European Community and the Challenge of the Future* (2nd Edition) (Ed. Lodge, J.) London: Frances Pinter.

Silvia, S. (1991), 'The Social Charter of the European Community: a defeat for European labour', *Industrial and Labour Relations Review*, 44, 4, pp. 626-643.

Streeck, W. (1994), 'European Social Policy after Maastricht: the 'Social Dialogue' and 'Subsidiarity', *Economic and Industrial Democracy*, 15, pp. 151-177.

Tett, G., Fisher, A. and Hill, A. (1995), 'When strength is a weakness: competitive devaluations are posing problems in Europe', *Financial Times*, Wednesday, 9th August.

Tomaney, J. (1994), 'Regional and industrial aspects of unemployment in Europe' in *Unemployment in Europe* (Eds. Michie, J. and Grieve Smith, J.), London: Academic Press, pp. 160-176.

Tomaney, J. (1995), 'The Utilities Directive, Public Procurement and Industrial Restructuring: the Case of the Railway Equipment Industry', unpublished paper, Centre for Urban and Regional Development Studies, University of Newcastle-upon-Tyne.

Vanhoven, N. and Klaasen, L. H. (1987), *Regional Policy: A European Approach*, Avebury: Aldershot.

5

ECONOMIC STRUCTURE AND CHANGE IN THE EU PERIPHERY

Frank Barry, John Bradley and Delma Duggan

5.1 INTRODUCTION

Our purpose in this chapter is to describe the similarities in economic structure that characterise the peripheral EU countries — Spain, Portugal, Greece and Ireland — and to analyse the structural changes that have taken place in these countries since their joining the EU.

We begin by looking at the convergence experience of the periphery, i.e. the extent to which these regions have caught up to the core in terms of GDP per capita. Although some convergence has occurred, these countries remain the poorest in the Union and it is not surprising therefore that they share many characteristics. Some of these are more apparent than others; the relative importance of agriculture and the underdevelopment of physical infrastructure in the periphery, for example. Less obvious, however, are features such as the extent of unemployment and underemployment; the relative share of producer and consumer services, and the relative lack of increasing-returns-to-scale (IRS) segments of the manufacturing industry. Section 5.3 of the paper looks at these issues.

Section 5.4 describes the macroeconometric model, derived from the HERMIN project, which is used to analyse the internal workings of the peripheral economies as well as their relationship with the encompassing world economy. The model throws up interesting differences between how the various peripheral economies operate at present, as well as suggesting the direction in which structural change is likely to proceed in the medium term.

Section 5.5 describes how the model has been used to analyse the likely impact of the Community Support Framework (CSF) (commonly known as the Structural Funds programme) and the development of the Single European Market.

A final section contains our conclusions.

5.2 THE CONVERGENCE EXPERIENCE OF THE EU PERIPHERY[1]

We use the term 'EU periphery' to denote those countries, all or most regions of which have 'Objective 1' status. These regions, with 75 per cent or less of the EU average GDP per capita, comprise the western and southern seaboards of the Union.

Have the relatively poor regions been converging on the richer regions, in terms of GDP per head, or not?

The conventional wisdom in economic growth theory is that regions should converge over time. The world data (depicted in Barro and Sala-i-Martin (1995) for example), however, shows divergence rather than convergence. These authors and many others argue, however, that, when the stock of human capital is controlled for, *relative* convergence appears.

Walsh (1993) and Ó Gráda and O'Rourke (1994) control for this, though, and still find Ireland to be a slow-growth outlier in terms of European convergence. Prados et al. (1993) report similar findings for the whole European periphery.

Many of these findings, however, depend strongly on the time period of the sample. Table 5.1 takes a broad look at the convergence experience and indicates fairly rapid convergence in recent years.

TABLE 5.1: RELATIVE GDP (GNP) PER CAPITA IN PURCHASING POWER PARITY TERMS (EU12 = 100)

	1960	1973	1980	1985	1990	1993
Ireland	61 (62)	59 (59)	64 (62)	65 (58)	71 (62)	77 (69)
Spain	60	79	74	71	75	76
Greece	39	57	58	51	47	49
Portugal	39	56	55	51	56	61

Source: European Commission Annual Report (1994).

---

[1] Further detail on the material in this section can be found in Barry (1994).

Using Barro and Sala-i-Martin's average convergence speed (2 per cent per annum), each country except Greece is found to have performed somewhat better than expected (in terms of GDP per head) since its accession into the EU.[2] This may be partly attributable to the Structural Funds programme,[3] though there is some empirical evidence that trade integration promotes convergence.

If living standards are more accurately measured by private consumption per capita, however, as shown in Table 5.2, relative living standards are found to have fallen in all four peripheral member states between 1973 and 1991.[4] (Ireland, on this measure, lies much closer to the lower levels of Portugal and Greece than to the relatively high level of Spain.) The convergence experience is not therefore unambiguous. It becomes of great interest to look at the structural differences between core and periphery, and to ask whether the two groups of regions have been becoming more similar in these respects or not.

TABLE 5.2: ECONOMIC INDICATORS IN THE PERIPHERY

	Gr	Irl	Port	Spn	EU
Unemployment Rate (%)					
1960	n/a	4.7	1.9	2.4	2.5
1973	2.0	6.2	2.6	2.6	2.6
1993	7.8	18.4	5.2	21.2	10.4
Private Consumption/Cap.					
1973	57	67	65	80	100
1991	54	62	58	76	100

Source: Eurostat National Accounts (1970-1991).

---

[2] Note that there is controversy in Ireland over the accuracy of recent GDP figures, many economists holding that they are overestimated due to the transfer-pricing behaviour of multinational companies.

[3] The Structural Funds programme was substantially reformed and expanded in 1988. The 1989-93 allocation, as a proportion of regional GDP, was 3.5 per cent for Portugal, 2.9 per cent for Greece, 2.3 per cent for Ireland, 1.2 per cent for the 70 per cent of Spain classed as Objective 1, and 0.8 per cent for the Italian Mezzogiorno. Funding was again increased substantially for the 1994-1999 period.

[4] Consumption is measured according to its own specific purchasing power parity (from Eurostat National Accounts, 1970-91).

5.3 STRUCTURAL SIMILARITIES BETWEEN PERIPHERAL REGIONS[5]

The European Commission's (1990a) 'One Market, One Money' report points out that the EU periphery is characterised by higher unemployment than prevails in the EU core. This is a statistical artifice however since Spain, the country with the highest unemployment rate, is also by far the largest peripheral economy. We argue here, however, that all the peripheral countries can be seen to suffer from either unemployment or underemployment (which does not show up in the standard data). We then focus on a number of shared characteristics that are likely to increase the burdens of adjustment on peripheral labour markets, factors such as the relative importance of agriculture, the difficulties of adjusting to free trade, and the relative underdevelopment of financial markets and of physical infrastructure in the periphery.

We then move on to analyse other structural similarities between peripheral countries: relative proportions of producer and consumer services, and the share of increasing-returns sectors within manufacturing.

5.3.1 Unemployment and Underemployment
The first shared characteristic of peripheral regions we will look at is unemployment and underemployment.

Table 5.2 illustrates that two of the peripheral countries, Ireland and Spain, have very high unemployment rates while Greece and Portugal have rates below the EU average. The minimal nature of the social welfare systems in Greece and Portugal, however, and the large proportion of the labour force engaged in agriculture in these countries suggest a substantial degree of underemployment.

This is further borne out by the fact that Portugal and Spain have exceptionally low productivity levels in agriculture — only about one-third of the already low national level in each case. The professional status of employment also points to agricultural underemployment in Greece and Spain, where 38 per cent and 19 per cent, respectively, of total agricultural employment is classified as unpaid family workers. While the proportion of unpaid family workers in Portugal and Ireland is much lower (less than 10 per cent in each case), in both these countries there are still

---

[5] For more on this material see Duggan, 1995.

many smallholders with no prospect of long-term viability. Furthermore, in Greece the exceptionally high proportion of non-agricultural employment classified as employer/self-employed (27 per cent) or unpaid family workers (5 per cent, with 11 per cent of females so classified) also suggests underemployment.

Ireland, Spain and Greece also have exceptionally high dependency rates. In Ireland in 1991 there were 21 dependants for every 10 workers, in Spain 20 and in Greece 17, as compared with an EU average of 14. This is due not only to unemployment but also to the very low labour-force participation rates in these countries. This in turn points to a relatively high incidence of discouraged workers.

There are several structural similarities between peripheral regions that are likely to increase the amount of absorption required of the labour market.[6] These include:

- the relative importance of agriculture

- the underdeveloped state of financial markets, and of both physical and human infrastructure

- the difficulties faced by the periphery in adjusting to free trade.

5.3.2 Agricultural Orientation
As the 'One Market, One Money' report (CEC,1990a) notes, Objective 1 regions have a relatively high share of employment in the inexorably declining agricultural sector. Of the four countries, Greece has the largest proportion of employees in agriculture (22.2 per cent of total employment in 1991). This compares with 17.4 per cent in Portugal, 14.0 per cent in Ireland and 10.9 per cent in Spain (Eurostat, 1993).

This factor adds to the number of workers who must be absorbed into the urban labour force, or else, as in Portugal and Greece, provides a refuge in the form of underemployment for those who in a more developed welfare system would add to the unemployment rolls.

---

[6] Of course, economies such as the US appear to be able to absorb labour relatively easily. For such pressures to result in unemployment, therefore, there must be other factors hindering the peripheral labour markets' ability to adjust.

5.3.3 Underdevelopment of Infrastructure and Capital Markets

Two further characteristics of peripheral regions appear likely to hinder the development of employment opportunities. One is the underdeveloped state of financial markets. Larre and Torres (1991), in a study of Spain, Portugal and Greece, make the following points, many of which apply to Ireland as well:

> In the mid-1980s financial markets were still in their infancy, with . . . little or no competition between banks and financial institutions; narrow capital markets; a limited range of savings instruments and a preponderance of public debt securities; credit controls (Greece and Portugal) and administratively fixed interest rates; compulsory portfolio requirements for banks, and a high proportion of subsidised credit.

This theme is echoed in 'One Market, One Money' (1990a), which reports that the high cost of credit and poor availability of risk capital are among the major factors that firms in peripheral regions identify as growth inhibiting.

The same report also notes that firms identify infrastructural deficiencies in the areas of education and training, transport and communications, and the supply and cost of energy, as more important impediments than geographic factors such as the proximity of suppliers and of customers. The available data on the stock of infrastructure in peripheral regions provides supporting evidence. Table 5.3 below, adapted from Martin and Rogers (1994), reports relative infrastructural levels for an aggregate of transportation, telecommunications, energy and education. It reveals that Ireland, Spain and Portugal fell further behind the EU average between 1979 and 1985, while Italy and Greece converged slightly.

TABLE 5.3: RELATIVE INFRASTRUCTURAL LEVELS IN EU COUNTRIES

	1979-80	1985-86
Italy	81.7	85.4
Spain	77.7	74.3
Ireland	71.1	67.1
Greece	54.5	56.0
Portugal	40.0	38.7
EU	100.0	100.0

5.3.4 Difficulties of Adjustment to Free Trade

Progressive trade liberalisation within Europe is likely to entail substantial industrial disruption in the periphery, while sectoral restructuring within core EU countries, which have fairly similar factor endowments, is more likely to take place through the development of market niches rather than through the wholesale disappearance of existing industries. Evidence in this regard is provided by Neven (1990) who shows that Greece and Portugal have less intra-industry trade than the other EU countries; Ireland, Spain and Italy have intermediate levels, while Germany, France, the Netherlands, the UK and Belgium are characterised by intense intra-industry trade. Adjustment problems are therefore likely to be greater in the periphery.

As Krugman (1987) notes with respect to the Southern periphery's accession to the EU:

> the trade expansion produced by EC enlargement is simply not likely to be as painless as the trade expansion produced by the formation of the Community and earlier enlargement. There will certainly be income distribution problems created by the changes, and also quite possibly some real costs in terms of unemployment.

A massive shake out of jobs in Irish and Spanish 'traditional' industry occurred as trade liberalisation progressed. The low productivity sectors in Greece and Portugal are also likely to face intense pressures in the next decade.

Further confirmation of the structural changes likely to be in store for Greece and Portugal is provided by the size structure of enterprises in peripheral regions, shown in Table 5.4. The National Economic and Social Council (1989) documents how the average size of establishments in Ireland declined in the wake of free trade as indigenous firms in increasing-returns sectors were wiped out. Something similar may have happened in Spain.[7] Portugal may therefore be thought to resemble the pre-free-trade Irish position, while the fact that nearly three-fifths of Greek non-agricultural employment is concentrated in micro-enterprises

---

[7] On the basis of Ireland's adjustment, we would regard small initial firm size in increasing-returns sectors as a competitive disadvantage, rather than as representing an opportunity for the exploitation of further scale economies in an integrated market, as in Neven (1990).

with less than ten employees probably does not augur well for their ability to compete internationally.

TABLE 5.4: NON-AGRICULTURAL EMPLOYMENT SHARES BY
ENTERPRISE SIZE, 1988

	Greece	Ireland	Portugal	Spain	EU
Micro (0-9)	59	34	36	36	30
Small (10-99)	21	30	27	30	25
Medium (100-499)	11	18	17	17	16
Large (500+)	9	17	20	17	30

Source: First Annual Report of the European Observatory for SMEs (1993).

5.3.5 The Structure of the Services Sector

The economic geographers Keeble, Offord and Walker (1988) noted that the structure of the services sector differed significantly between core and periphery, with the core being relatively more specialised in producer services.[8]

Table 5.5 below shows the ratio of employment in producer relative to consumer services. It shows, as Keeble et al. suggested, that there is a substantial difference between the relative proportions accounted for by producer and consumer services in the core *vis-à-vis* the periphery.

It is clear that the core-periphery distinction is significant and long-lasting. Ireland, however, seems to have extricated itself from its peripheral position, particularly between 1978 and 1983, while Greece appears as the periphery outlier, with a ratio of producer-to-consumer services more like that of the core. The latter is easily explained, however, by the fact that Greece, which contains a large number of islands, possesses an unusually large transport, communications and storage sector which is part of producer services. Keeble et al. (1988) suggest that Ireland's core-like characteristics appear to be evidence of successful industrial policies.

---

[8] Producer services are defined in the NACE and ISIC classifications as categories 7 (Transport and Communications) and 8 (Banking and Financial Services), while consumer services are categories 6 (Distribution, Hotels and Catering) and 9 (Community, Social and Personal Services).

TABLE 5.5: RATIO OF EMPLOYMENT IN PRODUCER VERSUS
CONSUMER SERVICES

	1968	1978	1983	1987
Belgium	.299	.33	.327	.332
Germany	.342	.316	.318	.314
France	.343	.351	.344	.343
Netherlands	.522	.308	.359	.362
Ireland	.241	.251	.354	.332
Italy	.40	.267	.262	.267
Portugal	n/a.	.259	.24	.225
Spain	n/a.	.294	.289	.269
Greece	n/a.	.457	.378	.345

Why does the core appear to be relatively specialised in producer
services? Hansen (1990) argues that:

> in an increasingly information-oriented economy, producer
> services play a pivotal role in the . . . expanding division of la-
> bour, which in turn creates productivity increases throughout
> the economy. Regions that have a high density of producer
> services are thus likely to have higher per capita incomes than
> other regions.

Causation can equally plausibly run in the opposite direction. The
fact that 'core regions almost always contain above-average concentrations of highly qualified workers' can be related to studies
by Beyers et al. (1986) and Wier (1992) which showed that the
producer-services sector is dominated by professional and technical employees, while consumer services are typically labour-
intensive low-productivity low-wage jobs.

Whichever direction of causation is more important, it is clear
that a high ratio of producer-to-consumer services jobs is
beneficial.

5.3.6 Increasing-Returns-to-Scale Manufacturing Sectors
Equivalently, it is beneficial for a region to have a high share of
the manufacturing sectors that exhibit increasing returns to scale
(IRS). As Heffernan and Sinclair (1990) note, average productivity
in the regions that capture these sectors rises relative to that prevailing elsewhere.

One of the potential difficulties that the periphery faced in adjusting to EU membership was the possibility that as trade barriers fell these industries would be attracted more to the core because of economies of agglomeration. Indeed, as Barry (1994) showed, this process *did* result in the decline of Irish indigenous industry in IRS sectors.[9] However, the influx of multinational companies in precisely these sectors more than dominated this decline, so the share of Irish employment in IRS sectors has increased substantially.

TABLE 5.6: DEVELOPMENTS IN IRS INDUSTRIES

	1973	1980	1993
Indigenous employment	25,209	27,440	22,565
Share of total manufacturing	12.46%	11.86%	11.64%
Multinational employment	32,735	50,114	59,055
Share of total manufacturing	16.18%	21.67%	30.46%

Source: IDA Employment Survey

Summing multinational and indigenous employment, we find the share of IRS sectors in total manufacturing employment has risen from 29 per cent in 1973 to 42 per cent by 1993. While this is still small relative to the equivalent share in the core EU countries (see Table 5.7 below), it has been increasing over time rather than decreasing.

Once again, we see a very clear core-periphery pattern emerging, with the periphery less specialised in IRS sectors. Unfortunately the paucity of data precludes an analysis of how this situation has changed over the course of the 1980s.

If the Irish experience is anything to go by, however, we can say that the periphery is likely to be capturing an increasing share of IRS industries. The data on foreign direct investment in manufacturing (from the *OECD International Direct Investment Statistics Yearbook*) reveal that while the Irish share of foreign direct investment (as a proportion of GNP) was twice as large as Spain's and three times as large as Portugal's in the early 1980s, the

---

[9] The IRS sectors are identified by O'Malley (1992) on the basis of Pratten's (1988) study of engineering economies of scale.

Portuguese and Irish shares had been equalised by the early 1990s, and the Spanish share was now twice as large as these. Only the Greek share remained low, and stagnant.

TABLE 5.7: EMPLOYMENT IN IRS SECTORS AS A PER CENT OF TOTAL MANUFACTURING EMPLOYMENT

	1968	1979	1983	1989
Germany	55	60	65	63
France	42	55	55	51
Netherlands	50	62	54	54
Belgium	42	57	55	53
Italy	49	54	56	55
Ireland	21	35	40	45
Spain	n/a.	38	39	37
Portugal	n/a.	n/a.	28	25
Greece	n/a.	n/a.	36	35

Source: Eurostat: Structure and Activity of Industry, various years.

5.4 MODELLING THE EU PERIPHERY[10]

For many purposes, such as analysing the impact on the periphery of the Single European Market or the Structural Funds programme, a formal macroeconometric model is required. In this section we describe the structure of the HERMIN model which has been constructed for these purposes, focusing on similarities and differences between the structures of the various peripheral countries.[11] The national HERMIN models differ not only in terms of numerical parameters within a uniform encompassing framework, but also in some more fundamental ways.

Each national HERMIN model consists of three broad parts: the supply side, the absorption side and the income distribution side. Most of the differences between national models appear on the supply side.

---

[10] Further detail on the HERMIN modelling project can be found in Bradley et al. (1995).

[11] The Greek HERMIN model is still at an early stage of development and we report only on the Irish, Spanish and Portuguese cases.

5.4.1 Tradable-sector Output Determination

Here the Irish and Portuguese models appear as polar opposites. The small size and extreme openness of the Irish economy, and the dominant position occupied by branch plants of foreign-owned multinational firms, dictates a particular approach to manufacturing-output determination, with consequences for the behaviour of manufactured exports. Domestic demand is found to play a relatively small part in the long-run decisions of Irish manufacturing firms, and output prices are almost completely determined abroad. Irish tradable-sector output is driven primarily by world demand and cost competitiveness.

In the Portuguese HERMIN model on the other hand, traded-sector output responds strongly to changes in both domestic demand and in world demand conditions. Unlike in the Irish case, then, the standard domestic-demand multiplier effects are strong. Portuguese prices are also more strongly affected by domestic costs, in contrast to the strong degree of externally-determined pricing behaviour found for Irish manufacturing.

These distinctions are crucial to understanding the behaviour of the three HERMIN models. While the Portuguese approach appears to offer a good explanation of past behaviour, however, the position may be changing very rapidly in the context of the Single European Market (SEM). If Portuguese indigenous manufacturing were to follow the much earlier pattern of Irish manufacturing in its process of opening to world trade, then it is likely that the influence of foreign-owned multinationals will rise and many of the less efficient indigenous Portuguese firms will decline. Hence, the Irish HERMIN model may illustrate one possible development pattern for the future Portuguese manufacturing sector.

5.4.2 Migration and Labour Supply

With respect to labour supply, the Irish and Portuguese models are also polar extremes, with the labour supply exogenous in the Portuguese model and both endogenous and highly elastic (because of the migration links between Ireland and the UK) in the Irish case. The Spanish model permits some endogeneity to enter via discouraged worker effects in the male and female labour force participation decisions.

In the Portuguese model there is a one-to-one relationship between employment and unemployment: at the margin, a job created means one less unemployed person. Once again, however, we argue that the Portuguese model may become more similar to Ireland's as the Portuguese labour market integrates with those of the European core economies.

5.4.3 Econometric Comparisons

We now turn to an evaluation of the econometric estimation of the three national HERMIN models. Again focusing on the supply side, we find three aspects of the national model estimations that generate interesting results: the specification of the production functions, and the processes by which producer prices and wage demands are determined.

Focusing first on production functions, we summarise in Table 5.8 the elasticities of substitution between capital and labour in the tradable (manufacturing) sector. The main finding that comes through is the fact that the Irish elasticity is much smaller than those for Portugal and Spain.[12]

TABLE 5.8: ELASTICITIES OF SUBSTITUTION IN TRADABLE-SECTOR PRODUCTION FUNCTIONS

Ireland	Portugal	Spain
0.34	0.80	0.77

The smaller elasticity for Ireland can be understood as follows. In a traditional and/or relatively closed economy, the substitution of capital for labour as a result of shifting relative factor prices normally takes place within the economy. However, in an economy dominated by multinationals this substitution will often involve a shift in production capacity to other countries, i.e., capital will not replace labour in the Irish factory but will instead seek out lower costs elsewhere.

Turning now to sectoral-output prices, the output price of non-tradable services in all three models is simply a mark-up on unit labour costs. In the determination of output prices in the traded sector on the other hand, Ireland stands out as a rather extreme case of price-taking. About 30 per cent of external price

---

[12] The volume of output is held constant in determining the values of these elasticities.

transmission originates from the UK sterling zone, while the remaining 70 per cent originates from the DM zone.

Mixed external-price-taking and price mark-up equations were estimated for Portugal and Spain. In Portugal the 'world' price had an elasticity of 0.70, with domestic unit labour costs having a value of 0.30. The Spanish results were 0.41 (external) and 0.59 (domestic costs) respectively. These can be rationalised in terms of the greater openness of the smaller Portuguese economy relative to Spain.

Finally, we turn to the determination of wages in the traded and non-traded sectors in the three countries. In all cases wage rates in the traded sector are modelled as the outcome of bargaining between employers and trades unions. However, the three countries produced different patterns of results.

In Ireland, a full pass-through of price increases was not rejected by the data, so bargaining was assumed to take place in real-wage terms. In Portugal only 89 per cent of increases in prices were compensated for by wage increases, while in Spain the degree of price indexation was found to depend on a move in 1978 to more centralised wage bargaining (the Moncloa Agreements). Post-Moncloa, there was only partial (92 per cent) indexation to price increases. All three countries exhibited a similar pass-through of productivity increases to wages, ranging from a low of 61 per cent in Portugal, through 69 per cent for Ireland, to 70 per cent for Spain.

In the Irish case the tax wedge is found to be a key driving variable. The tax wedge (the gap between the total cost of labour to employers and the real post-tax wage of employees) includes indirect taxes, direct taxes paid by labour, and social insurance contributions paid by employers. For Portugal and Spain, no direct income tax effects could be found.

It is in the impact of unemployment on wage demands (the 'Phillips Curve' effect) that the three wage equations differ most. Table 5.9 shows the effects on the wage rate of a one percentage point rise in the rate of unemployment.[13]

---

[13] In the case of Ireland, the figure presented is for the year 1989, since the Phillips curve term is entered in log rather than in linear form.

TABLE 5.9: PHILLIPS CURVE EFFECTS: IRELAND, PORTUGAL AND
SPAIN: PERCENTAGE CHANGE IN WAGES RESULTING FROM 1 PER
CENT RISE IN UNEMPLOYMENT

	Traded	Non-traded
Ireland	-1.63	-1.63
Portugal	-0.464	-2.76
Spain	-0.005	-0.006

It is clear that wage bargaining in the traded sector is least influenced by the level of unemployment in the Spanish case, Portugal is an intermediate case, and Ireland shows the strongest influence. However, it should be noted that the presence of an unemployment-sensitive migration mechanism in HERMIN-Ireland reduces the effective size of the Phillips Curve coefficient.

Turning to wage bargaining in the non-traded sector, wage inflation in the Irish case seems to be equal to that in the traded-goods sector. Separate sector-specific bargaining models are used in Portugal and Spain and one of the key differences relates to the Phillips Curve effect. In Portugal the power of unemployment to influence wage bargaining is six times stronger than in the traded sector, indicating, as pointed out earlier in this paper, that flexibility in this sector is enforced through the virtual absence of a social welfare system. No such flexibility is found in the Spanish case, offering further insights into that country's high unemployment.

5.4.4 How the Economies React to Exogenous Shocks

In all three models an attempt has been made to carry out comparable shocks to observe how each model reacts. We briefly review the responses of each model to world-demand and public-employment shocks.

In Table 5.10 below we tabulate the impact of a world-demand shock on traded output (Y_T), non-traded output (Y_N) and GDP at factor cost (Y), together with the sectoral wage effects (w_T for tradables and w_N for non-tradables) and the effects on the consumer price deflator (p). All table entries represent percentage deviations from the baseline.

The direct influence of the world-demand shock on traded sector output is greatest in the case of Ireland, reflecting the strong export orientation of the manufacturing sector. The Portuguese and Spanish effects are smaller and of about the same size in the long run (a rise of about 0.69). The long-run induced effects on non-traded sector output are also larger for Ireland (rising to just under 0.5 per cent, compared to around 0.25 for the other two countries). The aggregate effect on GDP at factor cost for Ireland is also about twice that pertaining to Portugal and Spain.

TABLE 5.10: EFFECTS OF WORLD DEMAND SHOCK (1 PER CENT SUSTAINED RISE)

	Y_T	Y_N	Y	w_T	w_N	P
Ireland						
1991	0.96	0.27	0.43	0.22	0.22	0.04
2010	0.97	0.45	0.58	0.13	0.13	0.00
Portugal						
1991	0.63	0.23	0.25	0.45	0.63	0.26
2010	0.69	0.29	0.30	0.64	0.77	0.36
Spain						
1991	0.28	0.11	0.13	0.13	0.13	0.10
2010	0.69	0.24	0.31	0.24	0.26	0.18

The inflationary consequences of this expansionary shock are modest for Ireland, intermediate for Spain, and much higher for Portugal. Various factors cause this: the domestic cost-push element in the traded-sector output prices of the latter countries compared with pure price taking in Ireland; the high Phillips Curve coefficient in the Portuguese non-traded sector wage equation (one and a half times larger than in the Irish case); the closed labour markets in Portugal and Spain compared to the very open Irish one.

The other shock we explore, an increase in public sector employment, investigates the role of the Keynesian (domestic-demand) multiplier in each model. In Table 5.11 we tabulate the short and long-run multipliers for the case where the extra public expenditure is debt financed. For comparison, in the Irish case we run the same shock with a policy-feedback rule that holds the public debt to GNP ratio constant. Similar results could be derived for the Portuguese and Spanish models.

TABLE 5.11: KEYNESIAN PUBLIC EMPLOYMENT MULTIPLIERS: 5 PER
CENT SUSTAINED RISE (POLICY-FEEDBACK-RULE RESULTS ARE IN
BRACKETS)

	Ireland	Portugal	Spain
Impact (1991)	1.202 (1.148)	1.48	1.45
Long-run (2001)	1.528 (0.560)	1.87	1.29

In the case of Ireland and Portugal, the results are very much in
line with our prior expectations. The leakages out of the Irish
economy are large and the impact multiplier is barely above unity.
In the long run it reaches 1.5, but it must be remembered that the
increase in public expenditure has been debt financed and the
debt/GNP ratio (not shown) rises by 11 percentage points by the
year 2010. Imposing the policy-feedback rule (where increases in
the direct tax rate are used to prevent any increases in the
debt/GNP ratio) produces a dramatically different result, where
the long-run fiscal multiplier falls to below 0.6 (the term in
brackets).

In the Portuguese case the long-run multiplier rises to about
1.9 but, as with the Irish case, the debt/GNP ratio increases by 8.6
percentage points above its baseline. The Spanish case is intermediate, with an impact multiplier of 1.45, almost identical to the
Portuguese case. However, over time it falls to 1.29 as the interaction of wages and prices, together with the Phillips curve,
erodes international competitiveness. If the fiscal policy rule were
imposed in both models the multipliers would be much lower, as
shown in the Irish case.

5.4.5 Overall Perspective on the HERMIN Models
In the Irish case the HERMIN model reflects an economy that
reacts very rapidly to movements in world demand, indicating the
close supply-side links with foreign multinational activity. The
very limited role for domestic fiscal expansion is reflected in the
low fiscal multipliers, which are less than unity when the national
debt is capped.

In the Portuguese and Spanish cases the HERMIN model reflects economies that are only partially exposed to international
competition. Increases in world demand bring only limited increases in domestic production, reflecting the more traditional
nature of their exports and the predominance of imports of

finished goods. The fiscal multipliers also appear to be quite large, though they probably characterise an era that has now passed, when Portugal was relatively insulated from world economic forces. The lack of homogeneity in the Portuguese labour market will also probably disappear in the future, since the Social Chapter of the Maastricht Treaty will lead to greater harmonisation of social welfare systems and labour legislation. We suspect that the Portuguese economy may become much more like the Irish economy in future years.

The Spanish results are interesting. Our prior belief was that Spain would behave as a semi-closed economy, given its large size relative to Ireland and Portugal. This is partially borne out in the world output shock. However, the fiscal multipliers were found to be rather smaller than expected. The combination of high competitiveness elasticities and the institutional rigidities of the labour market appear to be responsible for this.

5.5 ANALYSING THE IMPACT OF THE STRUCTURAL FUNDS AND THE SINGLE EUROPEAN MARKET

Many aspects of public investment policy in the peripheral countries now fall within the scope of the EU's Community Support Framework (CSF). The implementation of the first CSF covered the five-year period 1989-93. Moves towards EMU were accompanied by another expansion of the size and scope of the CSF by over 50 per cent, to compensate for the fact that many of the remaining areas of policy autonomy in the periphery will be further restricted. This second CSF programme runs for the six-year period 1994-99.

In this section we describe how the effects of this second programme, which amounts to 87 billion ECU in total for Ireland, Spain and Portugal, have been evaluated.[14]

In all cases, the beneficial demand-side effects of the policy shocks are likely to be transitory, particularly where an element of domestic financing is required and where domestic public sector finances must be kept in balance. The choking-off of these beneficial effects will arise mainly because of a loss of competitiveness in the traded sector brought about by the need to raise taxes, and

---

[14] Note that private expenditure makes up part of the total CSF funds, on top of EU and national public funds. Notice also that the domestic public cofinancing ratio varies from country to country.

the consequential impact of the bigger tax wedge on wage bargaining, unit labour costs, and international competitiveness.

In terms of supply-side effects of the CSF programmes there are two ways to proceed. The first approach — taken in the ESRI HERMES-based study of CSF 1989-93 — tries to estimate the cost savings using micro studies of the individual infrastructure programmes. Having introduced the projected cost savings directly into the model as a shock, the supply-side consequences were derived from model simulation (Bradley et al., 1992).

The 'pure' human capital effect of investment in human resources was incorporated in a similar way, by the assumption of a rate of return to human capital investment, in line with the (limited) empirical evidence.[15]

The conventional approach, however, ignores spill-over effects that might arise from state-of-the-art technology, clustering and agglomeration economies, so a second approach has been introduced which recognises that the basic effects are supplemented by spillovers which enhance the effects of well designed investment and training policy initiatives.

The first spillover effect (or 'externality') arises through the increased total factor productivity likely to be associated with improved infrastructure and a higher level of human capital.

The second type of externality is likely to be associated with the role of improved infrastructure and training in attracting productive activities to Ireland through foreign direct investment, and enhancing the ability of indigenous industries to compete in the international marketplace. This can be thought of as an industrial composition externality, since it is well known that the mix of goods produced becomes more technologically advanced as the development process proceeds.

It is likely that the factor productivity externality will be a two-edged process: industry and services become more productive and competitive, but labour demand is weakened. The role of the industrial composition externality is likely to be more unambigu-

---

[15] The measurement of rates of return is fraught with difficulty, however. The literature displays not only considerable differences in estimated rates of return but also considerable confusion between the concepts of 'social' and 'private' rates of return. Furthermore, it is difficult to relate quantitatively the expected benefits in terms of technical progress to the CSF expenditures on human resources.

ously beneficial: the higher it is, the faster the period of growth to a higher income plateau.

The values of these externality effects are now examined. For the case of physical infrastructure, Aschauer (1989) showed that there was a significant relationship between public capital and private sector output. In a survey of econometric results, Munnell (1993) shows that the elasticity with respect to public capital ranges from an upper bound of 0.39 for the entire US, through 0.20–0.15 for individual states, to lower bounds of 0.08–0.03 for individual metropolitan areas. In our empirical CSF analysis the lower-bound value of 0.05 was used for Ireland, an *ad hoc* value of 0.10 was assumed for Portugal and, on the basis of several Spanish studies, a value of 0.2 was used for Spain.

In terms of the relationship between human capital and growth, Psacharopoulos (1994) has recently surveyed the vast literature examining the private and social returns to education and training.[16] Once again there is a wide range of estimates for the social rate of return, from a high of 25 per cent to a lower rate of 5 per cent. Even for the richer OECD countries, however, the social rate of return for higher education (the worst case) he found to be over 8 per cent. In our empirical CSF analysis we use low values in the range 0.02 for Ireland (from Callan, 1993), 0.05 for Portugal (*ad hoc*), and 0.07 for Spain (on the basis of Spanish studies).

While a good case can be made for externalities in the case of physical infrastructure and human resources, areas of predominantly public sector activity, only a weaker case can be made in the case of investment aids to the private sector. Here, there is likely to be crowding out of private sector activity and considerable deadweight, i.e., state-aided private investment that would have gone ahead even in the absence of the state aids.

Table 5.12 below reports the estimated growth bonus of the CSF programmes agreed for Ireland, Spain and Portugal. The table presents three sets of columns. The first shows CSF expenditures (including associated private investment) on an annualised basis as percentages of national GDP. In 1994 these amount to 3.7 per cent for Ireland, 5.4 per cent for Portugal and 1.6 per cent for Spain.

---

[16] Callan (1993) represents an up-to-date treatment of this area for the Irish case.

TABLE 5.12: CSF GROWTH BONUS FOR THE EU PERIPHERY

	CSF Shock as % of GDP			GDP (Demand)			GDP (D+S)		
	1994	1999	2020	1994	1999	2020	1994	1999	2020
Irl	3.7	5.4	3.1	1.7	2.7	1.8	1.7	3.8	4.6
Port	6.4	6.2	5.8	7.0	8.1	7.6	7.0	9.1	8.9
Spn	1.6	2.0	1.2	1.9	2.9	1.9	1.9	4.3	8.7

The assumptions made about the time pattern of CSF expenditure in every country combined with the increase in nominal GDP that each national HERMIN model produces mean that the later figures follow different paths. In every case it was decided that after 1999, when the current CSF ends, the shock is sustained unchanged under the same co-financing arrangements as before.

The second series of columns, denoted GDP (Demand), shows the estimated impact on GDP of the CSF when only the conventional demand-side effects are taken into account. The relatively poor results for Ireland in these columns arise from the fact that, as described earlier, the Keynesian demand-side multipliers are small for this economy.

The third series of columns, denoted GDP (D+S), compute the full demand and full supply-side externality effects. Concerning these supply-side effects, the impact on both Spain and Ireland is much larger than is the case for Portugal; this arises because the externalities operate directly through manufacturing output for Ireland and Spain while they operate only indirectly, through the exports equation, for Portugal. Thus their impact on GDP is reduced in the latter case.

The CSF analysis just described takes the economic structure of the periphery as given. We now wish to describe briefly a methodology we have developed for trying to quantify structural change. This arises in the context of an ongoing study of the impact of the progressive development of the Single European Market (Barry, Bradley and Hannan, 1995). Recognising that a substantial proportion of the economy will be opened up to increased international competition, we model this as a shift from the non-(internationally)-tradable sector to the tradable sector.

Table 5.13 below describes our implementation of the methodology. The EU Commission identified 40 (out of 100+) manufacturing sectors which were likely to be affected by the development of

the Single European Market. On the basis of the Irish study in
the *European Economy* (1990b) special issue, and on subsequent
work by its author, O'Malley (1992), we classify these sectors by
three-digit codes as follows. The first digit, S (successful) or D
(declining), describes whether the sector is expected to be positively or adversely affected by the transition to the Internal Market (IM). S-sectors are therefore expected to grow, and D-sectors to
decline. The second digit can take a value of 1 or 2; these describe
whether the EU-wide sectors are likely to be strongly affected by
1992 (as is the case for those for which strongly restrictive public
procurement policies applied pre-1992) or are likely to be only
weakly affected (as is the case for those for which only low non-
tariff barriers applied). The third digit describes whether world
demand growth for the sector's products is strong (a value of 1),
moderate (a value of 2) or weak (a value of 3).

We describe our methodology for the Irish case only, since
similar considerations apply to Greece, Portugal and Spain
(though the proportions expected to shift from being non-tradable
to being tradable are lower for Spain, since it is a much larger
economy).

TABLE 5.13: CLASSIFICATION OF THE SECTORS TO BE AFFECTED BY
THE SEM

		NACE Sector	X/Y	NT/Y	L/LM	dl/LM	Dem. Adj.
S1	S11	330 Office and Data-processing Machinery	98	2	3.8	0.00	0.00
		344 Telecommunications Equipment	87	13	2.6	0.08	0.09
		341 Insulated Wires and Cables	40	60	2.1	1.05	1.16
	S12	421 Cocoa, Chocolate	62	38	1.2	0.34	0.34
	S13	372 Medical and Surgical Equipment	99	1	2.3	0.00	0.00
S2	S21	251 Basic Industrial Chemicals	43	57	1.2	0.34	0.38
		257 Pharmaceuticals	97	3	2.8	0.0Q	0.00
		345 Radios, TVs, etc.	38	62	1.1	0.34	0.38
		346 Domestic Electrical Appliances	78	22	1.3	0.14	0.16
		351 Motor Vehicles	33	67	0.4	0.13	0.15
		428 Soft Drinks	13	87	1.3	0.57	0.62
	S22	325 Plant for Mines, Steel	69	31	0.6	0.09	0.09

		NACE Sector	X/Y	NT/Y	L/LM	dl/LM	Dem. Adj.
		364 Aerospace Equipment	40	60	1.1	0.33	0.33
		413 Dairy Products	29	71	3.8	1.35	1.35
		427 Brewing, Malting	13	87	1.6	0.70	0.70
	S23	247 Glass and Glassware	55	45	1.9	0.43	0.38
		322 Machine Tools	69	31	0.6	0.09	0.08
		323 Textile Machinery	69	31	0.05	0.01	0.01
		324 Food, Chemical Machinery	69	31	0.2	0.03	0.03
		326 Transmission Equipment	69	31	0.1	0.02	0.01
		327 Other Machinery	69	31	0.04	0.01	0.01
		432 Cotton Industry	84	16	0.4	0.03	0.03
		481 Rubber Products	85	15	1	0.08	0.07
		491 Jewellery	50	50	0.9	0.23	0.20
		494 Toys and Sports Goods	85	15	0.3	0.02	0.02
Total					32.69	6.39	6.56
D1	D12	342 Electrical Machinery	90	10	1.1	0.00	0.00
		361 Shipbuilding	93	7	0.3	0.00	0.00
		417 Spaghetti, Macaroni	50	50	0.02	0.01	0.01
D2	D21	256 Other Chemical Products	77	23	0.7	0.08	0.09
		321 Agricultural Machinery	69	31	0.6	0.09	0.10
		493 Photographic Labs	29	71	0.1	0.04	0.04
	D22	431 Wool Industry	70	30	1.9	0.29	0.29
		453 Clothing	54	46	6.5	1.50	1.50
		455 Household Textiles	74	26	0.5	0.07	0.07
	D23	248 Ceramic Goods	91	9	0.4	0.00	0.00
		347 Electric Lamps	90	10	0.1	0.00	0.00
		438 Carpets, Floor Coverings	65	35	0.4	0.07	0.06
		451 Footwear	42	58	0.6	0.17	0.16
Total					13.22	2.31	2.30

The first column on the right-hand side of the table shows the current export to output ratio for each sector, the second column shows the proportion of sectoral output sold on the home market (i.e. 100 per cent minus the value in column 1), and the third column shows the proportion of total manufacturing employment operating in each sector. (The export to gross output data is available in some cases only for more highly aggregated sectors; for these cases we assume that these numbers apply also to the individual sub-sectors). The fourth and fifth columns (the derivation of which is explained below) show the proportion of manufacturing employment in each sector that we expect to be affected by the IM.

We proceed on the basis of assumptions about the likely impact of the IM on the sectors identified as being strongly affected (S1 and D1 sectors), versus those identified as likely to be only weakly affected (S2 and D2).

For the first group we assume that the export-to-output ratio (X/Y) will rise to at least 90 per cent. For a sector such as Data Processing Machinery, which we classify as S1 and which already exports a greater proportion of its output than this, its export orientation is not expected to rise further, and so no change is registered in Column 4. For Insulated Wires and Cables, which is also classified S1, however, we posit that the export ratio will rise from its current level of 40 per cent up to 90 per cent as restrictive public procurement policies disappear. Thus 50 per cent of employment in this sector (90 per cent – 40 per cent) successfully makes the transition from the non-tradable to the tradable category. Ten per cent of employment and output in this sector remains non-tradable and continues to depend on the level of domestic demand.

Now looking at some of the D1 sectors, those which *a priori* are expected to be strongly adversely affected by the IM, we see that since Shipbuilding (NACE 361) exports at present 90 per cent of output, our assumption implies that it will not in fact be affected by the IM. (The alternative would be to assume that the remaining 10 per cent of its output disappears under the rigours of increased competition; we prefer to work with the weaker assumption that a minimum of around 10 per cent of each sector's output remains non-tradable). Looking at another D1 sector such as Pasta Products (NACE 417), however, the implication for this sector is that domestic sales will fall from the current level of 50 per cent of output to 10 per cent. Thus 40 per cent of output in this sector will not successfully make the transition and this proportion of both sectoral output and employment will disappear in the face of increased competition within the IM.

For sectors likely to be less strongly affected by the IM (S2 and D2), we assume that increased international competition will reduce the proportion sold on the home market by 50 per cent. (Comparing Tables 4.5 and 5.3 of O'Malley (1989) we see that this occurred for Irish manufacturing other than Food, Drink and Tobacco as the economy opened up between 1951 and 1978).

For a sector such as Domestic Electric Appliances, then, which is expected to respond positively (S2), the decline in the proportion sold on the home market from its current level of 22 per cent to a new level of 11 per cent entails a successful transition of 11 per cent of output and employment from the non-tradable to the tradable category. Output and employment do not fall in this case; they shift from being driven by domestic demand to being driven instead by world demand. For a sector such as Clothing, however (NACE 453), which is classified as D2, the decline in the proportion sold on the home market from 46 per cent of output to 23 per cent does entail adverse output and employment effects. Twenty-three percent of output and employment in this sector (46 per cent – 23 per cent) does not make the transition from the non-tradable to the tradable category successfully.

The fourth column (entitled dL/LM in Table 5.13) summarises the change in sectoral employment (as a proportion of total manufacturing) that will result from these changes. We see that some 6 per cent of manufacturing employment is in sectors expected to make the transition successfully, and some 2 per cent is in sectors expected to be adversely affected by the process.

The fifth column, entitled 'adjusted for demand conditions', factors in data from the *European Economy* special issue on the state of demand for the output of individual sectors. For sectors for which EU demand is growing rapidly the numbers in column 4 are multiplied by 1.1; for average-growth sectors the numbers are unchanged, and for slow-growth sectors the numbers are multiplied by 0.9. This column reveals that the sectors into which Ireland is expected to specialise are growing more rapidly than the sectors Ireland is specialising out of.

The overall implications of the 1992 pro-competition shock, then, we calculate as shown in Table 5.14.

This arguably represents the proportion of the manufacturing labour force that shifts successfully versus those that shift unsuccessfully. These are in the nature of exogenous shocks. The overall employment and output implications obviously then clearly depend on the degree of flexibility of the various labour markets.

Since Greece appears to have a high degree of flexibility, as pointed out earlier, the adjustment will not be as traumatic as the above data suggest. For Spain, with highly rigid labour markets, the adjustment may in fact turn out to be more difficult.

TABLE 5.14: IMPACT OF THE SEM IN TERMS OF PROPORTIONS OF THE MANUFACTURING SECTOR THAT SHIFT FROM BEING NON-TRADABLE TO BEING TRADABLE

	Successful Transition (in per cent)	*Unsuccessful (in per cent)*
Ireland	6.56	2.3
Portugal	12.67	9.2
Spain	4.84	7.63
Greece	3.53	20

5.6 SUMMARY AND CONCLUSIONS

We have attempted in this chapter to highlight the similarities of the various peripheral EU economies in comparison with the core, as well as to highlight differences that exist between the various peripheral countries.

The shared characteristics of peripheral regions that we identified include the seriousness of the unemployment (and under-employment) problems that are arguably exacerbated by a set of common features that include:

- a relatively high share of agriculture in employment

- common difficulties faced in the adjustment to free trade, and

- relatively underdeveloped financial markets and both physical and human infrastructure.

Other shared characteristics of peripherality include a high share of consumer relative to producer services, and a relatively low share of increasing-returns-to-scale sectors of manufacturing industry. It is argued that neither of these aspects of economic structure is beneficial, although whether they are causes or consequences of peripherality is unclear.

The differences between the various peripheral countries become clearer once the economies are characterised in terms of the macroeconomic model. Focusing on Ireland, Spain and Portugal,

Ireland appears to be at the opposite end of the modelling spectrum to Portugal and Spain.

The extent to which Irish manufacturing output is dominated by multinational companies has a number of important consequences. Firstly, the prices of tradable goods are almost completely determined abroad. Secondly, Irish tradable goods output is largely independent of domestic demand, and thirdly, the proportions of capital and labour used in manufacturing tend to be determined by foreign blueprints rather than by domestic factor prices.

Portugal, on the other hand, still has a large number of traditional industries, whose prices are influenced by domestic cost conditions, while the much smaller role played by multinational companies there means that factor proportions in production are more strongly influenced by Portuguese relative factor prices.

Consequences of these differences include the much smaller domestic-demand multiplier for Ireland, and the substantially larger world-demand multiplier. Greece is likely to be more similar to Portugal and Spain in this regard.

Another important difference between Ireland and Spain, on the one hand, and Portugal, on the other, that shows up in the econometric modelling is the behaviour of wages in the non-(internationally)-tradable goods sector. Wage inflation in both tradable and non-tradable sectors proceeds at the same pace in Ireland, indicating that the service sector is not, as it is so frequently elsewhere, the 'employer of last resort'. In Spain, wage inflation in both sectors is equally impervious to the level of unemployment, while wages in the non-tradable sector in Portugal are strongly affected by unemployment. This goes a long way towards explaining the high levels of unemployment evident in Ireland and Spain, and the very low level in Portugal.

We strongly suspect that in the coming decades, as traditional industries decline in Portugal and Greece and are replaced by multinational companies, and as their social welfare systems become more like those prevailing in the rest of the EU, these countries will come more and more to resemble Ireland in terms of economic structure.

These likely structural changes, though they will be speeded up by the Structural Funds programmes, are not captured in our CSF analysis which instead takes each country's economic structure largely as given. Our brief discussion of our current research on the impact of the Internal Market, however, suggests how structural changes can be taken into account.

References

Aschauer, D. A. (1989), 'Is Public Expenditure Productive?', *Journal of Monetary Economics*, Vol. 23, pp. 177-200.

Barro, R. and Sala-i-Martin, X. (1995), *Economic Growth*, New York: McGraw Hill.

Barry, F. (1994), 'Peripherality in Economic Geography and Modern Growth Theory: Evidence from Ireland's Adjustment to Free Trade', forthcoming in *The World Economy*.

Barry, F., Bradley, J., Kennedy, K. and O'Donnell, N. (1994), 'Labour Market Performance in the EU Periphery: Lessons and Implications' in *Papers and Proceedings of the European Economic Forum* (Ed. Mortensen, J.), The Hague: Central Planning Bureau.

Barry, F., Bradley, J. and Hannan, A. (1995), 'An Evaluation of the Impact of the SEM on the EU Periphery with the Aid of Macroeconometric Models', ESRI Seminar, November.

Beyers, W., Tofflemire, J., Stranahan, H. and Johnson, E. (1986), *The Service Economy: Understanding the Growth of Producer Services in the Central Puget Sound Region*, Seattle, Central Puget Sound.

Bradley, J. (ed.) (1992), *The Role of the Structural Funds: Analysis and Consequences for Ireland in the Context of 1992*, Dublin: ESRI.

Bradley, J., Herce, J. A., Modesto, L. and Sosvilla Rivero, S. (1995), Modelling in the EU Periphery: The HERMIN Project, *Economic Modelling*, Vol. 12., No. 3.

Callan, T. (1993), 'Returns to Educational Investment: New Evidence from Ireland' in *The Community Support Framework 1989-93: Evaluations and Recommendations for CSF 1994-99*, Dublin: ESRI.

Commission of the European Communities (1990a), 'One Market, One Money: An evaluation of the Potential Benefits and Costs of Forming an Economic and Monetary Union', *European Economy*, Vol. 44.

Commission of the European Communities (1990b), 'Social Europe: The Impact of the Internal Market by Industrial Sector', *European Economy*, Special Issue.

Duggan, D. (1995), 'The Core and the Peripheral Regions of the European Union: Distinctive Characteristics and Core-Periphery Comparisons', unpublished MA Thesis, Department of Economics, University College Dublin.

Hansen, N. (1990), 'Do Producer Services Induce Regional Economic Development?', *Journal of Regional Science*, Vol. 30, No. 4, pp. 465-476.

Heffernan, S. and Sinclair, P. (1990), *Modern Industrial Economics*, Oxford: Basil Blackwell.

Keeble, D., Offord, J. and Walker, S. (1988), *Peripheral Regions in a Community of 12 Member States*, Brussels: Commission of the European Communities.

Krugman, P. (1987), 'Economic Integration in Europe: Some Conceptual Issues' in *Efficiency, Stability and Equity* (Ed. Padoa-Schioppa, T.) Oxford: Oxford University Press.

Larre, B. and Torre, R. (1991), 'Is Convergence a Spontaneous Process? The Experience of Spain, Portugal and Greece', *OECD Economic Studies*, 16, pp. 169-198.

Martin, P. and Rogers, C. (1994), 'Trade effects of Regional Aid', CEPR Discussion Paper 910.

Munnell, A. H. (1992), 'Infrastructure Investment and Economic Growth', *Journal of Economic Perspectives*, Vol. 6, pp. 189-198.

National Economic and Social Council (NESC) (1989), *Ireland in the European Community: Performance, Prospects and Strategy*, Report No. 88, Dublin: NESC.

Neven, D. (1990), 'EEC Integration Towards 1992: Some Distributional Aspects', *Economic Policy*, Vol. 10, pp. 14-62.

Ó Gráda, C. and O'Rourke, K. (1994), 'Irish Economic Growth, 1945-1988', CEPR Discussion Paper No. 975.

O'Malley, E. (1992), 'Industrial Structure and Economies of Scale in the Context of 1992' in *The Role of the Structural Funds: Analysis and Consequences for Ireland in the Context of 1992* (Ed. Bradley, J.), Dublin: ESRI.

Ortega, E. (1992), 'La Inversion Extrajera Directa en España', *Banco de España Estudios Economicos*, No. 51.

Prados de la Escosura, L., Daban Sanchez, T. and Sanz Oliva, J. (1993), 'De Te Fabula Narratur? Growth, Structural Change and Convergence in Europe 19-20th Centuries', Mimeo, Universidad Carlos III, Madrid.

Pratten, C. (1988), 'A Survey of Economies of Scale', Economic Paper No. 67, Directorate-General for Economic and Financial Affairs, Brussels: Commission of the European Communities.

Psacharopoulos, G. (1994), 'Returns to Investment in Education: A Global Update', *World Development*, Vol. 22, No. 9, pp. 1325-43.

Walsh, B. (1993), 'The Contribution of Human Capital Formation to Post-War Economic Growth in Ireland', CEPR Discussion Paper No. 819.

Wier, T. (1992), 'Service Sector Development in a Hierarchy of Central Places: A Regional Analysis of 7 Southern States', Unpublished Ph.D. thesis, University of Tennessee.

6

THE ROLE OF EXPORT PROMOTION ORGANISATIONS

Jim Bell

6.1 INTRODUCTION

This chapter explores the export promotion activities of three small peripheral nations: Ireland, a long-standing member of the European Union (EU); Finland, which recently joined the EU and Norway, which has declined membership of the EU on several occasions, most recently in 1995, but which, nevertheless, has considerable trade links with member states. In each case, valuable insights can be gained from their approaches to stimulating export activity among small indigenous firms. It also considers national export promotion within an EU context and speculates on its future shape and direction in light of the completion of the Single European Market (SEM) and EU competition policy.

In an increasingly global economy, most national governments place considerable emphasis on export promotion activities (Seringhaus and Rosson, 1990). As well as seeking to stimulate export-led growth, such measures are often aimed at reducing the trade deficits which have been experienced by many nations during the past two decades (Hibbert, 1991). This policy-focus is manifest in advanced and emerging nations alike (Seringhaus, 1986; Seringhaus and Rosson, 1991), but is particularly important in small open economies which have limited domestic markets and are often geographically isolated from their main trading partners. Additionally, predominantly small-firm economic bases and the relative absence of large indigenous enterprises to provide the engine for export growth mean that such nations must take cognisance of the specific needs of smaller firms seeking to export from peripheral location. Thus, as well as providing a standard range of offerings similar to those available in many other countries, they are also forced to adopt highly innovative small-firm approaches to export promotion.

Stimulating exports from within the small-firm sector is increasingly regarded as important for large and small nations alike. In the former, these activities are often viewed as incremental to the contributions of large internationally-oriented companies. In the latter, they play a more crucial role, for although the proportion of small firms (and their contribution to wealth creation and employment) is not significantly different from those in large economies (such as Germany, the UK or the USA) they are, of necessity, much more active in the area of exporting.

The issue of peripherality is also important. Many commentators contend that all countries outside the 'triad' regions of North America, Europe and the Far East are peripheral, insofar as they are outside the mainstream of international trade flows. However, it can also be argued that even countries within the 'triad' may be peripheral due to their location. Thus, for example, Ireland, Greece and Portugal, can be considered 'peripheral' because they are located at the geographical margins of the EU rather than at the centre. This fact is well recognised in the allocation of additional EU 'cohesion' funding. Similarly, even advanced economies, such as Finland and Norway are peripheral due to their location. Indeed, the definition adopted in this chapter is that 'peripheral' may be applied to any country which is geographically isolated from its major trading partners.

Thus, in terms of small-firm perspectives and peripherality, a study of government export promotion in Finland, Ireland and Norway is apposite. Moreover, as small advanced nations with widely-recognised reputations for proactive and innovative export promotion measures (Bell, 1994), they provide useful insights into 'state of the art' developments of value to 'peripheral' and 'mainstream' economies as well as emerging and advanced nations. However, prior to discussing offerings in the aforementioned countries, a broader discussion on the nature and scope of export promotion and a comparative review of national systems is desirable.

6.2 THE NATURE AND SCOPE OF EXPORT PROMOTION

Seringhaus (1986), one of the most authoritative researchers in the area, defines export promotion as 'all public policy measures that actually or potentially enhance exporting activity either from a firm, industry or national perspective'.

Seringhaus and Rosson (1990) conclude that such measures can be divided into direct and indirect programmes. The latter focus on the production and supply side and include government support which deals with issues such as; productivity, research and development, technology innovation support, manpower planning, regional or sectoral development and fiscal measures. They note that:

> All of these services and programmes have the purpose of improving competitiveness and performance through structural and/or process change at the company level. As the term 'indirect' implies, however, such change is not specifically for export activities. None the less, export benefits may be derived at some point in time.

In contrast, direct export promotion programmes focus on the market and demand side. According to Seringhaus and Rosson (1990), these include:

> an array of programmes that range from awareness-creating, interest-stimulating, research support, export preparation, export market entry, to export market development and expansion focused activities.

They conclude that direct measures aim to influence positively a firm's export competitiveness and that 'all of such activities are either information, learning- and experience-intensive, or both'.

As can be seen in Figure 6.1, Diamantopolous et al. (1993) classify these direct measures into three categories. Firstly, those which provide standardised or customised information and advice on exporting in general and export markets in particular. The latter may include experiential information gained by the firm through foreign market visits or participation in trade fairs. Secondly, programmes which render various types of assistance to firms, ranging from grant-aiding export market research to facilitating actual market entry (such as agent/distributor identification programmes). Thirdly, various measures which cover firms' financial risks through insurance and export financing. Increasingly, many of these facilities — for example, export credit guarantee schemes and export insurance — are provided by private rather than public sector organisations.

FIGURE 6.1: THE SCOPE OF GOVERNMENT EXPORT PROMOTION

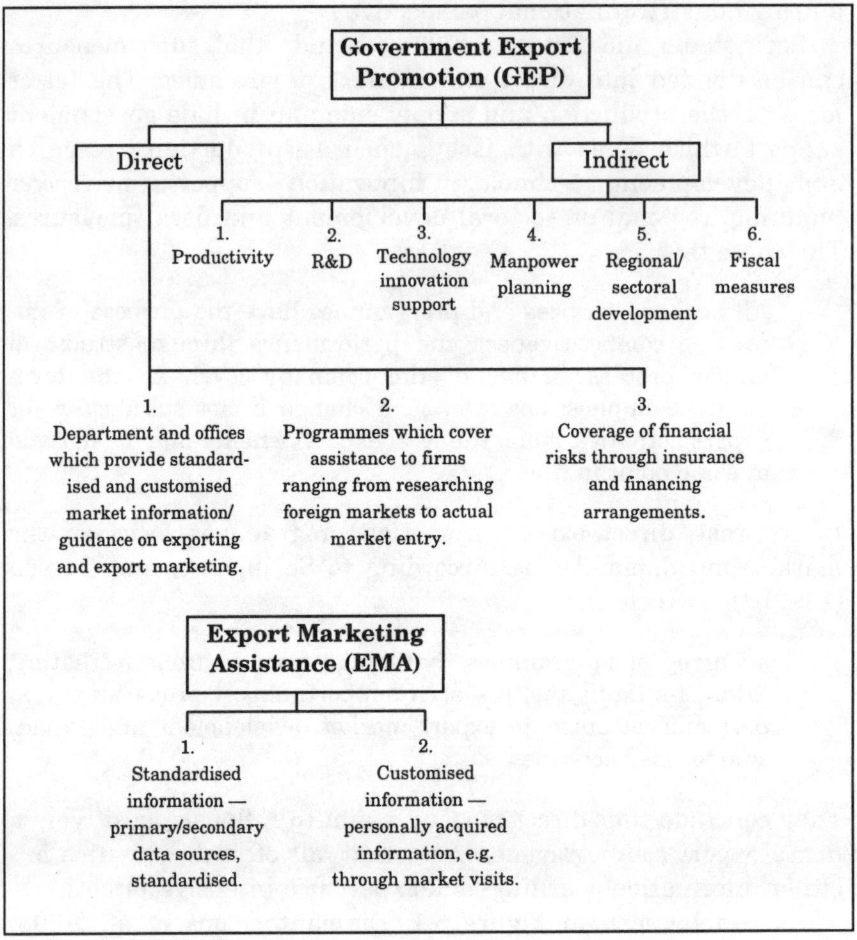

Source: Diamantopolous et al., 1993.

The value of indirect measures which develop infrastructures and improve the domestic and/or international competitiveness and efficiency of firms cannot be underestimated. However, differentiation between these and direct export promotion measures is important. In the case of the former, they are normally integral elements of industrial policy implemented by various central government agencies at national, regional or sectoral level. In contrast, the latter are generally the remit of export promotion organisations which are charged by government with the specific task of developing exports, either solely or, in some countries, in collaboration with the private sector. In consequence, enquiries tend to focus exclusively on the direct provisions of export promotion organisations.

Seringhaus and Botschen (1990) contend that specific goals underlying export promotion can be summarised as follows:

- to develop a broad awareness of export opportunities and to stimulate interest among the business community

- to assist firms in the planning and preparation for export market involvement

- to assist firms in acquiring the needed expertise and know-how to successfully enter and develop export markets

- to support foreign market activity tangibly through organisational help and cost-sharing programmes.

Seringhaus (1986) maintains that these goals hold particular relevance to under-resourced small and medium-sized firms. He further contends that:

> Stimulating such firms' interest and broadening their international scope and competitive competence seems to be the single most important objective for public export marketing assistance. The basic challenge for public policy-makers is to understand firms' needs relative to their export involvement and meet them effectively with assistance programmes. This understanding means providing the right information (assistance) to the right firm at the right time.

This view recognises that firms at the pre-export stage will have different support needs as they decide whether or not to initiate exports than will already active firms that are seeking to expand international operations. Furthermore, it indicates that different support programmes and services will be required to assist firms at various stages of export development. Indeed, researchers generally agree that the broad thrust of export assistance — and specific support measures — should recognise that firm's needs do change over time and with experience. (Czinkota and Johnston, 1981; Reid, 1981; Cavusgil, 1983)

However, Root (1974) cautions that it should not be the mission of an export promotion organisation to make an exporter out of every firm as this only dissipates scarce resources. Rather, they should seek to maximise incremental export sales by focusing on client-firms which 'have a product or products with high export sales potential and have a high support requirement'.

In practice, however, precluding firms which do not meet these criteria from seeking assistance is more problematic.

6.3 COMPARISONS OF EXPORT PROMOTION SYSTEMS

Given common goals and objectives in export promotion — as summarised by Seringhaus and Botschen (1990) in the preceding section — it is hardly surprising that the provisions of national Export Promotion Organisations (EPOs) are broadly similar (Bowen, 1986; Elvey, 1990; Camino, 1991). GATT regulations also impose a wide range of restrictions on the types of support that signatory states can offer indigenous firms, these too have led to substantial standardisation (Korth, 1985). In addition, EU regulations and those introduced within other trade areas (such as NAFTA) are increasingly 'harmonising' the activities of member states. Where differences occur is in the extent to which services are provided by the public and/or private sector. Seringhaus (1987) contends that these relationships vary considerably from country to country and that, as a consequence, export activities may be loosely co-ordinated or highly planned. The approach adopted also impacts on the funding of export promotion activities.

Thus, for example, while national governments administer and fund export promotion activities in many countries, in others, notably Denmark and Finland, national industry federations play a significant role. This is also the case in Germany where government provides export information but most other activities are organised by chambers of commerce and industry associations. In the US, the Department of Commerce provides general information to exporters, but there is evidence that the responsibility for implementing support programmes, such as outward trade missions, is increasingly being devolved to individual states.

In terms of funding mechanisms, some countries finance export promotion from a levy on exports (Austria, Iceland, Norway). Some rely in part on subscription fees from industry federations and/or income generated by the respective EPO (Denmark, Finland, Sweden). Others including Greece, Portugal and the UK, are funded solely by government, or generate a very small proportion of their income. For example, An Bord Tráchtála, the Irish EPO, obtains some 10 per cent of its revenues by charging for services and undertaking consultancy. The trend is to encourage EPOs to generate more of their own revenues. Arguably, the Finnish Foreign Trade Association (FFTA) is most advanced in this respect insofar as funds are obtained in equal proportions from government, industry subscriptions and EPO earnings.

In respect to export promotion systems in OECD countries, a number of broad patterns are discernible. First, that governments in smaller or more peripheral countries spend proportionately more on export promotion activities than those in larger, more centrally located nations. Second, that industry participation in, and financing of, export promotion is more prevalent in Germanic and Scandinavian countries, than elsewhere. Third, there is evidence that some governments are devolving aspects of export promotion to the private sector (particularly in respect to exporting finance) and that certain tasks are being co-ordinated at regional level (especially in terms of promotional activities).

However, countervailing patterns are also evident in the EU, with increased Brussels involvement in developing a cohesive strategy for member states. These include information provision via the Euro-Info centres, programmes such as SPRINT which focus on technology transfer between small firms within the EU, the development of client-supplier networks through initiatives such as the Europartenariat programmes, intra-regional initiatives and so forth. Clearly, all of these tend to focus on developing intra-community trade, but they, nevertheless, have implications for export promotion. Moreover, DGXXIII, the small-business directorate, has commissioned studies into small-firm barriers to exporting outside the EU (EIM/ESNR, 1993) with a view towards establishing and implementing appropriate support measures.

Despite differences in approaches to export promotion and alternative funding mechanisms, both Bowen (1986) and Seringhaus (1987) observe that offerings of the advanced industrial nations are broadly comparable. Bowen's (1986) study of EPOs and export credit agencies provides a useful overview of export promotion systems in OECD countries indicating the degree of interaction between public and private sector, the extent of national and international coverage, the spectrum of promotional activities and market intelligence support and the range of export credit services. Based on a detailed review of services and interviews with government officials, Bowen (1986) also attempts to rate respective national systems and concludes that Austria, France, Canada and the UK all provide highly-rated services. Lowest-rated are those of the US, Germany, Switzerland and Japan, al-

though the latter's performance reflects the fact that JETRO is
principally involved in promoting imports.

While a major limitation of Bowen's study is that it fails to reflect users' views, it does raise a number of interesting points
(Bell, 1994). Firstly, countries with highly-rated services, such as
Austria and France, adopt different approaches. The same is true
of countries where services are poorly rated. Thus, no firm conclusions can be reached on the relative merits of public versus
quasi-private export support systems. Secondly, the emphasis on
certain types of support is clearly different. This is notably the
case with trade fairs and overseas missions which are organised
either by chambers of commerce or industry federations in Austria, Denmark and Germany, but are generally government-
organised in Canada, France and the UK. Thirdly, highly-rated
services do not, necessarily, mean strong exports and vice versa.

Seringhaus' (1987) comparison of export promotion in twelve
advanced countries indicates that the main services available are
broadly similar (see Figure 6.2). However, inward visits by foreign
buyers are not supported by Austria, France, Italy or Germany as
they prefer indigenous firms to venture abroad.

Seringhaus and Rosson (1991) contend that most variations in
service are attributable to the economic size of the country and its
foreign trade sector, attitudes of the private sector towards foreign
market involvement and the ability and willingness of government and business to respond to areas of greatest need in the development of international competence. They conclude that the
similarity of programme portfolios suggests that advanced
nations:

> attempt to cover the full spectrum of export market involve-
> ment; differentiate services and programmes over different ex-
> port phases according to perceived need (and) recognise the
> relatively greater need for external assistance among small and
> medium sized companies.

Research conducted in emerging economies by the International
Trade Centre (ITC) in Geneva (1986, 1988) and extensively analysed by Seringhaus (1990) and Seringhaus and Rosson (1991),
also indicates that EPO activities in these countries are very
similar. These studies, based on data obtained from seventy developing countries, reveal that, in virtually every respect, national
EPOs' activities mirror those of their counterparts in the advanced economies. Most are heavily involved in overseas promo-

tion; undertake a wide spectrum of product and market development activities; provide export management support; and; offer support to other public/private institutions involved in export-related training and development initiatives. Indeed, Rosson and Seringhaus (1991) conclude that export promotion approaches are broadly adopted and fairly well organised in the developing world. Such similarities are not wholly surprising, given that the majority of these nations are GATT signatories and that many of their EPOs were initially advised by the ITC and modelled on those of the advanced nations.

FIGURE 6.2: EXPORT PROMOTION IN TWELVE DEVELOPED COUNTRIES

Stage of Exporting Process	Major Service Type	Australia	Austria	Belgium	Canada	France	Japan	Netherlands	Sweden	United Kingdom	United States	West Germany
Pre-export	Export Motivation Programmes	a	b	b	a	a	a	b	a	a	a	a
	Information Services	a	b	a	a	a	a	a	a	a	a	a
Market Entry	Market Research Programmes	a	b		a	a	a	a	a	a	a	b
	Trade Mission Programmes	a	b	a	a	a	b	a	a	a	a	b
	Export Financing/ Insurance Programmes	a	a	a	a	a	a	a	a	a	a	a
Export Operations	Foreign Buyer Programmes	a		a	a		a	a	a	a	a	
	Trade Fair Programmes	a	b	a	a	a	a	a	a	a	a	a

a Programmes offered by public sector/government

b Programmes available through or assisted by quasi-private institutions such as chambers of commerce, industry associations, etc.

Source: Seringhaus, 1987.

From the preceding discussion it can be concluded that the main issues concerning export promotion are now well understood and that policy measures are not only comprehensive but also considerably sophisticated in developing and advanced nations alike. However, attempting to assess the impact of export promotion programmes (and firms' usage and satisfaction thereof) remains a major concern for policy-makers seeking to demonstrate that public funds allocated to such activities are being properly and efficiently utilised. It is also recurring theme in the exporting literature and a topic which continues to attract considerable research interest and attention.

6.4 EVALUATION OF EXPORT PROMOTION ACTIVITIES

Previous studies have sought to measure the impact of export promotion in terms of cost-benefit analyses, aggregate improvements in the export performance of targeted sectors, actual or projected sales gained from participation in overseas trade fairs or outward missions, (Pointon, 1978; Brezzo and Perkal, 1983; Schwarting et al., 1982). Such quantitative approaches and the use of narrow or specific indicators of outcome have been criticised on several counts. Firstly, Root (1971) argues that export promotion is substantially an information-gathering and knowledge-dissemination activity, for which there is no satisfactory means of measurement. Secondly, Seringhaus and Rosson (1990) conclude that:

> Such numbers falsely suggest unequivocal and direct causality between programme expenditures and sales results. The principal difficulty with such indicators is that ... many factors influence company export behaviour and results, and therefore the aggregate export performance of an industry or a country.

However, Seringhaus and Rosson (1990) also criticise other attempts to evaluate export assistance. They argue that surveys which take a broad approach and collect profile, experience and performance characteristics of service-users also suffer from drawbacks such as incomplete questionnaires, partial representation of the target group of firms and, therefore, questionable representativeness of results regarding the impact of offerings. They further contend that measurement problems are exacerbated by vague notions of 'effectiveness', unclear and/or unspecific programme objectives and the absence of agreed-upon parameters

against which individual services can be measured. Diamantopoulos et al. (1993) argue that these problems are exacerbated by a
dominant use of global-construct measures which means that differences in the efficacy of specific services may not be detected
because they tend to be measured collectively.

These methodological problems have implications for both
academic enquiry and policy formulation. Indeed, Seringhaus and
Rosson (1990) argue that due to the difficulty of showing direct
causal links between export promotion offerings and micro-level
outcomes, unspecific programme/service objectives and quantifi-
cation problems, 'adequate measures of programme impact on
users are difficult to establish and very little can be said conclu-
sively about the effectiveness of export promotion'.

Nevertheless, they also conclude that numerous indirect, in-
visible and desirable effects may emanate from programme use.
For example, companies may learn of other forms of export support; awareness of specific programmes may provide other useful
sources of information; offerings may convince firms to rethink
their export approaches and strategies and perhaps, most significantly, export support may strengthen companies' commitment to
foreign markets.

However, the literature does reveals considerable user dissatisfaction with export services. Although various studies examine
different national structures and systems and, in spite of the
aforementioned methodological problems, there is a strong degree
of consistency in conclusions which, typically, concur that many
programmes are inadequate and unsuited to the needs of exporters; and, moreover, that firms' awareness of services tends to be
low (Albaum, 1983; Cavusgil, 1983; Kedia and Chhokar, 1986;
Bannock, 1987; De Mortage and Van Gent, 1991), that levels of
utilisation are variable (McFarlane, 1978; Buckley, 1983; Reid,
1984) and that users are, generally, less than satisfied with provisions (Simpson, 1981; Brady and Gill, 1987; Howard and Herremans, 1988).

The provision of export information is widely criticised
throughout the literature. Pointon (1978) considers British Overseas Trade Board (BOTB) information services to be more suited
to the market intelligence needs of larger firms. Buckley (1983)
finds that BOTB information on potential agents or distributors
was out-of-date and unhelpful. According to Kaynak and Stevenson (1982), many Canadian firms regarded ITC information as
'unimportant'. Walters (1983) contends that Department of

Commerce (DOC) information was only of moderate use to US firms. The statistical data and market research provided by the DOC was also deemed to be too general to be helpful. Cannon and Willis (1981) also find that the BOTB's highly generalised information was of limited value. These findings support Denis and Depelteau's (1985) view that services should 'focus on identifying and satisfying precise information needs and stop contributing to the already abundant and often redundant body of general information already available'. Nevertheless, a number of studies do in fact, conclude that small firms find export information services to be more beneficial than do larger companies (Czinkota, 1982; Seringhaus, 1986; Bannock, 1987).

Exporters' widely-acknowledged preferences for experiential information rather than that obtained from secondary sources (Cunningham and Spigel, 1971; Johanson and Vahlne; 1977; Khan, 1980; Reid, 1980; Seringhaus, 1987) contribute to the fact that the objective information provided by EPOs is not highly rated. However, they also lead to relatively higher perceptions of benefit and levels of satisfaction with programmes such as trade fairs and trade missions which enable firms to obtain market knowledge and experience first-hand (Reid, 1983; Walters, 1983). Most research indicates that firms tend to be more aware of, and rather more favourably disposed towards, government services which provide financial support for export activities and which require a high degree of involvement on the user's part (Seringhaus, 1987).

To add to the criticism of offerings which are available, research also indicates a lack of congruence between the services firms desire and those offered by export agencies (Czinkota and Ricks, 1981; Czinkota, 1982; Seringhaus, 1986). This discrepancy not only impacts on firms' usage of government services, but also on levels of satisfaction thereof. Indeed, Seringhaus (1986) argues that 'only a portion of the services offered by government may be needed, relevant or useful to a firm'. Albaum (1983) is even more scathing of US DOC services, contending that there is an urgent need to reappraise their effectiveness, as programmes 'that are not used and are not perceived to have much usefulness by those for whom they are intended really have little value to anyone.'

Criticism is most widespread in respect of the provision of export assistance to smaller firms. Many studies find that government attempts to stimulate export initiation are generally rather ineffective (Tesar, 1974; Tesar and Tarleton, 1983). In Bannock's

(1987) UK survey, only 1.18 per cent of respondents indicated that they began exporting as a result of government encouragement. Strandskov (1986) finds that external change agents were of minor importance in the decision and that less than 3 per cent of Danish firms had been influenced by government export programmes. However, the propensity of decision-makers and firms to internalise success and externalise failure may contribute to these findings.

In this context, the need for greater targeting of services is also a recurrent theme in the export promotion literature. Researchers have consistently criticised the lack of differentiated services and have argued that firms have different support needs at various export development stages (Czinkota, 1982; Cavusgil, 1984, Seringhaus, 1987). Indeed, Thomas and Araujo (1985) contend that:

> government policy designed to stimulate exports should not be confined to macro level inducements but should be aimed at directly influencing decision-makers in individual firms, and specifically tailored to the stage each firm has reached in the export process.

The thrust of these arguments is that the provision of standard export assistance packages results in low usage and satisfaction levels which are exacerbated by low awareness of offerings in the first place. If, as appears to be the case, much of this dissatisfaction stems from a failure to differentiate offerings, then the key to any improvements in provision is the ability of EPOs to tailor services more precisely to meet users' specific needs.

However, the provision of customised services presents problems for EPOs. Given their limited budgets, it remains unlikely that they will have the human and financial resources or the indepth product and market expertise to fully satisfy the diverse range of user needs. Nevertheless, with greater targeting of priority sectors/industries and more intensive support for smaller, less experienced firms the potential for greater tailoring of assistance to specific segments, and more differentiated support for particular firms therein, becomes more feasible. Such approaches may not, necessarily, lead to highly personalised packages for each and every firm seeking export assistance. They will, however, result in a better match between firm's needs and government provisions generally and a more effective allocation of scarce EPO resources.

In consequence, studies by Framnes and Welch (1982), Stenburg (1982), and Welch and Joynt (1984) highlight the need to

provide alternative support systems for SMEs While these enquiries focus on specific small-firm initiatives such as export
manager for hire schemes, group exporting and small-business
training and development programmes introduced in the Scandinavian countries, they reflect widespread recognition of the particular needs of the small-firm sector.

In the light of these conclusions, the remainder of this chapter
focuses on export promotion in Finland, Ireland and Norway. It
outlines provisions in each country and focuses particularly on
those initiatives which attempt to provide tailored support for the
small-business sector.

6.5 EXPORT PROMOTION IN FINLAND, IRELAND AND NORWAY

As Seringhaus and Rosson (1991) conclude, export promotion
services are broadly similar in advanced and emerging nations. In
this respect, Finnish, Irish and Norwegian export services are no
exception for they provide similar offerings, although they are
structured and financed differently from each other (see Figure
6.3 and Table 6.1).

Despite these differences, Bowen's (1986) study rates them
closely, with Finland ranked 9th overall, Ireland 10th and Norway
14th. Furthermore, provisions in all three countries, notably in
respect to the delivery of tailored advice and targeted marketing
schemes, are more highly rated than those of larger advanced nations which allocate greater public or private resources to exporting. In fact, it may be argued that Finnish, Irish and Norwegian
offerings are underrated insofar as the lower ratings obtained in
areas such as international coverage, trade missions, libraries and
publications reflect the size and scope of EPO operations and
smaller client bases, rather than the quality of these services *per se*.

FIGURE 6.3: EXPORT PROMOTION IN FINLAND, IRELAND AND
NORWAY

Stage of Exporting Process	Major Service Type	Finland	Ireland	Norway
Pre-export	Export Motivation Programmes	a	a	a
	Small Business Export Programmes/ Initiatives	a	a	a
	Information Services	a	a	a
Market Entry	Market Research Programmes	a	a	a
	Trade Mission Programmes	a	a	a
	Export Development Grants/Support	a	a	a
Export Operations	Export Insurance Programmes	b	b	b
	Foreign Buyer Programmes	a	a	a
	Trade Fair Programmes	a	a	a

a   Programmes offered by public sector/government
b   Programmes available through or assisted by quasi-private institutions

Source: Author's Research)

TABLE 6.1: PERCENTAGE OF PUBLIC/PRIVATE SECTOR FINANCE FOR
EXPORT PROMOTION

	Government Funding	*Subscr. Fees*	*EPO Earnings**	*Levy on Import/ Export*
Finland		34	33	33
Ireland	90		10	
Norway			10	90

* Including fees for services, consultancy and other income
Source: Unpublished ETPO Study Document, 1987.

6.5.1 Export Promotion in Finland
Suomen Ulkomaanka Uppalitto, the Finnish Foreign Trade Association (FFTA) promotes Finland's foreign trade. It is a semi-

governmental organisation which is maintained by the Confederation of Finnish Industries (with some 800 member firms), the state and the Finnish Furniture Exporters Association and serves all firms engaged in export trade. It employs about 150 staff, including 16 at regional offices outside Helsinki. Funding is obtained in a ratio of 34/33/33 from the Ministry of Trade and Industry (MTI), federation membership fees and charges for services.

In 1994 the FFTA's budget was approximately $15 million. However, the MTI also provide direct grant-aid, ranging from 40-75 per cent of total cost, to companies participating in export-related activities including establishing overseas facilities, hiring foreign consultants, market research, trade fairs and missions and training young export executives. Thus the overall expenditure on export promotion was almost $50 million and MTI's contribution to the FFTA was just over $5 million.

The FFTA makes export advisory services available to Finnish firms, provides information on export markets and trade opportunities, produces publications on Finland's export supply and offers services related to import trade. Clients outside Finland are furnished with information on Finland's industry and market as well as on prospects of doing business. On request, they are also introduced to Finnish exporters and importers. A computerised register of Finnish exporters and their products and services is available to clients at home and abroad.

The FFTA organises Finnish participation at over 120 international exhibitions and trade fairs, together with other promotional events and inward visits. It is also the operational liaison centre for commercial attachés stationed in some 50 Finnish diplomatic missions abroad. These attachés are recruited from the private sector for a five year period by the MTI. Among the many services these posts offer are agency/distributor identification and assessment.

Specific services provided by FFTA include: client-commissioned research projects and market reports; information on foreign market legislation and trade regulations; political risk assessment and; assistance for firms bidding for UN/IBRD development projects.

In addition to these standard provisions, FFTA offer a number of special programmes including:

- **Regional Export Advisers (REAs)** — A network of 16 advisers based in regional offices throughout Finland offer basic and specific advice to exporting firms. In addition REAs will actually seek out firms with export potential who are not currently exporting. They will help firms research foreign markets, select those which offer the best prospects and assist them develop a marketing and action plan. They will also help these firms establish contacts in the foreign market, identify buyers and recruit agents or distributors. Established in 1980, this scheme assists over 2000 firms each year and has a high re-use rate, providing evidence of considerable user satisfaction.

- **Export Consultants** — This provision was initiated in 1985 and the FFTA now provides some 25 consultants. One consultant is attached to 4 or 5 companies for a two year period and assists firms in the first intensive stages of exporting when expenditure is high, but firm resources and expertise are limited. Consultants provide a similar type of assistance to the REAs but on a more sustained and concentrated basis. After two years the firm should be sufficiently competent and confident to continue exporting on its own, however, many retain their consultant in an advisory capacity. No grants are available as fees are already heavily subsidised.

- **Group Export Managers** — The Export Consultants scheme also offers group export managers to assist in the formation and activities of export co-operation groups. In 1993, over 1000 firms belonged to 48 such groups. Counselling is provided to groups on both a market-and sector-specific basis. In terms of value for money this scheme ranks highly with both the FFTA and participating firms and is one which the FFTA are most keen to expand and develop.

- **Export Managers for Hire** — This service has been offered since 1976 and over 400 firms have benefited from the scheme. At any given time, between 5 and 10 experienced export managers, often seconded from industry, are employed by the FFTA. Each export manager is 'hired' by firms to carry out a specific task, rather than a general brief and usually carries out assignments for two or three firms concurrently. The scheme has not been an unqualified success, partly because of the difficulty of obtaining such expertise at salaries FFTA can afford to pay and also because firms are increasingly choosing to engage the services of commercial consultants.

The Finnish technology development centre (TEKES) is also involved in promoting the development of technologically-advanced, products and processes which are deemed to be internationally competitive. Individual SMEs and national programmes are supported via TEKES units throughout Finland.

Export credit in Finland is provided by Vientitakuulaitos (VTL) and by Suomen Vientiluotto OY (FEC). The former offers a conventional range of export insurance services to protect firms against non-payment due to political and other risks. The FEC (Finnish Export Credit) is a joint-stock company that promotes exports by granting medium- or long-term credits. It finances exports of capital goods, construction and consulting projects and also offers credits for consignment stocks abroad, foreign leasing of Finnish equipment and, in certain cases, equity investments abroad.

Export training is the remit of Vientikoulutussaatio, the Finnish Institute for International Trade (FINTRA) which is partly funded by the MTI and supported by the FFTA. It also generates income from fees and offers export training programmes, seminars and foreign language courses, some of which are specially designed for small firms. In addition, FINTRA provides in-house programmes for larger companies (a review of FINTRA activities is contained in Cellich et al., 1989).

6.5.2 Export Promotion in Ireland

The *modus operandi* of An Bord Tráchtála (ITB) is broadly similar to that of its predecessor Córas Tráchtála (CTT) which merged with the Irish Goods Council in 1991. It is a state-sponsored limited-liability company with major responsibility for promoting export services to firms. With over 70 per cent of enquiries coming from firms with less than 100 employees, the Board has a small-firm export department and a specific government remit to support the small business sector.

The ITB has a staff of over 300, some 30 per cent of whom are based in 3 UK offices and in 20 other key export markets (most EU countries, China, Japan, Russia, Singapore, Saudi Arabia and the US). It also employs a network of trade consultants in countries without direct EPO representation. As well as a head office in Dublin, it has offices in Cork, Limerick, Sligo and Waterford.

Funding is provided by central government, although the consultancy and fees for services account for some 10 per cent of revenues. Since late 1987, much greater emphasis has been placed on generating income from fees via chargeable services. In 1994 Bord Tráchtála's budget was some $52 million. About $2 million is generated from technical assistance programmes for developing countries funded by the EU, UN organisations, or Ireland's own Overseas Development Co-operation Programme.

The ITB provides information on export markets obtained from published sources and networks of overseas offices. It offers a special advisory service in which staff or regional officers proactively visit over 1000 firms annually, providing assistance on export matters. It also has a design advisory service to help firms develop — or modify — products, packaging and promotional material for export markets. In addition to an Irish exporters' handbook and export guides, it produces reports on opportunities in key export markets for specific industry sectors. A market information centre in Dublin contains published and on-line information and houses the European Business Information Centre (EBIC), one of over 40 set up in Europe by the EC SME Task Force.

Supplying foreign buyers with information on Irish goods is an important activity and an Irish Export Directory and various sectoral guides are published for overseas firms seeking to source Irish goods. These include CONNECT, a database of the electronics and software industries in Ireland. Overseas ITB offices also have annual targets for effecting introductions between foreign and Irish firms.

In terms of promotional activities, 40 to 50 Irish stands are organised at international trade fairs each year with 200 to 300 firms exhibiting their goods. Typically, 12 to 15 general or sectoral trade missions are organised annually with over 200 participating firms. Inward visits by groups of foreign buyers are also arranged on a regular basis which in any given year bring upwards of 1250 buyers to Ireland. In addition, as part of an export development programme reviewed hereafter, market study groups and exploratory missions, generally to the UK, are arranged for groups of first-time exporters.

Specific services provided by Bord Tráchtála include client-commissioned export market research, market introduction and agent assessment, foreign market contact lists, field assistance and overseas office facilities.

In addition to these standard offerings, CTT/ITB have been involved in a number of special initiatives which are outlined hereafter:

- **The Targeted Marketing Consultancy (TMC) Programme —** In January 1990, CTT launched a programme designed to provide marketing inputs and incentives to encourage firms to undertake major export development. Over 30 contracts were signed with specially selected firms, with the aim of generating an additional $600 million of exports. Under this scheme, consultants advise participating firms on the development and implementation of marketing plans, and support of up to $1 million is available to individual companies on the programme. Grants of 66 per cent are available, 50 per cent of which is repayable. Bord Tráchtála is currently working with some 50 firms, and thresholds have been lowered so that firms planning to spend $100,000 or more on export development are eligible for support. All available evidence indicated that participating firms are extremely satisfied with the TMC and the programme is currently being expanded. However, the ITB also appear to be selecting clients very judiciously to ensure that only those firms which can genuinely benefit from the support receive it.

- **Grouping for Exports —** In 1984, CTT began to promote group marketing as an effective method of exporting for small firms. The concept was that three or more companies would agree to co-ordinate some or all of their export marketing activities. These included sharing office facilities, sales representation, research and promotional material. Costs were shared and the 'groups' were eligible for grant-aid, CTT also engaged export staff on the group's behalf. Some 40 groups, involving over 150 firms, were established in sectors such as clothing, furniture and joinery, healthcare and pharmaceuticals. Target markets included Germany, the UK, the US and China. While there was a high attrition rate, especially during the first year of a group's formation, many have been successful. (A more comprehensive discussion of the scheme, together with case studies, is provided by Lennon (1988).)

- **Special Trading Houses —** Although not directly under CTT control, the government's 1988 initiative is worthy of mention. It sought to increase exports by encouraging the formation of licensed trading companies to wholesale Irish goods and services. Special trading houses qualified for a rate of 10 per cent corporation profits tax and investors in them would be eligible for tax relief under the business expansion scheme. Applications for licenses were vetted by CTT and approved by the Department of Industry and Commerce. While the scheme initially attracted over 200 applications and led to the rapid establishment of some 20 Special Trading Houses, it has not been an unqualified success. Adverse global economic conditions, the restriction of trading solely Irish goods and low uptake within the small-firm sector have been contributory factors.

The Irish government operates an export credit insurance scheme through the Insurance Corporation of Ireland. This provides Irish exporters with cover against non-payment due to sovereign/political or commercial risk, delays in payment due to documentation problems and so forth. It also offers a number of preferential finance schemes. The major banks and the Industrial Credit Corporation provide letter of credit arrangements, short- and medium-term finance and forfeiting facilities.

Unlike Finland and Norway, Ireland has no single organisation responsible for export training. Between 1986-90, AnCO the Irish industrial training authority (now FÁS), in conjunction with the Northern Ireland Training and Employment Agency, offered export marketing programmes which focused on European and North American markets. In these, young graduates were attached to small firms wishing to develop exports. After initial training, graduates spent up to six months conducting research in the firm's target market. A parallel programme provided a series of company development workshops (a detailed description and evaluation of programme is contained in Bell et al., 1990). These programmes were discontinued in 1990, ostensibly due to a change in the remit of FÁS which led it to refocus training provisions towards the needs of unemployed school-leavers. Since 1990, CTT/ITB have offered an Export Training Programme wherein recent graduates are attached to firms for a one-year period during which they undergo specialist export training. This programme is a revised version of one provided by CTT prior to the AnCO/FÁS offerings.

CTT/ITB has also been involved in a number of export development/training initiatives:

- **Export Development Programme(s)** each of which is of 18-24 month duration. These involve eight stages, including a series of export appraisal workshops, export development activities and exploratory sales visits to an export market. Thereafter, the Board assists firms to develop and implement export marketing strategies. Each stage acts as a filter so that support was increasingly targeted at highly-committed firms with good export potential. Since 1986, over 1,500 firms have attended export appraisal workshops and more than 200 have completed the programme and started exporting. A number of sectoral-specific programmes have been offered on this basis.

- **Export Development Programme(s) for Small Firms** provided by the Irish Management Institute with support from Bord Tráchtála and the Allied Irish Bank. Over a twelve-month period firms attend a series of two-day workshops, develop formal marketing plans and visit identified target markets in small groups. Each firm is allocated an experienced export counsellor who advises on conducting research and identifying agents for the duration. The fee of about $5,000 is subsidised, market visits are grant-aided and firms can avail of Irish Export Board assistance throughout. Over 100 small firms have completed these highly-rated programme.

Other marketing development programmes are offered by University College Dublin and University College Galway. In many cases these are supported by government agencies and, given the importance of exporting to firms and the economy, often contain a significant export development element. All of the aforementioned programmes demonstrate the government's commitment to assisting indigenous small firms to generate direct or indirect export business. Nevertheless, they also reflect policy-maker's concerns that Ireland has become over-reliant on the export activities of MNE subsidiaries.

6.5.3 Export Promotion in Norway

Norges Eksportrad, established in 1946, co-ordinates measures to develop Norwegian exports. A special unit, the Small- and Medium-sized Business Exports (SMB-E), was set up in 1985 specifically to assist smaller firms with less than 100 employees. In addition to the head office in Oslo, it has over 40 overseas posts and over 200 staff. It collaborates closely with Norway's foreign service and Norges Eksportrad staff are attached to diplomatic and con-

sular missions abroad. Important activities include the provision
of export information, establishing useful overseas contacts, and
support for promotional events such as trade fairs and missions.

Norges Eksportrad activities are funded by a 3/4 *per mille* levy
on commodity exports (excluding ships and oil platforms) together
with fees for services which account for some 10 per cent of revenues. In 1994 its total budget was $35 million. Direct grants and
loans to exporters are also provided by the Norwegian Industrial
Foundation which has a staff of sixty and an annual budget of
some $20 million. Companies can apply to the Foundation and/or
Norges Eksportrad for grants of up to 50 per cent of the costs of
setting up an overseas office, adapting products for export or visits to international markets. Grant-aid is also available to defray
losses incurred during the first year of export operations.

Specific services offered by Norges Eksportrad include: export
feasibility studies and market reports; product testing; agent/
distributor identification; information on tariffs and trade regulations and; legal advice and support.

Since it was established in 1985, the SMB-E department has
built a client base of over 400 small firms. Some 100 export managers have been hired to assist more than 200 companies and
about 15 to 20 firms a year have been encouraged to initiate exporting. To be eligible for SMB-E assistance, firms must have less
than 100 employees, a turnover of below $1.6 million and must
not be wholly-owned subsidiaries of large companies. They should
be financially sound, well-established in the domestic market,
possess products with export potential and have the capacity, desire and motivation to develop export activities. Two specific
SMB-E offerings merit further amplification:

- **Internationalisation Programme** — Small firms seeking to
  export can avail of this scheme. The process begins with firms
  completing a detailed questionnaire on their organisation,
  management, product range and possible target markets.
  SMB-E staff then visit the firm, complete a report on its product profile and export capacity and attempt to identify a suitable market. This report is forwarded to the Norges Eksportrad office in a selected foreign market where Overseas Promotion Officers (OPOs) conduct primary market research and
  identify at least three potential agents or distributors for the
  client firm, which has a final say in any appointment. While
  overseas offices charge for this service, client firms can apply
  for grant-aid from Norges Eksportrad for up to 30 per cent of

the costs of market research and agency identification undertaken by OPOs. They can also obtain up to 50 per cent of the cost of visiting the market.

* **Export Managers for Hire Scheme** — Through the SMB-E, small firms can hire an experienced export manager for a period of a year or two on a full- or part-time basis. In exceptional circumstances, the firm may retain the manager's services for three years. Part-time managers are usually local consultants, full-time ones can be recruited from a register of skilled professionals wishing to change jobs, but are more frequently individuals already identified by the firm. The role of the consultant/manager is to develop the firm's export strategy during the period of assistance, but many remain with the company thereafter. SMB-E financial support includes 50 per cent of the manager's salary or consultant's fee, 50 per cent of his business expenses and 100 per cent of his travel costs.

Export Credit in Norway is provided by the Guarantee Institute for Export Credits (GIEK) which covers a range of commercial and political risks. Firms can obtain export development loans from the Norwegian Industrial Foundation. These are repayable over an eight year period, with the first two years interest free and the remainder at levels below the commercial rate. The Foundation also offers foreign currency loans of up to $3 million for overseas acquisitions.

Export training is provided by Norges Eksportskole which, together with FINTRA in Finland, is part of the Organisation of Scandinavian Institutes of Export (NES). The Eksportskole is a non-profit organisation and part of Norges Eksportrad. Its offerings include the International Management Programme, the Export Graduate Programme and courses for export sales personnel and export secretaries. In addition, short courses, seminars and workshops are provided on export financing, negotiation skills and internationalisation strategies. Some 2,000 participants attend around 80 such programmes every year.

6.6 DISCUSSION

A number of pertinent points can be made from the preceding discussion. Firstly, despite differences in funding and organisation, the services offered in Finland, Ireland and Norway are remarkably similar. Although the exact nature of offerings vary, their objectives are broadly comparable.

As shown in Table 6.1, these services aim to stimulate export motivation, provide export market information and offer assistance in conducting export market research. Additionally, each EPO organises a range of promotional activities such as trade fairs and trade missions and assists participating firms financially. Finally, although export insurance in each country is provided by other organisations, the respective EPOs all provide grant-aid for a range of export activities. To this extent, services are comparable to those offered elsewhere (see Figure 6.2), albeit on a more limited scale due to lower overall demand.

Secondly, and especially noteworthy, is the extent to which programmes, such as Export Managers for Hire Schemes in Finland and Norway and the Targeted Marketing Consultancy Programme in Ireland, seek to provide proactive and small-firm orientated approaches with a strong emphasis on export development, rather than the provision of export information. Also manifest is a serious attempt to tailor services to the specific needs of individual firms. In this respect, these countries EPO offerings are better focused than those of larger nations whose services have been frequently criticised in the literature because of their lack of differentiation and inattention to small-firm needs.

Thirdly, and arguably of greatest significance, is evidence of a more holistic approach to export promotion in the countries in question. The use of consultants and the availability of financial assistance are well-integrated with other EPO services such as information provision, the grant-aiding of market research, and practical support from the EPOs' overseas offices. Offerings such as the product design advisory service in Ireland and Produkttest in Norway offer assistance of a very practical nature to small firms in critical export development areas. In this respect the national EPOs offer a much more comprehensive and all-embracing 'package' of export support to individual firms than appears to be the case elsewhere. However, it must also be recognised that smaller client bases in Finland, Ireland and Norway undoubtedly enable EPOs to provide a more personalised service to individual clients.

Evidence of the efficacy of such approaches is provided by Bell's (1994) enquiry into small computer software firms' awareness and utilisation of export services in these countries and their satisfaction with EPO provisions. This study reveals a number of interesting findings:

- First, awareness of most services is high in all countries, often at the 60 to 100 per cent level. In isolated instances where specific offerings are not well-known, there is generally a plausible reason, such as the programme's recent introduction, or the fact that it is selectively offered by the EPO.

- Second, use of specific services is acceptably high, with 30 to 60 per cent of firms in each country using the majority of services. Particularly high usage is reported for services which offer support and financial assistance, as opposed to those which only provide information. Again, there is lower usage for certain offerings which are not especially appropriate for smaller firms and/or those within the software sector.

- Third, where particular services are used, there is a high degree of satisfaction, ranging from 3 to 5 (on a scale of 1-5, where 1 = very dissatisfied and 5 = very satisfied). No Irish services and only two Finnish and Norwegian services are rated below the 3 threshold. Levels of satisfaction are particularly high for those services which offered practical assistance combined with an element of financial support. Conversely, satisfaction levels are lower for information-type services.

In many respects, these findings run contrary to the results of many previous studies into the inefficacy of export promotion measures, *vis-à-vis* smaller firms in particular. Nevertheless, they do confirm small-firm preferences for the types of programmes which enable small firms to develop 'experiential' knowledge and expand their networks of international contacts. Moreover, although Bell's (1994) investigation focuses specifically on computer software firms, it supports the findings of several confidential industry-wide consultant's reports commissioned by the Norwegian EPO in respect of their own services. Discussions with expert witnesses within each EPO also indicated that results were broadly in line with their own perceptions of services. All of these factors suggest that the Finnish, Irish and Norwegian EPOs may have succeeded where other EPOs appear to have failed in the past, by providing support for an increasingly important indigenous small-business sector.

In this context, it is interesting to observe changes which have been taking place in the provision of export promotion in the US in the past decade. Due to the widespread criticisms of US Department of Commerce services, individual states have become increasingly involved in providing export support, in terms of inward and outward visits, state-organised trade missions and export development programmes for smaller local firms (Chadwin, 1990; Goodnow and Goodnow, 1990; Lesch et al., 1990). A useful summary of the activities of individual states is contained in *Small Business Success,* Volume VI (1993). At the same time, the role of the DOC appears to have diminished to that of providing more general export information such as trade statistics. As will be discussed below, there is some evidence to suggest that similar patterns are emerging within the EU, especially in respect of greater provision of information from the centre via the Euro-info centres.

Finally, an underlying objective of EPO services in each of these countries is that of fostering international competitiveness. This is a broader perspective than simply seeking to stimulate greater export activity and is particularly manifest in initiatives such as the Irish Targeted Marketing Consultancy Programme and the Norwegian SMB-E programmes. This is particularly important in an increasingly global business environment and should constitute the key focus for export promotion organisations world-wide. However, it is especially critical for peripheral nations which increasingly find themselves marginalised and outside the mainstream of international trade flows.

Clearly, these nations include most of the developing countries in Africa and Latin America. They also include many Eastern European countries and the new republics of the former Soviet Union, many of which have expressed aspirations to join an enlarged European Union. However, as has already been observed, the notion of peripherality also pertains to existing EU member states which are located at the geographic extremities of EU and which consequently continue to be somewhat isolated from intra-community trade which tends to be concentrated in the centre.

Fostering international competitiveness is especially important in light of developments within the EU, as it may be argued that intra-community trade, within the 'single' market, can no longer be considered as 'exporting'. This has two major implications. First, although the European Commission has, thus far, adopted a fairly *laissez-faire* attitude towards national small-firm policies including export promotion measures, it may ultimately be forced to rigorously implement 'competition policy' legislation to prevent governments from providing support that distorts trade between member states.

In these circumstances current export support measures for small firms, which generate much of their sales within the EU, would have to be replaced by initiatives that focus on increasing competitiveness. Clearly, these would be consistent with EU policy of stimulating intra-community trade, particularly, in support of 'less advantaged' peripheral member states, and in line with current EU initiatives such as BC-Net, SPRINT, the Europartenariat programmes, the EBIC networks and so forth.

Second, despite greater integration, individual member states still need to provide export promotion measures for firms wishing to enter extra-community countries. Again, there is evidence that the EU is anxious to provide greater and more co-ordinated support in this respect, especially *vis-à-vis* the small-firm sector. It is difficult to speculate on any future relationship between centrally-co-ordinated EU trade policies and national export promotion strategies.

However, a potential scenario is that the European Commission may — increasingly — attempt to supply export information needs, leaving national EPOs to concentrate on the provision of more specific support measures. Indeed, there is no obvious reason why greater efficiencies could not be gained by centralising the provision of export information, thereby reducing the level of duplication which currently exists and enabling national EPOs to re-direct scarce resources towards the provision of targeted support and assistance.

Conceivably, this might mean a shift towards a US-style model which might well find favour given that Germany, the most influential EU member state, already operates a system where export information is provided by central government, but chambers of commerce or industry federations undertake a significant proportion of export support activities. It may also lead to a greater involvement by private sector institutions and/or quasi-government bodies in the provision export support. The 'privatisation' of export credit guarantees in many countries is a case in point.

In view of these potential developments, the need for peripheral member states to develop proactive and highly-targeted support measures for small indigenous exporters, such as those provided in Finland, Ireland and Norway, is paramount. However, the apparent success of the respective national EPOs in delivering the type of support that small indigenous firms require, provides object lessons for other peripheral economies elsewhere. Moreover, it offers useful insights for larger nations where export provisions for the small business sector have been severely criticised in the past.

6.7 CONCLUSIONS

This chapter has reviewed the activities of the Finnish, Irish and Norwegian EPOs in light of the criticisms of export promotion provisions which proliferate in the literature. It concludes that these countries provide examples of good export promotion practice which could be adapted and adopted by other peripheral nations, whether they are located within the EU or not. Furthermore, it contends that their pro-active, holistic and well-targeted approaches offer valuable insights for policy-makers in advanced and emerging economies alike.

References

_____ (1993), 'The Wide World of International Trade', *Small Business Success*, Volume 6, pp. 30-42.

Albaum, G. (1983), 'Effectiveness of Government Export Assistance for U.S. Smaller-Sized Manufacturers: Some Further Evidence', *International Marketing Review*, Vol. 1, No. 1, pp. 68-75.

Bannock, G. and Partners (1987), 'Into Active Exporting', BOTB Occasional Papers, HMSO. 8934782 J0229NJ, London: HMSO.

Bell, J., (1994), 'The Role of Government in Small-Firm Internationalisation: A Comparative Study of Export Promotion in Finland, Ireland and Norway, with Specific reference to the Computer Software Industry', unpublished PhD Thesis, University of Strathclyde.

Bell, J., Murray, M. and Madden, K. (1992), 'Developing *Exportise*: An Irish Perspective', *International Small Business Journal*, Vol. 10, No. 2, pp. 37-53.

Bowen, D. (1986), 'A World Guide to Export Services', *Business*, June, pp. 55-62.

Brezzo, R. and Perkal, I. (1983), 'The Role of Marketing Incentives in Export Promotion: The Uruguayan Case' in *Export Promotion: The*

Public and Private Sector Interaction (Ed. Czinkota, M. R.), New York: Praeger, pp. 51-65.

Buckley, P. J. (1983), 'Government-Industry Relations in Exporting: Lessons from the United Kingdom' in *Export Promotion: The Public and Private Sector Interaction* (Ed. Czinkota, M. R.), New York: Praeger, 89-109.

Camino, D. (1991), 'Export Promotion in Spain and other EEC Countries: Systems and Performance' in *Export Development and Promotion: The Role of Public Organisations* (Eds. Seringhaus, F. H. R. and Rosson, P. J.), Boston: Kluwer Academic Publishers, pp. 119-44.

Cannon, T. and Willis, M. (1981), 'The Smaller Firm in Overseas Trade', *European Small Business Journal*, Vol. 1, No. 3, pp. 45-55.

Cavusgil, S. T. (1983), 'Public Policy Implications of Research on the Export Behaviour of Firms', *Akron Business and Economic Review*, Vol. 14, No. 3, pp. 16-22.

Cellich, C. (1989), 'Export Training in Action: the Case of Finland' in *Managing Export Training: Strategies, Policies and Principles for Developing Countries*, Geneva: International Trade Centre, UNCTAD/GATT.

Chadwin, M. (1990), 'State Development Programs: Assessment and Recommendations' in *International Perspectives on Trade Promotion and Assistance* (Eds. Cavusgil, S. and Czinkota, M), Westport, CT: Quorum Books, pp. 39-52.

Cunningham, M. and Spigel, R. I. (1971), 'A Study in Successful Exporting', *British Journal of Marketing*, Vol. 5, No. 1, pp. 2-12.

Czinkota, M. R. and Johnston, W. J. (1981), 'Segmenting U.S. Firms for Export Development', *Journal of Business Research*, Vol. 9, pp. 353-365.

Czinkota, M. R. and Ricks, D. A. (1981), 'Export Assistance: Are we Supporting the Best Programs?', *Columbia Journal of World Business*, Summer, pp. 73-78.

Czinkota, M. R. (1982), *Export Development Strategies: U.S. Promotion Policy*, New York: Praeger.

De Mortanges, C. P. and Van Gent, A. P. (1991), 'International Marketing and Government Export Promotion in the Netherlands' in *Export Development and Promotion: The Role of Public Organisations* (Eds. Seringhaus, F. H. R. and Rosson, P. J.), Boston: Kluwer Academic Publishers, pp. 243-71.

Denis, J. E. and Depelteau, D. (1985), 'Market Knowledge Diversification and Export Expansion', *Journal of International Business Studies*, Vol. 16, No. 3, pp. 77-89.

Diamantopoulos, A., Schlegelmilch, B. B. and Katy Tse, K. Y. (1993), 'Understanding the Role of Export Marketing Assistance: Empirical Evidence and Research Needs', *European Journal of Marketing*, Vol. 27, pp. 5-18.

EIM/ENSR (1993), *European Observatory for SMEs: First Annual Report*, Economisch Instituut vor het Midden- en Kleinbedrijf, Zoetermeer.

Elvey, L. A. (1990), 'Export Promotion and Assistance: A Comparative Analysis', in *International Perspectives on Trade Promotion* (Eds. Cavusgil, S. T. and Czinkota, M. R), Westport, CT: Quorum Books, pp. 133-48.

Framnes, R. and Welch, L. S. (1982), 'An Evaluation of Recent Norwegian and Australian Policies to Increase Export Orientation' in *Developing Global Corporate Strategies* (Ed. Bonham-Yeaman, D.), Miami, FL: Florida International University.

Goodnow, J. D. and Goodnow, W. E. (1990), 'Self-Assessment by State Export Promotion Agencies: A Status Report', *International Marketing Review*, Vol. 7, No. 3, pp. 18-30.

Hibbert, E. P. (1991), *The Management of International Trade Promotion*, London: Routledge.

Howard, D. G. and Herremans, I. M. (1988), 'Sources of Assistance for Small Business Exporters: Advice from Successful Firms', *Journal of Small Business Management*, Vol. 26, No. 3, pp. 48-54.

ITC (1986), *Selected Export Promotion Organisations: Structures, Functions and Activities*, Geneva: International Trade Centre, UNCTAD/GATT.

ITC (1988), *Profile of Trade Promotion Organisations*, Geneva: International Trade Centre, UNCTAD/GATT.

Johanson, J. and Vahlne, J-E. (1977), 'The Internationalisation Process of the Firm: A Model of Knowledge Development and Increasing Foreign Commitments', *Journal of International Business Studies*, Vol. 8 (1), pp. 23-32.

Kathawala, Y., Judd, R., Monipallil, M. and Weinrich, M. (1989), 'Exporting Practices and Problems of Illinois Firms', *Journal of Small Business Management*, Vol. 27, No. 1, pp. 53-58.

Kaynak, E. and Stevenson, L. (1982), 'Export Orientation of Nova Scotia Manufacturers' in *Export Management* (Eds. Czinkota, M. R. and Tesar, G.), New York: Praeger, pp. 132-45.

Kedia, B. L. and Chhokar, J. S. (1986), 'An Empirical Investigation of Export Promotion Programs', *Columbia Journal of World Business*, Winter, pp. 13-20.

Khan, M. S. (1978), 'A Study of Success and Failure in Exports', unpublished PhD Dissertation, University of Stockholm, Stockholm.

Lennon, J. J. (1988), 'Group Marketing: Theory and Practice', *Irish Marketing Review*, Vol. 3, pp. 69-77.

Lesch, W. C., Eshghi, A. and Eshghi, G. (1990), 'A Review of Export Promotion Programs in the Ten Largest Industrial States' in *International Perspectives on Trade Promotion and Assistance* (Eds. Cavusgil, S. and Czinkota, M.) , Westport, CT: Quorum Books, pp. 39-52.

MacAuley, A. (1992), 'The Perceived Usefulness of Export Information Sources', *European Journal of Marketing*, Vol. 27, No. 10, pp. 52-64.

McFarlane, G. (1978), 'Scots Queen Award Winners Don't Excel', *Marketing*, April, pp. 29-32.

Pointon, T. (1978), 'Measuring the Gains from Government Export Promotion', *European Journal of Marketing*, Vol. 12, No. 6, pp. 451-62.

Reid, S. D. (1983), 'Export Research in a Crisis' in *Export Promotion, the Public and Private Sector Interaction* (Ed Czinkota, M. R.), New York: Praeger, pp. 129-53.

Reid, S. D. (1984), 'Information Acquisition and Export Entry Decisions in Small Firms', *Journal of Business Research*, Vol. 12, pp. 141-57.

Root, F. R. (1971), 'The Elements of Export Promotion', *International Trade Forum*, Vol. 7, pp. 11-30.

Root, F. R. (1974), 'Conceptual Foundations for the Strategy of a Government Export Promotion Agency', *Foreign Trade Review*, Jan-Mar 1974, pp. 326-38.

Rosson, P. J. and Seringhaus, F. H. R. (1991), 'Export Promotion and Public Organisations: Present and Future Research' in *Export Development and Promotion: The Role of Public Organisations* (Eds. Seringhaus, F. H. R. and Rosson, P. J.), Boston: Kluwer Academic Publishers, pp. 319-39.

Schwarting, U., Thoben, T. and Wittstock, M. (1982), Nachfrageverhalten halten Kleiner und Mittler Unternehmen nach Assenhandels Informationen Beitrage zur Mittel Standforschung, Heft 83.

Seringhaus, F. H. R. (1986), 'The Impact of Government Export Marketing Assistance', *International Marketing Review*, Vol. 3, No. 2, pp. 55-65.

Seringhaus, F. H. R. (1987), 'Export Promotion: The Role and Impact of Government Services', *Irish Marketing Review*, Vol. 2, pp. 106-16.

Seringhaus, F. H. R. (1988), 'Export Promotion Organizations in Developing Countries: Their Role, Scope and Function', paper presented at the International Symposium on Export and Public Organizations, Waterloo, Canada.

Seringhaus, F. H. R. and Botschen, G. (1990), 'Cross National Comparison of the Export Promotion Services and their Usage by Canadian and Austrian Companies', *Proceedings of the 19th European Marketing Academy Conference*, pp. 1563-82.

Seringhaus, F. H. R. and Rosson, P. J. (1990), *Government Export Promotion: A Global Perspective*, London: Routledge.

Seringhaus, F. H. R. and Rosson, P. J. (1991),'Export Promotion and Public Organisations: The State of the Art' in *Export Development and Promotion: The Role of Public Organisations* (Eds. Seringhaus, F. H. R. and Rosson, P. J), Boston: Kluwer Academic Publishers, pp. 3-18.

Stenberg, T. (1982), 'Systemamverkam — En Mojlighet for Svensk Industri?' (Systems Co-operation — A Possibility for Swedish Industry?), Sweden: Kompendiet-Lindome.

Strandskov, J. (1986) 'Towards a New Approach for Studying the Internationalization Process of the Firm', Working Paper No. 4, Copenhagen School of Economics, Copenhagen.

Tesar, G. (1974), An Empirical Study of Export Operations Among Small and Medium-sized Manufacturing Firms', unpublished PhD dissertation, University of Wisconsin-Madison, Wisconsin.

Tesar, G. and Tarleton, J. S. (1983), 'Stimulation of Manufacturing Firms to Export as Part of National Export Policy' in *Export Promotion, the Public and Private Sector Interaction* (Ed Czinkota, M. R.), New York: Praeger, pp. 24-36.

Thomas, M.J. and Araujo, L. (1985) 'Theories of Export Behaviour: A Critical Analysis', *European Journal of Marketing*, Vol. 19, No. 2, pp. 42-55.

Walters, P. G. P. (1983), 'Export Information Sources — A Study of their Usage and Utility', *International Marketing Review*, Vol. 1, No. 2, pp. 34-43.

Welch, L. S. and Joynt, P. (1984), 'International Small Enterprise Review: Scandinavian Developments in the Promotion of Small Business Internationalization', *Management Forum,* Vol. 10, No. 2, pp. 52-59.

Welch, L. S. and Joynt, P. (1987),'Grouping for Export an Effective Solution' in *Managing Export Entry and Expansion* (Eds. Rosson, P. J. and Reid, S. D.), New York: Praeger, pp. 54-70.

7

FOREIGN DIRECT INVESTMENT TO A PERIPHERAL COUNTRY: THE CASE OF IRELAND

James Wrynn

7.1 INTRODUCTION

Foreign Direct Investment (FDI)[1] as an explicitly-stated policy instrument of economic development, vigorously pursued, is of relatively recent origin. An understanding of FDI may be achieved from several interrelated perspectives including international trade and investment theory, economic development models, concepts of the nature and dynamics of transnational corporations (TNCs) and the strategies and policy objectives of host countries.

FDI in practice has a long history. Singer has been identified as the first modern US multinational, moving into the UK in the 1850s (Wilkins, 1970). Large-scale FDI commenced after the Second World War, with much of this dominated by US investment into Europe. FDI from Europe into the US is of more recent origin and has been more weighted towards acquisitions, rather than toward the greenfield projects which dominate US investment in Europe. Traditionally FDI has been stimulated by TNC strategy, rather than as a result of incentive policy by host countries. Indeed, in the past, many countries, both developed and less developed, have been suspicious of FDI. Recipients have expressed many fears, such as loss of control over important aspects of economic activity. However the comments of the Steuer Report on FDI in the UK (Steuer et al., 1973) represent a considered view on the effects of FDI in a developed economy:

---

[1] FDI is used to denote FDI in greenfield manufacturing projects or expansion of same. It does not include FDI for acquisitions or FDI in Financial Services except in Section 7.1 where the inclusive definition applies.

concerns over the multinational firm and inward investment on the grounds of monopoly power, technology and the balance of payments are not well founded. At the same time some drawbacks have been indicated.

Even countries with indigenous-based TNCs have expressed concerns about the investments of such companies taking place abroad rather than at home. This issue has been addressed in the Swedish context by Hornell and Vahlne (1986), but they concluded that:

> (foreign) direct investments of (Swedish) multinational companies contribute to a restructuring of Swedish industry in a direction which tends to enhance Sweden's international competitive position.

Inward FDI as a policy instrument of economic development is of more recent origin. The more significant examples of this are the Sunbelt states in the US and the less-favoured regions (LFRs) of the EU. More widespread use of FDI in this way has led to competitive bidding for FDI and accusations of unfair competitive advantage accruing to FDI projects because of capital and other subsidies. In Ireland's case, export profit tax relief (EPTR), which zero-rated tax on profits from exports and which largely benefited FDI in Ireland,[2] had to be abolished under EU anti-competitive rules. It was replaced by a nominal ten per cent tax on all profits from manufacturing industry in Ireland. Because of the growing importance of FDI and the associated competitive issues, the OECD has initiated discussions on a Multilateral Agreement on Investment, and FDI issues are now formally part of the remit of GATT/WTO as a result of the Uruguay Round agreements.

The discussion in this chapter focuses on the role of FDI in Ireland from the perspective of the host country. Section 7.2 deals with the political, historical and economic background to Ireland's economic development and economic policy in the early years of independence. The next section describes the sequence of events which led to a reversal of policy resulting in Ireland pursuing a most active policy of encouragement of FDI. Section 7.4 examines the details of FDI policy implementation and performance.

---

[2] Ireland is used to denote the Republic of Ireland except where the context obviously indicates the whole island.

Section 7.5 briefly discusses the source of FDI and Section 7.6 seeks to draw conclusions.

Ireland's economic development presents an interesting case, because policies of nominally restricting foreign investment were initially vigorously pursued and subsequently a complete policy reversal took place, initiating one of the most enthusiastic policies of attracting foreign investment. As with most areas of economics, policies and policy changes in this area of foreign investment were a product of a complex mix of historical, cultural, political and economic considerations.

7.2 POLITICAL, HISTORICAL AND ECONOMIC BACKGROUND

In 1922, 26 of the 32 counties in Ireland achieved independence from the United Kingdom. At that time the more industrialised part of Ireland was the area remaining as part of the UK. Nevertheless economic historians are of the view that there was little if any significant disparity in per capita income between these six counties and the newly independent southern state. In international comparative terms, Ireland ranked about middle way in European league terms in the early part of the century.

TABLE 7.1: RELATIVE GDP PER CAPITA, 1913

UK	164
Denmark	136
Belgium	125
Germany	118
Netherlands	113
Austria	107
France	103
Ireland	100
Sweden	97
Finland	80
Italy	70
Spain	61
Portugal	50
Greece	50

Source: Adapted from Kennedy et al. (1988), p. 18.

While economic data at the time lacked the comprehensiveness and accuracy of data today, there is reasonable agreement that the position of Ireland was approximately as set out in the above table.

However within Ireland, the political orthodoxy propounded a view that colonial Ireland under British rule had suffered terribly and that Ireland could prosper much more as an independent state. While there was broad agreement on the merit of independence, there was both confusion and diversity of opinion on the economic policies to be pursued. Griffith, founder of the independence movement, Sinn Féin, argued for tariff protection on the basis of what was a fundamental misinterpretation of Frederich List's infant-industry thesis. Thomas Davis, an important 19th century influence on the independence movement and a poet, regarded by some to be in the tradition of European romanticism, advocated small-scale domestic industry, rather than large-scale factory production, where, in the words of Lalor, another 19th century advocate of independence, 'workers spend their lives from the cradle to the coffin shut up from the sun and sky'. The Gaelic revivalists and other groups including such significant influences as Yeats saw the peasant or small farmer as representing an authentic Irish way of life.

However not all commentators subscribed to the evils of colonialism as the cause of economic misfortune or the simplicity and attractiveness of rural life as a panacea. James Connolly presented a Marxist analysis and argued that the structure of the Irish economy was determined by international capitalism. Horace Plunkett, the advocate and developer of the co-operative movement in Ireland, pointed to the role of education and the values derived from Catholicism as a factor in underdevelopment. (Plunkett, 1905, p. 18-19).

This diversity of vaguely-stated ideas, mostly under the common umbrella of nationalism, highlighted the view that 'the fledgling Irish state inherited a confused baggage of ideals' (Daly, 1992, p. 11) in relation to social and economic development.

7.2.1 Ireland Post-Treaty

Ireland's middle rank position somewhat obscures a weaker underlying position. Relative to its dominating neighbour, the UK, it was a much poorer country, with the UK at that time the leading country in the European economic league table. Its exports were solely dependent on the UK market. Strong British firms competed on the Irish market and the Irish government infra-structure was very weak following a war of independence and a bitter civil war. Even though its average European economic posi-tion appeared respectable, its economic structure was marked by a weak industrial base. Thus, from a developmental point of view, the economy was weak, under-developed and displayed many of the characteristics of a peripheral economy.

The government and civil service of the new state were lacking any distinctive ideas, and their judgements were cautious and tended towards favouring the status quo. Economic policy was de-termined by experts of broadly similar mind (Daly, 1992). The most significant commissions of experts were the Fiscal Inquiry Committee which looked at the effects of the existing fiscal sys-tem on industry and agriculture and the Banking Commission which determined currency policy.

Prior to 1922, Britain, Northern Ireland and the Irish Free State had operated as a single fiscal unit with the common selec-tive protective duties introduced by Britain during World War 1. The Fiscal Inquiry Committee now sought to establish an appro-priate fiscal policy for the new state. The committee received conflicting evidence. The Government Department of Industry and Commerce advocated tariff protection as a tool for industrial development while manufacturers with established markets in the UK argued for a tariff-free situation between Ireland and the UK. Industry and Commerce's main point in favour of tariffs was that they would lead to inward investment by 'some of the best organised external manufacturing concerns' (Daly, 1992, p. 24). Selective tariffs were imposed in the 1924 and 1925 budgets. Sub-sequently a Tariff Commission was established in 1926 to decide on a tariff regime. One of its first acts was to decide on a tariff for rosary beads, perhaps a reflection of the ethos of the new state.

While some foreign investment was stimulated by the nascent tariff protection, other foreign investment was stimulated by what we refer to today as globalisation. In the 1920s the brand names of Lever Bros. dominated the soap market and most tobacco sales were dominated by British brands. Such firms established over-seas plants to serve local markets and a number of other UK firms adopted this strategy in relation to Ireland. But political hostility to foreign investment grew, with criticism focusing on themes familiar to us today, such as minimum taxes and repa-triation of profits (Daly, 1992).

7.2.2 Import Substitution Industrialisation

The 1932 election brought to power the aggressively nationalist party Fianna Fáil, with some radical policies on industrialisation. Import substitution industrialisation (ISI) was to become their principal policy instrument. Tariff protection was greatly increased to protect manufacturing concerns located in Ireland, with the Department of Industry and Commerce effectively taking over decision making on tariffs. The Tariff Commission itself continued in existence until 1938, but with an insignificant role and its last decision echoed its first, being on the level of tariffs on prayer books. While Fianna Fáil policy was dressed up in strong nationalist self-sufficiency terms, the Minister responsible, Lemass, was in practice more pragmatic. While in 1929, in opposition, Lemass had lamented 'an estimated 459 foreign firms within the state' (Daly, 1992, p. 81), his officials told Dunlop (the tyre manufacturer) that 'in their own interest it (investment in Ireland) would be a judicious step to take' (Daly, 1992, p. 88) when they indicated they were considering Ireland as a manufacturing location.

The Control of Manufacturers Act (1932) was another key instrument of the new policy. This made it impossible to license new firms supplying sectors serviced by Irish manufacturers and required that a majority of shares in foreign investment in Ireland be Irish-held. However, this latter requirement was surmounted by complex share-capital structures often constructed with the tacit support of government officials.

In summary, a policy of industrial development, while articulated in quite extreme nationalist terms and perceived by the public as favouring Irish companies, in reality pursued industrialisation as the over-riding objective and recognised the necessity for foreign investment because of an absence of capital, entrepreneurial skills or technical knowledge. It is important to note of course that the primary purpose of foreign investment at this time was to provide for the home market. Retaliatory tariff protection by the UK prevented an export-driven sector from being established through the vehicle of inward investment. More importantly, it also hindered the development of larger Irish companies, as such companies were prevented from accessing their nearest substantial market, the UK, because of retaliatory tariffs. It was precisely for this reason that Guinness established a brewing facility in London to service that market with this move eventually contributing to a shift in the centre of gravity of the company to London.

Overall, it is argued that despite the veneer of nationalism 'the balance of experience favoured foreign business who drove hard bargains' (Daly, 1992, p. 89). The following table indicates the degree of success of the ISI policy pursued over the period 1932-38. Industrial employment rose by almost 50 per cent in the period 1931-37, but by 1937, the policy, as practised, had exhausted its potential.

TABLE 7.2: INDUSTRIAL EMPLOYMENT, 1926-1938

Year	Transportable Goods	Building	Other	Total
1926	57,237	9,852	35,426	102,515
1929	65,162	11,754	31,599	108,515
1931	61,380	12,530	36,678	110,588
1936	94,708	18,207	40,973	153,888
1937	98,973	15,009	47,230	161,212
1938	98,444	19,548	48,182	166,174

Source: Daly (1992).

The socio-cultural issues of development and of foreign investment during this period are worthy of consideration. Mjøset (1992) in his study of the Irish economy from a comparative institutional perspective, with countries such as Austria, Denmark, Finland, Sweden and Switzerland, argues that socio-economic development in Ireland may usefully be examined by locating the Irish experience in a context which posits two models of development, with Ireland located somewhere between the two. On the one hand, 'auto-centric growth' and development typically results from reinforcing factors such as technical change brought about by successful import substitution, rising living standards and modernisation of the way of life. On the other hand 'peripheral growth' with little development arises from little technical progress because of failure of import substitution, marginalisation of the standard of living and little modernisation of the way of life. These reinforcing factors may be significantly affected by external economic and internal socio-cultural factors. For example in Ireland's case, it was economically substantially dependent on Britain and consequently 'became a free rider on Britain's decline' (Mjøset, 1992, p. 9). Overall, within this framework, Mjøset concludes that Ireland in the 1920s had a weak system of national innovation.

It may be argued that the foreign investment stimulated by tariff policy could have been a mechanism for bringing much needed technical innovation, rising living standards and spill over effects of modernisation. However, despite the early promise of the vigour of the new policies, the developmental impetus had exhausted itself by 1936 as is clear from Table 7.2. The attachment and dependence on the British economy was reinforced by the almost exclusive British character of the foreign investment. Furthermore any general movement towards socio-cultural modernisation which might be expected from economic growth was firmly stifled by a number of factors. This included an increasingly dominant church ethos and a political system dominated by two catch-all parties which acted as barriers to real political discourse on developmental and societal issues generally. Thus some of the potential benefits of foreign investment were almost stillborn. Daly (1992) concludes that the new state chose native control of industry as the vehicle for building a new identity in the economic sphere. In this context, perhaps Deutsch's (1966) view on nation-building is revealing:

> Only the most carefully screened and selected influences from the outside world are henceforth to be admitted to the budding nation, and usually they are to be confined to narrowly technical economic or scientific matters in regard to which foreigners are to be 'overtaken and surpassed' without admitting any broader values, habits or cultural patterns (cited in Daly, 1992, p. 181).

It is a view that would have found a welcome resonance in Ireland in the 1930s. Attempts to corral foreign influences in this way may be a reason why the developmental objectives being pursued in this fashion were doomed to failure in the long-run.

O'Hearn (1993) in a radical critique of Irish peripherality, states that many peripheral countries like Ireland attempted strategies of ISI during the period 1914-45. Many of these experiments persisted for a considerable time, indeed until such time as they were beset by problems of insufficient foreign exchange and lack of access to capital equipment and technology. He argues that such peripheral ISI experiments were doomed to fail because of the monopoly of the most advanced techniques by developed countries. Furthermore, he points out that the collapse of ISI was blamed on the 'failure of peripheral people to become modern, their lack of respect for free market forces . . . and their affinity to outdated ideas like nationalism and protection'. He asserts that such arguments were later used to justify Ireland being incorporated into the US-dominated world system. This critique is made in the context of developing a historical backdrop to the argument that core-periphery disparities in Europe will continue in spite of current EU cohesion measures and reliance on FDI.

7.3 POLICY CHANGE

Ireland's neutrality during the Second World War resulted in the country's industrial structure being intact in 1945, when most other European countries were confronted with massive reconstruction problems. Gross domestic product (GDP) had fallen during the war years but rebounded immediately afterwards with an annual growth rate of 4.1 per cent between 1944 and 1950.

Despite its war-time neutrality, and its intact infrastructure, Ireland was offered Marshall Aid in 1948, as part of the overall Marshall Aid program for Western Europe. The level of aid was small but it had very significant repercussions in subsequent policy changes in relation to foreign investment. Acceptance of Marshall Aid required Ireland to become a member of the OEEC and to accept the thrust of US expansionist policy in the area of free trade, e.g. 75 per cent of all quantitative import restrictions were to be removed by 1951. Mjøset (1992) argues that within the Irish governmental bureaucracy, two opposing coalitions existed. One was deflationist and cautious and wished to retain the established tariff-regime while the other was expansionist and wished to encourage export-oriented investments. It can be argued that the acceptance of Marshall Aid and in particular its policy consequences (e.g. the reduction in the import quotas), was a victory for the expansionists. This event marked a very small, albeit an important change in policy in relation to industrial development, and later in relation to foreign investment. Nevertheless, the changes did not achieve widespread or formal acceptance or come to full practical fruition for another 10 years.

The expansionists were immediately successful in achieving the setting up of the Industrial Development Authority (IDA) in 1949. Its remit was to initiate proposals to attract foreign industry. In 1952, a new institution, An Foras Tionscail, was set up to give grants to new industry in depressed regions. Subsequently these institutional arrangements were developed and re-organised with the IDA emerging as a powerful promotional and grant-awarding authority. While important first steps in this process of establishing strong institutional arrangements to promote industrial development were taken in the 1950s, it was only in the following decade that these new policies began to bear fruit. Politically the 1930s protectionist self-sufficiency policy was still the accepted orthodoxy during the 1950s.

7.3.1 Foreign Direct Investment

Abysmal economic performance during the 1950s, when GDP rose by less than one per cent per year until 1958, coupled with a severe balance-of-payments crisis, forced a formal complete re-evaluation of policy in relation to economic development, industrialisation and foreign investment. This policy change was now based on, firstly, substantial capital grants and tax concessions to encourage export-oriented manufacturing; secondly, the attraction of foreign manufacturing enterprise aimed at exports, and finally the dismantling of protection in return for greater access to markets abroad.

The direct support for foreign investment included incentives such as direct capital grants, an attractive tax regime by way of very reduced levels of nominal corporate taxation and a generous equipment-depreciation regime, education and training assistance and a research and technical infrastructure provision.

This fundamental change in policy in relation to trade and tariff protection was quite significant. Most of the quantitative restrictions on imports had been phased out by 1960, but the more important tariff barriers posed a more serious issue. The new policy of attracting foreign investment which was export-oriented effectively required the country to introduce a free trade regime. Three international agreements gave effect to this. In 1965 the Anglo-Irish Free Trade Agreement was negotiated and this provided for the phased elimination of tariffs between Ireland and the UK. Ireland then subscribed to GATT in 1967 and finally became a member of the EEC in 1973. Thus, the country over a fifteen-year period between 1958 and 1973, had put in place a very wide range of policy initiatives, some of which constituted a fundamental reversal of previous policies. The over-riding objective was economic development and the key instrument of this development was overtly stated to be foreign investment. Furthermore, while the policy changes may be categorised as economic, they could only take place in the context of much broader political and socio-cultural change. Politically a nationalism which emphasised self-sufficiency and isolationism now readjusted its definition to emphasise economic growth by whatever means as an important political objective. The benefits which flowed from economic growth, such as higher wages, reduced emigration and improved social services, particularly in education, implanted the new departure firmly in the political landscape. Lemass, now the Prime Minister, fully appreciated that the new economic policy, largely driven by inward investment, was not just about economic change. He predicted in 1962, that the inefficient industrial producer, the traditional farmer and the trade union leader rooted in Victorian assumptions 'all of these by 1970 will have become anachronistic relics of a dead past' (Lee, 1992, p. 400). Significant anchor points of a society were to disappear.

7.3.2 Policy Review: Telesis

In 1977, Fianna Fáil returned to power on a policy platform of economic expansionism, partly in response to a temporary economic slowdown in 1976. As part of this expansionist policy, a review of industrial development was undertaken. A key element of this review was a major review of industrial policy conducted by the Telesis Consulting Group for the National Economic and Social Council (NESC, 1982). This review came to a number of important conclusions.

Firstly it argued that 'successful indigenously owned industry is essential for a high income economy. No country has successfully achieved high incomes without a strong base of indigenously owned resource-based or manufacturing companies in traded sectors' (NESC, 1982, p. 26). This raised the most fundamental questions in relation to excessive reliance on FDI. Secondly it argued that the incentive packages offered to attract FDI were overgenerous. Telesis advocated 'testing the water' by raising the price, i.e. reducing the level of grants. Subsequently a less generous direct grant regime, consuming less resources was put in place (see Table 7.7 and Figure 7.1) but this was compensated for by way of a more favourable corporate tax regime.

The report also highlighted the low level of linkages between foreign-owned companies and indigenous ones.

Overall, the response to Telesis by way of policy change was minimal. There was some shift in emphasis towards the indigenous sector and there was a reduction in the generosity of the grants regime. However the reliance on FDI, as the key policy instrument of industrialisation, continued.

7.3.3 Policy Review: Culliton

The 1980s was largely a period of great economic difficulty for Ireland, largely characterised by severe budgetary problems and very poor economic growth. One outcome at the end of the decade was a further review of industrial policy by the Industrial Policy Review Group chaired by Culliton. (Culliton, 1992).

This review argued, as did Telesis, that more reliance needed to be placed on indigenous industry, and in particular in developing Porterian clusters in the indigenous sector. However it sought to blur the dichotomy of indigenous investment and FDI. It emphasised the need for companies to be deeply embedded in the economy, but implied that this might well be achieved by FDI with strong linkages, while still having a strong emphasis on the objective of developing the indigenous sector. It even argued that 'the definition of indigenous industry must clearly encompass foreign industrial projects which locate core business functions in Ireland' (Culliton, 1992, p. 66). This proposition of defining a nation's prosperity partly in terms of the quantity and quality of employment in a country, regardless of nationality, is supportive of Reich's view on competitiveness, which regards nationality of firms as irrelevant. This subject is dealt with in detail by O'Donnell in Chapter 3.

Culliton also addressed other issues in relation to FDI. It argued that the basis of Ireland's attractiveness to FDI should move away from low corporate tax and cheap labour. The official response to this has, however, been at the least ambiguous. In the 1995 and 1996 government budgets, payroll taxes have been reduced, to facilitate wage competitiveness, even though such taxes are at the lower end of the European scale. This raises some issues in relation to competition for FDI within Europe. Streeck (1992) has argued that some EU countries which depend on low wages for inward investment may feel ambivalent about high common labour standards for the EU as a whole, as such standards may raise labour costs. While Ireland has officially supported the EU Social Charter, employer organisations have been less enthusiastic. The government's strategic approach on labour costs is ambiguous. On the one hand Culliton argues for a move-ment away from low wages as a basis of attractiveness, and the government supports the Social Charter, while on the other hand policy instruments such as payroll tax shifts policy in the opposite direction.

7.4 PERFORMANCE

The policy changes formally initiated in 1958 and continued with some modification to the present day brought about a sustained period of economic growth. In the 1960s most foreign firms were from sectors that were technically mature and labour-intensive such as textiles, plastics and light engineering. In the 1970s and 1980s there was a shift towards more sophisticated sectors such as chemicals and electronics. The following sections will examine the performance of FDI as a policy instrument from the varying perspectives of employment, economic growth, linkage develop-ment, foreign trade impact, costs, and the issue of profit repatria-tion which is particularly important in Ireland's case.

7.4.1 Employment
The increasing role of FDI in industrial employment is illustrated in Table 7.3. While the new FDI policy was formally initiated in the late 1950s, it did not become a central element until the early 1970s.

TABLE 7.3: CHANGES IN INDUSTRIAL EMPLOYMENT, 1973-94

	Irish	Non-Irish	Total
Total Employment 1973	145,815	69,388	215,203
Total Employment 1994	114,613	90,099	204,712
Net Change in Employment 1973-94	-31,202	20,711	-10,491
Total Job Gains 1973-94	231,999	161,866	393,885
Total Job Losses 1973-94	263,201	141,175	404,376

Source: O'Sullivan (1995), p. 369.

This data clearly illustrates the increasing importance of FDI in employment terms. It of course also illustrates, that while total industrial employment actually fell over the period 1973-94, there was considerable turmoil in the composition of that employment with the FDI sector accounting for 44 per cent of industrial employment by 1994.

7.4.2 Economic Growth

Despite falling employment, the overall economy continued to grow, greatly facilitated, of course, by the more productive foreign sector (Table 7.4).

TABLE 7.4: ANNUAL GROWTH RATE GDP

1960-73	1973-79	1979-86	1986-94
4.4%	4.1%	1.5%	4.3%

Source: Haughton (1995) p. 39.

Overall this represents an impressive performance. The difficult period in the 1980s was caused by necessary adjustments to the oil price changes of the 1970s, a general slowdown in the European economy and more significantly by the consequences of rather reckless fiscal policy, involving significant deficits, in the period 1977-82.

7.4.3 Linkages

The Telesis criticism of the low level of linkages with local sub-supply firms deserves scrutiny. The role of linkages in economic development as enunciated by Hirschman (1958) is well-established, with particular emphasis on the role of backward linkages. Much emphasis has been placed on linkages development as a mechanism for developing a more substantial and sophisticated indigenous sector and indeed it has been used to dampen criticism of reliance on FDI.

Lall (1978) has argued that the level of linkage is related to whether the FDI is focused on the home or export market, the level of technical sophistication and the rate of technical change in the investment and the level of sophistication of the indigenous sector. He suggests that FDI involving mature technologies, serving the local market and with a well-developed indigenous sector will establish much more significant linkages than export-oriented, high technology, dynamic companies operating alongside an under-developed indigenous sector.

Turok (1993) suggests two alternative linkage scenarios, one labelled a developmental scenario, the other a dependent scenario. In the development scenario, the vertical disintegration of large companies and decentralisation of decision-making may give rise to collaborative relationships with local suppliers that may lead to fairly sophisticated local supply clusters benefiting from technology and expertise transfers. In the dependent scenario, relationships are adversarial with cost-cutting a driving force and the local firms bear the burden of cyclicality in supply requirements.

There has been little examination of the variables described by Lall or of the texture of relationships posited by Turok, in the Irish context. However two studies in the area of technological sophistication and linkages in Ireland partially address Lall's arguments. The Sectoral Development Report (SDC) on Technological Capacity of Indigenous Irish Industry (1985) found low levels of process technology and skills in sectors such as mechanical and electrical engineering, chemicals and pharmaceuticals with electronics and plastics having a medium rating. Such sectors are important as potential supply sectors. The SDC Report on Linkages (1985) which ascertained the views of FDI companies, identified eight reasons why linkages were weak. In summary these reasons amounted to a lack of managerial, technological and skill sophistication of suppliers leading to poor quality and unreliable supply. There were, of course, purchasing-company constraints not related to the capacity of supply companies, such as policies on diversity of supply. Taken together, both studies suggest that basic weaknesses in potential supply companies act as a significant barrier to linkage development. This supports Lall's hypothesis that linkage development is dependent on the sophistication of the indigenous sector. It would be interesting to engage in a comparative study of the extent of linkage development where FDI is located in a developed and a weak indigenous context.

Much of the available analytical work on linkages has focused on the extent of linkages. Turok (1993) examines the composition of locally-sourced supplies to the Scottish electronics industry where the proportion of local sourcing is estimated at 12 per cent. He found that purchases are not technically sophisticated, and that most of the upward shift in sophistication which is taking place is due to foreign suppliers establishing local operations. Furthermore his analysis of some of the factors contributing to weak linkages identifies reasons very much similar to those identified in Ireland, namely inadequate quality and unreliable supply among other factors.

Returning to the position in Ireland, Table 7.5 confirms the disappointing level of performance with respect to linkages.

TABLE 7.5: IRISH ECONOMY EXPENDITURES (ALL FOREIGN INDUSTRY), 1990-94 (£IR MILLION, CONSTANT 1994 PRICES)

	1990	*1991*	*1992*	*1993*	*1994**
Sales	10,855 (100%)	10,767 (100%)	11,541 (100%)	12,427 (100%)	13,841 (100%)
Irish Economy Expenditure**	4,032 (37%)	4,162 (39%)	4,610 (37%)	4,855 (39%)	5,149 (37%)
Of which:					
Labour Costs	1,480 (14%)	1,532 (14%)	1,577 (14%)	1,590 (13%)	1,675 (12%)
Irish Raw Materials	1,153 (11%)	1,150 (11%)	1,300 (11%)	1,459 (12%)	1,533 (11%)
Irish Services	1,353 (12%)	1,392 (13%)	1,365 (12%)	1,571 (13%)	1,681 (8%)

Source: IDA.

* Estimate
** Totals of Labour, Raw Materials and Services may not agree with Irish Economy Expenditure due to rounding and other residual items.

Specifically, the low level of linkages in relation to raw materials, reiterates the lack of success of linkages from FDI as a developmental instrument. Kennedy (1991) has argued that low levels of corporate tax discourage backward linkage development. Companies seeking to maximise profit creation in Ireland will prefer to purchase supplies from within the corporate entity to utilise transfer pricing arrangements to maximise profit location in Ireland.

7.4.4 Trade
The contribution of FDI to Ireland's export trade performance is sharply illustrated by reference to the destination of exports (Table 7.6).

TABLE 7.6: PERCENTAGE DISTRIBUTION IN VALUE TERMS OF
EXPORTS BY DESTINATION

	1964	1974	1984	1994
UK	72	56	34	27
EU (excl. UK)*	11	18	34	41
US and Canada	7	11	11	9
Other	10	15	21	23

Source: Central Statistics Office, Trade Statistics

* France, Germany, Belgium, Netherlands, Luxembourg, Italy, Denmark, Spain, Portugal, Greece for all years

There is the very clear pattern of a lessening dependence on the UK market and the EU emerging as the dominant destination. This more widespread distribution of exports masks a more serious problem for the indigenous sector. While it is not possible to diagnose precisely from government data the pattern of exports between the indigenous sector and the FDI sector, it is possible to establish a pattern by examining those sectors where indigenous companies are dominant and the sectors where FDI is dominant. Such analysis (Bannon, 1996) suggests that over 65 per cent of exports of the indigenous sector go to the UK. This figure of 65 per cent is very close to the overall figure of 72 per cent pertaining in 1964. Thus it appears that there has been little learning or spill-over effect from the FDI sector to the indigenous sector and that the FDI sector is largely responsible for greater diversity in export destination.

7.4.5 Costs of FDI
While Telesis suggested a significant shift was required in industrial policy, the government did not respond in a substantial manner. There was a reining-in of the level of direct capital subvention to firms, but the overall thrust of relying on FDI, largely continued (Table 7.7).

While the data refers to total state aids and does not discriminate between aid to FDI and indigenous industry, it nevertheless indicates two interrelated factors. Firstly, there is a clear convergence between Irish levels of state aid and levels in other EU countries. Secondly, Irish levels of state aid have diminished, reflecting an acceptance of the Telesis comment, earlier referred to, on the generosity of Irish grants to FDI. This movement towards a less generous grant support regime is well illustrated by Table 7.7 and Figure 7.1.

TABLE 7.7: TOTAL STATE AIDS* IN THE EUROPEAN UNION (PER CENT OF MANUFACTURING GROSS VALUE-ADDED)

Country	1981-86	1986-88	1988-90
Belgium	4.5	4.3	4.1
Denmark	1.7	1.9	2.1
France	3.6	3.8	3.5
Greece	13.9	24.3	14.6
Ireland	**12.3**	**6.4****	**4.9****
Italy	15.8	6.2	6.0
Luxembourg	3.5	2.3	2.6
Netherlands	4.1	3.1	3.1
Portugal	n/a	2.2	5.3
Spain	n/a	6.8	3.6
UK	2.9	2.6	2.0
West Germany	2.9	2.7	2.5
EU 10 or EU 12	5.5	4.05	3.55

Source: O'Sullivan (1995) p. 383.

* Includes tax reliefs but excludes impact of differences in tax rates. Thus, Ireland's EPTR is included but the effects of her relatively low rate of taxation of corporate profits is not.

** After 1986 EPTR in Ireland was of declining importance prior to its phasing out in 1990. It was replaced by the 10 per cent manufacturing tax as the major fiscal incentive to manufacturing firms. The effects of the latter incentive are not included above.

The cost-per-job sustained is calculated by taking into account all IDA expenditure to all firms in the period of calculation. Only jobs created and sustained to the end of each seven-year-period are credited in the calculations. Obviously the cost-per-job is a function of the number of jobs created and the retention rate. These two elements are not dissaggregated in the data in Figure 7.1, nevertheless the overall significant downward shift does indicate a more selective approach as recommended by Telesis.

FIGURE 7.1: COST PER JOB SUSTAINED (CONSTANT 1995 PRICES)

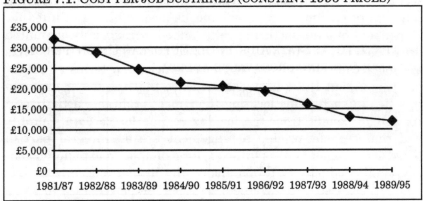

Source: IDA

7.4.6 Profits Outflow and Transfer Pricing

While FDI has contributed significantly to Irish economic growth, reservations have been expressed in relation to the true underlying contribution to the Irish economy. Multinational companies repatriate what are in some cases very significant profits, and the net output of such companies may be distorted by transfer-pricing mechanisms so that the real beneficial contribution to the Irish economy may be overstated. This effect of profit and related outflows is well illustrated by Table 7.8.

TABLE 7.8: OUTFLOWS OF PROFITS, DIVIDENDS AND ROYALTIES, 1980-92

	1980	*1986*	*1987*	*1988*	*1989*	*1990*	*1991*	*1992*
Profits, etc. Outflows (IR£m)	258	1,320	1,307	1,954	2,447	2,507	2,337	2,735
Outflows as a % of GDP	2.8	6.8	6.3	8.7	9.8	9.4	8.6	9.3

Source: O'Malley, et al. (1994)

In addition to the issue of profit outflows there is the related question of transfer pricing. Most of the recent industrial growth has occurred in sectors where FDI is the dominating influence. FitzGerald and Honohan (1994) point out that a handful of such sectors including pharmaceuticals, data processing equipment, software production and miscellaneous foods which accounted for 27 per cent of manufacturing value-added in 1990, only accounted for 10 per cent of employment. It might be argued that such firms are more capital-intensive and more efficient in terms of output per person, but there is strong evidence that the major explanation lies in such firms locating their most profitable activities in Ireland to benefit from the low-tax regime for corporate profits and that transfer-pricing arrangement are an integral part of these arrangements. It is difficult, for example, to explain on conventional productivity terms alone, why in pharmaceuticals, Ireland's measured gross value-added per employee in 1988 was 166,000 ECU per employee as against 52,400 ECU in Germany.

Murphy (1994) in a polemical work, addresses this issue of the true contribution of FDI to the Irish economy. He has focused on three sectors of foreign investment in Ireland (the three Cs) computers and related areas, chemicals (including pharmaceuticals) and cola concentrates (Pepsi and Coca Cola produce cola concentrate in Ireland). In 1990, these sectors had an aggregated gross output of £6.3 billion and a net output of £4.1 billion with a labour force of just over 24,000. This compares with total Irish-owned manufacturing which required a labour force of 106,000 to produce a net output of only £2.8 billion. Specifically, Pepsi Cola and Coca Cola had a turnover of £1.7 million and £1.6 million per employee respectively in their Irish operations. Smurfit, one of Ireland's most successful international companies had a worldwide turnover per employee of £73,000 in 1992, less than one-twentieth of that of the operations of Pepsi or Coca Cola in Ireland. It is interesting to note that Pepsi's global sales were $59,148 per employee in 1992. Of course, it is true that turnover per employee will vary from stage to stage of the overall business entity, but the discrepancies are nonetheless somewhat extreme.

7.5 SOURCES OF FDI IN IRELAND

Ireland's close traditional economic ties with the UK, as outlined earlier, meant that in the early years of pursuing a policy of encouraging FDI, UK firms were an obvious target. Table 7.9 illustrates the changing composition of FDI in terms of employment creation.

The increasing role in employment terms of US-originating FDI is very clear. Much of this US investment is concentrated in electronics and chemicals. The greatly diminishing role of UK investment indicates the further weakening of the dependence of the Irish economy on the UK.

O'Hearn (1993) argues that Ireland's attractiveness stems significantly from its position as a point of entry into European markets and thus FDI in Ireland will tend to be of US and of Asian origin rather than of European origin.

TABLE 7.9: NON-IRISH INDUSTRIAL EMPLOYMENT BY NATIONALITY OF OWNERSHIP OF PROJECT, 1973-94

	1973 Aggregate Employment	Share %	1994 Aggregate Employment	Share %
UK	31,459	45.3	11,806	13.1
Germany	4,735	6.8	9,674	10.7
Other European	5,943	23.0	14,130	15.7
US	15,678	22.6	47,429	52.7
Other non-European	1,573	2.3	7,051	7.8
Total non-Irish	69,388	100	90.099	100

Source: Adapted from O'Sullivan (1995), p. 369

However, change in Eastern Europe has created new opportunities for available mobile FDI. Table 7.10 provides an interesting profile of changes in the flow of FDI.

Figures relate only to greenfield projects which is the main focus of Irish policy in relation to FDI. In addition to the significant share of greenfield projects locating in Eastern Europe, there is very significant FDI in the privatised sector formerly under state ownership.

While the data deals with projects and thus may not indicate a pro rata weighting in terms of capital investment or employment, it nevertheless provides an interesting picture, particularly in relation to Eastern Europe. Nonetheless, to date Ireland's share has remained constant with the exception of 1992.

TABLE 7.10: DESTINATION OF FDI IN EUROPE (GREENFIELD PROJECTS) (%)

	1990	1991	1992	1993	1994
UK	33	29	28	26	33
France	21	22	19	23	10
Ireland	**14**	**13**	**8**	**14**	**14**
Netherlands	9	7	11	7	3
Germany	6	9	6	8	1
Belgium	4	7	13	7	4
E. Europe	n/a	n/a	5	7	25
Other	13	13	10	8	10

Source: IDA

7.6 CONCLUSIONS

FDI has become a central instrument of Irish industrial policy. Such investment is now the dominating element of new manufacturing employment in Ireland. Spill-over effects involving transfer or diffusion of managerial know-how or technology to the indigenous sector have been extremely weak. Backward linkages parallel the low level pertaining in Scotland. This implies, if one accepts the Telesis argument of the necessity for a strong indigenous sector as a basis for wealth, that current FDI-based policy is not a success from this perspective. However, it may well be argued that the development of the indigenous sector cannot be brought about as a by-product of FDI and that other policy instruments are required. FDI has brought about significant increases in GDP, but much lesser increases in GNP due to profit repatriation.

It is salutary to take a long-term historical scan of Ireland's position in terms of comparative economic development. Using 1913 as a base position as per Table 7.1, and selecting 1960 as a dividing point between the abandonment of the ISI policies and the systematic adoption of FDI policies, we can establish Ireland's comparative performance over the period 1913-1995 (see Table 7.11).

Ireland's comparative performance has been particularly weak. In the period 1913-60, all countries with a higher per capita income in 1913 widened the gap with Ireland. Furthermore the three countries with a lower income in 1913 — Sweden, Finland and Italy — outperformed Ireland, and in the case of Sweden and Finland (see Solvell & Zander (Chapter 14) and Ainamo (Chapter 15)) in a quite spectacular fashion. Only Spain and Portugal lagged Ireland in performance. The period 1960-95, the period of FDI policy, seems to provide a more optimistic picture. The gap between Ireland and other EU countries narrowed on the basis of the figures below. But the improvement is somewhat illusory and may partly be due to a very high-performing economy in the period between 1990 and 1995. The illusion relates to the GDP/GNP issue discussed earlier and while the picture indicates some convergence of GDP per capita with the average of EU countries, it must be noted that as recently as 1990 the figure was 65 per cent in contrast to the figure of 75 per cent achieved in 1995. The Irish economy has grown strongly in this period in contrast to the sluggishness of most other European economies. It is unclear if the high levels of economic growth in recent years are a temporary blip or represent the start of a real convergence between GDP in Ireland and the EU average.

TABLE 7.11: RELATIVE GDP PER CAPITA

	1913^1 (Irl=100)	1960^2 (Irl=100)	1960^2 (EU15=100)	1995^2 (Irl=100)	1995^2 (EU15=100)
UK	164	214	128	110	83
Denmark	136	202	121	195	146
Belgium	125	189	113	156	118
Germany	118	202	121	191	144
N'lands	113	160	96	148	112
Austria	107	138	82	169	128
France	103	207	124	153	116
Ireland	100	100	60	100	75
Sweden	97	292	175	143	108
Finland	80	177	106	143	108
Italy	70	122	75	107	81
Spain	61	59	35	81	62
Portugal	50	46	31	62	47
Greece	50	78	47	61	46

Source: (1) Adapted from Kennedy et al (1988) p. 18. (2). Adapted from European Commission (1995), p. 110.

While economic growth, or lack of it, is obviously due to a complexity of factors, it is clear that FDI has played a central role in economic performance since 1960. Overall, it may be argued that FDI policy has contributed to a halt in Ireland's relative decline. Of course as the above data focuses on the relative position of Ireland, it is important to acknowledge that in the period since 1960, the economy has grown broadly in line with other EU countries. The weakness of Ireland's position stems from the fact that the base year of 1960 was very close to the low point of Ireland's position relative to other European countries and that performance since then has broadly been one of holding that relatively weak position.

Earlier reference has been made to Mjøset's (1992) argument regarding Ireland's weak national system of innovation being responsible for its poor performance in the immediate post-colonial period. Since the late 1950s, Ireland has in effect tried to import a foreign system of innovation through FDI. But FDI has not generated sufficient spill-over effects to create an organic self-sustaining Irish system of innovation. The indigenous sector remains weak, characterised by small companies, with those engaged in exporting, still very reliant on the UK market.

Policy is ambiguous with regard to an appropriate response. Culliton emphasises national clusters, in areas such as agriculture and food processing, where Ireland has natural advantages. But Culliton also moves somewhat in the direction of Reich in relation to embedded FDI providing a basis for competitive advantage. Ultimately it is perhaps unfair to expect clarity of government policy given the unresolved as yet conflicts in the theoretical arguments.

References

_____ (1982), A Review of Industrial Policy (A Report Prepared by the Telesis Consultancy group), Dublin: NESC.

_____ (1992), A Time for Change — Industrial Policy for the 1990's (The Culliton Report), Dublin: The Stationery Office.

Cantillon, S., Curtis, J. and FitzGerald, J. (1994), *Economic Perspectives for the Medium Term*, Dublin: ESRI.

Bannon, S. (1996), *EMU and Ireland's Sterling Trade*, Presentation to Statistical and Social Inquiry Society of Ireland, Dublin.

Daly, M. E. (1992), *Industrial Development and Irish National Identity, 1922-1939*, Dublin: Gill and Macmillan.

Deutsch, K.W. (1966), *Nationalism and Social Communication: An Enquiry into the Foundations of Nationality*, Cambridge, MA: Harvard University Press.

European Commission (1995), *European Economy-1995*, Broad Economic Policy Guidelines, No. 60.

FitzGerald, J. and Honohan, P. (1994), *Where did all the Growth go?*. *ESRI, Medium Term Review 1994-2000*, Dublin: ESRI.

Haughton, J. (1995), "The Historical Background" in *The Economy of Ireland*, (Ed. O'Hagan, J.W.), Dublin: Gill and Macmillan.

Hirschman, A.O. (1958), *The Strategy of Economic Development*, London: Yale University Press.

Hornell, E. and Vahlne, J.E. (1986), *Multinationals: The Swedish Case*, London: Croom Helm.

Kennedy, K. A. (1991), "Linkages and Overseas Industry" in *Overseas Industry in Ireland* (Eds. Foley, A. and McAleese, D.), Dublin: Gill and Macmillan.

Kennedy, K. A., Giblin, T. and McHugh, D. (1988), *The Economic Development of Ireland in the Twentieth Century*, London: Routledge.

Lall, S. (1978), 'Transnationals, Domestic Enterprises and Industrial Structure in Host LDC's; A Survey', *Oxford Economic Papers*, Vol. 30, pp. 217-248.

Lee, J. J. (1992), *Ireland 1912-85*, Cambridge: Cambridge University Press.

Murphy, A. (1994), *The Irish Economy, Celtic Tiger or Tortoise*, Dublin, Money Markets International.

Mjøset, L. (1992), *The Irish Economy in a Comparative Institutional Perspective*, Dublin: National Economic and Social Council.

O'Hagan, J. W. (1995), *The Economy of Ireland*, Dublin: Gill and Macmillan.

O'Hearn, D. (1993), 'Global Competition, Europe and Irish Peripherality', *The Economic and Social Review*, Vol. 24, No. 2, January, pp. 169-197.

O'Malley, E. and Scott, S. (1994), *Profit Outflows Revisited, Economic Perspectives for the Medium Term*, Dublin: ESRI.

O'Sullivan, M. (1995), "Manufacturing and Global Competition" in *The Economy of Ireland*, (Ed. O'Hagan, J.W.), Dublin: Gill and Macmillan

Plunkett, H. (1905), *Ireland in the New Century*, London: John Murray.

Sectoral Development Committee (1985), 'Key Factors Determining the Achievement of Linkages in Certain Industrial Sectors', SDC Report No. 10.

Sectoral Development Committee (1985), 'Technological Capacity of Indigenous Irish Industry', SDC report No. 8.

Steuer, M. D. (1973), *The Impact of Foreign Direct Investment on the United Kingdom*, London: HMSO.

Streeck, W. (1992), 'National Diversity, Regime Competition and Institutional Deadlock: Problems in forming a European Industrial Relations System', *Journal of Public Policy*, Vol. 12, No. 4, pp. 301-330.

Turok, I. (1993), 'Inward Investment and Local Linkages: How Deeply Embedded is "Silicon Glen"?', *Regional Studies*, Vol. 27, No. 5, pp. 401-417.

Wilkins, M. (1970), *The Emergence of Multinational Enterprise: American Business Abroad for the Colonial Era to 1914*, Cambridge, MA: Harvard University Press.

Young, S., Hood N. and Hood, C. (1996), "Transatlantic Perspectives on Inward Investment and Prospects for Policy Reconciliation" in *International Business and Europe in Transition*, (Eds. Burton, F.N., Yamin, M. and Young, S.), London: Macmillan.

8

A HIGH CAPITAL STRATEGY FOR THE PERIPHERY? INWARD INVESTMENT AND HUMAN RESOURCE DEVELOPMENT IN THE REPUBLIC OF IRELAND

Alastair McPherson

8.1 INTRODUCTION

This chapter considers the relationship between investment in the human capital of the periphery,[1] inward Foreign Direct Investment[2] and changing human resource and industrial relations practices. Specific reference is made to the Republic of Ireland, an area of the periphery that increasingly recognises the virtue of fully developing and utilising human capital as a source of competitive advantage.

The premise underlying this strategy is a recognition of the need to compete on the basis of quality and innovation as a source of economic advantage rather than relying upon a low-cost environment for relatively low-skill functions. This 'High Capital' route is driven by competition for a low-cost trajectory from the Newly Industrialised Countries and the emerging economies of Eastern Europe. In addition, technological and structural changes are commonly viewed as increasing the level, and altering the

---

[1] For a detailed definition of peripherality readers are referred to earlier chapters. In this chapter peripherality is defined as those countries or regions displaying significant economic disparities in comparison with the EU average and being located at the geographical extremities of the EU, namely Greece, the Mezzogiorno of Italy, Northern Ireland, Portugal, the Republic of Ireland, and Spain.

[2] Foreign Direct Investment represents investment in foreign assets whereby a company purchases assets that it manages directly.

nature, of skills required within the labour market (European Commission, 1994). Globalisation of labour markets in key occupations is another factor which peripheral locations must consider in the development and utilisation of appropriate skills.

In considering the factors underpinning a high capital strategy, the chapter examines the argument that national economies that do not adjust their industrial relations arrangements to a more co-operative model will be unable to compete. On the one hand, the model of union-management co-operation to be found in the German automobile industry is often viewed as an example of recommendable practice. This is a system which favours training and re-training leading to a highly skilled workforce engaged in high-technology production and in which the unions are intimately involved within the workplace and at a centralised level. On the other hand, union-management developments in the UK are often cited as the antithesis of the German model where competition is based on inferior terms and conditions of employment and more flexible industrial relations, and which indicates a short-term strategy aimed at cost cutting (Veersma, 1995).

Two possible outcomes of the development of such different industrial relations trajectories within Europe are an increased level of 'social dumping', where companies transfer their production activities and employment in order to exploit lower wages and inferior working conditions in peripheral countries, and 'regime competition', with industrial relations policies competing for investment on the basis of different employment and working conditions.

This chapter explores the extent to which inward investing firms are involved in shaping the development of the industrial relations system. In particular, what is the role of overseas investors as a factor in stimulating human resource development. The chapter reflects on whether strategies for human resource development are likely to fit with emerging trends in the organisation of production. The merits of the 'flexible specialisation' approach as an industrial model conducive to peripheral human resource development objectives are considered in the light of more critical appraisals of organisational and human resource trajectories. A factor that emerges from the discussion is the role of institutional structures in shaping the course of industrial relations models.

In examining the argument that the institutional parameters of a country or region have a key role in facilitating firms to pursue a 'high capital strategy', the chapter considers the case of the

Republic of Ireland. The competitive status of the Republic of Ireland, and the objective of human resource development strategies in boosting this position, are examined alongside the status of overseas-owned operations and the institutional context in which these have operated.

8.2 INWARD INVESTORS AND HUMAN RESOURCE DEVELOPMENT

Debate on the relationship between skill, training and work organisation has addressed the issue of whether technological trends in industry demand greater skills or not (Blauner, 1964; Bell, 1973; Braverman, 1974 cited in Osterman, 1995). Initially this debate focused on the de-skilling effects of modern industry. Increasingly the question has arisen of whether 'flexible work systems' and the development of the 'High Performance Work Organisation'[3] has created an inherent demand for skills (McDuffie, 1991; Kaufman, 1992; Ichniowski, Shaw et al., 1993; Applebaum and Batt, 1994 cited in Osterman, 1995) (See Table 8.1).

Osterman notes that case study approaches to examining this issue, as well as more extensive survey work, have not produced conclusive findings (Flynn, 1988; Howell and Wolff, 1991 cited in Osterman, 1995). These studies (and others that seek to combine elements of both strategies) have not successfully related skill factors to the broader character of firm strategy and structure. Thus the link between training and work organisation remains obscured. Nonetheless the contention exists that High Performance Work Organisations have an in-built emphasis on improving competitiveness through training and skill development. Osterman notes a trend towards 'upskilling' in US firms, especially for technical and professional jobs which is explicitly connected with new forms of work organisation but also to corporate structure, strategy and the industrial relations context (Osterman, 1995). The issue is, for what organisational practices and in what circumstances does this model hold true? In particular, how relevant is the 'High Performance Work Organisation' model for branch plant activity in the European periphery?

---

[3] Readers are referred to (Applebaum and Batt, 1994 cited in Osterman, 1995, p. 126) for a discussion of the definition and usage of the term.

TABLE 8.1: CHANGES IN INDUSTRIAL SKILLS PATTERNS

Traditional Patterns	*Emerging Patterns*
Single discipline skills	Multiple and multi-functional skills, wide range of skills and qualifications
Predominance of manual and operational skills (manual workers, admin. staff)	Loss of unskilled workers, more qualified workers, technicians, engineers, managers etc.
Long skill lifetime, limited needs for skill updating, new skills by recruiting	Rapid obsolescence of skills. More use of education and training to advance competence
Technology limited to a few key people, large focus on specialisation	More need for technologists, technology skills needed from many staff, more generalist and integrators
Communication and social skills of minor importance	New skill need high communications and co-operation, creativity and flexibility

Source: Adapted from IRDAC 1994 cited in Government of Ireland, 1995b, p. 13.

While Osterman cautiously asserts that work systems drive training, it could as easily be suggested that training and high performance work organisation are two related aspects of a quality driven production ethos that is likely be developed over a period of time. In a study conducted for FÁS (Foras Áiseanna Saothair/The Emploment and Training Authority) the skill implications are assessed for the introduction of World Class Manufacturing (WCM) in the Irish engineering industry (FÁS, 1993). This study emphasises training at all levels as a catalyst for WCM implementation. Further, adoption of WCM is viewed as dependent on the development of organisation, attitudes and processes together. For peripheral locations it is important to determine the mechanisms and contexts through which skills and training, along with work organisation, affect productivity and quality levels.

However, the mechanisms and contexts which influence attitudes to skills, training and work organisation are not factors which operate in isolation behind the doors of particular firms. A number of authors emphasise that skill and training standards are inescapably linked to cultural, institutional and political factors (Olson, 1982; Barnett, 1986; Porter, 1990 cited in National Economic and Social Council, 1993). Others have emphasised the principal role of training institutions in understanding the role of human resources as a crucial factor in the competitiveness of firms and of the national economic systems (Kern and Schumann, 1984; Dore, 1987; Marsden, 1987; Finegold and Soskice, 1988; Streeck, 1989 cited in Regini, 1995). In turn, the model of union-management co-operation and how this relationship interacts with training institutions within and outside the workplace is of crucial importance. Thus the scope for the High Performance Work Organisation to generate a positive feedback in skills, training, quality and competitiveness must be set against the peripheral economies' ability to encourage conducive corporate strategies by transnational corporations (TNCs) and to develop conducive industrial relations regimes within the wider economy.

8.3 THE HIGH CAPITAL ROAD TO COMPETITIVE ADVANTAGE

In developing the role of the labour process in economic development, Le Heron and Van Der Knapp (1995) depict changes in international growth regimes and the integration of these into a 'revised labour perspective'. They characterise two extreme strategies for dealing locally with global pressures: a low capital approach and a high capital approach (See Table 8.2). The approach is useful in considering the development trajectory of the periphery. However, Le Heron and Van Der Knapp's indication that this schema represents a historical and developmental ladder is questionable. Regini, for example, emphasises that labour process characteristics are deeply embedded within regional and national production systems and industrial relations contexts and that human resource patterns reflect the capital-labour traditions of particular places rather than the differential working out of aspatial trends (Regini, 1995).

A more refined European model is presented by Regini (1995) where firms are distinguished by their product market strategy which in turn corresponds with patterns of human resource utilisation. It is asserted that specific regions can be distinguished by predominant patterns of product market strategy. Thus different locations are configured with different production regimes, specific structuring of the labour market and a given set of training institutions. Two broad types of training and education system are identified. The first is 'oriented to redundancy' with skills supplied qualitatively and quantitatively in excess of demand, as in Germany, France and Italy. A second system is 'oriented to appropriateness' with supply matched to demand. The system is characterised by a reactive nature and a focus on particular groups within the workforce. This system of 'lean training' is best typified by the UK and the US but is also characteristic of the Irish system.

TABLE 8.2: REVISED LABOUR PERSPECTIVE

Environment to Achieve Employment and Social Outcomes		
	Strategy 1 Low Capital	Strategy 2 High Capital
Goals	Internationally competitive industries	Interventions of industries in health, housing, environment, welfare, etc.
Worker qualities	Superficial training	Education is a high priority
Emphasis	Contractible residuals of welfare state	Social primacy of living standards industries

Source: LeHeron and Van Der Knapp, 1995, p. 16.

It has been argued by some authors that 'flexible specialisation' offers the opportunity for branch plant activity to become increasingly integrated with the regional economy in accord with a high capital strategy. One of the main means through which economic development is to be achieved, within this perspective, is via the development of clusters of firms within regions (Piore and Sabel, 1984; Sabel and Zeitlin 1985; Hirst and Zeitlin, 1991; Sabel, 1994). This approach envisages an industrial model in which competitive advantage is gained by increased reliance on 'skills, flexibility and networking between task-specialist units in order to produce changing volumes and combinations of goods without incurring productivity losses (resulting from not utilising sections of the workforce or the productive apparatus at any given moment)' (Amin and Thrift, 1994 pp. 20-21). It is argued that this paradigm encourages the geographical clustering of productive activity and is associated with the emergence of locally integrated regional economies (Storper and Scott, 1989; Sabel, 1994; Scott, 1995).

The organisational principles sustaining flexible specialisation are found in 'technopoles', such as Silicon Valley; craft-based industrial districts as in the 'Third Italy'; and in innovative, hi-tech, high skill German, Italian and Scandinavian firms. These are also

viewed to embody the new industrial relations of flexible specialisation emphasising labour-management co-operation, decentralised management, worker participation, polyvalence and high
skills (Grahl and Teague, 1991). These perspectives assert a prescriptive opportunity for defining strategies for the creation of
'industrial spaces' based on private-public sector investment in
human resources and industrial and service infrastructure. Along
with technological opportunities for new industrial geographies,
and local policy efforts aimed at boosting human resource capaci-
ties, 'is a search for new 'models' of human resources relations
which will give special advantage to local areas and their activities' (Le Heron and Van Der Knapp, 1995 p. 6). Such a scenario
would make the aim of human resource development in a peripheral setting a plausible and fitting contribution to evolving organisational trajectories.

   However, debates of the 1980s on the shape of economic restructuring and particularly those surrounding the concept of industrial districts are portrayed as flagging amidst theoretical uncertainty and empirical constraints (Le Heron and Van Der
Knapp, 1995). International corporate strategies point to a
globalisation of production (Amin and Malmberg, 1992), and while
this does not necessarily diminish the potential role of regional
economies (as is suggested by Castells, 1989; Sassen, 1991), there
is little strong evidence to suggest that 'inward investment in a
diversity of regional contexts has become sufficiently 'locally embedded' to constitute local growth poles' (Turock, 1993; Dicken,
Forsgren et al., 1994 cited in Amin, 1994, p. 25).

   Storper's industrial geography perspective and his characteri-
sation of 'industrial districts' has been criticised as a partial explanation of integrative tendencies in the global economy
(Storper, 1992 cited in Le Heron and Van Der Knapp, 1995). One
area that receives too little attention is the role and quality of labour in the development of industrial districts. More generally, in
considering the links between inward investment and the organisation of work, primacy is commonly given to 'investment linkages
and patterns, ahead of, for instance, transformations in labour,
employment and work that might ensue in localities as a result of
restructured investment' (Le Heron and Van Der Knapp, 1995, p.
18).

   An important issue is whether the 'flexibly specialised-high
capital-soft HRM' strategy, which embodies themes such as teamwork, flexibility and continuous improvement, implies that the

'boundaries of interaction connected with labour' are extended beyond the firm, thus tying the transformation of the labour process into the 'spatiality' and 'place-boundedness' of capitalist development. While it may be relatively easy to assess the adoption of human resource ideas, the influence of these on 'industrial spatiality' is less clear. Yet 'the whole import of the human resources movement is to create new arrangements and this may be a historical basis for the creation of quite new geographies of interaction and investment' (Le Heron and Van Der Knapp, 1995 p. 23). However, there is little evidence to suggest 'whether the human resource initiative is a necessary condition or merely a contingent aspect of restructuring' (Le Heron and Van Der Knapp, 1995, p. 23).

8.4 LIMITS TO THE HIGH CAPITAL ROAD

A less promising prospect is envisaged by French regulationist writers (Aglietta, 1979; Coriat, 1979; Aglietta, 1982; André and Delorme, 1982; Lipietz, 1985; Boyer, 1986; Mistral, 1986; Lipietz, 1987; Boyer, 1988b; Boyer, 1988a; Boyer, 1991; Coriat and Petit, 1991; Lipietz, 1992; Lipietz, 1993). This more critical appraisal recognises variants on 'Fordist' systems of industrial relations rather than new models, with for instance, Lipietz identifying continued scope for 'Taylorist' practices. In a similar vein, taken from a German perspective, Streeck, along with Esser and Hirsch, question the prospects for the emergence of the 'soft HRM' of the flexible specialisation model (Streeck, 1992; Esser and Hirsch, 1994). These authors view a 'defensive' industrial strategy based on low and flexible wages and limited labour involvement as a strong contender for future patterns of organisational flexibility.

The benefits of such a model of flexibility, it is argued, lie in: greater national competitiveness; firm level efficiency and adaptability; and advantages to individuals in adopting flexible working methods (CBI, 1994). On the other hand, the main disadvantages involve: less commitment to training of flexible workers on the part of employers; changes in technology may result in a reduction of skill levels for some flexible workers, e.g. administrative staff; there is a possibility that some flexible workers will be unable to engage in self-development and be caught in a cycle of deprivation; cost benefits of flexible workers could shrink through moves to equalise rights of different status employment groups; and the employment infrastructure may need to adapt to new demands. The pursuit of a 'low capital' strategy may be beneficial to employers in providing for much more flexible employment. However, it could threaten to undermine the European periphery's skills base if employers are less likely to take responsibility for employee who are not at the 'core' of the business or are not working full-time. It has been argued that the Republic of Ireland exhibits a defensive 'low skills equilibrium' similar in many respects to that identified in the United Kingdom (Mjøset, 1992). This reflects a negative feedback scenario where poorly trained managers and workers are involved in the production of low quality goods and services. This is a status perpetuated via 'a self reinforcing network of societal and state institutions' (Finegold and Soskice, 1988).

Nonetheless, authors such as Lipietz and Streeck illustrate the variability of regional and national solutions in determining the shape of work organisation and industrial relations (Streeck, 1992; Lipietz, 1993). Indeed, while German regulationists view the less benevolent and defensive trajectories of new systems of work organisation as somewhat built-in to post-Fordist models, the French regulationists view the pursuit of 'offensive' or 'defensive' economic and industrial relations trajectories as a contested process strongly influenced by prevailing sectoral or national contexts. This point has been reinforced in an Irish context, where the receptivity of firms or regions to new Human Resource Management (HRM) and industrial relations practices can be fragmentary and subject to the powerful inertia of local institutional traditions (Roche and Geary, 1994; Roche and Turner, 1995).

8.5 THE INSTITUTIONAL BASIS FOR COMPETITIVE ADVANTAGE

Consequently, there exists a 'continued salience of places as settings for social and economic existence, and for forging identities, struggles, and strategies of both a local and global nature' (Amin and Thrift, 1994. p. 9). This statement reflects a shift of attention from economic reasons for self-reproducing growth in local areas to the social and cultural basis. Attention has moved from factors such as product specialisation and vertical disintegration of the division of labour to levels of inter-firm collaboration; institutional support for local business; and structures encouraging innovation, skill formation and the circulation of ideas.

Of particular significance is the conceptualisation of local institutions and the ways in which these have scope to shape 'self-
governed development paths in an era of global interdependencies' (Amin and Thrift, 1994, p. 1). Social and cultural factors,
summarised in terms of 'institutional thickness', are central to the
pursuit of development paths (See Table 8.3). Institutional thickness is constituted by a strong institutional presence, representing many different organisations and leading to a range of desired
outcomes: institutional persistence; construction of an archive of
commonly-held knowledge; institutional flexibility; high innovative capacity; ability to extend trust and reciprocity; and consolidation of a sense of inclusiveness (Amin and Thrift, 1994). Hence,
'in those industrial contexts which are heavily reliant on the production of knowledge, innovation, and information for competitiveness, institutional thickness can have a decisive influence on
economic development, notably in local situations in which such
assets are not, as it were, 'locked into' individual firms' (Amin and
Thrift, 1994, p. 16). However, it is cautiously noted that 'the vast
majority of cities and regions will continue to occupy specific
functional positions within a global division of labour — a status
which is not likely to promise self-reproducing growth at the local
level' (Amin and Thrift, 1994, p. 2).[4]

The institutional thickness described below represents an environment which establishes legitimacy for the structures for human resource development and develops notions of trust between
employers and employed. The importance of these factors for the
development of inward investment and the pursuit of a high-skills
equilibrium is central when it comes to co-operative mechanisms
within the workplace. In turn, the development of institutional
forms which promote a stable dialogue between employers and
employed is strongly influenced by the regulatory trajectory of the
European periphery. An instance of this is the adoption of works

---

[4] Institutional thickness may not always be necessary or sufficient, indeed
'thickness' may be a hindrance to development if it represents the institutions of a prior industrial structure. Furthermore, the issue of local institutional thickness is made redundant if 'it were possible to retain a context of
strengthened national and supranational regulatory regime capable of
safeguarding the interests of "weaker" local economies' (Amin and Thrift,
1994, p. 19).

councils legislation by EU member states and, more generally, the promotion of a social dimension to European integration.

TABLE 8.3: THE BASIC ELEMENTS OF INSTITUTIONAL THICKNESS

A strong institutional presence	Comprised of different types, e.g., firms; financial institutions; local chambers of commerce; training agencies; trade association; local authorities; development agencies; innovation centres; clerical bodies; unions; government agencies providing premises, land, and infrastructure; business service organisations; marketing boards
High levels of interaction amongst institutions in the local area	High levels of interaction, co-operation and information exchange often embedded in shared rules, conventions and knowledge which constitute the 'social atmosphere' of a particular region
Development of high levels of domination and/or patterns of coalition	Resulting in collective representation of what are normally sectional and individual interests and serving to socialise costs or to control rogue behaviour
Mutual awareness of a common enterprise	Almost certainly meaning a commonly-held industrial agenda which the collection of institutions both depends upon and develops

Source: Adapted from Amin and Thrift, 1994, pp. 14-15.

In considering the likely impacts of the greater labour market regulation which would be entailed in a high capital strategy, Marsden concludes that while regulation in the European labour market does have detrimental employment effects on lower paid segments of the labour market, it can benefit other key labour market segments where 'co-operative exchange' is important for developing employee-employer interaction (Marsden, 1994). In particular, 'co-operative exchange between skilled and professional workers and their employers is critical to achieving high productivity levels and good quality output' (Marsden, 1994, p. 3). Job demarcation, rigid working patterns and ineffective information-sharing act against continuous adaptation within firms. However, the ability to achieve flexible working and information-sharing through co-operative exchange depends on a level of trust between the groups involved. In turn, the regulatory and institutional environment influences the mechanisms through which trust is developed and sustained. An appropriate institutional framework is necessary to sustain trust and to police grievances, with employer organisations and unions backing-up enterprise level co-operation.

One view is that national economies that do not adjust their industrial relations arrangements to a more co-operative model will be unable to compete and that economic prospects depend on the system of worker participation. The model of recommendable union-management co-operation is seen as the 'co-determination complex' of the German automobile industry. It is characterised as possessing a cohesive union movement with centralised strength combined with shop-floor decentralisation. This is accompanied by strict legislation on worker participation and union involvement in training programmes, within the workplace and outside (Slomp, 1995). In addition, the German management strategy favours training and re-training leading to a highly skilled workforce engaged in high-technology production. The unions are intimately involved in this strategy which continuously improves employment conditions and job protection.

Instead, countries such as the UK and the US can be viewed in terms of cost reduction strategies. The response of the these countries to technological change and international competition 'consist of a monopoly of management-imposed forms of worker participation, and (further) decline in union influence, wage restraint, and, ultimately, either serious wage cuts or, as the only other alternative, mass redundancies due to disinvestment and an exodus to low-cost countries' (Slomp, 1995, p. 316).

Where agreements between unions and employers at a national or sector level operate, a 'sheltered niche' is created for worker participation, which at the same time is absolved from enterprise-level bargaining conflicts and able to adopt a co-operative role. Where enterprise-level regulation of the terms and conditions of employment is the norm, trade union representatives and works councils are likely to diminish the scope for co-operation by virtue a stronger bargaining responsibility.

However, Regini argues that training regimes differing from the German model are best suited to the predominant product and market strategies in other locations (Regini, 1995). In turn, while the skill-surplus-oriented system in Germany is suited to the quality-driven patterns of production, this is not necessarily an efficient approach to human resource development under other product-market strategies favouring more 'traditional' Fordist approaches. Following this line, the well-developed and extensive skills produced by the institutional framework in Germany may not be suitable to the form of production in the periphery. One problem with this perspective is that Regini assumes that all product-market strategies are of equal value and that competitive advantage comes from tuning the education and training system to the dominant product-market strategy. However, not all product-market strategies are equal in terms of the ability to provide the desired social outcomes or to sustain competitiveness in the long term against low-cost competitors outside Europe.

Therefore it remains important to consider the institutional basis for the development of quality driven production strategies. As indicated, an important dimension of any such institutional foundation is its ability to foster co-operative exchange. When it comes to considering mechanisms of co-operative exchange, one manifestation, at a firm level, is the development of work-teams. In the Republic of Ireland, efforts at work reorganisation have been modest and confined to a small number of overseas-owned enterprises (Geary, 1995). There is a greater interest in these initiatives on the European Continent. For example, a third of firms surveyed in France pointed to the use of 'multi-disciplinary work groups' or 'project groups', and 11 per cent to the use of 'self-regulating work groups' (Coutrot and Parraire, 1994 cited in Geary, 1995). However, this interest is strongly shaped by employers, as opposed to being a union- or employee-led initiative, and is associated with the employers agenda for productivity and corporate culture.

For the Foreign Direct Investment-Labour Process relationship in the periphery, a deregulatory, low-skill path will not foster a climate of co-operative exchange, necessary to provide the productive, high-quality, high-wage jobs sought from this sector. While co-operative exchange may be observable in a number of cases, enterprise-level initiatives are unlikely to be sustainable if adverse economic conditions and increased levels of competition are combined with a range of opportunities for deregulatory practices. A key to maintaining the level of commitment to co-operative exchange is a regulatory framework which supports employer-employee co-operation and a forum for co-operative exchange within the firm, preferably backed-up by employer associations and union agreements.

The sort of dialogue for continuous improvement that becomes possible under these conditions makes deregulation in other areas less important. Still, a deregulatory environment may weaken the

resolve of employers to stick to a 'high-wage, high-skill' trajectory
and to establish effective forums for dialogue in the first place.
The case for de-regulation in some areas remains strong and may
be the best-fit for some industries and sectors in the periphery. In
addition, relatively low-wage, low-skill sectors fulfil a need by creating footholds into employment for new entrants into the labour
market and opportunities for part-time workers.

Given that co-operative exchange is a desirable objective and
that the development of work-teams is an important example of
this tendency, the role of consultation between management and
unions on the regulation of team-working and the degree of willingness of both parties to co-operate remains an area of contention, as is the manner in which employee representatives become
involved. A need for 'institutional separation' is evident, where a
works-council-type forum exists independently from traditional
collective bargaining arrangements. The idea of establishing a
new forum to regulate the introduction of new work structures
(and this refers not necessarily to just team-working) creates potential problems for both employers and unions. On the one hand
there is a loss of autonomy for managers. Thus, 'where collective
bargaining is separated out from joint-decision-making, management faces a fundamental choice of whether union involvement
should be confined to joint consultation or should be extended to a
right of joint regulation' (Geary, 1995). On the other hand is the
possibility of work councils stealing the traditional role of the
unions.

8.6 HUMAN RESOURCE DEVELOPMENT IN A
PERIPHERAL ECONOMY

The chapter has argued that the institutional basis of co-
operative exchange forms a key part in the establishment of a
high capital strategy for competitiveness. This section considers
the situation in the Republic of Ireland with regard to human resource development, setting this position in its industrial and institutional context. As the demand for skills increases across
Europe, there is evidence that parts of the periphery are struggling to meet this demand. The EC-commissioned Industrial Research and Development Advisory Committee (IRDAC) report
outlines a number of likely skill-needs across the European
Union: an increased demand for highly educated and skilled
workers; a reduced demand for unskilled workers; a change in the

nature of jobs due to technological change and changed organisational structure; enhanced employment opportunities for multi-skilled workers; a move from manufacturing employment to the services sector (Industrial Research and Development Advisory Committee cited in Government of Ireland, 1995b). In particular, for the Republic of Ireland, a number of studies testify to the weakness of training in Irish firms.

The European Social Fund Programme Evaluation Unit's Survey of Employers indicates a low commitment to training in Ireland (cited in Government of Ireland, 1995b, p. 85). Despite the fact that in, 1993 some 23,000 persons in employment benefited from FÁS-financed training programmes (Walsh, 1995), and that 86 per cent of firms engage in training, some 73 per cent had no training budget, 62 per cent had no employee appraisal system and 57 per cent only monitor employee performance on an informal, ad hoc basis (cited in Government of Ireland, 1995b).

Sectoral studies carried out by FÁS bear witness to a restricted training commitment on the part of employers and point to the human resource development needs of the Irish economy, as do the conclusions the National Economic and Social Council (NESC) investigations into the status of human resources in Ireland and the findings of the Industrial Policy Review Group (IPRG) (Industrial Policy Review Group, 1992; FÁS, 1993; National Economic and Social Council, 1993) (See Table 8.4). In particular the IPRG report pointed to a significant gap in skills levels between the Republic of Ireland and competitor countries (Industrial Policy Review Group, 1992). The response has been an increase in the level of resources devoted to skills and training. For instance, the European Union Community Support Framework for Ireland (1994-99) sets aside 1,672 million ECU for human resources, just over one-third of Irish Community Support Framework funds (Economist Intelligence Unit, 1994).

Underlying the gap that has been exposed between Irish skill levels and those of competitors, is the recognition of the need for greater innovation within the economy. As summarised by the Science, Technology and Innovation Advisory Council (STIAC) report, Irish industrial policy has in the past entailed a continuous relative neglect of the potential of science, technology and innovation for economic and industrial development (Government of Ireland, 1995a). A vicious circle of decline has persisted since the last century (Mjøset, 1992). This has led to both high unemployment and emigration combined with a dual industrial sector divided between overseas-owned and indigenous firms (Government of Ireland, 1995a, p. 51) (See Table 8.5).

TABLE 8.4: HUMAN RESOURCE DEVELOPMENT NEEDS FOR MAIN
LEVELS OF DEFICIENCY

Level	Development Needs
Management	Need for higher proportion of managers with formal management skills, especially in small and medium-sized enterprises.
Supervisors	Need for system for formal, recognised training in the supervisory and technical aspects of their jobs.
Technicians	Need to facilitate craftspersons to progress to technician-level; need to combine practical craft experience with theoretical knowledge of technician.
Skilled workers	Need for continual up-dating of skills and addition of new skills and qualifications. Training of semi-skilled operatives to higher skill and multi-skill levels so as to perform wider range of tasks and take greater responsibility in workplace.

Source: Adapted from Government of Ireland, 1995b, pp. 86-87.

TABLE 8.5: MANUFACTURING, NATIONALITY OF OWNERSHIP

	Establishments (%)	Employment (%)	Net Output IR£ '000's (%)
Irish	3,805 (82.68)	105,884 (54.53)	2,810,916 (31.54)
EC	378 (8.21)	31,257 (16.10)	1,364,057 (15.31)
Non-EC	419 (9.11)	57,036 (29.37)	4,736,600 (53.15)
Total Foreign	797 (17.32)	88,293 (45.47)	6,100,657 (68.46)
All Estabs.	4,602 (100.0)	194,177 (100.0)	8,911,574 (100.0)

Source: Census of Industrial Production 1990, CSO, 1993 cited in (Government of Ireland, 1995a, p. 65).

Despite the increased recognition of the economic role of smaller, indigenous industry, a large commitment still exists towards inward investment activities (See Figure 8.1). Since the 1960s Irish industrial development has been predominantly based on Foreign Direct Investment. However, the production units established add little in terms of sub-supply linkages to the Irish economy and the embededness of overseas firms remains low in terms of local-supplier linkages which suggests limited value added (Kennedy,

1991). The most common manufacturing process is assembly and only a small proportion of firms engage in research and development, product development or marketing (FÁS, 1993).

FIGURE 8.1: OPERATIONAL PROGRAMME FOR INDUSTRIAL DEVELOPMENT, 1994-99, TOTAL PROGRAMME EXPENDITURE (IR£M)

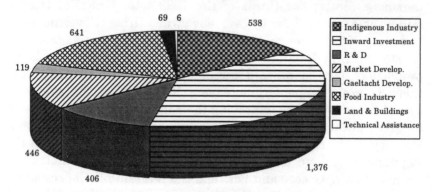

Source: Adapted from Government of Ireland, 1994, p. 13.

Concern with human resource development as a competitive force for the periphery has to be viewed alongside a recognition of the importance of inward investment as a source of productive employment; as a means of transferring industrial technology, marketing and management skills to Irish industry; as a source of new capital investment; and as a means of providing significant market opportunities for indigenous industry (Government of Ireland, 1994). It is noted that in 1991 expenditure by overseas-owned firms in Ireland on wages, raw materials and services was estimated at IR£4.3 thousand million, a 37 per cent increase on 1985 levels (*ibid.*). Overseas-owned firms support around 110,000 people in other parts of the economy as well as the 95,000 directly employed (*ibid.*).[5]

---

[5] The two main means for achieving continued inward investment in the Republic of Ireland are fixed-asset support and human resources development. The former provides grants of up to 60 per cent of the cost of a project's eligible fixed assets. Funds for 1994-99 are to be split equally between new and existing projects. The latter measure provides recruitment incentive grants up to IR£10,000 for each additional employee. Training grants are also available for both general and company-specific training. Grants of up to 100 per cent of eligible training courses are available.

Given a continuing commitment to overseas investors, can the goals of human resource development and a high capital strategy for competitiveness, really go hand-in-hand with the branch-plant economy? While there may be an increase in the order of activity of some overseas-owned firms, in comparison with similar small countries, the Republic of Ireland's overall Business Expenditure on Research & Development (BERD) is low (see Table 8.6). Furthermore, almost two-thirds of the 1993 total BERD of IR£235 million is accounted for by overseas-owned firms (Government of Ireland, 1995a). Though, only 24 per cent of TNCs engage in any R&D within the Republic of Ireland. On top of this an even lower proportion have significant autonomy from their parent. Thus, there is great scope for increasing R&D within the overseas-owned firms as well as improving their innovation performance. A further indication of the need for a human resource development strategy is given by the low level of skilled R&D personnel in the Republic of Ireland labour force (see Table 8.7). Nonetheless, in Ireland, Spain, Greece and Portugal the total number of researchers, scientists and engineers has more than doubled over the last ten years (European Commission, 1994, p. 119).

TABLE 8.6: BUSINESS EXPENDITURE ON R&D (PER CENT OF GDP)

	1987	*1991*
Sweden	1.99	1.95
Finland	1.03	1.18
Norway	1.13	1.00
Denmark	0.79	0.99
Ireland	0.48	0.65
New Zealand	0.28	0.28
Portugal	0.12	0.16
Greece	0.10	0.12

Source: Government of Ireland, 1995a, p. 38.

TABLE 8.7: R&D MANPOWER INTENSITY OF THE BUSINESS
ENTERPRISE SECTOR IN SELECTED OECD COUNTRIES, 1991

Country	Total R&D Personnel*/ Labour Force (per thousand)
Sweden	11.9
Finland	11.6
Netherlands	9.5
Belgium	9.3
UK	9.2
Denmark	8.8
Ireland	6.1
Italy	5.8
Spain	4.7
Greece	2.7
Portugal	2.5

* in full-time equivalents
Source: OECD, 1994 cited in Government of Ireland, 1995a, p. 74.

As would be expected, as R&D levels are relatively low, so are measured levels of innovation[6] (FitzGerald and Breathnach, 1994). Electrical/electronics and chemical/pharmaceutical sectors have the highest share of innovating firms and these innovative firms are disproportionately represented by overseas-owned firms. The biggest area of innovation expenditure is in R&D itself (See Table 8.8). This is followed by product design; work on trial production, training and tooling-up; market analysis; and the purchase of patents and licences. From available evidence, the role of process innovation within each of these sub-areas is not clear. All the same, innovations possibly reflect not just new products but new labour processes and hence changes in human resource patterns. An important question is the extent to which new labour processes have permitted overseas-owned firms to adopt a higher level of innovation within a peripheral location.

---

[6] Innovation includes both product and process innovation: 'A process innovation is the adoption of new or significantly improved production methods. These changes may involve new equipment of production origination or both. Process innovations may be introduced in order to make new products, or to increase efficiency with which existing products are produced' (FitzGerald and Breathnach, 1994, p. 34).

TABLE 8.8: ALLOCATION OF EXPENDITURE ON INNOVATION

	All Firms
Research and development	36%
Product design	28%
Trail production, training and tooling-up	22%
Market analysis	10%
Purchase of patents and licences	4%

Source: FitzGerald and Breathnach, 1994, p. 15.

Other studies highlight the changing skill requirements of Irish industry. For the Irish engineering industry 'intermediate production skills', such as skilled operatives, craft-workers, and technologists as well as management, are required to integrate overseas investors, to attract skill-based TNCs and to develop indigenous firms (FÁS, 1993). Indeed, the Republic of Ireland would appear to exhibit a similar difficulty to the UK in terms of production skill weaknesses and restricted management capabilities. Roche and Tansey (1992), in a study of Irish firms, note a complacency about the needs for technology training, with the accountancy aspects of the firm shown greatest concern. Starkly put, a 'lack of training in the past has resulted in a pool of Irish managers and supervisors who do not appreciate the importance of training or know how to implement training for themselves and their subordinates' (FÁS, 1993).

Evidence suggests attention has to be directed at a 'failure to provide technical and vocational training and education of a standard comparable with that achieved in other industrial economies' (National Economic and Social Council, 1993, p. 51). Only some 21 per cent of employees receive off-the-job training, with 35 per cent of managers and 11 per cent of craftspeople receiving off-the-job training (Roche and Tansey, 1992). Skills issues are at the heart of a number of weaknesses identified in the Irish engineering sector.[7] Further, differences exist in the quality of training

---

[7] Key weaknesses in the Irish engineering sector have been identified as: lack of supply chain infrastructure; lack of commitment to training; poor knowledge of market structures; over-reliance on a small number of large customers; limited scope for breakthrough technological innovation due to lack of tradition in innovation and low R&D spend; inadequately skilled workforce in certain key areas; lack of language skills; shortage of people

under different ownership, with Irish firms more concerned with manual and health and safety training and overseas-owned firms devoting more effort to management, supervisory and strategy issues, along with customer service (see Table 8.9). Thus, while the status of a high-skill strategy within overseas-owned firms in Ireland is limited, this sector retains the greatest levels of innovation and the most sophisticated approaches to human resources and business development.

TABLE 8.9: GRANT-SUPPORTED TRAINING AND DEVELOPMENT BY COMPANIES IN IRELAND

Type of Training / Development Activity	Per cent Training and Development Grants Supported by Ownership (n=115)		
	Ireland	US / Japan	Europe
Business strategy	3%	16%	8%
People management and supervision	6	11	19
Customer service quality	10	15	21
Health and safety	22	6	11
Management development	10	20	14
Manual skills training	48	32	27

Source: Garavan, Costine et al., 1995, p. 87.

Given the goal of improved peripheral competitiveness through quality, enterprise and innovation, and the weaknesses identified in Irish industry, the issue of an adequate labour supply is viewed as increasingly important by Irish policy makers. The recognition amongst Irish policy makers for a systematic approach to human resource development has been a sporadically recurring theme since the establishment of the state. The Government-appointed Commission on Technical Education established in 1926 was highly critical of the existing system and highlighted its inability to meet the development needs of Ireland (Garavan, Costine et al., 1995). It was not until the 1960s, however, that the need for a more thoroughgoing reassessment of the training system was recognised. Until this time a largely voluntaristic approach to skill development had been adopted. The increasingly pressing

---

with a mix of technical and marketing skills; limited home market; and slow to adopt new cultures or strategies (adapted from FÁS, 1993).

economic circumstances highlighted the weakness of a training
system that was largely confined to the apprenticeship system,
which itself was relatively narrow in conception. The International Labour Organisation (ILO) report on vocational education
in 1962 summarised many of the inadequacies of the system at
that time (See Table 8.10).

TABLE 8.10: CONCLUSIONS OF THE ILO REPORT ON VOCATIONAL
EDUCATION (1962)

The voluntarist system facilitated the perpetuation and enhancement of the familiar problems and allowed them to continue untackled.
There was no effective national body to keep apprenticeship and other training activities under review.
There was an insufficient number of skilled workers to meet the growing demands of the developing Irish economy.
A small number of employers trained well, for example, Guinness and Bewleys, and their skilled workers were often poached by those who invested little in training.
The state itself provided a poor example in this regard with inappreciable investment in training in the public sector.
Training methods were also poor, with few formal qualifications, and the training situation was in considerable need of improvement.

Source: Adapted from Garavan, Costine et al., 1995, p. 66.

A Government White Paper of 1965 followed the ILO report and
adopted many of its recommendations. In turn the Industrial
Training Act of 1967 set about establishing a national Industrial
Training Authority/An Comhairle Oiliúna (AnCO). However,
throughout the 1970s and 1980s the body was the focus of considerable criticism from industry and other training providers. The
main concerns were inefficiency, lack of co-ordination and lack of a
clear remit. Subsequently, the Government's White Paper on
Manpower Policy provided the stimulus for significant reform and
streamlining of the training system. A major contribution to this
was the formation of FÁS (Foras Áiseanna Saothair/The Employment and Training Authority) out of the National Manpower
Service, AnCO and the Youth Employment Agency. However, FÁS
inherited many of the criticisms of its predecessors (Roche and
Tansey, 1992).

The IPRG report maintained that provision for training at work remained inadequate (Industrial Policy Review Group, 1992). A clear distinction between training activities for the unemployed and industry-relevant training was called for along with more attention on the latter. These criticisms are reinforced by the Irish Business and Employers' Confederation (IBEC) who make a number of criticisms of the training system, and which over thirty years on, echo many of the conclusions of the 1962 ILO report (IBEC, 1994).

In order to respond to trends in industry and the weakness of the national training system, the role of the education and training system is vital. In the Republic of Ireland a number of policy statements have recognised this position, as outlined in detail by the NESC report on education and training policies for economic and social development (National Economic and Social Council, 1993).[8] Nonetheless, measures in relation to adaptation to industrial change and improvements in the quality of training provision, are explicitly viewed as taking second position to the efforts of employers themselves, 'the need to increase training of those in employment is recognised and the primary responsibility in this respect rests with employers' (Government of Ireland, 1995b, p. 85). Thus an important dimension in human resource develop-

---

[8] Human resource measures undertaken through the current operational programme for human resource development focus on three areas: the provision of management development grants, particularly for small and medium firms, concentrating on strengthening existing skills and building up the management team; the provision of training grants for both general and company-specific training of existing workers, where appropriate aimed at facilitating their adaptation to industrial changes and changes in the production system; and the provision of training grants towards the training of operatives in new start-up companies to facilitate the development of essential industrial skills (Government of Ireland 1994, p. 8). Where the objectives of the operational programme are met, grants may be made for the recruitment of new or additional staff. In addition, specific assistance will be available to assist companies in the implementation of World Class Manufacturing (WCM). WCM is the term applied to a set of techniques and attitudes aimed at increasing productivity by reducing manufacturing defects and delays and includes: the general philosophy and attitude of WCM; Just-in-Time; Total Quality Management; Team-working, flexibility and multi-skilling; Flexible Manufacturing System; Training of operatives to be more involved in decision taking at the shopfloor; Cross-training of staff for multi-job assignment; Work simplification; Customer service; Cost reduction; and Design, particularly design for manufacturing and assembly (FÁS 1993, pp. 2-6, 12-15).

ment as a competitive force for the periphery are the strategies of Irish employers with respect to education and training.

However, it is acknowledged that 'the relative passivity of Irish employers in this regard has led to inadequate training provision, an imbalance in State support, a supply-driven approach to training, and a failure to influence and lead national training policies for the employed' (Irish Business and Employers Confederation, 1995, p. 3). Nevertheless, the Irish Business and Employers' Confederation, with regard to social policy, also makes clear their opposition to 'over-regulation' of the labour market.

Employers assert that training for industry should be business-driven, which contrasts with the present state of affairs in the Republic of Ireland where national policy on the training of the employed is driven mainly by the state agencies. Notwithstanding a restructuring of state support for industry aimed at more targeted and co-ordinated support for industry, employers still only have a consultative role in determining training needs and priorities. Despite representation on the board of FÁS and on Industry Training Committees (ITCs) the main player in training action is FÁS itself, albeit with stronger industry/social partner involvement. While, employers are represented on an equal social partnership basis with trade union representatives, 'the ITCs . . . role is clearly consultative. . . . They do not drive initiatives, are not generally pro-active and were never expected to lead the way to a reform of the design and delivery of training initiatives' (IBEC, 1994, p. 8).

Irish employers argue that employer organisations are better placed to interact with individual companies in setting up schemes, monitoring effectiveness and co-ordinating education and training provision. In many other European states employer organisations and employer-led training bodies are formally and actively involved in the planning and organisation of training. This involvement is often at national, sectoral and local/company level. However, where employer organisations do have a more active role, this is accompanied by dedicated units on training policy development and co-ordination, something that is absent in the Republic of Ireland.

While Irish employers have not encouraged a Foreign Direct Investment-Labour Process based on a well-developed mechanism of co-operative exchange, at the same time, training and development have been low-priority issues for Irish trade unions. The unions having traditionally adopted a passive or neutral stance to the provision of training for members despite unions having long had a stake in the Irish official policy-making bodies in the area of training since the Apprenticeship Act of 1931. Training activities are viewed as a managerial concern and outside the remit of union activity. Rather, unions have concerned themselves mainly with pay and work conditions. In adopting such a stance the Irish trade unions were sustaining an old-style model of industrial relations and, 'in this understanding of what good industrial relations entailed, trade unions, collective bargaining and adversarialism were seen to be intrinsic to the process' (Roche 1994, p. 5). This approach was dominant into the 1980s, with adversarial collective bargaining accepted as the underpinnings of a healthy industrial relations structure.

However, the stability of this system has been undermined by several factors. Irish management has become increasingly professionalised, bringing new ideas into the business of employee relations and accompanied by a growth in management and industrial relations education. Within the Republic of Ireland the relationship between unions and overseas-owned firms under the traditional industrial relations institutional framework was assured by Government support. As inward investment entered Ireland from the late 1950s most firms were encouraged to recognise local unions, most often in the form of single-union deals. Nevertheless, a retreat from union recognition in the 1980s, especially within the electronics industry, sanctioned by government agencies and facilitated by employers' organisations, has further undermined the old adversarial model of industrial relations.

An additional pressure on the old system is a new model of industrial relations which expressly seeks to combine Human Resource Management with collective bargaining based on strong unions as a means of counteracting a competitive environment which militates against the uncompetitive practices associated with established industrial relations. Success is increasingly envisaged as springing from greater co-operation and commitment between employers and employed. Thus, collective bargaining may no longer be the most important or only significant point of contact for organised representatives of employers and employed.

Under this set of rules 'trade unions and collective bargaining remain the cornerstone of good industrial relations; but unions take on new responsibilities for the operation of the business and collective bargaining to coexist with joint union-management decisions making based on consensus' (Roche, 1994, p. 19). This vision has not been unanimously accepted by unions. An alternative interpretation of these events is one of an increasingly deregulated labour force, operating under increasingly intensified conditions. Where Irish unions have moved away from the old-model, the response has been termed 'defensive'. That is, training is actively supported where this is associated with the defence of members' pay and conditions of employment, and with the upgrading of members' skills. However, a further broadening of unions' attitudes is suggested and reflected in policy pronouncements of the Irish Confederation of Trade Unions (ICTU) in which the 'need to ensure adequate skills training, as well as promising opportunities for personal development, is associated with the introduction of new work organisation strategies' (cited in Garavan, Costine et al., 1995, p. 92).

A future path of union activity embodies the development of coherent training policies and proactive collective bargaining intervention, in search of training agreements and the establishment of joint trade union/management training structures.

> If the apparent increase in Irish trade union awareness and interest in training and development is to be transferred into future active intervention, the mechanisms of training policies, agreements and committees will become important . . . and may be considerably strengthened if embodied within a legislative framework (Garavan, Costine et al., 1995, p. 94).

The benefits from the unions' point of view are represented in Table 8.11.

TABLE 8.11: BENEFITS TO UNIONS FROM PARTNERSHIP-BUILDING

More cordial employee relations, through agreement on the benefits of a training and development ethos for all organisational stakeholders
Members' perceptions of trade unions becoming more congruent with their broadening expectations
Opportunities opening up for trade unions to gain a more secure foothold on the participatory ladder, through involvement in joint training structures
Trade unions having a more radical influence on national training, especially by their pursuit of legislative measures to support training and development opportunities for employers

Source: Adapted from Garavan, Costine et al., 1995.

8.7 CONCLUSION

The chapter has discussed changes in work organisation, and policies for human resource development in the context of overseas investors as important catalysts for the development of skills, training and high-quality production in the Republic of Ireland. The promotion of a 'High Performance Work Organisation' or a 'World Class Manufacturing' ethos has had little impact on the value added of overseas-owned industry in Ireland. Furthermore, the scope for employers to foster new work systems through development of their own corporate strategies, work organisation and in dialogue with the training and skills policies of public agencies, employers' organisations and unions, remains unclear.

The development of appropriate 'institutional thickness' is important for the pursuit of a model of sustainable economic growth based on high skills and high quality. While it may benefit some firms, flexibility without skill does not promote the competitive position of the Republic of Ireland, or is it likely to advance other peripheral locations. A pivotal issue is the institutional structure of co-operative exchange and the effective split between this and collective bargaining and the extent to which union-employer co-operation outside the arena of collective bargaining is balanced. Within the Republic of Ireland, the regulation of this area cannot be left unattended but requires a structure which can set the ground rules for firm level activities. Firm-level initiatives are less likely to succeed or even be attempted without the development of industry-level frameworks for co-operative exchange in which to anchor firm-level initiatives.

References

Aglietta, M. (1979), *A Theory of Capitalist Regulation*, London: New Left Books.

Aglietta, M. (1982), 'World capitalism in the eighties' *New Left Review*, Vol. 136, pp. 3-41.

Amin, A. (1994), 'Post-Fordism: models, fantasies and phantoms of transition' in *Post-Fordism: A reader* (Ed. Amin, A.), London: Blackwell, pp. 1-39.

Amin, A. and A. Malmberg (1992), 'Competing structural and institutional influences on the geography of production in Europe', *Environment and Planning A*, Vol. 24, pp. 401-416.

Amin, A. and N. Thrift (1994), 'Living in the Global' in *Globalisation, Institutions and Regional Development in Europe* (Eds. Amin, A. and Thrift, N.), Oxford: Oxford University Press, pp. 1-22.

André, C. and R. Delorme (1982), *L'Etat et L'Economie*, Paris: Seuil.

Applebaum, E. and R. Batt (1994), *The New American Workplace*, Ithaca, NY: Cornell University Press.

Barnett, C. (1986), *The Audit of War: The Illusion and Reality of Britain as a Great Power*, London: Macmillan.

Bell, D. (1973), *The Coming of Post-industrial Society*, New York: Basic Books.

Blauner, R. (1964), *Alienation and Freedom*, Chicago: University of Chicago Press.

Boyer, R. (1986), *La théorie de la régulation: une analyse critique*, Paris: La Découverte.

Boyer, R., Ed. (1988a), *The Search for Labour Market Flexibility: The European Economies in Transition*, Oxford: Clarendon Press.

Boyer, R. (1988b), 'Technical Change and the Theory of Regulation' in *Technical Change and Economical Theory* (Eds. Dosi, G., Freeman, C., Nelson, R., Silverberg, G. and Soete, L.), London: Frances Pinter.

Boyer, R. (1991), 'The Eighties: The Search for Alternatives to Fordism' in *The Politics of Flexibility* (Eds. Jessop, B., Kastendiek, H., Nielsen, K. and Pedersen, O.), Aldershot: Edward Elgar.

Braverman, H. (1974), *Labour and Monopoly Capital*, New York: Monthly Review Press.

Castells, M. (1989), *The Informational City: Information Technology, Economic Restructuring and the Urban Regional Process*, Oxford: Blackwell.

CBI (1994), *Flexible labour markets. Who pays for training?*, London: Confederation of British Industry.

Coriat, B. (1979), *L'atelier et la chronomètre*, Paris, Christian Bourgois.

Coriat, B. and P. Petit (1991), 'Deindustrialisation and tertiarization: towards a new economic regime?' in *Towards a new Europe?* (Eds. Amin, A. and Dietrich, M.), Aldershot, Edward Elgar.

Coutrot, T. and J. L. Parraire (1994), *Le Développement Recent des Politiques de Motivation de Salaires. Premières Synthèses DARES*. Paris, Ministry of Labour, Employment and Vocational Training.

Dicken, P., M. Forsgren, et al. (1994), 'The Local Embeddedness of Transnational Corporations' in *Globalisation, Institutions and Regional Development in Europe* (Eds. Amin, A. and Thrift, N.), Oxford: Oxford University Press.

Dore, R. (1987), *Taking Japan Seriously: A Confucian Perspective on Leading Economic Issues*, Stanford, CA: Stanford University Press.

Economist Intelligence Unit (1994), *Country Report, Ireland*, 4th Quarter, London: EIU.

Esser, J. and J. Hirsch (1994), 'The crisis of Fordism and the dimensions of a 'post-Fordist' regional and urban structure' in *Post-Fordism: A Reader* (Ed. Amin, A.), London: Blackwell, pp. 71-97.

European Commission (1994), *The European report on science and technology indicators 1994*. Brussels: Office for Official Publications of the European Communities.

FÁS (1993), 'Sectoral study of the mechanical engineering, electrical engineering and electronics industry', Dublin: FÁS.

Finegold, D. and D. Soskice (1988), 'The failure of training in Britain: analysis and prescription' *Oxford Review of Economic Policy* , Vol. 4, No. 3, pp. 21-53.

FitzGerald, A. and M. Breathnach (1994), 'Technological innovation in Irish manufacturing industry. Preliminary findings from the Irish Innovation Survey Evaluation and Statistics Unit', Forfás, Dublin.

Flynn, P. (1988), *Facilitating Technological Change*, Cambridge, MA: Ballinger.

Garavan, T. N., P. Costine, et al. (1995), *Training & Development in Ireland: Context, Policy and Practice*, Dublin: Oak Tree Press.

Geary, J. (1995), *Working at Teamwork: Lessons from Europe*, Dublin: Centre for Employment Relations and Organisational Performance.

Government of Ireland (1994), *Operational Programme for Industrial Development 1994-1999*. Dublin: Stationery Office.

Government of Ireland (1995a), *Making knowledge work for us. A strategic view of science, technology and innovation in Ireland*, Dublin, Science Technology and Innovation Advisory Council.

Government of Ireland (1995b), *Operational Programme for Human Resources Development 1994-1999*, Dublin: Stationery Office.

Grahl, J. and P. Teague (1991), 'Industrial relations trajectories and European human resource management' in *International Comparisons of Human Resource Management* (Eds. Brewster, C. and Tyson, S.), London: Pitman, pp. 67-91.

Hirst, P. and J. Zeitlin (1991), 'Flexible specialisation versus post-Fordism: theory, evidence and policy implications', *Economy and Society* , Vol. 20 ,No. 1, pp. 1-156.

Howell, D. and E. Wolff (1991), 'Trends in the growth and distribution of skill in the US workplace, 1960-1985', *Industrial and Labour Relations Review*, Vol. 44, No. 3, pp. 481-501.

Ichniowski, C., K. Shaw, et al. (1993), 'The effects of human resource management practices on productivity', Carnegie Mellon University.

Industrial Policy Review Group (1992), *A time for change: industrial policy for the 1990s (Culliton Report),* Dublin: Stationery Office.

Irish Business and Employers Confederation (1994), *The training of people in employment*, Dublin: IBEC.

Irish Business and Employers Confederation (1995), *Annual Review 1994-1995*, Dublin: IBEC.

Kaufman, R. T. (1992), 'The effects of IMPORSHARE on productivity', *Industrial and Labour Relations Review*, Vol. 45, January, pp. 311-22.

Kennedy, K. A. (1991), 'Linkages and overseas industry' in *Overseas Industry in Ireland* (Eds. Foley, A. and McAleese, D.), Dublin: Gill and Macmillan, pp. 85-102.

Kern, H. and M. Schumann (1984), *Das Ende der Arbeitsteilung? Rationalisierung in der industriellen Produktion*, Munich: Beck.

Le Heron, R. and B. Van Der Knapp (1995), 'Industrial spaces as contexts for human resource development' in *Human Resources and Industrial Spaces* (Eds. Heron, R. L. and Van Der Knapp, B.). Chichester: John Wiley and Sons, pp. 3-27.

Lipietz, A. (1985), *The Enchanted World: Inflation, Credit and the World Crisis*, London: Verso.

Lipietz, A. (1987), *Mirages and Miracles: Crises of Global Fordism*, London: Verso.

Lipietz, A. (1992), *Towards a New Economic Order: Post-Fordism, Ecology and Democracy*, Oxford: Oxford University Press.

Lipietz, A. (1993), 'The local and the global: regional individuality or inter-regionalism?', *Transactions of the Institute of British Geographers* , Vol. 18, pp. 8-18.

Marsden, D. (1987), 'Collective bargaining and industrial adjustment in Britain, France, Germany and Italy' in *Managing Industrial Change in Western Europe* (Eds. Duchene, F. and Shepherd, G.), London: Pinter, pp. 178-209.

Marsden, D. (1994), *Regulation vs. de-regulation: which route for Europe's labour market*, London: Employment Policy Institute.

McDuffie, J. P. (1991), 'Beyond mass production, flexible production systems and manufacturing performance in the world auto industry'. Sloan School of Management, MIT.

Mistral, J. (1986), 'Régime internationale et trajectories nationales' in *Capitalisme Fin de Siecle.* (Ed. Boyer, R.). Paris: Presse Universitaires de France.

Mjøset, L. (1992), *The Irish Economy in a Comparative Institutional Perspective*, Dublin: National Economic and Social Council.

National Economic and Social Council (1993), *Education and Training Policies for Economic and Social Development*, Dublin: NESC.

Olson, M. (1982), *The Rise and Decline of Nations*, New Haven, CT: Yale University Press.

Osterman, P. (1995), 'Skill, training and work organization in American establishments', *Industrial Relations*, Vol. 34, No. 2, pp. 125-146.

Piore, M. and C. Sabel (1984), *The Second Industrial Divide: Possibilities for Prosperity*, New York: Basic Books.

Porter, M. (1990), *The Competitive Advantage of Nations*, New York: The Free Press.

Regini, M. (1995), 'Firms and institutions: the demand for skills and their social production in Europe', *European Journal of Industrial Relations*, Vol. 1, No. 2, pp. 191-202.

Roche, F. and P. Tansey (1992), *Industrial training in Ireland*, Dublin: Department of Industry and Trade.

Roche, W. K. (1994), *Trade Unions and Industrial Relations*, Dublin: Centre for Employment Relations and Organisational Performance.

Roche, W. K. and J. Geary (1994), 'The attenuation of "host-country effects"? Multinationals, industrial relations and collective bargaining in Ireland', UCD Graduate School of Business, Dublin.

Roche, W. K. and T. Turner (1995), 'The human resource policy sophistication of organisations in Ireland: institutions, markets and internal influences', UCD Graduate School of Business, Dublin.

Sabel, C. and J. Zeitlin (1985), 'Historical alternatives to mass production: politics, markets and technology in nineteenth century industrialisation', *Past and Present* , Vol. 108, pp. 133-76.

Sabel, C. F. (1994), 'Flexible specialisation and the re-emergence of regional economies' in *Post-Fordism: A Reader* (Ed. Amin, A.), London: Blackwell, pp. 101-156.

Sassen, S. (1991), *The Global City: New York, London, Tokyo*, Princeton: Princeton University Press.

Scott, A. J. (1995), 'The geographic foundations of industrial performance', paper presented at Economic Geography Study Group: Society, place, economy: debates and directions-states of the art in economic geography, Institute of British Geographers Annual Conference, University of Northumbria at Newcastle, 3-6 January, 1995.

Slomp, H. (1995), 'National variations in worker participation', in *International Human Resource Management* (Eds. Harzing, A. W. and Ruysseveldt, J. V.), London: Sage, pp. 291-317.

Storper, M. (1992), 'The limits to globalization: technology districts and "international trade"', *Economic Geography*, Vol. 68, No. 1, pp. 60-93.

Storper, M. and A. J. Scott (1989), 'The geographical foundations and social regulation of flexible production complexes' in *The Power of Geography: How Territory Shapes Social Life* (Eds. Wolch, J. and Dear, M.), Winchester, MA: Unwin Hyman.

Streeck, W. (1989), 'Skills and the limits of neo-liberalism: the enterprise of the future as a place of learning', *Work, Employment and Society*, Vol. 3, No. 1, pp. 89-104.

Streeck, W. (1992), 'National diversity, regime competition and institutional deadlock: problems in forming a European industrial relations system', *Journal of Public Policy*, Vol. 12, No. 4, pp. 301-330.

Turok, I. (1993), 'Inward investment and local linkages: How deeply embedded is "Silicon Glen"?', *Regional Studies* , Vol. 27, No. 5, pp. 401-417.

Veersma, U. (1995), 'Multinational corporations and industrial relations: policy and practice', in *International Human Resource Management* (Eds. Harzing, A. W. and Ruysseveldt, J. V.), London: Sage, pp. 318-336.

Walsh, J. A. (1995), *Regions in Ireland. A statistical profile*, Dublin: Regional Studies Association (Irish Branch).

9

SMALL FIRMS, UNIVERSITIES AND TECHNOLOGICAL DEVELOPMENT IN A PERIPHERAL ECONOMY: THE CASE OF THE REPUBLIC OF IRELAND

Dylan Jones-Evans

9.1 INTRODUCTION

Peripheral regions in Europe have different economic problems from those experienced in the core of Europe, problems that require quite different economic solutions. This, however, is no easy task, as the long-run processes of regional economic development are extremely complex phenomena, and currently policy-makers are unable to provide an adequate explanation of the conditions under which economic activities grow and decline and change their locations, industrial composition and relationships within a specific region. Whilst governments in the past have attempted to formulate some types of regional policy programme, such as the promotion of branch plants, support of large industries and protection of agriculture, none of these policy measures (that are still being pursued by some governments on both a national and regional level) have succeeded in laying the basis for self-generated regional growth. Whilst there is a growing awareness of the importance of technological networks at a regional level, especially networks between different actors such as government, universities and entrepreneurial small firms, much of the development of such linkages in Europe, especially within peripheral regions, remains considerably underdeveloped.

Through examining the economy of the Republic of Ireland, this paper will discuss the role of technology in the development of the peripheral regions of Europe, concentrating, in particular, on the role that can be played by small technology-based firms and the university sector. It will demonstrate that the indigenous technological capability of industry within a peripheral economy such as the Republic of Ireland remains low, mainly as a result of a weak entrepreneurial high technology sector, and the under-utilisation of the university sector in developing linkages with this indigenous industry.

9.2 TECHNOLOGICAL DEVELOPMENT

9.2.1 Technology and National Competitiveness

Rapid technological advance within a region or country can give competitive advantages in local, national and international markets, which can result in increased industrial output, employment and prosperity (Saxenian, 1994; Smilor et al., 1990; Nijkamp, 1986; Amin and Goddard, 1986; Cooke, 1985; Ewers and Wettmann, 1980). Indeed, the future competitiveness of industry, and success in accelerating growth and increasing employment, depends on the capacity of firms to innovate in response to changing external conditions, including the continuing rapid pace of technological development (NESC, 1993). In the medium to long term, sustained competitiveness in the global economy will depend on technological or innovation-based strengths, such as the ability to develop new products, to access successfully new markets, to apply new technology, to incorporate best practice in the management of enterprises, and to develop skill levels across the full spectrum of the labour force. Consequently, a plethora of different approaches have been developed to initiate and sustain the development of technological innovation, which include the concept of regional industrial complexes such as 'technopoles' (Castells and Hall, 1994), i.e. planned technology-based developments such as science and technology parks which are planned by central or local government, often in association with both universities and private industry; highly specific financial incentives to support product development within small firms (Moore, 1993), and training programmes to develop the potential of small technology-based firms (Klofsten and Jones-Evans, 1996).

9.2.2 Technology and the Development of Peripheral Regions

Commentators have noted that the dependency on technological development for future national competitive advantage may be particularly pronounced within peripheral regions of Europe, such as Greece, Ireland, Spain and Portugal, which need to have a much broader spectrum of R&D capabilities if they are to successfully exploit technologies in industry, even within medium-technology sectors (Walsh, 1987). This is because it is becoming generally accepted that small peripheral countries cannot sustain a development strategy based on relative-factor costs (wages, labour, etc.) and must increasingly develop a comparative advantage based on the enhancement and exploitation of the national knowledge base, as in other developed, progressive countries, where science and technology is at the top of the national agenda. As the recent report of the Science, Technology and Innovation Advisory Council (STIAC, 1995) in the Republic of Ireland stated, many small advanced countries (especially those in the Nordic countries) have appreciated that every economy must build a capacity to create, absorb, and apply new technologies, whether developed locally or elsewhere. A failure to innovate or, more precisely, to establish a national system of innovation is a significant barrier to the long run competitiveness of peripheral economies (NESC, 1993).

Therefore, the increasing emphasis by economists and policy-makers on the importance of the generation and availability of new technologies has considerable implications for the promotion of economic growth within the peripheral regions of the European Union (Bradley et al., 1993). As Malecki (1991) points out, the allure of high technology has sparked a number of policies to create or generate innovativeness of peripheral regions, and to upgrade the technological capabilities of local firms through regional innovation centres. Despite this, however, success in the development of innovation at a regional level has eluded peripheral regions, mainly because of their low innovation potential, which is an outcome of the relative scarcity of R&D carried out there (Ewers and Wettmann, 1980). As such, the knowledge of available technologies and how to use them may be comparatively poor. Indeed, there may be only one way of increasing the technological capability and potential of a peripheral region, as Malecki suggests:

> In the context of most small peripheral regions, however, innovative development may be too good to be true. The human capital of such regions is limited and mobile, so it can be expected that many talented people will simply leave. Historically, indeed, outmigration selects the most productive subset of the population of rural regions. In addition, the industrial and

personnel structure of peripheral countries and regions is a result of their dependence on branch plants of large, multinational corporations. The evidence is clear that such plants tend to have lower levels of highly trained and skilled personnel, certainly lower levels of R&D, and little attention to nonroutine activities or new products. Such a regional structure is unlikely to be innovative, especially in a setting of short product cycles, which require a continuous flow of up-to-date information and knowledge. It is the entrepreneurial spin-off process which is the principal local route of technology transfer. Indeed, new ideas enter an economy primarily through the identification of opportunities by entrepreneurs. The local nature of entrepreneurship poses great challenges, but it is such a process which was the basis of the successes which national and regional S&T policies are trying to imitate. The process of entrepreneurship may be a more important one to regional and local economies than the process of technological change (Malecki, 1991, p. 314).

If these processes of technological change and entrepreneurship can be linked, then it may benefit the peripheral regions within the European Union. To date, policy-makers in peripheral regions have tended to neglect the role that a vibrant indigenous technology-based sector can play in the development of the economy. This reflects much of recent innovation policy undertaken by peripheral regions in the EC, which has been aimed towards the attraction of the R&D facilities of large firms, with the hope that there will be subsequent spin-off activity, rather than the development of a strong indigenous technological sector. Peripheral regions have tended to attract only branch plants, with little or no R&D activity, and their subsequent possible contribution to regional innovation growth has been minimal. As the recent paper on growth, competitiveness and employment (European Commission, 1993) recognised, one of the significant potential sources of growth firms in Europe are small businesses working in high technology sectors.

9.3 SMALL TECHNOLOGY-BASED FIRMS

9.3.1 The Importance of Small Technology-based Firms
With the growing appreciation of the contribution of small firms to a healthy national and regional economy, and the concomitant growth in the diversity and complexity of technology, attention

has been focused on this relatively new type of small business — the small technology-based venture — which is based on the technical skills and experience of its owner-managers (Jones-Evans, 1992). The emergence of such firms, it has been argued, has been mainly due to changes in both industrial and cultural values, which has encouraged the rapid development of a vibrant small firm sector within technology-based industrial sectors in most developed economies. For example, the increasing use of flexible specialisation and customisation within high technology manufacturing has led to the growth of many small specialist businesses (Aydalot and Keeble, 1988), especially within high value-added niche markets such as computing, medical instrumentation and biotechnology. In some cases, these firms have been established to maximise the competitive advantages offered by the decreasing costs of microprocessor technologies, enabling them to compete directly with larger organisations (Green and Howells, 1988). Recently, such businesses have gained economic significance for the following reasons:

Employment

Technology-based small firms have become increasingly important to future national industrial employment in both Europe (Oakey, 1991) and the United States (Phillips et al., 1991). For example, a recent analysis of employment within the UK high technology industrial sector in the period 1987-1991 found that while total employment in firms with 100 or more employees decreased by 83,419 jobs, total employment in firms with 1 to 99 employees increased by 26,766 jobs (Jones-Evans and Westhead, 1996).

Technological Innovation

Generally, various researchers have demonstrated the valuable contribution of small technology-based firms to technological innovation within a number of high technology industrial sectors (Acs and Audretsch, 1988), particularly because of the increased productivity and efficiency demonstrated by such organisations in the use of R&D resources (Monck et al., 1988; Cooper and Bruno, 1977). Such industrial sectors are usually characterised by fast-changing markets, low capital intensity and small dependence on economies of scale, and are thus better suited to smaller firms, due to the entrepreneurial nature and lack of bureaucracy in decision making within such organisations (Rothwell, 1994). For ex-

ample, in the UK, comprehensive research into the relationship
between firm size and the level of innovation has revealed that
small firms' share of innovations, during the period 1945-1983,
had increased by over 50 per cent and now accounts for over a
quarter of the total number of innovations in the UK (Robson and
Townsend, 1984). Moreover, in many new industries, such as computing services, their contribution is highly significant, as new
advances in particular niche areas has presented entrepreneurs
with the opportunity to develop many new innovatory and market
opportunities.

Wealth Creation

A number of studies show that technologically-innovative SMEs
have a higher than average growth in assets, retained profits and
exports (Wynarczyk and Thwaites, 1994). Moreover, such firms
tend to have lower closure rates than businesses in other sectors
(Westhead and Storey, 1994).

9.3.2 Small Technology-based Firms in Peripheral Regions

Thus, small technology-based firms, in general, make a valuable
contribution to competitiveness, employment and innovation
within high technology industries. Indeed, the European Commission (1993) have gone so far as to state that this sector holds
the key to the future growth and renewal of the EC.[1] However, the
development of small technology-based firms within the peripheral regions of Europe remains somewhat limited (Fontes, 1995),
mainly because the existing industrial structures within peripheral regions have characteristics which are very different from
those that can be observed in more advanced regions, as demonstrated in other chapters in this book. Indeed, as Tsipouri (1994)
indicates, whilst new technology-based firms are a recent, but not
negligible trend in less-favoured regions, they tend either to remain small and struggling for survival, or lose their markets and
disappear in relatively short periods of time. There are exceptions
— for example, a recent report examining the peripheral regional
economy of Wales showed that the innovative strength of the
technology sector came from its dominant SME sector, rather than

---

[1] There is currently very little data available on the number of small technology-based firms in the different European regions, although there is currently a major project being undertaken to ascertain this (Cogan, 1995).

larger branch plants (CASS, 1995), although this, as Fontes (1995) suggests, may be due to the fact that firms of peripheral regions of more advanced countries, such as the UK, are already inserted into the context of an industrialised country.

One of the main reasons for the relative lack of development of the small-firm technology sector within peripheral regions in Europe may be the lack of interaction with the local science and technology infrastructure (Fontes, 1995). Indeed, a major obstacle to the general development of a vibrant technological base of industrial firms is the lack of co-operation in the exchange and absorption of knowledge, especially with third-level institutions such as universities. This is despite increasing evidence of the importance of universities in developing the technological potential at a regional level.

9.4 UNIVERSITIES AND TECHNOLOGICAL DEVELOPMENT

9.4.1 Universities as Facilitators for High Technology Firms

The feedback within the innovation process, and the frequent and intermittent need for new scientific knowledge has led to an increasing focus on links between industry and academic institutions (Malecki, 1991), especially on the flows of knowledge between the two partners, which may lead to considerable diffusion of scientific and technical knowledge, particularly into the small-firm sector. Indeed, universities and other higher educational institutions (HEIs) have, in recent years, become regarded as facilitators of growth for high technology firms. There are a number of reasons for this:

Sources of New Firms

HEIs concentrate a large critical mass of scientifically sophisticated individuals who can generate new technologies which, in turn, can lead to innovative ideas (and technological knowledge) which can be channelled and diffused by new ventures. Various studies have recognised that a significant number of new technology-based businesses in both the USA and Western Europe had been established by scientists emerging from different types of academic-based organisations, such as non-profit research institutes, government research centres and universities (Klofsten,

1994; Giannisis et al., 1991; Roberts, 1991; Samsom and Gurdon, 1990). One example of this can be found in one of the fastest growing regions of Sweden, namely Linköping. The region contains a strong high technology industrial environment, which includes the presence of Saab's Aircraft Division, Ericsson Radio and the Swedish Defence Research Establishment, and is at the forefront in the creation and development of new technology-based firms in Sweden. Academics from Linköping University have played a leading role in this — of the 350 small technology-based spin-offs established in the region to date, approximately 70 of these have emerged directly from academic research activities at Linköping University (Klofsten and Jones-Evans, 1996), with a high number of the others using or developing university research findings as the basis for their products or services. Similarly, in the UK, a study of the 'Cambridge Phenomenon' found that nearly all of the 350 high technology businesses in the area had ultimately been generated from Cambridge University, especially the departments of physics, engineering and computing (Segal, 1985). The role of universities in creating these milieus of innovative firms within different regions has led to a proactive approach by universities, usually supported by regional or national government, in adopting a direct entrepreneurial role. This can range from the establishment of university-owned holding companies to promote fledgling academic entrepreneurs (Gibson and Smilor, 1991) to the development-specific centres of research and training which promote and assist the process of spin-off of academic research into a network of industrial firms and business ventures (Klofsten and Jones-Evans, 1996).

Employment Opportunities

As stated earlier, local and national governments view the high technology sector as a source of direct and indirect employment opportunities, and HEIs are seen as crucial to facilitating the growth of the local high technology sector. The development of a centre of academic excellence in a certain field can create or enhance a favourable public image and reputation. As a result, additional jobs can be created not only in a HEI, but also in the wider community surrounding the HEI, because of its enhanced economic and social status. For example, a recent study by Acs et al. (1995) of 37 American cities and six high technology groupings found a positive relationship between university research and increase in high technology employment of a city. Similarly, in East

Anglia in the United Kingdom, where much of the emphasis has been on utilising the University of Cambridge as a catalyst in linking academic research, entrepreneurs and financial institutions to create a seedbed for new industry, there has been considerable growth in employment in high technology manufacturing, as well as other knowledge-based services activities such as R&D and computer services (Jones-Evans and Kirby, 1994).

The Generation of New Basic and Applied Scientific Knowledge

As Castells and Hall (1994) point out, research-oriented universities are to the informational economy what coal mines were to the industrial economy, and they argue that universities are better suited to this role than private or public research centres. In an era of increased competition, industry has appreciated the need to increase its knowledge base, and in technology-intensive industries, links with HEIs can result in early access to scientific or technological knowledge. For example, a recent study by Mansfield (1994) demonstrated that in the USA, academic research has become a major underpinning for industrial innovation in many science-based industries. In information processing, pharmaceuticals and instruments, among others, more than 10 per cent of new products and/or processes in recent years could not have been developed (without substantial delay) in the absence of recent academic research.

Sources of Technical Expertise and Knowledge for Local Firms

The technical expertise available in HEIs can be used by existing local businesses to solve production process problems and to supplement their commercial advantage. This can particularly benefit small firms, who usually cannot afford the relevant technical expertise or equipment, especially as HEIs have computing, testing and analysis and library facilities which are an incentive for small firms to engage in a HEI-industry based relationship. As a result, local firms can become more technologically sophisticated, thus enhancing their competitive performance and, in some cases, their survival (Westhead and Storey, 1995).

Sources of Skilled Employees for Technology-based Firms

HEIs are increasingly seen by high technology businesses as a crucial source of skilled graduates whom they can employ after graduation. Universities are also involved in training, in both requisite quantity and quality, of the labour force of scientists, engineers and technicians, which will provide the key ingredient for the growth of technologically advanced industrial centres. Indeed, the presence of a large research university with its thousands of potential highly educated technical personnel can be a factor in attracting firms to a particular region, as firms can only easily recruit their workforce if they are already located in an advanced urban-industrial area. For all start-up technological centres, the ability to build a local labour market of good quality engineers and scientists is critical, and the university can play an important part in this through the supply of highly trained science and technology graduates. One example of this can be found in Austin, Texas, where the decision by a number of large technology-based businesses to locate in the region was due to the availability of high-quality graduate students in the fields of computer science and electrical engineering (Gibson and Smilor, 1991). Moreover, students can also be used, through placements and assignments, by local small businesses to develop critical management and technical competences which they could not otherwise afford (Kirby and Mullen, 1991).

Therefore, universities can play an important role in the development of indigenous technological development, which can range from being a source of well-trained manpower to a direct involvement in the imaginative matching of potential technologies to economic and social needs (McBrierty and O'Neill, 1991). However, within peripheral regions there is evidence that they are still particularly under-utilised, despite arguments that one of the chief impediments to economic development in these regions has been the failure to efficiently and effectively utilise the output of the education system (Kennedy et al., 1988).

9.4.2 University-industry Linkages within Peripheral Regions

As Table 9.1 shows, there has been considerable growth in the expenditure on R&D by universities in peripheral regions, with Ireland (102.4 per cent), Greece (187.1 per cent), Portugal (250 per cent) and Spain (234.3 per cent) increasing their R&D expenditure in higher education by a higher amount than the European Community (74.6 per cent) in the period 1985-91.

TABLE 9.1. RESEARCH AND DEVELOPMENT EXPENDITURE,
PERFORMED BY HIGHER EDUCATION (MILLION ECU — 1994 PRICES
AND EXCHANGE RATES)

	1985	1986	1987	1988	1989	1990	1991	% Change 1985-91
Belgium	333	353	386	382	608	—	696	109.0
Denmark	234	268	301	335	367	390	402	71.8
Germany	3,008	3,346	4,025	4,233	4,457	4,800	5,734	90.6
Greece	31	29	34	40	81	86	89	187.1
France	2,345	2,505	2,626	2,739	3,039	3,313	3,528	50.4
Ireland	41	50	52	52	62	72	83	102.4
Italy	1,209	1,371	1,580	1,756	1,935	2,317	2,470	104.3
N'lands	809	872	919	902	943	1,061	1112	37.5
Portugal	34	41	50	60	83	104	119	250.0
Spain	248	268	307	402	531	671	829	234.3
UK	1,987	1,918	2,072	2,370	2,509	2624	2,882	45.0
EC	10,276	11,020	12,352	13,270	14,615	—	17,944	74.6

Source: European Commission (1994).

An analysis of further data from the European Report on Science
and Technology Indicators (European Commission, 1994, p. 255)
suggests that this increase in R&D spending, as well as a corresponding increase in R&D personnel in universities within peripheral regions, may be largely due to involvement in European
Commission Research and Technological Development (RTD) in-
ternational-based programmes (mainly with other universities
and private/public research centres) rather than specific links
with indigenous firms. In the three less developed countries of the
European Union, namely Ireland, Portugal and Greece, RTD
funding from the EU accounts for between 10 per cent and 35 per
cent of total civil R&D spending.

Within many peripheral regions of the European Union, there
is evidence that the structure of universities is 'endogamic' and
therefore do not favour the establishment of relevant links with
industry. This 'link gap' constitutes yet another impediment to the
development of technology-based entrepreneurship (Castells and
Hall, 1994). The reason for this relative lack of co-operation with
indigenous small firms may, in part, be a symptom of the culture,

especially within academia, that does not encourage the development of links with small-scale industry. As Louis et al. (1989) suggest, universities are not traditionally viewed as leaders in entrepreneurship. In fact, they suggest that there is often a tendency to distinguish between the search for truth in science — which is considered a legitimate function of the university — and the search for invention — which is considered an inappropriate focus on ideas that have potential commercial or practical applicability. Indeed, it has been indicated that many academics are concerned that research collaboration with industry was against the central ethics of universities, which focused on fundamental research and the education of students, and that links with industry not only detracted from this but could, in some cases, restrict the free flow of information between academics and institutions (Charles and Howells, 1992).

There is also evidence of a reluctance by small technology-based firms within peripheral regions to become involved in relationships with their local universities (Fontes and Coombs, 1994), although large companies regularly access universities for external sources of technological expertise (Chatterji and Manuel, 1993; Link and Rees, 1990). Whilst small firms were aware that university departments could provide advanced inputs in favourable conditions, it was generally considered that the knowledge generated by universities was less likely to be targeted to their needs. This is despite evidence from Mansfield (1994) that initiatives such as technical consultancy by an academic scientist for an industrial organisation may be one of the most effective forms of technology transfer. This general apathy — by universities and small firms alike — towards closer collaborative links, may be one of the greatest weaknesses of Europe's research and technology base, which has resulted in a comparatively limited capacity to convert scientific breakthroughs and technological achievements (from university research) into industrial and commercial success (European Commission, 1993).

The next section will consider some of the issues raised above in the context of a peripheral country in the European Commission, namely the Republic of Ireland.

9.5 THE REPUBLIC OF IRELAND

9.5.1 Technology-based Industry in Ireland

As in other peripheral countries in Europe, a shift in the Republic of Ireland's indigenous-industry structure towards industries with long term international growth prospects (such as technology-based sectors) is long overdue. To date, remarkably little progress has been made in this direction over many years, with a general lack of technological capability within Irish industry, which has not been compensated for by a relatively weak indigenous sector. As Table 9.2 shows, the contribution of indigenous firms to technology-based sectors remains low, with overseas (mainly large multinational) plants providing the bulk of exports and over 90 per cent of high technology exports which originate in Ireland (Foley and Griffith, 1992). Such firms also account for more than 75 per cent of high technology employment.

TABLE 9.2: INDICATORS OF SCALE OF IRISH INDIGENOUS MANUFACTURING, 1990

Indigenous share of manufacturing	
Employment	54.33
Exports	24.4
Indigenous share of employment in:	
Chemicals	23.45
Pharmaceuticals	13.98
Office and data processing equipment	7.19
Electrical engineering	22.66

Source: Foley and Griffith (1994).

Similarly, the annual Irish innovation study (FitzGerald and Breathnach, 1994) suggested that the typical profile of an innovating firm in Ireland was that of a large foreign-owned enterprise operating in the high technology sector with the contribution of small firms to innovation and employment in Ireland being relatively low (Table 9.3). As O'Brien (1985) suggests, there are a number of reasons for this:

- as Ireland is a late-industrialising country, firms do not have a local base of sophisticated users, nor ready access to the range of suppliers and services available to firms in more advanced countries

- Irish firms are generally late entrants to technology-based industries, and have to compete with existing sophisticated firms abroad

- as a peripheral region of Europe, Ireland faces problems of access to information on technology, markets and competitors, as well as higher transport and selling costs

- Ireland has a small home market which makes it difficult for new industries to grow and learn in an environment unprotected from abroad.

This differs from the profiles of core countries such as the UK, where technology-based small firms have become increasingly important to future national industrial employment, especially within high technology industries.

TABLE 9.3. PROFILES OF THE INNOVATORS AND ALL FIRMS IN THE REPUBLIC OF IRELAND (%)

	Innovators	*All Firms*
Ownership		
Irish	66	83
Foreign	34	17
Number of employees		
10-49	52	61
50-99	19	21
100+	29	19
Sector*		
Low tech	50	66
Medium tech	20	22
High tech	30	12

* High tech: electrical and electronic equipment (including software), pharmaceuticals and instruments; medium tech: chemicals (including plastics), machinery, transport equipment; low tech: all other sectors.

Source: FitzGerald and Breathnach, 1994.

9.5.2 Technology-based Small Firms in Ireland
The relatively poor performance of indigenous medium and large firms, coupled with the mixed performance of foreign-owned firms, may serve to increase the Irish government's dependence on the indigenous small firm as a key element in its approach to economic development (Walsh and Anderson, 1994). As the Department of Industry and Commerce (1990) pointed out in their review of industrial performance, small firms have a role to play in establishing a seedbed of industrial enterprises from which larger internationally-trading enterprises can develop. However, most of the firms established in Ireland are small concerns which are very unlikely to expand into even medium-sized enterprises selling overseas (O'Farrell and Crouchley, 1984). While the indigenous small firm sector in Ireland has increased its employment in recent years, this has been mainly as a result of the creation of new business (which remain small) rather than through the growth of those businesses after they had been established (Walsh and Anderson, 1995). Indeed, only 1 per cent of firms established in Ireland since 1973 have grown to employ more than fifty employees (Department of Industry and Commerce, 1990) and, as the Task Force on Small Business (1994) points out, this is considerably less than in other countries, and there remains the need to develop sectors of Irish industry with substantial growth potential (Duijnhouwer, 1992; O'Farrell, 1986), especially within vibrant and entrepreneurial technology-based industries. This is no easy task, even within relatively successful sectors such as the Irish electronics industry, which has demonstrated considerable growth, especially in the areas of automation, communication technology and instrumentation (Orsenigo and O'Siuchrú, 1991). Indeed, there is still some doubt as to the electronics industry's future potential, with few firms being able to achieve penetration in their export markets that would enable them to reap the benefits of being leaders or near-leaders in their respective niches (Government of Ireland, 1989).

Despite this, one of the few options open to Irish technology-based industries is to develop a base of indigenous firms with sufficient scale and resources to compete internationally from a peripheral location. However, unlike most advanced economies, where most small technology-based firms have emerged as spin-offs from large industrial organisations, mainly as a result of recessionary forces, fragmentation and flexible specialisation

(Jones-Evans and Westhead, 1996), there is little evidence of a similar trend occurring in a peripheral economy such as Ireland, with no history of an indigenous high technology sector. As indicated earlier in Table 9.2, modern and growing high technology activities such as pharmaceuticals, chemicals, electrical engineering and instrument engineering, are dominated by foreign companies, with Irish firms to be found in more traditional sectors, such as food processing and the manufacture of metal articles. A recent study by Cogan (1995) suggests that there may be less than fifty small growth-oriented technology-based firms in the Republic of Ireland, which suggests an imperative need to develop this sector further. This small number of new technology-based firms within a peripheral region has also been reflected in a study of this type of organisation in Portugal (Fontes, 1995). Therefore, the question remains — how can the small technology-based firm sector within a peripheral region be aided to grow and develop?

As Rothwell (1994) indicates, the main strengths of small innovative firms are flexibility, dynamism and responsiveness, and this is borne out by the studies of such firms in Ireland (Cogan, 1995) and Portugal (Fontes, 1995). However, their main disadvantage and impediment to further growth is associated with a lack of access to financial and technological resources. The recent STIAC report (1995) recognised that Irish small technology-based firms are critically dependent on the emergence of new financing structures, especially in the development of indigenous seed and venture capital funds. This issue of financing for small technology-based firms is discussed in further detail by Kinsella and McBrierty (1994).

With regard to access to technological resources, there is little evidence of formal links between large and small technology-based firms in Ireland, except in a purely subcontracting capacity. This is not surprising, as the development of innovation within peripheral regions such as Ireland is characterised by an industrial structure in which there are relatively few large companies with sufficient resources to invest in Research and Development (R&D). Therefore, it is inevitable that other sources of technological expertise, such as the university sector, will play an increasingly pivotal role in a peripheral nation's knowledge base and research effort, including the training of scientists and technologists, services to industry, and industrial testing, as well as the creation and interpretation of knowledge for commercial exploitation.

9.5.3 Universities and Industry in Ireland

The Irish higher education system is broadly divided between the university sector (which consists of six universities: University College Dublin, Trinity College Dublin, Dublin City University, University College Cork, University College Galway, University of Limerick) and the Regional Technical Colleges (RTCs), which also includes the Dublin Institute of Technology. However, as Table 9.4 shows the majority of research is actually carried out within the university sector, although RTCs are geared to work with industry on a more localised level.

TABLE 9.4: RESEARCH OUTPUT OF THE HIGHER EDUCATION SECTOR IN IRELAND (1993-94)

	Universities	DITs	RTCs	Total
No. of research contracts	2,242	206	233	2,681
Annual research budget (£million)	44.3	1.4	3.0	48.7
Patents filed	58	2	15	75
Campus companies formed	146	1	31	30
Jobs created in campus companies	1,708	30	145	1,883
Research jobs sustained by contracts	1,689	120	147	1,956
Total jobs in research or campus companies	3,397	415	292	4,104

Source: Kinsella and McBrierty (1994)

Gross expenditure on R&D by the higher education sector in Ireland has increased by 380 per cent in the period 1982-1992, with over IR£73 million now being spent on R&D within the university sector (STIAC, 1995). Moreover, as the OECD (1987) have recognised, the research carried out in many Irish universities is often of a world-class standard, and the R&D capability of the Higher education sector has become a central element in the development of indigenous technological industry. For example, the Faculty of Food Science and Technology at University College Cork is at the forefront of the development of scientific and technology facilities for the food industry and has maintained close links with industry for over 70 years (Orsenigo and O'Siuchrú, 1991). It also houses the National Food Biotechnology Centre, which was established as a contract-research facility to commercialise Irish biotechnology research. In addition, the establishment of the Plassey Technological Park on the campus of the University of Limerick during the early 1980s has actively promoted university-industry linkages in the Mid-West Region of Ireland.

During the last ten years, the Irish government has developed a number of specific policy initiatives such as the creation of industrial liaison offices and incubators for campus companies. This has been relatively successful, with 178 companies formed, creating over 1800 jobs in the process (Table 9.4). However, many of these firms will remain small consultancy or 'lifestyle' firms, and will tend not to grow beyond a few employees, reflecting the trend found in other Irish industrial sectors. There have also been other national initiatives to promote academic-industry co-operation, including programmes in advanced technologies, applied research programmes, promotion of industrial liaison offices, and placement programmes (Frain, 1992), as well as high involvement in international research and technological development programmes.

Despite such initiatives, and the fact that Irish universities are as well organised as other international institutions in the provision of technology transfer to industry (McBrierty and O'Neill, 1991), the data still points towards a relative under-utilisation of universities as sources of knowledge and innovation, with very little evidence of this R&D being accessed directly by Irish industry. Universities are not solely to blame for this situation. As Table 9.5 demonstrates, indigenous firms are themselves reluctant to become involved with funding of research in academic institutions, with Irish businesses responsible for only 7 per cent of all R&D spending in Ireland. Moreover, a recent survey for the STIAC report showed that less than one-third of Irish R&D performing companies that responded were involved in a collaborative agreement with the higher education sector, which compares unfavourably with the foreign-based firms that responded, where over 40 per cent had research links with HEIs (see Table 9.6).

TABLE 9.5: EXPENDITURE ON R&D IN THE HIGHER EDUCATION
SECTOR, IR£'000S, 1992

Source	Total	% of Total
HEA Indirect Funds	28,960	40
Direct Government sources	19,797	27
European Commission	12,580	17
Irish Business Sector	5,351	7
Other funds	3,175	4
Foreign sources	2,004	3
Irish Private Funds	1,101	2
Total	72,968	100

Source: STIAC (1995)

TABLE 9.6: NUMBER OF R&D PERFORMING COMPANIES INVOLVED IN
R&D CONSORTIA WITH THE HIGHER EDUCATION SECTOR IN
IRELAND, 1991.

	Yes	No	No Response	Total
Irish	82*	272	125	479
Foreign	45**	106	41	192
Total	127	378	166	671
% Total	18.9 %	56.3 %	24.8%	

* A sectoral breakdown shows that the indigenous sectors best represented
are Food, Drink and Tobacco; Chemicals, Software, and Engineering Services

** A sectoral breakdown shows that the foreign-owned sectors best represented are Electronic Equipment, Fabricated Metal Instruments; Food Drink
and Tobacco, and Chemicals

Source: STIAC (1995)

Thus, there are still considerable gaps in the development of university-industry relationships in Ireland, where the evidence suggests a piecemeal approach to developing closer university-
industry relationships (although as Table 9.4 suggests, the university sector is having some success through patenting and the
development of campus companies). This problem was highlighted
by the recent STIAC (1995) report, which recognised that knowledge is the key to innovation-led development, and much of

modern industry is now 'knowledge-based'. As such, the knowledge-generating system in Irish colleges and universities must be strengthened and it must be ensured that it reaches areas where it will be most productive, especially the small firm sector, which seldom has in-house research resources, but can instead rely on university centres of excellence, such as biotechnology or polymer technology, for problem-solving and advanced level help with innovation.

However, one of the main obstacles to increased co-operation between indigenous industry and the higher education sector in Ireland may stem from the general lack of enterprise culture at all levels of industry and society within Ireland, as highlighted in various reports (World Economic Forum/IMD, 1994; OECD, 1987). This apathy towards enterprise may be especially the case within the higher education sector, where there is little or no tradition of an enterprise culture within universities in Ireland. The STIAC report has suggested a number of measures at university level which may begin to address this problem. These include:

- the adoption of a new research charter by universities which promulgates, for the benefit of all research staff, a proactive attitude towards research activities and, in particular, towards interaction with commercial users of research expertise, and which deal with policies relating to the career prospects of researchers involved in commercial-contract   research

- a campaign to create a greater awareness and understanding throughout the knowledge base of the concept of intellectual property, especially between the knowledge producer and the knowledge user. Indeed, a model should be established between representative bodies of both industry and third-level institutions to deal with this matter

- a formal mechanism to ensure collaboration and co-ordination between the main participants in the STI skills system

- all state-sector and third-level institutions involved in research or technological development should devote sufficient resources to a specific function for technology transfer, aimed at identifying those firms which can benefit from currently available technology

- a third-level/industry understanding, setting out the rights and obligations of industry and institutions in relation to research contracts, should be formulated in order to improve the prospects for increased research collaboration and technology transfer.

These proposed policy changes reflect the concerns of industry in other peripheral regions (Fontes and Coombs, 1994), as discussed earlier, as well as the policies of entrepreneurial universities in more advanced economies where factors such as the positive attitude of both administrators and departmental heads towards non-traditional academic activities, and the development of entrepreneurship courses specifically designed for university scientists and researchers have positively aided the links between university and academia (Klofsten and Jones-Evans, 1996; Albert et al., 1991). When such policies are in operation, it has been seen to be beneficial to both the university and the technology-based venture (Samsom and Gurdon, 1990). It remains to be seen whether Irish universities can develop the right environment in which internal academic entrepreneurship can thrive.[2]

9.6 CONCLUSION

The future competitiveness of peripheral economies in Europe, such as those of Ireland, Portugal and Greece depends, to a large extent, on the development of technologically-innovative sectors. With the absence of strong indigenous medium and large firms, policy-makers have increasingly begun to turn their attention towards small technology-based firms, which have been shown to have made significant contributions to employment, innovation and the competitiveness of technology-intensive sectors within the more advanced economies. However, evidence indicates that there are currently relatively few small technology-based firms in the peripheral regions of Europe, and there is a need for various policy initiatives to stimulate their formation and development. As Fontes (1995) suggests, these must concentrate on addressing critical elements in the creation of small technology-based firms, such as the emergence of technological opportunities, the people with the capacity to identify them, and market opportunities

---

[2] The author is currently co-ordinator of a European Commission research project to examine university-industry relationships within the peripheral regions of Europe — the regions/countries to be studied include the Republic of Ireland, Finland, Sweden, Wales, Scotland, Spain, Portugal and Northern Ireland.

which permit to turn them into a successful business. Any policy intervention, to be effective, must address the root of the problems identified in these areas, namely the supply and demand for technology. With the absence of industrial R&D facilities within many small economies, universities are one of the few sources of technical knowledge and expertise available to industry and to small technology-based firms, although evidence from one peripheral economy, the Republic of Ireland, suggests that many firms choose not to form close links with academia. In addition, there is a general apathy, on the part of universities, to form close links with industry, although this may be associated with the general lack of an enterprise culture within the Irish economy. This is despite recognition by the European Commission White Paper (1993) that one of the major problems facing the growth and competitiveness of European industry, particularly within peripheral regions, is the ability to translate R&D capability within the academic sector into commercial applications.

Future research should examine the mechanisms which exist for transferring technology between university departments and industry. Indeed, as Geisler and Furino (1993) states, there is an urgent need to explore selected dimensions of university-industry relationships in detail, such as technology transfer and knowledge acquisitions, especially their impact on participating organisations. The evidence presented in this paper suggests that this need is imperative within peripheral regions such as Ireland.

References

Acs, Z. J. and Audretsch, D. B. (1988), 'Innovation and firm size in manufacturing', *Technovation,* Vol. 7, pp. 197-210.

Acs, Z. J. and Audretsch, D. B. (1987), 'Innovation, market structure and firm size', *Review of Economics and Statistics,* Vol. 69, pp. 567-75.

Acs, Z. J., FitzRoy, F. and Smith, I. (1995), *High technology employment and university R&D spillovers: Evidence from US cities.* Paper presented at the Babson College-Kauffman Foundation Entrepreneurship Research Conference, London Business School, April.

Albert, P., Fournier, R. and Marion, S. (1991), 'Developing entrepreneurial attitudes and management competence among scientists: the Groupe ESC Lyon's experience', *Entrepreneurship and Regional Development*, Vol. 3, pp. 349-62.

Amin, A. and Goddard, J. B. (1986), *Technological Change, Industrial Restructuring and Regional Development,* London: Allen and Unwin.

Aydalot, P. and Keeble, D. (1988), *High Technology Industry and Innovative Environments — The European Experience,* London: Routledge.

Bradley, J., Whelan, K. and Wright, J. (1993), *Stabilisation and Growth in the EC Periphery,* Aldershot: Avebury.

CASS (1995), *South Wales Technopole Project*, Second Interim Report to the European Commission DGIII/SPRINT, University of Wales College, Cardiff.

Castells, M. and Hall, P. (1994), *Technopoles of the World — The Making of 21st Century Industrial Complexes*, London: Routledge.

Charles, D. and Howells, J. (1992), *Technology Transfer in Europe: Public and Private Networks*, London: Belhaven Press.

Chatterji, D. and Manuel, T. A. (1993), 'Benefiting from external sources of technology', *Research-Technology Management*, Vol. 36, No. 6, pp. 21-26.

Cogan, D. J. (1995) 'Irish New Technology-Based Firms', paper presented at the first Irish Entrepreneurship Research Conference, University College Dublin, November 3rd-4th.

Cooke, P. (1985), 'Regional Innovation Policy: Problems and Strategies in Britain and France', *Environment and Planning C: Government and Policy*, Vol. 3, pp. 253-267.

Cooper, A. C. and Bruno, A. V. (1977), 'Success among high technology firms,' *Business Horizons,* Vol. 20, No. 2, pp. 16-22.

Department of Industry and Commerce (1990), *Review of Industrial Performance*, Dublin: Stationery Office.

Duijnhouwer, A. (1992), *Competitiveness, autonomy and business relationships*, Zoetermeer, Netherlands, Research Institute for Small and Medium Sized Business.

European Commission (1994), *The European Report on Science and Technology Indicators 1994*, Luxembourg: European Commission.

European Commission (1993), *Growth, competitiveness, employment: The challenges and ways forward into the 21st Century — white paper*, Luxembourg: European Commission.

Ewers, H-J and Wettmann, R. W. (1980), 'Innovation-oriented regional policy', *Regional Studies*, Vol. 14, pp. 161-79.

FitzGerald, A. and Breathnach, M. (1994), *Technological Innovation in Irish Manufacturing Industry: Preliminary findings from the Irish Innovation Survey*, Dublin: Evaluation and Statistics Unit, Forfás

Foley, A. and Griffith, B. (1992), 'Indigenous manufacturing enterprises in a peripheral economy and the single market: the case of the Republic of Ireland', *Regional Studies*, Vol. 26 No. 4 pp. 375-386.

Foley, A. and Griffith, B. (1994), Education, training and the promotion of high quality entrepreneurs in the Republic of Ireland, *Proceedings of the 4th Internationalising Education and Training Conference*, Stirling, Scotland.

Fontes, M. (1995), 'New technology based firms and national technological capability: the case of Portugal', Unpublished Ph.D. thesis, University of Manchester Institute of Science & Technology.

Fontes, M. and Coombs, R. (1994), 'NTBFs in less favoured environments: the problem of technology access confronted by Portuguese NTBFs', *Proceedings of the 2nd Annual High Technology Small Firms Conference*, Manchester Business School, 19-20th September.

Frain, P. (1992), 'Multiplicity in action: Co-operation between higher education and industry in Ireland,' *European Journal of Education*, Vol. 27, No. 4, pp. 349-64.

Geisler, E. and Furino, A. (1993), 'University-industry-government co-operation: research horizons,' *International Journal of Technology Management*, Vol. 8, Nos. 6/7/8. pp. 802-11.

Giannisis, D., Willis, R. A. and Maher, N. B. (1991), 'Technology Commercialisation in Illinois' in *University Spin-off Companies: Economic Development, Faculty Entrepreneurs and Technology Transfer* (Eds. Brett, A. M., Gibson, D. V. and Smilor, R. W.), Savage, MD: Rowman and Littlefield Publishers, pp. 197-221.

Gibson, D. V. and Smilor, R. W. (1991), 'The role of the research university in creating and sustaining the US Technopolis' in *University Spin-off Companies: Economic Development, Faculty Entrepreneurs and Technology Transfer* (Eds Brett, A.M., Gibson, D. V. and Smilor, R. W.), Savage, MD: Rowman and Littlefield Publishers, pp. 31-70.

Government of Ireland (1989), *Strategy for the Irish-owned electronics industry*, Dublin: Department of Industry and Commerce.

Green, A. E. and Howells, J. R. (1988), 'Information services and spatial development in the UK economy', *Tijdschrift voor Economische en sociale geografie,* 79, Nr 4, pp. 266-277.

Jones-Evans, D. (1992), 'Technical entrepreneurship in the UK — an examination of the relationship between the previous occupational background of the technical entrepreneur and the management of the small technology-based venture', PhD Dissertation, Aston University.

Jones-Evans, D. and Kirby, D. A. (1994), 'The growth and development of technology-based services in the United Kingdom — the decline of large-scale high-technology manufacturing and the rise of the technical consultant', Durham University Business School Working Paper Series.

Jones-Evans, D. and Westhead, P. (1996), 'High technology small firm sector in the United Kingdom', *International Journal of Entrepreneurial Behaviour and Research*, Vol. 2, No. 1, (forthcoming).

Kennedy, K. A., Giblin, T. and McHugh, D. (1988), *The Economic Development of Ireland in the Twentieth Century*, London: Routledge.

Kinsella, R .P. and McBrierty, V. J. (1994), *Economic Rationale for an Enhanced National Science and Technology Capability*, Dublin: EOLAS.

Kirby, D. A. and Mullen, D. C. (1991), 'Education support for the growth company' in *Recent Research in Entrepreneurship* (Eds. Davies, L. G. and Gibb, A. A.), Aldershot: Avebury, pp. 258-65.

Klofsten, M. (1994), 'Technology-based firms: Critical aspects of their early development', *Journal of Enterprising Culture*, Vol. 2, No. 1, pp. 535-57.

Klofsten, M. and Jones-Evans, D. (1996), 'Stimulation of technology-based small firms — a case study of university-industry co-operation', *Technovation*, Vol. 16, No. 4, pp. 187-193.

Link, A. N. and Rees, J. (1990), 'Firm size, university-based research and the returns to R&D', *Small Business Economics*, Vol. 2, No. 1, pp. 25-32.

Louis, K. S., Blumenthal, D., Gluck, M. E. and Stoto, M. A. (1989), 'Entrepreneurs in Academe — an exploration of behaviours among life scientists', *Administrative Science Quarterly*, Vol. 34, pp. 110-31.

Malecki, E. J. (1991), *Technology and Regional Development,* Harlow: Longman.

Mansfield, E. (1994), 'The contributions of new technology to the economy', presented at the American Enterprise Institute Conference on the Contributions of Research to Economy and Society, Washington, DC, October.

McBrierty, V. and O'Neill, E. (1991), 'The college role in innovation and entrepreneurship: an Irish experience', *International Journal of Technology Management,* Vol. 6, Nos. 5/6, pp. 557-67.

Monck, C. S. P., Porter, R. B., Quintas, P., Storey, D. J. and Wynarczyk, P. (1988), *Science Parks and the Growth of High Technology Firms,* London: Croom Helm.

Moore, I. (1993), 'Government finance for innovation in small firms — the impact of SMART', *International Journal of Technology Management*, Special Issue on small firms and innovation: the external influences, pp. 104-108.

NESC (1993), 'A strategy for competitiveness, growth and employment', Dublin, National Economic and Social Council.

Nijkamp, P. (1986), *Technological change, employment and spatial dynamics*, Berlin: Springer-Verlag.

O'Brien, R. (1985), 'Technology and Industrial Development: the Irish Electronics Industry in an International Context' in *Perspectives on Irish Industry* (Eds. Fitzpatrick, J. and Kelly, J.), Dublin: IMI.

O'Farrell, P.N. (1986), *Entrepreneurs and industrial change: the process of change in Irish manufacturing*, Dublin: IMI.

O'Farrell, P. N. and Crouchley, R. (1984), 'An industrial and spatial analysis of new firm formation in Ireland', *Regional Studies*, Vol. 18, pp. 221-36.

Oakey, R. P. (1991), 'Government policy towards high-technology' in *Paths of Enterprise: The Future for Small Business* (Eds. Curran, J. and Blackburn, R.), London: Routledge, pp. 128-148.

OECD (1987), *Economic Survey — Ireland*, Paris: OECD.

Orsenigo, L. and O'Siuchrú, S. (1991), *Archipelago Europe — Islands of innovation. The cases of Italy and Ireland*, Vol. 20-21, Prospective Dossier No 1, Commission of the European Communities.

Phillips, B. D., Kirchhoff, B. A. and Brown, H. S. (1991), 'Formation, growth and mobility of technology-based firms in the US economy,' *Entrepreneurship and Regional Development*, Vol. 3, pp. 129-144.

Roberts, E. B. (1991), *Entrepreneurs in High Technology: Lessons from MIT and Beyond*, New York: Oxford University Press.

Robson, M. and Townsend, J. (1984), 'Trends and characteristics of significant innovations and their innovators in the UK since 1945', (mimeo) Science Policy Research Unit, University of Sussex, August.

Rothwell, R. (1994) 'The changing nature of the innovation process: implications for SMEs' in *New Technology-based Firms in the 1990s* (Ed. Oakey, R.), London: Paul Chapman, pp. 11-21.

Samson, K. J. and Gurdon, M. A. (1990), 'Entrepreneurial scientists: Organisational performance in scientist started high technology firms' in *Frontiers of Entrepreneurship Research*, Babson College, MA, pp. 437-51.

Saxenian, A. (1994), *Regional Advantage: Culture and Competition in Silicon Valley and Route 128*, Cambridge, MA: Harvard University Press.

Segal, N. (1985), 'The Cambridge Phenomenon,' *Regional Studies*, Vol. 19, No. 6, pp. 563-78.

Smilor, R. W., Gibson, D. V. and Dietrich, G. B. (1990), 'University spin out companies: technology start-ups from UT Austin', *Journal of Business Venturing*, Vol. 5 pp. 63-76.

STIAC (1995), *Making Knowledge Work for us — a strategic view of science, technology and innovation in Ireland,* Dublin: Stationery Office.

Task Force on Small Business (1994), *Task Force on Small Business*, Dublin: Stationery Office.

Tsipouri, L. (1994) 'The Challenge to Less-favoured Regions — Adapting Technology Infrastructure to Improve Absorptive Capabilities of SMEs', European Workshop *Research and Technology Management in Enterprises: Issues for Company Policy*, Brussels, 9 November.

Walsh, J. S. and Anderson, P. H. (1994), 'Education, training and the growth of the owner-managed firm: recent evidence from Ireland. Proceedings of the 4th Internationalising Education and Training Conference, Stirling, Scotland.

Walsh, J. S. and Anderson, P. H. (1995), 'Industrial policy and indigenous small firm employment growth in Ireland: empirical evidence and recommendations', paper presented at the 15th Annual Babson Entrepreneurship Research Conference, London Business School, April 9-13th.

Walsh, V., (1987), 'Technology, Competitiveness and the Special Problems of Small Countries', *STI Review*, Vol. 2, No. 2, pp. 81-133.

Westhead, P. and Storey, D. (1994), *An assessment of firms located on and off science parks in the United Kingdom*, London: HMSO.

Westhead, P. and Storey, D. (1995), 'Links between higher education institutions and high technology firms,' *Omega, International Journal of Management Science*, Vol. 23, No. 4, pp. 345-360.

World Economic Forum/IMD (1994), *World Competitiveness Report,* Geneva, WEF/IMD.

Wynarczyk, P. and Thwaites, A. (1994), 'The financial performance of innovative small firms in the UK'. Proceedings of the 2nd Annual High Technology Small Firms Conference, Manchester Business School, 19-20th September.

10

CROSSBORDER MERGERS AND ACQUISITIONS IN EUROPE: HOST COUNTRY IMPACT AND POLICY

Jim Hamill

10.1 INTRODUCTION

One of the main consequences of the trend towards closer economic co-operation and integration within Europe has been a wave of crossborder mergers and acquisitions (M&As). The years since the late 1980s have witnessed a boom in crossborder takeovers within Europe as companies attempt to strengthen product and geographical market positions in the Single Market. In the period 1989 to 1995, there were more than 6,000 crossborder M&As in Europe valued in excess of £100 billion (*Acquisitions Monthly* various). These included both crossborder deals within the EU and a large number of European acquisitions by non-EU firms.

The host country impact of foreign direct investment has been extensively covered in the literature, with several chapters of this book contributing to the debate concerning whether foreign multinationals are 'good or bad' for host country economies. A major criticism of this literature is its failure to distinguish the economic impact of 'greenfield' FDI from that of FDI which takes the form of external acquisitions of domestic companies. This is a serious omission in the literature for two main reasons. First, crossborder acquisitions have become the dominant mode of FDI. Almost 60 per cent of the increase in FDI flows since 1986 has been accounted for by crossborder takeovers (United Nations, 1994). Second, the balance of positive and negative host country effects will be significantly different in the case of foreign acquisitions compared to 'greenfield' FDI. While the literature points to generally positive effects in the case of the latter, the economic impact of foreign acquisitions is less clear. Particular concerns have been expressed regarding the possible negative effects associated with post-acquisition integration and rationalisation (e.g. employment losses, transfer of HQs functions etc.).

In the context of this book, the most important issue to arise is the impact of the recent boom in crossborder M&As on national competitiveness. In Chapter 3, O'Donnell correctly points out that national competitive advantage cannot be assessed using simple measures of international trade, but rather, must encompass the full range of international business activities, including FDI by MNEs. Dunning's (1992, 1993) extension of Porter's (1990) Diamond Model is used to explain the impact of inward direct investment on national competitiveness. Little recognition is given, however, to the nature of this inward investment; whether 'greenfield' or in the form of external acquisitions of domestically-based companies. This chapter extends the previous discussion of FDI impact by examining the host country effects of the recent boom in international takeovers, based on the experience of the UK. The choice of the UK is particularly relevant given its pole position as the leading target country for crossborder acquisitions in Europe. Over 40 per cent of the total value of all crossborder acquisitions in Europe in recent years have been accounted for by the foreign acquisition of British companies. This has led to public concerns regarding the economic impact of such takeovers and has resulted in demands for a reassessment of current merger control legislation in the UK.

The host country impact of external acquisitions is examined in five main areas including resource transfer effects; impact on market structure, conduct and performance; trade and balance-of-payments effects; employment and sovereignty effects (see Figure 10.1). Each of these areas can have a major impact on the three main measures or dimensions of national competitiveness mentioned by O'Donnell and based on Buckley's (1988a and 1988b) work — competitive performance; competitive potential; and competitive processes. Thus, external acquisitions may impact on competitive performance by changing the export propensity of the newly-acquired subsidiary. Competitive potential will be affected by any changes in the operational efficiency of the subsidiary after acquisition. The introduction of innovative management practices by the new parent company will impact on competitive processes.

10.1.1 Foreign Takeovers in the UK

The full effects of any acquisition will normally take between 3 and 5 years to work through. The chapter, therefore, focuses on foreign acquisitions in the UK up to and including 1992.

The boom in foreign takeovers in the UK from the mid-1980s is shown clearly in Table 10.1. Between 1985 and 1992, foreign companies made a total of 1,278 acquisitions in the UK valued at almost £60 billion. The years 1989 and 1990 were particularly active with a total of 558 deals valued at £31 billion. Many of the UK's largest industrial and commercial companies have passed into foreign ownership as a consequence of being externally acquired, with Table 10.2 showing the 20 largest acquisitions by value. In total, there have been 101 foreign acquisitions, over the period, valued at £100 million or more; with 21 deals in excess of £500m. Public interest has quite naturally focused on these mega-acquisitions. Foreign acquisitions of UK companies, however, have not been confined to such mega-deals. A large number of small and medium-sized (SMEs) British companies have been externally acquired; with some 548 acquisitions (43 per cent of the total) valued at £1 million or less (Table 10.3). This is a legitimate source of concern from an economic impact and policy perspective given the importance attached to SMEs as generators of economic growth.

TABLE 10.1: FOREIGN ACQUISITION IN THE UK: 1985-92

Year	Number of Acquisitions	Acquisition Value (£m)
1985	82	796
1986	102	3950
1987	108	4299
1988	198	8,877
1989	253	17,460
1990	305	13,873
1991	141	4, 478
1992	89	5,642
Total	1,278	59,375

Source: Derived from *Acquisitions Monthly*, various editions.

Competing from the Periphery

TABLE 10.2: TWENTY LARGEST FOREIGN ACQUISITIONS IN THE UK: 1985-92

Acquired Company	Acquiring Company	Nationality of Acquiring Company	Sector	Acq. Value (£m)	Year
Beecham	SmithKline	US	Pharma-ceuticals	4,509	1989
Midland Bank	Hong Kong & Shanghai Bank	Hong Kong	Banking	3,600	1992
Rowntree	Nestlé	Switzer-land	Confectionery	2,622	1988
STC plc	BCI Inc.	Canada	Electronics	1,836	1990
Jaguar	Ford Motor	US	Motors	1,560	1989
Courage	Elders IXL	Australia	Brewing	1,400	1986
Inter-Continental	Saison	Japan	Hotels	1,350	1988
Occidental Petroleum	Elf Aquitaine Oil	France	Mineral Oil and Gas	1,350	1991
Pearl Group	Australian Mutual Provident Society	Australia	Insurance	1,243	1989
Nabisco RJR	BSN	France	Crisps, Snacks, Biscuits	1,064	1989
Reedpack	Svenska Cellulosa	Sweden	Packaging & Paper	1,050	1990
Yorkshire Bank	National Australia Bank	Australia	Banking	977	1990
Morgan Grenfell	Deutsche Bank	Germany	Banking & Fin. Services	950	1989
Smiths/Walkers	Pepsico	US	Potato Crisps	856	1989
Guinness	Louis Vuitton Moët Hennessy	France	Brewing	821	1990
Metalbox Packaging	Carnaud	France	Metal Packaging	780	1988
ICL	Fujitsu Ltd.	Japan	Computers	743	1988
Mount Charlotte	Brierley Investments	New Zealand	Hotels	644	1990
DRG	Pembridge Associates	US	Stationery & Packaging	641	1989
RTZ Chemicals	Rhône-Poulenc	France	Fine Chemicals	568	1989

Source: Derived from *Acquisitions Monthly*, various editions.

TABLE 10.3: FOREIGN ACQUISITIONS IN THE UK BY ACQUISITION
VALUE: 1985-92

	<£1m	£1m <10m	£10m <20m	£20m <50m	£50m <100m	£100m <500m	>£500m
Number of Acquisitions	548	276	128	141	83	80	21
% of Total Number	43	22	10	11	6	6	2
Acquisition Value (£m)	26	1,208	1,816	4,418	5,755	17,047	29,105
% of Total Value	<1	2	3	7	10	29	49

Source: Derived from *Acquisitions Monthly*, various editions.

The nationality-of-ownership distribution of foreign acquirers in
the UK is shown in Table 10.4. US companies have been the most
active acquirers accounting for 22 and 25 per cent respectively of
the total number and value of deals; followed by French (13 per
cent and 16 per cent) and Australian (4 per cent and 9 per cent)
companies. A particularly interesting aspect to note from Table
10.4 is that non-EU based companies have been the most active
foreign acquirers in the UK. Over 70 per cent of the total value of
all foreign acquisitions in the UK during the period covered have
been accounted for by non-EU firms. For many of these companies, UK acquisitions have been used as a 'beach head' into European markets in the run-up to '1992'.

Finally, in terms of industry distribution, foreign acquisitions
in the UK have occurred across a wide range of sectors, both
manufacturing and non-manufacturing (Table 10.5). Almost half
of the total value of all deals, however, is accounted for by just
three sectors — banking, insurance and financial services; food
and drink; and chemicals.

TABLE 10.4: FOREIGN ACQUISITIONS IN THE UK BY NATIONALITY OF ACQUIRING FIRM: 1985-92

Nationality	Number of Acquisitions	% of Total Number of Acquisitions	Acquisition Value (£m)	% of Total Acquisition Value
Non-EC				
US	279	22	14,787	25
Australia	55	4	5,505	9
Hong Kong*	17	1	3,862	7
Switzerland	51	4	3,762	6
Sweden	85	7	3,699	6
Japan	58	5	3,318	6
Canada	29	2	3,107	5
New Zealand	11	1	1,715	3
South Africa	15	1	835	1
Other Non-EC	155	11	2,083	4
All Non-EC	738	58	42,673	72
EC				
France	167	13	9,330	16
Germany	83	6	2,634	4
Netherlands	70	5	1,891	3
Eire	128	10	1,342	2
Belgium	17	1	768	1
Denmark	33	3	419	1
Italy	26	2	192	---
Spain	10	1	149	---
Luxembourg	6	---	97	---
Portugal	2	---	10	---
Greece	---	---	---	---
All EC	542	42	16,641	28
Total	1,278	100	59,375	100

* Most of this value due to one acquisition of £3.6 billion, i.e. Hong Kong & Shanghai Bank's takeover of Midland.

Source: Derived from *Acquisitions Monthly*, various editions.

TABLE 10.5: FOREIGN ACQUISITIONS IN THE UK BY INDUSTRY: 1985-92

Sector	Number of Acquisitions	% of Total Number of Acquisitions	Acquisition Value (£m)	% of Total Acquisition Value
a) Manufacturing				
Food, drink & tobacco	69	5	9,497	16
Chemicals & pharmaceuticals	71	6	6,878	12
Paper, printing & publishing	135	11	4,048	7
Electrical & electronic engineering	108	8	4,023	7
Vehicle manufacturing	52	4	2,032	3
Mechanical engineering	83	6	1,608	3
Other manufacturing	114	8	2,676	5
Total manufacturing	632	48	30,762	53
b) Services				
Banking, insurance & finance	168	13	13,384	23
Hotels & catering	34	3	2,457	4
Management & marketing services	78	6	1,713	3
Wholesale distribution & transport	148	12	1,956	3
Retail distribution	23	2	848	1
Other services	44	4	2,311	4
Total services	495	40	22,669	38
c) Water & Energy				
(Oil & gas)	49	49	2,963	5
Construction	12	12	83	0
Other	90	90	2,898	5
All Industries	1,278	100	59,375	100

10.2 IMPACT OF FOREIGN ACQUISITIONS IN THE UK

While the economic impact of 'greenfield' FDI on the UK has been extensively covered in the literature (Dunning, 1958, 1976 and 1986; Steuer et al., 1973; Brech and Sharp, 1984; Stopford and Turner, 1985; Panić and Joyce, 1980; Panić 1991; Hood and Young, 1976, 1982, 1983, 1984; Hood, Young and Hamill, 1988), very little work has been done on the impact of inward acquisitions. What little there is largely predates the recent boom in foreign take-overs in the UK (e.g. Hood and Young, 1983). There has been some related work which has examined the impact of external acquisitions on regional economies within the UK. The foreign-owned dimension, however, has not been specifically examined in these studies (Ashcroft, 1988; Ashcroft and Love, 1988, 1990 and 1993; Ashcroft, Love and Scouller, 1987; Coppins, 1989; Hughes, 1989; Leigh and North, 1978; Smith 1979 and 1982).

The literature on the host country impact of 'greenfield' FDI can be used to develop a framework for evaluating the impact of external acquisitions. The host country impact of 'greenfield' subsidiaries is normally examined in five main areas covering resource-transfer effects; impact on market structure, conduct and performance; trade and balance-of-payments effects; employment; and sovereignty effects (see Hood, Young and Hamill, 1988). These can be used as a basis for hypothesising concerning the impact of foreign acquisitions. Figure 10.1 summarises the range of potential positive and negative effects of foreign acquisitions in the UK in each of the five areas. Thus, foreign acquisitions in the UK would have positive effects when:

- new or advanced technology is transferred to the recently acquired subsidiary

- new management practices are introduced in the areas of finance, marketing, human resources etc.

- the subsidiary gains access to new sources of capital

- the acquisition overcomes market-entry barriers; reduces industry-concentration levels; and stimulates competition

- subsidiary exports are increased through gaining access to wider international distribution channels and the introduction of new products

- as a consequence of the above (increased exports; new technology etc.), both the level and quality of employment is enhanced and labour relations are improved

- the recently acquired subsidiary is given enhanced decision-making responsibility, perhaps as a European Regional HQ.

There are, of course, opposing scenarios in each of these areas. Thus, negative effects would occur when:

- technology transfers are limited and there is a loss of indigenous technology capability through the centralisation of R&D

- the introduction of new management practices leads to conflict between parent and subsidiary

- access to funding is restricted

- the acquisition strengthens the existing UK market position of the foreign acquirer, thereby increasing industry concentration and reducing competition

- the newly acquired subsidiary is allocated a restricted product/market status thereby reducing exports

- post-acquisition rationalisation leads to major job losses and reduced job security

- there is a significant transfer of head office functions from subsidiary to parent resulting in the loss of decision-making autonomy.

FIGURE 10.1: POTENTIAL EFFECTS OF FOREIGN ACQUISITIONS IN THE UK

Impact	Positive Effects	Negative Effects
Resource Transfer	• Transfer of new technology from acquiring to acquired company • Transfer of new management practices • Acquired company gains access to new sources of capital	• Access to new technology restricted • Centralisation of R&D at parent company leading to loss of indigenous technology capability • Capital funding restricted to reinvested earnings

Trade and Balance-of-Payments Effects	• Capital account gain through initial purchase price • Increased exports through access to international distribution channels and international marketing knowledge of parent • UK subsidiary granted wide product/geographical market mandate, e.g. Europe	• Subsequent repatriation of profits, royalties, interest, etc. • Increased imports of intermediary products from other subsidiaries/parent company • Subsidiary role restricted to UK market/narrow product line
Market Structure, Conduct and Performance	• Acquisition stimulates competition through breaking existing oligopoly • Improved efficiency and performance through transfer of resources (as above) and competitive reaction of rivals • Increased international competitiveness	• Acquisition strengthens existing market position of acquirer and increases industry concentration • Further increase in industry concentration through rival acquisitions
Employment Effects	• Increased employment and job security as a consequence of higher exports, wide product/market mandate, etc. • Improved quality of employment through technology transfers, international marketing responsibilities, etc.	• Large-scale job losses as consequence of post-acquisition rationalisation; reduced job security • Lower quality of employment due to restricted role of subsidiary
Sovereignty and Autonomy Effects	• Transfer of some HQ functions to acquired company	• Loss of autonomy through transfer of HQ functions to new parent

Source: The author.

The above list covers mainly the first-order effects of an inward acquisition. There will, however, be important second-order effects associated with foreign takeovers. For example, the foreign acquisition of a UK company may result in reduced local linkages as the newly-acquired subsidiary becomes integrated with the global or Euro-wide strategy of the acquirer. Important second-order effects may arise, too, in terms of the impact of the acquisition on indigenous companies. Where a foreign acquisition stimulates competition, this may be expected to lead to improved efficiency. On the other hand, a foreign acquisition which results in a dominant market position may have adverse effects on indigenous companies who lack the scale economies necessary to compete with the new industry leader. Finally, it is worth noting that the balance between positive and negative effects may differ considerably depending on the motivations underlying the acquisition. Hamill (1993) explained the boom in crossborder mergers and acquisitions since the mid-1980s as an attempt by TNCs to create a sustainable competitive advantage in industries which were becoming increasingly global or regional in scope. Two main types of competitive advantage can be sought through crossborder acquisitions; first, acquisitions which seek to strengthen product and geographical market portfolios; second, acquisitions which seek to achieve lower costs and greater efficiency through resource sharing and scale economies. Clearly, elements of both may be present in any specific deal since acquisitions are multi- rather than uni-causal (Hamill, 1993).

The importance of this distinction between acquisitions which are primarily product/market expansion-driven and those which are cost/efficiency-driven is that the nature of post-acquisition change, and therefore the economic impact of the acquisition, may differ radically. Foreign acquisitions in the UK which are primarily cost/efficiency-driven are likely to have greater negative effects than those which are product/market expansion-driven. The former is likely to be accompanied by significant post-acquisition rationalisation and integration leading to major job losses, reduced subsidiary status, the transfer of HQ functions out of the UK and so on. In product/market expansion-driven acquisitions, on the other hand, the UK company acquired may play a much more important role in the overall international market development of the new parent company.

10.3 METHODOLOGY

In order to examine the economic impact issues identified in the previous section, a postal questionnaire was sent to a large sample of British companies externally acquired since 1985. A total of 325 companies were surveyed, covering all acquisitions valued at £20 million or more (see Table 10.3). Thirty-eight companies replied that the survey was inappropriate, mainly because there had been a further change in ownership since the original acquisition. From the 287 remaining companies, a total of 73 completed questionnaires were returned giving a response rate of 25 per cent. Given the highly sensitive nature of the topic, this was a very satisfactory response level. The respondent companies were highly representative of the total population by sector, nationality of acquirer, date and value of acquisition (see Table 10.6). Over 90 per cent of the acquisitions examined were described as being friendly rather than hostile takeovers. Again this is representative of acquisitions in general. Despite the extensive media coverage of hostile deals, the vast majority of acquisitions are friendly takeovers.

TABLE 10.6A: SAMPLE CHARACTERISTICS

Year of Acquisition	Number of Companies	% of Sample
1985	3	4
1986	6	8
1987	4	5
1988	7	10
1989	18	25
1990	19	26
1991	12	16
1992	4	5
Total	73	100

TABLE 10.6B: SAMPLE CHARACTERISTICS

Nationality of Acquirer	Number of Companies	% of Sample
France	18	25
US	13	18
Germany	9	13
Japan	6	8
Australia	4	6
Sweden	4	6
Finland	3	4
Others	16	20
Total	73	100

TABLE 10.6C: NUMBER AND PER CENT OF SAMPLE COMPANIES BY
ACQUISITION VALUE

	£20<50m	£50<100m	£100<200m	>£200m
Number of Companies	43	10	12	8
% of Sample	59	14	16	11

TABLE 10.6D: SECTORAL DISTRIBUTION

	Number of Companies	% of Sample
Oil, gas, mining water utilities	7	10
Manufacturing	37	51
Non-Manufacturing	29	40
Total	73	100

TABLE 10.6E: NATURE OF ACQUISITION

	Number of Companies	% of Sample
Friendly	67	92
Hostile Bid	6	8
Total	73	100

Source: Postal Survey

The questionnaire itself was divided into five main sections covering background information on the company and the acquisition
(company name, principal activities, year of acquisition, acquisition value, nationality of acquirer, friendly or hostile takeover, pre-
acquisition and current sales, pre-tax profits, exports and employment); acquisition motivations (with a list of motivating factors being presented derived from the acquisition literature — see
Hamill, 1992); post-acquisition change covering subsidiary product strategy, R&D, export volume and export markets supplied,
imports, technology transfers, capital investment, changes in employment levels and personnel; the locus of post-acquisition decision-making covering financial, production, marketing, personnel

and R&D decisions; finally, general comments covering post-acquisition integration and performance.

Before summarising the main findings of the survey it should be noted that there are a number of methodological problems in attempting to assess the economic impact of takeovers. These have been examined in detail by Ashcroft and Love (1993) and include the appropriate balance between quantitative (financial ratios) and qualitative (structural changes in products/markets supplied, etc.) measures; data sources (e.g. company reports, postal surveys, company interviews, etc.); the choice of indicators; the time-period covered and so on. A particular problem is the counterfactual difficulty of distinguishing between 'what happened after the acquisition' and 'what happened because of it'. Clearly these difficulties apply to the research reported here. The postal survey was the first of a two-stage research programme evaluating acquisition impact; and will be followed-up with detailed personal interviews with the companies concerned. The counterfactual position was at least partly established by asking respondents to explain why certain post-acquisition changes had taken place in order to assess whether they were a direct consequence of the takeover per se.

10.3.1 Acquisition Impact: Survey Results

As stated previously, acquisition impact may vary significantly with acquisition motivations (e.g. product/market expansion v. cost/efficiency-driven acquisitions). Before presenting the main findings of the survey concerning acquisition impact, the motivations underlying foreign acquisitions in the UK need to be examined. These are summarised in Table 10.7. The results support the proposition advanced earlier that the boom in crossborder mergers and acquisitions since the mid-1980s has been a consequence of the attempt by MNEs to improve their competitive position in increasingly global markets. For foreign acquisitions in the UK, 76 per cent of the companies surveyed stated that improving international competitiveness was a 'very important' or 'important' reason underlying the acquisition. This increases to 83 per cent for the non-EU-based firms surveyed. Table 10.7 also shows that product/market expansion-driven acquisitions were more common than cost/efficiency-driven acquisitions. A much higher proportion of the sample companies claimed that factors such as 'extending geographical market coverage in Europe'; 'acquiring market share'; 'product/market diversification', and 'acquiring products, brands, marketing and management skills' were important motivating factors compared to cost/efficiency motivations such as economies of scale in marketing, distribution, R&D, production and HQ activities. The relative importance of product/market expansion motivations needs to be borne in mind when considering the results presented below.

TABLE 10.7: ACQUISITION MOTIVATIONS (CITED AS VERY IMPORTANT/IMPORTANT)

	% of Total Sample	% of EC Acquirers	% of Non-EC Acquirers
Improve international competitiveness	76	68	83
Extend geographical market coverage in Europe	73	78	66
Acquire large market-share in UK	69	73	60
Product/market diversification	67	59	74
Gain foothold in UK market	65	73	60
Gain access to management/ marketing skills	61	58	60
Acquire products or brands	59	51	60
Achieve instant growth	56	68	40
Strategic response to competitors' actions	55	54	51
Acquire large market-share in EC	51	54	46
Gain access to technology	47	51	43
Gain foothold in the EC	46	49	43
Economies of scale in mktg/dist.	43	38	46
Increase short-term profits	42	49	31
Economies of scale in R&D	36	41	29
Exchange-rate influences	34	22	9
Acquire undervalued assets	28	27	26
Economies of scale in production	26	19	31
Increase share price	26	35	11
Acquire a competitor	22	16	29
HQ economies of scale	16	16	11
Other economies of scale	11	8	6

Source: Postal Survey

The following sub-sections present the main findings of the survey covering the five impact areas identified earlier. The sections draw from Tables 10.8a and 10.8b which provide a concise summary of the main findings.

TABLE 10.8A: POST-ACQUISITION CHANGE: SUMMARY TABLE

	% of Sample				
	Significant Increase	*Some Increase*	*No Change*	*Some Reduction*	*Significant Reduction*
R&D Expenditure	14	25	52	5	4
Product Range	14	33	13	11	29
Export Markets Supplied	17	28	45	6	4
Export Volume	13	31	48	4	4
Import Volume	12	26	59	2	2
Employment Levels	4	16	12	30	37

TABLE 10.8B: PER CENT OF SAMPLE CLAIMING SIGNIFICANT CHANGE IN SELECTED AREAS

	Yes	*No*
Technology transfer	40	61
Management practices transfer	55	45
Capital transfers	44	56
Executive changes	69	31
Market structure changes	45	55
Personnel and industrial relations practices	58	42

Source: Postal Survey.

Resource Transfer Effects

Figure 10.1 identified a range of potential positive and negative resource transfer effects associated with the foreign takeover of British companies. The results of the survey support net overall benefits in this area, particularly in terms of increased subsidiary R&D and technology transfer.

Thirty-nine per cent of the sample companies claimed a 'significant' or 'some' increase in UK R&D expenditure post-acquisition. This increases to 47 per cent in the case of manufacturing companies. Only 9 per cent of the sample (2 per cent of the manufacturing companies surveyed) stated a post-acquisition reduction in subsidiary R&D. Therefore, the evidence does not support the often expressed fear that foreign acquisitions in the UK will lead to a loss of indigenous technology capability through the transfer of R&D activity to the new parent company. Indeed, the evidence supports the opposite case, with 40 per cent of the sample (Table 8b) reporting significant transfers of technology from the new parent company to the UK subsidiary post-acquisition. This increases to 51 per cent for manufacturing companies.

In addition to increased subsidiary R&D expenditure and technology transfer, other resource transfer effects associated with foreign acquisitions in the UK include the transfer of management practices and capital. As regards the former, 55 per cent of the sample stated that new management practices had been transferred post-acquisition (Table 10.8b). This increases to 61 per cent for the manufacturing companies surveyed. The areas in which management practices were transferred were wide-ranging including financial reporting and planning procedures; quality control techniques; new product development and production planning; distribution and logistics systems; communication procedures; and management culture. Regarding capital transfers, 44 per cent of the sample (45 per cent of the manufacturing firms surveyed) had received a significant injection of capital investment post-acquisition.

The general conclusion emerging from the evidence presented above is that the resource transfer effects of foreign acquisitions in the UK have been in many cases positive, and in others neutral. In very few cases has the resource transfer impact been negative. It is worth noting, however, that there are significant variations in the results by nationality of ownership of the acquiring company. Forty-nine per cent of the non-EU-based acquiring companies, compared to only 30 per cent of EU-based parents, claimed a 'significant' or 'some' increase in R&D post-acquisition. For management and capital transfers the respective percentages were 60 and 57 per cent for non-EU-based parents compared to 51 and 32 per cent for EU firms. Thus, the positive resource transfer effects are greatest in non-EU acquisitions of UK companies. Such nationality of ownership differences are examined in more detail later.

Trade and Balance-of-payments Effects

As in the case of resource transfer effects discussed above, both positive and negative hypotheses can be established concerning the trade and balance-of-payments effects of foreign acquisitions in the UK. These relate to the nature and extent of post-acquisition integration of the newly-acquired subsidiary into the overall global operations of the new parent company (see Figure 1). Positive trade effects would arise when increased subsidiary exports result from access to the wider international distribution channels of the new parent and/or the UK subsidiary is granted a wide product/geographical market mandate. Negative effects would arise from increased imports of intermediary products and in cases where the newly-acquired UK subsidiary is granted a narrow product/geographical market mandate.

Several questions in the survey addressed these issues covering changes in the product role of the subsidiary post-acquisition, export volume and markets supplied, and subsidiary imports. The empirical evidence highlights significant changes in each of these areas post-acquisition (i.e. significant changes in product/market responsibilities). For example, only 13 per cent of the companies surveyed stated that the acquisition had no effect on the product role of the UK subsidiary. By contrast, 47 per cent stated that there had been a 'significant' or 'some' increase in the product range of the subsidiary post-acquisition, with 40 per cent claiming a 'significant' or 'some' decrease. The evidence, therefore, highlights important subsidiary product role changes post-acquisition. Concerning export markets, 45 per cent of the sample stated a broadening of geographical markets supplied, compared to only 10 per cent stating a narrowing of geographical focus. As a consequence, 44 per cent of the sample claimed a 'significant' or 'some' increase in export volume post-acquisition, compared to only 8 per cent stating a 'significant' or 'some' reduction in exports. The survey estimated the direct impact of these changes on the total value of exports in the sample companies. The post-acquisition value of exports in the 73 companies was £623 million compared to pre-acquisition exports of £458 million, i.e. an increase of 36 per cent in value terms.

As in the case of resource transfer effects examined in the previous section, the evidence presented above supports net benefits overall in terms of the trade and balance-of-payments impact of foreign acquisitions in the UK; especially in terms of increased export volume and access to wider geographical markets. There are, however, two main qualifications to this conclusion. First, the increase in subsidiary export propensity post-acquisition must be balanced against a much higher import propensity. Thirty-eight per cent of the companies surveyed claimed a 'significant' or 'some' increase in post-acquisition imports compared to only 4 per cent stating a decrease. This is consistent with post-acquisition integration of the UK subsidiary into the wider global operations of the parent company and implies reduced local linkages. Second, there were significant variations in the results discussed above by nationality of ownership of the acquiring company. As in the previous section, the trade and balance-of-payments effects of foreign acquisitions in the UK were generally more favourable in the case of non-EU-based acquirers compared to EU companies. Forty-nine per cent of non-EU acquirers claimed a 'significant' or 'some' increase in export markets supplied post-acquisition, compared to only 28 per cent for EU acquirers. In terms of export volume, 57 per cent of non-EU acquirers claimed a 'significant' or 'some' increase post-acquisition compared to only 31 per cent of EU acquirers. This is consistent with the UK acquisition being used to gain entry into EU markets. For imports, 36 per cent of non-EU firms, compared to 40 per cent for EU firms claimed an increase. Thus, it may be concluded that UK acquisitions by non-EU firms have generally positive effects on UK trade; the opposite is the case for EU acquisitions of UK companies.

Market Structure, Conduct and Performance Effects
A detailed analysis of the market structure effects of the recent wave of foreign acquisitions in the UK is largely beyond the scope of this paper since this would require an in-depth study of changing industry concentration levels. In order to gather some preliminary evidence, however, respondents were asked to state whether there had been any significant change in the competitive structure of their UK industry in recent years as a consequence of mergers and acquisitions. Forty-four per cent of the sample claimed that significant changes in market structure had taken place. The two principal changes identified were, first, increased competition from non-UK based companies as a consequence of foreign acquisitions in the UK (especially in the water supply,

electronics and financial services industries) and second, an increase in industry concentration levels as a consequence of M&As (especially in chemicals, financial services, publishing, food and drinks).

Employment and Related Effects

The employment and related effects of foreign acquisitions in the UK have become an issue of major concern given the persistence of high UK unemployment.

As in previous sections, both positive and negative propositions can be advanced in terms of employment impact. Negative employment level effects would arise from post-acquisition production rationalisation and from the transfer of certain functions out of the UK. On the other hand, to the extent that the foreign acquisition widens export distribution channels (see earlier), total employment levels may increase post-acquisition. Foreign acquisitions of UK companies may have other significant employment effects on UK managers and workers through changes in executive personnel post-acquisition and the transfer of parent company personnel and industrial relations practices.

Regarding employment level effects, two-thirds (67 per cent) of the companies surveyed reported a 'significant' or 'some' decline in employment levels post-acquisition. Total pre-acquisition employment in the sample was 101,826 employees compared to 91,061 employees currently, i.e. an 11 per cent reduction in employment pre- and post-acquisition. Leaving aside the 20 per cent of firms who reported 'some' increase in employment, the 47 firms reporting an employment decline recorded job losses from 80,087 to 70,653 employees; i.e. a reduction of 12 per cent. Clearly not all of these job losses were a direct consequence of the acquisition 'per se', with other causes being the recession, technology change and so on. It was clear from the explanations given that approximately 80 per cent of the jobs lost were a direct consequence of post-acquisition rationalisation. The conclusion to be drawn from the above results, therefore, is that foreign acquisitions in the UK have, in general, a net negative effect on employment levels. There was only minor variations by nationality of acquirer. Seventy-two per cent of EU based acquirers compared to 63 per cent of non-EU based acquirers reported employment losses.

Regarding the other employment and related effects identified earlier, foreign acquisitions of UK companies are generally accompanied by major changes in executive personnel post-acquisition. Sixty-nine per cent of the sample reported major changes in this area. In the majority of cases, this involved the appointment of new senior executives (often from the parent company) and non-executive directors, across a range of functional areas. The survey also highlighted significant transfers of personnel and industrial relations practices post-acquisition. Fifty-eight per cent of the companies surveyed reported 'significant' or 'some' transfers in this area with the main reason given to achieve standardisation of practices across subsidiaries.

Sovereignty and Autonomy Effects

A major concern relating to the boom in foreign takeovers of UK companies is the potential loss of national sovereignty associated with the transfer of decision-making power out of the UK. The survey examined the locus of post-acquisition decision-making across a range of functional areas with the results summarised in Table 10.9. Clearly, UK companies which have been externally acquired are granted a large degree of decision-making autonomy in terms of day-to-day operational issues covering production, marketing and personnel decisions. A much higher level of centralisation is evident in financial decision-making, consistent with the transfer of long-term strategic control out of the UK. R&D decisions were also centralised in a significant proportion of the companies surveyed.

10.4 DISCUSSION OF RESULTS

The problems involved in attempting to evaluate the host country impact of external acquisitions were discussed earlier. With these in mind, the evidence derived from the postal survey at least allows some preliminary conclusions to be drawn concerning the economic impact of foreign acquisitions in the UK and these are summarised below.

The survey highlighted a mix of positive and negative effects. There was little evidence to support fears that foreign takeovers will lead to a loss of indigenous technological capability. Only 9 per cent of companies (2 per cent of manufacturing companies) reported a reduction in post-acquisition R&D expenditure. A significant proportion of the sample (40 per cent overall and 51 per cent for manufacturing companies) reported an increase in R&D expenditure post-acquisition. The position regarding other resource transfer effects (management practices, capital) was also generally positive.

Probably the most important area of impact concerns changing subsidiary product/geographical market roles post-acquisition. The evidence highlights significant post-acquisition integration of acquired UK subsidiaries into the overall global operations of the new parent, resulting in major changes in products and markets supplied. The positive trade and balance-of-payments effects associated with the subsequent increase in export volume need to be balanced against increased imports of intermediary products and reduced local linkages. The most significant negative effects of foreign acquisitions relate to post-acquisition employment losses (some) loss of decision-making autonomy and increased industry concentration levels.

Significant variations emerged in acquisition impact by nationality of ownership. Generally, UK acquisitions by non-EU firms have a more favourable (less negative) effect than acquisitions by EU-based firms. These differences are related to the initial motivations underlying the acquisition. For non-EU-based companies, UK acquisitions have acted as a major channel for establishing market share in the Single European Market. As argued earlier, such product/market expansion-driven acquisitions may have positive effects if the acquired UK operation is given an important role to play in the overall European strategy of the parent company. This is much less likely in the case of UK acquisitions by EU-based firms which are more cost/efficiency-driven. Such acquisitions will have certain negative effects on the UK particularly concerning increased imports and employment losses.

10.5 POLICY IMPLICATIONS

Previous sections of this paper have shown that the boom in foreign takeovers of British companies since the mid-1980s raises important issues concerning the impact of external ownership on the UK economy. The results of the survey highlight a mix of both positive and negative impacts. These are of sufficient magnitude that the overall net impact of external acquisitions should be a legitimate area of concern for policy-makers. This, however, has not been reflected in the conduct of UK merger policy which has been characterised by an almost total lack of concern with the effects of external acquisitions. There is a residual power under the Industry Act (1972) to block foreign takeovers of UK companies of strategic importance (e.g. national security and defence) and this has been invoked on a few occasions (e.g. Westland Helicopters). Generally, however, the issue of foreign ownership has not been in the forefront of the debate on merger control in the UK.

Three main phases in the evolution of UK merger policy relevant to the debate on the impact of external acquisitions can be identified. Prior to the early 1980s, the public interest criteria predominated. The Monopolies and Mergers Commission assessed proposed mergers referred to it by the Secretary of State on the grounds of whether the merger would operate against the public interest. The latter was defined in extremely broad terms to include the potential impact of the proposed merger on competition and on consumers in terms of the price, quality and variety of goods available; questions of industrial efficiency, costs, technology and international competitiveness; employment and related effects; and issues concerning the regional distribution of industry.

This broad definition of the public interest was both a strength and a weakness of UK merger policy during the 1970s. The major strength was that it allowed a detailed investigation to be made of all aspects of the proposed merger taking into account both macro- and micro-economic effects. The major weaknesses were the length of time taken to investigate proposed deals (six to nine months on average) and the absence of clearly defined criteria on when a deal was or was not against the public interest. By the early 1980s, UK merger policy had degenerated into a confusion of ad hoc and inconsistent precedents. This led to the second main phase in policy evolution namely, the 'Tebbit dictum' under which the sole criteria for assessing mergers became their impact on competition. For most of the last decade or so, proposed mergers have been defined as being against the public interest only when they restrict, distort or prevent competition. This reflects the Conservative government's belief in the benefits of free competition and the use of market forces over government intervention. The main strength of this policy is its clarity and certainty deriving from an unambiguous definition of the public interest as being equal to competition. The main weakness is the almost total lack of attention paid to the wider macro- and micro-economic effects of mergers and acquisitions, including questions of foreign ownership.

The third main phase in the evolution of UK merger policy has been imposed externally. As a member of the EU, the UK is subject to EU merger control procedures which require that all proposed deals with a 'Community dimension' have to be notified to the European Commission for approval before they are put into effect. Included in the definition of 'Community dimension' are mergers and acquisitions where the companies involved have worldwide sales of ECU 5,000 million (approximately US $6,000 million); at least two of the groups to which the companies involved belong have sales in the European Community of ECU 250 million (approximately US $300 million); and the companies involved do significant business in more than one EC Member State. Companies achieving more than two-thirds of their EU sales in one Member State are exempt from the legislation, since these cases are considered essentially national in character. The legislation covers both cross-border acquisitions within the EU and EU acquisitions by non-EU firms. More contentiously, the legislation also covers mergers and acquisitions between two non-EU firms. For example, a merger or acquisition between two US companies would have to be notified to the Commission if either had more than ECU 250 million sales within the EU. As in the UK, the dominant criteria used by the EU in evaluating mergers and acquisitions is their effects on competition. A deal will only be prohibited when it 'strengthens a dominant position as a result of which effective competition in the market would be impeded'.

It can be concluded from the above review of UK and EU merger policy that the question of external acquisition of UK companies has not been a major concern of policy-makers and that existing merger control legislation is inadequate to deal with the issue. The concerns raised earlier in this paper indicate that this is a serious weakness in current UK merger policy and that there may be a strong case for a more proactive approach — one which would lead to a more detailed evaluation of the economic impact of foreign acquisitions in the UK. At least four main arguments can be advanced for this approach: First, the scale of the phenomena, with a total of 1,278 British companies being externally acquired in the last eight years valued at £60 billion. Second, the fact that over 40 per cent of the total value of all cross-border acquisitions in Europe is accounted for by the foreign acquisition of UK companies reflecting an 'unlevel playing field' which puts British companies at a major disadvantage in attempting to establish the scale necessary for competitiveness in the Single European Market. Third, the fact that foreign acquisitions may have certain detrimental effects on the UK economy, especially in the case of acquisitions by EU-based firms. Finally, while the volume of foreign takeovers has declined significantly over the last year or so in line with the recession and the slump in the acquisition market generally, this is likely to be only a temporary interruption. The continuing globalisation of markets and competition and the trend towards further European integration are likely to lead to a further upsurge in activity over the next few years. As a consequence key British enterprises and sectors of the UK economy could pass into foreign ownership without any attempt to assess the net effects of such deals on the UK.

The need for a reassessment of current policy was clearly illustrated at the end of January, 1994 with the announcement of BMW's £800 million takeover of the UK's only remaining volume car producer, the Rover Group. The takeover was warmly welcomed by the UK government as being evidence of the confidence of foreign investors in the UK economy. No account was taken of the fact that the economic impact of inward direct investment in the form of acquisitions may be radically different from that of greenfield FDI. Given the strategic importance of Rover to the UK engineering industry, it is surprising that no attempt was made to assess the long-term economic impact of the acquisition.

There is a strong case, therefore, for a change in UK government policy in relation to foreign acquisitions of British companies. As to the type of policy to be introduced, however, the government's room for manoeuvre is severely limited by policy at an EU-wide level. In addition, returning to the pre-1980 (see earlier) position is not a solution given the problems in defining 'public interest' criteria and the time involved in investigating proposed deals. Moreover, the introduction of tight controls might lead to retaliatory measures being imposed on British acquirers abroad. At a very minimum, the government should encourage foreign acquirers in the UK to make public their short- and long-term plans for the newly acquired subsidiary. This would at least lead to some degree of public debate and accountability in the post-acquisition period.

10.6 CONCLUSIONS

The argument advanced above should not be interpreted as one in favour of autarky or for imposing stringent controls on foreign ownership. Rather, it is based on a realistic assessment that a continuation of past trends in foreign acquisitions could have a profound effect on the future, long-term well-being of the British economy. This should be a legitimate area of concern for policy makers. In the context of this book, there is an urgent requirement for further empirical-based studies which evaluate the long-run effects of external acquisitions on the international competitiveness of UK industry.

References

Acquisitions Monthly, The Merger and Acquisition Magazine, various editions.

Ashcroft, B. (1988), 'External Takeovers in Scottish Manufacturing: The Effects on Local Linkages and Corporate Functions', *Scottish Journal of Political Economy*, Vol. 35.

Ashcroft, B. and Love, J. H. (1988), 'The Regional Interest in UK Mergers Policy', *Regional Studies*, Vol. 22.

Ashcroft, B. and Love, J. H. (1990), *Corporate Takeovers and the Interests of Regions and Local Communities*, Hume Occasional Paper No. 17, David Hume Institute, Edinburgh.

Ashcroft, B. and Love, J. H. (1993), *Takeovers, Mergers and the Regional Economy*, Scottish Industrial Policy Series 5, Edinburgh University Press.

Ashcroft, B., Love, J. H. and Scouller, J. (1987), *The Economic Effects of the Inward Acquisition of Scottish Manufacturing Companies 1965 to 1980*, ESU Research Paper No. 11, Industry Department for Scotland, Edinburgh.

Brech, M. and Sharp, M. (1984), *Inward Investment: Policy Options for the UK*, Chatham House Papers 21, London: Routledge and Kegan Paul.

Buckley, P. J., Pass, C. L. and Prescott, K. (1988a), 'Measures of international competitiveness: A critical survey', *Journal of Marketing Management*, Vol. 4, No. 2, pp. 175-200.

Buckley, P. J., Pass, C. L. and Prescott, K. (1988b), 'Measures of international competitiveness: Empirical findings from British manufacturing companies', *Journal of Marketing Management*, Vol. 6, No. 1, pp. 1-13.

Coppins, B. (1989), 'The Spatial Dimension of Takeovers and Geographical Transfer of Corporate Control: Evidence from the UK, 1968-85', Mimeo, Department of Economics and Financial Studies, Napier Polytechnic.

Dunning, J. H. (1958), *American Investment in British Manufacturing Industry*, London: Allen and Unwin.

Dunning, J. H. (1976), *US Industry in Britain*, EAG Business Research Study, London: Wilton House.

Dunning, J. H. (1986), *Japanese Participation in British Industry*, London: Croom Helm.

Dunning, J. H. (1992), 'The competitive advantage of countries and the activities of transnational corporations', *Transnational Corporations*, Vol. 1, No. 1, February, pp. 135-168.

Dunning, J. H. (1993), 'Internationalizing Porter's diamond', *Management International Review*, Vol. 33, special issue 1993/2, pp. 7-17.

Hamill, J. (1992), 'Crossborder Mergers, Acquisitions and Alliances in Europe' in *Europe and the Multinationals: Issues and Responses for the 1990s* (Eds. Young, S. and Hamill, J.), London: Edward Elgar.

Hamill, J. (1993), 'Crossborder Mergers, Acquisitions and Strategic Alliances' in *Multinationals and Employment: The Global Economy of the 1990s* (Eds. Bailey, P., Parisotto, A. and Renshaw, G), Geneva: ILO.

Hood, N. and Young, S. (1976), 'US Investment in Scotland: Aspects of the Branch Factory Syndrome', *Scottish Journal of Political Economy*, Vol. 23, No. 3.

Hood, N. and Young, S. (1982), *Multinationals in Retreat: The Scottish Experience*, Edinburgh: Edinburgh University Press.

Hood, N. and Young, S. (1983), *Multinational Investment Strategies in the British Isles: A Study of MNEs in the Assisted Areas and in the Republic of Ireland*, London: HMSO.

Hood, N. and Young, S. (1984), *Industry Policy and the Scottish Economy*, Edinburgh: Edinburgh University Press.

Hughes, A. (1989), 'The Impact of Merger: A Survey of Empirical Evidence for the UK', in *Mergers and Merger Policy* (Eds. Fairburn, J. A. and Kay, J. A.), Oxford: Oxford University Press.

International Labour Office (1993), *Multinationals and Employment: The Global Economy of the 1990s* (Eds. Bailey, P.; Parissoto, A; and Renshaw) Geneva: ILO.

Leigh, R. and North, D. J. (1978), 'Regional Aspects of Acquisition Activity in British Manufacturing Industry', *Regional Studies*, Vol. 12.

Panić, M. and Joyce, P. L. (1980), 'UK Manufacturing Industry: International Integration and Trade Performance', *Bank of England Quarterly Bulletin*, March.

Panić, M.(1991), 'The Impact of Multinationals on National Economic Policies', in *Multinationals and Europe 1992* (Eds. Bürgenmeier, B. and Mucchielli, J. L.), London: Routledge.

Porter, M. (1990), *The Competitive Advantage of Nations*, London: Macmillan.

Smith, I. J. (1979), 'The Effect of External Takeovers on Manufacturing Employment Change in Northern Region Between 1963 and 1973', *Regional Studies*, Vol. 13.

Smith, I. J. (1982), 'Some Implications of Inward Investment Through Takeover Activity', *Northern Economic Review*, February.

Steuer, M. D. (1973), *The Impact of Foreign Direct Investment on the UK*, London: HMSO.

Stopford, J. M. and Turner, L. (1985), *Britain and the Multinationals*, Chichester: John Wiley.

United Nations (1994), *World Investment Report: Transnational Corporations, Employment and the Workplace*, Geneva: United Nations Centre for Trade and Development.

Young, S., Hood, N. and Hamill, J. (1988), *Foreign Multinationals and the British Economy*, London: Croom Helm.

11

SUBSIDIARY STRATEGIES FROM THE PERIPHERY

James H. Taggart and Jenny Taggart

11.1 INTRODUCTION

Other things being equal, economic activity and economic confidence are closely linked, never more so than when core-periphery aspects are considered (Van Hove and Saunders, 1990). The purpose of this chapter is to assess how the perspectives of multinational subsidiaries in a peripheral region of the European Union (EU) compare with an analysis of subsidiary strategy, and how the two might interact with the core-periphery tension to impact on the subsidiary's degree of independence from headquarters control. In the first section, the basic economic parameters that affect the core-periphery continuum are reviewed; this is followed by an appraisal of the concepts underlying our understanding of strategy-making at subsidiary level, and a brief survey of evidence from one peripheral unit — Scotland. Following a concise overview of the Irish economy, the position of five multinational manufacturing subsidiaries in Ireland are analysed with specific reference to the strategic factors that affect subsidiary independence. Finally, some conclusions are drawn, together with brief prescriptions for future strategic direction.

11.2 CORE-PERIPHERY ECONOMIC EFFECTS

The completion of the Single European Market (SEM) will bring many economic benefits to the European Union (EU) as a whole, though some commentators detect the emergence of a core-periphery effect. Core and periphery are key concepts in the spatial analysis of economic activity. The core is not necessarily represented by the geographical centre, but is defined by those regions in which economic activity is concentrated; the periphery is described by the economically less-favoured regions. Welford and

Prescott (1992) identify the EU core as including Northern France, Southern Germany and Northern Italy. The periphery of the EU is less easily defined; however those areas eligible for structural funds under Objective 1 status may be considered as peripheral. These include the whole of Portugal, Ireland and Greece, parts of the UK including the Highlands and Islands of Scotland, Italy and Spain. From 1989, four-fifths of all structural funds have been allocated to those regions to promote 'the development and structural adjustment of the regions whose development is lagging behind' (Welford and Prescott, 1992, p. 28). These authors contend that firms located in Ireland and the UK are particularly competitively-disadvantaged due to sea barriers. Thus, it is possible the competitive forces released by the creation of the SEM will prove to be centripetal not centrifugal in nature.

The Cecchini Report (1988) on the 1992 Treaty of European Union asserts economic gains to be made by the single internal market may be considerable. Estimates of the overall gain to the EU could amount to 200 billion ECU or 5 per cent of the EU GNP, price deflation of 6.1 per cent, increased external trade of 1 per cent, and the creation of 1.8m new jobs (Welford and Prescott, 1992).

Cecchini's estimates, arising from 'a virtuous circle of expansion', are developed from a traditional approach to the theory of international trade, and consider only the gains to be made in the EU as a whole. Traditional theory argues that in the long run the free movement of labour and capital between states will tend to equalise returns across the regions. Any disparities that exist will be the result of rigidities in the market or intervention in the market system. El-Agraa (1990) classifies the economic evidence that lends support to Cecchini's SEM gains and 'level playing field' thesis into five main areas:

- specialisation in accordance with the laws of comparative advantage

- economies of scale leading to increased production

- improved international bargaining power leading to better terms of trade

- allocative and X-efficiency gains due to enhanced competition

- increased dynamic efficiency brought about by technological advances.

Cecchini concludes that smaller and newer states 'have proportionately the biggest opportunities for gain from market integration' — presumably on a one-off basis as the process of equalisation feeds through. The viability of these forecasts will become clear in due course. The more important question for policymakers is whether the removal of the EU's internal barriers to trade will, on the one hand, generate perfect flexibility and mobility in the market leading to economic equality throughout, or on the other hand, exacerbate the inequalities that already exist between core and periphery regions.

A number of commentators (Padoa-Schioppa, 1987; NESC, 1989; El-Agraa, 1990; Cuddy and Keane, 1990) suggest that disparities in economic prosperity will increase. This alternative view is developed from the perspective of a new approach to international trade theory developed, most notably, by Helpman and Krugman (1985). This perspective argues that the 'perfectly competitive environment' assumed by classical economic theorists does not exist; not only is there a wide variety of market structures in the modern trading environment, but each country has its own distinctive features that contribute to the international competitiveness of that country. In Helpman and Krugman's view, both factors contribute significantly to the pattern of trade; in particular increasing returns to scale, external economies, monopoly power and barriers to entry created by high capital and R&D requirements are all considered to contribute to the emergence of differences between regions.

Within a defined trade area, such as the EU, the economically vibrant core region will experience economies of scale coupled with economies of agglomeration and have an initial advantage. This is reinforced as capital and labour are drawn from the weaker regions and adds to the initial competitive edge. Economies of scale require the construction of good infrastructure; this, in turn, offers external economies to the firm that also contribute to lower costs and greater efficiencies. The development of skills, ease of exchange of knowledge and information all lead to a self-perpetuating growth structure. The OECD (1993), in terminology that recalls Kaldor's (1970) 'cumulative causation' effect, notes that innovation and manufacturing expertise tend to grow by a 'cumulative effect of scale and cross-fertilisation'. Krugman (1983) argues this 'economic rent' effect is a key determinant of competitive advantage, and must further benefit core-based firms. Further, it is known that the greater share of foreign direct

investment (FDI) is directed towards industrialised central regions, not to third world or peripheral regions (EC Commission,
1993). The increasing popularity of Japanese working practices
and the move away from vertically-integrated firms towards
subcontracting and joint projects will only add to increasing
centralisation.

A number of commentators have adopted a 'new trade theory'
approach to their interpretation of the future development of in-
tra EU trade patterns. In a critique of the Cecchini (1988) estimates, Padoa-Schioppa (1987) states 'spatial distribution of such
gains is less certain and is unlikely to be even'. This opinion is
shared by the National Economic and Social Council of Ireland
(NESC, 1989) who conclude 'completion of the internal market
should not be expected to narrow the income disparities between
regions in the EC, let alone bring about convergence'. El-Agraa
(1990) argues that the entry of low-income countries Spain and
Greece to the Community will exacerbate the problems associated
with peripherality. Cuddy and Keane (1990) observe that distance
from markets is the key problem for firms located in peripheral
regions but they argue it is not the sole issue; the type and quality
of infrastructure and the nature of the product to be transported
are critical. High stock levels on the input side become necessary
to guard against failure of delivery; as a result 'just-in-time' systems of management become impractical. Further, Cuddy and
Keane find that international division of labour will result in a
concentration of skilled personnel in core economic regions, particularly those involved in R&D. As a result, the mature product
at the end of its life cycle is the typical manufacture of the peripheral region. This assertion may arise from an earlier report by the
European Commission (1981) that finds greater innovative and
technological dynamism existing in EU core countries and concludes the gap will increase with the rate of innovation.

In summary, new trade theories are felt to offer a more realistic
interpretation of trade patterns in a modern economy. Thus,
strong economic arguments support the view that benefits provided by the SEM will not be distributed evenly throughout all
regions, and that the existing core-periphery effect within the EU
will be exacerbated.

11.3 CORPORATE AND SUBSIDIARY STRATEGY

11.3.1 Concepts

The task of the multinational manager is becoming increasingly complicated as competition becomes sharper, consumer demands change, technology advances, and as progressive globalisation leads to intensification of the international business environment. While managers at corporate level have long ago learned the advantages of managing strategically, executives at subsidiary level are becoming more aware that proactive strategising on their part not only improves the position of the affiliate itself, but often improves the parent's overall competitive edge.

The contingency approach to firms operating in rapidly changing environments was first explored by Burns and Stalker (1961), and subsequently by Lawrence and Lorsch (1967). While neither of these contributions focused on the multinational corporation, they did suggest that this type of firm tended to adopt more informal methods of control and co-ordination than those working in more stable environments, thus anticipating two of the more important concepts in current international business research. Within a few years the spotlight had turned to problems specific to multinational corporations and Aylmer (1970), for example, had concluded that extensive headquarters preoccupation with subsidiaries' marketing decisions was positively correlated with the degree of international experience enjoyed by the corporate parent. In a study of 24 subsidiaries of six large Swedish multinational corporations, Hedlund (1981) identified the key role of integration, typified by product flows to and from the subsidiary, and its effect on autonomy of affiliates. He found that the extent of subsidiary independence was directly correlated with the degree of informality in the headquarters-affiliate relationship. In trying to explain these relationships, he suggested that relevant determinants might include the size of the multinational corporation relative to its component subsidiaries, linkages and dependencies between the subsidiaries, and even the historical manner of Swedish internationalisation.

Perlemutter (1984) took a somewhat different tack, looking to executives and corporate behaviour patterns to classify the strategy of multinational corporations, though his paradigm is also relevant to the subsidiary. He distinguished four broad strategies:

1. **Ethnocentric.** This calls for the acceptance of home-country values and standards throughout the multinational corporation, thus implying centralised control and very limited notice taken of the views of subsidiary managers in the various host countries.

2. **Polycentric.** In this case, the multinational's headquarters accepts that local managers have a clearer view of what is best for each subsidiary, or in each country. Therefore, the subsidiary tends to maximal localisation in terms of behaviour and identity.

3. **Regiocentric.** This is less well-defined, but may be regarded as a working attempt to squeeze the best from ethno- and polycentric philosophies, or as a transitional phase between them. It calls for the establishment of regional headquarters, which becomes a focus for the strategy-making and implementing processes.

4. **Geocentric.** Collaboration between headquarters and subsidiaries is called for here, so that broad and universal standards may be established that have an acceptable degree of variation depending on where particular strategic decisions are being taken.

By the mid-1980s, multinational corporate and subsidiary strategy had become two clearly defined fields of research. In respect of the former, two principal paradigms emerged. Porter's (1986) paper suggested that the imperative of a successful global strategy is to establish and sustain a balance between the configuration (dispersion or concentration of activities) and co-ordination of international activities. The ability of firms to co-ordinate globally an array of value-chain activities is improving rapidly with the application of modern information technology; the need to co-ordinate is also increasing to respond to differentiated buyer needs throughout the world and to offset greater dispersion of international activities. Concentrating activities in one or a few locations is now less necessary in economic terms, and is becoming less feasible as government regulation forces more international dispersion. Thus Porter's two dimensions impact on one another and his model (see Figure 11.1) gives multinational strategists a way of creating a sustainable balance between them. This paradigm yields four strategy prescriptions: when combined with low co-ordination needs, concentration of activities suggests an export-based corporate strategy, while dispersion leads to a country-centred strategy; with high co-ordination, dispersion gives a strategy of high foreign investment with extensive co-ordination among subsidiaries, while concentration yields a 'purest global strategy'.

FIGURE 11.1: TYPES OF INTERNATIONAL STRATEGY

Co-ordination of Activities	*Geographically Dispersed*	*Geographically Concentrated*
High	High foreign investment with extensive co-ordination among subsidiaries	Purest global strategy
Low	Country-centred strategy by multinationals or domestic firms operating in only one country	Export-based strategy with decentralised marketing

Configuration of Activities

Source: Porter, 1986.

The model developed by Prahalad and Doz (1987) also has two dimensions; the first is local responsiveness, and the second is an amalgam of the global integration of activities and global strategic co-ordination (see Figure 11.2). Local responsiveness is represented by aspects of customers' needs in international markets, the global nature of competition and technology within the industry, and the overall 'personality' of the subsidiary's executive team. Global integration reflects strategy-related decisions about manufacturing capacity and inter-plant linkages, the nature of international customers, and the degree of control exerted by headquarters. Strategic co-ordination relates to quality and product specifications, and to aspects of international marketing; it resembles some aspects of Porter's co-ordination, but is really a different dimension. In terms of strategy prescription, this model describes a continuum from high integration/co-ordination and low responsiveness (they term this 'integrated product strategy, world-wide business management') to high responsiveness, low integration co-ordination ('locally responsive strategy, autonomous national subsidiaries'). Between these two extremes are the intermediate multifocal strategy (product emphasis) and multifocal strategy (locational emphasis).

FIGURE 11.2: THE INTEGRATION-RESPONSIVENESS GRID

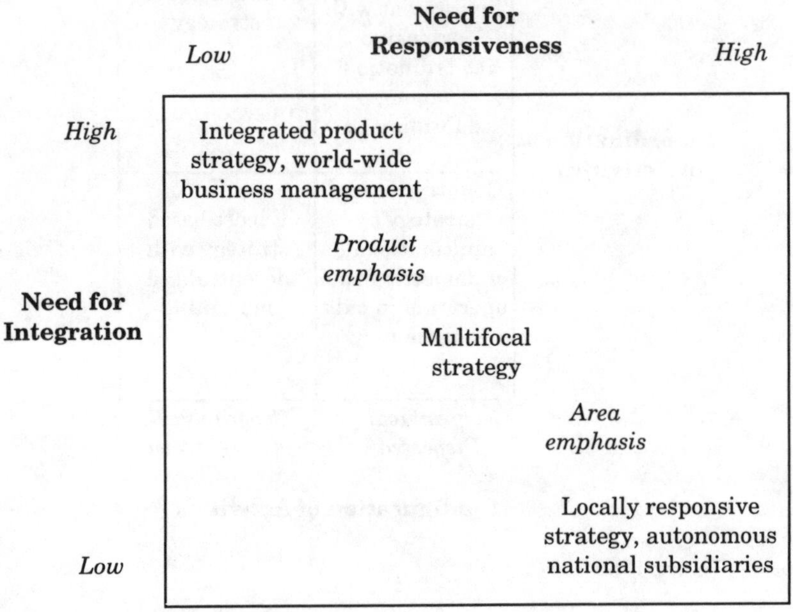

Source: Prahalad and Doz, 1987.

Both the Porter and the Prahalad and Doz paradigms have good analytical and descriptive power, and relate to the way international managers think about strategy. The strategy outcomes of the two models cover a wide spectrum of options and are therefore helpful tools for conceptual probing of problems and scenarios. Finally, both have been extensively assessed in empirical surveys, and expanded in detail and prescriptive power (see, for example, Roth and Morrison, 1990; Kobrin, 1991; Martinez and Jarillo, 1991).

Turning now specifically to subsidiary strategy, two models have had a powerful impact in recent years. The first was developed by White and Poynter (1984) who assessed the situation of multinational subsidiaries located in Canada. They developed an analytical model (see Figure 11.3) based on three dimensions: market scope (the degree of freedom the subsidiary has to determine which markets it sells into and which not), product scope (subsidiary autonomy in terms of additions and subtractions from the product line offered), and value-added scope (the subsidiary's freedom to add value to its output by additional investments in product and process technology, and in advanced marketing techniques). These dimensions yield two four-box models (market scope is common to both) with five strategy prescriptions:

1. **Miniature Replica.** Here, the subsidiary operates as a small-scale replica of the parent, and produces some of its product lines locally. Depending on the degree of product scope the affiliate has, this strategy has three sub-divisions: Adopters, which take products and marketing programmes and introduce them locally, making only minor changes; Adapters, which take products and programmes from the parent, and make changes to suit local conditions; and Innovators, that develop new but related products for local distribution.

2. **Marketing Satellite.** No manufacturing is involved here; the affiliate imports from the parent or other affiliates, carries out only minimal processing (e.g. re-packaging), and delivers the required range of distribution activities.

3. **Rationalised Manufacturer.** Here, the subsidiary produces a set of components for a multi-country or global market. Successful implementation of this strategy depends on the subsidiary's ability to deliver lower manufacturing costs.

4. **Product Specialist.** This type of subsidiary uses similar technologies to the parent but uses them specifically to develop, manufacture and market a limited product line to multi-country or global markets. It has substantial strategic control over its product range and is usually self-sufficient in R&D, manufacturing and marketing.

5. **Strategic Independent.** These affiliates are autonomous in R&D, manufacturing and marketing, and are allowed almost complete strategic freedom. The only links to the parent are financial and administrative, and the parent performs the role of passive investor.

FIGURE 11.3: TYPES OF SUBSIDIARY STRATEGY

	Product Scope		
	Limited		*Unconstrained*
Global	Product Specialist		Strategic Independent
Market Scope			
Local	Adopter	Miniature Replica Adapter	Innovator

	Value Added Scope		
	Narrow		*Broad*
Global	Rationalised Manufacturer		Strategic Independent
			Product Specialist
Market Scope			
Local	Marketing Satellite	Adopter	Miniature Replica Adapter	Innovator

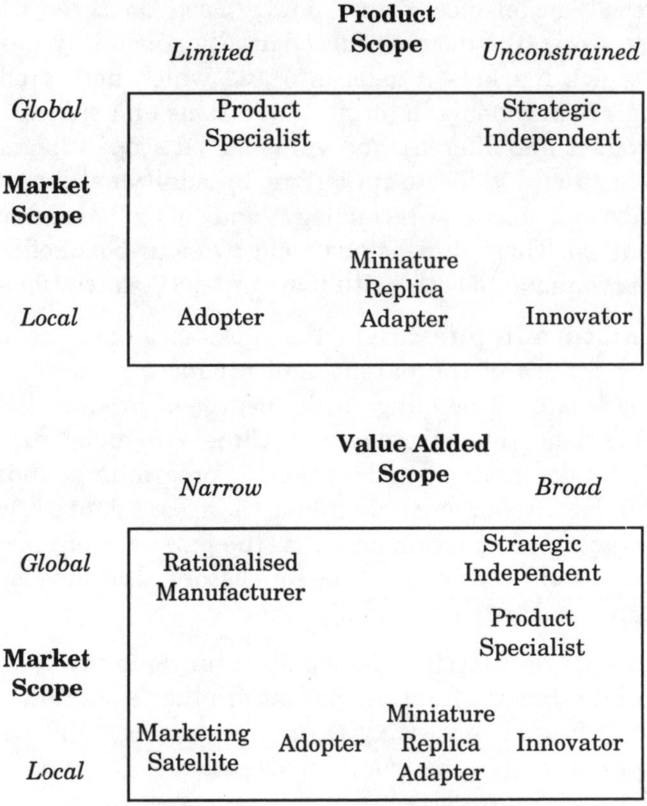

Source: White and Poynter, 1984

The second prominent model of subsidiary strategy was developed by Jarillo and Martinez (1989), and carries much of the thinking of Prahalad and Doz down to affiliate level. The two strategic dimensions they use (see Figure 11.4) are the geographic localisation of value-chain activities and the degree of integration of those activities that are carried out locally with the same activities performed by sister affiliates in other countries. Again, these dimensions give rise to a number of subsidiary-strategy prescriptions:

1. **Autonomous Affiliate.** This strategy is characteristic of the type of international firm that Bartlett (1986) terms 'multinational', and of the type of industry that Porter (1986) describes as 'multidomestic'. Here, the subsidiary carries out a

broad range of value-chain activities quite independently of both parent and sister affiliates.

2. **Active Affiliate.** Here, by contrast, the wide range of activities is tightly integrated with other parts of the multinational corporation, and this is a typical role within the 'transnational' firm described by Bartlett and Ghoshal (1989).

3. **Receptive Affiliate.** This type of subsidiary performs a limited range of activities (e.g. marketing of manufacturing), but these are highly integrated within the multinational corporation. This strategy is followed by most affiliates of what Bartlett (1986) describes as 'transnational' and 'global' firms.

FIGURE 11.4: THE INTEGRATION-LOCALISATION GRID

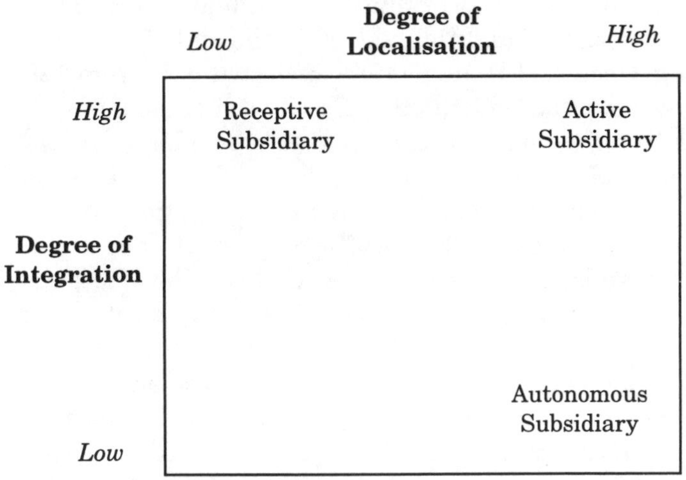

	Degree of	
Low	**Localisation**	*High*

High	Receptive Subsidiary	Active Subsidiary
Degree of Integration		
		Autonomous Subsidiary
Low		

Source: Jarillo and Martinez, 1989.

The conceptual linkages between the Prahalad and Doz model and Jarillo and Martinez have already been noted, but the latter also shared some of its abstract underpinning with Porter's paradigm. Also, White and Poynter's strategy classification has some relationship to co-ordination and integration on the one hand, and with localisation and aspects of configuration on the other. Between the strategy paradigms themselves, certain similarities may be indicated: namely, between Autonomous Affiliates and Strategic Independents/Product Specialists, between Receptive

Affiliates and Rationalised Manufacturers, and between Active
Affiliates and Miniature Replicas. Thus the two subsidiary models
of strategy yield a powerful and coupled system for analysing and
interpreting the strategic roles of multinational affiliates under a
range of different circumstances.

11.3.2 Evidence from Scotland

The relationship of the Scottish economy to the English is not unlike that of the Canadian to the US. Certainly, in the case of the
former, there is a long-established customs union and a common
currency, but both Scotland and Canada have all the disadvantages and benefits of having a large, dominant economy as a next-
door neighbour. Thus, it is not surprising that a substantial part
of the follow-up work to White and Poynter's research has taken
place in Scotland. Along with an initial focus on the White and
Poynter paradigm, this work has also evaluated and extended the
studies of Prahalad and Doz, and of Jarillo and Martinez.

Young, Hood and Dunlop (1988) collected data from 129 manufacturing subsidiaries located in Scotland including variables like
nationality of ownership, period of establishment, market areas
supplied, R&D capability, intra-multinational movement of components and sub-assemblies, nature of production operations, locus of decision-making, and width of product ranges. Despite a
somewhat ambiguous use of cluster analysis, the White and Poynter paradigm was broadly supported, and the clusters tended to
conform fairly closely with the expected strategy classifications.
Thirteen per cent of the sample had characteristics that suggested the Miniature Replica type; these tended to be small firms
of recent origin, with a very high proportion of non-US parents.
Another 13 per cent showed much more definite characteristics of
the Miniature Replica; these also tended to be small and fairly
new firms, with significant non-US representation. Affiliates with
characteristics of the Rationalised Manufacturer represented
about 39 per cent of the sample (the largest single group); these
were larger, well-established firms with predominantly US ownership. The fourth group, comprising 35 per cent of the sample,
consisted mainly of US-owned affiliates; they tended to be the
largest and longest-established firms and demonstrated characteristics of both Product Specialist and Strategic Independent
classifications, though the analysis could not easily differentiate
between these two strategies. Other results from this research
showed that 28 per cent of Scottish affiliates were supplying

world-wide markets, a quarter of firms were obtaining between 25 and 50 per cent of material inputs from other plants within their respective internal networks, and 53 per cent were carrying out significant R&D (with only 15 per cent recording no R&D whatsoever). Thus, at least from the policy-maker's point of view, these results demonstrate substantial international integration, innovative capacity, autonomy, and access to a wide range of world markets. From the perspective of the multinational corporations and their Scottish subsidiaries, they suggest some form of deterministic strategy evolution, though the imperatives driving these developments are not made clear.

This last point has been taken up and developed in a series of studies aimed at establishing linkages between corporate and subsidiary strategies, and how these linkages interact with the business environment to determine the nature, rate and direction of strategy evolution at subsidiary level. By means of a case analysis of two particular affiliates (Compaq and Caledonian Paper), Taggart (1992) postulated the existence of an 'affiliate learning curve' whereby the thrust of corporate strategy is tempered by subsidiary-level imperatives as the subsidiary becomes well-established within its markets and within its internal network.

This critical question of subsidiary-strategy development over time has recently been at the centre of another research survey (Taggart, 1995a, 1995b) of 121 manufacturing affiliates located in Scotland. A test of the Prahalad and Doz integration/co-ordination/responsiveness model indicated some support for the original two-dimensional approach, but suggested that a three-dimensional paradigm (i.e. integration, co-ordination and responsiveness taken as distinct and orthogonal variables) yields a substantive and rigorous approach that is more realistic and robust. However, in terms of evaluating strategy evolution over a ten-year period among the sample firms, a simple two-dimensional model was found to be adequate. The first dimension was similar to Prahalad and Doz 's approach to responsiveness and consisted of an amalgam of homogeneity of customers and their needs, the extent to which competitive strategies are easily identified, and the stability of technology (particularly where it involves manufacturing sophistication). The second dimension was an integration/co-ordination-type of variable and included aspects of market area strategy decisions, geographical specificity of product and quality specifications, and the extent of centralisation of pricing decisions.

Cluster analysis led to a four-group solution, three of which corre-
sponded to the strategy spectrum of Prahalad and Doz. Firms in
the exceptional fourth cluster were characterised by high levels of
both responsiveness and integration/co-ordination, a result that is
not predicted by Prahalad and Doz. With regard to strategy development over time, all of the clusters evolve substantially along
the responsiveness dimension over the ten-year period of the
study, while three move only marginally along the other dimension. The substantial negative movement in integration/co-
ordination illustrated by one of the clusters is difficult to explain
without further research. Finally, 57 per cent of the sample were
involved in higher levels of R&D compared to 53 per cent in an
earlier survey (Young, Hood and Dunlop, 1988), and only 13 per
cent were doing no R&D at all.

In summary, it can be concluded that multinational manufacturing subsidiaries in Scotland show significant development of
strategy in terms of complexity and international linkages, and
that these developments — while undoubtedly associated with a
number of important organisational factors, are also linked to the
age of the subsidiary and its decision-making relationship with
headquarters. Thus, it may be that the worst of the peripheral effects in Scotland have been mitigated, at least for the multinational-subsidiary sector, by the nature and form of the strategies
pursued by firms within this sector.

11.4 THE IRISH ECONOMY AND MULTINATIONAL SUBSIDIARIES

11.4.1 Concepts
At first glance, Ireland does not seem to be a country ideally
placed to attract inward investment. Located on the periphery of
the EU, it has a small domestic market of 3.5 million that is the
third poorest in Europe. Wage costs are high relative to some
European countries, there is little in the way of natural resources
and the Irish Punt can make no claim to importance as an international trading currency. It is the only European country without
direct rail and road links; the Irish-based exporter must rely on
air and sea transport. Yet from the 1960s, Ireland has been
successful in attracting inward investment by multinational
corporations.

Over this period investment by foreign firms has been a cornerstone of Irish industrial policy. Manufacturing exports have increased from 10 per cent of GDP in the early 1960s to 45 per cent in 1992 (OECD Economic Survey, 1993). This growth has been primarily as a result of the establishment of multinational corporation (MNC) subsidiaries that now provide 75 per cent of all manufacturing exports. By 1988, US investment was estimated at one-third of all foreign direct investment in Ireland, followed by the UK at approximately one-fifth of total investment. Japanese firms accounted for only 2 per cent (19 manufacturing firms), although the trend in Japanese foreign direct investment in Ireland is upwards (Jacobson and Andreosso, 1990).

Ireland offers three further key areas of advantage as a location for the multinational subsidiary; all are government-induced. Firstly, Ireland has a stable macroeconomy and is a long-standing member of the EU. The need to avoid EU external tariff barriers has encouraged multinationals from non-member states to establish manufacturing capacity within the boundaries of the trade area. This explains why a multinational corporation should locate within the EU, not specifically within Ireland; however, language and networking by expatriate Irish are seen as providing two significant locational advantages, given a straight choice between Ireland and a number of other small stable EU states.

The practice by Irish governments of providing fiscal advantages in the form of grants and tax incentives to inward investors has created the second and most effective area of advantage to Ireland as a preferred location for multinationals. Capital grant allocations provide the main financial incentive. These account for approximately 70 per cent of total grant assistance to overseas companies and may amount to 30 per cent of the cost of eligible fixed assets. These tax levels may seem generous but are less so than in the early days of Ireland's industrial development programme, at which time capital grants alone could amount to 40 per cent. Further, capital grants are now not automatic but discretionary in nature and are tied to the creation of employment. As a result they are less attractive to multinational corporations. For the overseas-owned manufacture, 10 per cent corporation tax has proved the most enduringly popular government 'sweetener'. This level of taxation may have to be adjusted due to harmonisation regulations introduced within the EU in 1992 that set limits on the extent to which individual states may offer aid to domestic industries. However, certain derogational provisions favour

Ireland. Those EU regions with low standards of living and high unemployment are permitted to promote 'economic development' within their own borders. The practice of enticing multinational subsidiaries by government 'sweeteners' looks set to continue in Ireland, at least in the medium term. From the viewpoint of the Irish economy, low taxation has had an unfortunate side-effect. Multinationals are often motivated to carry out R&D in a particular country (all other things being equal) if the costs can be set against high taxation rates; in Ireland, this internal incentive is weakened by the low level of corporation tax, which may go some way to explain why so few multinational subsidiaries there have associated R&D activity. This lack of R&D facilities has tended to generate a 'branch factory syndrome' in the Republic.

Ireland's third key locational advantage is the skills level of its workforce. A sea change has occurred in education over the last decade, with a pronounced swing from traditional study in the arts towards business, electronics and computing. It is unclear whether this change has been supply- or demand-driven, or whether the government can be given credit for having the foresight to create a skills base that compares favourably with any in the EU. Regardless of the cause, the effect is that Ireland has a workforce which may prove to be a critical determinant in the multinationals' locational decisions in the longer term. However, a considerable threat to Ireland's ability to continue attracting inward investment in the long run is posed by the emergent East European nations that have highly-educated workforces and low wage levels. The government has recognised this potential threat, and successfully introduced a five-year incomes policy in 1991 (Programme for Economic and Social Progress, PESP) that aims to make Ireland's wage rates more competitive. The combination of the right skills and the right price should allow Ireland to continue to be a preferred option for foreign direct investment.

Thus, it is likely that Ireland will continue to provide a favourable location for the multinational subsidiary within the EU. The Regional Fund has provided the means to improve internal road networks and ferry links with the UK and continental Europe. A major international airline network operates out of Shannon on the west coast. Serious unemployment problems coupled with the government's incomes policies seem likely to drive wage costs down, at least in the short term. Lack of recognition of the Punt by international money markets has been turned to advantage in that financial controllers in Irish firms are at ease trading in a multitude of currencies. This not only suits the customer, but often allows the cost of imported inputs to be offset by the invoicing currency of the exports. Irish awareness of the potentially tenuous nature of a multinational subsidiary encourages a trend towards a hard-working labour force and efficiently-run organisations.

11.4.2 Evidence from Ireland

In order to explore the strategic factors that affect subsidiary independence, in-depth interviews were conducted with the chief executives of five multinational manufacturing subsidiaries located in Ireland. The main findings are presented in the following sections.

Logstrup, Tuam

Logstrup is a Danish firm, privately-owned by one family, that commenced business in the early 1950s. Originally, the firm manufactured electrical equipment but found that the existing methods of producing steel enclosures for electrical switchgear left something to be desired. Logstrup developed a meccano-like system so that, with a basic stock of parts, a very large number of combinations of switchgear and enclosure could be quickly put together. This allowed it to sell modular enclosure systems to smaller firms that did not have the appropriate design or manufacturing facilities. A substantial export business to the rest of Europe developed until, in 1982, Logstrup took over a factory occupied at that time by another Danish engineering firm that was about to close down. In the early days the factory was managed by the Danish owner, but gradually the control of operations passed to the Irish management team, and there are now no Danes on site. The present employment level is 46, though that has moved from a peak of 55 in 1990, and a low point of 35 in 1993. Employment is likely to grow over the next few years, tied directly to expansion in the construction industry but, in times of recession, the market shrinks to replacement and refurbishment. Since 1993, both turnover and profit have increased, and efficiency gains have also pushed up turnover per employee.

The plant manufactures one complete range of products and exports back to Denmark and to sales companies in the UK and Sweden; it also sells and distributes on the Irish market (including Northern Ireland). Decisions about the product range sold in Ireland are made by the subsidiary, as are most of the investment and operating decisions; full budget responsibility is retained in Ireland with minimal monthly reporting to headquarters. Further, the subsidiary exercises substantial influence over the design and development of the product range, and there is virtually complete freedom of action with the items marketed at home. How advantageous this has been can be seen from the much poorer overall performance of the UK subsidiary, which does not have this autonomy or capability in terms of re-design and adaptation; in fact, with a market of around one-tenth the size, Logstrup sells more product in Ireland than in the UK.

The parent firm manufactures about 2,500 product lines in total; the Irish subsidiary manufactures around 1,000 of these though, in terms of overall volume, it accounts for around 70 per cent of the corporate total. There is no overlap of customers; the subsidiary is responsible for its customers in the Irish market, while headquarters is responsible for Denmark and all other export markets. Product sold into the Danish warehouse must be price-competitive, and headquarters makes regular open-market comparisons with other contractors to ensure that this is so. Difficulties are being experienced with increasing raw materials costs, and customers are most unwilling to accept price increases. The subsidiary sources steel, its main input, from Germany, France, Sweden and the UK; shortage of EU steel capacity is encouraging cost inflation (15-20 per cent in twelve months). Input costs of copper and plastics are also rising quickly, by over 30 per cent in the case of the latter.

Exports have fallen from 75 to 60 per cent of turnover during 1990-95, mainly because the subsidiary is selling substantially more on the Irish market. Over the next five years the export proportion is expected to rise again as penetration of the Irish market reaches a peak; additionally, the export market is expected to grow faster than the domestic. The parent firm has much wider market responsibility than the subsidiary, marketing and distributing in every major European country. Eighty per cent of the plant's exports to the parent are of finished product; the remainder is represented by a recent addition to the product line that is manufactured in Ireland and shipped to the parent for final painting. Successful new products designed for the Irish market are subsequently offered to the parent, which is generally less active in product R&D.

Much of the plant output is converted directly from raw materials, but some subcontracting takes place for high-volume turned parts, electro-plating, and some painting. As well as metal fabrication, a wide range of skills is exercised including injection moulding, milling, turning, punching, bending and welding. Government training schemes and company apprenticeships are used in combination to develop the range of skills required. In addition, the workforce is highly flexible and this helps in meeting tight delivery deadlines; some of the production plant is permanently on 24-hour shift working.

In terms of overall subsidiary development, the chief executive believes that most inward investors see Ireland primarily as a cheap manufacturing location, but often change their views when exposed to the quality of the Irish workforce and management cadres. Eventually the parent firm will evaluate the situation and allow a movement of autonomy to the Irish plant. This is particularly the case in customer-related matters, thus reflecting a substantial emphasis on the importance of local responsiveness. This, in turn, means that the Irish subsidiary is more closely involved in the development of aspects of corporate strategy as it develops its own abilities and its profile within the corporate network.

Apple Computer (Cork)

Apple Computer Inc. is one of the world's major personal computer manufacturers, and has sales and service subsidiaries in every developed economy. Apple Computer Ltd. (Ireland) is one of the multinational's three major manufacturing plants, the others being in California and Singapore. The latter looms large in the consciousness at Cork, as the plant's tactical objective is to produce computers at a lower landed price in European markets than the Singapore factory can achieve. The plant was established in Cork in 1980 and the workforce had increased to 700 by 1990; it is currently at 1,200. In 1990 turnover per employee was £715,000 rising to £833,000 in 1995, and is expected to be £1,000,000 by the end of the decade. Exports throughout have been at a steady 95 per cent of output.

Decision-making is subsidiary-oriented in human resources, finance, manufacturing technology and production; it is strongly parent-oriented for market area and product range supplied, and for advertising and promotion. In the early years, R&D was carried out entirely in California, but in recent years some product development (mainly software-linked) has been carried out in Cork; this trend is expected to accelerate in the future. The plant has increasingly transferred process technology and production know-how to other group plants; co-ordination with these plants of the purchase of common items is virtually complete, though this subsidiary is responsible for the bulk of its own purchasing requirements. Since its inception, and particularly in the last five years, the perception has been that an increasing level of strategic skills and resources has been located within the Cork plant.

The principal market for the plant's output is Europe, though other selected markets are serviced from time to time. Up to 10 per cent of the output goes to other group plants for final assembly; though this is a fairly small proportion, it has increased substantially in the last five years, indicating a growth in certain linkages within the international Apple network. However, over the same period the proportion of material inputs obtained from other group plants has fallen from over 15 per cent to under 5 per cent. Conversely, the proportion of material inputs sourced in Ireland has increased from around 8 per cent in 1990 to over 30 per cent in 1995, and this proportion is likely to increase further over the next five years.

Comparing 1990 with 1995 and looking forward to 2000, the local responsiveness variable is a difficult one to evaluate for the Cork plant. On the one hand, customer needs are becoming less well identified and their motivations more complex, while competitors are becoming more diffuse and their strategies more difficult to evaluate. On the other hand, the basic technology is becoming more stable, manufacturing sophistication is increasing, products are becoming mature, and much greater emphasis is being put on production technology improvements, capacity utilisation and cost minimisation.

Despite the operational and strategic changes that have occurred, the bond of trust between the Cork plant and corporate headquarters remains strong. In the view of the chief executive, the formulation of parent company strategy is characterised by increasingly effective two-way communication involving the Cork facility, and the subsidiary has full and legitimate opportunity to challenge the strategic views of headquarters during the formulation process. Corporate executives demonstrate a high level of knowledge and understanding about the market situation of the Irish subsidiary, and it is provided with a very full account of corporate strategic decisions. Finally, corporate decision-making is rated as fairly consistent across all subsidiaries within the international network, so far as the Cork perspective is concerned.

The development of this subsidiary in terms of both operations and strategy has been along fairly standard lines, but this is perhaps all the more surprising given the vicissitudes of the computer industry and, especially, of the Apple corporation since 1980. The subsidiary is a vital contributor to the Irish economy, and is crucial to employment in south-west Ireland, particularly in view of recent plant closures. The plant would not have survived if it had not offered steadily increasing added-value to its parent throughout the years, though there have been times when the spectre of the Singapore plant has offered a threatening capacity alternative. Perhaps it is not without significance that, in the original locational decision and in the constant economic evaluations and assessments that have transpired since, the Cork plant has had a champion in the higher corporate levels in California whose family tree is — at least — tinged with green.

Stafford-Miller (Ireland) Ltd., Dungarvan

Stafford-Miller is a subsidiary of the Block Drug Co. Inc. of New Jersey; the parent company is a market leader in dental care products and was founded in the early 1900s. Expansion into Europe came in 1938, and production locations were established in Belgium and England. The Irish unit was established in 1981 and has since doubled its factory area; it manufactures dental paste and denture cleansers, virtually all of which is exported. Employment at the factory has steadily risen from 140 in 1990 to 180 in 1995; it is forecast to grow to 200 over the next five years. Staff turnover is very low and quality is excellent at all levels from top management to the shop floor. Turnover per employee has increased from £107,000 to £178,000 since 1990, and will probably rise to £200,000 by the end of the century.

Decisions regarding market area and product range supplied, and advertising and promotion, are decided mainly by the parent without consulting or seeking the advice of the Irish subsidiary. There is more consultation in the case of R&D and manufacturing technology decisions, while for production, finance and human resources, the decision-making processes are significantly more subsidiary-oriented. The degree to which Stafford-Miller's activities are co-ordinated internationally within the Block network is unclear; marketing activity and product development are carried out with little regard for the needs or requirements of other subsidiaries, but there is increasing co-ordination in the case of purchase of common material inputs and in the inter-subsidiary transfer of process technology and production know-how. Since 1990, Stafford-Miller has developed substantial strategic skills and resources, and this trend is expected to continue over the next five years. Thus, the plant is becoming less reliant on the skills and resources based at headquarters, and perhaps even less so on those located in other subsidiaries.

In 1990 the Irish affiliate's sales efforts were confined to European markets, but exports are also now made to selected markets in other parts of the world. Over the same period there has been an increase to around 10 per cent in the proportion of output going to other group plants for further processing. Similarly, the proportion of material inputs obtained from other group plants has risen from 8 per cent to around 15 per cent, but this is expected to fall back again by the end of the century. The subsidiary is engaged in a high level of manufacturing operations and has sufficient R&D capability to adapt manufacturing technology to meet developing needs.

Overall, the degree of international integration within the Block group appears to be rising and subsidiaries are becoming increasingly dependent on one another, with the specific exception of strategic skills and resources indicated above. In 1990, capacity and process decisions involving Stafford-Miller were made by the parent on a project-by-project basis with a view to the subsidiary serving specific market areas. By 1995, such decisions reflected a move towards creating multiplant linkages and multiplant sourcing potential, and this trend is expected to continue aggressively over the next five years. Similarly, the product and quality specifications developed and co-ordinated at the Irish plant are increasingly aimed at serving the corporate parent's geographically-defined markets. The subsidiary's local responsiveness is generally fairly high, especially in technology-related aspects. Products are relatively mature, manufacturing sophistication is high, and the emphasis has swung heavily to production technology improvements and cost minimisation. This encourages the subsidiary to become more customer-oriented in its search for competitive advantage.

There have been significant advances since 1990 in this subsidiary's perception of the fairness of the corporate strategy formulation process, and this is forecast to continue over the next five years. The parent has always been relatively knowledgeable about Stafford-Miller's market situation, but the effectiveness of two-way communication between subsidiary and corporate levels during the strategy formulation process has improved remarkably since 1990. A similar improvement has been experienced in

Stafford-Miller's perception of the consistency of the corporate decision-making process as it affects all subsidiary units. In addition, satisfactory improvements have occurred in two other areas; first, the subsidiary now has better opportunities to offer legitimate challenge to the views and assumptions that drive corporate strategy formulation; second, the subsidiary is more satisfied with the account given of final strategic decisions at headquarters.

Stafford-Miller's original location in Ireland came about after a new vice-president, who had previous experience of Ireland, joined the parent corporation at a time when it was looking to further international expansion of facilities. The Irish subsidiary has developed uniquely within the Block group, as it is the only subsidiary that is manufacturing only; all others also have a marketing function. All of Stafford-Miller's output is exported to other subsidiaries who are responsible for marketing and distribution. This unusual situation has its obvious drawback in that the subsidiary has nowhere to hide its costs, they are there for all (particularly headquarters) to see. There is, however, a corresponding advantage in that, if the factory is run effectively, then its overall cost efficiency is the best protection against plant closure. It is currently Block's most efficient European plant, though this has taken six years of intense effort to achieve; it is also the group's most modern plant anywhere in the world. The Irish affiliate survives and expands entirely on the basis of service to the market place, and its competitive advantage depends ultimately on the high quality of staff and management referred to above. Perhaps this is best illustrated by reference to Block's sales to Japan; these are currently manufactured entirely by the Irish affiliate since even the US factory cannot achieve the required zero-defect standard (product and packaging); the Dungarvan factory is now accomplishing this as a matter of routine.

Henkel (Ireland) Limited, Cork

Henkel is a world-wide specialist in applied chemistry and its market segments include oleochemicals, adhesives, metal chemicals, detergents and household cleaners, cosmetics and toiletries, and industrial and institutional hygiene products. The company was founded in Germany in 1876, and it now employs some 40,000 in factories in 53 countries around the world. The Cork factory was originally opened and owned by General Mills Chemicals, a division of the American multinational General Mills Inc. Henkel bought the division in 1977, and the Cork facility thus passed into German ownership. The original business was the manufacture of liquid ion exchange reagents supplied to various segments of the metal-mining industry; these reagents enable the extraction of semi-precious metals in a very pure state and in an environmentally sound manner with, in the right circumstances, a pronounced cost-advantage. Virtually none of this product range is sold in Ireland or anywhere else in Europe. The main markets are South America, Africa, Australia and, most recently, China. The subsidiary also manufactures a low temperature bleach activator that is a key ingredient of washing powders (Henkel is the owner of the Persil brand in Germany and certain other markets). This product is sold throughout Europe, primarily to other Henkel subsidiaries in Germany, Spain, Italy, France and Belgium; none is sold in Ireland, where the Persil brand name is owned by Lever Brothers. These internal sales are made in competition with outside contractors, so Cork has to be price-competitive at all times.

Employment at the Cork plant has increased from 100 to 160 since 1990, and may reach 200 by 2000. Turnover per employee has risen from £180,000 to £312,500 in the last five years, and may reach £400,000 in five years time. Human resource decisions are wholly devolved to the subsidiary, and the parent plays a consultative role only in decisions relating to product range, R&D, production, manufacturing technology and finance. There is significantly more corporate involvement in market area decisions, and in advertising and promotion. Co-ordination of activities is highest in developing products that are responsive to the market needs of other subsidiaries, but otherwise is of little consequence. The corporate parent is deeply involved in R&D, but there has been a substantial increase in this activity at the Cork plant in the last five years; a full range of product and process work is now being implemented for the liquid ion exchange business, and there is a growing level of process engineering activity on detergent additives. As noted earlier, market areas supplied are either European or world-wide, depending on the product group. Other group plants provide virtually no raw materials to Cork, but a growing proportion is sourced in Ireland, perhaps as much as 20 per cent by the end of the decade.

This plant demonstrates a low level of integration within the Henkel international network, and this is in line with earlier remarks on co-ordination. Capacity and process decisions, product and quality specifications, customers and technology development are all highly subsidiary-specific. It is largely independent of other affiliates in terms of product flows, and headquarters plays little part — other than providing guidelines — in production planning and control of inventories, quality and costs. However, it should be noted that all customer support and marketing of the liquid ion exchange product group is carried out by the Henkel subsidiary in Tucson, Arizona. This occasionally causes some problems for stock control and production runs. Henkel (Ireland) is also locally responsive to a high degree, being very aware of customers and their needs, of competitors and their strategies, and of the maturity of products and associated technologies. The relationship with headquarters is good, especially in terms of the ability to challenge corporate views and assumptions during the strategy formulation process. There have been some misgivings concerning headquarters' understanding of the local situation of the subsidiary, but this has improved in the last five years.

Liquid ion exchange reagents constitute the larger part of the Cork output, and this sector of the business is also growing faster. In fact, present and projected output of copper (copper ore refiners are the main user of Henkel's product) suggests that growth will be very healthy for some time to come. The subsidiary management team are very confident about this whole area of the business and clearly revel in the problem-solving associated with open market competition. Perhaps the key competitive advantage is the concentration on improving the environmental aspects of the product at a time when environmental costs for the mining and extractive sector are soaring. The attitude is somewhat different on the detergent-additives side, where most of the sales are transfer-price deals within the Henkel network. However, there is a clear recognition that the cut-throat aspect of this sector provides all the necessary encouragement to cut costs and constantly improve plant and operational efficiency. In summary, this subsidiary is a curious amalgam of two elements of the conceptual typology. On the detergent-additives side, the plant is highly integrated with Henkel's international network, and operates very much as a Rationalised Manufacturer. On the liquid ion exchange side, there is much more freedom to develop and much less contact with headquarters; both aspects are typical of the Strategic Independent. This side of the Cork subsidiary gives the impression of having never been fully accommodated within the parent corporation, even though 18 years have passed since the original acquisition from General Mills.

Ascom Timeplex, Dublin (Tix)

This firm (which refers to itself as 'Tix International') was originally a subsidiary of Timeplex Inc. of New Jersey, a multinational
corporation involved in manufacturing data communications
equipment. Timeplex was acquired by Unisys, then sold three
years ago in its entirety to Ascom A. G. of Berne, a European
multinational in broadly the same line of business. Tix's main
business line is the manufacture of networking equipment, and is
the only factory within a complex European organisation that is
involved in this sector, although there are another two of the
original Timeplex factories in America (one in New Jersey, one in
Puerto Rico) that also manufacture networking equipment. The
Dublin plant currently employs 80, well down from the 1990 figure of 120. This fall, put down entirely to recession, is forecast to
be more than recovered by 2000 when the employment level
should approach 150. Turnover per employee was £333,000, but
managed to rise to £375,000 by 1995, despite recession; it is forecast to reach £533,000 by the end of the century. All but 2 per cent
of the output of the factory is exported.

Much of the decision-making is concentrated at corporate level
including aspects of market area, product range supplied, advertising and promotion, and R&D. Production and finance decisions
have become more subsidiary-oriented in recent years, but the
Dublin plant is only consulted about changes in manufacturing
technology. Full autonomy is only retained in the area of human
resource management. The chief executive makes full use of this
particular freedom of action to emphasise good selection, training
and motivation of people, from his office down to the shop floor.
Thus, when he claims that quality workers and quality managers
are a prime source of competitive advantage, it is unlikely to be
an idle boast. This subsidiary is fairly well co-ordinated with
other group affiliates, particularly in terms of transferring process
technology and production know-how, and also in the purchase of
common items of material input. In addition, the subsidiary carries out very little purchasing for itself as this is done at a regional level. The same is true of R&D, with none being carried out
locally. Altogether, the picture that emerges is one of high co-
ordination and high configuration of activities within this multinational, with a great deal of emphasis on cost control, cost reduction, aggressive control of overhead, and plant efficiency. With
regard to the latter, Tix regard themselves as being a world-class
manufacturer; in the semi-automatic process used, the failure

rate has been pushed below 150 parts per million, against a recognised 'world class standard' of 200 parts per million.

For the last five years the plant's output has been exported
primarily to Europe with a smaller proportion going beyond
Europe; the forecast for the next five years is that the latter proportion will increase, possibly substantially. Most of the output is
of finished product, with less than 5 per cent going to other group
plants for final assembly. By contrast, the bulk of material inputs
come from other plants, with less than 10 per cent being sourced
in Ireland. As might be expected from the observations on international co-ordination (above), this plant is highly integrated
within the parent's network; the only real exception to this is that
capacity and process decisions tend to be specific to the Dublin
plant and the particular market area it serves, which is linked to
the fact that this affiliate is basically independent of the others in
terms of product flows. Not surprisingly in view of the nature of
the market and the organisation of the parent, this subsidiary is
not particularly locally-responsive, though there is clearly a sensitivity to customer needs and competitor behaviour.

The subsidiary has a fluctuating and somewhat negative perspective on how fairly it is judged in terms of the corporate strategy-making process. Effective two-way communication seems to
be at a five-year low, though the position is forecast to improve
substantially by 2000. The same is true for Dublin's opportunity
to challenge the parent's views and assumptions during strategy
formulation, although both the decline and the forecast improvement are even more pronounced. The parent is judged to have a
reasonably accurate knowledge of the affiliate's local situation,
but is seen to act inconsistently across its family of subsidiaries
when making strategic decisions. Finally, the corporate mechanism for rendering an account of final strategic decisions to the
Dublin plant is not impressive. However, despite the rather negative impression created here, the subsidiary believes that these
'procedural justice' variables are unimportant in evaluating the
strategic relationship with headquarters, laying much more stress
on co-ordination and decision-making as befits a firm that manufactures a technical product with a virtually global specification.

11.5 DISCUSSION

These five case studies of Irish firms competing from the periphery can be assessed in two ways: first, by comparing them with

five broadly similar MNC subsidiaries in Scotland and, second, by assessing their strategy evolutions over time in terms of what seems necessary to survive and develop. Some of the evidence presented earlier on MNC affiliates in Scotland might suggest that, as a group, they are somewhat further advanced in the life-cycle than Irish subsidiaries; this may provide broad pointers to future development.

Logstrup was originally very much a 'slave' subsidiary but has increased its autonomy and its product development activity in fair measure in recent years. Uniroyal Englebert is the Scottish subsidiary of a European parent; like Logstrup, it was acquired by its present MNC parent from a previous multinational. Very little of the production is aimed at satisfying local needs, and exports to Europe in particular have grown rapidly in recent years. Expenditure on production technology is high, though product R&D is virtually absent; there is some local decision-making autonomy, but very little marketing activity. Thus, unlike Logstrup which is developing as an innovator-type Miniature Replica, Uniroyal Englebert has become a Rationalised Manufacturer.

As with Logstrup, Apple was originally significantly less autonomous but, as the parent corporation's need for tight world-wide integration has reduced, this position has changed. Autonomy of the Irish subsidiary has increased, software R&D has been introduced indirectly, and the bonds of trust and confidence have improved between parent and affiliate. The Scottish subsidiary of Compaq also has an American parent and has a similar focus on low-cost manufacturing. It has little real autonomy and this is unlikely to change while the 'low-cost producer' corporate strategy is in place. Unlike Apple in Cork, Compaq's Scottish affiliate has added nothing significant in the way of R&D capability and this is not likely to change in the medium term.

Stafford Miller is a producer of basic chemical products whose major focus is on high-quality, defect-free manufacturing with no local R&D or marketing, and high and increasing integration within its parent's international network. Despite its relative lack of autonomy, the parent-affiliate relationship has improved markedly in recent years, perhaps in line with the need for closer integration. Silberline is a US multinational whose Scottish affiliate produces basic chemical additives for the paint, plastics and printing ink industries. It has considerable latitude within overall corporate strategy and a good working relationship with the parent, probably not unconnected with good future prospects for the affiliate's various businesses. Local autonomy is particularly important in marketing and R&D, where a small team carries out a wide range of technical developments for world markets.

Henkel is a producer of high technology chemicals for specific applications, and belongs to a European parent with broadly-based world-wide chemical interests. It has a very high degree of autonomy and an excellent relationship with its parent. The subsidiary works within the Henkel corporation's overall low level of integration and, because its products have global application, there is little need for local responsiveness. There is a very high level of local technology development, supported by an able local R&D team. Ciba-Geigy Pigments, based at Paisley in Scotland, also produces high technology chemical additives to serve a global market, and also belongs to a European chemicals multinational with world-wide interests. The Scottish affiliate is highly autonomous, with virtually total responsibility for marketing and R&D. While acknowledging the place of the parent corporation, Paisley is effectively the headquarters of a world-wide business.

Tix International was, until recently, owned by a US multinational, but is now under Swiss control. It operates within the electronics industry with a low need for local responsiveness, and is highly integrated within the Ascom corporation. It carries out neither marketing nor R&D, and does very little of its own purchasing. Tix depends on 'world standard' manufacturing for its competitive edge and, indeed, for its very survival as an element of the Ascom network. Hewlett-Packard Ltd, based in east-central Scotland, is part of the well-known US electronics MNC. As a corporation, HP has a well-deserved reputation for openness and informality, with a non-authoritarian working environment. The Scottish subsidiary is over thirty years old and, in common with other HP affiliates, has a clearly-defined range of products to design, develop, manufacture and market in designated countries. Apart from major capital expenditures, the subsidiary enjoys a high degree of autonomy and — unlike Tix — has always had a very satisfactory working relationship with HQ.

The manner in which the strategies of the five Irish subsidiaries are evolving over time can be assessed by using versions of Figures 11.1 and 11.3. The first step is to compare how corporate strategy has developed; in the interviews, the overall corporate strategy of the parent corporation was discussed and assessed as it was five years ago (1990), as it appeared to be at the time of interview (1995), and as it seems likely to be in five years time

(2000). The future forecast was based, as far as possible, on the respondent's knowledge of future corporate plans. Figure 11.5 shows this evolution of MNC strategy, using Porter's (1986) typology.

FIGURE 11.5: TYPES OF INTERNATIONAL STRATEGY

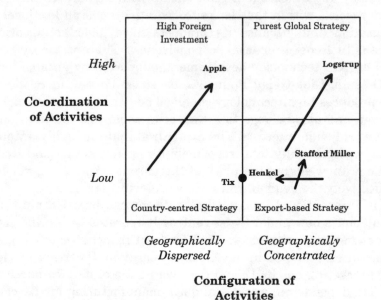

Over the ten-year period, Logstrup moves strongly from Export-based to Purest Global strategy, although its success in doing so might rest with HQ's ability to develop appropriate control mechanisms for its subsidiaries while allowing free reign to creative and ambitious local management. Apple also makes a very strong move from Country-centred to High Foreign Investment strategy; in common with others in its industry, the overall achievement of such an evolution will depend primarily on rapidly-changing competitive conditions and on Apple's ability and flexibility to position itself to take full advantage of such changes. Stafford Miller and Henkel stay within the Export-based strategy area, with both making adjustments to fine-tune strategic position to environment; Stafford Miller increases co-ordination of activities and Henkel moves carefully in the direction of increased geographical dispersion of activities. In both cases, the MNCs seem to be prudently altering an already

successful international strategy to take account of varying customer requirements and changing competitive imperatives. Only
Tix International's parent seems to be adopting an unvarying aspect in its corporate strategy. In the general case, this may occasionally be the correct prescription, but it is more likely to be akin
to opposing an advancing squadron of heavy tanks with a platoon
of riflemen immobilised in trenches.

In terms of subsidiary strategy, Figure 11.6 shows the movements determined during the interviews. Logstrup remains as a
Miniature Replica, but moves strongly from adopter-type to
innovator-type, principally through increased added-value
brought about by expanded technological capability, though adding to the product range also has a part to play. However, this affiliate's static position in terms of market scope is somewhat dis-
turbing. Apple is also strictly limited in market scope, but moves
strongly towards the innovator-type of Miniature Replica by dint
of increased added-value through the addition of software R&D at
the Cork plant. Stafford Miller is static in its product scope, but
makes a pronounced move in the direction of Product Specialist
mainly because of increments in added-value, and less so through
increases in market scope. Henkel has a strong position as a
Product Specialist, and does not see the need to change. It is not
often profitable to attempt to second-guess a successful firm but,
in this case, the exigencies of customer requirements coupled with
the need to retain a significant technological edge in its mining
market may show this strategy stasis to be an untenable position.
Tix shows minor changes in market scope, but insufficient to
move significantly from its adopter-type Miniature Replica strategy. This may well be the result of rapid changes of ownership
coupled with the strategic outlook and corporate culture of the
latest parent but, coupled with a rooted corporate strategy, it is
not persuasive of future success.

FIGURE 11.6: TYPES OF SUBSIDIARY STRATEGY

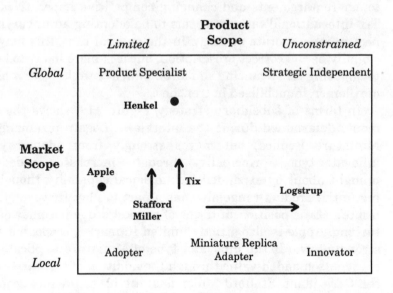

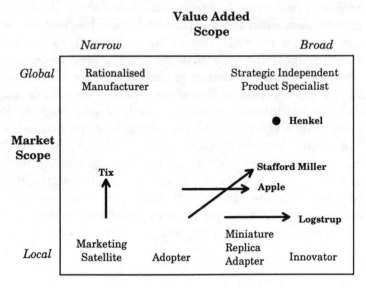

11.6 CONCLUSION

This chapter set out to assess subsidiary strategy within the bounds of the core-periphery concept, specifically by looking at the Irish experience. The review of corporate and subsidiary strategy coupled to comparison with the case of Scotland, suggests three lessons. The first is that Irish subsidiaries seem to be moving along the same kind of development life-cycle as followed by Scottish affiliates, albeit a generation behind. The emphasis on added-value, particularly through advanced R&D activities, must be given the same priority by Irish managers and policy-makers as has been the case in Scotland. Second, relaxed and positive relations with HQ seems to be coupled (without defining causation) with increased autonomy at subsidiary level and this, in turn, is not unconnected with subsidiary longevity. While this should be a particular focus for affiliate managers, it is also an important factor for policy-makers in general, and IDA Ireland in particular, to consider when developing 'after-care' programmes for inward investors. Third, evolution of subsidiary strategy over time, particularly in light of corporate strategy elaboration, must be given significantly more attention by subsidiary managers and policy-makers who wish to improve global or regional competitive advantage from within fringe economies. The techniques used here are exploratory, but indicate clearly what can be done.

It seems, then, in keeping with economic theory that Ireland is experiencing increasing effects of its peripherality. The multinational-subsidiary sector is, however, showing signs of awareness of the need to develop specific strategies to deal with the situation. Lessons may be learned from observation of the Scottish experience. This is not to imply that either country may be complacent; both are peripheral within the EU and the peripherally-located MNC affiliate must be constantly aware of the continuing fragility of its competitive position.

References

Aylmer, R. J. (1970), 'Who makes marketing decisions in the multinational firm?', *Journal of Marketing*, October 1970, pp 25-39.

Bartlett, C. A. and Ghoshal, S. (1989), *Managing across Borders: The Transnational Solution*, Boston, MA: Harvard Business School Press.

Bartlett, C. A. (1986), 'Managing and building the transnational: the new organisational challenge' in *Competition in Global Industries*, (Ed. Porter, M. E.) Boston, MA: Harvard Business School Press.

Burns, T. and Stalker, G. M. (1961), *The Management of Innovation,* London: Tavistock.

Cecchini, P. (1988), 'The cost of non-Europe', Brussels: Commission of the European Communities.

Commission of the European Communities (1981), 'The region of Europe: first periodic report on the social and economic situation of the regions of the Community', Brussels: Commission of the European Communities.

Commission of the European Communities (1993), 'Inward and outward foreign FDI in western Europe', special feature in *Panorama of EC industry*, Luxembourg: Commission of the European Communities.

Cuddy, M. P. and Keane, M. J. (1990), 'Ireland: a peripheral region' in *The Single European Market,* (Eds. Foley, A. and Mulreany, M.), Dublin: Institute of Public Administration, pp. 381-405.

El-Agraa, A. M. (1990), *Economics of the European Community*, (3rd ed.), London: Philip Allan, p. 13.

Hedlund, G. (1981), 'Autonomy of subsidiaries and formalization of headquarters-subsidiary relationships in Swedish MNCs' in *The Management of Headquarters-subsidiary Relationships in Multinational Corporations*, (Ed. Otterbeck, L.) Aldershot, Hants: Gower.

Helpman, E. and Krugman, P. (1985), *Market Structure and Foreign Trade*, Cambridge, MA: MIT Press.

Jacobson, D. and Andreosso, B. (199), 'Ireland as a Location for Multinational Markets' in *The Single European Market,* (Eds. Foley, A. and Mulreany, M.), Dublin: Institute of Public Administration, pp. 307-334.

Jarillo, J. C. and Martinez, J. I. (1990), 'Different roles for subsidiaries: the case of multinational corporations in Spain', *Strategic Management Journal*, Vol. 11, pp. 501-12.

Kaldor, N. (1970), 'The case for regional policies', *Scottish Journal of Political Economy*, Vol. 17.

Kobrin, S. J. (1991) 'An empirical analysis of the determinants of global integration', *Strategic Management Journal*, Vol. 12, pp. 17-31.

Krugman, P. (1983), 'New theories of trade among industrial countries', *American Economic Review*, Vol. 73, May.

Lawrence, P. R. and Lorsch, J. W. (1967), *Managing differentiation and integration*, Boston, MA: Harvard Business School.

Martinez, J. I. and Jarillo, J. C. (1989), 'The evolution of research on co-ordination mechanisms in multinational corporations', *Journal of International Business Studies*, Vol. 10, No. 3, pp. 489-574.

Martinez, J. I. and Jarillo, J. C. (1991), 'Co-ordination demands of international strategies', *Journal of International Business Studies*, Vol. 22, No. 3, pp. 429-44.

NESC (1989), *Ireland in the European Community: Performance, Prospects and Strategy*, Dublin: Government Publications Office, p. 343.

OECD, (1993), *Economic survey: Ireland*, Paris: OECD Publications.

Padoa-Schioppa, F. (1987), *Efficiency, Stability and Equity: A Strategy for the Evolution of the Economic System of the European Community*, Oxford: Oxford University Press.

Perlemutter, H. V. (1984), 'Building the symbiotic societal enterprise: a social architecture for the future', *World Futures*, Vol. 19 Nos. 3/4, pp. 271-284.

Porter, M. E. (1986), 'Changing patterns of international competition', *California Management Review*, Vol. 28, pp. 9-40.

Prahalad C. K. and Doz, Y. L. (1987), *The Multinational Mission*, New York: The Free Press.

Roth, K. and Morrison, A. J. (1990), 'An empirical analysis of the integration-responsiveness framework in global industries', *Journal of International Business Studies*, Vol. 21, No. 4, pp. 541-64.

Taggart, J H. (1992), 'Multinational subsidiaries in Scotland', *Multinational Business*, (Summer), pp. 6-15.

Taggart, J. H. (1995a), 'The integration-responsiveness grid: an alternative approach', *SIBU Working Paper 95/7*, University of Strathclyde.

Taggart, J. H. (1995b), 'Strategy development in multinational manufacturing subsidiaries', *SIBU Working Paper 95/8,* University of Strathclyde.

Van Hove, N. and Saunders, G., (1990), 'The single market: an overview' in *The Single European Market and the Irish Economy* (Eds. Foley, A. and Mulreany, M.) Dublin: Institute of Public Administration, pp. 307-334.

Welford, R. and Prescott, K. (1992), *European Business: An Issue-based Approach,* London: Pitman, pp. 62-63.

White, R. E. and Poynter, T. A. (1984), 'Strategies for foreign-owned subsidiaries in Canada', *Business Quarterly* (Summer), pp. 59-69.

Young, S., Hood, N. and Dunlop, S. (1988), 'Global strategies, multinational subsidiary roles and economic impact in Scotland', *Regional Studies,* Vol. 22, No. 6, pp. 487-497.

12

LOGISTICS, PERIPHERALITY AND MANUFACTURING COMPETITIVENESS

Alan McKinnon

12.1 INTRODUCTION

Logistics is the management function responsible for the movement, storage and handling of materials at all stages in the supply chain. It is fundamental to all manufacturing operations and is a major determinant of their competitiveness and profitability. In Western European countries manufacturers spend an average of between 4 and 8 per cent of sales revenue on logistical activities (Touche Ross, 1995), though in some sectors, they account for more than 20 per cent. Such cost estimates, however, do not adequately establish the true importance of the logistics function. By controlling the inward flow of supplies and the outward distribution of finished product, logistics can strongly influence the efficiency of the production operation and the quality of customer service. This means that the performance of a firms' logistical operation is reflected in both the price and availability of its products.

One of the many factors influencing logistical performance is the location of the production point. Where this is in a 'peripheral' area, one would expect transport costs to be higher and transit times to be longer than if the plant were more centrally located with respect to suppliers and customers. It is often argued, therefore, that manufacturers in peripheral regions incur a logistical penalty and that to be competitive they must derive compensating benefits from their remote location. Peripherality can, nevertheless, be a handy excuse for a weak trading position in national and international markets.

This paper examines the logistical implications of manufacturing in peripheral regions. It begins with a discussion of the concept of peripherality and shows that it needs to be adapted to take account of the complexity of modern logistic networks. The second section assesses the logistical penalties associated with peripherality, supplementing an analysis of transport-cost differentials with a more broadly-based review of the logistical challenges confronting 'peripheral' manufacturers. This analysis and review are based largely on the experience of Scottish manufacturers. Current trends in logistics are creating new problems and opportunities for these manufacturers. These trends are reviewed in later sections and an assessment made of their effect on the attractiveness of peripheral regions to manufacturing investment.

12.2 THE CONCEPT OF PERIPHERALITY

Much of the academic work on peripherality has been conditioned by two theoretical frameworks: the core-periphery model and classical industrial location theory.

The former divides the 'space economy' into a well-developed core region, where economic activity and demand are concentrated and accumulating, and a less-developed periphery which has limited indigenous demand and productive capacity and which supplies much of its output to the core region. The extent to which an area is peripheral is then judged relative to the position of the prosperous core region. This distinction between core and periphery has become blurred, however, as a result of the expansion of market areas, the formation of trading blocs and the general globalisation of business activity. Surveys of large samples of European manufacturers have shown that the proportions of supplies sourced from outside the home country and outside Europe have risen sharply in recent years and this trend is forecast to continue (A. T. Kearney Ltd., 1992). This process is not confined to more central regions. As Phelps (1993a) acknowledges '. . . peripheral region branches and subsidiaries are being integrated into a spatial division of labour which is becoming increasingly international'. The geographical expansion of supply and distribution networks has made it necessary to redefine core regions at an ever-larger spatial scale. Regions which are considered to be remote at a national level, can become less peripheral at a continental scale and even quite favourably located in global terms. Dicken (1992) neatly summarises the new situation when he states that:

> The complexity of global change has rendered simplistic notions of 'core' and 'periphery' less useful or capable of capturing the

nature of today's global economy. The world is a 'mosaic of un-evenness in a continual state of flux' rather than a simple di-chotomous structure of core and periphery.

The classical industrial location theory of Weber (1909), which has underpinned much of the subsequent work on the subject, was based on the assumption that factories would be positioned with respect to raw material sources and markets, at points which minimised transport costs. Weber's hypothetical factories were embedded in very simple supply chains comprising one tier of suppliers upstream and one tier of customers downstream. The implication was that there would be a simple linear flow of prod-uct from raw material source to final point-of-sale via a single processing plant. Peripherality tends to be similarly conceptual-ised in terms of a basic, uni-directional flow towards a core mar-ket. This grossly over-simplifies the pattern of freight movement in many industrial sectors, in which factories are entwined in complex networks linking them to many tiers of suppliers, sub-contractors and distributors. Where these networks are geo-graphically extensive, for example, as in the case of the electronics industry, the relative peripherality of individual plants becomes much more difficult to define and measure. Within these net-works, products often follow circuitous routes, shuttle back and forth between plants at different stages in the production process and are switched between final markets in response to short-term variations in consumer demand. When set against the total dis-tance a product travels between raw material source and final point-of-consumption, its routing via a peripheral region for in-termediate processing may only marginally increase the total transport requirement.

As manufacturing systems, particularly in high technology sec-tors, have become increasingly complex and transport-intensive, it has become less meaningful to assess peripherality on a regional basis. Furthermore, differences in the logistical requirements of manufacturing enterprises have widened both within and be-tween sectors making it much more difficult to generalise about the logistical consequences of locating in a peripheral area. In ex-amining these consequences, it is important to distinguish be-tween different types of production operation.

12.3 CLASSIFICATION OF PERIPHERAL MANUFACTURING

Firms manufacturing in peripheral areas can be crudely classified in terms of logistical advantages and disadvantages. Some firms actually derive a logistical advantage from locating in a peripheral region where:

- most of their sales are within that region

- a large proportion of the supplies originate in the region and much or their weight/volume is lost during the production process

- their main competitors are located in more peripheral locations.

For most manufacturers, however, a peripheral location imposes a logistical penalty. The magnitude of this penalty partly depends on the cost and quality of the logistical resources available in the region, such as road haulage and warehouse space, and partly on the geographical extent of the firm's procurement and distribution operations.

Several of the classificatory schemes that have been devised for manufacturing plants take account of their pattern of industrial linkage. For instance, key criteria in the classification of branch plants presented by White and Poynter (1984) are their degree of inter-connection with the parent company's other plants, the size of their market area and the degree of autonomy granted to local managers in matters of sourcing, product design and marketing. Plants in their 'miniature replica' category, for example, are characterised by long supply lines, though distribute finished product relatively short distances into local markets. 'Product specialist' plants, on the other hand, source materials from a smaller catchment area, but serve a much wider market.

Cooper (1993) has developed a similar classification (see Figure 12.1), which relates more explicitly to the logistical requirements of global manufacturers.

- *Invader*: Manufacturer setting up branch plant in a foreign market where it assembles kits obtained from the 'parent' and from which it distributes finished product to national or continental markets.

- *Settler*: Firm undertaking more fundamental processing at a branch plant and sourcing a much larger proportion of its supplies locally. Invaders typically evolve into settlers, especially where regulatory pressures exist to increase local content.

- *Cloner*: Firm establishing similar branch plants around the world which draw heavily on local sources of supply from the start. They require large inputs of local raw materials and, because of the nature of the finished product (e.g. soft drinks), serve only a limited market area, probably a single national or regional market.

FIGURE 12.1: PRODUCTION PROCESS AND GLOBAL LOGISTICS REQUIREMENTS

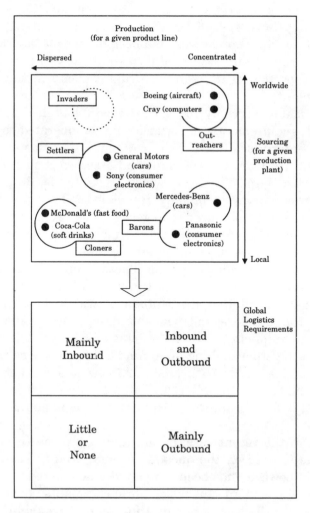

Source: Cooper, 1993.

- *Baron*: Manufacturer which concentrates its production capacity in the home country and continues to rely heavily on local suppliers. Finished products are delivered world-wide from this base.

- *Outreacher*: This type of manufacturer also centralises its production, often at a single location, but sources and distributes products world-wide.

In recent decades, invaders' have been evolving into 'settlers' and 'barons' into 'outreachers', dramatically altering their logistical requirements.

Neither the White and Poynter nor Cooper typologies make specific reference to the location of the production operation, though they have special relevance for peripheral regions. The aggregate logistical pressures on a peripheral area, and hence the potential scale of any locational disadvantage, will partly depend on the proportion of its manufacturing capacity in the different types of plant.

Empirical research by Young et al. (1988) has shed light on the logistical requirements of branch plants operated by multi-national enterprises (MNEs) in Scotland. Using cluster analysis, they identified four types of plant and assessed their relative importance. The largest category, which accounted for 39 per cent of the factories surveyed, broadly resembled White and Poynter's 'rationalised manufacturer' category. These were 'true branch plants . . . closely integrated into the manufacturing networks of the parent MNE'. As a result of strong inter-company links, supply lines would be relatively long. These plants also served wide market areas. The second largest group, with 35 per cent of the plants, also distributed their products widely but, conforming more to the 'strategic independent' designation, could exercise much more autonomy over the sourcing of supplies. The other two categories, together making up around a third of the sample, comprised smaller plants with much more limited market areas. A large proportion of the MNE-affiliated plants based in Scotland, therefore, had geographically-extensive sourcing and distribution operations.

Much of the recent research on manufacturing in peripheral areas has focused on the question of industrial linkage. Most of this work, however, has been motivated much more by a desire to measure the extent to which branch plants have become 'embedded' in the local economy, thus generating spin-off benefit, than by a concern for the logistics of sustaining a competitive manufacturing operation in a remote location. Those studies which have addressed the latter issue, have tended to take a narrow view of logistics, concentrating on regional differences in freight transport costs.

12.4 INTER-REGIONAL COMPARISONS OF MANUFACTURERS' EXPENDITURE ON FREIGHT TRANSPORT

It is often alleged that manufacturers located in peripheral areas have to pay significantly more for their transport and that this impairs their competitiveness. This is well illustrated by the following quotations:

> The main disadvantages of peripherality stem from the higher costs of communications and of market access. Unless there are sufficiently lower factor costs in peripheral areas, it would be expected that such economic activities would tend to gravitate towards the core of the EC (Begg, 1990).

> The North and Scotland are perceived to be remote regions of the UK when viewed from Europe. This peripherality brings its own handicaps of distance from international markets, customers and suppliers....If transportation is the lifeblood of modern industry, the North and Scotland are badly in need of a blood transfusion (Charles Barker Assocs., 1992).

Sometimes the claim is backed by statistical evidence. For example, in a joint report (cited by Barrett, 1994), the Irish Government and European Commission claimed that 'Transport costs for Irish exporters to mainland Europe (at over 9 per cent of export sales values) are approximately twice those incurred by Community countries trading with one another on the European mainland. The disadvantages of peripherality have a particularly serious impact on Ireland because it is a small open economy.' This claim has, nevertheless, been disputed by Durkan and Reynolds-Feighan (1990) who conducted a survey of 147 Irish-based firms and on this basis calculated the ratio of international transport costs to foreign sales revenue to be 3.6 per cent for exports to other EC countries, a lower figure than for trade flows between mainland EC members.

This apparently anomalous result is by no means unique. Four studies conducted over the past 25 years of Scottish manufacturers' expenditure on freight transport have yielded similar results (Logan, 1971; Industry Department Scotland, 1981; PIEDA, 1984 and Steedman and Vickerman, 1993). They have shown that, when expressed as a percentage of value-added (or net output), their transport expenditure is not significantly higher than that of UK manufacturing as a whole. Indeed, the most recent study, based on input-output data collected in 1989, indicated that Scottish firms paid only 1.02 per cent of their sales revenue on road transport, while their counterparts elsewhere in the UK paid an average of 1.30 per cent. This differential is likely to be strongly reflected in total freight transport expenditure by manufacturers as, in 1989, road accounted for 71 per cent of freight tonnage lifted in Scotland and 68 per cent across the UK as a whole (Scottish Office 1994; Department of Transport 1994a) Even a matched pair survey of small manufacturers in a peripheral region (Scotland) and a core region (south east of England) could find no 'systematic inter-regional difference' in freight transport costs (O'Farrell and Hitchens, 1989).

The apparent absence of a significant transport cost penalty can be explained with reference to three factors:

- structural adaptation

- strategic adjustment

- transport market conditions.

12.4.1 Structural Adaptation
It has been argued that, at a macro-level, manufacturing industry in a peripheral region can adapt to its location in ways which minimise the associated transport cost penalty (Chisholm, 1985). These include:

1. *Disproportionate development of sectors producing high value products, which are characterised by low ratios of transport cost to sales.* This is well illustrated by Scotland, whose export trade is overwhelmingly dominated by high value-density products. In 1993, electronic equipment and whisky, accounted for over 60 per cent of total export sales (Scottish Council Development and Industry, 1994). This is reflected by the fact that the average value per tonne of Scotland's manufactured exports is approximately 25 per cent higher than the UK average (Department of Transport, 1993).

2. *Heavier dependence on international trade, particularly in deep-sea markets, because relative peripherality can diminish as trading links become more geographically extensive.* This argument has been advanced by Chisholm (1987) and endorsed by Hoare (1993). Scotland again provides supporting evidence for this hypothesis. International trade represents a significantly higher proportion of its GDP than that of the UK as a whole and a much larger share of its exports (by value) go to deep-sea destinations (Department of Transport, 1993).

3. *High degree of regional self-sufficiency.* This minimises firms' exposure to higher inter-regional and international transport costs. Although Scotland exhibits an above-average propensity to trade with other regions and countries in value terms, freight transport statistics suggest that in tonnage terms it is relatively self-contained. Approximately 92 per cent of road freight tonnage lifted in Scotland moves internally within the region, whereas elsewhere in the UK only around 73 per cent of road freight is intra-regional (Department of Transport, 1994b). Even when one allows for intra-regional movement of export and import traffic to local ports and airports, there remains a wide disparity.

12.4.2 Strategic Adjustment

At the micro-level, there are several measures that firms located in peripheral areas can take to ease or offset any transport cost penalty. These measures can be divided into two general categories: those which confer a genuine benefit and those which merely transfer responsibility for logistics to other organisations, often to the detriment of the peripheral manufacturer.

The beneficial measures are as follows:

1. *Purchase supplies at uniform delivered prices.* Many suppliers, particularly within the domestic market, charge uniform prices across the country as a whole or within wide zones covering several regions. By purchasing supplies from such firms, peripheral manufacturers can effectively have their delivery cross-subsidised by other more centrally-located customers.

2. *Maximise value-added in a low cost, peripheral location.* Manufacturers must recover the cost of their transport operation from the value they add to products. To be economically attractive, a location in a peripheral area must offer a higher

ratio of value-added to manufacturing cost than can be achieved elsewhere. In peripheral regions, the cost of factor inputs is generally lower and financial support, in the form of grants and/or tax concessions, made available by local and central government. As explained in an earlier paper:

> Having established a manufacturing operation in a remote location, a firm is likely to want to exploit these cost advantages to the full by maximising the amount of processing carried out there, especially where, as in the case of Scotland, the region has a skilled labour force capable of performing high value-adding operations. This can ensure that the ratio of value added to manufacturing cost is sufficiently large in the remote location to offset the higher transport costs.' (McKinnon, 1993)

3. *Make more efficient use of transport.* Firms based in peripheral areas have a greater incentive than their more centrally-located counterparts to use transport resources efficiently. This might encourage them, for example, to select transport modes and carriers more carefully, consolidate loads to a greater extent and plan vehicle routes and schedules more rigorously. The study by PIEDA (1984) indicated that manufacturers in Scotland and Northern Ireland attached greater importance to transport costs and reviewed their transport operations more frequently than firms in the South East of England. No research has yet been done, however, to establish whether this greater concern for transport has been translated into more efficient freight movement.

The following measures are more questionable:

4. *Selling products on an ex-works or FOB[1] basis.* This allows a manufacturer to avoid paying all or part of the delivery charge, thus reducing the ratio of transport cost to value-added. It may be a more attractive option for peripheral manufacturers, given the longer distances to customers. As no research has yet been done on regional variations in manufacturing pricing schemes, this remains an untested hypothesis. It is generally agreed, however, that selling *ex works* tends to reduce the competitive-

---

[1] When a product is sold on a Free-on-Board (FOB) basis, responsibility is divided between the supplier and customer. The latter usually arranges and pays for carriage as far as a depot, port or airport within the country of origin.

ness of a firm's products (Davies et al., 1988), particularly where the transport arranged by the customer is inferior in terms of cost and service quality.

5. *Selling and/or purchasing via local intermediaries.* Manufacturers in peripheral areas can also shed responsibility for inbound and outbound transport to wholesalers and dealers. This also tends to narrow regional differentials in the ratio of transport cost to net output. The PIEDA (1984) survey suggested that manufacturers in peripheral regions made slightly greater use of wholesale intermediaries than more centrally-located firms. Very little research has been done, however, on the extent to which peripherality can influence the channel decisions of manufacturers. If it were to cause over-reliance on intermediaries, overall competitiveness and profitability might be adversely affected.

12.4.3 Transport Market Conditions

There are several ways in which the nature of the freight transport market can be advantageous to peripheral manufacturers.

1. *Uniform rate structures.* Many airfreight rates and deep-sea container rates tend to be standardised at the national level, with firms paying approximately the same rate regardless of location. Research in the UK on air cargo services used by the electronics industry, for example, suggests that there is 'little difference between the average freight rates to and from Scotland and to and from London' (Forster and Peters, 1994). Even when analysed on a 'generalised cost' basis, allowing for differences in transit times, the data indicate that 'manufacturers in Scotland do not suffer a significant cost disadvantage compared to manufacturers in South East England'. In the case of deep-sea shipping, the 'grid system', operated by the major conference lines, subsidises the overland feeder movement of containers from Scotland to the major English 'hub' ports of Southampton, Tilbury, Felixstowe and Liverpool. For Scottish firms, the overland transport costs are calculated with respect to Greenock or Grangemouth (which are no longer visited by deep-sea vessels) despite the fact that their containers travel much longer distances to the English hub ports. Similar overland container charging systems exist in other European countries.

2. *Tapering of transport costs over distance.* Even in the absence of these uniform-charging regimes, freight rates seldom increase in direct proportion to distance. The existence of a large element of terminal/vehicle standing cost, which is unaffected by the distance travelled, causes total transport cost per km. to 'taper' as the length of haul increases. For example, in the case of the average 38-tonne articulated lorry in the UK, only around 51 per cent of total vehicle operating costs is sensitive to the distance travelled (*Motor Transport,* 1994).

3. *Traffic imbalances.* The volumes of freight moving to and from peripheral regions are often unbalanced and this can depress freight rates on outbound journeys, to the benefit of exporters. For instance, in the case of Scotland, roughly twice as much road freight tonnage enters the country as leaves it (Scottish Office, 1994). This does not mean that Scotland is running a large trade deficit! It is largely due to differences in the modal split and value-density of flows in the two directions. The surplus of outbound road haulage allows Scottish-based manufacturers to distribute their products at more favourable rates (TecnEcon, 1994).

In summary, it appears that peripherality need not impose a significant transport cost burden. Research on the transport operations of Scottish-based manufacturers, for example, appears to challenge the traditional view of peripheral regions as being severely handicapped by their location. It is necessary, however, to issue several caveats.

First, although the transport cost differentials are small relative to manufacturing value-added, they will represent a much larger proportion of the profit margin. As transport costs account for only a very small proportion of sales revenue though, the sensitivity of profits to these regional cost differentials is likely to be very low. This was confirmed by an analysis of geographical variations in industrial profitability in the UK undertaken by Tyler et al. (1988). In their assessment of industrial cost elements contributing to the geographical 'profit gradient' outward from London, transport cost was one of several residual items collectively responsible for only 8.4 per cent of the variation in profit.

Second, while the average level of manufacturers' transport costs in a peripheral region may be broadly in line with that elsewhere, this need not apply at the sectoral level. In the case of Scotland, for example, firms in the metal manufacturing, mechanical engineering and transport equipment sectors, appear to suffer a notable transport cost penalty (Steedman and Vickerman, 1993). In Northern Ireland, the mechanical engineering, furniture and carpet industries are believed to be vulnerable to higher transport costs (Sheehan, 1993). For a peripheral region to retain a diverse industrial base, the transport needs of particular sectors must be addressed.

Third, research on the effect of peripherality on manufacturing has been pre-occupied with the cost of transport and given little consideration to the *quality* of transport services. This ignores the fact that, in many industrial sectors, much greater emphasis is placed on the speed and reliability of transport than its cost. Ironically, it is those sectors producing high value-density products, which can withstand the costs of long distance freight movement and which are essential to the process of structural adaptation, whose transport operations tend to be the most time-sensitive (McKinnon, 1993). For them, logistical disadvantage is more a function of the length and variability of transit times than the cost of movement. Although these variables are inter-related, with faster services commanding premium rates, the volume of traffic moving to and from a peripheral region is unlikely to support as wide a range of transport options and as frequent services as more central regions. Firms' freedom to trade-off service quality against cost in their choice of mode and carrier may also be constrained by the nature of the product and pattern of freight flow. The issue of service quality is discussed more fully in section 12.5.

Fourth, peripherality has so far been examined in purely transport terms and not with respect to the broader logistical framework within which transport is organised. This framework also encompasses the range of inter-related activities, including inventory management, materials handling, warehousing, order-processing, procurement and even production scheduling. By ignoring these other activities, one overlooks the possibility that firms in peripheral areas minimise their transport expenditure at the expense of other aspects of their logistics operation. For example, in an effort to consolidate loads for expensive hauls to distant markets, they might accumulate larger inventories and offer customers a less responsive delivery service. Also, as a result of the longer feeder distances to hub ports and airports, vehicles often have to leave earlier than from more centrally-located plants, imposing a tighter constraint on production schedules. As transport is now widely planned and managed within the context of logistics, it is necessary to take a much broader view of the logistical penalties associated with peripherality.

12.5 THE INTEGRATION AND ELEVATION OF LOGISTICS

The restructuring of logistics management began in the US in the early 1960s. Since then the general principles of logistics have diffused both sectorally and geographically (Bowersox et al., 1986). One of the key principles is that the management of interrelated logistical activities should be closely co-ordinated in such a way as to optimise the complete system of material movement, storage and handling. This is reflected in the large numbers of firms which have created logistics departments with wide-ranging control of material flow (Cooper et al, 1991).

As recognition has grown that logistics can make a major contribution to competition, the status of the function has risen within the corporate hierarchy. Logistics issues are now being accorded greater importance in strategic decision-making on matters such as plant location. For example, in evidence to the House of Commons Scottish Affairs Committee (1993), the American electronics firm Compaq claimed that distribution requirements had 'become its over-riding consideration in plant location decisions'.

When seen in a broader logistical context, the relative importance of any transport cost penalty diminishes. Across a sample of 381 manufacturers in seven European countries surveyed in 1994, transport accounted for roughly 30 per cent, on average, of total logistics costs and 1.5 to 2.0 per cent of sales revenue (Touche Ross, 1995). Between 1987 and 1992, transport costs declined as a percentage of both logistics costs and sales revenue (A. T. Kearney Ltd., 1992). As pointed out earlier, a large part of this transport cost element (around 50 per cent in the case of road haulage) is not distance-related and hence unlikely to be subject to a 'peripherality' effect. Any additional transport costs a firm incurs by locating in a peripheral area can be offset by the lower cost of other logistical 'inputs', such as labour and warehouse space.

The transit time penalty which peripheral manufacturers often experience also needs to be reassessed within a wider logistical context. One of the dominant trends in logistical management in recent years has been the acceleration of material flow and consequent reduction in inventory levels. This has placed much greater emphasis on the speed and reliability of delivery.

12.6 ACCELERATION OF MATERIAL FLOW

One of the most potent business ideas of recent years has been that of 'time-based' competition. As Stalk (1988), one of its main exponents, has observed:

> Today, time is the cutting edge. The ways leading companies manage time — in production, in new product development and introduction, in sales and distribution — represent the most powerful new sources of competitive advantage.

A key element in time-based competition is the speed with which material flows through the business. The time elapsing between the arrival of inbound supplies and the delivery of the finished product to the customer is often called the 'logistical cycle' time. Companies are under intense pressure to reduce this time, particularly in sectors experiencing a rapid rate of technological change. Having greatly accelerated the development of new products, companies are obviously keen to minimise the 'time to market' by physically distributing new ranges as quickly as possible. The corresponding shortening of product life-cycles is forcing firms to accelerate the flow of materials right across the logistical channel (or 'pipeline') to minimise the risk of being left with large amounts of inventory when a particular product is superseded (Christopher, 1992).

Increasing numbers of firms are employing 'lead-time management' to identify and eliminate sources of delay in their procurement, production and distribution operations (Braithwaite and Christopher, 1989). The application of the just-in-time (JIT) principle in manufacturing and the adoption of 'quick response' in retail distribution are compressing order lead times at different levels in the supply chain. The benefits, mainly in reduced inventory, increased responsiveness and reduced risk of obsolescence, have been impressive.

Order lead time, however, should not be confused with transit time. The time taken to transport goods contributes to the overall order-lead time, but, for most products, usually accounts for only a small proportion of the total time expended. Its share of the total logistical cycle time, which includes the time spent in the production process, can be very small indeed. There is a large amount of 'idle time' in the typical logistical channel, when products, in their original material/component form, as sub-assemblies or finished items, lie around as 'static inventory'. For example, an analysis by Cranfield School of Management of the logistical cycle time of a video recorder manufactured in Japan and distributed to a British retailer revealed that of the 190 days that elapsed between the arrival of the first component at the assembly plant to the delivery of the finished product to the retailer only 45 days were required for manufacture and transport. Transit times can be short relative to the amount of time that materials and components spend on factory sites awaiting processing. An analysis by a Scottish-based electronics company of lead times within the factory found that one class of components was spending on average 11 days in the plant, but only 4 hours actually on the production line undergoing assembly. Prior to the adoption of a 'lean logistics' programme, the ratio of value-adding time to idle time for materials in a Microsoft plant in Ireland was even greater (Fynes and Ennis, 1994).

While transit times are important, they must be seen in perspective. Relative to a product's total logistical cycle time slightly longer transit times to and from more peripheral areas may be of little significance. Regional differences in transit times can also be obscured by variability within firms' logistical systems. Logistical cycle times can vary widely, even for a particular product. The time taken at each stage in the channel can vary and when added together can produce wide fluctuations in total lead time (Stock and Lambert, 1993). Research by Philips, the Dutch electrical firm, indicated the extent to which transit times can vary by consignment (Farmer and Ploos van Amstel, 1992). They tracked the movement of a sample of consignments between Japan and their main plant in the Netherlands. The total transit time varied between 6 days and 22 days. Transit time variability tends to increase with the number of transport modes used and number of international frontiers to be crossed, but not necessarily with distance *per se*. While, in theory, the globalisation of firms' logistical operations should be increasing this variability, major carriers, freight forwarders and the shippers themselves are trying to standardise on the minimum possible transit time. This may have the effect of magnifying any transit time penalty associated with the routing of products via peripheral regions for processing.

Although the redefinition of 'lead times' to encompass the full spectrum of activities involved in procurement, production and distribution makes any additional transit time penalty associated with a peripheral location appear small, two points should be borne in mind:

- Firms often consider it easier to cut transit times than to reduce lead times in other parts of the business, particularly as responsibility for transport usually resides with outside agencies.

- As the time expended on non-transport activities is reduced, especially with the development of IT systems, the relative importance of transit times may increase, making manufacturers' logistical operations more sensitive to inter-regional variations in delivery times.

To minimise any transit time disadvantage peripheral regions must, therefore, try to:

1. *Maximise the range, frequency and convenience of direct services.* Often the development of transport services to and from peripheral regions is constrained not only by remoteness but by the relatively small and unbalanced flows of freight traffic. Moreover, where direct services do exist, they are often less conveniently scheduled than those to more central regions and less well synchronised with production and distribution cycles.

2. *Offer easy access to hub ports and airports outside the region.* The development of global sourcing and marketing has made access to global air and sea networks an important criterion against which to assess a region's relative peripherality.

3. *Maximise the reliability of direct and indirect services.* Most of the research done on supplier and carrier selection suggests that the most important requirement is reliability. This usually takes precedence over speed and price. Sharp reductions in inventory levels have reduced the tolerance of production and distribution systems to transport deficiencies.

As peripheral areas tend to suffer a transit time penalty, it is possible that manufacturers based there will try to modify their logistical systems to minimise its impact on the efficiency of their production operations and quality of their customer service. Peripherality might therefore distort the trade-offs that manufacturers make between transport and other logistics variables, particularly inventory and information.

12.7 THE EFFECT OF PERIPHERALITY ON INVENTORY LEVELS

To compensate for longer transit times, peripheral manufacturers might be expected to hold larger inventories. In the case of inbound supplies, this would involve holding larger buffer stocks of 'materials, stores and fuel' (MSF) at, or in the vicinity of, the factory. For outbound distribution, it might entail either holding larger stocks of finished product (i.e. 'goods on hand for sale' (GHS)) at the plant to ensure that it was readily available for despatch whenever an order arrived or dispersing inventory to depots within easier reach of the main markets. As explained in a later section, the dispersal of inventory generally increases the total amount of inventory that needs to be held, inflating both stockholding and storage costs. Any tendency by peripheral manufacturers to decentralise inventory to a greater extent than their more centrally located competitors might, therefore, achieve parity on customer service at the expense of significantly higher logistics costs. No research has yet been done on matched samples of manufacturers in peripheral and core regions to establish whether or not such a tendency exists.

It has, nevertheless, been possible in the UK, using Census of Production data, to conduct an analysis of the amounts of inventory held by manufacturers at their production facilities (McKinnon, 1991). This revealed that in the three most peripheral regions in the UK (Scotland, Northern England and Northern Ireland), the ratio of manufacturing inventory to net output was 30 per cent or more above the national average. More detailed analysis of the Scottish data attributed around half of the over-stocking to the long-term storage of whisky, but this still identified several other important sectors, such as electronics, electrical engineering and transport equipment, significantly overstocked by national standards. Further investigation revealed that almost all the excess stock was in the 'work-in-progress' category, i.e. within the production process. Stock levels at either end of the production process interfacing with the external supply and distribution systems were broadly in line with national averages. This indicated that 'the relative overstocking was largely intrinsic to the production process and not a consequence of long supply and distribution links' (McKinnon, 1991).

The apparent absence of a distance-related peripherality effect on factory-based inventory levels may be explained in several ways:

1. Peripheral manufacturers try to minimises the transit time penalty by using faster transport services. These would also be more expensive, however, and, as pointed out earlier, there is no evidence to show that Scottish manufacturers incur significantly higher transport costs than their counterparts elsewhere in the UK.

2. A larger proportion of finished stock is dispersed to depots in other regions/countries. This requires further investigation.

3. Transit times exert only a minor influence on the amounts of MSF and GHS inventory that a manufacturer holds. Other factors such as purchasing policy, production scheduling, seasonal and promotional variations in demand and IT systems can be much more important and these are unlikely to be subject to the same degree of geographical variation as transit times. In the case of IT, firms in peripheral areas have an added incentive to communicate and process commercial information rapidly so as to minimise the non-transport element of the order lead time. By so doing they would effectively be substituting IT resources for higher inventory levels and/or faster, more expense transport (Christopher, 1992). It is not known if peripheral manufacturers exhibit this bias as no comparison has yet been made of inter-regional differences in logistics information systems.

4. Peripheral manufacturers are more heavily dependent on local suppliers and distributors. It was noted earlier that in terms of freight volumes the Scottish economy is more self-contained than that of other UK regions. When measured in value terms, however, its external trade its relatively high and it is in value terms that variations in manufacturing inventory levels have been analysed. For example, in 1989 71 per cent, by value, of the purchases made by Scottish manufacturers came from outside Scotland, while 66 per cent of their output, again by value, was sold outside the region (Vickerman, 1992/3).

The management of inventory in many manufacturing sectors has been transformed over the past 10 to 15 years by the application of the JIT principle. This has been of particular relevance to Scotland as a large share of its manufacturing output is from sectors, such as electronics and electrical engineering, in which the principle has been widely adopted. In theory, JIT can present both a threat and an opportunity to a peripheral region. The threat is that by compressing lead times JIT will magnify the transit time penalties that peripheral regions suffer making them less attractive locations for manufacturing investment and making it difficult for factories already based there to enjoy the full benefits of JIT. The potential opportunities are that JIT will promote a higher degree of local sourcing within the peripheral region and that more component suppliers will be drawn to the region by the need to meet the needs of peripheral assembly plants at short notice. In practice, however, JIT appears so far to have had much less effect on manufacturing activity in peripheral regions than was predicted.

12.8 JIT AND PERIPHERALITY

In the early stages of JIT adoption in Western economies, it was anticipated that it would stimulate local economic development in the vicinity of major assembly plants, particularly in the electronics, consumer electrical and automotive sectors (e.g. Estall, 1985). The clustering of JIT suppliers around such plants in Japan was reckoned to provide a model of what would happen in the West. It was hoped that JIT might provide the basis of a new local economic strategy leading to the development of 'just-in-time regions' characterised by strong local bonding and the emergence of 'spatially-concentrated growth poles' (Mair, 1993). In a study of the 'spatial dynamics of JIT manufacturing systems', Reid (1995) claims to have detected evidence, at county level, of a JIT-related agglomeration effect around Japanese branch plants in the United States. This finding is fairly exceptional, however. Most research on the subject has been unable to establish clear evidence of JIT either increasing the proportion of supplies drawn from local firms or causing a clustering of plants in JIT complexes. This conclusion appears to apply both cross-sectorally and to central regions as much as those on the periphery.

The failure of JIT to induce a geographical shift in procurement patterns towards local suppliers is clearly illustrated by the Scottish electronics industry. Despite this industry's commitment to JIT sourcing, the proportion of supplies (by value) obtained by Scottish-based electronics firms from within Scotland has remained fairly stable at around 12 per cent since the mid-1980s (Turok, 1993; SPEED Ltd, 1994). Indeed, during the 1990s there has been a sharp increase in the proportion of supplies originating outside the UK, up from 60 per cent in 1990 to 74 per cent in

1994. This recent trend provides support for the view that, as a result of increasing manufacturing specialisation at inter-regional and international levels, 'the adoption of JIT supplier relations, far from engendering a localisation of backward linkages, may undermine existing levels of local sourcing in many industries' (Phelps, 1993b).

Several reasons can be offered for the absence of a pronounced JIT effect on the pattern of industrial linkage. Firms sourcing large quantities of supplies tend to attach limited importance to the location of the vendor. In a survey of 40 such firms in the US, Ansari and Modarress (1990) found that only 9 per cent considered this to be a major sourcing criterion, while 56 per cent regarded it as being of little or no importance. The purchasing decision is still dominated by other factors such as design, quality and price, particularly in the case of the higher-value components which collectively make up a large proportion of total material costs. Because of their high inventory costs and tight quality specifications, these parts can justify expensive express delivery. Where transport infrastructure and services are fast and reliable, any JIT localisation effect is likely to be weakened (Linge, 1991). This leads Mair (1993) to suggest that:

> Highly localised spatial concentration in Japan may be uniquely related to that country's poor transportation infra-structures. Places with good infrastructures can, paradoxically, expect less local supplier company investment.

Good transport links are one of three reasons that Milne (1990) offered for suppliers of components not gravitating to plants assembling consumer electrical products on a JIT basis. The others were that:

- no single assembly plant was big enough, and therefore, by implication, took a large enough share of an individual supplier's output, to exert the necessary locational pull

- by drawing closer to one assembly plant, a supplier might lengthen the backward linkages to its own suppliers, thus impairing its own ability to operate a JIT production system.

On the whole, most manufacturers' JIT sourcing policies have not put suppliers under pressure to relocate closer to their premises. On the contrary, it appears that, in the pursuit of 'world-class' suppliers, they are often prepared to make concessions where sourcing over long distances compromises their JIT operation. As Clarke and Beaney (1993) observe in a study of the Scottish electronics industry, 'most major information-system companies in Scotland claim to operate JIT sourcing, but it is clear that its manner of operation is designed around the perceived capabilities and cost structure of suppliers in different parts of the world'. Advances in communication and the development of closer supply chain liaison have also made it possible for distant suppliers 'to establish the experience of local engineering and manufacturing without actually locating facilities close to their customers' (Angel, 1992).

Although JIT has not significantly increased the relative value of purchases from local suppliers, it may have increased the degree of local sourcing in terms of freight volumes. It is now common for firms, particularly in peripheral areas such as Scotland and Wales, to obtain bulkier, lower value materials, such as packaging and plastic mouldings, on a JIT basis from local suppliers (Turok, 1993; Munday et al., 1995). They can thus avoid the high cost of transporting these products long distances and of meeting their heavy warehouse space requirement.

The implementation of JIT is one of several factors that have caused manufacturers to reappraise their sourcing policies and redefine their relationships with suppliers. The implications of these changes for peripheral regions extend well beyond the issue of JIT delivery.

12.9 CHANGING RELATIONSHIPS WITH SUPPLIERS

Many firms have realised that it is not enough simply to overhaul the logistical operations that they directly manage. The efficiency of these internal operations can be impaired by the actions of firms above and below them in the supply chain. Supply chain management aims to improve the quality of the external relationships with suppliers and distributors and affects many aspects of their operations, including product design, quality control and production scheduling. One of the key elements in any supply chain management programme is the improvement of transport links between the participating companies (Carter and Ferrin, 1995). In some sectors, particularly electronics, this has resulted in assembly firms assuming more control over the inward flow of supplies. This has occurred for several reasons:

1. *To increase the reliability of deliveries to the standard required for JIT operation.* Sharp reductions in buffer stocks have increased the vulnerability of production operations to the late delivery of supplies. By more closely monitoring and controlling inbound flows firms can help to reduce the risk of disruption.

2. *To consolidate in-bound supplies.* The adoption of JIT and more flexible forms of manufacturing has resulted in supplies being ordered more frequently in smaller quantities. To help maintain the efficiency of the inbound transport operation and relieve pressure on factory reception facilities many manufacturers now employ contractors to consolidate supplies, often for delivery directly to the production line. This sometimes involves a 'milk run' around several suppliers to collect supplies for later consolidation. The Scottish-based assembly plants of firms such as IBM and Digital have demonstrated that it is possible to operate such a collection system effectively from a peripheral region.

3. *To obtain return loads for delivery vehicles and thus improve the overall efficiency of the transport operation.* The proportion of lorry-kms. run empty in the UK declined from 32.8 per cent in 1980 to 28.5 per cent in 1994, partly as a result of firms making greater effort to backload their vehicles (McKinnon, 1996). By extending their influence back along the supply chain, firms have been able to co-ordinate more closely inbound and outbound movements, thereby increasing opportunities for return loading.

4. *To minimise the risk of being overcharged for delivery by suppliers.* It is now quite common for suppliers to be asked to provide two quotations, an *ex works* price and a price inclusive of delivery. This has increased the 'transparency' of inbound transport costs. Many manufacturers now have a better idea of the cost of transporting supplies to their plants than in the past. This will have increased awareness of any 'peripherality effect' particularly in the case of purchases from suppliers whose delivery charges reflect the distance travelled. On the other hand, a purchasing firm based in a peripheral area may now be able to find more efficient means of conveying its supplies, thus effectively reducing their bought-in price.

It is not only the nature of the relationship with suppliers that is changing. The boundaries of manufacturing enterprises are being redefined, with increased sourcing of goods and services from outside agencies. A broad consensus has developed over the past decade that firms should concentrate on their 'core competencies' and buy-in goods and services that can be produced more cheaply and to a higher quality by outside suppliers. Western countries appear to be moving towards the Far Eastern pattern of industrial organisation which is characterised by a high degree of subcontracting and external sourcing. In Britain, the branch plants of Far Eastern manufacturers have exhibited a much greater propensity to source components externally than indigenous firms (Turok, 1993). This is partly because their UK branch plants draw many of their supplies from the parent company and because of 'dissatisfaction with local suppliers over quality, price and delivery' (Trevor and Christie, 1988). It also reflects the tradition in the home country of relying heavily on outside suppliers. The high level of inward investment by these firms, particularly from Japan, in sectors such as electronics and car assembly, has, nevertheless, had a major impact on the structure of the UK supply network.

The vertical 'disintegration' of manufacturing operations is adding more links to the supply chain and generating more movement of freight at intermediate stages in the production process. Activities that were previously concentrated at the main manufacturing site are now performed elsewhere by subcontractors. In some cases, sub-assemblies go out for processing and/or testing and are then returned to the main plant. The traditional view of firms' freight transport requirements as comprising inbound flows of materials and outbound movements of finished product often over-simplifies the true situation.

From a logistical standpoint, it is obviously beneficial to have contract operations performed locally. In optimising plant location, firms are increasingly taking account of the local availability of subcontractors and the ability of transport links to support intermediate movements to more distant contractors. Within the UK, major 'subcontractor complexes' have developed in peripheral areas such as Scotland and Wales (Clarke and Beaney, 1993; Munday et al., 1995), although in a study of branch plant development in the North East of England, Phelps (1993a) concludes that, 'intra-corporate trade remains a powerful constraint upon processes of vertical disintegration in peripheral regions.'

An additional, often intra-corporate, link has been added to many manufacturing supply chains by the separation of product customisation from the main assembly operation. As customisation is usually performed close to the market, it is of particular relevance to firms with major production facilities in peripheral regions.

12.10 GROWTH OF CUSTOMISATION

An increasing proportion of manufactured products are being tailored to the requirements of particular customer groups or even individual consumers. In an effort to retain scale economies in production, while greatly increasing the degree of market segmentation, manufacturers have had to restructure their production and distribution operations. A common strategy has been to concentrate the mass production of standard units in low-cost locations and then to customise products to local requirements at plants closer to the regional markets. This allows firms to apply the 'principle of postponement' and thus avoid committing product to particular markets until a late stage in the logistical cycle. As Cooper (1993) notes, 'the postponement aim is to retain product commonality as long as possible in the production process.' By customising close to the final demand, in both geographical and scheduling terms, firms can reduce inventory levels and increase their responsiveness to short-term variations in market conditions.

Customisation can involve a wide range of activities varying in the amount of value that they add to a product. Normally, however, it adds relatively little value and offers limited opportunity to exploit a peripheral region's advantages as a manufacturing base, such as low labour costs and property prices. Many firms would, therefore, derive little benefit from routing products via a peripheral region solely for customisation, except where they already have a major production facility there. Customisation work can usefully bolster these existing plants, as exemplified by OKI's plant at Cumbernauld in Scotland which supplements its main activity of printer manufacturing with the tailoring of fax machines produced in Japan to the varying technical requirements of European telecom systems. It can also expand the volumes of international freight moving to and from a peripheral region, thus promoting the development of more frequent and direct services.

Changes in the geography of customisation operations has been closely related to re-organisation of distribution in the European market. Much of the responsibility for final preparation and packaging, which was previously devolved to national sales and distribution centres across the continent, has now been concentrated at 'pan-European' warehouses and factories, some of which are located on the periphery of the Single Market. For example, with concentration of IBM's and Digital's European production and distribution operations at plants in Scotland has come a range of customisation activities previously undertaken at numerous locations across the European mainland.

12.11 CENTRALISATION OF INVENTORY

A major motive for the restructuring of distribution systems at national and international levels, has been the desire to centralise inventory. Centralisation enables firms to exploit the 'square root law of inventory' and thus reduce substantially the total amount of stock they need to hold (Maister, 1976). Although, in practice, the inventory savings are seldom as great as those predicted by this 'law', they can still be large. For example, a leading distributor of chemicals and pharmaceuticals recently achieved a 30 per cent reduction in stock levels by closing its eight UK depots and replacing them with a single warehouse in the East Midlands.

The centralisation of inventory within the UK, which has been underway for over 20 years and has been largely facilitated by the development of the motorway network, has resulted in the closure of many distribution depots in more peripheral parts of the country (McKinnon, 1989). Firms, such as Lever Bros. and ICI Paints, for example, no longer hold stock in Scotland and supply the Scottish market directly from English factories or distribution centres.

A similar process of inventory centralisation is now occurring at a European level within the Single Market (O'Laughlin et al., 1993). Companies such as Rank Xerox, Apple Computers, Sony and Polaroid, have been closing national warehouses and concentrating their inventory at European Distribution Centres (EDCs). According to research by Buck Consultants (1991), the vast majority of the EDCs used by US and Japan companies are located in the Netherlands, Belgium and Northern France.

This process of centralisation could pose a threat to the economies of Europe's more peripheral regions if multinationals already based there shifted their storage and distribution capacity to the core of the European market and this led to a gradual erosion of other more value-adding activities. The experience of Scotland, however, suggests that this is a very pessimistic scenario, for several reasons:

1. Several foreign-owned companies with large production and distribution operations in Scotland, including IBM, Digital, OKI and Mitsubishi, have recently reviewed their European logistical strategies, taking account of the creation of the Single European Market, and decided to retain and, in some cases, expand their distribution facilities in Scotland.

   IBM and Digital, for example, have closed down many of their national distribution centres and now supply European customers directly from their Scottish plants. The plants' 'customers' are no longer sales/distribution subsidiaries in other European countries but rather outside distributors and end users. The decision to 'direct ship' from Scotland has been made despite the fact that:

   • The removal of buffer stocks from each of the national markets has made the standard of delivery to customer much more dependent on the speed and reliability of direct transport services from Scotland. Firms that have made this change insist that the standard of the delivery service has not been compromised and, if anything, improved.

   • Delivery direct to customers, rather than via a national distribution centre, usually requires adherence to much tighter delivery schedules. This is because many customers now specify booking-in times for delivery vehicles. If a vehicle fails to arrive within the specified 'time window' at a customer's premises (typically 30-60 minutes), it is often turned away and delivery postponed until the following day. In the past, deliveries from Scottish plants to national distribution centres were not so strictly disciplined and it was easier for local delivery vehicles to meet customer book-in times over the shorter distances from these distribution centres.

   • Direct shipment to customers has also entailed some loss of efficiency in international transport operations. When the trunk movement from Scotland was to a national distribution centre, traffic could be consolidated into full loads. Direct deliveries to customer are often of smaller quantities and the need to supply these consignments quickly limits the possibility of holding back orders until a full load accumulates (Picard, 1982). The decline in vehicle utilisation has increased unit transport costs from Scotland, although this appears to have been more than offset by the benefits of centralising distribution at Scottish plants.

- While this restructuring of European distribution operations has been underway, many companies have been expanding their sales area, mainly into Eastern Europe. There is no evidence that this has weakened firms' commitment to using Scotland as a major, if not the main, base for European distribution.

2. Predictions made in the late 1980s about the centralisation of European distribution systems within the Single Market appear to have exaggerated the process. While most companies have been reducing depot numbers, very few have concentrated their storage and distribution operations at a single point. Many regard this as a high-risk strategy and do not believe that they could satisfy customer service requirements reliably throughout Europe from a single point. It has also proved more difficult to co-ordinate centralised distribution operations with nationally-based sales activities than was anticipated.

3. Advances in information technology are making it possible for firms to enjoy much of the benefit of inventory centralisation without physically concentrating it at a single warehouse. This development is well summarised by Christopher (1992):

> Whilst the logic of centralisation is sound, it is becoming increasingly recognised that there may be even greater gains to be had by not physically centralising the inventory, but rather by locating it strategically near the customer or the point of production and managing and controlling it centrally. This is the idea of 'virtual' or 'electronic' inventory. The idea is that by the use of information the organisation can achieve the same stock reduction that it would achieve through centralisation whilst retaining a greater flexibility by localising inventory.

This may weaken or even arrest the trend to greater inventory centralisation, particularly if concentrating it in fewer locations is made more difficult and costly by increases in traffic congestion, oil prices and environmental taxes.

12.12 CONCLUSION

Traditional theories of industrial location and regional development provide a poor basis for assessing the logistical implications of manufacturing in a peripheral region. They place too much emphasis on transport costs, model these costs in a rather simplistic way, under-estimate the complexity of modern supply chains and fail to consider the interaction between transport and other logistical variables, such as inventory, warehousing and information processing. As a result of the fundamental changes that have occurred over the past twenty years in the way that production and distribution operations are managed, it is necessary to re-appraise the relative costs and benefits of a peripheral location within a broader logistical framework.

This chapter has shown, with reference mainly to Scotland, how a peripheral location need not impose a serious logistical handicap. At a macro-scale, the economy of a peripheral region can adapt to its geographical location by, for example, relying more heavily on intra-regional freight movement and specialising in the production of products with a high value-density. At the micro-scale, there are measures that individual firms can take to minimise the effects of remoteness. Any remaining logistical penalties can be more than offset by other locational advantages, such as lower labour costs, cheaper property and the availability of government financial incentives.

The experience of Scotland suggests that recent trends in logistics, such as the adoption of JIT, the growth of subcontracting and the centralisation of inventory, need not adversely affect the development of a peripheral region. On the contrary, the fact that major corporations have recently decided to concentrate their European distribution activities in Scotland and that, over the past few years, the country has enjoyed one of the highest *per capita* levels of foreign inward investment in Europe suggests that some of these trends might even have worked to its advantage.

This positive view of logistics' role in the regional development process requires several qualifications, however. First, it is largely based on the Scottish situation, which need not be representative of that of other peripheral regions. Scotland benefits from having quite a high standard of transport infrastructure, a favourable factor endowment and government regional support. Its main industry, electronics, produces high-value products and is now sufficiently large and diverse to generate valuable agglomeration effects. Its second largest industry, whisky, relies mainly on indigenous raw materials, adds value mainly through long-term storage and also produces a finished product of relatively high value-density. Only by conducting a cross-sectional study of a broad range of peripheral regions will it be possible to establish if Scotland is a special case, or if the logistical tendencies and trends that it has exhibited also exist elsewhere.

Second, there is a danger that the compression of logistical cycle times will magnify differences in transit time between peripheral and more central regions. This effect could be compounded by increasing traffic congestion on the trunk road network. In some sectors, it may become difficult to maintain a competitive level of delivery service from a peripheral region without switching traffic to premium airfreight services and thereby incurring much higher transport costs.

Third, it is anticipated that the cost of freight transport, particularly by road and air, will rise steeply over the next decade as governments internalise, through fuel taxes and network user charges, more of the environmental costs of freight movement. Such distance-related environmental taxes will discriminate against businesses in more remote regions. Firms serving the European market from the periphery are heavily reliant on long-distance transport. As their logistical systems are more transport-intensive than those of companies located in more central regions, sharp increases in transport cost may impair their competitiveness. The implementation of an environmentally-sustainable transport policy may, therefore, conflict with regional policy goals and create a new set of logistical challenges for peripheral manufacturers.

References

Angel, D. P. (1994), 'Tighter Bonds? Customer-Supplier Linkages in Semiconductors', *Regional Studies*, Vol. 28, No. 2, pp. 187-200.

Ansari, A. and Modarress, B. (1990), *Just in Time Purchasing*, New York: The Free Press.

A. T. Kearney Ltd. (1992), *Achieving Customer Satisfaction Leadership in Europe*, London.

Barrett, S. (1994), 'The Effects of European Integration on the Industrial Policies of Peripheral Regions' in *Peripherality and Logistics in the New Europe* (Ed. Vainio, J.), Turku, Center for Maritime Studies, University of Turku, pp. 68-89.

Begg, I. (1990), 'The Single Market and the UK Regions' in *Cambridge Economic Review: The Outlook for the Regions and Countries of the United Kingdom in the 1990s* (Eds. Cameron, G. et al.), Cambridge Economic Consultants/Department of Land Economy.

Braithwaite, A. and Christopher, M. (1989), 'Managing Strategic Lead Times', *Logistics Information Management*, Vol. 2, No. 4, pp. 192-7.

Bowersox, D. J., Closs, D. J. and Helferich, O. K. (1986), *Logistical Management*, New York: Macmillan.

Buck Consultants (1991), *Holland: Europe's Distribution Centre,* The Hague: Holland International Distribution Council.

Carter, J. R. and Ferrin, B. G. (1995), 'The Impact of Transportation Costs on Supply Chain Management', *Journal of Business Logistics*, Vol. 16, No. 1, pp. 189-212.

Charles Barker Ltd (1992), *The North and Scotland — Poorer and Distant Cousins: A Review of Transport and Distribution in Northern Britain,* London.

Chisholm, M. (1985), 'Accessibility and Regional Development in Britain: Some Questions Arising from Data on Freight Flows', *Environment and Planning A,* Vol. 17, pp. 963-80.

Chisholm, M. (1987), 'Regional Variations in Transport Costs in Britain, with Special Reference to Scotland', *Transactions of the Institute of British Geographers*, Vol. 12, pp. 303-14.

Christopher, M. (1992), *Logistics and Supply Chain Management* Pitman: London.

Clarke, T. and Beaney, P. (1993), 'Between Autonomy and Dependence: Corporate Strategy, Plant Status and Local Agglomeration in the Scottish Electronics Industry', *Environment and Planning A*, Vol. 25, pp. 213-32.

Cooper, J. C., Browne, M. and Peters, M. (1991), *European Logistics: Markets Management and Strategy*, Oxford: Blackwell.

Cooper, J. C. (1993), 'Logistics Strategies for Global Businesses', *International Journal of Physical Distribution and Logistics Management*, Vol. 23, No. 4, pp. 12-23.

Davies, G., Fitchett, J. and Gumbrell, K. (1988), 'The Benefits of Delivered Pricing', *European Journal of Marketing*, Vol. 21, No. 1.

Department of Transport (1993), *Origins, Destinations and Transport of UK International Trade 1991*, London: HMSO.

Department of Transport (1994a), *Transport Statistics Great Britain* London (annual publication), London: HMSO.

Department of Transport (1994b), *The Transport of Goods by Road in Great Britain* London (annual publication), London: HMSO.

Dicken, P. (1992), *Global Shift: The Internationalisation of Economic Activity*, London: Paul Chapman, 2nd Ed.

Durkan, J. and Reynolds-Feighan, A. (1990) *A Survey of Irish Manufacturers' Transport Costs*, Dublin: ESRI.

Estall, R. C. (1985), 'Stock Control in Manufacturing: The Just-in-Time System and its Locational Implications', *Area*, Vol. 17, No. 2, pp. 129-33.

Farmer, D. and Ploos van Amstel, R. (1992), *Effective Pipeline Management*, London: Gower.

Forster, M. and Peters, M. (1994), 'An Assessment of Air Cargo Service Costs and Capacity for Electronic Manufacturers in Scotland', *International Journal of Logistics Management*, Vol. 5, No. 2, pp. 81-94.

Fynes, B. and Ennis, S. (1994), 'From Lean Production to Lean Logistics: The Case of Microsoft Ireland', *European Management Journal*, Vol. 12, No. 3, pp. 332-30.

Hoare, A. G. (1993), 'Domestic Regions, Overseas Nations, and their Interactions through Trade: The Case of the United Kingdom', *Environment and Planning A*, Vol. 25, pp. 701-72.

House of Commons Scottish Affairs Committee (1993), *The Future of Scotland's Transport Links with Europe*, London: HMSO.

Industry Department for Scotland (1981), 'Transport Costs in Scottish Manufacturing Industries', *Scottish Economic Bulletin*, No. 22.

Linge, G. J. (1991), 'Just-in-Time: More or Less Flexible?', *Economic Geography*, Vol. 67, No. 4, pp. 316-32.

Logan, R. (1971), *Transport and Communications in Industrial Mobility: The UK Experience with Particular Reference to Scotland and Northern Ireland*, Unpublished PhD thesis, University of Glasgow.

Maister, D. H. (1976), 'Centralisation of Inventories and the "Square Root Law"' *International Journal of Physical Distribution*, Vol. 6, No. 3, pp. 124-34.

Mair, A. (1993), 'New Growth Poles? Just-in-Time Manufacturing and Local Economic Development Strategy', *Regional Studies*, Vol. 7, No. 3, pp. 207-21.

McKinnon, A. C. (1989), *Physical Distribution Systems*, London: Routledge.

McKinnon, A. C. (1991), 'Regional Variations in Manufacturing Inventory Levels', *International Journal of Physical Distribution and Logistics Management,* Vol. 21, No. 6, pp. 4-14.

McKinnon, A. C. (1993), 'Manufacturing in a Peripheral Location: An Assessment of the Logistical Penalties', *International Journal of Logistics Management,* Vol. 3, No. 2, pp. 31-48.

McKinnon, A. C. (1996), 'The Empty Running and Return Loading of Road Goods Vehicles', *Transport Logistics*, Vol. 1, No. 1 (forthcoming).

Milne, S. (1990), 'New Forms of Manufacturing and their Spatial Implications: The UK Electronic Consumer Goods Industry', *Environment and Planning A*, Vol. 22, pp. 211-32.

Motor Transport (1994), *Cost Tables*, June.

Munday, M., Morris, J. and Wilkinson, B. (1995), 'Factories or Warehouses? A Welsh Perspective on Japanese Transplant Manufacturing', *Regional Studies,* Vol. 29, No. 1, pp. 1-17.

O'Farrell, P. and Hitchens, D. M. (1989), 'The Competitiveness and Performance of Small Manufacturing Firms: An Analysis of Matched

Pairs in Scotland and England', *Environment and Planning A*, Vol. 21, pp. 1241-63.

O'Laughlin, K. A., Cooper, J. and Cabocel, E. (1993), *Reconfiguring European Logistics Systems*, Oak Brook, IL: Council of Logistics Management.

Phelps, N. A. (1993a), 'Contemporary Industrial Restructuring and Linkage Change in an Older Industrial Region: Examples from the Northeast of England', *Environment and Planning A*, Vol. 25, pp. 863-82.

Phelps, N. A. (1993b), 'Branch Plants and the Evolving Spatial Division of Labour: A Study of Material Linkage Change in the Northern Region of England', *Regional Studies*, Vol. 27, No. 2, pp. 87-101.

Picard, J. (1982), 'Typology of Physical Distribution Systems in Multi-National Corporations', *International Journal of Physical Distribution and Materials Management*, Vol. 12, No. 6, pp. 26-39.

PIEDA (1984), *Transport Costs in Peripheral Areas*, ESU Research Papers No. 9, Edinburgh, Industry Department for Scotland.

Reid, N. (1995), 'Just-in-Time Inventory Control and the Economic Integration of Japanese-owned Manufacturing Plants with the County, State and National Economies of the United States', *Regional Studies*, Vol. 29, No. 4, pp. 345-55.

Scottish Council Development and Industry (1994), *Survey of Scottish Manufacturing and Exports, 1992-3*, Glasgow.

Scottish Office (1994), *Scottish Transport Statistics 1992/93*, Edinburgh.

Sheehan, M. (1993,) 'Government Financial Assistance and Manufacturing Investment in Northern Ireland', *Regional Studies*, Vol. 27, No. 6, pp. 527-40.

SPEED Ltd (1994), *1994 Survey of Distribution and Logistics in Scottish Manufacturing Industry*, Edinburgh.

Stalk Jnr., G. (1988), 'Time — The Next Source of Competitive Advantage', *Harvard Business Review*, July-August.

Steedman, J. and Vickerman, J.M. (1993), 'Road Transport Costs in Scottish Industry and the Impact of a Carbon/Energy Tax', *Scottish Economic Bulletin*, No. 47.

Stock, J. and Lambert, D. (1993), *Strategic Logistics Management*, Homewood, IL: Irwin.

TecnEcon (1994), *Road Haulage Industry in Scotland: Final Report*, Glasgow, Scottish Enterprise.

Touche Ross (1995), *European Logistics: Comparative Costs and Practice 1995*, Corby: Institute of Logistics.

Trevor, M. and Christie, I. (1988), *Manufacturers and Suppliers in Britain and Japan*, London: Policy Studies Institute.

Turok, I. (1993), 'Inward Investment and Local Linkages: How Deeply Embedded is "Silicon Glen"?', *Regional Studies*, Vol. 25, No. 5, pp. 401-17.

Tyler, P., Moore, B. C. and Rhodes, J. (1988), 'Geographical Variations in Industrial Costs', *Scottish Journal of Political Economy*, Vol. 35, No. 1, pp. 22-50.

Vickerman, J. M. (1992/3), 'Trade in the Scottish Manufacturing Sector', *Scottish Economic Bulletin*, No. 46, pp. 27-33.

Weber, A. (1909), *Theory of the Location of Industries*, Chicago: University of Chicago Press.

White, R. E. and Poynter, T. A. (1984), 'Strategies for Foreign-Owned Subsidiaries in Canada', *Business Quarterly*, Summer, pp. 59-69.

Young S., Hood, N. and Dunlop, S, (1988), 'Global Strategies, Multinational Subsidiary Roles and Economic Impact in Scotland', *Regional Studies*, Vol. 22., No. 6, pp. 487-97.

13

INDUSTRIAL MARKETS AND NEO-MODERN PRODUCTION: THE VIEW FROM THE EDGE

Paul A. Ryan

13.1 INTRODUCTION

The globalisation of business has been one of the most discussed economic phenomena of recent decades (Levitt, 1983; Porter, 1986, 1990; Ohmae, 1990; Bartlett and Ghoshal, 1990). Global corporations have the capacity to manufacture and sell their products in all parts of the world. It is possible for many of these corporations to organise production on a truly global basis by sourcing worldwide, often from low-cost-labour countries. The objective of this chapter is to show that, although it is possible to organise production on such a global scale through advances in technology which have facilitated the international division of labour on the basis of cost and quality, mitigating factors such as trade restrictions, the emergence of just-in-time production systems in industrial markets (that is networks of firms producing goods for ultimate sale in consumer markets), and the need for closer supplier relations, frequently prompt producers to organise production within a defined economic or geographic region. This regionalisation of manufacturing can, and frequently does, occur within a global framework with global corporations operating production plants within each significant global region. A region generally has an industrial core and periphery. This chapter examines how firms supplying into industrial markets from a peripheral location within the region are coping with the changed conditions of neo-modern production and outlines the trade-offs which exist between on the one hand, the benefits of geographic proximity in terms of shorter delivery lines and times and more frequent customer contact for firms at the core of the industrial market and, on the other hand, the gains from lower input costs, higher investment incentives and greater availability of labour accruing to firms located at the periphery.

Such is the case in the global automobile industry, one of the most visible sectors in the world economy. Lamming (1989) found that in the case of the European automobile industry 'less than 5 per cent of parts are imported from outside the EC. In North America the spend is similarly restricted'. This chapter reports on an exploratory investigation of the European automobile industry, which encapsulates most of the conditions of regional production and neo-modern production methods. It examines whether peripherally-located supplier firms in the sector employ just-in-time delivery systems and are endeavouring to develop closer relations with their powerful assembler customers or are dismissed as distant and unviable and thus are expelled from the supply chains of the assemblers. The following section will illustrate the potential for global sourcing prior to an examination of the factors which militate against the deployment of such an organisational form in most sectors.

13.2 THE ORGANISATION OF INTERNATIONAL PRODUCTION

Advances in communications and transport technologies have created the potential for the global organisation of production. Firms can locate or source from plants manufacturing parts, components and final product where the factor advantages are greatest, for example where raw material or capital costs are lower, but usually where labour costs are minimised.

13.2.1 The New International Division Of Labour
The potential now exists for corporations in many sectors of modern industry to split production into a much larger number of separate activities, each of which can be performed in separate plants, often located in different countries. Under this rationalised process form of international manufacturing the choice of location will depend on the factor proportions required for each separate activity. The more labour intensive stages of production will tend to be located where the necessary labour is available and cheap, and vice versa. For this reason, such rationalised international production is referred to as the 'new international division of labour' and is typical of the 'global' model of production (Grimwade, 1989). There are a number of factors which permit

this new rationalisation of production. The first is technology. It is possible to design products to permit subdivision of the production process into the assembly of a larger number of standardised components. Each component can be produced separately in quantities which allow the exploitation of economies of scale. Components themselves are designed as multi-component goods creating a hierarchy of components which are assembled at various stages before final assembly. The second is transport. The most important improvements have been the introduction of jet aircraft, the development of much larger ocean-going vessels, and containerisation which greatly simplifies transhipment from one mode of transport to another. The third factor is communication. Information technologies have reduced the costs of co-ordinating global communications associated with separated plants. In this respect, the key element is the linking together of computer technologies with information transmission technologies over vast distances (Dicken, 1992).

The key locational consideration is the trade-off between the economies of large-scale production at one or a small number of large plants and the additional transport and co-ordination costs involved in assembling the necessary inputs and in shipping the final product to a geographically-extended market from a large number of smaller plants.

13.2.2 Global Subcontracting and Sourcing
Rather than manufacturing parts and components themselves, corporations have the opportunity to engage in global subcontracting. The major factors influencing the location of the sources of global subcontracting are:

- the labour-intensity of the product or process: wages and labour unrest tend to be higher in developed countries as, however, are productivity and skills

- the degree of standardisation of the production process: high repetitiveness is more suited to unskilled, low-cost labour

- the extent that production process can be fragmented into individual, self-contained operations and the importance of additional transport costs. Critical factors are weight and bulk

- government policies towards offshore processing and export production (Dicken, 1992).

However, the following discussion will illustrate that, albeit possible on a global scale, international production is most commonly organised around regional manufacturing clusters.

13.3 REGIONALISATION OF PRODUCTION

Frequently the most feasible way to serve global markets is with a regional-production approach (MacCormack et al., 1994). Such regions tend to be quite large, encompassing a defined economic trading bloc such as the European Union (EU), or even extend to the geographic region of Europe as a whole. Firms may operate a regional rather than purely global manufacturing strategy for a variety of reasons. Some reasons are strategic; others are macroeconomic, political or trade-related and usually outside the control of the organisation.

13.3.1 Insiderisation

The first motive behind the regional organisation of production is the need for a presence in a region to respond to customer needs. Ohmae (1990) recommends companies to be 'insiders' in each of the triad regions, North America, Western Europe and South-East Asia. The most structured trading bloc is the EU. NAFTA links the USA, Canada and Mexico. Although technically not a free trade area, South-East Asia has become the fastest growing economic region in the world on the back of the trading success of Japan, the 'four tigers' (South Korea, Hong Kong, Taiwan and Singapore), and more recently the members of the ASEAN economic grouping. Schwab and Smadja (1994) point to a 'new world economic order' and suggest that an overall redistribution of economic power has resulted in a fully tripolar world with Western Europe, North America and East Asia in a position of parity. Regions differ in terms of customer needs and wants. Hence firms need to be 'insiders' to properly identify and understand these differing tastes and preferences. This approach to organising international operations has also been termed 'glocalisation' as it incorporates local needs within a global perspective.

13.3.2 Trade Restrictions

The second set of factors militating against purely global manufacturing are the new forms of protectionism in world trade such as voluntary export-restraint agreements (VER) and local-content rules. A VER is a non-tariff intervention to restrain the flow of trade. It is similar to an import quota except that the restriction is enforced by the exporting, and not the importing, country. VERs are generally bilaterally negotiated. Since they are not unilaterally imposed restrictions on trade they are not covered by GATT rules. To avoid such restrictions, firms will locate manufacturing plants in the country or region of imposition. For example, the EU has restricted the sales of Japanese cars produced outside the Community to 16.6 per cent of the car market until 1999. This has prompted the major Japanese auto assemblers to establish manufacturing operations within the EU, where local-content rules attempt to ensure that they do not become mere 'screwdriver plants' engaging in the simple assembly of parts and components imported from the home nation.

Hence, one can depict the evolution of a world trade system based on regional blocs which encourages final product manufacturing firms to become 'insiders' in each significant region to identify customer needs and to avoid trade penalties and administrative hurdles by following direct investment strategies. This move toward regionalism in manufacturing has been alluded to by Dunning (1988), who claims that 'a reduction in transport costs and the formation of customs unions or regional trading blocs have prompted greater regional specialisation of multinational enterprises (MNEs)'. Therefore in many industry sectors it is necessary to consider emerging manufacturing practices in the context of regional-based production rather than the more commonly discussed global context.

The next section will illustrate that such regional production organisation would appear to be a more apt context for the newer organising philosophy of lean production developed by the Japanese and increasingly in evidence in the West, which depends on closer relations along the supply chain, timeliness of delivery and total quality production and management systems. These systems are considered more amenable to the contraction rather than expansion of geographic space and the implications of this for firms distant from their industrial customers are examined.

13.4 LEAN PRODUCTION

Since the mid 1970s, the Japanese have succeeded economically against the West in several manufacturing sectors. (It is worth noting that although these successful Japanese manufacturers were located at a great distance from their customers, the industrial clusters which produced the consumer goods were very compact with almost all major production activity carried out at the core of the industrial market, for example car production at Toyota City). The focus of this chapter is on peripherality within the industrial market itself and thus the compact situation in Japan does not represent an apt 'comparison other'. The discussion is chiefly concerned with the impact on Western operations of the adoption of Japanese manufacturing practices within the context of a larger geographic map (in this case Europe), and hence an expanded production environment, and in particular the impact of such diffusion on suppliers distant from the core of the industrial market.

The origins of lean production are to be found in the Japanese automobile industry. In an effort to identify the reasons for the success of the Japanese automobile companies the MIT International Motor Vehicle Programme (IMVP) was undertaken in the late 1980s. Its aim was to measure the performance of both the traditional Western production system and the newer Toyota production system, and its derivatives in other Japanese car-makers. The researchers called the newer system in evidence in Japan 'lean production' (Womack et al., 1990) because 'it uses less of everything' (Jones, 1992). The conclusion was that the system is fundamentally lean in its avoidance of problem-hiding buffers (Krafcik and MacDuffie, 1989). Combining the 'best' features of both craft production (product variety), and mass production (high volume output), it allows the user to provide a wide range of products while reducing costs per unit (Womack et al., 1990) and at the same time maintain high levels of quality and productivity (Krafcik, 1988).

The development of leaner production is in great part due to the production engineering and organisation efforts of Toyota's long-time (now deceased) production manager, Taiichi Ohno. Ohno reasoned that the mass production practice of passing on errors to keep the line running caused errors to multiply endlessly. He instructed workers to stop the whole assembly line immediately if a problem emerged that they could not fix. The whole team would subsequently work on and solve the problem. Krafcik (1988) reports that 'at Toyota inventory levels were kept at an absolute minimum so that costs could be shaved and quality problems quickly detected and solved; bufferless assembly lines assured continuous-flow production. If a worker was absent without notice, the team would fill in; repair areas were tiny as a result of the belief that quality should be achieved within the process, not within a rectification area'. Eventually the principles of lean manufacturing were applied throughout the manufacturing chain from assessing the needs of customers, to design, development, engineering, manufacturing, the components supplier network, final assembly and distribution. Lean production presents higher risks since any hiccup will stop production totally. However, much of the risk can be neutralised given an experienced and well-trained workforce. The supplier is integral to the system as zero-defect quality is expected of incoming parts and component systems.

Jones (1992) summarises the essential characteristics of the whole lean production system as follows:

- it is customer-driven, not driven by the needs of manufacturing

- there is a high level of information exchanged and a transparent cost structure

- the discipline necessary for the system to function and expose problems is provided by JIT and TQM in the plant and supply chain

- whenever possible, responsibility is devolved to the lowest level in the plant or to suppliers

- the system is based on stable production volumes but with scope for flexibility

- relations with employees, suppliers and dealers are based on reciprocal obligations.

13.4.1 Lean Supply

It is clear that lean production is not simply a function of efficient plant operations but a manifestation of the efficient operation of the entire supply chain. It seems that 'world class plants are embedded in world class supply chains' (Oliver et al., 1993). Just as the IMVP study of the global automobile industry found a two-to-one difference in performance between Japanese lean producers and western mass producers, a recent study of direct suppliers to the assemblers (Andersen Consulting, 1993) found similar productivity gaps. Thus the system has less inventory, fewer defects, higher quality, lower cost structures and is 'in control' (Oliver et al., 1993).

Lean supply is an integral part of a lean production system. It depends on the proper working of a JIT system of production and delivery (Lamming, 1993). JIT principles recognise that co-ordinating maximum efficiency of individual units within the supply chain is the route to efficiency of the system as a whole. The goal of JIT manufacturing is to eliminate buffer stocks on both sides of a dyadic relationship (Nishigushi, 1989) by eradicating all forms of waste from the production process and keeping inventory at a minimum (O'Neal, 1987). Schonberger (1982) describes JIT as the production and delivery of finished goods just in time to be sold, sub-assemblies just in time to be assembled into finished goods, fabricated parts just in time to go into sub-assemblies and purchased materials just in time to be transformed into fabricated parts. The alternative traditional western model of supply chain management has been based on holding stocks of raw materials and bought-in parts as insurance against disruption to the supply chain. Oliver (1990) terms this a 'just-in-case' operating system. The main drawback is that materials, parts or sub-assemblies, which are stationary as they queue to enter the next stage in the system, accumulate cost but gain no value.

13.4.2 Peripherality and Lean Production and Supply

There are several implications of lean production and supply for firms supplying over extended distance. The move to a leaner system of production, with a greater dependence on suppliers employing just-in-time production and delivery, has brought with it a commensurate need for increased geographic proximity, or at the very least, reliable and timely delivery. Under a lean supply system 'there are obvious benefits to synchronised manufacture of components and vehicles involving 'door-step' plants', i.e. plants located next to the final assembly plant (Lamming, 1993). Locating at the edge of an economic region is commonly considered to adversely affect competitiveness due to the added transport costs associated with distance from markets and customers. Furthermore, transit may be considered another form of stock-holding, and is wasteful under the precepts of lean production since it does not add value. Begg and Mayes (1994) conclude that, because of these factors, firms in remote areas *may* be 'off the map' as potential suppliers of certain goods.

Ultimately, Lamming concludes that 'there will be "door-step" plants, just-in-time (but at a convenient distance) plants, and "out-of-area" plants' and, ominously, for the latter he suggests that 'it is possible that the last category will become uneconomic'. However, he contends that 'there is no evidence to suggest that close geographical proximity is (always) a requisite part of lean supply: several companies in Japan, the USA and Europe are achieving just-in-time deliveries over considerable distances ... it is clearly not the distance but the travel time between supplier and customer which is important — a factor which presents a particular challenge when the goods must flow across international borders'. Thus it can be concluded that although distance does increase travel time it does not necessarily militate against timeliness of delivery.

Even more positive for peripheral supplier firms is the fact that JIT, and its companion TQM, involve the worker in the production process to an extent which requires motivated skilled or semi-skilled workers rather than purely low-cost labour. There is little or no room for error in this fragile system. Thus the requirement is increasingly for a well-educated, multi-skilled and involved workforce. A new model of low-medium cost, high-skilled labour may be emerging, rather than the more traditional low-cost/low-skilled or high-cost/high-skilled models. Such a model is very applicable to the peripheral economies of the EU which, assisted by EU funds, have invested heavily in their education infrastructures and thus have a ready and available supply of skilled labour available at a fraction of the cost of the core economies where skilled labour is in much shorter supply.

Input costs (e.g. labour costs, property prices) tend to be lower in remote locations. Thus contrary to their 'off-the-map' premises, Begg and Mayes (1994) warn that 'the standard presumption that remote location will necessarily be damaging to competitiveness because it implies higher costs is, therefore, open to question'. Government grants and tax incentives can also influence the location decision and lessen the negative effects of peripherality. The fact is that there are many contingent issues and factors at play in resolving the impact of peripherality on industrial suppliers. It is not a 'black-and-white' negative. Hence, there are trade-offs as to which parts of the system need to be located proximate, where input costs tend to be more expensive and vice versa.

13.4.3 Industrial Buyer-Supplier Relations: Classification and Models

JIT manufacturing involves the operation of a system which produces the exact quantity, at required quality, of raw materials, parts or sub-assemblies just in time for the next stage of the manufacturing process. This inevitably requires a high level of interaction between industrial customers and suppliers. Thus lean supply incorporating the just-in-time exchange concept is an operational philosophy which epitomises the relational model of buyer-supplier interaction (O'Neal, 1989). Viewed broadly, supply chain management can be seen to consist of a series of interactions between buyers and sellers. To achieve the high level of interaction required for small-lot production and delivery there needs to be frequent contact between buyer and supplier. Good working relations must be cultivated in a climate of trust and commitment. The key question for the supplier firms at the periphery is whether distance between interacting parties impinges on the development of such close relations. The next section will address this question in the context of buyer-supplier relations in modern industrial markets, the nature of which are initially outlined and described.

Helper (1991) suggested that a useful way to classify an industrial buyer-supplier relationship is to examine the methods used to resolve problems that arise between the parties. In an 'exit' relationship, a customer who has a problem with a supplier finds a new supplier. On the other hand, in a 'voice' relationship, the customer works with the supplier to resolve the problem. The relationship has two dimensions, information exchange and commitment. Information exchange includes both the nature and mutuality of the information flow between supplier and buyer. At the lowest level, the only information exchanged is the price of the product. At the intermediate level, the parties may share information about finances, plant and equipment. At the highest level, customer and supplier provide continuous feedback and suggestions for improvement of each other's operations. Commitment is the importance that a seller or buyer attaches to the other party and is measured by a willingness to invest time and resources in their dealings (Ford, 1984). For Helper, commitment refers to the supplier's degree of certainty that the customer will continue to buy its products for some length of time.

Akin to Helper, Sako (1992) also employs a continuum to classify relations between buyers and suppliers. At one extreme she places Arms' Length Contractual Relations (ACR), wherein the buyer changes suppliers as prices dictate. At the other extreme is Obligational Contractual Relations (OCR), where dealings are based on trust and commitment. Trust stems from a growing confidence in a firm's expectations of the future This increases the likelihood of co-operative exchange over multiple rounds, an extension of the exchange horizon, and a subsequent reduction in incentives for uncooperative behaviours (Axelrod, 1984). Commitment to the relationship is a consequence of the party's investments in it and the level of satisfaction felt (Wilson and Mummalaneni, 1986). OCR does not deny competition and pressure on the relationship. A mechanism exists for ranking core suppliers on the basis of their regular performance leading occasionally to marginal shifts in sourcing.

Going beyond classification researchers have developed models of industrial buyer-supplier relations. Two examples of these will be briefly discussed here. The first is the Industrial Marketing and Purchasing (IMP) Group's 'Interaction Model' (Ford, 1984). The IMP assume in their interaction approach that the buying process is not one of action and reaction as in consumer marketing, but one of interaction. This interaction between buying and selling firms in an industrial market is seen by the researchers as occurring within the context of a relationship between the firms. This relationship may be distant and impersonal, but is often close, developing through a number of stages as the parties gradually and mutually commit themselves to business with each other (Ford, 1980; Hallen et al., 1987). The type of relationship that evolves is often affected by the anticipated duration of the exchange (Heide and John, 1990).

A second version of the nature and character of buyer-supplier relations in an industrial market is Lamming's 'Partnership Model' (1993). Lamming developed a relational model which is strongly rooted in the buyer-supplier practices evident in the Japanese automotive industry. Key among its premises are: the recognition of the specialist abilities of the supplier as crucially important; a tier of suppliers provides the optimum combination of complementary assets in subcontracting firms; co-operation, both with other suppliers (including competitors) and with customers is essential; costs should be discussed openly and reductions shared; efficient information exchange is of fundamental importance; despite largely collaborative behaviour the dependence upon commitment from both buyer and supplier leads to high levels of pressure to perform, rather than complacency.

Partnerships thus involve customers and suppliers within industrial markets committing to continuous improvements through joint efforts resulting in shared benefits. Principally, this is achieved through open communication and the exchange of relevant information. Problems are resolved jointly rather than by finding a new trading associate. Commitment and trust are again core elements. Over time, costs are reduced and quality improved. Such co-operative relations are very common in Japan and becoming more so in the USA and UK (Sako, Lamming and Helper, 1994). For the most part the Japanese view the ability to maintain a loyal long-term relationship as more important than a new technology or cost saving presented by a newcomer (Lamming, 1989).

Distance can reduce the closeness of relations between buyer and seller. Obviously, the closer parties are geographically the more accessible they are. This may be vital when crises arise. However, in the normal course of events relations can develop over time if cultivated appropriately, even over extended distance. Telecommunications and transport improvements serve to narrow the gap, both real and perceived by enhancing the opportunities for personal contact.

At the operational level, the principal factor mitigating the adverse impact of distance is information technology (O'Laughlin et al., 1994). Electronic Data Interchange (EDI), which involves the exchange of information between computers about trading transactions, reduces the time taken to process orders along the supply chain (Ojala and Suomi, 1992). It allows the minimisation of stock held and permits small-scale production planning. Thus the shorter order lead times essential for effective JIT operations are attainable. Promisingly for peripheral supplier firms, Ojala and Suomi (1992) conclude that:

> the introduction of EDI will benefit firms operating in peripheral regions more than those operating in central regions since EDI will enable these firms to gain better control over their material flows ... we believe it is not the speed of transport but the control and timing of the material and information flow which is crucial for effective logistics management.

13.5 PERIPHERAL SUPPLIERS IN THE EUROPEAN AUTOMOBILE INDUSTRY

The European automobile industry is a regional-based production cluster encompassing trade sanctions, neo-modern production practices, regional clustering and extended supply lines with less than 5 per cent of parts imported from outside the EU. The Japanese assemblers have established manufacturing bases within Europe since the mid- to late-1980s and are demanding, and achieving, leaner operations from their European suppliers, incorporating JIT and zero-defect quality. In response, the incumbent European assemblers are moving toward leaner methods of production. Hence this sector represents an apt example of the impact and effects of the change to neo-modern manufacturing within a defined region.

13.5.1 Tiering And Logistics In The European Automobile Industry

The European motor industry represents almost 10 per cent of the area's manufacturing output (Rhys, 1995). Indeed, as Table 13.1 shows, Europe is the first world's largest passenger car market.

TABLE 13.1: FIRST WORLD PASSENGER CAR SALES

	Jan-Sep 1995 (000s)	%	Jan-Sep 1994 (000s)	%	Jan-Sep 1993 (000s)	%
W Europe	9,355	48.3	9,306	47.9	8,813	47.6
USA	6,635	34.3	6,891	35.5	6,473	35.0
Japan	3,375	17.4	3,220	16.6	3,228	17.4

Source: Automotive Industry Data Ltd. (AID), 1995

Extensive shifts in the industry's structure are occurring as efforts are made by the assemblers to cut costs and introduce leaner manufacturing systems to meet the twin challenges of reduced demand since 1993 (see Table 13.2) and the arrival of the Japanese assemblers in the market. Competition is intense as production exceeds demand, and although the forecast to the end of the decade is for improved sales, they are not expected to reach the levels of the late 1980s and early 1990s. Consequently this

intensely competitive situation is likely to continue for the foreseeable future.

TABLE 13.2: TOTAL NEW REGISTRATIONS OF PASSENGER CARS IN
WESTERN EUROPE/PASSENGER CAR PRODUCTION IN WESTERN
EUROPE (1988-95; FORECAST 1996-97)

	New Registrations (000s)	*Production (000s)*
1988	13,019	13,846
1989	13,424	14,545
1990	13,214	14,423
1991	13,500	13,914
1992	13,497	14,216
1993	11,250	12,033
1994	11,904	13,546
1995 (forecast)	11,930	14,325
1996 (forecast)	12,311	14,634
1997 (forecast)	12,573	14,720

Source: Economist Intelligence Unit, 1995.

Conscious of the Japanese successes in the US car market and the
restricted nature of Japan's own market some European nations,
in particular Italy and France, have convinced the EU to put in
place measures to ensure a similar infiltration of the European
car market does not occur. The EU has imposed Voluntary Export
Restraints (VERs) which will restrict the Japanese share of the
European car market to 16.6 per cent until 1999 despite the provisions of the Single European Act of 1992. The response of the
Japanese to the implementation of trade barriers has been to become 'insiders' by setting up assembly plants within the EU,
mainly in the UK where they feel, and are made feel, most welcome. By the end of the decade, Japanese production in Europe is
likely to amount to 1 million units, representing about 8 per cent
of the total EU manufacturing capacity (EIU, 1995). Nissan commenced production in the UK in 1986 and Toyota and Honda
commenced production there in 1992. Approximately 65 per cent
of Nissan's 200 European suppliers are UK-based. Half of Toyota's
160 suppliers are UK-based. Honda's UK facility sources from 150

European suppliers of which around 100 are UK-based (IBEC, 1994).

The first-tier direct suppliers to the auto assemblers must currently operate within the parameters of macroeconomic trade battles, nationalistic tendencies and geographic logistical challenges, frequently supplying over great distances in this pan-European industry. The incumbent assemblers, feeling the pressure of the intense competition and the threat created by the entry of the Japanese, are endeavouring to acquire components at ever-reduced cost. At the same time the production systems employed under the more wasteful system of mass production are being adapted in response to the leaner manufacturing systems pursued by the Japanese assemblers. It appears that quasi-Japanese systems, more applicable to the European situation, are being adopted.

The Boston Consultancy Group (BCG) (1993) found that while only a handful of automotive component companies were using what it defined as 'true' JIT production methods some 40 per cent had adopted JIT-style delivery systems involving new logistical solutions. Rather than achieving synchronous production, European suppliers are building up substantial inventories out of which small quantities of components are delivered on a 'just-in-time' basis, or suppliers were delivering to distribution centres rather than the assembly plant, and from there a series of 'timed deliveries' are made direct to the production line. These problems are compounded by the actions of European assemblers which, Jones (1992) claims, have been unwilling to give up the power-based bargaining with suppliers that they have relied on for so long. He points to the fact that these assemblers have reduced their parts' inventory to two to three days stock while the suppliers still carry anywhere between eight and sixteen days supply leading to a scepticism about the true merits of the just-in-time system on their part.

However, certain changes towards a proper emulation of Japanese-style practices are underway. Chief among these are changes in the relationship between the car manufacturers and their suppliers, as more is learned of the Japanese approach to buyer-supplier relations (Turnbull et al., 1993). Close inter-relationships between Japanese suppliers and their auto-maker customers form a central feature of the Japanese auto industry (MEMA, 1990). As Lamming's 'partnership model' illustrates, in Japan, the actual contract between manufacturer and supplier is based on co-operation, a full exchange of information, a commitment to improve quality and a recognition that costs can, and will, be reduced each year to their mutual benefit. Such relationships constitute the 'glue' that holds Japan's long-term auto-maker-supplier structure together. Affiliated companies (*keiretsu kigyo*) operate in close co-ordination with their auto-maker parent almost as subsidiaries. The looser supplier associations (*kyoryokukai*) primarily assist in promoting efficient communications with, and among, an auto-maker's suppliers.

European assemblers, who have amassed very large supply bases are currently reducing the numbers in an effort to form better relationships with fewer companies (Lamming, 1993). Only a select few are likely to survive as 'preferred suppliers'. Many firms have, or will, become second-tier suppliers of lower-value parts and materials supplying to first-tier suppliers who deal directly with the final auto-assemblers. This new relationship between first-tier suppliers and final assemblers involves the delivery of component systems rather than individual parts. The change from individual components to systems purchasing and the increased level of outsourcing is forcing the tiering of the European automotive components industry. The tiering of the industry is creating several layers of companies with very different structural and capability characteristics. For the European sector, Lamming (1993) forecasts that 'fewer, larger and more talented suppliers will emerge'. He claims that 'the work now done by small suppliers will be carried out for first-tier companies as part of their systems integration role. These developments will thus lead to the gradual removal of supply base 'tails''.

BCG (1993) has similarly forecast a huge restructuring in the European autocomponents industry as first-tier suppliers enlarge their operations and smaller operations drop to second-tier status, assembling parts for first-tier systems integrators or being forced out of the industry through acquisition or liquidation. Individual car-makers have already taken drastic action to cut the number of their direct suppliers from around 1,250 on average in 1988 to 900 in 1993, but the number is expected to drop again to around 400 by 1997, creating what Turnbull (1993) describes as a, Japanese-type 'pyramid structure'.

13.5.2 Peripherality and Industrial Markets: The Case of Ireland's Autocomponent Sector

As there is no automobile assembly plant in Ireland, 100 per cent of autocomponent production must ultimately be exported so all Irish-based supplier firms are peripheral to this major industrial market. The autocomponent sector in Ireland currently employs upwards of 10,000 people (IBEC, 1994) and across a series of economic measures such as sales, imports and exports, ranks as Ireland's seventh most important industrial sector (CSO, 1995). By international standards most of the firms currently in the sector would be considered small to medium-sized enterprises but by Irish standards they represent some of the largest manufacturing operations in the country. The products manufactured range from low-tech, labour-intensive items such as wire harnesses to high-tech electronic parts entailing high-skilled labour input. All the major assemblers are supplied, to varying degrees, by the Irish-based component manufacturers. The majority of the assembler customers are based in Germany and the UK (see Table 13.3). Irish component companies have cornered just £10 million of the new Japanese transplant market and may have to settle for a position in the second tier of suppliers since the Japanese assemblers tend to remain loyal to their direct suppliers.

TABLE 13.3: EXPORT DESTINATION AND THE MAJOR BUYERS OF AUTOMOTIVE COMPONENTS MADE IN IRELAND (1994)

Country	(£IRm)	%	Company	(£IRm)	%
Germany	98.9	42.3	GM/Opel	76	32.5
UK	44.9	19.2	Mercedes-Benz	52	22.2
France	25.7	11.0	Audi/VW	42	17.9
US	10.0	4.3	Ford	20	8.5
Spain	7.5	3.2	Renault	15	6.4
Italy	7.0	3.0	BMW	12	5.1
Belgium	5.1	2.2	Nissan	4	1.7
Sweden	3.3	1.4	Toyota	4	1.7
Others	31.4	13.4	Honda	2	0.9
			Others	7	3.1
Total	234.0	100.0		234.0	100.0

Source: Irish Trade Board.

Crowley (1990) has documented the logistical problems encountered by exporters located in Ireland in getting their product to the market. First, Ireland is an island on the periphery of Europe and now, with the completion of the channel tunnel, will be the only European Union (EU) member state without a land link to Europe; and second, Ireland is impeded geographically from the European mainland by Britain, so single mode straight-line routings to central European markets cannot be followed.

Currently the foremost threat to Irish suppliers comes from Eastern Europe and other non-EU countries such as Turkey. For example, on a labour cost per hour basis, Hungary has a 33-50 per cent advantage over Ireland (Irish Trade Board, 1995). Where Ireland has maintained business is through the use of modern manufacturing methods to achieve higher quality, greater efficiency, and flexibility of operations. Hence, the low-skill low-cost manufacturing model appears to be failing, but the high-skill medium-cost model is apt.

13.5.3 Research Findings

In order to gain a fuller understanding of this sector a series of personal, in-depth interviews with production and customer service managers from the five largest Irish-based first-tier auto-component manufacturers (which between them account for over 65 per cent of total exports in the sector), was conducted by the author. The aims were, first, to investigate the reasons why auto-component firms would locate distant to the assembly plants and, second, to assess the impact of the new conditions brought about by the industry movement towards leaner production methods incorporating just-in-time delivery and closer customer contact on firms peripheral to this neo-modern industrial market. The main findings were:

Reasons for Location Choice

1. **Government support** through, firstly, *tax incentives* (a low tax rate of 10 per cent for manufacturing industry), and secondly through *capital grants* (fixed assets costs eligible for grants include sites, buildings and new equipment).

2. **People**: One of the major driving forces behind the decision of firms to locate in Ireland, as identified by the interviewees, is the availability and skills of low- to medium-cost labour.

3. **Labour availability** is related to demographic factors such as the country having the youngest population in Europe with half its population under eighteen years of age (CSO, 1994). This provides a steady flow into the labour market.

4. In **education**, Ireland spends in excess of 20 per cent of the national budget on education with technical training receiving a high priority (CSO, 1994). More than 78 per cent of the Irish 16-year-olds stay on in full-time education. Approximately 120,000 students are currently participating in full-time third level courses, and some 55 per cent of these are pursuing business, engineering or science disciplines.

5. Finally, Ireland's **labour costs** compare favourably with other European countries (see Table 13.4). However, it is interesting to note that in the case of low-tech parts production one supplier rhetorically inquired 'no matter how lean you get how do you compete with India's labour costs'.

TABLE 13.4: COMPARATIVE LABOUR COSTS: AVERAGE HOURLY COMPENSATION (US $)

Europe — High	1993	1994	1995
West Germany	25.67	27.16	29.74
Sweden	23.52	24.69	27.11
Italy	19.87	21.43	23.86
Netherlands	20.49	21.52	23.44
Denmark	21.10	21.19	23.20
Europe — Medium	1993	1994	1995
France	17.17	18.08	19.83
UK	15.33	16.42	18.17
Spain	13.57	14.56	16.21
Ireland	13.32	14.02	15.35
Europe — Low	1993	1994	1995
Greece	7.42	7.80	8.65
Portugal	5.23	5.68	6.34
Non — Europe	1993	1994	1995
US	16.42	17.11	17.73
Japan	16.79	18.43	20.63

Source: US Bureau of Labour Statistics.

Impact of the Shift to Neo-Modern Production Methods.

The movement towards leaner production in the sector has resulted in the following developments in the key areas of leaner supply and closer customer contact which impact upon peripherally located suppliers:

Quasi-JIT: Just as Jones (1992), BCG (1993), and Oliver (1993) reported, evidence from the interviews suggested that 'true' just-in-time was not practised in the European automobile sector except in the case of 'door-step' plants, an example of which are car seat production plants which manufacture and deliver seat systems which arrive at the assembly line in the exact order in which they are needed. This sequential delivery of a component is the most elaborate form of just-in-time. Thus *'sequential just-in-time'* depends on the nature of the product or part. As Karlsson and Ahlstrom (1995) also report, when parts are standardised and relatively inexpensive this highest level of just-in-time is not essential. Neither is it essential for smaller parts which can be transported on pallets in high volumes and require minimal storage space. Thus, the principal study finding is that, aside from the few situations where 'sequential' or 'true' just-in-time is required, the opportunity affords itself to peripheral firms to be integral parts of the supply chain.

Even where just-in-time delivery to the assembly plant is sought, variations exist to satisfy the practicalities of the situation. Lamming (1993) described three variations on just-in-time which typify the delivery methods employed by the supplier firms in the research population. The first he termed *'apparent just-in-time'*. The assembler demands, and receives supplies just-in-time for use on the assembly line but the supplier manufactures the parts in batches and delivers as required from finished-goods stores. The levels of materials held by the assembler are reduced to a minimum and, since the supplier is not producing just-in-time, the cost of holding inventory remains in the chain, but one stage back. This model of JIT is quite common in the peripheral supplier plants visited. One supplier interviewed claimed that 'the onus is from the car company on the supplier to hold stock'. The second form of quasi-JIT involves *'in-line warehouses'*. Several interviewees in the Irish-based component manufacturers alluded strongly to this as the currently prevailing situation. One described their logistical arrangement: 'a warehouse is used by the assembler to co-ordinate all suppliers' deliveries and forwarded to the assembly plant on a just-in-time basis'. This gives the impression of just-in-time operation at the assembler's site with no real benefit accruing to the supply chain usually with a rental cost for warehouse space to the supplier. The third type Lamming calls *the milkround, or ex-works delivery system*, wherein the assembler collects the parts from the suppliers and delivers to consolidation points from where delivery to the plant along with aligned parts occurs on a just-in-time basis. In the case of the Irish-based suppliers they simply became part of a European-wide collection service on the part of the assemblers which employed this form of just-in-time delivery to the assembly plant.

Although not 'true' just-in-time as in evidence at Toyota in Japan, these systems seem to suit the wider European map since not all products, component systems or parts require sequential just-in-time delivery, and frequently do not need any form of quasi-just-in-time. These views are reflected in the realistic comment of one of the distanced suppliers interviewed who claimed that 'just-in-time is fine but at some level common sense intervenes'.

Buyer-Supplier Relations: The trust and assurance developed with existing customers by the respondents' firms has assisted greatly in maintaining business. According to the interviewees, the bases of this trust are to some extent the personal relations developed over the years, but for the most part they are a result of a good performance record (flexibility, high quality and reliability), rather than mutual trust or obligation. Firms at the periphery have been overlooked to a great extent by the Japanese transplants thus far. Most of their suppliers are UK-based. Although acceptance of the importance of close relations to the Japanese was evident there was also a level of scepticism about its extent and motive. One interviewee felt that to the Japanese 'relationship is the "icing on the cake". Price comes first.' Another interviewee stated that one of the cornerstones of the 'partnership' model, open-book access to cost structures was 'dangerous. They'll identify your margin and drag you down to it. If they insist on it , it's best not to show the truth'.

Nevertheless, the potential for a strengthening of relations with distanced assemblers is felt to be improving. Technological developments have lead to further advances in oral and visual communication systems and a reduction in transport times enabling increased contact opportunities. Albeit in the opinion of most interviewees that EDI is still some way off, it was felt that in the medium-to-long term, this form of communications technology will permit enhanced operational communication in particular over extended distance, enabling better control over the material flows from peripheral regions.

13.6 CONCLUSION

Modern manufacturing, for the most part, is organised in regional clusters. For even the largest corporations many factors such as trade restrictions, differing customer requirements and preferences, and neo-modern manufacturing methods dictate that, for most industry sectors, the global company must establish a manufacturing presence in each region of significant market demand. Industrial supply chains are created within the region to produce parts and component systems for assembly into the final product. The location of these supplier plants depends on the trade-off between scale benefits, position in the supply chain, transport costs, labour costs and availability, and government incentives.

Within these parameters, manufacturing can be configured with some suppliers located close to the assembly plant and others at a greater distance. This chapter has focused on the conditions pertaining to those supplier firms located at a long distance from the customer within these neo-modern industrial manufacturing configurations. The first message of the chapter is that as long as quasi-JIT is the norm, firms at the edge of regional manufacturing clusters have a role to play in the production of certain component systems and parts. Sequential JIT delivery would be virtually impossible to operate over extensive geographical distances. With distanced-delivery systems transport costs increase and transit is certainly considered a waste under the principles of lean production but these limits to peripheral operations can in many cases be outweighed by the benefits of lower input costs, the availability of skilled and/or low-cost labour and government investment incentives. In any case, timely delivery is quite achievable over distance, particularly when co-ordinated by the use of information technologies.

Secondly, the production of component systems rather than' individual parts, for example, a full control panel rather than simply the steering mechanism of a car, increases the amount of value-added prior to transit. Manufacturing clusters utilising 'true' JIT can produce such systems within the peripheral region.

The idea is for sub-regional clusters to combine to form pan-European regional clusters. Thus transport becomes an even smaller percentage of total manufacturing cost and many of the benefits of lean production can be attained in the early stages of the supply chain.

Likewise, the production of high-tech parts requires skilled labour. This input is generally more expensive and in shorter supply at the core of an industrial region. Such products can be more economically produced in a peripheral region with an educated workforce. A newer model of low-medium-cost high-skilled labour, rather than the simple low-cost low-skilled or high-cost high-skilled models, is emerging in many industrial sectors. This is a favourable development for peripheral economies in the EU which can no longer compete at the low-tech levels with competition from Eastern Europe, Turkey or even India, but have invested heavily in their education systems.

Third, neo-modern production calls for greater supplier input in the production process to avoid waste along the supply chain. This necessitates closer relations between industrial buyers and sellers. If both parties are keen to achieve a type of relationship based more on trust, obligations and commitment than mere price and bargaining, distance should not unduly militate against it. Transport improvements which reduce time and space make face-to-face contact more convenient. Telecommunication advances permit video-conferencing, computer link-ups and cheaper phone contact. Hence in the long term relations can be cultivated, nurtured and cemented. Crises and emergencies can be more difficult to deal with over distance but this is a short-term price which again needs to be weighed against lower input costs, higher incentives and increased labour availability. It may be that the greatest difficulty is one of perception. The feeling that the supplier is far away in a backward land, out of quick contact, may be more in the mind of managers than in reality.

Industrial policy implications suggest an important role for Government in mitigating the adverse impacts of peripherality on suppliers. Some considerations from a policy perspective include the need to build a positive economic view of the location by promoting lower input costs, tax incentives and availability of cheaper high-quality labour and by turning 'drawbacks' into advantages (for example, one supplier positively asserted that 'there are no traffic jams on the Irish Sea'). In addition, Government can support continued infrastructural development in transport and communications, continue to spend on education, provide training grants and support internal linkages to produce systems rather than simple parts to nurture sub-regional manufacturing clusters.

Further research is required into a trade-off model of manufacturing at the periphery which attempts to balance the extra costs of transit, the need to hold some emergency stock, the reliability of delivery, the closeness of buyer-supplier relations, the level of product technology, the lower input costs, the cost and quality of labour, and the availability of Government incentives. A proper understanding of the true nature and real practices and potential of neo-modern manufacturing and supply is essential to guide and inform such research.

References

Andersen Consulting (1993), 'The Lean Production Enterprise Project', published report findings.

Axelrod, R. (1984), *The Evolution of Co-operation*, New York: Basic Books.

Automotive Industry Data Ltd. (1995), *Newsletter no. 9523*.

Bartlett, C. and Ghoshal, S. (1990), *Managing Across Borders: The Transnational Solution*, Boston, MA: Harvard Business School Press.

Begg, I. and Mayes, D. (1994), 'Peripherality and Northern Ireland', *National Institute Economic Review*, pp. 90-99.

Boston Consulting Group (1993), 'The Evolving Competitive Challenge for the European Automotive Components Industry', Report prepared for The Commission of the European Communities, Directorate General for Industry.

Crowley, J. (1990), *1992 and the Transport Sector*, Dublin: Europen.

Dicken, P. (1992), *Global Shift: The Internationalisation of Economic Activity*, London: Chapman.

Dunning, J. (1988), *Explaining International Production*, London: Harper Collins.

Economist Intelligence Unit (1995), 'Europe's Automotive Components Business', 4th quarter.

Ford, D. (1980), 'The Development of Buyer-Seller Relationships in Industrial Markets', *European Journal of Marketing*, Vol. 14, No. 5, pp. 339-354.

Ford, D. (1984), 'Buyer-Seller Relationships in International Industrial Markets', *Industrial Marketing Management*, Vol. 13, pp. 101-112.

Grimwade, N. (1989), *International Trade: New Patterns of Trade, Production and Investment*, London: Routledge.

Hallen, L., Johanson, J. and Mohamed, N. (1987), 'Relationship Strength and Stability in International and Domestic Industrial Marketing', *Industrial Marketing and Purchasing*, Vol. 2, No. 3, pp. 22-32.

Heide, J. and John, G. (1990), 'Alliances in Industrial Purchasing: The Determinants of Joint Action in Buyer-Supplier Relationships', *Journal of Marketing Research*, Vol. 27, pp. 24-36.

Helper, S. (1991), 'How Much Has Really Changed Between U.S. Automakers and Their Suppliers?', *Sloan Management Review*, Summer, pp. 15-28.

Helper, S. and Sako, M. (1995), 'Supplier Relations in Japan and the U.S.: Are They Converging?', *Sloan Management Review*, Spring, pp. 77-84.

IBEC (1994), 'Growth or Gridlock?', Report on Irish Automotive Components Industry.

Jones, D. (1992), 'Beyond the Toyota Production System: The Era of Lean Production' in *Manufacturing Strategy — Process and Content* (Ed. Voss, C.), London: Chapman and Hall.

Karlsson, C. and Ahlstrom, P. (1995), 'Assessing Changes Towards Lean Production', *International Journal of Operations and Production Management*, Vol. 16. No. 2, pp. 24-41.

Krafcik, J. (1988), 'Triumph of the Lean Production System', *Sloan Management Review*, Vol. 30, No. 1, pp. 41-52.

Krafcik, J. and MacDuffie, J. (1989), 'Explaining High Performance Manufacturing: The International Automotive Assembly Plant Study', International Motor Vehicle Programme (IMVP), MIT.

Lamming, R. (1989), 'The International Automotive Components Industry: The Next Best Practice' for Suppliers', IMVP Policy Forum, MIT.

Lamming, R. (1993), *Beyond Partnership: Strategies for Innovation and Lean Supply*, Hemel Hempstead: Prentice Hall.

Levitt, T. (1983), 'The Globalisation of Markets', *Harvard Business Review*, Vol. 61, No. 3. May-June, pp. 94 -104.

MacCormack, A., Newman, L. and Rosenfield, D. (1994), 'The New Dynamics of Global Manufacturing Site Location', *Sloan Management Review*, Spring, pp. 69-80.

MEMA. (1990), Keiretsu: 'The Effects of Inter-Relationships on Japanese OEM Sourcing', Report of the Motor and Equipment Manufacturers Association, USA.

Nishigushi, T. (1989), 'Is JIT Really JIT', IMVP International Policy Forum, May.

Ohmae, K. (1990), *The Borderless World*, New York: Harper Collins.

Ojala, L. and Suomi, R. (1992), 'EDI: An Advantage or Disadvantage for Remotely-Situated Countries?', *International Journal of Physical Distribution and Logistics Management*, Vol. 22, No. 8 pp. 35-42.

O'Laughlin, K., Cooper, J. and Cabocel, E. (1993), *Reconfiguring European Logistics Systems*, Oak Brook, IL: Council of Logistics Management.

Oliver, N. (1990), 'JIT: Issues and Items for the Research Agenda', *International Journal of Physical Distribution and Logistics Management*, Vol. 20, No. 7, pp. 3-11.

Oliver, N., Delbridge, R. and Lowe, J. (1993), 'World Class Manufacturing: Further Evidence from the Lean Production Debate', Paper submitted to the British Academy of Management Conference.

O'Neal, C. (1989), 'JIT Procurement and Relationship Marketing', *Industrial Marketing Management*, Vol. 18, No. 1 pp. 55-63.

O'Neal, C. (1987), 'The Buyer-Supplier Linkage in a Just-in-time Environment', *Journal of Purchasing & Materials Management*, Vol. 23, No. 1, pp. 7-13.

Porter, M. E. (1986), 'Changing Patterns of International Competition', *California Management Review*, Vol. 28, No. 2 (Winter), pp. 9-40.

Porter, M. E. (1990), *The Competitive Advantage of Nations*, New York: The Free Press.

Rhys, G. (1995), 'The European Motor Industry', Paper presented at Autotech Conference, NEC, Birmingham.

Sako, M. (1992), *Price, Quality and Trust: Interfirm Relations in Britain and Japan*, Cambridge: Cambridge University Press.

Sako, M. , Lamming, R. and Helper, S. (1994), 'Supplier Relations in the UK Car Industry: Good News-Bad News', *European Journal of Purchasing and Supply Management*, Vol. 1, No. 4, pp. 237-248.

Schonberger, R. (1982), *Japanese Manufacturing Techniques*, New York: The Free Press.

Schwab, K. and Smadja, C. (1994), 'Power and Policy: The New Economic World Order', *Harvard Business Review*, Vol. 72, No. 6, pp. 40-50.

Turnbull, P., Delbridge, R., Oliver, N. and Wilkinson, B. (1993), 'Winners and Losers — The Tiering of Component Suppliers in the UK Automotive Industry', *Journal of General Management,* Vol. 19, No. 1, pp. 48-63.

Turnbull, P., Oliver, N. and Wilkinson, B. (1992), 'Buyer-Supplier Relations in the UK Automotive Industry: Strategic Implications of the Japanese Manufacturing Model', *Strategic Management Journal*, Vol. 13, pp. 159-168.

Wilson, D. and Mummalaneni, V. (1986), 'Bonding and Commitment in Buyer-Supplier Relationships', *Industrial Marketing and Purchasing*, Vol. 1, No. 3, pp. 44-58.

Womack, J., Jones, D. and Roos, D. (1990), *The Machine That Changed the World*, New York: Rawson MacMillan.

14

SUCCESSFUL COMPETITION FROM THE PERIPHERY: THE CASE OF SWEDISH MULTINATIONAL ENTERPRISES

Örjan Sölvell and Ivo Zander

14.1 INTRODUCTION

If Europe is defined in terms of where the political centres or largest markets are located, this chapter on the evolution of Swedish multinational enterprises (MNEs) is clearly about successful competition from the periphery. However, peripherality in terms of political developments or markets does not preclude centrality in terms of industrial and innovative activity. Indeed, as the chapter illustrates, Sweden being a small country in northern Europe has developed many world-class centres of industrial activity. Such centres, or clusters of interrelated industries, have played a critical role in creating a range of Swedish MNEs that successfully compete in today's international markets.

The importance of world-class clusters of interrelated industries for the development of international competitiveness is illustrated by Hollywood — the home of film, video and TV production. Hollywood provides a cluster of key players in the industry, including actors, directors, distributors, producers, technical consultants, studios, script writers, stunt men and so on. It has for several decades proved a conducive environment for innovation and upgrading through specialised education and research facilities, and has managed to attract new financial and human resources from around the world. Products from Hollywood movie producers have reached a level of competitiveness which allows them to be distributed world-wide.

Hollywood is of course not unique, and the regional agglomeration of economic activity and its effects on innovation and technological upgrading has experienced a renaissance in recent years (Freeman, 1987; Porter, 1990; Krugman, 1991; Nelson, 1993; Malmberg and Sölvell, 1995). Indeed, empirical observations confirm the trend towards increased international specialisation of technological activity (Pavitt, 1988; Cantwell, 1989, 1991; Archibugi and Pianta, 1992a, 1992b). Germany and the United States, and regions within these countries, are world-leading centres for automobiles and many chemicals, Japan for home electronics and office machinery, Switzerland for insurance services and pharmaceuticals, Sweden for paper products and heavy trucks, Italy for segments of the machine tool industry and ceramic tiles, and so on.

All industrialised countries display a selection of dynamic and world-leading industry clusters, including competing firms, specialised education and research facilities, advanced suppliers, consultants, firms in related technologies, and sophisticated customers. The 'Hollywoods' are also sufficiently dynamic to attract new talented people and investments from MNEs based in other nations (see Figure 14.1). With market integration and increased European and global competition, the industry clusters of different countries are increasingly matched against each other, and fewer of these 'Hollywoods' will exhibit the power of staying in the centre of technological development.

FIGURE 14.1: HOLLYWOOD — A LOCAL INDUSTRY CLUSTER WITH GLOBAL REACH

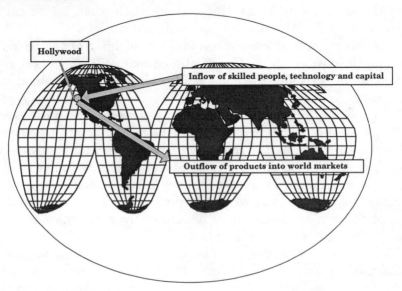

This chapter starts with an overview of the emergence of industrial activity in Sweden and the growth of Swedish MNEs. From that base we then describe the growing industry clusters, or industrial Hollywoods, in Sweden and how they have promoted the international competitiveness of Swedish firms. The pulp and paper and automotive clusters are used as illustrations of the large number of interrelated industries that might support innovation and technological upgrading in a well-established industry cluster.

In the sections that follow, we suggest that the importance of innovation and upgrading of competitive advantage in local industry clusters has not diminished as markets globalise — rather the contrary. Particular reference is made to the internationalisation of technological activity in Swedish MNEs and the development of multi-centre structures for innovation and upgrading of competitive advantage. In the final section, we discuss the integration of the European market and what it implies for the competitiveness of firms based in the periphery of political and market developments.

14.2 THE EVOLUTION OF SWEDISH INDUSTRIAL ACTIVITY AND MNEs IN THE PREWAR PERIOD

Initial sources of competitive advantage among Swedish firms were strongly associated with the existence of abundant natural resources, in particular copper and iron ore and vast forests. Foreign capital, expertise and direct investments related to mining, metal production and forestry were attracted into Sweden, thus supporting the advancement of industrial activity in the Swedish economy (Heckscher, 1935). The evolution of leading firms in raw material-intensive industries such as steel products and pulp and paper built on imported technologies in combination with local innovation activity. Sandvik, for example, today a world-leading specialty steel and materials technology firm, successfully exploited and improved upon the Bessemer patent which was acquired from Great Britain in the 1860s.

The inflow of skills and technologies was also notable in mechanical engineering, which nurtured the development of a number of indigenous mechanical engineering workshops in the early 19th century. These mechanical workshops became instrumental in the growth and development of the Swedish shipyard and railway industries. Improved mechanical engineering skills also

became an important input into a range of other Swedish industries, including pneumatic and hydraulic equipment, precision-
based instruments, bearings and various forms of production
equipment (Table 14.1).

Starting from favourable access to raw materials and imports
of foreign skills for their exploitation, Swedish industrial activity
moved beyond factor dependence in the late 19th century. The establishment of two technical institutes, the Royal Institute of
Technology in Stockholm (1827) and Chalmers Institute of Technology in Gothenburg (1829), was instrumental in facilitating this
process. Other important training institutes included the Falu
mining school (1820), the Filipstad mining school (1830) and the
Forestry Institute (1820). Another achievement which would
prove significant for the development of more advanced industries
in later periods was the establishment of compulsory popular
education in 1842 and the foundation of a series of technical secondary schools in the mid-19th century. Growing Swedish industries frequently came to draw upon the same specialised pools of
educated people and research institutions, which cut across successful Swedish product areas. The strength of these clusters of
technologies was reinforced by university curricula aimed at supporting the growing needs of industry.

The progress of industrialisation was followed by the formation
of tighter linkages across the emerging Swedish industries. The
first wave of mechanical workshops in the 1830s and 1840s
formed the backbone of the evolving shipyard and railway industries. The growth of these industries in turn created demand for
iron and steel components, welding equipment and improved diesel engine technology. In a similar way, forestry, mining, metal and
pulp and paper production demanded increasingly advanced materials as well as mechanical and power-generating equipment
such as saws, rock drills and rock-drilling machinery and tur-
bines. Energy-intensive processes in the iron and steel and pulp
and paper industries promoted the exploitation of hydro-electric
power and furthered the development of techniques to distribute
electricity over long distances.

TABLE 14.1: EXAMPLES OF IMPORTANT INFLOWS OF TECHNOLOGIES
AND SKILLED PEOPLE INTO SWEDEN

Inflow of Technologies through Licensing:			
Technology	*Origin*	*Firm*	*Period*
Precision sawing	Holland	Ekman	Mid-19th cent.
Forging	England	Lesjöfors	1830s
Steel processes (Bessemer, Martin, Thomas)	England, France	Sandvik	1850-1870
Separator (Alfa-pat.)	Germany	Alfa-Laval	1889
Diesel engine	Germany	Scania	Early 20th cent.
Aircraft assembly	Germany	Saab	1920s
Pharmaceuticals	Germany, Switzerland	Astra	1910s and onwards
Jet engines	England, US	Volvo Flygmotor	1950s and onwards
Thyristor technology	US	ASES	1959
Healon for eye surgery	US	Pharmacia	1970s
Inflow of technologies through immigration:			
Family	*Origin*	*Technology*	*Period*
Steffens, Grissbach, others	Germans	Mining, forging	1600s
Firbrandt	Germans	Textile	1624
Rademacher	Balt-Germ.	Steel products	1654
DeBesch, DeGeer, others	Walloons	Forging, steel, weapons	1600s
Peyron, Meaurin	French	Silk weaving	Mid-18th cent.
Mulder	Dutch	Fine paper	1758
Owen	English	Steam technology	1809
Hall, Carnegie, Dickson	English	Trading houses	19th cent.
Barclays, Davies, others	English	Textile	1850s
Bechman, others	Germans, Norwegians, Germans	Breweries, Sawing, Window glass	Mid-19th cent.
Gibson, Keiller	Scottish	Mechanical engineering	1830s
Versteegh	Dutch	Steam saws	1880s
Cassel	English	Railroads, mining	1880s
Mazetti	Danish	Confectionery	1883

Source: Sölvell (1994)

The growing clusters of industrial activity, together with the establishment of private banks and more efficient capital markets, supported the emergence of a critical mass of entrepreneurial activity. Around the turn of the century, several Swedish inventions became instrumental in transforming the raw material-based economy, and promoted the subsequent development of an unusual number of large industrial firms (Gustavson, 1986). The three-phase electrical motor, the lighthouse, the spherical ball-bearing and dynamite promoted the growth of firms like Nitro Nobel, ASEA (today ABB), AGA, and SKF. Other inventions, such as the safety match and match manufacturing machinery, electric arc welding, and the adjustable wrench figure prominently in Sweden's technological history, furthering the expansion of the firms Swedish Match, ESAB and Bahco (today part of Sandvik Saws and Tools). In many cases, inventions were significant improvements of ideas which had been picked up elsewhere. This was particularly the case with the separator and the telephone and telephone switches, which became the bases of Alfa-Laval (today part of the Tetra Laval Group) and Ericsson.

While technical departments appear to have been established in many firms already in the late 19th century, the following decades saw the development of formalised research and development departments among the major Swedish firms (Ahlström, 1993). Increasingly, in-house research and development and firm-specific knowledge became the basis for further international expansion. With few exceptions, technological activity of Swedish MNEs was concentrated at home, and a majority of all newly-introduced technologies appear to have had their origin in the Swedish units (Zander, 1994).

As a complement to skilled engineers and in-house technological activity, industry associations to an increasing extent provided an opportunity to carry out joint research programs and continued to disseminate new technological findings among the associated firms. For example, the Royal Swedish Academy of Engineering Sciences (Ingenjörsvetenskapsakademien, IVA), the Wood Pulp Research Association (Pappersmassekontoret), and the Swedish Institute for Metals Research (Metallurgiska Institutet) were all established between 1917 and 1920.

As the inventions and subsequent innovations were strongly associated with the development of more advanced engineering skills, they were also instrumental in the internationalisation of Swedish firms. For many Swedish MNEs, the 1920s and 1930s were the most important periods of internationalisation (some of the firms which developed rapidly during this period were AGA, Alfa Laval, ASEA, Ericsson, SKF and Swedish Match). Some important firms also experienced considerable development after the second world war, stimulated by growing domestic demand, such as Electrolux in home appliances and Volvo in transportation equipment.

Many of the foreign investments took the form of sales subsidiaries, some of which later developed into manufacturing units. Various types of tariff and non-tariff trade barriers were the most important drivers behind the geographical dispersion of manufacturing operations. Also, fears of losing foreign sales in an increasingly protectionist world supported the transfer of manufacturing technology to foreign units just before the second world war (see Wohlert, 1981; Gårdlund and Fritz, 1983). Foreign subsidiaries were predominantly established in Europe, in particular in Germany, France, and Great Britain while in the interwar period investments became more frequent in Latin America and the United States.

14.3 COMPETITIVE ADVANTAGE AND INTERNATIONALISATION IN THE POSTWAR PERIOD

As the Swedish economy and its firms entered the postwar period, the basic industry clusters had become more firmly established. These clusters involved many linked industries which sustained development in a mutually reinforcing way, in particular within materials/metals, forest products, multiple business components, transportation equipment, power generations and distribution systems, and telecommunications (see Figure 14.2).

Throughout the postwar period, the development of more advanced industrial products was accompanied by increasing research and development efforts, which were primarily carried out in Sweden. Most of the research and development was accounted for by the large Swedish MNEs, which came to rely heavily on in-house development. Only a small part of their total research and development expenditure seems to have been related to the purchasing of licences, patents, and other know-how (Granstrand, 1981; Vahlne and Hörnell, 1986; Swedenborg, 1992).

A few new Swedish firms were able to build international positions on the basis of continuous innovation, including Astra and Pharmacia in pharmaceuticals, Tetra Pak in liquid packaging

machinery, Gambro in artificial kidneys and related equipment,
IKEA in furniture retailing and Inter Innovation in automatic
teller machines. There was also new business formation within
the established MNEs, frequently based on follow-up innovations
within or connected to established areas of technological activity,
such as Ericsson Radio Systems and ABB Robotics (Wallmark and
McQueen, 1986). These 'second-hits' sustained international expansion and investments through the transfer of manufacturing
technology to foreign countries (Zander, 1991).

FIGURE 14.2:   MAIN CLUSTERS OF INTERNATIONALLY COMPETITIVE
SWEDISH INDUSTRIES (SHADED)

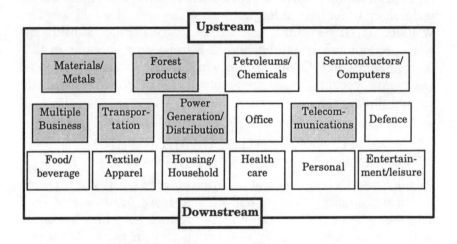

As Swedish industry emerged intact from the Second World War,
it was in a favourable position to supply the growing needs for
industrial products throughout Europe. Many Swedish firms were
able to consolidate their international positions in the immediate
postwar period, involving the establishment of an increasing
number of foreign sales and manufacturing units. The importance
of foreign sales in Swedish MNEs continued to grow throughout
the postwar period (Swedenborg, 1979), and as a result a large
number of these firms had achieved more than 80 per cent of total
sales in foreign countries already by the 1970s (see further Swedenborg, Johansson-Grahn and Kinnwall, 1988; Andersson, 1993).

As many of the industrial products of the Swedish MNEs required service and modifications according to local demand, the
postwar period saw a continuous expansion of foreign assembly

and manufacturing subsidiaries. The setting up and expansion of foreign manufacturing operations increased gradually but significantly throughout the 1960s and 1970s (Lund, 1967; SOU, 1975; Swedenborg, 1979, 1982, 1985; Swedenborg et al., 1988; Ghauri, 1990). As the trend continued in the 1980s, both among established MNEs and those that were less experienced internationally, the share of foreign manufacturing had reached beyond 60 per cent in several important firms by the late 1980s (Andersson, 1993). As production in foreign subsidiaries expanded, so did their share of total sales.

In the postwar period, many of the established MNEs consolidated their domestic industries through mergers and acquisitions. This went hand-in-hand with increased research and development expenditures and the economies of scale developed by the firms that internationalised their operations most forcefully. Firms like ASEA, ESAB and Electrolux all assumed dominant roles in their respective industries. Efforts to consolidate the domestic industry also spilled over to international markets. The 1970s and 1980s saw a major change in the mode of foreign expansion among Swedish MNEs, as much of their internationalisation efforts became based on foreign acquisitions (Swedenborg, 1982; Forsgren, 1989; Forsgren and Larsson, 1984).

Towards the end of the 1980s, foreign acquisition programmes took on even more substantial proportions, as some Swedish MNEs became involved in industrial restructuring at an international level. In 1988, ASEA merged its core operations with Brown Boveri et Cie in Switzerland to form ABB. A few months later, ABB announced the acquisition of Westinghouse's Transmission and Distribution operations in the United States. With the acquisition of the US firm Combustion Engineering in 1989, ABB formed the world's largest electro-technical group. Also, Volvo had far developed but never realised plans of merging operations with Renault in France, and Tetra Pak acquired Alfa-Laval in 1991, forming the Tetra Laval Group.

Swedish pulp and paper manufacturers, especially Stora and SCA, consolidated their leading positions throughout Europe through major acquisitions. Also, the Swedish steel industry became involved in large pan-European mergers and acquisitions. In 1991, Avesta merged with the British firm Sheffield into Avesta-Sheffield. In the pharmaceutical industry, Pharmacia acquired Italian Farmitalia Carlo Erba in 1992 and merged with American Upjohn in 1995, forming the Pharmacia-Upjohn Group.

The chemicals producer Nobel was acquired by Dutch Akzo and operations merged into Akzo Nobel in 1992.

14.4 SWEDISH INDUSTRIES AND FIRMS IN THE PULP AND PAPER CLUSTER

While innovations and the capability to upgrade technology over time has been instrumental in the internationalisation of Swedish multinational firms, it should be emphasised that innovation to a large extent remains the outcome of close interaction between related industries and firms. Firms that manage to sustain technological upgrading and to compete successfully from the periphery are based in leading industry clusters — or 'Hollywoods' — where they draw extensively on the exchange of knowledge with suppliers, customers, related firms and universities. As indicated in the preceding section, Sweden has built up many such industry clusters since the industrial revolution: pulp and paper products, upgraded steel products, power generation and distribution equipment, cemented carbide tools for machine tools, heavy trucks and cars, pharmaceuticals, and so on (see Sölvell, Zander and Porter, 1993).

The Swedish pulp and paper cluster is a good illustration of how Swedish firms have built world-leading positions throughout a large number of related industries, including a dense network of manufacturers of specialty inputs, machinery, and services as well as buyer industries such as liquid packaging. The multitude and diversity of competitive industries in the cluster is shown in Figure 14.3.

The leading Swedish pulp and paper groups include SCA, Stora, MoDo, AssiDomän, and Södra Skogsägarna. Independent specialty manufacturers include Munkedal, Munksjö, Rottneros, Tumba, Klippan, and Lessebo.

Swedish pulp manufacturers have been on the forefront in developing new pulp qualities, for example, as the result of the TMP (thermomechanical pulp) and CTMP (chemi-thermomechanical pulp) processes. In paper products, Swedish firms have developed particularly strong positions in newsprint, kraft paper (kraft liner, sack kraft paper) and paperboard, while fine paper (woodfree printing and writing paper) and tissue paper (toilet paper and other cleaning tissue) historically have been relatively less important.

FIGURE 14.3: THE SWEDISH PULP AND PAPER CLUSTER

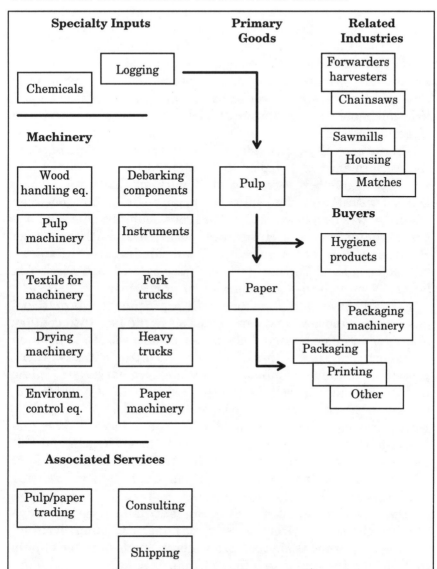

Today, SCA is the second-largest pulp and paper manufacturer in Europe, and has strong positions in printing paper and corrugated board. SCA has acquired a number of paper mills throughout Europe since the 1980s, including Italcarta (Italy), Peaudouce (France), Laakirchen (Austria), Reedpack (UK), and PWA

(Germany). Stora, being number three in Europe, offers a wide range of paper, and is a leading producer of printing paper, especially newsprint (Stora News), paperboard and wrapping paper. Stora took a major step to establish itself among the leaders in Europe by acquiring Feldmühle Nobel in Germany in 1990. This acquisition was the largest foreign acquisition ever made by a Swedish firm. MoDo concentrates on fine paper (MoDo Paper), printing paper such as newsprint (Holmen Paper) and paperboard (Iggesund Paperboard).

On the specialty-input side, efficient logging has contributed to the performance of Swedish pulp manufacturers. Sweden has produced a number of leading machinery manufacturers, which evolved with the mechanisation of logging. The lighter, one-man chainsaw was developed in the late 1950s. Major Swedish producers of chainsaws were Husqvarna, Jonsered and Partner. After Husqvarna had been acquired by Electrolux in 1978, the two rivals Jonsered and Partner were also incorporated, and Electrolux became a world leader in chainsaws for professional use.

Sandvik Saws and Tools has built a prominent international position in handsaws and saw blades since the late 19th century, and later in guide bars and chains for chainsaws. Mechanisation of logging continued with specially-designed tractors, forwarders, processing machines (limbing and ducking), log harvesters (felling and processing), as well as thinning and planting machines. A number of Swedish firms evolved in these fields, including ÖSA, Bruun System, Umeå Mekaniska Verkstad, Laxo Mekan and Kockum, today all part of the two Finnish firms, Repola and Valmet. Other Swedish industries linked to logging include cranes and other machinery, technical consultants, and firms specialising in fertilisers.

The development of the Swedish pulp industry spawned a number of manufacturers of pulp machinery. Leading firms included Götaverken (soda-recovery boilers), Sunds (a range of pulp machinery), Defibrator (a range of pulp machinery) and Kamyr (continuous digesters, bleaching plants). Sunds, a subsidiary of SCA, acquired Defibrator in 1979, forming Sunds Defibrator. Other machinery industries linked to pulp production include wood handling machinery (Valmet KMV, Söderhamns Verkstäder, Skega) and conveyors (Consilium Bulk, Kone Wood). Sweden developed strong positions in drying machinery (today ABB Flakt) and fabric and felts (Nordviror, Nordiska Filt and Bruzaholms Viror).

Pulp and paper plants utilise distribution, control and drive systems, and have been important customers to ABB throughout history (ABB Drives, ABB Process Automation, ABB Motors and ABB Distribution). Furthermore, various instruments, image-processing systems and other equipment are used to control and monitor the production process. In this field, many Swedish firms developed international positions, e.g. Scanpro, EKA Nobel, Boliden Kemi and Innovativ Vision. Scanpump is a leading supplier of pumps to the pulp and paper industries.

The forest products cluster is also linked to the transportation equipment cluster in several important ways. Heavy trucks are used to transport timber and paper. Volvo and Scania are known for their reliability and sturdiness for log transports. Heavy-duty forklift trucks (Kalmar Heavy Lift Truck) are used to improve logistics within pulp and paper plants. On the specialty-input side, the pulp and paper industries are major users of chemicals. Sweden historically hosted a number of leading suppliers of chemicals for the pulp and paper industry. However, during the last few years the industry has consolidated. Stora Kemi (including Alby after Stora's acquisition of Swedish Match) and EKA Nobel became the two leading firms. In 1990, EKA Nobel (today part of Akzo Nobel) acquired Stora Kemi and established a dominating position in Sweden.

Historically, the forest cluster was tightly linked to trading houses, which developed in the mid- and late-19th century, some of which specialised in forest products. The owners of trading houses were the leading capitalists at the time, and supported the establishment of new pulp and paper manufacturers. The major shipping port was Gothenburg on the Swedish west coast. Leading Swedish trading companies with a history in trading forest and paper products include Elof Hansson and Ekman Liebig, both located in Gothenburg. The need for international pulp and paper transports has spawned specialty shipping lines such as Gorthon Lines, and by the 1960s SCA had developed special cargo ships for paper shipments.

The Swedish pulp and paper cluster has been sufficiently dynamic to maintain and strengthen its position in Europe, and represents a good example of an established 'Hollywood'. Interestingly enough, the surviving leaders in Europe have their home bases in the 'periphery', most importantly in Sweden and Finland (Table 14.2).

TABLE 14.2: LEADING PULP AND PAPER FIRMS IN EUROPE, 1995 (MILLION SEK)

Firm	Home Base	Est. Revenues
Kymmene UPM	Finland	76,000
SCA	Sweden	68,000
Stora	Sweden	59,000
KNP BT	The Netherlands	56,000
Enso Veitsiluoto	Finland	51,000
Arkp Woggoms Appleton	Great Britain	34,000
Metsäliito	Finland	30,000
Bowater	Great Britain	28,000
MoDo	Sweden	23,000
AssiDomän	Sweden	23,000
Jefferson Smurfit	Ireland	20,000

Source: Dagens Industri 1995-09-12

The current state of the Swedish pulp and paper cluster reflects decades of continuous improvement and upgrading, involving competing pulp and paper manufacturers, suppliers of specialised inputs, machinery and services, buying industries, and various research and educational institutions. This cluster has evolved over time, with changes in demand conditions and specialisation of factors of production, including the establishment of training centres, changes in the curricula of universities and the like. It has grown with the consolidation into larger firms, but also through the entry of new firms whereby rivalry and experimentation was enhanced. This has not been a smooth process, but rather a process of continuous tension where firms were pressured to innovate and upgrade competitive advantage in order to survive and prosper.

14.5 SWEDISH INDUSTRIES AND FIRMS IN THE AUTOMOTIVE CLUSTER

The Swedish automotive cluster provides a second illustration of how Swedish industries and firms have built world-leading positions from a dense network of manufacturers of specialty inputs, machinery and buying industries. This cluster began to take full shape after the Second World War, supported by the existence of a number of related industries, such as bearings, high-quality steel, engines, manufacturing equipment, and so on. The establishment of Volvo and Saab-Scania, belonging to two different groups of owners, enhanced dynamic rivalry and has sustained pressure for innovation throughout the postwar period (Figure 14.4).

FIGURE 14.4: THE SWEDISH AUTOMOTIVE CLUSTER

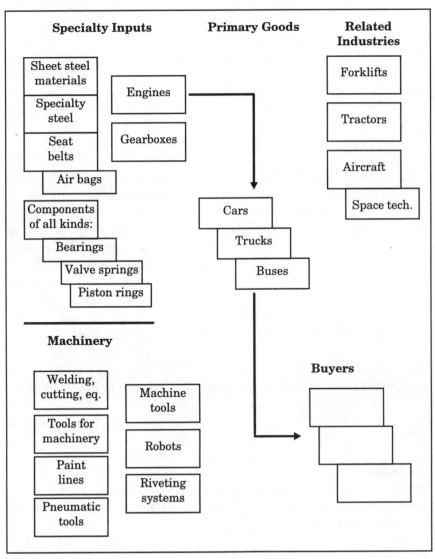

Manufacturing of automotive products combines a range of materials, components and systems, such as steel, aluminium, machine tools, welding equipment, bearings, engines and electrical systems. Even the wood-working industry was linked to the manufacturing of trucks and automobiles in the early days, when car bodies and truck cabs were built from wood.

Several Swedish mechanical engineering workshops entered into automobile production in the early 1900s, although none survived as an automobile manufacturer. Some firms tried to build trucks and buses. VABIS (in Södertälje) presented its first automobile in 1897, Scania (in Malmö) in 1901, and Tidaholms bruk in 1903 (liquidated in 1934). In 1902, both Scania and VABIS produced their first trucks. The two companies merged in 1911, forming Scania-Vabis, which became one of Sweden's two large truck and bus manufacturers. Thulinverken (in Landskrona) went from production of aircraft engines to automobile production after World War I, but went bankrupt in 1927.

Volvo entered the industry in 1927, beginning with passenger cars, but soon moved into truck manufacturing — a light truck based on the same chassis as the automobile. In the process of building up automobile and truck manufacturing, Volvo was helped by a number of advanced suppliers and low-cost labour compared to other automobile-producing countries. Important Swedish suppliers in the cluster included SKF (bearings, castings for engines and brakes), Bofors (steel), Pentaverken (engines), Köpings Mekaniska Verkstad (gearboxes), Åtvidabergs Industrier (wooden parts for the body and spokes) and Svenska Stålpressnings AB Olofsström (pressed sheet steel and pressed parts). Volvo later acquired Pentaverken (1930), Köpings Mekaniska Verkstad (1942) and Olofsström (1969). Nyströms Mekaniska Verkstad in Umeå had introduced the first self-supporting steel cab in the world in 1948, and joint development together with Volvo resulted in the introduction of a new design in 1960. In 1964, Volvo acquired Nyströms, which was renamed Volvo Umeverken. Likewise, Scania acquired its main supplier of cabs, Be-Ge Karosserifabrik in Oskarshamn in 1966. Volvo developed a global orientation, both in cars, trucks and buses. In cars, increased competition in the standard segment forced Volvo to develop specialty cars.

Saab (Svenska Aeroplan AB) was a manufacturer of military aircraft, set up in 1937, which subsequently diversified into production of automobiles. The first prototype was exhibited in 1947, and the first series was introduced in 1949. In 1969, Saab acquired Scania-Vabis, forming the Saab-Scania group. In addition to military aircraft, Saab-Scania now came to include production of cars, trucks and buses. The car division developed its international position much more slowly than Volvo, and did not develop an internationally-competitive product until the 1970s. After a few difficult years in the 1970s, a merger between Volvo's and Saab's car businesses was proposed. Strong resistance inside the two companies prevented the merger. The two manufacturers continued on their own, and were forced to develop niche products in order to survive competition in the world market. Positions were built up with the introduction of new car generations, especially in the US. However, in the late 1980s, Saab-Scania experienced difficulties in the car division, and decided to sell out 50 per cent to General Motors, forming Saab Automobile. Later the Saab-Scania group was split up altogether and Scania became an independent manufacturer of trucks and buses in 1996.

Swedish suppliers to the automobile industry form a large and heterogeneous group. They include many small domestic-oriented firms, but also a few internationally-competitive suppliers. Industries which have been the most innovative have been pushed by anticipatory demand, such as Electrolux Autoliv in seat belts and airbags. Diesel engines for trucks and buses were refined by Scania-Vabis and Volvo. Scania-Vabis' first internally-developed diesel engine came in 1936, whereas Volvo produced its own engine in 1944. The world's first turbo-charged diesel engine for trucks was developed by Scania-Vabis in 1951. After the Saab-Scania merger, the company began to develop car engines, which were manufactured by the Scania division in Södertälje. In the late 1970s, Saab-Scania developed a reputation of being an innovative manufacturer of engines. The first turbo passenger car was produced in 1977, the APC system in 1980, and direct ignition in the late 1980s. Pentaverken (Volvo Penta from 1930) developed gasoline engines for use in cars and boats. Today, Volvo Car manufactures engines for trucks and buses.

A key industry contributing to the evolving automotive cluster was the machine tool industry, including lathes, milling cutters, drilling machines, planes, bending machines, stamping machines, shearing machines and presses. Only a few Swedish machine tool manufacturers developed international positions. SMT Machine Co. and Pullmax had extensive foreign sales, but experienced years of financial difficulties and were eventually taken over by the government and merged. The two companies were later split up. Lidköping Machine Tools is a highly-advanced machine tool manufacturer, which is used as an in-house supplier to its owner, SKF. Computer systems for machine tools are produced by Pullmax, Saab-Scania and ABB (the latter two for general purpose systems). The machine tool industry is linked to the materials and metals cluster through its use of tools. Tools for machines tools include both steel tools and hard-material tools. SKF Tools and Uddeholm Tooling are both international leaders in steel tools, and Sandvik Coromant and Seco Tools have developed strong international positions in hard material tools.

In the 1970s, the automobile industry began to use industrial robots. The first industrial robot prototypes in Sweden were developed in the early 1970s. ASEA presented the world's first electrical microprocessor-controlled industrial robot in 1973, working in close contact with the Swedish car manufacturers. A special welding robot was developed jointly with ESAB. Today, ABB Robotics offers a broad range of robots, with emphasis on heavy robots — the area where Swedish industry has its main advantages.

Finally, Swedish forwarding companies and transporters of timber to the Swedish pulp and paper industry, have been key customers of Volvo and Scania trucks. Heavy timber transports created an early focus on heavy vehicles and promoted the development of high-performance engines and high-quality trucks. Swedish forwarding companies followed Swedish industry into international markets, and leading firms with international positions include Bilspedition (including Scansped Group), Inter Forward and ASG.

As in the case of pulp and paper, the experience of the Swedish automotive sector reveals that peripheral countries can play a dominating role in international competition. Both Volvo and Scania are among the top ten producers of heavy trucks in the world (see Table 14.3).

14.6 NEW SOURCES OF COMPETITIVE ADVANTAGE AMONG SWEDISH MNEs

The growth of Swedish MNEs also created new sources of competitive advantage which were intimately linked to the increased presence in foreign markets and enhanced economies of scale. As foreign sales were increasingly supported by the transfer of manufacturing technology to foreign units, it was also possible to provide better service to local customers and to respond more effectively to new local business opportunities. Other potential benefits came with the increased possibilities of integrating international operations, by which some manufacturing subsidiaries were given regional and global product responsibilities. This has led to cost reductions following from specialisation and cross-flows of components and products within the international network of subsidiaries.

TABLE 14.3: LEADING TRUCK MANUFACTURERS, 1994 (> 15 TONNES)

Firm	Home Base	Production
Daimler-Benz	Germany	98,000
Volvo	Sweden/US	64,000
Paccar	US	51,000
RVI	France	44,000
Navistar	US	42,000
Scania	Sweden	32,000
Hino	Japan	28,000
Ford	US	25,000
MAN	Germany	20,000
Iveco	Italy	18,000
Nissan Diesel	Japan	18,000

Source: SvD 96-02-05

Furthermore, over time the international growth of Swedish MNEs created a secondary source of firm-specific advantages which derived from research and development in foreign countries. The share of foreign research and development in Swedish MNEs increased gradually from the 1960s and onward, and had reached an average of about 30 per cent in the period 1985-90 (Zander, 1994; Håkanson, 1981; Håkanson and Nobel, 1993). A large part of the increase appears to have followed the general growth in foreign direct investment and the need to support increasingly sophisticated foreign manufacturing operations.

However, during the 1970s and 1980s increased foreign technological activity was related to the more frequent use of foreign acquisitions. These acquisitions added both similar and new technological capabilities which have been further developed by the foreign units. It appears that the common approach to organising the additional foreign technological capabilities is a relatively strict division of labour, by which one unit has taken the leading role in technological development in each individual technology (Zander, 1995a, 1995b).

There are good reasons to believe that the geographical dispersion of technological capabilities has not fundamentally changed the process of innovation and upgrading of competitive advantage among the large Swedish MNEs. Both the costs and lengthened development times associated with internationally-integrated innovation activities, as well as the difficulties in exchanging technological knowledge across geographically-dispersed units, suggest the continued importance of knowledge exchange within the local industry cluster. This suggests the development of multi-centre or multi-home-based structures among Swedish MNEs (Forsgren, 1990; Holm, 1994; Forsgren, Holm and Johanson, 1988; Sölvell and Zander, 1995), whereby firms draw strength from an increasing number of industry clusters around the world, with relatively little co-ordination in between such centres.

14.7 SUMMARY

In this chapter, we have suggested that successful competition from the periphery is indeed possible if the firm is established in a strong and dynamic industry cluster. We used two particularly strong Swedish clusters to illustrate how industrial 'Hollywoods' have emerged in the periphery of Europe and supported the international success of its firms.

With increased market integration in Europe we expect to see not only increased competition between firms, but also between industry clusters in different parts of Europe. When clusters from various countries compete under increasingly equal conditions, fewer centres of innovation and technological upgrading will more clearly emerge, concentrating investments into the most dynamic clusters. In this process, peripherality in terms of political influence or market size is not the deciding factor. Instead, the ability to maintain dynamism and technological upgrading, supported by the attraction of resources from the outside, will continue to be significant importance for the international success of multinational firms.

References

Ahlström, G. (1993), 'Industrial Research and Technical Proficiency — Swedish Industry in the Early 20th Century', *Lund Papers in Economic History*, No. 23, Lund University, Department of Economic History.

Andersson, T. (1993), 'Utlandsinvesteringar och policy-implikationer' in SOU 1993:16, Stockholm: Norstedts.

Archibugi, D. and Pianta, M. (1992a), 'Specialisation and Size of Technological Activities in Industrial Countries: The Analysis of Patent Data', *Research Policy*, Vol. 21, No. 1, pp. 79-93.

Archibugi, D. and Pianta, M. (1992b), The Technological Specialisation of Advanced Countries — A Report to the EEC on International Science and Technology Activities, Kluwer Academic Publishers and The Commission of the European Communities.

Cantwell, J. (1989), *Technological Innovation and Multinational Corporations*, Oxford: Basil Blackwell.

Cantwell, J. (1991), 'Historical Trends in International Patterns of Technological Innovation' in *New Perspectives on the Late Victorian Economy — Essays in Quantitative Economic History 1860-1914* (Ed. Foreman-Peck, J.), Cambridge: Cambridge University Press.

Forsgren, M. and Larsson, A. (1984), 'Foreign Acquisitions and the Balance of Power in Transnational Enterprises: The Swedish Case', *Working Paper No. 2*, Centre for International Business Studies, Uppsala University.

Forsgren, M., Holm, U. and Johanson, J. (1988), 'Divisional Headquarters Go Abroad — A Step in the Internationalisation of the Multinational Corporation', *Journal of Management Studies*, Vol. 32, No. 4, pp. 475-491.

Forsgren, M. (1989), 'Foreign Acquisition: Internationalisation or Network Interdependency?' in *Networks of Relationships in International Industrial Marketing* (Eds. Hallén, L. and Johanson, J.), Greenwich, CT: JAI Press.

Forsgren, M. (1990), 'Managing the International Multi-Centre Firm: Case Studies from Sweden', *European Management Journal*, Vol. 8, No. 2, pp. 261-267.

Freeman, C. (1987), *Technological Policy and Economic Performance*, London: Frances Pinter Publishers.

Gårdlund, T. and Fritz, M. (1983), *Ett världsföretag växer fram — Alfa-Laval 100 år*.

Ghauri, P.N. (1990), 'Emergence of New Structures in Swedish Multinationals' in *Advances in International Comparative Management* (Ed. Prasad, S. B.), Greenwich, CT: JAI Press Inc.

Granstrand, O. (1981), 'The Role of Technology Trade in Swedish Companies', RP 81/3, Stockholm: Institute of International Business.

Gustavson, C. G. (1986), *The Small Giant — Sweden Enters the Industrial Era*, Athens, OH: Ohio University Press.

Heckscher, E. F. (1935), *Sveriges ekonomiska historia från Gustav Vasa*, Stockholm: Albert Bonniers Förlag.

Holm, U. (1994), *Internationalisation of the Second Degree*, published doctoral dissertation, Department of Business Studies, Uppsala University.

Håkanson, L. (1981), 'Organization and Evolution of Foreign R&D in Swedish Multinationals', *Geografiska Annaler*, 63B, pp. 47-56.

Håkanson, L. and Nobel, R. (1993), 'Foreign Research and Development in Swedish Multinationals', *Research Policy*, Vol. 22, pp. 373-396.

Krugman, P. (1991), *Geography and Trade*, Cambridge, MA: MIT Press.

Lund, H. (1967), 'Svenska företags investeringar i utlandet' in *Sveriges industri*, Stockholm: Industriförbundet.

Malmberg, A. and Sölvell, Ö. (1995), 'Spatial Clustering, Accumulation of Knowledge and Firm Competitiveness', paper presented at the 1995 Residential Conference of the IGU Commission on the Organization of Industrial Space, Seoul, August 7-11.

Nelson, R. R. (ed.) (1993), *National Innovation Systems — A Comparative Analysis*, Oxford: Oxford University Press.

Pavitt, K. (1988), 'International Patterns of Technological Accumulation' in *Strategies in Global Competition* (Eds. Hood, N. and Vahlne, J.-E.), London: Croom Helm.

Porter, M. E. (1990), *The Competitive Advantage of Nations*, New York: The Free Press.

SOU (1975), Internationella koncerner i industriländer — samhällsekonomiska aspekter.

Swedenborg, B. (1979), *The Multinational Operations of Swedish Firms — An Analysis of Determinants and Effects*, Stockholm: The Industrial Institute for Economic and Social Research.

Swedenborg, B. (1982), *Svensk industri i utlandet — En analys av drivkrafter och effekter*, Stockholm: Industriens Utredningsinstitut.

Swedenborg, B. (1985), 'Sweden' in *Multinational Enterprises, Economic Structure and International Competitiveness* (Ed. Dunning, J. H.), Chichester: John Wiley and Sons.

Swedenborg, B., Johansson-Grahn, G. and Kinnwall, M. (1988), *Den svenska industrins utlandsinvesteringar 1960-1980*, Stockholm: IUI.

Swedenborg, B. (1992), 'Svenska multinationella företag' in *Sveriges industri*, Stockholm: Industriförbundet.

Sölvell, Ö., Zander, I. and Porter, M. E. (1993), *Advantage Sweden* (2nd ed.), Stockholm: Norstedts.

Sölvell, Ö. (1994), 'Sveriges framtid finns i historiska "Hollywoods", Stockholm, *MTC Kontakten*, Jubileumstidskrift.

Sölvell, Ö. and Zander, I. (1995), 'Organization of the Dynamic Multinational Enterprise — The Home-Based and the Heterarchical MNE', *International Studies of Management and Organization*, Vol. 25, Nos. 1-2, pp. 17-38.

Vahlne, J.-E. and Hörnell, E. (1986), *Multinationals: The Swedish Case*, London: Croom Helm.

Wallmark, T. and McQueen, D. (1986), *100 viktiga svenska innovationer under tiden 1945-1980*, Lund: Studentlitteratur.

Wohlert, K. (1981), *Framväxten av svenska multinationella företag — En fallstudie mot bakgrund av direktinvesteringsteorier Alfa-Laval och separatorindustrin 1876-1914*, Uppsala, Almqvist and Wiksell International.

Zander, U. (1991), *Exploiting a Technological Edge — Voluntary and Involuntary Dissemination of Technology*, published doctoral dissertation, Stockholm, Institute of International Business.

Zander, I. (1994), *The Tortoise Evolution of the Multinational Corporation — Foreign Technological Activity in Swedish Multinational Firms 1890-1990*, published doctoral dissertation, Stockholm, Institute of International Business.

Zander, I. (1995a), 'The Organization of Technological Capabilities in the Multinational Corporation — Evidence from Swedish Multinational Firms', paper presented at the 1995 Academy of International Business Annual Meeting, November 15-18, Seoul.

Zander, I. (1995b), 'Technological Diversification in the Multinational Corporation — Historical Evolution and Future Prospects', paper presented at the 21st Annual EIBA Conference, Urbino.

15

THE EVOLUTION OF THE FINNISH SYSTEM OF INNOVATION: THE CONTRIBUTION OF NOKIA

Antti Ainamo

15.1 INTRODUCTION

For an economy, being peripheral means not being fully integrated into the global economy. The intellectual and economic rewards of participation in global industrial networks are greatest at the 'core' of the networks. The mission of peripheral economies in modern times has been to 'catch up' (Hampden-Turner and Trompenaars, 1994) or 'undertake' (Freeman, 1995) with the more developed or advanced economies at the core. The strategy of the public policy makers in most peripheral economies has been to implement a broad range of policies designed to accelerate, or to make possible, industrialisation and economic growth.

This chapter describes, from a historical perspective, Finland's strategy of catching up with the core. In viewing Finland's industrial strategy of competing from the periphery as a series of stages of economic development, the chapter describes its economy-wide strategic changes, illustrating these changes with a description of the impact of Nokia Corporation's firm-level strategy on the Finnish economy as a whole. Implications for public policy of other economies are also suggested.

15.2 STAGES OF ECONOMIC DEVELOPMENT

A peripheral economy is usually isolated from the core by geographical distance; by a lack of transportation infrastructure; by a unique or rare language or cultural heritage that is unknown to the outside world; by a lack of education, political stability, globally incompatible industrial standards; or by the small size of its

market. All these factors contribute to other economies giving little consideration to the economy's needs or desires.

Yet peripherality is not a simple on/off feature that an economy
either has or has not. Peripherality is a variable that is dynami-
cally contingent on the situation of the economy. There is wide
agreement (e.g. Vernon, 1966; Porter, 1990; Freeman, 1995) that
the various degrees or of peripherality can be seen as 'stages' of
economic development (see Figure 15.1).

FIGURE 15.1: FOUR STAGES OF NATIONAL COMPETITIVE
DEVELOPMENT

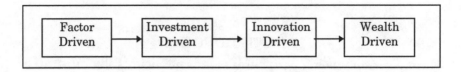

Source: Porter, 1990, p. 546.

According to this view, the growth of economies is, typically, initially driven by natural endowments. Porter (1990) has found that
peripheral economies can successfully compete on the basis of
natural endowments, as long as natural endowments last and
costs do not rise. When either of these contingencies occur, there is
an imperative for the economy to progress towards the core
through investments and innovation.

In the investment-driven stage, investments in foreign manufacturing technology and methods are applied to the local setting,
adapted to suit the particular circumstances of those settings, and
improved upon. The purpose of investing is to develop a superior
accumulated base of investments: here, consistency and continuity of investments are the key. The longer the duration of
continuous investment, the greater the barrier to entry for rivals.
A national strategy driven by investment results in an accumulation of up-front investment as a competitive advantage because
rivals find it difficult or impossible to match decades or centuries
of investment.

However, markets may change or technology may be updated
or radically improved by others. Such sources of turbulence may
decrease the value of accumulated investment: policy makers
would then be wiser to move gradually towards the next stage.

The innovation-driven stage is characterised not only by the application and improvement of technology, but also by the creation of new technology that is new not only to the periphery, but also to the core. This stage provides superior incentives and rewards in comparison to the factor-driven and investment-driven strategies.

Yet, like the factor-driven and the investment-driven stages of development, the innovation stage also requires a caveat. For this stage to be sustainable, wealth that is generated through innovation should be invested in industry to further increase competitiveness; however, wealth sometimes degrades the cost-competitiveness of labour and technology and motivation for innovation.

The wealth-driven stage is triggered when wealth created by innovation ceases to be the medium that makes further innovation and wealth creation possible. When wealth becomes the central end in itself, investment accumulation and innovation degenerate or cease altogether. Porter cites the experience of Britain as an example of an economy that became a 'service economy' where industrial innovation effectively for a long time ceased to take place. Britain, a first-mover at the core of global industrial networks during the 19th century, digressed from its core positions towards the periphery.

Diversity of new ideas is an essential requirement of innovation but attainment of the wealth-driven stage degenerates the intent of original ideals. Attention to the intensity of market selection at the dense core of competition roots out the new ideas that do not immediately contribute to innovation and wealth creation. The wealth-driven stage, in this respect, equals short-termism.

One conclusion that can be drawn from the experience of Britain is that competitive advantage can only be sustained in a competitive niche where the economy remains isolated from the core by the virtue of being peripheral. Within Porter's evolutionary framework of economic development, economies need to develop unique systems of languages, and skills for two-way communication with development at the core.

There is a large variety of alternatives to configure such a 'national system of innovation' (see Freeman, 1995). The system itself is a collective effort of national or regional education systems, industrial relations, technical and scientific institutions, government policies, cultural traditions, and many other institutions. The optimal alternative fits with the particular circum-

stances of the particular economy. It provides the economy with
industrial innovations that can be applied to industry in order to
maintain and increase competitiveness. How the system works in
reality is explored in the following sections with reference to the
case of the Finnish national system of innovation and the role of
Nokia in shaping that system.

15.3 THE FINNISH SYSTEM OF INNOVATION

15.3.1 Finland in the Historical Context

Historically, the peripherality of the Finnish system of innovation
has many roots. Finland shares the collectivist culture of other
Nordic countries (Sweden, Norway, Denmark, and Finland). These
four Nordic countries were shaped from the 19th century onwards
by social-democratic ideals (e.g. serving the safety and comfort of
the human being). Where Finland is different from the other
countries is that its location at the north-eastern corner of Western Europe is geographically more peripheral than its neighbours
and, indeed, it was once a Grand Duchy of Russia. In addition, the
Finno-Ugrian language is somewhat obscure when compared to
those of the Scandinavian Peninsula and Denmark.

Finland became independent in 1917 and there followed a civil
war between right- and left-wing factions. Much of the subsequent
internal strife remained latent under the cover of Scandinavian
collectivism and consensus.

Developments during World War Two further underline Finland's greater attention to relations with Russia/the Soviet Union
than has been the case in the other Nordic countries. Denmark
and Norway were quickly occupied and Sweden succeeded in
staying neutral, but Finland fought both the Soviet Union and
Germany. Finland was one of the few countries in Europe that did
not benefit from American aid. Instead, Finland found itself paying heavy war reparations to the Soviet Union.

Finland is historically the poorest of the four Nordic countries,
resulting in a lack of financial capital for investment, innovation
and wealth accumulation. Historically, the country has a high
level of economic dependence on its natural endowments, from
which it has had difficulties in freeing itself. Natural endowments
(mainly forestry) have remained the most significant exports. After World War Two, a heavy-metal industry was established to

conform to the requirements of the reparations to the Soviet Union.

A few established Finnish firms in forestry and heavy-metal were, in the late 1940s and early 1950s, able to sponsor the international marketing of crafts-manufactured consumer products (in such product classes as furniture and glassware). But there was little or no scope to build up critical volume in these 'new exports' so as to provide a platform through which further domestic volume expansion through internationalisation could take place. The reasons for this were two-fold. Firstly, a lack of standardised technology kept industrial-scale volumes from being reached. Secondly, Finland lacked endogenous economic demand for its new consumer products. There was simply not enough affluence within Finland to create any meaningful scale of production for these 'new exports' (as industrial products not building on natural endowments were labelled) as long as the country was run as a war economy. Thus these consumer products remained showpieces for export promotion rather than truly commercial products.

15.3.2 How Finland Competed from the Periphery in the 1950s and 1960s

Finland finished paying its war reparations to the Soviet Union between 1951 and 1952. At the same time, remaining wartime industrial material and ideological structures provided direction for economic development. The Finnish combination of a low standard of living (i.e. low wages) and earlier investments into the heavy-metal industries resulted in some economic growth.

As a result of that growth, Finland had by the 1960s progressed to a stage where it was as much at the periphery as it was at the core. Gradually, the country began to experience improvements in wage levels, as well as catching up with the leading Western countries in terms of living standards and endogenous consumer demand.

Given that Finland needed to maintain its path towards increasing affluence, its policy-makers and industrialists perceived a material need for new products and export markets that were appropriate for this objective. They believed that a rising wage level strengthened the need to steer the economy away from dependence on natural wood resources. There was concern that the supply of wood was already causing problems (see Finnovation, 1970).

Because Finland historically had a weak economy, there was a lack of financial capital for investment. Thus there a is saying in Finland: 'our country is poor, and thus it will stay'. As the paths towards both further exploitation of natural endowments and investment accumulation were blocked, the belief was that innovation would, for Finland, have to be more important in the 1970s than during any previous decade in its economic history. There was also a belief that the decade would internationally, too, be the 'the product innovation decade'. Finnish industry began to invest in new sectors, such as electronics.

The Western world met Finland half-way in her attempt to internationalise. Student revolts and labour unrest in 1968 signalled internationally the diffusion of the Nordic-type ideals into Western popular culture. The concept from the earlier decades to expand 'new exports' now received broad interest in Finnish industry. The idea was that showpiece consumer products for export promotion could be a direct basis for new exports. However, the real business reality was that Finnish success stories in terms of new exports remained few in number and isolated from one another.

15.3.3 How Finland Retreated into a Uniquely Protected Niche in the 1970s

The 1973 oil crisis took most of the Western world by surprise. Most Western European economies experienced a decline in economic growth. Only welfare and social security systems buffered the appearance of social unrest in Western Europe, particularly among traditional craft-based and smokestack industries. Yet the case of the Nordic countries is a notable example of the oil crisis not being experienced uniformly by all economies. Denmark may have had some difficulties but Norway had oil. Sweden found that there was sufficient wealth accumulated in its multinationals to withstand the crisis. Finland's way was perhaps the most interesting of all.

In Finland the dominant industrial sectors, forestry and heavy metal, were evolving towards maturity (Normann, 1976). The national innovation system was still characterised by a lack of financial capital directed towards innovation, which made movement into new products and markets difficult. This was seen as a reason for a concern in most countries. Yet global concern was not highly regarded in Finland but considered to be a Western managerial 'fad'.

Finland also developed a good working relationship with the Soviet Union. The bilateral trade based on exchange of quotas of products rather than fluctuating market prices provided an enormous new export market for Finnish industry. As a result, Finland was one of the spectacular success stories of post-war Europe.

15.3.4 How Finland Re-experienced Peripherality from the Late 1980s

The sudden decline of the Soviet Union in the mid-1980s developed a momentum which subsequently led to a downturn in industrial growth in Finland. There emerged a willingness to re-participate in the developments in Western Europe, and there was much debate about reconfiguring the national innovation system (e.g. Lemola and Lovio, 1984). The Confederation of Finnish Industries became a prime advocate for high-tech electronics industry in Finland. In a seminal move, the Finnish telephone monopoly in 1981 co-operated with other Nordic telephone monopolies to set up a joint Nordic mobile telecommunications (NMT) network. From 1985, the Finnish telephone monopoly initiated deregulation of the Finnish telephone markets, as did the telephone monopolies of the other Nordic countries.

Of even greater significance than telecommunications deregulation was that Finnish authorities deregulated the country's financial markets in one bold swoop in 1986. With the global boom of the financial markets at that time, the worth of Finnish stocks and shares spiralled upward. As the financial markets grew, more and more people were employed in the sector, and began to share in exceptional profits. With such easy profits to be made, the relative significance of investments in industrial production and innovation declined. The whole concept of industrial progress from the periphery to the core ran into serious controversy in Finland. Finland was now wealth-driven.

The major global downturn in the international financial markets in 1987 caused such concern globally that it was generally feared that the outcome would be similar to the stock market crash of 1929 that began a global economic depression. Such concern was not felt by the majority of Finns who believed that the breadth and size of the Finnish participation in financial markets meant that, while some sold stocks and shares, others were still willing to buy. The global financial markets was, from the Finnish perspective, such a large cake that the Finns never expected it to diminish suddenly.

Finns as a whole were still buying, while foreigners were selling. Finland's financial sector soon declined even faster than its Soviet-based industry. The Finnish economy as a whole plunged into a recession in 1990/1991. There were many bankruptcies, a major bank collapsed, and unemployment soared from a level of well under five per cent to over twenty per cent.

15.3.5 Crisis and Innovation in the 1990s

The Finnish recession acted as the trigger for the reorientation of its industry, as well as the revitalisation of its whole national system of innovation. Finland took steps towards the process of European integration in the early 1990s, joining the EU at the beginning of 1995. It reconfigured and documented its new national competitive strategy (National Industrial Strategy of Finland, 1993). In accordance with the earlier aspirations (Finnovation, 1970, Lemola and Lovio, 1984), new exports were developed in the electric and electronics industries and outside the dominant forestry and heavy-metal sectors.

Furthermore, there was a labour force ready and willing to reorient themselves towards the telecommunications industry. These reorientations of the Finnish national system of innovation and of its labour force proved a successful combination. Most measures of national competitiveness have, since 1992, shown major improvement (even if unemployment and foreign debt have remained problems). Finnish authorities have continued the process of deregulation, including additional markets in the 1990s (e.g. agriculture, transportation and retailing).

With success in the telecommunications industry, the national system of innovation included electronics as the third cornerstone of the economy along with forestry and heavy metal industries. The future will tell whether current deregulatory steps will cause new crises and new reorientations in the economy as a whole. Candidates for new cornerstones of the Finnish industry include medical electronics and environmental know-how.

15.4 NOKIA'S ROLE IN THE FINNISH SYSTEM OF INNOVATION

One individual Finnish firm has been at the cutting edge of the new institutionalised national system of innovation (Lovio, 1993).

The Nokia Corporation has emerged as a number two supplier in global sales of mobile phones and also remains a world leader in the building of telecommunications networks. Nokia developed in a very short time in the 1980s from a predominantly Finnish firm into a leading European company and has become a benchmark model for other firms to follow. How was this rapid leap from the Nordic periphery to the core of the European market possible?

15.4.1 How Nokia Developed an Early Involvement in Electronics in the 1960s

Nokia as a name dates back to 1865, when a wood-processing firm of that name was established. That firm was acquired in 1918 by Finnish Rubber Works, which in 1966 merged with Finnish Cable Works. This new conglomerate became known as the Nokia Corporation. Nokia was already at that time one of the biggest companies in Finland.

Electronics in the current Nokia Corporation — mobile phones, telecommunications and other communications products — date back to the establishment of an electronics department at Nokia Cables Works. Nokia Cables Works was, in 1960, the second largest manufacturing company (after Lohja) in Finland in electronics.

Nokia's history differs from those of other Finnish electronics firms, at least from the 1970s. By 1960, it was already a first-mover in Finland in importing and hiring out computers and providing data processing services, remaining the country's largest provider of such services throughout the 1960s. It also manufactured telecommunications devices and industrial electronics.

15.4.2 How Nokia Expanded Domestically in the 1970s

Despite consistent losses early on, Nokia's electronics division initiated an ambitious program for pioneering development and application of new technology. In 1972 the Nokia Corporation commenced the manufacture of a small microcomputer, and also developed data automation systems and instruments for the pulp and paper industry.

Nokia endeavoured at this point in time to become a generalist mass producer. It diversified its product portfolio, entering such new fields as plastics, metals and chemicals divisions and defeated rival private firms that attempted a similar strategy to its own. With such a strategy, Nokia became the largest privately-owned company in Finland.

Nokia benefited from managerial tenacity. Despite consistent losses in electronics, Nokia acquired a French license in order to expand into the telephone exchange domain. This proved to be a successful move. In both 1978 and 1979 Nokia's electronics division was the most profitable division of the Group.

The Nokia Corporation has also shown considerable courage. It has consistently focused on those business technologies it believes to be core technologies and has left its rivals to focus on the often, on superficial examination, more profitable product applications of these core technologies (e.g. Valmet and Strömberg in power electronics, Instrumentatium in medical electronics, Salora and Lohja in consumer electronics).

15.4.3 How Nokia Internationalised Aggressively in the 1980s

In 1981 Nokia took the lead in the Finnish electronics industry by acquiring Televa, a business nurtured by the Finnish government as the country's leading manufacturer of telephone exchange systems. This acquisition contributed to Nokia benefiting from public investments in the development of telecommunications technology. As a result, Nokia came to share in the development of the Nordic mobile telephone network through the Televa acquisition.

Nokia's mobile phone and telecommunications devices businesses began to grow, as did its personal computer business. A programme of further internationalisation was undertaken, even though exports already amounted to 40 per cent of net sales. In 1983 Nokia acquired two television manufacturers: the Finnish Salora and the Swedish Luxor. With these acquisitions, the electronics division became the largest division in the corporation. The integration of these acquisitions was very successful. In 1984 Nokia was the global first-mover in launching a light portable telephone. With Nokia's success in industrial reorientation, Nokia's CEO was made the President of the Confederation of Finnish Industries in 1986. There, he was well placed to influence the public policy makers, whose responsibility it was to devise the industrial strategy of the Finnish economy as a whole to fit Nokia's strategy.

Nokia was the first Finnish electronics firm that had successfully followed a generalist strategy to manufacture a series of diverse products and was intent on further internationalisation. It was involved in almost all electronics product groups that were manufactured in Finland. In 1986 and 1987 the corporation acquired the computer business of Swedish LM Ericsson and the consumer electronics business of ITT-owned Standard Elektronik Lorenz.

By 1988 Nokia was the second largest Nordic electronics company after LM Ericsson. It was the world's largest manufacturer of mobile phones, the third largest television manufacturer in Europe and the seventh largest supplier of computers and information systems in Europe. Half of Nokia's employees worked outside Finland.

15.4.4 Calculated Risk-taking at Nokia in the 1990s

The profitability of Nokia's electronics businesses declined rapidly in the late 1980s: the success of Nokia's strategy of rapid expansion met its limits. After changes in management, business operations were streamlined. Nokia divested its basic industries (paper and rubber) and the Nokia Data Division was sold to ICL/Fujitsu in 1991. Reallocation of resources from these sales into mobile phones and telecommunications increased the share of these businesses to more than half of net sales.

The costs of developing new technology became ever greater. Nokia's strategy was to take risks on the shape of future technologies: R&D expenditures remained well below 10% of the Group's net sales. This strategy proved highly profitable as Nokia's product for the 'global standard for mobile phones' (GSM) in 1991 proved to be a phenomenal success. Nokia's business success became internationally apparent. The company's share price skyrocketed on the Helsinki, New York and London stock exchanges, increasing more than tenfold in value in a matter of only a couple of years.

The phenomenal growth in Nokia's sales, profits and share prices has stabilised in recent years. One reason was that the corporation had bet on the success of TDMA technology as a successor to GSM, whereas a rival CDMA technology has more recently received institutional support in many international markets, most notably in the United States. Nonetheless, Nokia has firmly established itself as a key player in the global electronics industry. The Corporation now has the resources necessary for making multiple bets as to the direction of future technologies.

15.5 DISCUSSION

15.5.1 Analysis of Nokia's Role in the Finnish System of Innovation

The peripheral economy of Finland has historically lagged international developments and trends: the war economy ended roughly five years later in Finland than elsewhere in Western Europe. This peripherality was an advantage to the Finnish economy, as long as it could be maintained. Thus, when the global economy infiltrated the Soviet Union in the 1980s, it was no longer possible for Finland to practice innovation in a well-protected local environment where modest improvement and innovation was noticed and appreciated. It became apparent that Finland had jumped from factor and investment-driven stages of development to a wealth-driven stage without experiencing the innovation-driven stage in between.

Nokia Corporation has been a key influence on the shape of Finnish industrial structure. The company developed in a very short time during the 1980s into one of Europe's leading electronics producers by diversifying internationally into related sectors. Many factors — being the Finnish first mover in the evolution of Finnish system of innovation, a relatively large size by Finnish standards, commitment to electronics, and close relations with domestic institutions — improved its operational capability in comparison to its domestic rivals. Also, Nokia's ownership structure was more balanced and diversified than that of its rivals. Nokia's historical rivals were family-owned (Salora), state-owned (Valmet and Televa), foreign-owned (LM Ericsson) or companies owned by other firms (Strömberg, ICL), where capacity for quick and aggressive strategic change was considerably less than that of Nokia.

Despite being nationally dominant, Nokia long remained a small pioneering firm from an international perspective. It could go unnoticed by its rivals when it took advantage of the new business opportunities emerging from the microelectronics revolution of the 1970s. The most obvious example in hindsight is mobile phones. This provided it (as it did to a lesser extent Swedish LM Ericsson) with a first-moving advantage of a considerable time duration, which is another reason for its success.

Nokia has established close relationships with the key actors at the core of the global economy, which the rest of the Finnish electronics industry has used as a platform for penetration of international markets (e.g. the privately owned Polar-Elektro and Suunto, as well as the state-owned Telecom Finland). Nokia's co-operation with other Finnish firms remains a key factor in the growth of the Finnish electronics industry as a whole.

15.5.2 The Global Dynamic of Core and Peripheral Economies

The case of Finland suggests that the global economy can be viewed as a complex industrial network governed by a two-party system where each peripheral economy tries to formulate a convincing alternative to the predominant strategy of economies at the core, while the core group collectively manages the existing one. In other words, the peripheral economy has the inherent advantage in being the professional revolutionary in the global economy: peripheral economies at 'election time' (e.g. the collapse of the colonial empires, the collapse of the Soviet Union) convince those at the core that its alternative strategy is better than that of the ruling core.

The Finnish economy has historically entered the global economy at its peripheral fringes and worked itself towards the core. The economy has made market investments principally only on the basis of positive financial feedback. Cumulatively, it has developed a great number of 'weak ties' (see Håkansson, 1987). Over time, some of these weak ties have become strong ties. This can be categorised as competing from the 'outside-in' within the global industrial network.

However, Finland has used more than one basic way to compete. The competitive strategy of the Nokia Corporation has provided a spearhead for the Finnish economy by diverging from the 'outside-in' strategy. Nokia has entered global industrial networks at their very core. This corporation has forced itself to the core of a network by co-operating with counterparts that are at the core and then has worked itself towards the edges. It has advanced within the network from the 'inside-out'.

The inside-out strategy is faster than moving from the periphery towards the centre of the network. With the help of Nokia and its partners at the core, Finland has explored larger risks than it could have explored on the level of the economy as a whole. Historically Nokia as an individual firm with limited resources has been able to participate in only a few networks with intensity. Its strategy of competing from the inside-out has required large up-front or accumulated investments before effective networks have been put in place. If Nokia's existing relationships are to break down before new ones are created, much will be lost by Nokia, while Finland as a whole will be also be faced with problems..

15.6 IMPLICATIONS FOR OTHER ECONOMIES

In addressing how a peripheral economy could progress from the periphery towards the core, several tentative implications can be considered. Firstly, the optimal way to compete from the periphery depends to a large extent on the opportunities and threats that prevail: it is not necessarily stable nor predictable. An outside-in strategy is effective when it helps a peripheral economy to push or pull itself toward the core in a way where positive bandwagon effects spread across the economy as a whole. The strategy favours peripherality because the core of the global economy is turbulent. The closer an economy is to the core, the stronger the turbulence is felt.

In the more complex inside-out strategy, an individual innovative firm is directed towards the establishment of focal basic relationships that may be useful for the economy as a whole. If the firm is successful, its strategy can be put in place in the economy as a whole in order to reset the kind of learning that is needed to withstand turbulence at the core.

Furthermore, timing and entry strategy is important. Global industrial networks tend to offer entry points at some points in time for one strategy rather than another. As the case of the Finnish system of innovation suggests, reliance on any one strategy is a risky strategy. Finland's industrial performance lagged with an over-reliance on the outside-in approach to Soviet trade in the early and mid-1980s and even more on an over-reliance on the inside-out approach to the financial sector in the late 1980s. Finland pulled out of the resulting recession with the help of Nokia's inside-out strategy in the telecommunications sector.

The future belongs to economies competing from the periphery that learn to be masters in the game of catch-up and to economies competing from the core that learn to be masters in the game of continuous innovation. But no peripheral economy can effectively change everything at once.

The challenge is to remain sufficiently peripheral to be isolated from turbulence at the core and to be sufficiently close to introduce peripheral ideas at the core that are new to the core. Incremental economy-wide changes, on the one hand, and courageous and tenacious first-mover firms that prepare the ground for other firms to follow, on the other, are a promising avenue for competing from the periphery. In this way, the economy competes from the periphery in a way where it combines the two strategies. Constraints to being peripheral are reversed and shaped into a pathway for sustainable competitiveness.

These implications are contingent on the national system of innovation, industries and time-period chosen for study. This chapter calls for comparative studies in other research settings.

References

Finnovation, (1970) *Man and Product Planning,* edited by Lahden-pää, M. Kyriiri, Helsinki (in Finnish).

Freeman, C. (1995) The 'National System of Innovation in Historical Perspective', *Cambridge Journal of Economics*, Vol. 19, pp. 5–24.

Håkansson, H. (Ed.) (1987), *Industrial Technological Development: A Network Approach,* London: Croom Helm.

Hampden-Turner, C. and Trompenaars, F. (1994), *The Seven Cultures of Capitalism*, London: Piatkus.

Lemola, T. and Lovio, R. (1984), *Perspectives on Industrial Innovation and Technology Policy in Finland in the 1980s*, Valtioneuvoston kanslian julkaisuja, Finland (in Finnish).

Lovio, R. (1993), *Evolution of Firm Communities in New Industries: The Case of the Finnish Electronics Industry,* The Helsinki School of Economics and Business Administration, Helsinki.

National Industrial Strategy of Finland, (1993), The Finnish Ministry of Trade and Industry.

Normann, R. (1982), Introduction to the Finnish translation of *Management for Growth*, W&G. Espoo, Finland.

Porter, M. (1990), *The Competitive Advantage of Nations*, New York: The Free Press.

Vernon, R. (1966), 'International Investment and International Trade in the Product Cycle', *Quarterly Journal of Economics,* Vol. 80, Number 2, May, pp. 190-207.

16

EASTERN EUROPE: A SOURCE OF ADDITIONAL COMPETITION OR OF NEW OPPORTUNITIES?

Kenneth N. Bernard

16.1 INTRODUCTION

The fundamental nature of the changes which have taken place in the countries of the former Communist bloc — frequently, if somewhat simplistically, referred to collectively as 'Eastern Europe' — has prompted many reassessments of the validity of previously unquestioned tenets, in the socio-business and management spheres as well as in the political environment.

Nowhere is this more true than in the world of Marketing, where the change in the business environment has prompted a need not simply to explain the concepts of marketing, or to demonstrate their universal applicability, but also to re-evaluate the validity and the relevance of these principles in circumstances where the subsumed infrastructure of a market economy is far from being a practical reality — however widely the notion has been discussed as an academic or political ideal. Initially, a great deal of this re-assessment of the principles of a 'free market society' was carried out in academic cloisters or in uneasy meetings of businessmen who were anxious not to let slip the supposed benefits of the change in environment with which they were presented. The new scenarios have led many to examine the extent to which the apparent practices of Marketing do indeed match with what have come to be regarded as the universal truths of its theoretical constructs, and to consider the significance of and the responsibility for any mismatches which exist (see Thomas, 1994, for example). The emergence of the notion of Relationship Marketing, for example, has been — albeit coincidentally — more or less contemporaneous with the opening of 'Eastern Europe' to market-driven economics. The recognition that Marketing does not simply comprise the manipulation of a mix of managerial variables is as important to developed markets as it is crucial in the evolution of a whole market orientated society (see McKenna, 1991 for example).

The constructs of a 'market economy' are taken so much for granted by many 'Westerners' that they are rarely thought about and still less often defined, yet this concept is taken as the underlying premise of the goal to which the ex-Communist world has been aspiring. It is almost as if the notion of market freedom is seen as a divinely-given norm and the existence of any other approach to society and business is some form of exception or aberration. There has emerged a belief that just because some sort of system of socio-politico-economic cultures and beliefs has evolved and survived for longer in some countries than others have elsewhere, it must therefore be 'right'. Such is Western European or Euro-American arrogance.

Of course, others have developed similar prejudices at other times — it is a salutary shock to many Europeans venturing to North America or Asia for the first time to encounter maps of the World where Western Europe is *not* in the centre and thus is not portrayed as its natural hub. Not without some present-day irony, the Chinese imperial dynasties considered themselves to be at the centre of the world, referring to China as 'the Middle Kingdom'. Major cultural, racial, religious, political and economic groupings have continually emerged and declined but during their period of importance have regarded themselves as the norm by comparison with which, by definition or implication, everything or everyone else has been seen as exceptional or abnormal. However, the political, social and economic changes which have taken place 'east' of the erstwhile 'Iron Curtain' since 1989 have caused many of these cosy preconceptions of normality and desirability to come increasingly under fresh scrutiny from 'within' as well as from outside.

16.1.1 Rationale and Structure of the Discussion

Much of this present consideration of competitive strategies applicable to relationships with the countries of the former Eastern bloc is based on the results of a programme of research undertaken in 1992-94 under the aegis of the EU ACE (Action and Co-operation in Europe) programme, which focused primarily on the development of business relationships and joint ventures between companies located in Poland and Hungary on the one hand and the UK and Germany on the other. The prime focus of the research was on the extent to which SMEs have been developing international business links and on the efficacy of those links. While the operations of multinationals and other large organisations could not be ignored, they were of only secondary significance in the research project itself.

It must be recognised from the outset that a research base of just two countries in this region may produce findings which are not fully applicable accurately to the region as a whole, given the large number and diversities of the countries involved. However, the research programme was among the earliest to explore the issue of business relationships with the region at a micro-level and was significant in that it was specifically not directly focused on the activities of large and/or multinational enterprises. The subsequent discussion does however attempt to address the extent to which the research findings may be generalisable and to offer pointers for the region as a whole.

Rationale

Perhaps not surprisingly, available evidence suggests that in Poland and Hungary — and perhaps through the region as a whole, including the former Soviet Union — there is insufficient reliable data to support the view that any real sense of 'best practice' of marketing can be deduced, particularly among indigenous players in the SME segment. That is not to imply that there is or has been no appreciation of marketing theory or principles — far from it — Budapest University of Economic Sciences, for example, has had a Department of Marketing since 1973. The theoretical aspects of the subject have been studied there and elsewhere in great depth but what was, for a long time, lacking was the diffusion of this appreciation into the business community at large. Many managers have been keenly aware of *what* they have needed to achieve, but have needed assistance and direction in *how* to proceed and progress.

Several consequences have been observed, of which three principal facets may be considered as significant indicators for the adoption of marketing concepts and practice in the foreseeable future:

1. The emphasis of business development programmes has been on skills development and training rather more than on the evolution of strategic approaches to market development. That,

however, is widely considered unlikely to remain the case in-
definitely.

2. The recent business, social and industrial history of much of
   the region has revealed capabilities for production (albeit often
   based on outmoded and/or inefficient practices and technologies) and for consumption of wide ranges of imported as well as
   indigenously-produced goods and services — to a level of sophistication which frequently surprises visitors from outside
   the region. There is an apparent propensity for at least some of
   the markets in the region to adopt 'Western' branded goods in
   preference to locally-produced merchandise (Becker and Baker,
   1995).

3. The weak points in the economic systems are frequently perceived to be those concerned with physical distribution and logistics management; with effective market identification and
   marketing orientation, and with marketing competitiveness at
   all levels, but especially with respect to quality standards,
   consistency and reliability. This has allowed several 'Western'
   distribution and retail organisations to establish significant
   bridgeheads in the region, to the potential detriment of indigenous business development.

Several of these structural and infrastructural issues have attracted attention and action at a macro level, both by inter-
government and supra-government initiatives and also by interventions in the region by multinational companies making either
investments in or acquisitions of local companies, or indeed by
new greenfield developments. To date, there has been little real
evidence or discussion of the extent to which these activities are
benefiting the economies at a micro-level, and in particular, of the
extent to which there is any 'trickle down' effect of the 'new' skills
and philosophies which have been introduced by the large
players.

In this chapter, it is not proposed to focus on issues of macroeconomic policy, nor seek to offer any radically new models of
marketing theory, nor to offer purported solutions to specific
problems — not least because of the wide variety of circumstances
and the uneven but rapid pace of change across the region. This
chapter does, however, reflect on the applicability and application
of perceived models of international business development in
markets which are developing, re-industrialising and located in

the heart of Europe. It also considers the conundrum of the extent to which the liberalisation of political and economic relationships will produce more opportunities than threats for the rest of (particularly European) business and whether those changes will be seen more in the form of new customers, or of competitors or of suppliers/subcontractors.

Structure

The chapter is built around these themes and is constructed around the following headings:

1. *Eastern Europe — A Peripheral Region?:* A discussion of the applicability of various of the interpretations of peripherality to the countries of the region

2. *The Marketing Environments:* An overview of the business situations in the region; of the areas of perceived management deficiency and of barriers to/sources of competitiveness, focusing discussion around particular micro contexts

3. *Privatisation Operations:* An appraisal of the impact of the various privatisation programmes on strategies of small and large companies in the region

4. *The SME Sector in Poland and Hungary:* A discussion of the recent research project and the attitudes, motivations and expectations of actual and potential business partners; discussion of the British and German SMEs' aspirations and experiences in the formation of business associations with Eastern European partners

5. *Discussion of Research Findings and Prospects for the Future:* A consideration of the extent to which the development of relationships between SMEs in Eastern and Western Europe and the interactions between them conforms to the norms of academic literature; market entry strategies and barriers to entry with some further reflections on the issues of peripherality.

16.2 EASTERN EUROPE — A PERIPHERAL REGION?

The existence of various approaches to and interpretations of peripherality is of significance to students of the region conventionally known as 'Eastern Europe' and to those who may be contemplating conducting business there. These differences only serve to highlight the essential physical, cultural and economic diversities of the region as well as its strategic significance for Europe as a whole.

Other contributors to this book have discussed in some detail the nature and practical significance of peripherality (see, for example, Chapter 2, De Burca). In discussing the roles of the re-emerging countries of the erstwhile Council for Mutual Economic Assistance (CMEA), including the former Soviet Union, the entire notion of peripherality appears ripe for re-examination. This is necessary in order to assess the impact of perceived peripherality on the development of business relationships with and by companies in those countries, bearing in mind that, for most potential partners, these countries have been effectively beyond reach for many years. Key aspects which have been discussed include perceptions of marginality based on *psychological criteria* related to 'image' or 'impressions of relevance' to the operations of organisations who perceive themselves to be more 'centrally' involved in major business activity as well as the more usual issues of *cultural distinction* and of *geographic location à propos* major markets and/or principal competitors and suppliers.

16.2.1 Geographic Peripherality

Of the three groups of criteria, geographic considerations are the most frequently discussed and, apparently, most readily appreciated. Remoteness is, of course, dependent upon the standpoint of the perceiver.

Taking the case of the swathe of countries between the former 'Iron Curtain' boundary and the Urals, they might realistically be treated as being remote from almost everywhere except, perhaps from states such as Germany, Austria, Italy and the members of the former Soviet Union. Separation from other European countries is maybe not all that dramatic, neither should it be unmanageable either mentally or physically — Europe is, after all, a small continent and travel and communication are simpler now than they ever have been previously. Historically, the physical separation between so-called Eastern Europe and North America has been still less significant in business contexts, whilst involvement with the emerging nations of the Pacific Rim was not even a hypothetical issue pre-1948. The simple fact is that until recent years, the opportunity and the need for Eastern European countries to play an active role in the economic life of the rest of the world was largely unrecognised — by either side. Thus, the issue of Eastern Europe's peripherality did not really arise. Quite simply: no-one thought about it!

In today's world, given the almost universal availability of affordable air travel, considerations of distance are, of themselves, of much less importance than at any time in the past. Electronic communication is virtually instantaneous and almost universally available in consumer as well as in business contexts. While diffusion of state-of-the-art communications technology through Central/Eastern Europe may still lag behind the levels achieved in South East Asia or, indeed, parts of Western Europe, it comes as a shock to many first-time visitors to discover that modern telecommunications facilities are widely available, especially in commercial contexts, but increasingly amongst individual consumers. The most crucial limiting factor in the growth of the use of these facilities has been the state of the basic infrastructure: that problem has been swiftly tackled and the fundamental bottlenecks removed. Poland and Hungary, for example, have introduced almost entirely new telecommunications networks and switching systems within just four or five years, thanks to major collaborative ventures with partners including AT&T and France Telecom. The end result is that it is as simple a matter for people in Bratislava to see and hear what others in Brisbane or Brighton are doing or buying as it is for them to form an impression of Berlin or Budapest. Mass communication has moved on from the potentially controllable arena of terrestrial television to the domains of satellite television and the Internet, which are more or less beyond the effective control of individual governments. Customer awareness of and interest in happenings in physically remote environments is now commonplace but that does not mean that distance and location are now irrelevant — rather that the nature of their significance has changed.

From the points of view of those located in the belt of land from the Baltic Republics to the Balkans, these countries are not peripheral at all — indeed there is a growing trend for them to refer to themselves as being 'Central' rather than 'Eastern' European countries. This is not simply a matter of semantics or a geographical nicety but rather a reflection of perceived physical and psychological reality. Likewise, from the perspective of would-be investors from outside Europe, distinctions between 'Western' and 'Eastern' European geographical remoteness or marginality are merely matters of degree — as witnessed by the apparent readiness of South East Asian manufacturers to invest in Hungary,

Poland and the Czech Republic as bases in their development of global supply chains, in preference to alternative sites further west.

16.2.2 Cultural Peripherality

There are, of course, many aspects to and ingredients of culture, of which the most obvious are perhaps habits, traditions, history, language and the arts.

To the casual observer, it may appear that all countries and even regions within countries exhibit differences from other locations. Conversely, it is frequently contended that the whole world is at risk of some sort of submersion in a mid-Atlantic pop culture, dominated by fast foods, television game shows, indifferent Hollywood movies and an 'easyspeak' derivative of the English language. Similar contradictions arise in the world of business. For example, although every country and trading group has its own legal and customary framework for the governance of activity, there is a perception that the community at large is dominated by the mores of the London-New York-Tokyo axis.

Where do the countries of Eastern or Central Europe stand in this regard? Once again, there seem to arise a mass of contradictory signals, some of which are clearly matters of subjective interpretation, depending upon the culture and traditions of the percipient. Just to itemise a selection of the more obvious examples is sufficient to make that point — it also serves to demonstrate that far from Eastern Europe being some sort of fringe entity, in cultural terms the region is at the very centre of European history and culture and is, therefore, a region of truly global significance.

Linguistically, almost all the countries of the region differ significantly from each other and from what the rest of the world has come to see as normality. Almost every country has its own language, which in most cases bears little resemblance to any other of the mainstream world languages. Communication is fragmented across Polish, Czech, Hungarian, Serbo-Croat, Romanian, to such an extent that the peoples and governments have for centuries found it a matter of practical expediency to 'adopt' a second language to facilitate international contact. The 'common' language adopted has frequently been that of a military or economic dominator — German, Russian, French or, latterly, English. However, the *linguae francae* of the region show no signs of dying out, being regarded as symbols of national identity.

In terms of the *Fine Arts*, and especially music and architecture, the region has a long and distinctly mainstream European heritage. World-renowned composers include Smetana, Lizst, Bartok, whilst Russia has contributed a school which in the 19th and 20th centuries has been as influential as was the Austro-German school of the 17th and 18th centuries. Warsaw, Prague and Budapest are home to three of the world's leading opera houses of the 19th century. Budapest was remodelled in the 19th century as a miniature of Paris, and in the 20th century was recognised by UNESCO as one of the very first cities to be designated as a World Heritage site. The catalogue could go on and on.

Historically, far from being on the fringe of Europe, the countries of the region have been at its very heart — physically, economically and politically. They have commanded positions of importance even when reviewed against the background of the two centuries or so from the beginning of the processes of industrialisation.

Poland, for example, had a chequered history for centuries. Until the end of the 18th century, it was a country larger than France, who sought to use it as a political counterweight to the influence of Prussia, Russia and Austria. That affinity endured after Polish partition, through to its re-emergence in 1919, with momentous consequences in 1939. Over the centuries, Poland has been regarded as being of crucial military strategic significance, being fought over by the Swedes, Prussians, Russians and Germans — often more than once — scarcely an argument for being regarded as a peripheral entity.

The Austro-Hungarian Empire, as successor to the Holy Roman Empire, endured until 1918 and at the beginning of the 19th century still extended to embrace almost all of what later became Germany, as well as Austria, Hungary, and present-day Belgium, Luxembourg, Slovakia, and the Czech Republic. This Empire contained great mineral and agricultural resources which would eventually lay the foundations for the industrial power of Germany and then the Soviet empire. In political as well as geographic terms, the territory of the Empire could well be said to be the cradle of Europe — far less its periphery.

The Balkan states have played central roles in the political shaping of the modern world throughout the 19th and 20th centuries, as did the Baltic Republics briefly in 1939/40 and again in 1989-91.

Against this varied, vibrant albeit often turbulent background, how is it that the countries of Eastern or Central Europe have come to be regarded as peripheral or marginal? There are perhaps several reasons.

1. In the era of imperialist, global expansion from 1850 onwards, the geographic location of most of the countries in question and, in particular, their difficulty of access to the world's oceans, acted as a barrier to any ideas that they may have had to expand their influence beyond their own borders. At the same time, their Western and Eastern neighbours did not have such limitations and exploited their potential influence accordingly.

2. The first two waves of industrialisation increased the economic influence firstly of Britain and then of Germany, reliant upon indigenous resources and on external commercial links with colonies and with the emergent United States. Once again, location worked against Eastern Europe. This was accompanied by rapid population expansion in the industrialising countries, which bypassed the countries of the East, so that their perceived socio-political significance declined as the economic influence of the West increased.

3. Political/military occupation or domination firstly by Germany and then by the Soviet Union completed the process of economic subjugation, relegating the countries, in varying degrees, to being mere sources of raw materials, food and industrial production for their political overlords. While this process did give the countries some skills and expertise, it restricted them to the whims of their masters, did not provide circumstances conducive to social growth, and — because of their isolation from world circles — progressively and severely restricted the countries' ability to acquire contacts and technologies which would enable them to compete in world markets, even had they wished to do so.

16.2.3 Psychological Peripherality
The cumulative effect of the politico-economic limitations outlined above has been to foster the psychological perceptions of peripherality — both within and outside the region. People and governments within the region began to feel isolated from the rest of the world, but the state ideologies maintained that this was a

temporary and largely irrelevant phenomenon. For as long as the Soviet Union's economy and its political machinery could provide the sheer muscle to provide some form of subsistence for the countries which it controlled, the politicians would be able to maintain control over the aspirations and movements of the population at large.

The fact of the matter was that many of the peoples of Eastern Europe did genuinely feel aggrieved, deprived, deserted and forgotten by the rest of the world. Two hundred years of history had already demonstrated that it takes far more than redrawing lines on a map or imposing a political infrastructure to eliminate perceptions of nationhood. Successively, people in Warsaw, Budapest and Prague had experienced real disillusionment at the failure of the Western democracies to come to their aid when they rebelled against political oppression. Furthermore, with the advent of modern mass communications and despite the best efforts of the politicians to prevent it, populations at large became increasingly aware of the widening gulf in living standards between Western and Eastern Europe.

On the other hand, to most people in Western Europe, the countries to the east of the 'Iron Curtain' were virtually a closed book. Very few had first-hand experience of travel there, and even fewer had any real experience of doing business there. Such experience as did exist was frequently fraught with difficulties and frustrations of dealing with monolithic, corrupt and incompetent government ministries. Experience tended to become somewhat embellished in the reporting to companies who were less than interested in doing unprofitable business with unreliable partners who rarely had enough acceptable currency to honour their contractual obligations. Not only were most individuals and companies in the West ignorant of the real state of affairs in the East, they did not want to find out because they did not see any actual or potential benefit in doing so.

The psychological barriers between East and West were probably the greatest contributors to the perceived peripherality of the region. That they were demolished on a wave of emotion was almost as irrational as the basis for their existence in the first instance. However, the manner and speed with which the official barriers have been removed has encouraged the formation of other misperceptions which, in the short term at least, have proved no less difficult to handle by all concerned. Both 'sides' saw the elimination of political barriers to trade as opening a world of new opportunities but in most cases, both 'sides' were operating under a series of critical and serious misperceptions of the other 'side's' aspirations and capabilities.

It is against that background that the redevelopment of business relationships, the re-equipment of much of eastern Europe's industrial base with modern technologies and the establishment of modern philosophies and practices of management must be viewed. The aim of all concerned has been to narrow the perceived gaps between Eastern and Western industries and societies — perhaps their ideas of the appropriate processes to achieve that aim and their motivations for doing so are varied — and perhaps sometimes to the point of irreconcilability.

That is the focus of the rest of this chapter.

16.3 THE MARKETING ENVIRONMENTS

The process of environmental scanning is generally held to be a fundamental first step in any programme which might lead to internationalisation of business (Young et al 1989). Without that, it is argued that objective evaluation of suitable entry strategies is impracticable and thus that there is a risk that decisions will be illogical or otherwise seriously flawed. While many supposedly analytical models have been devised and deduced — such as the traditional SWOT approach to evaluation of Internal and External environments; or the PEST approach to a range of largely external variables or indeed Porter's 5-Forces model (1980) and his Diamond model of 1989 — the entire process of environmental scanning, analysis and evaluation is still hazardous, approximate and largely subjective. The fundamental problem is the completeness, dependability and currency of the available data — the classic marketing research problem!

In the context of the Central/Eastern European region, it must always be remembered that databases and collection methods have not conformed to Western norms until very recently and, even where there has been acceptance of Western methodologies, there has also been a fairly steep conceptual, methodological and practical learning curve to surmount. Data collected before 1989 or so was collected for different ends from that required since — thus there are fundamental problems of incompatibility and incompleteness as well as of credibility. Indeed one of the key difficulties encountered by early Western entrants to the Eastern European business environment was an almost complete lack of understanding of the significance of 'profit' and financial accountability. It was not just that data was unavailable or unreliable: most managers did not understand the concepts and terminologies.

Discussions of the business environment therefore rest heavily upon popular perceptions and received wisdom rather than being based solely or largely on objective analysis of empirical fact. This sort of scenario is perhaps more familiar in respect of industrialising countries than one might expect to find in sophisticated European markets: it presents an extra dimension of complexity to those who wish to do business in the region and are constrained by 'normal' criteria of risk assessment, payback projections and credit security.

In the context of the present discussion, it is sufficient to outline the main areas for consideration rather than to attempt to provide a definitive picture of the entire market situation, especially since the position varies in so many dimensions and continues to change and evolve rapidly. Recognising that any would-be supplier, purchaser or investor would have individual criteria to satisfy, it would be reasonable to expect environmental appraisal to be based on the application of a mix of methods, such as those suggested above. A conventional academic starting point might well be a formal or informal examination of the firms' strengths, weaknesses and objectives and to combine a SWOT analysis with a PEST appraisal, covering in turn the *Political, Economic, Social* and *Technological* environments. In any context, these four elements are closely inter-related, but especially so in the former Eastern Bloc where for 50 years or more, the entire environment had been state-controlled and -directed. Always at the forefront of any such evaluation must be the recognition that to treat the region as a single entity is a dangerous and unsustainable oversimplification of a geographical environment comprising upwards of a dozen sovereign states with a total population of more than 300 million.

A brief resumé may serve to illustrate the complexity of the problems of re-orientation which have been and are being faced by indigenous organisations and individuals: these same problems face any would-be market entrants and would-be purchasers from suppliers in the region.

16.3.1 The Political Environment

There has been a popular approach in the Western media that has treated all the countries in the region as 'communist' and therefore as being politically homogeneous. While there were similarities, there were significant differences even under communist rule; those differences have tended to become magnified in the variety of strategic approaches to political, economic and social transition which have been adopted. There was a noticeable difference between the approach to communism adopted in, for example, Hungary from the versions found in Albania or Romania. Similarly, the approaches to such issues as privatisation differ significantly between Poland, Hungary and the Czech Republic, as do proportions of individual national outputs which have been transferred from the public to the private sectors.

Nominally, almost all of the countries of the region have turned their backs on state communism of the Stalinist or the Marxist-Leninist varieties and have submitted to at least the theory of parliamentary democracy. The political turmoil of the early 1990s suggests that the democratic transformation is still a matter of lip-service in many instances — perhaps exacerbated by inability of incoming regimes to deliver fundamental social and/or economic improvements 'at the drop of a hat'. It is a matter of record that parliamentary and/or presidential elections held in Hungary, Poland and Russia in between 1994 and 1996 showed a resurgence of the former Communist parties, albeit under new banners and with apparently modified approaches to personal and social freedoms and without insistence on state control of all production — at least in the initial instance. Similarly, in some parts of the former Soviet Union, (for example in Belarus and in several of the Caucasian republics), there has never been a move away from the communist philosophy by the group in power — simply a move to more decentralised authority.

Even during the period 1945-90, the countries of the region were markedly different. The populations came from different racial/ethnic origins and fell under communist regimes by different means, for different motives and at different times. Whereas the Russian Federation annexed the Ukraine, what is now Belarus, Georgia and the Caucasian Republics by force during the 1920s and acquired control of the Baltic republics as a result of Stalin's notorious deal with Hitler in 1939/40, the development of the ring of 'satellite' states from Poland southwards to the Balkans had a very different origin in the series of popular uprisings after the fall of Nazi Germany, and the military occupations which followed.

Despite direct Soviet military intervention in Hungary in 1956, in Czechoslovakia in 1968 or their open support of General Jaruzelski's maintenance of a state of martial law in Poland throughout the 1980s, there was no *overt* political take-over of these satellite states by Moscow, although economically, they were tightly integrated into the fabric of the CMEA. Production and skills were strictly rationalised so that each state had responsibility for supplying the whole Bloc with a part of their economic and industrial requirements, but that none was totally self-sufficient. Thus Czechoslovakia specialised in armaments and munitions; Hungary in railway equipment and buses; Poland in shipbuilding and repair and so on. The motive was not so much to exploit instances of Comparative Advantage, as to ensure security of supplies for the Soviet Union itself and to maintain a situation of economic dependence among the satellites.

Such a situation did not, of itself, provide much incentive for technological advancement, neither was there in any sense a free market where supply and demand had to balance in the long term. Indeed, there was virtually no internal accounting for trade or movements of goods between the CMEA states. At the time of the break-up of the CMEA 'empire', the Ikarus company in Hungary was 'owed' the equivalent of over £400 million for past deliveries of buses to the Soviet Union and was forced to accept that that debt was unlikely ever to be paid. In former days, that would have been almost immaterial because the relevant government ministries would simply have signed authorisations to continue to requisition raw materials and labour and to go on producing. On the other hand, Hungary was able to take an early and somewhat independent lead in reforming its economy on to more or less market-based principles as early as 1968. The only difference from Western European models was that the market was created and controlled by the state (Boote and Somogyi, 1991). Nevertheless, the experience of being self-accounting gave Hungarian organisations a distinct psychological and practical advantage over their colleagues in other countries when, eventually, political controls were loosened.

The one element of historical significance that the years of Soviet hegemony failed to reduce was the perception of nationality among the various members of the Eastern Bloc: indeed arguably that sense of national self-awareness may be considered to have been increased rather than the reverse. Certainly to even the most casual observer, that is one of the first and strongest impressions to be borne in on visitors and partners. The artificial creation of Yugoslavia only survived because of strong centralised control, since the demise of which, more basic, primitive urges have come to the fore, perhaps exaggerated by years of forced suppression. Ethnicity is a powerful motivating force and one which some members of the Eastern Bloc have still to learn to harness for productive ends — without antagonising potential partners, customers and suppliers.

The critical lesson to emerge from this review is that despite apparent similarities of experience during the Soviet era, and despite outward similarity of experience since 1989/90, the countries of the region have always been very different politically and continue to be so. As noted earlier in this chapter, many of the countries have had long and proud histories; many have been at the forefront of European affairs and have been influential in the evolution of the Europe which we now see — quite apart from having played pivotal roles in the global conflicts of the twentieth century. It would be a grave over-simplification to regard them as being, in any real sense, uniform.

It remains to be seen how their futures will develop: at the present time, it seems likely that some (especially the Visegrad Four — Poland, the Czech Republic, Hungary and Slovenia) will pursue policies of increasing integration with the European Union and perhaps with NATO. If their overtures were to be rejected, it is an open question whether they have sufficient political strength and commonality of purpose to form an independent caucus or whether social and economic pressures would force them back into some Russian-dominated sphere. That is the politician's current dilemma; it is also the investor's and the would-be customer's biggest nightmare. Fear of political instability has long been noted as a key deterrent to investment and to involvement in external purchase relationships, especially where these may evolve into strategic dependence (see, for example, Robock and Simmonds, 1983; Czinkota and Ronkainen, 1993). While, as Globerman (1986) has noted, it may be possible to forecast and to assess the likelihood and potential impact of future political change, experience in Europe over the past six or seven years indicates the imprecision of the tools available: it may be that the political pendulum may swing just as violently in the other direction, no matter how illogical or unlikely that might seem to an external observer.

16.3.2 The Economic Environment

As has already been noted in several contexts above, it is somewhat artificial and simplistic to attempt to treat the economic scenarios of the whole of Central and Eastern Europe in one uniform section and to see them as independent of political history or social ambitions. Again, as well as considering the diversity of the countries which make up the region and indeed its sheer physical scale, it is important to recall the unreliability of historic statistics and thus to remember the inherent subjectivity of any judgements which most companies are likely to be able to make.

Academic authors generally evaluate countries' economic attractiveness to suppliers and customers by reference to such benchmarks as demographic development and change; gross national product per capita; propensity to consume; fiscal policies and stability; wage levels and inflation and employment patterns (Czinkota and Ronkainen, 1993). Gathering of such data in respect of the countries of Eastern Europe is still very patchy and somewhat unreliable; furthermore, these conventional indicators do not reveal a complete picture, given the enormous structural changes which are in train. While it is possible to tabulate some of these criteria, data on others barely exist and furthermore, much more data is available for some countries than for others.

In general, there is a greater variety and depth of reliable information available for the Visegrad countries than for the others, whilst data for Russia is often sketchy and inseparable from other elements of the former Soviet Union, despite the size and significance of the country. At the extreme, the political turmoil in the former Yugoslavia and the perpetuation of secretive regimes in countries such as Romania place real limits on the volume and value of information emerging. One of the greatest stimuli to the provision of realistic data has been the need for several countries in the region to seek assistance from international bodies such as the World Bank, the International Monetary Fund and the European Bank for Reconstruction and Development. Furthermore, the political aspirations of some countries with regard to the EU has helped to focus their attention on the desirability of evolving and maintaining reasonably impartial and accurate economic statistical records.

Table 16.1 below provides a summary of the most easily accessible data in the public domain for the principal countries of the region, from which two things will be readily appreciated:

- how great are the deficiencies in factual and reliable knowledge, and

- how great are the gaps between even the most dynamic and advanced economies of the region and the countries of the EU.

The varied nature of the data presented in Table 16.1 illustrates dramatically the dilemma of the business analyst. Other data is available for some countries from published sources, and may be generated by some large commercial companies or government legations but that does not necessarily help greatly in the formulation of economic appraisals by the average small or medium-sized business. While there are regular publications of such items of data, as exemplified above, the time delays involved have obvious implications for strategic planning, especially when economic activity is going through a period of volatile adjustment.

TABLE 16.1: READILY-AVAILABLE ECONOMIC INDICATORS, SELECTED COUNTRIES

Country	Population (millions) 1990/91 est	Annual % Growth in GDP (to 12/95)	Retail Price Inflation % (to 04/96)	Unemployment (%)
Poland	38.3	+7.0	+20.4	
Hungary	10.3	+1.5	+24.4	10.9 (to 12/94)
Czech Rep	10.2	+5.0	+ 8.5	3.2 (to 12/94)
Slovakia	5.3	+4.8 (to 12/94)	+10 (est)	
Romania	22.8	+3.5 (to 12/94)	+34 (est)	
Bulgaria	9.0	+1.4 (to 12/94)	+62 (est)	
Slovenia	2.0	+5.0 (to 12/94)	+13 (est)	
Russian Fed	148.8	−4.0	+68.3	
Ukraine	51 5	−23.7 (to 12/94)	+329 (est)	
Belarus	10.3	−20.2 (to 12/94)	+737 (est)	
Switzerland	6.9	−0.2	+0.9	4.5 (04/96)
Germany	80.4	+1.0	+1.5	10.4 (04/96)
UK	57.6	+2.0 (to 03/96)	+2.4	7.8 (04/96)
Portugal	10.6	+2.8	+2.4	

Sources: The Economist, May, 1996; Whitaker's Almanac, 1994; IMF World Economic Outlook, October, 1995.

Despite the limitations of the data presented, it will be immediately apparent just how great a performance gap there is between the economic health of the Visegrad countries and, for example, the major members of the former Soviet Union. Even so, it is well to remember that even such a brief summary can and does conceal many variations which have been of great, albeit temporary, significance, such as the more or less uniform decline of about 20 per cent in real output during the period 1990 to 1993 inclusive, as the restructuring programmes took initial effect (Banerjee et al., 1995). By the end of 1994, it appeared that that trend had been halted, but it would be some time after that before the population at large would actually notice any real individual, corporate or societal improvement in economic well-being — the so-called 'feel good' factor.

Furthermore, even the most comprehensive of 'standard' economic data do not convey a complete picture of the health of a country's economy. Much greater analysis is usually required to discover, for example, the extent to which national wealth is diffused throughout the population. As noted by authors such as Kinsey (1988), one characteristic of an industrialising country is the existence of a dual economy where there is uneven distribution of wealth, buying power, education, social status and political power. These features may well have been evident under the communist regimes; they are, perhaps, still evident at levels above those which would be considered normal or acceptable in more-established industrialised countries.

16.3.3 The Social and Cultural Environments
Throughout the two previous sub-sections, there has been continual reference to social impacts of the policies of transformation and economic/political development. Aside from the comments which have already been made on the heterogeneity of the countries and societies of the region, one or two other points are noteworthy.

Firstly, one should remember that, despite the redrawing of political boundaries, the re-emergence of nationalism and ethnic consciousness, there are numerous instances where ethnic minorities exist within other countries' boundaries. In several cases, this situation produces linguistic differences as well as less obvious cultural divisions. A good example are the ethnic Hungarian minorities which exist within the boundaries of Serbia, Slovakia, the Ukraine and Romania. To date, this has posed little real difficulty, but in view of events in nearby Bosnia and Croatia, many politicians and potential investors are extremely sensitive to the risks which are perceived to exist. Furthermore, several countries in the region have been victims of what in the 1990s has euphemistically been called 'ethnic cleansing' but on a larger and still more vicious scale. Poland, Slovakia, Hungary and Romania had sizeable gypsy and Jewish populations — both of which suffered terribly during World War II. It is only with the post-communist liberalisation that people have begun to contemplate granting real personal freedom to such minorities and even then with a good deal of suspicion.

At a business level, the 1990s have introduced to the region a totally new phenomenon — competition. This promises to be more fundamental and far-reaching than any of the social changes arising from purely political causes. Since competition affects individuals' ability to enjoy a given standard of living, the consequences of competition are seen as being more dramatic and personal than perhaps most other aspects of economic life. On the one hand, competition can produce a greater range of consumer choice and can drive prices down; on the other, it can threaten individuals' livelihoods by eliminating their sources of employment. These scenarios have both been evident in most of the major centres of population in the region, but their negative consequences have allegedly been felt almost universally. In the industrial centres, ageing technologies have come under pressure from more advanced alternatives from outside, whilst agricultural and traditional 'cottage industries' have had to learn to compete with the more mechanised industries of the West. This might be regarded as a living case example of globalisation — or at least regionalisation — of procurement, where even within a domestic customer market, producers have a much wider choice of suppliers and are no longer confined to one local segment of the economy.

The local economies of many of the countries of the region have, in effect, had to make the transition from a selling orientation to a customer-driven marketing environment almost instantaneously, rather than over a period of years as the norm in Western Europe. One of the outward symptoms of liberalisation has been the growth in availability of imported consumer goods. Sometimes, these have been products previously unexperienced by the local consumers in Eastern Europe; on other occasions, Western products have displaced goods produced either locally or obtained hitherto from elsewhere in the CMEA region. In either eventuality, there are obvious impacts on countries' balances of payments, not to mention on indigenous industries. For how long will it be socially as well as economically practicable to stock the retail outlets with expensive imported goods? For how long will industrial buyers find it acceptable to think in terms of importation of materials and components in preference to seeking or developing a viable local source of supply?

It is often claimed that external technological superiority overrides any such issues of sentiment, but such arguments are often short-lived. One of the most common spurs to technological transfer and innovation is the desirability of import reduction, whether for purely economic or socio-economic reasons. From the point of view of both suppliers and customers, it is important that such a process of rationalisation and adjustment should take place without generation of any backlash, xenophobia or discrimination — even along the lines practised successfully by the emerging countries of South East Asia, who are frequently taken as role models by other would-be industrialising countries.

When it comes to selecting trading partners, the countries of Eastern Europe have some delicate choices to make, especially in the light of the military occupations, annexations and political partition that most of them have endured within the past century, if not more. There is a not surprising reluctance by many organisations in the ex-satellite states to trade with partners to their east, as a reaction against past domination and in the perception that Western customers will pay better and that dealing with Western suppliers will offer advances in technology. On the other hand, forty years or more of at least partial 'russification' have left legacies of linguistic, personal and cultural familiarity, which are at least as strong as the older ties with Western Europe. Such ties have been demonstrated to be effective factors in choice of trading partners.

One cannot overlook issues of simple geography. It is only 100 miles from Budapest to Vienna; or 350 miles from Berlin to Warsaw or 400 miles from Warsaw to Budapest. On the other hand, Moscow is less than half the distance from Warsaw than London is from any of the Eastern European capital cities and is no further away than Stuttgart is from Budapest or Warsaw. On the basis of both physical distance and socio-cultural distinction, it would be more logical for the countries of Eastern Europe to trade with Germany or Russia than it would with either France or the United Kingdom. Conversely, Western European countries have many reasons for seeking to overcome such socio-cultural barriers and to seek new markets and supply sources in the East.

Perhaps one key to the solution of this problem, from both 'side's' point of view might rest in the importance attached to technological re-equipment of Eastern Europe, although once again, there is less than complete unanimity as regards the extent, direction or control of the changes to be made.

16.3.4 The Technological Environment

One of the driving forces behind the investment development programmes which have been a feature of the early 1990s has been a perception that Eastern Europe required massive external assistance with the process of re-equipment if it was to become a viable region in a competitive market-driven global society. Allowing for the existence of a certain element of political double-talk, it was abundantly clear that many industries were saddled with outdated process technologies which were both financially outclassed and ecologically disastrous. Perhaps the Chernobyl disaster opened many eyes in the West: it also appears to have had a similar effect in the East.

The task of carrying out a technology audit is usually regarded as an integral part of an environmental analysis. In the context of the region in question, it was seen as a task so large that it could only be approached progressively, with government support and funds from supra-governmental sources. Practical implementation of any investment was always seen as being a private-sector responsibility. At a very early stage, however, a key need for re-education was identified and resources made available both by individual governments and by the EU, UN and other agencies. This was seen as a prerequisite for the introduction of many Western technologies and was directly consistent with the concept of ensuring the appropriateness of any transferred technology (Stewart, 1978; Bhalla and James, 1986). Technology is not, of course, an end in itself, but rather a key element in the determination of a company's and a country's ability to be competitive. Nevertheless, 'possession' of a certain level of technological competence is generally seen as a symbol of national or corporate maturity.

During the 1970s, there were several attempts by Poland and Hungary in particular to upgrade their competencies and their hard currency-earning potential through the conduct of joint ventures with Western partners. Most of these came to little, partly because of their inappropriateness and partly because of the incompatibility of the objectives and/or capabilities of the partners (Fonfara and Bernard, 1989). Those experiences did not dim the dreams of many potential partners on both sides of the 'line'. A popular perception — or misperception — among Eastern European businessmen and politicians, quite apart from the general public, is that Western investors have bottomless purses and are queuing up to give away their state-of-the-art technological secrets without strings. While to the person who has nothing even a few pence constitutes a fortune, the misinterpretation of the resources made available has hindered the effective operation of many potential joint ventures. The fault is not all one-sided: many potential investors have eyed Eastern partners solely as sources of cheap materials and/or labour, to be exploited for the sole benefit of Western market satisfaction in the worst traditions of economic colonialism (Kinsey, 1988).

One feature which does differentiate many parts of Eastern Europe from industrialising countries elsewhere in the world is the historical fact that many of them do have some previous industrial tradition, skills and capability. Indeed, some of the countries have been seen as world leaders, as was the case for example of Czechoslovakia in the armaments industry and several countries in the field of scientific and medical research. The marketer in or to the region must ask the same questions as anywhere else in the world:

• Is there a need for the product or service on offer?

• Is there a possibility of achieving a mutually satisfying transaction and/or of building a beneficial relationship with future potential?

• Does the supplier have the technological skills necessary and appropriate to the task in hand?

• If new technological investment is required, does the recipient have a level of basic and/or technical education necessary to operate, maintain and develop the plant and equipment after the period of basic familiarisation is completed?

Unless all of these can be answered affirmatively, any technology transferred will at best be transplanted and remain *de facto* under the control of the external investor: it is most unlikely to become integrated into the fabric of the economy and thus will not contribute measurably to further development. Such is the nature of technological inappropriateness and wastage as arose in Poland in the 1970s, for example (Fonfara and Bernard, 1989; Bhalla and James, 1986). Similarly, it came as a nasty shock to many Eastern producers to discover that, despite the undoubtedly low prices of many of their products, they were not readily acceptable externally on the grounds of perceived or real quality deficiencies and non-conformance to Western or accepted international standards.

All of these factors have tended to emphasise the apparent need for a major overhaul of the educational infrastructure through the region, with particular reference to modern financial management, marketing, procurement and quality. What customers, suppliers and competitors alike should bear in mind is that many of the countries of the region, having already had technological experience, the application and assimilation of new technologies from the West or elsewhere is likely to entail a shorter learning curve as the process is to some extent one of *re*-development rather than first-time industrialisation. Furthermore, as Western colonial powers learned in the past and as is now becoming evident in the case of China, the creation of a viable consumer market generates so much latent economic energy that it can lead quickly to the generation or regeneration of productive capability and the emergence of a new and competitive source of supply.

This brings the analysis full circle with the key questions:

- Is the re-industrialisation of Eastern Europe an opportunity or a threat to the countries of the West?

- How can the challenges be met most satisfactorily for all concerned, in the long term as well as in the short run?

The political and macroeconomic aspects of this debate are beyond the scope of this present discussion, but the evaluation of market opportunities and the development of trading links at a micro-level are generally perceived as being essential activities and contributors to the growth of a healthy and dynamic economy.

Having at least identified some of the structural and environmental issues for discussion, it is practicable to consider some of the specific business problems and scenarios which condition the region as a source of demand and/or of supplies. Entry strategies are conventionally determined in the light of the environmental appraisal exercise: experience suggests that, in the case of

Eastern Europe as a whole, sentiment and political fashion played at least as large a part in the early decisions as did cold rationality. The period since 1989 has seen a massive and continuing rise in the number of equity joint ventures established in Hungary and Poland especially, partly to overcome local barriers of language and bureaucracy and partly as a means of sharing financial risk whilst gaining local market knowledge in return for marketing know-how and Western product technology.

16.4 THE GROWTH OF THE PRIVATE SECTOR

Another of the popular Western misperceptions of pre-1990 life in Eastern Europe was that everything was owned by the state and that there was no scope for private enterprise. This was as false a premise as any suggestion that in a free market economy there is no scope at all for public sector participation.

Certainly, in pre-1989 Eastern Europe, the means of production was firmly in public sector control and all economic planning was carried out centrally with the driving force being the generation or maintenance of the facade or fiction of lifetime employment, income and prosperity for all. Two of the key facets of the transition to a market economy were seen to be the freeing of prices from state control and the liberalisation of business and industrial ownership such that commercial organisations needed to justify their existence in terms of customer satisfaction and profitability.

Some aspects of the economies were already in private hands before 1989, but in general these were small operations of a retail nature, where individuals were free to sell on the open market any surplus goods which they were able to produce above their state quota. In practice, this free enterprise culture was largely concentrated in the agricultural sector and even in countries like Poland and Hungary did not amount to a major part of the economy, although there are few reliable statistics on the matter.

As far as privatisation of public sector assets has been concerned, whilst there has been widespread agreement on the desirability of such an objective, strategic approaches have varied widely. In the early stages of liberalisation, Poland opted for a large-scale dispersal of state assets, with preference given to worker ownership. Hungary sought large-scale disposal to external purchasers as a means of generating official balances of hard currency. The Czech Republic was anxious to avoid inflationary pressures and was keen to preserve as much local control as possible: it opted for a complex voucher-based system of ownership entitlement and transfer which was slower to take effect but which to date has apparently proceeded more smoothly and with fewer social or political drawbacks than have emerged elsewhere.

Table 16.2 shows the extent to which the private sector was contributing to some of the key economies as early as 1992 — just a couple of years after the process had begun.

TABLE 16.2: WHERE THE WEALTH CAME FROM

Country	Private Sector Output as % of GDP, 1992
Poland	42
Hungary	40
Slovakia	22
Czech Republic	15

Source: Based on *The Economist,* March 13, 1993; National Statistical Offices.

The same source pointed out that the countries concerned had also adopted different solutions to the question of who was going to be required to take responsibility for the restructuring of the state firms — the state itself; foreign consultants or investors; existing managers; the banks or other financial institutions, or the new owners themselves. Perhaps a little surprisingly, given the other complexities of the process, this appeared to be a relatively trouble-free process. (Economist 1993).

Subsequent progress with privatisation has been very much more erratic. Not only has it become more difficult to identify and attract investors now that flagship disposals have already taken place; there has also arisen public debate about the prices obtained and the extent to which national economies are passing into foreign control, if not outright ownership. This in turn mirrors some of the risks perceived in the evolution of many of the partnerships, alliances, joint ventures and investments made by Western firms in and with indigenous organisations, where the outcome has appeared to be the demise of the Eastern partner — albeit for a variety of reasons or motives.

The pattern of investment has been most uneven, both as between the various countries of the region (Hungary is generally

perceived to have received the greatest share of inward investment, due in some degree to large undertakings by Ford, General
Motors and Suzuki among others), whilst the great bulk of investment has been the preserve of a relatively small number of
external multinational companies. It remains a matter of conjec-
ture and debate how far these investments are intended to benefit
the host country and how far they are just opportunistic moves in
the grand global game, the rules of which may well change without notice.

16.5 INTERNATIONAL BUSINESS ACTIVITY BY SMEs

There emerged a perception in the early 1990s that in the period
immediately following the formal abolition of centrally-planned
socialist government in much of Eastern Europe, the prime focus
of attention had been on programmes of investment and privatisation in which the active players were governments and large,
often multinational, corporations.

Although the market economy countries of Western Europe are
frequently considered to depend on large numbers of small and
medium-sized enterprises (SMEs) for much of their innovation
and entrepreneurial drive, there was little direct evidence that
such organisations were taking an active interest in developing
links with countries in the East. Similarly, although there was
considerable press reportage in the West regarding the emergence
of 'small business' and 'private business' in the East, there also
existed a suspicion that the nature of these developments was not
fully understood — either by many of the major players or by even
those SMEs who might have been potentially interested in developing external business links, of whatever type.

A research programme was therefore conceived as an attempt
to explore just what was, or was not, taking place in the SME environment in the period immediately post-1989 and to consider
the extent to which SMEs in Eastern and Western Europe were
adopting proactive roles in developing business links 'across the
line'. The initial concept focused on purely inter-SME relationships and linkages, but from a very early stage in discussion, it
became clear that investigations would probably also need to encompass relationships between small and larger companies —
and vice versa.

While the subject of SME development and operation is generally credited as being of critical strategic significance in

dynamic competitive economies and while there have been several studies of SMEs' contributions to the world of technological innovation (e.g. Rothwell, 1986), it remains a paramount impression that the international business literature is dominated by analyses of the large company environment. Somehow, this is regarded as being the norm.

Within the United Kingdom, statistics have consistently indicated that since the early 1980s, if not for longer, in terms of numbers, SMEs account for over 95 per cent of firms registered in the country, and contribute in excess of 30 per cent of GDP. Such figures tend to be consistent with general experience in Europe, North America, Singapore and Hong Kong, for example, but it is necessary to add a qualifying comment in that the basic definitions of 'Small', 'Medium-Sized' and 'Large' organisations vary considerably from country to country (Hughes, 1990; Peattie, 1985; Chin, 1994, among others). Nevertheless, despite all the caveats and limitations, the SME segment clearly has an important role in market-driven economies.

It also seemed to be a reasonable proposition that, in their drive to establish or re-establish market economies of their own, the public authorities in the major countries of Eastern Europe would not find it feasible, desirable or necessary to implement economic and social reform on the basis of progressive liberalisation and/or the promotion of market-orientated business education on a 'trickle-down' basis from or through large companies. Indeed, it seemed probable that many large organisations would find it more difficult to initiate changes of orientation and/or to adapt to new environments than might smaller businesses. Even in the very early days of liberalisation in 1989 and 1990, the economies of Poland and Hungary were conspicuous for the rate at which new enterprises were established: most were small; a great many would probably have only a short life, but all would, in some way or other, have a contribution to make to the process of experiential education in business management and survival in a dynamic, competitive and relatively uncontrolled market environment.

Many organisations — commercial, educational and quasi-governmental — in Western Europe and further afield were poised to offer aid, investment and know-how in order to help the develop both industrial and management technological skills throughout the region. Some of the motives may have been idealistic or altruistic; others may have been more overtly commercial.

Whatever the principal stimulus, there was widespread recognition that:

- the countries of the former Communist bloc had much to offer in terms of materials, resources and also advantageous labour skills and costs — provided that fundamental investment or reinvestment decisions were implemented

- there were strong cultural, ethnic and linguistic ties between several of the countries in the region and several individual countries in the EU, and many of these links long pre-date the 1930s, 1940s and 1950s

- several countries and industries in Western Europe were actively seeking new markets for existing products and technologies at least as a short-term expedient, especially given the fragile state of economic stability in Western Europe and ever present competition from SE Asia

- it appeared to be in everyone's interests to help actively in the redevelopment of Eastern European markets, as quickly as possible, not only to minimise local destabilisation brought about by social change — and especially by the collapse of the USSR in 1991 — but also to enable all partners to benefit from a net growth in overall economic demand, from the circulation of materials, goods and money and to consolidate the politico-economic benefits of the reform process.

Against this background, the project was conceived in late 1991 and commissioned by the EU in 1992, to evaluate the role of SMEs in the development of international business links between two EU countries (UK and Germany) and two ex-CMEA countries (Poland and Hungary).

The aim was to establish whether the accepted advantages of SMEs (decreasing unemployment, wealth creation, innovativeness, flexibility, market closeness) were capable of overcoming problems of capital shortage, experience deficiency and so on, to become a proactive engine of international business development in this unique politico-economic environment.

This programme covered findings gathered from quantitative and qualitative investigation. The information was gathered from SMEs in manufacturing industry, which was selected as the most nearly common denominator between all four countries, and the segment where investment barriers (to entry or exit) were likely

Competing from the Periphery

to be most significant. Thus pure opportunism as a business motive was likely to be less significant than might apply in services
for example. Furthermore, this appeared to present a logical focus,
given the then current perception that the key requirements in
Eastern Europe were for the upgrading of manufacturing technologies and for the creation of viable local markets for consumer
and industrial merchandise, rather than for pure services.

16.5.1 The Research Approach

Secondary data from the region was sparse and inconsistent between the countries involved. For example, in Hungary, there was
an available publication which provided details of many, but not
all, firms registered as having external shareholdings, but at the
time of the project, there was nothing comparable in respect of
Poland. Likewise, in both Germany and the UK it would have
been a physical impracticability to have tried to establish a comparable database within the time and resources available. However, such information as was available suggested that there was
likely to be a greater propensity for trade links to exist between
Germany and the countries of Eastern Europe than would exist
vis à vis the UK, for reasons of geography, culture/history and bias
towards manufacturing industries. This appeared to be borne out
by data in respect of Hungary as early as 1990, which showed
that some 300 manufacturing companies had German equity as
against only 23 with UK involvement. On the other hand, some 40
other companies had UK investment — primarily in the areas of
consultancy and export/import trading.

Three working hypotheses were adopted as a basis for a programme of field research, as follows:

1. That companies have a greater motivation to commence business operations if they have perceived specific market potential in the target countries

2. That the depth or extent of business involvement in the target
   country is directly influenced by the degree of prior familiarity
   with the country

3. That companies are prepared to extend or expand their business activities if they are content with the business environment.

An ambitious survey plan was devised involving a total of 5,600
manufacturing firms employing between 50 and 500 people across

the four countries, who were contacted with a written question-naire in their own languages. From this exercise a total of 950 usable responses was received, an overall response rate of almost 17 per cent, which was sufficiently evenly distributed to be con-sidered representative of all four countries. These questionnaires were supplemented by in-depth interviews with actively involved companies in all four countries: a total of some 75 interviews were conducted which cast further light on attitudes and future inten-tions beyond what was evident from the written responses.

16.5.2 Key Findings

The mass of data was analysed using SPSS software and revealed a remarkable degree of consistency between the perceptions in the countries as far as perceived problems of market entry and the prerequisite conditions for establishing business relation-ships.

Table 16.3 summarises the main perceived barriers to entry, whilst Table 16.4 shows the preconditions considered by respon-dents to be fulfilled before they would be prepared to enter inter-national markets.

TABLE 16.3: SUMMARY OF PERCEIVED BARRIERS TO ENTRY

Barriers (Rank Order)	British Companies	German Companies	Eastern Companies
1	Language	Availability of staff	Availability of staff
2	Availability of staff, distribution and logistics	Product prices	Availability of market information
3	Pricing and exchange risks	Language	Language
4	Competition	Distribution and logistics	Distribution and logistics
5	Availability of market information	Institutional structures	Competition

Against the background of these perceptions and preferences, it is perhaps not surprising that the overwhelming majority of com-panies from all locations have opted to enter the markets by the Direct Export route, with only a very small minority (less than

5 per cent) of SMEs from any source favouring direct investment, whether by joint venture, licensing or acquisition.

TABLE 16.4: KEY FACTORS FOR CONSIDERING STARTING A BUSINESS ABROAD

Factor (Rank Order)	British Companies	German Companies	Eastern Companies
1	Presumed market potential	Flexible credit facilities	Positive market data
2	Positive market data	Comprehensive country information	Specific competitive opportunity
3	Specific competitive opportunity	Flexible trading partners	Presumed market potential
4	Positive economic outlook	Favourable tariff conditions	Positive economic outlook
5	Potential location for production		Potential location for production

On the other hand there was some divergence in respect of future intentions as regards possible expansion of relationships. Some 20 per cent of Eastern companies intend to expand their trading associations with Western European countries as compared with over 50 per cent of the German respondents and only 15 per cent of UK respondents intending to increase their operations eastwards, lending support to the perceived importance of geographical proximity.

The issue of 'familiarity' was addressed by asking the respondents to rate their perceived familiarity with a list of 16 countries world-wide on a scale of 1 to 6, where 1 denoted total unfamiliarity/lack of confidence in doing business. The results were dramatic. In almost all cases, British and German companies professed almost complete unfamiliarity with both Poland and Hungary: the converse was also found to be true. More surprisingly, perhaps, Polish and Hungarian respondents also expressed unfamiliarity with each other's countries.

The in-depth interviews revealed several interesting points, some of which were both unexpected and sources of potential difficulties in future development of business relationships. Respondents confirmed the received wisdom that Eastern companies perceived Western partners to be cash-rich and keen to invest in technological renewal in the East. Conversely, Western companies indicated that they were more interested in supplying goods to the Eastern countries and/or in exploiting the perceived potential

of low-cost sources of supply for their own domestic markets. Indeed two of the UK companies interviewed stated that they had
formed joint ventures with Eastern manufacturing partners in
order to gain market entry, but had subsequently declined to rein-
vest in their partners, had closed down the manufacturing operations in the East and retained a presence solely for marketing
purposes. There appeared to be little interest in investing in
either Poland or Hungary with a view to establishing a spring-
board for further exploitation of other Eastern European markets.

Overall, the results of the research tended to confirm all three
of the operating hypotheses and, moreover to suggest that Western companies in particular were proceeding on a distinctly opportunistic basis in considering involvement in Eastern Europe.
Eastern companies, on the other hand were apparently more dynamic and constructive in their approach to doing business with
the West — not least by force of circumstances arising from the
changed political environment, the collapse of the ex-Soviet markets and the desire to both modernise and to ally themselves with
the EU.

16.6 CONCLUSIONS

It is always dangerous and difficult to deduce general conclusions
from the basis of a single research study, no matter how large, especially when the premises for that study rest on so many weak
foundations. This review has helped to clarify some of the popular
perceptions of the potential for Western and Eastern European
companies to develop trading relationships, but it also tends to
illustrate that pure logic is frequently modified by prejudices and
habits.

Considerations of geographical and cultural proximity have
been shown to be significant for SMEs, but that may not hold
equally good for large multinational organisations, where there is
in any case likely to be a much greater depth and breadth of
knowledge, quite apart from greater levels of resources. There appears little doubt that British companies consider Eastern Europe
to be remote — peripheral — to an extent that German companies
for example do not, and that the concept of peripherality in this
context is a combination of distance, language and culture, as well
as of unfamiliarity.

Thus the perception of peripherality is essentially as much
subjective as it is real and objective. The danger is that by giving

significant weight to peripherality as a business motive, opportunities will be lost and that — in the context of the subject of this chapter — others may refocus their attentions. The centre of gravity of European business long ago shifted away from the United Kingdom: the re-emergence of the countries of Eastern Europe into the world market environment will inevitably shift that centre of gravity still further eastwards, as this research has shown is already happening. The data acquired in respect of SMEs' approaches in the course of the recent research suggests that, despite the apparent emergence of an 'enterprise culture' in the 1980s, UK firms' attitudes towards conducting business internationally remains somewhat ambivalent and insular. Culture differences and geographical remoteness from the shifting centre of gravity undoubtedly will not assist in overcoming these problems, but the increasing universality of the English language might be expected to soften their impacts, given in particular the avidity with which Eastern Europeans seek to learn and to re-integrate themselves within mainstream European affairs.

It seems clear that the concepts of peripherality have changed little, in themselves: the key consequences remain, perhaps more strongly than hitherto, in the psychological rather than in the physical arenas. SMEs have been characterised as being more innovative and flexible than their larger counterparts: it remains to be seen how far they will employ these attributes constructively in the establishment and development of new relationships with partners at a greater physical distance than 'just the other side of the Channel', but with whom there is still the strong cultural affinity of being 'European'.

German counterparts may not be expected to face the same decisions and perceptions and thus do seem to see Eastern European business as much more local in context, albeit they may also face perceptions of peripherality of a linguistic nature. Ultimately, perhaps the choice for British competitors is between dealing with the issues of peripherality in selecting customers and suppliers and becoming seen as peripheral themselves.

References

Becker, S. H. and Baker, M. J. (1995), 'Hungary: A Market Ready for Western Brands?', *Journal of East-West Business*, Vol. 1, No. 2.

Bhalla, A. S. and James, J. (1986), 'New Technology Revolution — Myth or Reality for Developing Countries?' in *Technology, Innovation & Economic Policy* (Ed. Hall, P.), London: Philip Allen.

Boote, A. R. and Somogyi, J. (1991), *Economic Reform in Hungary Since 1968,* International Monetary Fund, Occasional Paper No 83.

Chin, S. F. (1994), 'Challenges in Managing and Developing a Small and Medium Scale Manufacturing Business', unpublished MBA Project Report, University of Strathclyde, UK.

Czinkota, M. R. and Ronkainen, I. A. (1993), *International Marketing* 3rd edition, London: The Dryden Press.

Fonfara, K. and Bernard, K. N. (1989), 'Co-operative Development and Commercial Internationalisation: An Appraisal of Recent Transfers of Technology Between Poland and Industrialised Countries', proceedings of the 18th Annual Conference of the European Marketing Academy, pp. 295-313.

Globerman, S. (1986), *Fundamentals of International Business Management*, Englewood Cliffs, NJ: Prentice Hall.

Hughes, I. (1990), 'Marketing for Small Businesses', unpublished MSc Dissertation, University of Strathclyde, UK.

Kinsey, J. (1988), *Marketing in Developing Countries,* Basingstoke: Macmillan

McKenna, R. (1991), *Relationship Marketing*, London: Century Business Books.

Peattie, L. R. (1985), 'Small Enterprises in the Development Process', Department of Urban Planning, Working Paper No. 2, University of Hong Kong.

Robock, S. H. and Simmonds, K. (1983), *International Business and Multinational Enterprises*, 3rd edition, Homewood, IL: Irwin.

Rothwell, R. (1986), 'Small firms contributions to Industrial Innovation: small or large?', *Science and Public Policy*, Vol. 13, No. 3, June, pp. 170-72.

Thomas, M. J. (1994), 'Marketing — In Chaos or Transition?' *European Journal of Marketing*, Vol. 28, No. 3, pp. 55-62.

Stewart, F. (1978), *Technology and Underdevelopment*, 2nd edition Basingstoke: Macmillan.

Whitaker, J. (1994), *Whitaker's Almanack of the World*, 126th edition, London: J. Whitaker and Sons.

Young, S., Hamill, J., Wheeler, C. N. and Davies, J. R. (1989), *International Market Entry and Development: Strategies and Management*, Hemel Hempstead: Harvester Wheatsheaf.

17

COMPETING FROM SOUTHERN EUROPE: THE CASE OF PORTUGAL

Michael McDermott

17.1 INTRODUCTION

The purpose of this chapter is to consider the case of Portugal in the context of core-periphery dynamics. It only became a member of the European Union in 1986 (along with Spain), some 13 years after other peripheral economies (e.g. Denmark, Ireland, and Scotland). It joined at a time when its participation in the global economy had declined dramatically from the days when navigators left its shores to discover the new world and build an empire that covered all continents.

For much of this century, this once major trading nation chose to withdraw from the world economy. Protected from international competition, and with a small domestic market (i.e. a population of just over 10 million today) indigenous firms lacked the incentive to become world-class. Politically, the country was only emerging from decades of dictatorship (i.e. 1928–74) when it joined the EU. Thus, economically and politically, it is perhaps best to view Portugal in the final quarter of the 20th century as a nation in transition from a closed, stagnant economy under dictatorial rule to an open, buoyant, mature democracy. Simultaneously, its larger neighbour, Spain has undergone a similar metamorphosis. It has benefited from staging global events (e.g. the 1982 soccer World Cup, Expo in Seville in 1988, and the Barcelona Olympic Games in 1992), but it has also seen an attempted coup in the Cortes (i.e. the Spanish Parliament). Portugal's transformation has avoided such extremes, but nevertheless the results have been impressive. In 1998 Portugal will host the World Exposition which is expected to attract almost 9 million visitors.

Managing such a transition requires consummate skill. Economic growth without economic development can trigger political instability which makes it difficult to achieve even the former. Portugal's economic and social indicators point to steady if unremarkable progress. The Socialist Party won the general elections of 1976 and 1995, and formed a coalition government after the 1983 election which it led until 1985. Cavaco Silva, then leader of the centre right Social Democrat Party, became Prime Minister in 1985 and won successive elections in 1987 and 1991.

Portugal today is quite different from the country in 1974/5. In terms of economic development strategy, the IMF and World Bank have exhorted nations world-wide to toe the line and focus on three major planks — 'Democratisation, Liberalisation and Privatisation'. Portugal now adheres to these guidelines. Its economy has been transformed under astute political leadership from democratically elected governments and presidents. Multinationals now choose to site strategically important, capital-intensive operations in the country because of its favourable domestic environment and its excellent international links. Indigenous companies are also responding to the unprecedented opportunities they now face. Many have already addressed the product quality issue, and now seek to conquer international markets. Admittedly, in many key industries Portuguese firms suffer a country-of-origin disadvantage. This, though, cannot and should not be used as justification for weak performance. Instead, just as other countries have overcome this problem, so too must Portuguese manufacturers.

This chapter begins by providing an overview of Portugal. It then considers the concept of national competitiveness. It highlights too the huge challenges which still have to be met in Portugal, and the initiatives underway to ensure they are overcome. It will be seen that a number of industries have recently been accorded priority status. It is premature to assess the impact of measures taken to nurture these sectors, but an overview of such initiatives is provided.

Seven industries have already been accorded priority status, ranging from traditional industries (e.g. wine) to new sectors growing largely because of and in response to inward investment (e.g. automotive components). The performance of three indigenous firms in three quite different sectors (i.e. wine, plastic moulds and auto components) is considered. The auto components sector or cluster is expected to play a crucial role in transforming

Portugal's industrial structure away from the traditional, basic, labour-intensive industries towards modern, capital- and technology-intensive sectors.

17.2 COUNTRY BACKGROUND AND THE SILVA REFORMS

A nation state since the 12th century, Portugal ranks as one of the world's longest established countries. Its borders have remained consistent since the 13th century, an indication of its stability domestically and internationally. Its historic and cultural links are reflected in the fact that Portuguese is the first language of nearly 200 million people throughout the world. Its geographic location provides not only ready access to the European market but also relative proximity to the east coast of the USA and the African continent.

It will be shown in this chapter that geographical location *per se* does not represent a competitive disadvantage to enterprises based in Portugal. Indeed, an examination of post-war economic development in developing nations suggests that geographical location is much less important than a commitment to export-oriented growth and domestic policies which maximise the potential of human resources (World Bank, 1993). However, one of the themes of this book is to examine the significance of location for the competitiveness of economies lying on the periphery of Europe, and for the enterprises headquartered in such countries.

During the period 1986-91, Portugal's growth rate was the highest in the EC. It slowed down in the early 1990s, but looks set to recover. Prime Minister Silva (1985-95) encouraged free enterprise, and investment in infrastructure (e.g. transport and communications), education and training. He reformed the tax system and abolished restrictions incompatible with a dynamic, open economy. The privatisation programme launched in 1987 has been a great success. Plans are afoot to sell off other state-owned enterprises (SOEs), including the loss-making national airline (TAP). The policy appears highly reminiscent of Mrs Thatcher's privatisation programme which has resulted in BT and British Airways emerging as global champions.

In 1986 Portugal had one of the highest unemployment rates in the EC. Today, with just 4.4 per cent unemployment, it has one of the lowest, and each year 100,000 new jobs are being created.

17.3 COMPETITIVE STRUCTURE AND STRATEGY

17.3.1 Overview
Restructuring of the economy has resulted in the service sector accounting for 49 per cent of the active population today, while it represented just 35 per cent in 1986. The importance of the agricultural sector has been steadily declining. Within the manufacturing sector, the basic traditional industries (i.e. textiles and clothing, footwear, cork, wood and paper pulp) are of diminishing importance. Labour-intensive processes are being transferred overseas. With strong Government support, many companies are changing their generic strategy from low cost to differentiation, and paying closer attention to marketing management policy.

17.3.2 Competitive Structure
Sectorally, Portugal's international image is as a manufacturer of traditional consumer products, notably apparel, shoes, textiles and wines. In terms of Porter's five-forces model, it can be seen that these are highly competitive industries (see Table 17.1). Moreover, these sectors are characterised by a strong country-of-origin effect which sees Portugal trail behind France and Italy in the areas of fashion and wine. In terms of apparel and textiles, Portugal also faces intense competition from lower-cost manufacturers from East Asia, Eastern Europe and North Africa. The vast majority of Portuguese firms (i.e. more than 95 per cent) are SMEs.

TABLE 17.1: SUMMARY OF PORTER'S FIVE-FORCES MODEL AND PORTUGAL'S TRADITIONAL AND NEW INDUSTRIES

Industry	Buyer Power	Supplier Power	Threat of New Entrants	Threat of Substitute Products	Intensity of Rivalry
Apparel	Strong	Weak	Strong	Weak	Strong
Shoes	Strong	Weak	Strong	Weak	Strong
Textiles	Strong	Strong	Strong	Weak	Strong
Wines	Strong	Weak	Weak	Strong	Strong
Moulds	Strong	Neutral	Strong	Weak	Strong
Auto Components	Strong	Weak	Strong	Weak	Strong

Source: Author.

17.3.3 Competitive Strategy

Portuguese producers need to develop a focused strategy to win market share by providing customer-responsiveness and flexibility at relatively low cost. Currently, though, too many enterprises are characterised by a *reactive* approach rather than a *proactive* approach. This weakness is compounded by a lack of product differentiation (i.e. weak brand identity) and limited access to suitable distribution channels.

Local manufacturers are moving to more capital-intensive production processes, and diversifying into more technology-intensive sectors with greater scope for value-added activities (e.g. auto components, chemicals, consumer electronics, machine tools, mouldings, non-metallic minerals). In future the most dynamic sectors are expected to be automation, electronics components, and information products. These sectors are compatible with Portugal's strategic intent of switching towards those sectors which are capital-intensive, have low energy consumption levels, and are environmentally-friendly.

17.4 INTERNATIONALISATION AND THE ROLE OF ICEP

Internationalisation plays a vital role in the economic development process of countries. It covers a range of activities, most notably:

- the development of international trade, especially exports by indigenous firms

- the attraction of inward investment

- the attraction of foreign visitors.

The significance of these areas is often reflected in the formation of national bodies to oversee such activities. For example, in the peripheral economies of Ireland and Scotland separate organisations are responsible for these activities. This division of responsibility has its downside. Those responsible for tourism may promote an image of geographic remoteness and tradition, when those charged with the promotion of inward investment wish to communicate ease of market access and modernity. Such conflicting messages may undermine the efforts of each body.

By concentrating control of all international activities in one body (i.e. ICEP — Investment, Trade and Tourism of Portugal), Portugal seeks to ensure conflicting messages are avoided and instead a consistent one is communicated to the global market. As far as is known, it is the *only* country in the world where responsibly for these three areas rests with the one authority. This is very much a deliberate strategic decision because it is recognised that 'Portugal' represents a brand which needs to be carefully managed. Moreover, as this brand is used for three quite different purposes, care needs to be taken in order to ensure that the goals of each activity are achieved without prejudice to the others.

Cost savings also serve as an additional reason for concentrating the three activities in one body. ICEP is competing in a global market against rivals that have far greater resources. On the other hand, it is best placed to allocate limited resources to maximise returns. *Corporate Location* awarded ICEP the 1995 prize for best inward-investment promotion material in the EU.

In terms of export promotion, ICEP provides assistance to firms seeking to attend international fairs and in the preparation of export catalogues. Ireland's Export Promotion Board is seen as an exemplar of efficiency. However, in terms of industrialisation, Italy is seen as the most suitable role model due to cultural convergence and similarities in the industrial structure of the two countries. ICEP also offers incentives to assist corporate internationalisation through outward investment when the purpose is to facilitate market access.

It is active in promoting inward investment projects which will contribute to regional development, technological modernisation, a positive foreign exchange balance, the provision of high added-value products, and the creation of new quality job opportunities. It emphasises that it is not aiming to deliver 'jobs at any price'. It regards Ireland's inward-investment attraction agency, the Industrial Development Authority, as its toughest competitor.

17.5 INTERNATIONALISATION AND THE OUTWARD DIMENSION

17.5.1 Export Growth

Exports are accounting for an increasingly high proportion of GDP, rising from 33 per cent in 1990 whereas Ireland's already represented 60 per cent. Moreover, Portugal has seen its share of total OECD exports rise from 0.54 per cent in 1985 to 0.71 per cent in 1992. More than 90 per cent of exports are destined for OECD countries, mainly to other EU countries.

17.5.2 Geographical Distribution of Exports

Germany remains the main export market, followed by Spain, France and the United Kingdom. These four together account for nearly 60 per cent of national exports. Trade with Portuguese-speaking Africa has been increasing, and further progress is expected due to the greater political stability offered in the priority markets (i.e. Angola, Mozambique, South Africa).

17.5.3 Sectoral Distribution of Exports

Although the structure of Portugal's exports is changing, it still relies mainly on indigenous SMEs in its basic, low-tech, low-growth sectors (see Table 17.2). They are, however, increasing their Gross Added Value by turning out higher quality products with improved design. Electric machinery and equipment and motor vehicles are displaying strongest growth (OECD, 1995). Portugal's machinery exports include mainly moulds for the plastic industry. Electronics is also a growing export sector, especially those for use in the automotive industry, as well as chips and microchips. Table 17.3 provides some summary details of Portugal's leading traditional consumer product exports.

TABLE 17.2: COMPARATIVE ANALYSIS OF EXPORT STRUCTURE IN SELECTED EUROPEAN PERIPHERAL ECONOMIES (1992)

Rank	Portugal	Italy	Spain
First	Clothing (22%)	Industrial machinery Motor vehicles (both 8%)	Motor vehicles (23%)
Second	Footwear (9%)	Clothing, specialised machinery (both 7%)	Fruit and vegetables (8%)
Third	Textiles (8%)	Textiles, electrical machinery and equipment, manufactured goods (all on 6%)	Electrical machinery and equipment, iron and steel, other transport equipment, other machinery (all 4%)
Fourth	Electric machines and equipment (7%)	Metallic manufactured goods, footwear, non-metallic mineral industries (all on 4%)	Non-metallic industries, oil and derivatives, other manufactured goods, metal manufactured goods (all 3%)
Fifth	Motor vehicles (6%)		

Rank	Greece	Scotland	Ireland
First	Clothing (22%)	Information technology	Information technology equipment (16%)
Second	Fruit and vegetables (13%)	Whiskey	Other manufactured goods (9%)
Third	Vegetable oils (6%)		Organic chemical products (8%)
Fourth	Textiles, tobacco, oil and derivatives, cereals, iron and steel, non-ferrous metals (all 5%)		Meat, milk, cheese and eggs (both 6%)
Fifth	Non-metallic mineral industry (4%)		Medical and pharmaceutical products, other food products, electrical machinery and equipment (all 5%)

Source: Author, using where appropriate OECD's *Foreign Trade Statistics*, 1994.

TABLE 17.3: SUMMARY DETAILS ON SOME OF PORTUGAL'S LEADING CONSUMER PRODUCT EXPORTS

	Textiles	Footwear	Ceramics and Glass
Industry Structure	Mainly SMEs	1,100 companies 50K employees	SMEs (350 exporters)
Values of Exports (bn Esc)	757.6		54.77
Export Rank		2nd in Europe 9th in World	
Share of Output Exported		90%	90%+
Share of Total Exports	26.12%	9%	
Geographical Location	the North (cotton) the Centre (wool and clothing		Ceramics Caldas da Rainha, Alcobaça, Coimbra, Aveiro, Águeda\n\nGlass Marinha Grande

	Textiles	*Footwear*	*Ceramics and Glass*
Export Items	Knitting wear (38%) Clothing (32%) Household textiles (13.5%) Fabrics (8.5%)		
Export Markets	UK (23%) Germany (16%) Spain (11%) France (10%) USA (6%)	Germany UK France Denmark	Ceramics Germany (21%) France (16%) USA (15%) UK (13%) Glass Germany (25%) Spain (13%) France and USA (12%) Holland (7%)
Brand Names			Vista Alegre

Source: Author

17.5.4 Comparison of Export Performance with Other Peripheral Economies

Table 17.2 provides a comparison of the differences in export structure between selected peripheral European economies. High levels of foreign ownership are indicated by italics. It appears that in manufacturing terms, the Iberian countries will consolidate their position in the automobile and components sectors, whilst the peripheral economies of Ireland and Scotland will remain leading production centres and export bases for firms in the information products industry. Northern Ireland's position is less clear, but it has achieved some success in both sectors.

The success of Ireland, Scotland and Spain in attracting inward investment, combined with the low levels of internationalisation of indigenous firms, results in their dependence on a small number of large, foreign-owned MNEs, in a narrow range of businesses for a high level of exports (Figure 17.1). This problem is particularly pronounced in the case of Scotland.

Figure 17.2 provides an indication of the position of Portugal and its peripheral European and global rivals in terms of business diversity and rate of export growth. As it shows, export growth is greater amongst its rivals in East Asia and the 'new world'. While it reflects their lower starting point, it reinforces the

fears expressed by the Forum that Portuguese firms are confronting a much harsher global market.

FIGURE 17.1: COMPARATIVE ANALYSIS OF PERIPHERAL ECONOMY
EXPORTS

**Extent of Indigenous Firms
Contribution to Exports**

	Low	*High*
High	Italy	Ireland Spain
Low	Portugal Greece	Scotland

**Degree of
Business Diversity
of Exports**

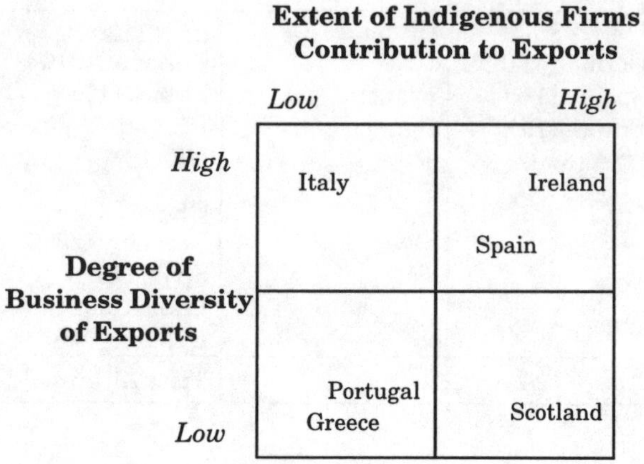

FIGURE 17.2: COMPARATIVE ANALYSIS OF PERIPHERAL ECONOMY
EXPORTS AND EMERGING ECONOMIES

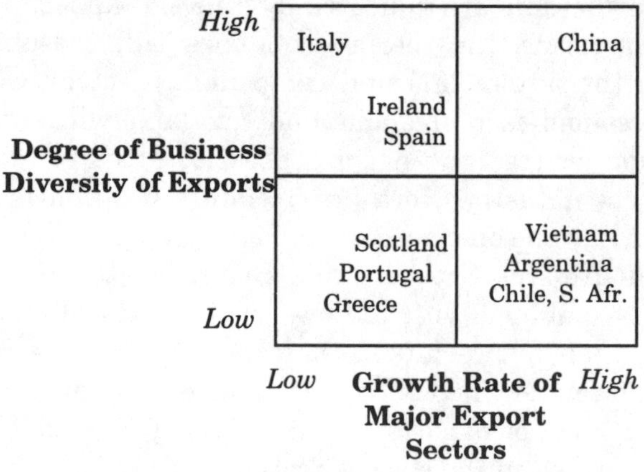

High	Italy	China
	Ireland Spain	
Low	Scotland Portugal Greece	Vietnam Argentina Chile, S. Afr.

**Degree of Business
Diversity of Exports**

Low **Growth Rate of** *High*
**Major Export
Sectors**

Figure 17.3 shows that the *high-growth* export sectors in Portugal
are characterised by high levels of *foreign ownership*. Conversely,
the *low-growth* sectors are characterised by *domestic ownership*.

This underlines the fundamental importance of inward investment in the short and medium term. In the long term, indigenous enterprises need to:

- revive selected traditional sectors (e.g. wine)

- expand more modern sectors (e.g. moulds)

- respond to opportunities presented as a consequence of inward investment and create new viable, indigenous sectors (e.g. auto components)

- withdraw from low-added value segments of traditional sectors (e.g. in apparel, footwear and textiles.

FIGURE 17.3: ANALYSIS OF PORTUGAL'S EXPORTS BY GROWTH RATE AND PATTERN OF OWNERSHIP

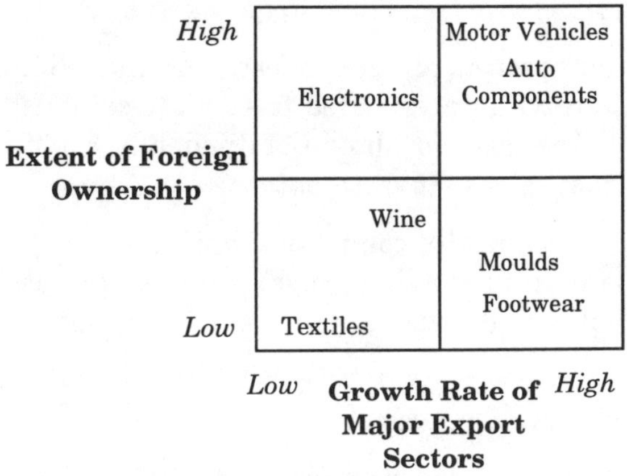

17.5.5 Outward Foreign Direct Investment (FDI)

Although small by international standards, outward direct investment has grown substantially in recent years, thus reflecting the increasing involvement of the national companies in the global market. Spain alone accounts for more than half of the total stock of outward FDI. During the mid-1990s, France and the UK emerged as other important destinations. Despite the rapid growth of outward investment, the international strategic positioning of most Portuguese companies is still weak.

17.6 INTERNATIONALISATION AND THE INWARD DIMENSION

17.6.1 Reasons for Growth of Inward Investment

Portugal is totally dependent externally on energy products, but in recent years import growth has been in manufactured products and equipments. This is hardly surprising in that inward investment has soared, peaking in 1991 (see Table 17.4). This investment boom was not peculiar to Portugal, as during this period the prospect of '1992' encouraged a wave of FDI throughout the EU. On the other hand, Portugal offered the following location-specific advantages:

- a presence in the EC market, with its population of 340 million

- political and social stability

- one of the lowest rates of industrial disputes in Europe

- favourable policy towards foreign investment, including financial and tax incentives, unrestricted freedom to establish in all sectors and the free transfer abroad of dividends, capital gains and proceeds from sales of investments

- availability of a technically competent work-force, with international competitive productivity levels and labour costs, supported by a nationwide network of centres for professional training

- mineral and forestry resources

- rapid modernisation of infrastructure, and

- substantial tourist development potential.

Since 1991, Portugal, along with most EU members, was unable to sustain the record levels achieved prior to 1992. In 1994 inward FDI amounted to 238 million escudos (see Table 17.4).

TABLE 17.4: FOREIGN DIRECT INVESTMENT IN PORTUGAL (IN MILLION ESC.)

Year	Value
1986	24,498,926
1987	61,226,568
1988	138,052,908
1989	349,532,161
1990	479,396,543
1991	798,490,812
1992	590,667,702
1993	279,164,233
1994	238,073,634

Source: ICEP

17.6.2 Sources of Inward Investment

The main sources of inward FDI cases during the period 1986-94 were the UK (583), France (330), Spain (326), Belgium (231), and the USA (180). The ostensible importance of the UK disguises the fact that apparently MNEs from the USA and Japan invest in Portugal via existing UK subsidiaries. Portugal fortunately appears to have began to impress potential investors from Japan and other East Asian economies witness the large recent investments by Pioneer and Samsung). Other sources of investment have also been targeted. In 1994 the fifth largest investor was Brazil.

17.6.3 Regional and Sectoral Distribution of Inward Investment

Inward investment is still strongly concentrated in the greater Lisbon area, but manufacturing industries are now being attracted to the Setubal area, in the south of Lisbon, which has received a number of important investments in the last years, such as Delco Remi (General Motors), Ford Electronics and Auto-Europa, the Ford/Volkswagen project, the country's largest ever foreign investment project — approximately US$3 billion in total assets. The new plant near Setubal, opened in 1995. By 1998 it will produce 180,000 vehicles per year, and employ 5,000 direct and 10,000 indirect jobs.

Since 1986 services have attracted the largest chunk of inward investment, mainly in real estate, banking and other financial services, business services, wholesaling and tourism. Industry accounts for around one-fifth of total inward investment. Its most significant areas are chemicals, and equipment and machinery. Many large-scale projects have been set up in Portugal, from the motor industry to high-precision moulds, through to components and electronics.

17.6.4 Tourism
In 1992 ICEP assumed responsibility for tourism. It recognised that there was a need for a clear identity for the country as a tourist destination. A local artist, de Guimaraes, was commissioned to design a suitable symbol. A year later he had completed his task and attention turned to logotype. The final product appears in all Portugal's tourism-related materials. ICEP's 'Thrill of Discovery' campaign has been a spectacular success, attracting more tourists, and at the top end of the market. Moreover, ICEP's marketing activities provide an important demonstration effect to the private sector.

In 1980 Portugal received only 7 million visitors and 2.7 million tourists. In 1995, it received more than 20 million visitors, and 9.5 million tourists. According to the World Tourism Organization, Portugal's share of the European tourism market has doubled in recent years.

Within the national economy, tourism has played an important role over the last decade, representing about 8 per cent of GDP. Nowadays, 250,000 people are employed in the sector (approximately 5 per cent of the working population) and regional development and consequently economic and social cohesion have increased with investments in tourism (ICEP, 1995)

17.7 NATIONAL COMPETITIVENESS: A GLOBAL OBSESSION
Undoubtedly, the concept of competitiveness is of enormous importance at the macro and micro levels. Individual countries are allocating more and more resources to identify actual and potential opportunities for boosting their competitiveness. Since the publication in 1990 of Michael Porter's *The Competitive Advantage of Nations*, its author and the Monitor Company have undertaken studies of economies other than the ten featured in his book

(i.e. Denmark, Germany, Italy, Japan, Singapore, South Korea, Sweden, Switzerland, the UK and the USA). Others have examined economies using his models.

National concern over competitiveness is evident (e.g. the US has established a Competitiveness Council), as is that of regional bodies (i.e. the EU has a Competitiveness Advisory Group). Portugal is no exception and in 1993 Monitor completed the project *Building the Competitive Advantage of Portugal* (see Table 17.5). This in turn led to the formation of the Forum for Competitiveness, a non-profit making body dedicated to promoting the competitiveness of Portuguese enterprises by stimulating intercompany co-operation and productivity growth.

17.8 SOURCES OF NATIONAL COMPETITIVENESS: THE DIAMOND

Porter (1990, p. xi) addressed a question which many social scientists have tackled: 'Why do some social groups, economic institutions, and nations advance and prosper?' His answer contradicts the conventional view of national competitiveness, with its emphasis upon economies of scale, exchange rates, interest rates, and labour costs. Furthermore, he argues, state subsidies and relaxed anti-trust laws to encourage formation of larger firms undermine rather than promote competitiveness.

Instead, he contends that irrespective of country or industry, nations are more likely to succeed in industries where the national 'diamond' — the determinants as a system — is the most favourable (see Figure 17.4 which applies the diamond to the auto components industry). The diamond consists of four variables which are discussed below:

- *Factor conditions*. The inputs necessary to compete in a given industry, such as labour, natural resources, capital and infrastructure — and how efficiently and effectively they are deployed. Indeed, innovation to offset weakness is more likely than innovation to exploit strengths (e.g. Japanese companies faced extremely high land costs and severe factory space constraints; to circumvent these difficulties, they created just-in-time and other space-saving techniques that also dramatically reduced inventory).

TABLE 17.5: SUMMARY OF THE BUILDING COMPETITIVE ADVANTAGE
IN PORTUGAL PROJECT

Phase I (Feb-July 1993)	Competitiveness Audit: survey of the context and constraints on competitiveness of Portuguese companies	Conference by Professor Porter
Phase II (July 1993-Feb 1994)	Action Initiatives: selection of a small number of representative clusters and horizontal policies for the process of generating change	*September 1993*: Meeting for the first time between Working Committee on Clusters, and Advisory Committee for Horizontal Policies; Conference held by Prof. Porter *January 1994*: Formal creation of the Forum for Competitiveness *February 1994*: Task Forces (TFs) established
Phase III (April 1994-July 1995	Design and implementation of plans	*April 1994*: TFs begin work under the co-ordination of the Forum; specialist industry organisations assume responsibility for footwear, tourism and wine *May 1994*: Launch pilot of BCAP Project methodology in new sector, fresh fruit and vegetables Phase II Final Conference *November 1994*: Relaunch of the Forestry Management Initiative, leading to creation of three TFs *January 1995*: Work starts on the report The Competitiveness of the Portuguese Economy *March 1995*: Meetings at Forum of specialists and opinion leaders to discuss structural policies relevant to the competitiveness of Portuguese companies. *July 1995*: Annual Conference for the Forum of Competitiveness, and presentation of the report on The Competitiveness of the Portuguese Economy.

Source: Forum for Competitiveness

- *Demand conditions*. The nature of home demand for the industry's product or service; quality of demand is more important than quantity. Italian consumers are very sophisticated and demanding in their purchase of shoes and designer fashion.

- **Related and supporting industries**. The presence or absence in the nation of supplier industries and related industries that are internationally competitive. The arrival of Japanese transplants has revitalised the UK auto industry, and has resulted in massive investment programmes by *all* producers and component manufacturers responding to the new environment.

- **Firm strategy, structure and rivalry**. The conditions in the nation governing how companies are created, organised and managed, and the nature of domestic rivalry. Nations with leading world positions often have a number of strong local rivals: Switzerland in pharmaceuticals, Germany in chemicals, the USA in computers and software, Japan in CNC machine tools, South Korea in consumer electronics and automobiles.

FIGURE 17.4: PORTUGAL'S AUTOMOTIVE CLUSTER AND THE DIAMOND OF COMPETITIVENESS

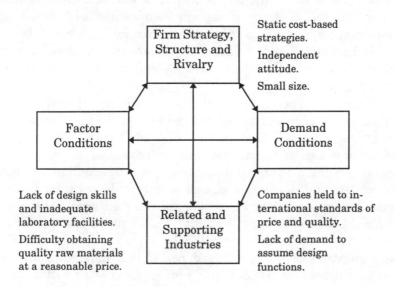

The effect of one determinant is contingent upon the state of the others. Favourable demand conditions, for example, will not lead

to competitive advantage unless the state of rivalry is sufficient to cause companies to respond. A nation need not always have advantages in all determinants to succeed internationally. Where a nation has a disadvantage in one determinant, national success normally reflects unusual advantage in others. Two additional variables can influence the national system in important ways: chance and government. Government's real role is in influencing the four determinants.

17.9 IMPACT AND MEASUREMENT OF NATIONAL COMPETITIVENESS

Most of the nations in Porter's study were competitive in more than one industry. This can be explained by the fact that the diamond creates an environment that promotes *clusters* of competitive industries. Linkages (i.e. horizontal and vertical) between competitive industries reinforce the cluster's strength and encourages geographical concentration.

According to Porter (1990), the only meaningful concept of competitiveness at the national level is national productivity. Productivity is the value of the output produced by a unit of labour or capital. Seeking to explain 'competitiveness' at the national level require a focus not on the economy as a whole but on specific industries and industry segments. International advantage is often concentrated in narrowly defined industries and industry segments.

National prosperity, he argues, is closely linked to the 'upgrading' of competitive advantage and sustained competitive advantage requires that firms upgrade their advantage(s) through innovation and investment in 'advanced' factors of production. At the national level, these processes enhance labour productivity and so there is an increase in real *per capita* income. A nation's industry may be considered internationally successful if it *possesses competitive advantage relative to the best worldwide competitors*. This is demonstrated by high levels of exports to many countries over a prolonged period, and/or significant outward investment based on skills and assets created in the home nation.

Porter (1990) concludes that national prosperity is created not inherited. Indeed, the competitive advantages of some nations are rooted in their need to overcome disadvantages (e.g. in natural resources). These countries have generated their own competitive advantage by creating new strengths such as highly skilled and dedicated workers or top-class infrastructure. Ultimately, nations gain competitive advantage in particular industries because their environment is the most forwarding-looking, dynamic and challenging. He identifies four stages of development. Portugal would appear to be a recent addition to the second stage, having progressed to the investment-driven stage (see Figure 17.5).

FIGURE 17.5: THE FOUR STAGES OF NATIONAL COMPETITIVE DEVELOPMENT

Stage of Development	Factor-Driven Stage	Investment-Driven Stage	Innovation-Driven Stage	Wealth-Driven Stage
Source of Advantage	• Normally low-cost labour or natural resources • Only factor conditions are present, other three parts of diamond are absent • Firms compete on price, technology (process and product is limited) and technology is imported	• Two elements of diamond are now present (i.e. factor plus strategy structure and rivalry • Firms improve technology to enhance their products and processes	• Completion of the industry diamond. Technology not just improved but developed within the nation • Competitive disadvantages stimulate innovation • Industry clusters are well-developed	• Leads to decline; economy driven by past wealth • Firms lose their competitive advantage due to diminishing rivalry, low investment and government support • Increase in numbers of senior managers, but decline in number of entrepreneurs
Examples	Developing nations, centrally-planned economies, Australia, Canada	Hong Kong, Singapore, Spain	Germany, Sweden, USA	UK

Porter's framework has attracted strong general criticism (e.g. Dunning, 1992a, 1992b; Grant, 1991; Van Den Bosch, 1994). It is not the purpose of this paper to enter into this debate. Indeed, some authors (e.g. Krugman, 1996) argue that firms, not nations, are competitive. Again, this is somewhat contentious. What is indisputable is that when league tables are compiled of economies' competitiveness, European economies — irrespective of location — are in the main slipping down 'the charts'.

17.10 PORTUGAL: THE ROAD TO WORLD COMPETITIVENESS

17.10.1 Indicators of Malaise

The *World Competitiveness Report, 1994* for the first time since its original publication in 1980, ranked 44 economic regions without making the traditional distinction between industrialised (mainly OECD countries) and industrialising ones. It defines world competitiveness as 'the ability of a country or a company to, proportionally, generate more wealth than its competitors in world markets'. The World Competitiveness scoreboard is based on:

• the statistical indicators of competitiveness as recorded by international organisations and national institutes, and

• the perceptions of business executives on the competitiveness of their countries drawn from the yearly Executive Opinion Survey.

It is worthwhile stressing that this methodology therefore produces results which measure reality (i.e. assuming statistics are accurate) and image (i.e. executives' perceptions).

The World Competitiveness scoreboard showed that for the first time since 1985, the USA was the world's most competitive economy whilst Japan slipped to third place after eight years in pole position. Table 17.6 reveals Portugal's score for a number of key variables, and Table 17.7 translates these into the 'competitive disadvantages' of Portugal. They makes depressing reading for those striving to build competitive advantage in the country.

TABLE 17.6: APPLICATION OF PORTER'S DIAMOND TO LEADING
INDUSTRIES IN PORTUGAL*

Industry	Factor Conditions	Firm Strategy, Structure and Rivalry	Related and Supporting Industries	Demand Conditions
Apparel	✓✓	✓	✓✓	✓
Footwear	✓✓	✓	✓✓	✓
Ceramics, glass	✓✓	✓✓	✓✓	✓
Textiles	✓✓	✓	✓	✓
Wine	✓✓	✓✓	✓✓	✓
Fresh fruit, veg	✓	✓	✓	✓
Plastic moulds	✓✓	✓✓	✓✓	✓✓✓
Auto components	✓	✓✓	✓	✓✓✓
Electronics	✓	✓✓	✓	✓✓✓

* On scale of 1-3 (i.e. poor to good), how would Portugal score? (Assumes Italy
is benchmark and would score ✓✓✓.)

Source: Author

TABLE 17.7: PORTUGAL AND ITS COMPETITIVE DISADVANTAGES

Competitive Disadvantages	Comment
Management	• Lack of entrepreneurship • Lack of organisational skills
Technology	• Absence of privately-funded R&D • R&D activities in public sector • Lack of technology dissemination from public to private sector
Production	• Low levels of investment • Low utilisation of optimum manufacturing techniques • Product quality suffers
Education	• Lack of co-ordination between education system and employers, to ensure needs of latter are met • Compares poorly with other EU economies, and some in Eastern Europe • Results in shortage of skilled human resources to solve other weaknesses
Role of the State	• State intervention is high, but counterproductive • High costs resulting from excessive bureaucracy • Inefficient fiscal collection

Source: Derived from *The Competitiveness of Portuguese Economy*, The
Forum for Competitiveness, July 1995.

17.10.2 The Troubleshooters: The Forum for Competitiveness

The first step in solving any problem is to diagnose accurately its source and then identify actions which lead to its solution. This situation faces all nations, irrespective of their level of development. The Forum has identified a number of weaknesses in the Portuguese economy which require addressing urgently (see Table 17.7). It also believes that the future offers an even more hostile environment due to:

- further trade liberalisation measures which may adversely effect Portugal's textiles industry

- enlargement of the EU to integrate Eastern European economies

- competition from East Asian economies which have a better-educated population, a more-advanced technological base, and relatively low costs.

In terms of macro-economic policy the Forum highlights the difficulties facing Portuguese businesses, especially those in the private sector. These include:

- a higher and more volatile inflation rate than virtually all other EU member countries

- capital is limited and real interest rates high

- rising public expenditure but no increase on spending in education and social welfare

- costly but poor transport infrastructure and telecommunications

- relatively high energy costs

- lack of labour mobility.

The Forum for Competitiveness aims to influence positively education, forestry management, management capabilities, science and technology and company financing (see Tables 17.8–17.12). These areas it classifies as horizontal policies. These are developed from following the 'Monitor methodology' (see Figure 17.6).

TABLE 17.8: ACTION INITIATIVES FOR HORIZONTAL POLICIES —
EDUCATION

ASSESSMENT AND CURRENT SITUATION
Consists of five distinct sub-systems (pre-school, *compulsory*, secondary (years 10-12): general & technological, university; *vocational*) — those in italics are the focus of Phase II of the BCAP Project. The text of this chapter discusses the major weaknesses of Portugal's education system.
VISION
Compulsory Schooling
• Develop a set of coherent policies to enhance the professional status of teachers, and seek to prevent decline in motivation and responsibility within the teaching profession
University Education
• Institutions must have clearly-defined objectives and must be endowed with sufficient autonomy to carry out their mission • There must be a system which ensures that assessment produces a reliable indicator of performance
Vocational Education
• Overall objective is 'to support and stimulate the development of education policies and structures that will contribute to the competitiveness of the Portuguese economy' • Vocational training is the priority sub-segment of the education system because actions directed at it are expected to have greatest impact in the short term • Vocational Education Task Force (VCTF) established in early 1994 • VCTF is undertaking audit on vocational training situation in the six target clusters of Phase II of the BCAP Project (i.e. automotive components, footwear, textiles, wood products, wine and tourism) • Pass legislation which encourages companies to concern themselves with the quality of vocational education, including the importance of the choice of curricula.

TABLE 17.9: ACTION INITIATIVES FOR HORIZONTAL POLICIES —
FORESTRY MANAGEMENT

ASSESSMENT AND CURRENT SITUATION

• Forests are the country's most renewable resource
• They cover 34% of the country — much lower than their potential
• Forest-based industries are responsible for:
  ◊ around 12% of industrial GDP
  ◊ 11% of exports
  ◊ 9% of manufacturing employment
• Industry faces shortage of supply in all species, but especially pine and eucalyptus, unless urgent action taken
• Traditionally, the focus has been simply on inputs (i.e. level of investment) but insufficient attention has been paid to outcomes (e.g. hectares planted, yields, etc.); the sector lacks a strategy
• There are 400,000 land-owners but many are absentee landlords or display low levels of commitment

VISION
• 'to build a sustainable large-scale forest which balances explicit economic, social and environmental needs'
ACTION
• To increase area of forest under-co-ordinated management • To prepare industry policy with involvement of participants • To raise national awareness of forestry problems

TABLE 17.10: ACTION INITIATIVES FOR HORIZONTAL POLICIES —
MANAGEMENT CAPABILITIES

ASSESSMENT AND CURRENT SITUATION
• Portugal has the weakest management capabilities of the 22 OECD countries featured in the *World Competitiveness Report* • Even in comparison with the NIEs in East Asia, Eastern Europe and South America, Portugal has a poor record (weakest of 41 countries in entrepreneurship, achieving a top 20 place in only four dimensions: labour costs (11), unemployment (16), working hours (18), and in-company training (20) • SMEs represent 99% of Portugal's corporate universe, a higher proportion than in any other EU country • Their strengths tend to be those now seen as critical success factors in global competition: speed, innovation, flexibility, customisation • Of the working population in the period 2000-2010, 70% are currently working, highlighting the need for on-job training/retraining
ACTION
• Establish a manager's sector-based pool, and an integrated consultancy system for SMEs • Co-operate with industry associations and industrial financial institutions to develop management capabilities.

TABLE 17.11: ACTION INITIATIVES FOR HORIZONTAL POLICIES —
SCIENCE AND TECHNOLOGY

ASSESSMENT AND CURRENT SITUATION
• There is no co-ordination of effort between companies, educational institutions and Government • Family-owned firms are often managed by founder's descendant(s), and normally have 'little in the way of management qualifications . . . and who consequently manages the company on the basis of the minimum knowledge necessary for its day-to-day operations' • Lack of technological knowledge of managers is a barrier to dialogue with R&D bodies • R&D bodies focus on theoretical rather than applied research, and do not meet companies' needs; moreover, this situation exacerbates the shortage in supplying managers qualified in technical disciplines • The best researchers are promoted within their institutions to management posts, leaving the less-gifted to perform the actual research • Technology is seen as means of overcoming competitive disadvantages rather than as a source of competitive advantage, and is invariably imported and targeted at the production process • Resources are spread too thinly, reflecting the lack of a coherent R&D policy to achieve concerted action

VISION FOR THE SCIENCE AND TECHNOLOGY SYSTEM
1. **Raising the awareness among businessmen of the benefits of science and technology**
Forum need to identify and publicise indigenous enterprises whose success is largely attributable to a positive attitude towards R&D
2. **Human resources mobility**
  • Transfers from institutions to companies and vice versa need to be facilitated
  • Focus on graduate recruitment by industry through establishment of specific projects and programmes
  • Prepare a Guide to Incentive Systems for companies so that they can take full advantage of programmes available
  • Develop a Teaching Company system, based on the UK model, which aims to carry out technological development and even research by meeting part of the cost of hiring suitable technical and scientific staff
3. **Permanent technological education**
  • To ensure that those already with higher degrees have the opportunity to constantly upgrade their knowledge
  • Conduct an audit of the 'Advanced Technology Training Market', and identify its suitability for the clusters earmarked for development

TABLE 17.12: ACTION INITIATIVES FOR HORIZONTAL POLICIES — FINANCE

ASSESSMENT AND CURRENT SITUATION
• Difficulty in gaining access to capital is a major barrier to improving the competitiveness of a large number of Portuguese companies, especially SMEs • Low level of interaction between companies and financial institutions and weak market mechanism • Companies are more indebted than those from other European countries; average debt ratio (i.e. outside capital/equity) is 1.42, whereas in UK manufacturing sector the average is 0.42 • Short-term borrowing (especially of bank overdrafts and credit lines) dominates the structure of debts • Nominal and real interest rates are higher than in most EU countries • Intensity of rivalry in banking sector is weak, leading to conservative lending policy • SMEs are in a 'catch-22' or a vicious circle: they won't receive loans until they produce accurate financial statements to potential lenders, but they fail to produce such statements
VISION FOR FINANCING SMES
'Four major objectives have been defined with the aim of encouraging the transformation of vicious circles into virtuous circles: • Financial institutions will provide SMEs with an efficient and diversified supply of capital • Public bodies and the legal and tax systems will encourage competitive lending to SMEs • SMEs will take appropriate investment and borrowing decisions and will supply financial agents with the necessary credible information • SMEs will become attractive investment opportunities.' (The Forum for Competitiveness, 1995)
ACTION FOR FINANCING SMEs
May 1994 — report submitted to the Ministry of Finance and the Ministry of Justice. It contained a series of proposals focusing on fiscal and legal-administrative framework: • Simplify administration and ensure equitable procedures • Encourage investment and modernisation • Encourage the creation and reinforcement of corporate groups • Support the internationalisation of companies and groups • Invigorate procedures for the recovery/reorganisation/rendering viable of companies • Contain public expenditure and state productivity Initiatives also proposed for the capital market to optimise savings: • Creation of more stable fiscal, procedural and regulatory environment, which is coherent, competitive and stimulates supply and demand • Enhance management skill of companies • Promote SME access to the equity market • Invigorate the capital market to make it more efficient • Make information available for investment decisions and management of securities portfolios.

FIGURE 17.6: THE MONITOR "THREE-STEP" METHODOLOGY FOR
CHANGE MANAGEMENT

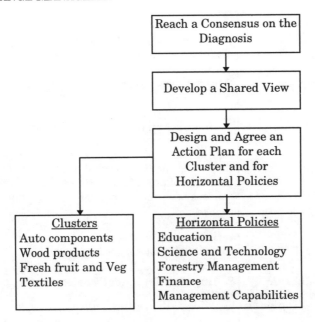

The intention is to bolster these for the benefit particularly of the
seven clusters (a cluster is a group of industries and organisations
whose inter-relationships or linkages enhance competitive advantage) which Portugal's future development will focus on. These are
automotive, footwear, textiles, tourism, fruits and vegetables, wood
products and wine.

These sectors were identified by Monitor as affording Portugal
the best opportunity to become internationally competitive. Table
17.13 provides the Forum's analysis of problems and recipes for
the fresh fruit and vegetable sector.

TABLE 17.13: OVERVIEW OF PORTUGAL'S FRUIT AND VEGETABLES
SECTOR

The Current Dilemma	Vision for the Cluster
Sectoral Status 24% of Final Agricultural Product, 1991-93 Vegetables comprised 11.5%, Fruit, 7.1%, Potatoes, 5.4%	**Solution based on three elements**: 1. Economic organisation 2. Technical-professional skills 3. Sector-based policies
Geographical Scope Nationwide due to suitable climate	**1. Strengthen Economic Organisation** *Aim*: To overcome some of the main short-comings detected by the diagnosis, namely the lack of corporate weight at all points in the chain of production and distribution and the lack of co-operation between companies *Actions*: • Improve organisation of production • Define zones and products • Establish professional organisations around common interests
Nature of Production • Dominated by inefficient SMEs, and absence of co-operation • Low productivity, and often poor quality product, especially in fruit • Serious water shortages • Lack of technical knowledge, import foreign know-how	**2. Improve Technical-Professional Skills** *Aim*: To address sector's limited capacity to develop specialised professional skills, and generate and disseminate market informa-tion and scientific knowledge to its members *Actions*: • Establish technical centre • Promote R&D activities
Marketing Disbanding of Junta Nacional das Frutas (National Fruit Board) as it did not comply with EU rules has had a negative impact	**3. Adapting and Co-ordinating Sector-based Policy** *Aim*: To make a contribution in areas where the action of public institutions or their dia-logue with the sector is felt to be insufficient *Actions*: • Institutional support • Interprofessional framework

Source: Derived from *The Competitiveness of Portuguese Economy*.

In industrial products, Portugal suffers from a lack of image
rather than from a negative image. Plastic moulds is seen as the
sole sector where 'made-in-Portugal' is seen as an advantage. Car
components and plastic moulds are the leading industrial products. The former has grown rapidly since the late 1970s when
Renault established its plant at Setubal, near Lisbon. Further

stimulus to this sector has come from the AutoEuropa project, the joint venture between Ford and Volkswagen to produce a multi-purpose vehicle. In terms of business-start-ups, a number of companies have been established in the software industry. They are focusing upon basic product adaptation, whereby existing software is modified to gain acceptability in Portuguese-speaking countries.

In consumer products, Portugal apparently suffers from a negative country-of-origin effect. It is regarded as a low-cost producer of, at best, average-quality goods. Ironically, Portuguese wines are unique to the country. They therefore have a unique selling point, but one at odds with industry trends which emphasise the type of wine (e.g. Cabernet Sauvignon, Chardonnay etc.).

Increasingly wine menus are compiled by wine type, rather than the country-of-origin. Most other wine-producing countries (e.g. Argentina, Australia, Chile, South Africa, the US) offer their own varietal wines. Some other countries face the same dilemma as Portugal (e.g. Germany, Italy, and Spain) and appear to have been more successful at promoting their own distinctive types of wine (e.g. Riesling; Chianti, Frascati, Lambrusco, Rioja). Italian wines in particular have benefited from Italian emigration and the popularity of Italian restaurants worldwide. By contrast, in most countries it is very unusual to discover a significant number of Portuguese restaurants.

Portuguese wine producers need to overcome two hurdles: the country-of-origin effect and to convert the uniqueness of their product from a disadvantage into a competitive advantage. They need to create the same level of product awareness once enjoyed by the Port industry, which traditionally has been British-controlled. This requires a concerted effort by wine producers which until recently was conspicuously missing. This tactic has been employed to great success by the 'new world producers'. For example, the Australian Wine Bureau was established to promote the generic product, rather than individual brand names.

In recent years, the industry has recorded major progress on the production front, leading to a more consistent and higher quality product, but effort is only now being made to address the marketing dimension. A consortium of seven leading wine producing companies — the 'G7' — was formed in 1993 to undertake joint international promotion efforts. More recently, Vini Portugal has been established and ICEP is playing a key role in furnishing

the wine producers with the support required if they are to pene-
trate international markets.

As one would expect, the Portuguese companies focus their international marketing activities in non-wine-producing countries
with potential for sales growth. The Scandinavian countries, especially Sweden, are the largest export markets. Box 1 explains
how Sweden (population 8.5 million) came to become such a vital
export market.

Box 1: Drink Up Sweden

The success in this market can be explained by political considerations. In 1974, immediately after the revolution, the Socialist Prime Minister, Mario Soares recognised that political
stability could be undermined by a weak economy. He thus
used his own contacts to try and boost Portuguese industry. He
approached the Swedish Prime Minister of the day, Olaf
Palme, also a Socialist. At the time the state had a monopoly
on the distribution of alcoholic drinks, and Soares urged
Palme to support Portugal and buy its wines. Palme obliged.

A closer look at the wine industry is provided in the case study
below by examining Portugal's oldest wine-producer, Fonseca. This
is followed by a review of Iberomoldes, Portugal's leading plastic
moulds maker, before looking at the automotive sector and
Autosil.

17.11 FONSECA

17.11.1 Evolution of the Company

Founded in 1834 by 30 year-old Mr Fonseca, the company is the
oldest producer in Portugal of table wine. Today the business is
run by the sixth generation of his descendants. The evolution of
the business is better understood by looking at four distinctive
cycles.

1834-1884 — The Founder's Marketing Philosophy

A mathematics graduate from Quimbra, Portugal's oldest university, Fonseca was a marketer by instinct. His huge library acted as
his Marketing Information System. He pioneered agricultural reforms which improved productivity and quality. A Gold Medal

winner at the 1855 Paris Universal Exhibition indicated that world class standards were being met.

Fonseca was a marketing pioneer too. In the 1850s he introduced his first branded product (i.e. Perequita). He was the first Portuguese to bottle wine rather than sell in oak casks. Each bottle was individually wrapped to protect the labelling. Fonseca understood clearly the importance of relationship marketing. He enjoyed good relations with the Duke of Palmela in whose region his main vineyards were found. As early as 1851 the company was already exporting to distant Singapore.

1885-1935 — The Brazilian Cycle

Fonseca was survived by one child, a daughter. Neither she nor husband shared her father's passion for wine and the business. During this period, the business grew mainly through exports to Brazil. Each year 100,000 cases or 60-70 per cent of total production was shipped there and Fonseca had its own representative office in Rio. In the 1930s a ban was imposed on all wine imports. Overnight Fonseca lost its largest market. Faced with bankruptcy, its most valuable assets were sold. It retrenched and focused on the Lisbon market where the trends was for bulk wine sales. The sophisticated marketing philosophy of Fonseca was way ahead of the local market. The company was poorly positioned to serve the less demanding, more competitive domestic market. Fortuitously, the company was saved by launching a new product.

1930s-mid-1980s — The Rosé Period

In 1936/37, Fonseca introduced its rosé wine under the brand name *Faisca* (translated as Lightening), which was packaged in an unusual bottle. *Faisca* proved an immediate success. In 1942, Sográpe, a rival producer, launched a rosé, Mateus Rosé. The following year Fonseca was approached by an American, Mr Behar, who wanted to sell Faisca in the US market. He indicated that the brand name was unsuitable because it sounded like 'fiasco'. An art enthusiast, and particularly fond of Velasquez, he suggested the name Lancers after one of the Spanish painter's best known works 'Les Lancers'. He also suggested that the company distinguish the product by using a terracotta bottle rather than glass.

Lancers was a great success in the US market, and in the late 1950s Mr Behar sold out to Heublein which took an 89 per cent stake in the company. Fonseca International was established to focus solely on Lancers rosé. Fonseca's hope was that as Lancers' sales expanded globally, other brands would be pulled through distribution channels. In 1986 Heublein was acquired from RJR Reynolds Nabisco by Grand Metropolitan for $1.2 billion. Subsequently, Heublein took full ownership of Fonseca International and thus assumed total responsibility on a global basis for Lancers.

Mid-1980s-Present — Starting Over

Fonseca had lost its flagship brand and access to Grand Met's global distribution network. The sixth generation (i.e. Antonio and Domingos Franco, the current president and vice-president) were committed to rebuilding Fonseca. They already had a sound knowledge of the business, and appreciated that modernisation and expansion were necessary if the business were to prove viable. All proceeds from selling the outstanding stake were reinvested in new equipment and purchasing other vineyards (i.e. José de Sousa). Today, Fonseca is Portugal's largest vine holder, with 500 hectares, which can meet 75-80 per cent of the company's annual needs.

17.11.2 International Marketing Management

International Product Policy

The company's most important export markets (in descending order of importance) are Scandinavia, the UK and Holland, Canada, Brazil, and the USA. It has already made some critical decisions regarding product policy:

- It refuses, despite repeated requests from Europe's leading supermarket chains, to offer wine for sale under the retailer's own label. The company is deeply committed to building brands. Again, this is a brave decision which runs against the trend in some leading markets (e.g. the UK).

- In Denmark, the company was selling large quantities of a particular wine, which was subsequently withdrawn because Fonseca did not believe it achieved a quality consistent with its strategic intent of being recognised globally as a purveyor of top-quality products.

From the producer's perspective, it is clearly preferable to achieve sales under its own brand name, but major MNEs in the food and drinks industry are losing market share to own-label products. The myth of consumer loyalty to particular brands has at last been exposed. Nevertheless, Fonseca and Sográpe remain resolutely committed to brand development. The latter is best known for its Mateus Rosé brand, but it faces stiff competition from own-label brands.

International Pricing Policy

Not only has Fonseca been able to raise the level of output, but more significantly, it has achieved a significant qualitative improvement. In terms of product policy, the only viable option was to return to its classic portfolio. A range of new wines were launched, aimed mainly at export markets. By 1995 the volume and value of exports represented around 40 per cent and 30 per cent respectively of total sales. The aim is to achieve by the year 2000 an even divide between domestic and international sales in volume terms, and a 60/40 split in value terms.

These figures reveal that its wines command a higher price in the domestic market. This price discrepancy can be best understood in terms of buyer perception. In Portugal, the buyers are knowledgeable about local wines and appreciate their quality. Overseas, buyers are not so knowledgeable of Portuguese wines and therefore many do not appreciate their unique qualities.

International Distribution Policy

Overseas, Fonseca relies on distributors, normally one per national market, the large US market being the exception. However, these distributors often import wines from many other countries. For example, Fonseca's UK distributor is the Ehrmann Group which has just acquired Beloni, the UK's largest importer of Italian wines. This situation is compounded by Ehrmann's questionable commitment to brand development, understandable though it may be due to the current trends in UK wine sales (i.e. greater proportion of wine sales made through large supermarkets, demise of independent wine merchant, switch to own-label).

Fonseca's organisational culture reflects its long-standing traditions. Despite changes in its competitive environment, it still regards the business as one where 'a gentleman's agreement still means something'. Its business dealings are based upon trusting long-term partners, rather than legal obligations.

International Promotion Policy

If Portugal's wine producers are to succeed in developing their own brands they have to indulge in creative marketing. They lack the resources to compete along conventional lines. However, many companies from other countries in different sectors have confronted a comparable situation. They succeeded by identifying radical alternatives. The fact that the promotion budget for a Spanish regional wine (i.e. Rioja) exceeds ICEP's budget for all Portuguese wines underlines the fact that Portuguese producers need to demonstrate a stronger commitment to flexible, intelligent relationship marketing. They also need to recognise that they must address domestic issues if they are to succeed in international markets. It is argued that the co-operative wine producers — representing half the industry — are inefficient due to their ownership structure. Whatever the cause of their reputed inefficiency, a solution needs to be found. Otherwise, the prospects are bleak.

17.12 IBEROMOLDES

17.12.1 Introduction
The origins of Portugal's mould-making industry dates to 1945 when Mr Anibal H. Abrantes recognised that the traditional skills utilised in the local glass-making industry in Marinha Grande could with adaptation be transferred to the emerging plastics industry. He founded Portugal's first mould-making company, which was subsequently nationalised in 1974, but purchased by Iberomoldes in 1986. The combination of this skills-base and low wages provided the source of competitive advantage, and Portuguese mould-makers were highly export-oriented. Moreover, Portugal was recognised globally as a centre of excellence in mould-making.

By the mid-1980s, the industry structure worldwide had been transformed by a wave of new entrants with cost-advantages, mainly from Asia's emerging economies, and rivalry intensified. This section focuses on the strategic response of one relatively youthful Portuguese mould-maker, Iberomoldes, which has overcome this hostile environment by adopting a strategy of focused differentiation. As is demonstrated below, the company is well-positioned to enjoy further market penetration of the higher priced, better quality niche in the market for mould-making.

17.12.2 Group Background

The company was founded in 1975 by Henrique Neto and Joaquim Menezes, who each invested $1,500 to launch Ibero-moldes as a design and marketing company for plastic moulds. In their rented office accommodation, and with no other employees, their assets amounted to basic telecommunications equipment. From such inauspicious beginnings they created the world's largest mould engineering group.

Previously, Messrs Netto and Menezes were the marketing and production managers respectively with a major mould-making company that was nationalised in the wake of the 'Revolution of the Carnations'. Ironically, the Group includes the company which the founders quit in 1975, having been bought over by them in 1986 in Portugal's first privatisation.

Iberomoldes SA is the holding company for the Iberomoldes Group. In all its 15 member companies have around 600 full-time employees, most of whom (around 480) are involved in manufacturing. The Group is a mould-making and engineering organisation which specialises in the marketing, engineering and manufacturing of moulds for injection, compression and blow-moulding of thermoplastics and thermoset resins, as well as die-casting tools for injection of light metal alloys. Sales now stand at $30 million and around 80 per cent are exports, mainly to the UK, the USA, Belgium and Sweden. This distribution of exports reflects a dependence on a small number of large multinationals.

Iberomoldes SA is located 100 miles or two and half hours drive north of Lisbon in the sleepy town of Marinha Grande. Appearances can be deceptive, however, and this region has emerged as a leading centre for the plastic-moulding industry, and Iberomoldes is the driving force.

17.12.3 A New Source of Competitiveness

From the outset Iberomoldes was a design and marketing company, and this alone distinguished it from its production-oriented rivals. In 1990 it formed a new subsidiary, Simultaneous Engineering Technology (SET). This concept, as the name implies, means that the producer of the plastic injection mould works in conjunction with the client to design the final product. For example, normally a company presents its designs to the plastic mould producer who then prepares the mould. Then the mould is dispatched to the client company for it to consider whether the mould offers the desired aesthetics and functionality. If not, and any alterations are required to the original mould, then adapting the tool results in quality deterioration. Apart from this adverse factor, this trial-and-error approach is a costly and timely process. In short, it takes longer and costs more for the client company to obtain an inferior product.

Previously, mould users (i.e. customers) dealt directly with mould manufacturers (i.e. member companies of the Iberomoldes Group). At first sight, this may appear desirable from the customers' perspective. But for the reasons described above, this proved a cumbersome relationship. SET overcomes this situation by involving from the outset the mould toolmaker in the customers' new product development process. SET focuses on design but also the practical dimension of the product. It was the first European mould company to use computer-aided design and manufacturing (CAD/CAM). Using state-of-the-art engineering modules, all conception, modelling, prototype production, design, tooling and plastic flow testing of moulds is performed on computer screens in three dimensions. It can thus determine which design affords maximum performance of the product under design.

SET has established close relationships with a number of major multinationals in a wide range of industries (e.g. automobiles, consumer electronics, domestic appliances, gardening equipment, luggage, office equipment, telecommunications equipment and toys). Currently, it is particularly involved with industry leaders such as Electrolux in vacuum cleaners, Flymo — part of the Electrolux group — in garden trimmers and Samsonite in luggage. The strength of its relationship is confirmed by the location of its sales offices (i.e. in Sweden and in Luton in the UK, where Electrolux has a major manufacturing operation). SET undertakes detailed analysis of products from Electrolux's rivals in order to ensure that all bases for product improvement have been covered.

The major multinationals that are clients of SET know that if they are to succeed in the marketplace they need to offer aesthetically pleasing products which do not compromise performance, and do so consistently and regularly to stay ahead of rivals. Delays in a product launch can prove disastrous. Iberomoldes has succeeded by ensuring its innovation is matched by a commitment to a reliable, world class service which benefits customers. Iberomoldes recognises that its customers' success is its success. In short, Iberomoldes clearly is committed to relationship marketing with its customers.

Iberomoldes seeks to gain customers' trust by focusing on three key areas: Quality, Delivery, and Communication (QDC). Its formula is produced and discussed below:

$$QDC = \text{Customers' Trust} = \text{Customer Loyalty}$$

- In order to produce Quality moulds it uses the best materials, and ensures that components are produced rapidly without interruption for maintenance over a long period to required tolerances, are precision-machined, and involve minimum consumption of energy and other raw materials.

- As for Delivery, the company should conform exactly to delivery dates. Pre-mature delivery is as unwelcome as late delivery, in that it may undermine customers' trust, giving the impression that the business was secured without Iberomoldes committing itself to optimum performance.

- Communication by whatever means needs to be unambiguous, and all contact with customers is documented and supplied to them so that both parties have records of their discussions.

Unfortunately, some businesses worldwide confuse brands and trust. Iberomoldes is correct to emphasis the importance of trust in winning customer loyalty. Significantly, branding was not an issue in the course of our discussions with the company. The company is ruthless in its self-assessment of gaining customer loyalty. Its benchmark is permanent customers (i.e. those who at any given time have a tool in production with Iberomoldes). By 1996, it had 32 such customers.

It is equally committed to its 600 employees, with an average age of just 29 years. Indeed without them it would fail to satisfy its customers. Thus, the company has established its own training organisation (i.e. Instituto de Tecnologia de Moldes ACE) which is regarded as 'an essential weapon' in developing a world-class labour force, capable of taking full advantage of the company's innovative technology. For each project, teams are custom-built to achieve the appropriate blend of creativity and application. Labour costs represented 30 per cent of the company's sales in 1990. By 1996, this proportion had fallen to 23 per cent.

Iberomoldes has also adopted a novel approach to mould-making. Its growth led to adversity in the form of a labour skills shortage. Traditionally, employees at Iberomoldes were toolmakers who received training in line with industry norms, and were thus expert in making a complete mould. The skills deficit encouraged the company to seek an alternative way of organising production. Hence, it began to train employees to perform a specific task in the mould production and, recognising this move towards specialisation, established six different companies to maximise this focus.

These specialised companies act as subcontractors, and thus vertical integration was achieved whilst retaining strong internal competition. They also have autonomy to undertake external work. Indeed, their target is to secure 50 per cent of their sales externally in order to ensure that they remain cost competitive. This situation requires careful scrutiny to ensure that sales to Iberomoldes are not cross-subsidising external sales. Another critical business relationship is with suppliers and Iberomoldes' organisational structure reinforces this dimension.

In terms of internationalisation, the company has two joint-venture manufacturing operations, in Mexico and Tunisia. Both are SMEs with only 25 employees.

Although the company's growth can be attributed to its empathy with its customers and its efforts to exceed their expectations, this is an essential part of its product (i.e. its service). There needs to be greater commitment to strategic analysis and planning, and a more proactive approach in its strategic marketing effort. Although its technology has unlimited applications in plastics, it needs to identify those segments and companies it wishes to serve and to consolidate.

17.13 THE AUTOMOTIVE SECTOR

17.13.1 Overview of Industry Trends
The automotive sector is characterised by a number of trends:

- the integration of components in 'functions'

- reduction in the number of direct suppliers — this is encouraging industry concentration and globalisation, as the Autosil case demonstrates

- drastic reduction of component stocks due to implementation of JIT

- increased supplier involvement in design and engineering of components and assemblies.

The automobile sector competes in the economy of globality (Garelli, 1996), whereby companies exploit the different comparative advantages of nations worldwide and integrate them into a global management of the value chain. This is a highly competitive industry because competition between nations is intense as technological revolution in communications and transportation essentially renders all nations potential participants. Winning locations must offer, simultaneously, cost efficiency and value-added benefits.

17.13.2 A Situation Analysis of Portugal in the Auto Component Industry

Strength(s)

The Forum, in conjunction with the component manufacturers, is seeking to foster partnerships and dissemination of information. At the vanguard of this initiative is Autosil and the AutoEuropa. The indigenous company operates in a mature, low technology sector, from a relatively old plant, but is enjoying success in international markets due to its long-standing commitment to relationship marketing.

The presence of AutoEuropa confirms Portugal's recently acquired status as an internationally competitive location. The political environment has been transformed. Between 1963 and the early 1980s, legislation prohibited the importation of Completely Built Up Vehicles. This import-substitution policy resulted in the establishment of small assembly operations with a local content level of 25 per cent. In 1980 Renault agreed to establish a larger, highly labour-intensive operation in Setubal, provided it was guaranteed 40 per cent of the domestic market. By the 1990s, this plant under Renault was an anachronism in export-oriented Portugal that attracted mobile inward investment on its location-specific advantages.

Not surprisingly, the French car producer has decided to terminate this operation, and it has reached agreement with the Portuguese government to sell the facility as a going concern. A South Korean auto producer is expected to acquire the operation.

Weaknesses

In the auto component industry, buyers are looking for suppliers that are internationally competitive on price, quality, design capability and global reach. Most component manufactures in Portugal believe that they are competitive on the first two dimensions, but weak in the latter two. Just over one-fifth provide OEMs with a comprehensive service, with the rest dependent on buyers for technical specifications and product development.

In terms of the average size of independent component suppliers (based upon number of employees), they are the third smallest in the EU, ahead only of their counterparts in Holland and Ireland, and lagging well behind those found in the large car-producing countries of Germany, France, Britain and Spain. Size, though, is not a source of competitive disadvantage. Instead, the problem rests with producers' reluctance to co-operate and their static, cost-based strategies.

Opportunities

Mobility is a key feature of this industry, providing economies with the relevant advantages and excellent opportunities for attracting inward investment. Producers' concern lies with *control* rather than *ownership* of the value-chain. Thus, leading car producers increasingly outsource. These two trends favour Portugal. The challenge is to provide an attractive location with a suitable cluster of activity for indigenous and foreign investors.

Strategic gap analysis points to a gulf between the current and desired situation. Without industry-wide co-operation the industry diamond is likely to remain incomplete (see Figure 17.4) and the competitive position of the players in the industry will remain weak. Portugal can draw comfort from the fact that an economy of globality is one where flexibility and speed are vital. The twin pillars of success have been identified — industry co-operation and sophistication (see Figure 17.7). Thus as Figure 17.8 shows, Portugal should emulate the North East of England, the European production base for Nissan cars since the mid-1980s, and an area without any previous involvement in the auto industry.

Threat

The downside is that Portugal has a limited time-frame to seize this opportunity. If it fails then it will lose out to other regional national economies seeking to participate fully in this sector.

Northern Ireland, for example, has also decided to target auto components as part of its development strategy, and its ability to attract inward investment may have increased dramatically due to the peace process and President Clinton's high-profile visit in late 1995. Eastern European economies, especially Poland, also stand to attract investment in this sector.

FIGURE 17.7: DEVELOPMENT OF A WORLD CLASS AUTOMOBILE COMPONENT INDUSTRY

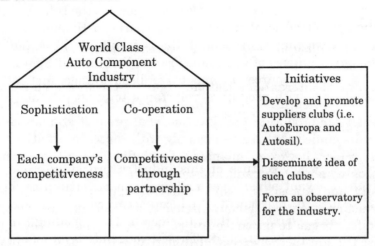

FIGURE 17.8: AUTOMOTIVE CLUSTER VISION

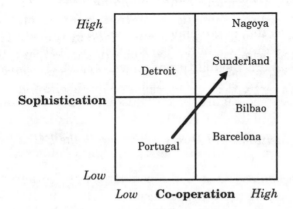

17.13.3 The Indigenous Producer — Autosil

Founded in 1925 as an import business, the company entered the motor trade in 1936. Its garages specialised in providing spare parts for all the leading component manufacturers. Its focus was on customer service. After the war, it began importing batteries from leading suppliers. In 1950, it acquired its present site and began construction of the office complex and manufacturing facility. By 1952 it had a nation-wide distribution network. Its focus throughout this period, however, was on the replacement market.

17.13.4 Company Evolution

Internationalisation — Passive Exporter, Indirect Exporting (1979-92)

In terms of internationalisation, arguably the first step came in the 1960s when it began to supply the OEM market in Portugal. Foreign car producers had international product standards, and they demanded that Autosil comply with these. Internationalisation proper, however, emanated from the Renault investment (discussed above). Renault had to source a number of components locally, and Autosil was an attractive supplier because battery production then was labour-intensive, and labour was cheap. It therefore began to purchase Autosil batteries, and moreover, purchased quantities in excess of that required to meet the output level of the Setubal plant. Batteries sold to Renault were non-branded.

Surplus batteries were exported by Renault to its plants in France. The French company had demanding product specifications and introduced the company to international markets, albeit only to plants owned by itself and Citroën. Even by the late 1980s, Autosil still relied primarily upon its domestic market, and these sales were in jeopardy because the local content regulations governing Renault's activities in Portugal were beginning to be phased out.

Proactive — Acquisitions and Direct Exporting in the EU (1993-1994)

Management recognised that if the company were to survive it had to adopt a much more *proactive* approach to international markets, rather than simply be *reactive*. It already had a 25 per cent market share in Portugal and languished in second place behind Tudor, a Spanish manufacturer (recently acquired by

Exide), which had a market share approaching 40 per cent. Autosil calculated that it would be very costly to win even a marginal increase in domestic market share. By contrast, it believed it could win international sales at relatively low cost.

Thus the next stage in Autosil's internationalisation came in 1993 when the company expanded into France and Spain focusing on the replacement market. This international expansion, however, highlighted the limitations in Autosil's production capacity. The company decided to increase manufacturing capacity by building a small manufacturing facility in France, near Brive. The choice of location was strongly influenced by the company's local distributor and the availability of attractive incentives. However, this plant alone did not offer the scale required to be a major global player.

Three options faced the company:

1. *Maintain the status quo*: maintain current production capacity levels of between 400,000 and 600,000 units per annum. This would result in the death of the company, as there was a trend towards decreasing margins.

2. *Sell the business*: this was indeed an option, as the battery industry in Europe was highly fragmented, and a number of players were seeking to become major players on a pan-European basis. This was unattractive to shareholders, however.

3. *Grow the business*: this required a substantial increase in production capacity. This was the preferred option.

An opportunity to attain this goal arose when the competition policy authorities in France ruled that Fiat, which had just acquired CEAC, one of the leading battery manufacturers in France — famous for its Steco brand name — reduce its dominance of the country's battery market. Autosil paid 4.5 billion escudos to acquire SEAC. In return it obtained:

- a total manufacturing capacity of 2.2 million batteries per annum

- the Steco brand name

- direct access to all of France's leading indigenous car manufacturers

- valuable technical know-how in the area of sealed batteries. Non-sealed batteries are predominantly used in the automobile industry whereas sealed batteries are increasingly used in rapid growth industries such as telecommunications.

The acquisition saw Autosil quadruple in size, measured in terms of assets and turnover.

Global Ambitions: 1995-Present

Autosil believes that it has to become a global player simply to survive. It can only do so through strategic alliances. It has formed a joint venture with an Indian group, and an alliance with a leading battery manufacturer in Brazil. For the time being, it regards China as too risky for a company of its size.

17.13.5 Prospects

Autosil faces an image problem arising from its country-of-origin effect. It has examined the leading brands of several other manufacturers. In a number of cases, some brands enjoy a higher level of perceived quality than is justified by reality. Unfortunately, consumers and buyers continue to underestimate the quality of Autosil's product.

17.14 CONCLUSIONS

This chapter has shown that organisations in the public sector and companies in the private sector are focusing attention on boosting the competitiveness of Portugal. However, this single-minded approach on creating competitive advantage is relatively recent and it is unrealistic to expect immediate benefits. Despite recent changes in the domestic political environment, the newly-elected government and president do not seem intent on radical change but, rather, appear to offer continuity. The political challenge is to remain popular with the electorate without pandering to demands for immediate rises in incomes that ultimately could prove damaging in the long term. The country needs to allocate more resources to human resource development and infrastructural projects.

At the corporate level, foreign investors based in Portugal are enthusiastic about the performance of their plants. Some of the leading US and European investors were interviewed for this chapter and in each case the operation in Portugal was one of the best-performing plants in the MNE's global production network, and had often attracted subsequent investment in the face of direct competition from other locations in the EU, or in one case ahead of a rapidly growing Asian economy. The message from these investors was that Portugal offered an excellent location for serving the European market.

In the case of indigenous companies, the geographical location of Portugal does not represent a weakness, but certainly buyers and consumers tend to underestimate the quality of products made by Portuguese companies. Moreover, in certain industries in Portugal (e.g. auto components), companies need to be committed to full-scale internationalisation if they are to become significant suppliers. From the perspective of Portuguese enterprises, the key motive for outward investment should be market access rather than cost reduction. However, in other industries (e.g. cork, fruits, wine), the nature of the product restricts Portuguese companies to an export marketing strategy. In terms of overall strategy, the key drivers need to be the imperatives of the 1990s rather than simply a desire to emulate producers from more-developed countries, whose strategy may have been driven by different imperatives.

ICEP has developed a strategy and structure that is best-suited to its environment rather than simply seeking to copy the best practices of other countries. The corporate sector needs to be equally courageous and far-sighted.

References[1]

Dunning, J. H. (1992a), 'The Theory of Transnational Corporations', in *UNCTC Library on Transnational Corporations, International Business and Development of the World Economy*, 1, London: Routledge.

Dunning, J. H. (1992b), 'The competitive advantage of countries and the activities of transnational corporations', *Transnational Corporations*, Vol. 1, No. 1, February, pp. 135-168.

---

[1] The author acknowledges generous support from ICEP which made this research possible. In particular, he wishes to thank Professor Miguel Athayde Marques, until recently President of ICEP, and his staff for kind assistance. Various ICEP publications were also made available to the author.

Forum for Competitiveness (1995), *The Competitiveness of the Portuguese Economy*, English version and summary of the report *A Competitividade da Economia Portuguesa*, July.

Grant, R.M. (1991) 'Porter's "Competitive Advantage of Nations": An Assessment', *Strategic Management Journal*, Vol. 12, pp. 535-548.

ICEP, (1995), *O Impacto do Investimento Directo Estrangeiro em Portugal entre 1986 e 1994*, Lisbon.

Krugman, P. (1996), 'A Country is not a Company', *Harvard Business Review*, January-February, pp. 41-51.

OECD (1994), *Foreign Trade Statistics*, Paris.

Porter, M. E. (1990), *The Competitive Advantage of Nations*, New York: The Free Press.

Van Der Bosch, F. A. (1994), 'The Competitive Advantage of European Nations: The Impact of National Culture — A Missing Element in Porter's Analysis', *European Management Journal*, Vol. 10, No. 2, pp. 173-178.

The World Bank (1993), *The East Asian Miracle: Economic Growth and Public Policy*, Oxford: Oxford University Press.

The World Competitiveness Report, (1994).

INDEX